Sparks

61- 13154

3-29-62

EUROPE IN THE
NINETEENTH CENTURY

VOLUME I

EUROPE IN THE NINETEENTH CENTURY

*A Documentary Analysis
of Change and Conflict*

VOLUME I

1815-1870

By

Eugene N. Anderson
Stanley J. Pincetl, Jr.
Donald J. Ziegler

Preface

THE two volumes presented here contain contemporary documents chosen to discuss changes during the nineteenth century in the institutional structure of European life. The first volume offers sources relating to the period from about 1815 to 1870, the second volume from 1870 to 1914. The documents analyze basic issues treated in every standard textbook and have been selected to elucidate the matters of what was at stake and why an event had historical importance.

The criteria for including the materials may reveal the nature of the objective toward which the editors have aimed. (1) The documents illustrate major developments in all important aspects of society. (2) Each document illustrates a fundamental development in more than one country. (3) Each reveals the significance of the subject for other aspects of social life than that with which it is directly concerned. (4) In the case of foreign relations only documents are used which discuss the issues in connection with internal affairs as well. Questions of diplomatic policy alone are excluded as too restricted in scope. (5) Since basic changes during the century occurred to a greater extent in France and Germany than elsewhere, a larger number of documents relates to the history of each of these two countries than to that of any other country. (6) Each document is selected from the history of a state closely involved in the issue under discussion. (7) The documents are written by persons active in affairs rather than by men of pure theory. The authors of documents include representatives of royalty, the nobility, the bourgeoisie, several professions, handworkers, and industrial workers. The only major group not represented is that of the peasantry, for this social group has left few first-hand records of its reactions. (8) Since the reader has easy access to many sources relating to British history, documents pertaining directly to the life of England have been excluded. Wherever relevant and practicable, materials have been selected that compare conditions in the continental countries with those of Great Britain and, at times, of the United States. (9) Since the documents have to do with changes in the structure of European life, they discuss ideas in relation to institutional change and may be read as intellectual history. (10) They are spread chronologically over the century so that except for the 1820's every decade is represented. (11) Approximately an equal amount of material is offered about social and economic aspects and about political and constitutional life. (12) Each selection is interesting in itself.

The length of any one of the sources brought together in these volumes is determined by the needs of its writer. Some subjects are treated in much briefer compass than others. In a number of instances the editors have omitted the parts of a document which seemed irrelevant or unimportant for understanding the whole.

Many more documents were rejected than were approved for inclusion in this publication. Suitable materials proved difficult to find, and, when they were on occasion abundant, lack of space compelled the editors to reproduce only one or two points of view. The pleasure of imagining for himself other attitudes and comments is usually left to the reader.

The documents are arranged in chronological order for the sake of convenience and because of the difficulty of finding any other organization that would not mislead the reader. Since the documents are few in number the reader should be able to relate any one to the relevant topic of study. Yet each is so rich in content that it may be related to several subjects within its chronological period. The impact of the selections upon the reader's thinking is and should be cumulative; thus arrangement of the documents under general headings has been avoided lest the reader be confused or discouraged from using each item as variously as it should be used.

Most of the documents are translated for the first time. Translations from the French and German languages are the work of the editors and Pauline R. Anderson. Stanley J. Pincetl has assumed general responsibility for translations from the French, Donald J. Ziegler for those from the German; but each of the translations has been checked for accuracy by two other persons. Professor Lenore M. Breslin translated the selection by Donoso Cortes, and Paul Sonnino the essay by

Preface

Baron Sonnino. Mrs. Jean Hanchett and Mrs. Stanley Pincetl have aided in translating a number of the French documents. Professor Harold Lionetti has advised in the selection of Italian and Spanish materials, and Neal Brogden placed his special knowledge at our disposal in the choice of documents relating to French military reform. To all of them the editors express cordial thanks.

The editors hope that use of the materials will justify the unexpected amount of time and energy which they have devoted to the preparation of these volumes.

EUGENE N. ANDERSON
University of California, Los Angeles
STANLEY J. PINCETL, JR.
San Diego State College
DONALD J. ZIEGLER
Carroll College

Contents

EUROPE IN THE
NINETEENTH CENTURY

VOLUME I

Introduction

THE nineteenth century of European history lies between two long periods of war and revolution. Much of the character of the century derives from the continued reaction of society to the French Revolution and the Napoleonic expansion and from the complications leading to the wars and revolutions of the present century.[1] Since the conflicts of 1789 to 1815 had affected all aspects of life, the way to reorganize society continued to be argued, especially before 1870, within the framework of the ideals and practices of the French Revolution and its opponents. At about the same time that Germany and Italy completed their political unification and the Balkan peoples asserted their national independence, the industrial revolution began to expand on the continent, modifying and often aggravating older sources of controversy, creating new bonds of social unity, engendering profound problems. Change and resistance to change in the internal affairs of each country characterize the century. The brief continental wars were as much civil wars as international conflicts; social reform was often both cause and effect.

1. THE PERIOD FROM 1815 TO 1870

The issues provoked by the French Revolution dominated European society before 1870, and even after the events associated with 1870 their influence persisted. The servile peasantry demanded emancipation and in this period, legally speaking, gained its freedom (Readings 1, 12, and 13). Many landed aristocrats struggled to preserve the way of life of the Old Régime, including serfdom and privilege (Reading 2). Royalty, many nobles, and members of other social groups endeavored to maintain the status quo by preventing further revolution (Readings 3 and 4). To achieve their end they compelled the services of the bureaucracy, the church, and the educational system, thereby rendering crucial to all reformers the issue of civil rights (Reading 5). Many conservatives gravely doubted the wisdom

13

of permitting widespread change in industrial production, transportation, and communication. Although desirous of the material benefits flowing from change, they feared the effects upon their own political and social status. On the other hand most of the bourgeoisie and many aristocrats welcomed material change as likely to improve their own role in society, and they saw it as an exponent of emerging liberalism and nationalism (Readings 1 and 7). Handicraftsmen and others whose world seemed disappearing found themselves constrained to adjust to a society in rapid transition (Reading 6). Some members of the passing order sank into the proletariat; others rose to be successful members of the bourgeoisie; still others formed a new lower middle class or status group for skilled services. Liberals and nationalists, forced to search for new institutions and procedures for carrying out their ideals and ambitions, were experimenting with constitutional forms (Readings 1, 8, and 9) and with economic forms (Reading 14). As pressure for reform increased decade by decade, conservatives sought ways of preserving what they called orderly society (Readings 10 and 11). Some of them recognized the need for concessions and devised means of preserving authoritarian government and society behind a liberal, national, constitutional façade (Reading 15B), thereby frustrating the liberals (Reading 15C).

By 1870 Europe sustained a greater variety of ways of life, standards of living, forms of government, and social organizations than ever before in its history, even though common trends appeared to a greater or lesser extent in all countries. The Old Régime, still strong in most of Europe, had clearly weakened, its leading forces everywhere fighting a rearguard action. The peasantry slowly awakened to a sense of its social importance. The industrial proletariat, newly conscious of its numerical power, began to form a class or social group of its own (Reading 16). The bourgeoisie, aided by some of the nobility and, in varying forms, by other social groups, in some countries took the lead in experiments with social, economic, and political institutions; in countries where the social power of the bourgeoisie was still weak its intellectuals by their writings stimulated the demand for change. European society, transformed at varying speeds according to country and area, evolved organizations hitherto unimagined.

II. THE PERIOD FROM 1870 TO 1914

Many of the forces and sources of friction which had dominated prior decades continued after 1870 to characterize European life. Two additional factors appeared that basically affected the course of society, namely the expansion of industrialism and the greatly augmented significance of power politics and the power state.

Europe now harbored a larger number of power states than this small continent had ever beheld. Spreading competition in internal and international affairs imposed responsibilities upon government which were comparable in nature to those under absolute monarchy but different in that they had a popular basis. Awareness of governmental responsibility in the several states varied with the level of culture. The level of culture in turn depended to a major extent upon the expansion and social maturity of modern industrialism, although —significant of the complicated life of the century—the prestige in international affairs of a power state was not yet entirely correlated with the degree of industrialization within its borders. A country of large geographic expanse and numerous population like Russia enjoyed respect from a preceding age which by material and social standards this empire did not then merit.

In 1914 standards for judging conditions appeared as confused as they had been at the beginning of the nineteenth century, so that control of internal and international affairs suffered from the inconsistency of criteria. The varied cultural stages of Europe's nations or regions resembled a Dadaist collage; yet all nations shared in the effort to industrialize and to impose upon government a burden of social responsibility, for which few governments were prepared. A close correlation existed as well between stability in government and society on the one hand and industrialization on the other, which entailed increased economic opportunities and a rising standard of living. Or conversely, where industrialism largely or entirely failed to develop, where opportunities for material improvement had not increased and the condition of the masses had improved but little, government employed physical coercion most. Autocracies (Reading 11) or countries of inefficient authoritarianism employing extreme means of protection evoked radical countermeasures (Reading 6). A spectrum analysis would show that a majority of countries possessed conditions somewhere between Russian autocracy and British liberalism.

In the period after 1870 certain problems resembled those of previous decades; thus the examples found in succeeding pages may be applied to many earlier situations. First, nationalistic issues, involving the use of native language (Reading 5), or concerning the total reform of society (Reading 13), recall similar ones in Germany and Italy before these countries were unified. In the later period, however, these issues affected the life of empires and the aspirations of small states which considered themselves torsos. Second, the forces of the Old Régime continued the effort to retain their position of political and social leadership in the new industrial culture, in some cases—irrespective of country—by adjusting to new conditions and accepting the bourgeoisie as allies, in others by refusing to adjust and deploying the physical force of government in their defense (Reading 11). Third, the power state continued to require the acceptance of at least the new sources of strength created by industrialism and the ideal of popular participation in a minimum of public affairs (Readings 1A and B). Here one sees an age-old process in a new stage, the power state imposing its demands upon the groups of the Old Régime (Reading 3) and upon those of industrialism, although doing so nationally with different degrees of awareness and response. Military service (Readings 1A and B) and education (Reading 4) came especially into question, as did also the kind of economic and social structure most conducive to the creation of state power (Reading 9).

Industrialism, already emergent in the previous period, began to transform the structure of society. Should the industrial working class become a proletariat or a lower middleclass group? At first neither lower nor upper classes knew where the new mass fitted into the social structure, and professors (Reading 2), trade union leaders

(Reading 8), socialists (Reading 6), and bourgeois politicians (Reading 12) debated the problem and sought a practical solution. It became evident likewise that political unification alone did not satisfy popular demand in respect to the efforts of the nation-state. Popular constitutional government, insofar as it failed to improve the social and economic life of the people, became of doubtful value (Reading 7), and on the eve of World War I authoritarian constitutional monarchy supplied the prevailing form of government and society. Germany furnished the model, Russia offered a caricature, Baron Sonnino chose constitutional monarchism for Italy; France alone among the powers held to the popular republic. Where local government was corrupt (Reading 10) the central government, no matter how ostensibly parliamentary, could not escape contamination.

By 1914 Europe had scarcely begun to achieve the new society made possible under industrialism. The documents from the years after 1870, like those of the preceding period, exemplify the range of problems discussed and of solutions proposed; but nowhere is it certain that the author of a document has found a solution, and often he does not even pose what subsequently proved to be the essential question. Reading the documents may make the American student reared in the tradition of the eighteenth-century Enlightenment aware of the great variety of beliefs and ways of life possible at any one time in the life of a continent with three thousand years of history. It may lead him to consider whether this Europe should have dared to risk its civilization in a world war, whether the kind of society that Europe experienced in the nineteenth century did not bear within it the explosive forces of the twentieth century.

1. The Social Impact Abroad of the French Revolution and Napoleon

Baron von Altenstein: *Basic Organization of Internal Constitutional Relations* (September 11, 1807)[*]

The crushing defeat of Prussia by Napoleon at Jena in 1806 forced Prussian leaders to come to grips with the measures needed to reform and revive their country. Baron von Altenstein, a member of one of the oldest Prussian families and a high official, in a long memorandum submitted September 11, 1807, to his superior Minister von Hardenberg, provided one analysis of Prussian weakness and proposals for reform. A section of the memorandum, that dealing with internal affairs, is quoted below. Altenstein called this section that of the internal constitution, a term to him comprehending economic and social as well as governmental structure and practices. His comparison of conditions in Prussia with those in France after the changes caused by the French Revolution points up for the reader the difference between two societies based upon antithetic principles—in the case of Prussia, those of a society of estates and privilege; in the case of France, those of liberty, equality, and fraternity. Altenstein addressed himself to the measures Prussia might take to maintain itself against a state with a new order or constitution like France, and he offered one course of action. His peer the Junker von der Marwitz, author of the next selection, advocated another plan. Both Altenstein and Marwitz attempted to describe existing conditions; but each interpreted the situation in a different way and proposed a different course of action.

One may use the statement by Altenstein to illustrate essential problems of a time of crisis in any country during the past two centuries; that is, one may examine the relation between

[*] Georg Winter, *Die Reorganisation des Preussischen Staates unter Stein und Hardenberg* (Leipzig: S. Hirzel Verlag, 1931), Pt. I, Vol. I, pp. 389-412.

war and internal reform, the reality behind the concept of nation, the contrast between a society or polity based upon
estates and a society embracing a true nation, the interdependence of the governmental, economic, and social aspects of
a society, and the relation between freedom and state power.
Not only Prussia but all countries under the conqueror found
themselves examining such matters, and Altenstein's ideas as
well as Marwitz's occur in many national contexts. Altenstein
did not yet have a fully developed concept of "nation" and
"nationalism," and he does not even employ the concepts
"liberalism" and "conservatism," which in England and France
already defined social realities. His problem was to change a
society of nobles, peasants, and a small middle class largely
composed of guildsmen in a way that would make it modern
and hence strong enough to exist in the world of nations.
Since most of Europe, like Prussia, had a society of the Old
Régime, Altenstein's analysis can be applied to subsequent
decades of European history while offering a fitting introduction to the century.

General Remarks

When the spirit of the times or the progress of humanity strives
mightily toward a higher goal, and works from within or without
forcefully for change, when the spirit seeks other forms—and without a change of form no new impetus toward a higher goal is possible—the constitution changes of its own accord, unless chains are
put upon it which make such change impossible. To loose these
chains is the responsibility of the highest power in the state. A
change in the basic constitution is merely an acquiescence in what
the spirit of the time demands. The art lies in understanding correctly the slightest expression of the *Zeitgeist* and giving it its due.
The highest ideal of the constitution lies in its offering in every provision not only the possibility for but even an impetus toward
progress.

All the constitutions of primitive peoples are erected for eternity
and are maintained unchanged until force overthrows them. En-

lightened and progressive peoples in their constitutions have always provided for further development and the possibility of change in accordance with improved understanding.

A high regard for this branch of government and a very noble point of view proceed from the above fact. He who is to lead this government must accept this elevated view. Then he will look upon the basic constitution of the state as a step in development, one taken freely by the nation but entered upon according to eternal laws; the entire plan of development becomes clear to him. He tests the constitution against the condition of the world, by the changes in the continually advancing spirit of the times or the total culture, and by the demands upon the state of external relations in the light of internal conditions. It becomes clear to him how far everything accords with demand, and to this end he looses the chains and lets the constitution develop in the conditions which he freely chooses but which are the result of necessity, since his insight allows him no other choice. He does not interfere in the constitution thoughtlessly, or needlessly destroy what can be retained. But he will not spare anything if it is no longer suitable merely because it is old and traditional, or exclude from his plans anything merely because it is new and strange and does not accord with current prejudices. Where he does not consider it advisable to stand fast, he will at least indicate the limits of advance.

. . . .

The French Revolution, the most forcible and repeated change of a constitution, ought to be convincing evidence of the truth of the foregoing remarks to anyone who cannot or will not believe the above. Experience has taught us this great lesson. It has shown us how preservation of old or outmoded constitutions cripples and finally completely destroys. It is evidence of how a change of constitution brings new life. Revolution is like deep cultivation of the soil when everything seems buried: the most luxuriant vegetation springs from the raw and apparently unformed earth.

Changes coming in the wake of the French Revolution have recently shown that such reform can take place not only by force but in an orderly fashion. The first revolution alone was brutal. Other changes, directed by able men, occurred more easily. We are beginning in fact to regard the Revolution from this point of view but still too unconvincingly to bring about much result. Nowhere has the constitution been voluntarily altered according to need and thus been made the means to higher goals. Continuation of the Revolution, the forcible imposition of the French system, however, even though it has already brought much progress, could not be generally enlightening. The constitution of states usually makes it very difficult for the voices of the wise to be heard and for the more deserving to gain control of reform with the necessary power.

Survey of the Conditions of the Prussian State in Recent Times in Respect to the Fundamental or Internal Constitution of the State

If we examine carefully the internal constitution of the Prussian state in the recent period, we find that in this regard it has remained far behind the advances of the spirit of the age and the demands which the progress and external relations of other states have made so irresistible. It would lead us too far afield to give a true picture of the constitution; a few main lines will suffice; anyone who is in a position to examine such a picture, after the following discussion, and especially after the proposals for changing the constitution, will be able to fill in the details.

For a long time the best minds in Europe, representatives of the true *Zeitgeist,* preached loudly in every possible way the need for and importance of a reform of all those conditions conducive not to respecting man as an individual but to regarding him as the possession of other men in the state, and not designed for using every possible force to achieve the appointed goal. They did this in writings, secret organizations, individual proposals in different states, and by more or less serious steps in these states. All the time, however, everything within the Prussian state has remained the same; not even the least essential reform has been undertaken.

In France a terrifying, long-anticipated revolution finally broke out, destroying everything in order to maintain equality of the rights of man and to effect the union of the forces of all for the common good, insofar as these rights are compatible with the greatest possible personal freedom. In Prussia, nevertheless, everything remained as of old, even when an unsuccessful war against this venture was tried, a war in which many Prussians from all classes learned to know this reform perfectly.

When France completed what it had begun and gave consistency to the constitution, and finally Napoleon developed with increasing refinement his purpose of destroying with the concentrated and new-found power of France everything that was too weak to oppose him; in fact, after many states had succumbed in the unequal struggle, and Napoleon had adapted to his purpose at least formally everything that had to succumb to him—still nothing in Prussia changed.

One can explain this fact only by the indifference and weakness which characterized recent times in all branches of thought and action, at least as a whole, and by the higher level of achievement which Prussia reached before other states, producing a feeling here of security and carefreeness and, if one looks carefully, of great pride in purely negative virtues. The harmful political system that Prussia followed for a long time—or rather the complete absence of system—favored this condition of the internal constitution. A compelling incentive for making an effort was lacking, and it indicates how important it is to estimate correctly the conduct of foreign affairs.

Thus it came about that in this period in Prussia all the vestiges of the cruder constitution were maintained. Sharply defined castes or status groups were to be found that had acquired increasingly bad characteristics in modern times. A nobility existed with many essential privileges, namely the exclusive possession of everything that gave it unearned honor and respect; a burgher group with urban rights, guilds, monopolies, etc., apparently valuable to it but actually crippling its own powers; and a large part of the nation unable to own property and in a condition of personal slavery. Originally these groups had a purpose in the state; but, sundered and isolated, they now formed hostile, mutually harmful forces directed more or less against the state. The state, or rather the government, had kept the nobility, the middle class, and the serfs in their constitutional place and sought to rise above the limitations of such status groups. The evil was increased by the fact that every status group isolated itself in order to contend with the others and to assure its existence against attacks from the state. If this could not occur openly, it occurred in secret, and obstacles were put in the way of everything which seemed to each group from its restricted point of view harmful to its own individual interest. There was no nation in the state, and not even in the provinces, but only individual status groups in individual provinces, each with a special interest, without any point of union except the general desire to preserve the traditional as conveniently and effortlessly as possible. This was true even for the oppressed class, since it was for the most part so coarsened by long oppression as to seem no longer to wish for anything better. Enormous difficulties stood in the way of any reform, and no means existed to bring all to cooperate in a communal effort. The remains of barbarism, feudal rights, which restricted natural freedom without benefiting the state, inadequate administration, lack of civil rights, curtailment of industry and so of trade, etc.—all persisted.

RESULTS OF THIS SITUATION

The results of this situation can be easily surveyed and in part are already revealed in the description itself. Again, it would take us too far afield to enumerate the individual results; all are comprehended in the chief result: decline of the state; for these results have more or less brought about decline. It is not difficult to develop them individually. Here are the most important:

The state lacked the energetic cooperation of all individual forces for a common goal. In part these forces were not even aroused. The existing ones were not sufficiently exploited, for they were divided and wasted in fruitless opposition. The result was that the state was much weaker than it should have been.

The constitution had nothing within it that might have drawn the nation together to advance toward a goal not as yet clearly in view. The several status groups were accustomed to leave all responsibility for the whole to the government. The government had assumed all duties and put them into the hands of paid servants, even including the administration of corporative property, apparently in order to abolish in some measure the evil of privileged social groups not connected with the constitution as a whole. Each of these groups sought only for its own preservation and its own exclusive advantage. Therefore complete indifference to the administration of the state had developed. Without being especially ordered and remunerated, no one felt that he had any responsibility for the civil administration. Few persons ever protested, whether superficially or otherwise, and these were usually persons who had suffered directly, or they were journalists seeking copy; they had little knowledge of the subject and its ramifications, which not even an official could compass. And what was true of individuals was true of status groups and corporations. The nature of administration by paid servants, the inferior position they held or were placed in, and the impossibility of giving the nation an understanding of administration—these aggravated the evil. Not only indifference but even bitterness toward the administration arose, especially if one of its regulations seemed to contradict public opinion or demand sacrifice. This indolent indifference on the one hand—often considered contentment—and bitterness on the other hand meant that even when public opinion expressed itself, no one listened to it, and it was likely to be denounced as the spirit of unrest. Means of bringing public opinion to express itself, or to correct it if it should be wrong, did not exist—using "public opinion" in the higher sense of the voice of the better forces. Then the spirit of the nation, or rather the nation itself, suffered, and gossip and rumor, which destroy the good and weaken every force, took control, nourished by bad journalism and thoughtless reading. The momentary attraction of resounding phrases was taken for knowledge and power.

Lately, in the political conditions of 1805 and 1806, all these results have come to light. Public opinion declared itself unambiguously. It was partly right and partly wrong. In 1805 it demanded forceful measures, later essential reforms in the conduct of affairs, and finally, although not unanimously, war again. The first two were right, the last quite wrong, since this opinion was produced merely by the false idea that conditions were as before and by the hope that the constitution would be reformed by such means. The more correct opinion did not penetrate. The incorrect one was not corrected but was used to support false views.

Many forces belonging to the state were absorbed by individuals who, regarding their fellow citizens as objects and their powers as property, exploited the condition of oppression of the rural subjects, the difficulties about owning property, and the oppression of compulsory services, all of which prevent the free use of the powers of others. Nonetheless, the privileged members of society did not increase their resources to the extent that the state lost its resources, nor were they able to provide the state with a relatively greater amount of valuable service. Failure to achieve greater progress in population, culture, and national income inevitably resulted.

Every new institution promising even a little improvement was opposed as soon as it implied loss of rights and privileges. The rights of the privileged hindered the administration on every hand. The administration, manned by salaried servants only, in the face of open or secret opposition could not impose its will, and every effort to do so was merely a harmful waste of strength.

The value of many means capable of operating as a powerful lever in the state declined, since their possession was left to chance. The nobility thus remained in possession of almost everything which according to the usual view entails honor. It became indifferent to the means for deserving honor, and the power inherent in the means disappeared. Envy on the part of other status groups operated to isolate the nobility even more. The results have perhaps been especially painfully evident in the case of the military.

The results of the condition of the internal constitution, only briefly touched on here, would inevitably have led to the overthrow of the state as soon as the state engaged in war with another state whose constitution had produced exactly the opposite results, namely an increase of strength; and this will continue to be the case if the constitution is not reformed in such a way as to produce still greater power than can be achieved in other neighboring states.

The Present Situation ·

The situation today is differentiated from the immediate past described above only by the fact that the misfortune suffered by the Prussian state is recognized as the result of a defective constitution. This point is extremely important.

Misfortune itself has destroyed much that was harmful. The question is how to guard against its reappearance. Many persons have become more convinced through failure and will not only acquiesce in reform that they previously opposed but will even favor it. A large number dully despairs and will submit to anything that seems to provide a ray of hope. In this state of opinion the stronger and more enlightened will feel a double duty to be beneficially effective.

Even if the present situation in this respect is favorable, we need to act quickly, before the old order reestablishes itself, indifference takes control, and opposition awakens.

Proposals for Changing the Constitution

The general principle underlying reform of the constitution flows from the idea of the whole as the guiding principle.

General Principle

Everything that weakens the fullest use of the resources of the state and makes it difficult for humanity to achieve the highest ends must be abolished.

This principle makes it possible for the state to have an internal revolution and to reap the beneficial results of such a revolution without the painful convulsions of a self-generated revolution.

More Specific Proposals

PRELIMINARY PRINCIPLES HERE

Of the more specific proposals to achieve reform the following are preliminary:

1. We should not hesitate to recognize and loudly proclaim the need for reform of internal conditions and the institutional structure.

Not only does this forthrightness not disparage the cause, but it calls attention to it and creates confidence. Unrest is not provoked but rather is obviated. Expression itself forces one to have a clear idea of the subject, and this has irresistible drawing power.

2. Nothing in the constitution which has collapsed or has been weakened should be recognized further and protected. Whatever cannot stand upright by its own power must fall.

3. All the powers needed by the state which individuals have assumed and used for their own advantage to the disadvantage of the state should be seized for the state without further consideration or, even better, left to operate freely.

4. We must be firmly convinced that such a rebirth cannot occur without pain, that the pain is no reason for avoiding the matter but rather should be regarded as a challenge to lessen the pain by means of the policy adopted for carrying the matter through—insofar as it can be done without sacrificing the goal.

5. We should not only allow the better, stronger, unprejudiced view to arouse opinion but should be attentive to it and so further arouse such opinion. It will be hard at first to maintain even a few organs in favor of reform of the constitution, but as soon as we seek them seriously, we shall find them.

FURTHER EXPLANATION

In accordance with these principles and the principal idea the following measures are requisite.

Establishment of Greatest Possible Freedom and Equality for All Citizens in Their Relations with the State

All citizens must be given the greatest possible freedom and equality in their relationship to the state. By recognizing inequalities the state itself renounces the forces—which thereby are necessarily lost—that hold one part in subjection to another part.

The main rule of politics is, therefore, to decrease inequality by raising the oppressed, with as little pain as possible to the formerly privileged, and with as little destruction as possible. Reform should proceed gradually and evenly. Only where this is impossible and the entire existing structure deserves to be abhorred should the state act quickly to show clearly its disapproval. Then the following should be done:

a. Nobility

It would take too long to discuss the value and need of the nobility. Such an inquiry, even if it were only moderately thorough, would be very extensive. It can be expressed only in formulae. The point of view must necessarily change with the condition of the whole and the progress of the *Zeitgeist*, since everything in this world changes. This assertion suffices to answer affirmatively the question of whether the Prussian aristocracy must change with the whole. If the nobility accepts a constitution in which it acts in a way not harmful but useful to the commonwealth, no one will want it abolished. It is not by chance that the nobility exists, any more than is the case with any other part of the constitution. Any effort to do away with it without overwhelming conviction that it does not harmonize with the social body as a whole would only cause harm and not be feasible. France can serve as an example. Nor can we humiliate the nobility and depose it; for to do so would decrease one resource of the state. We must try to elevate and improve it so that it ceases to be a liability to the state and becomes a beneficial force.

Napoleon expresses himself at every opportunity about the need for the nobility, asserting that misfortune ensues wherever one is not attentive to it. Apart from the fact that he might wish to be misunderstood and to have the nobility remain as it is in countries which he hopes to conquer and so have it continue to oppress and cripple the body social, from what he has done in France and the countries he has conquered one can see the principle at work that the aristocracy must be made more useful to the whole and thereby elevated. Accordingly Napoleon has bestowed nobility or what amounts to the same thing only for merit. The fact that what Napoleon recognizes as merit is not what is ordinarily recognized as true merit is explained by the tendency to subordination. This tendency causes him to recognize as a merit any manifestation of power, even that in evil, if

only it is not directed against him or the state. Napoleon has therefore sought everywhere to abolish whatever might make the nobility harmful to the state, both in the case of the imperial knights
and in that of the provincial nobility. It is very important in this respect, as in all his dealings, to understand Napoleon correctly. If he
is to be overcome, it can be done only by surpassing his best and not
just by slavishly imitating the good in his work.

The principal former privileges of the Prussian nobility were as
follows:

(1) INHERITANCE OF THE POSITIONS WHICH CONFER HONOR

The nobility was born into both honor and the possession of all
those positions in the state which confer honor or at least according
to popular belief are connected with honor. All positions requiring a
sense of honor, as well as all positions needing distinguished education, fell to the aristocracy. Non-nobles as a rule were excluded from
these positions, and in the case of the nobility, noble birth was more
a requirement than was proof of ability.

Especially was this the case with positions for officers, with court
and ambassadorial positions, and for presidents and ministers.

The basis for this favoritism was said to be that only the nobility
actually possesses or possesses to special degree the sense of honor
proceeding from its training and from the palpable scorn felt for him
who lost the sense of honor. It was overlooked that these reasons are
in part mistaken and at most possessed validity only at a very remote
time, and that they would prove nothing but the harmful effects of an
aristocracy, because it could only be disadvantageous to have all
sense of honor concentrated in one class. The concept of honor was
entirely misunderstood and the so-called false *point d'honneur* substituted for it; it was not noticed that the denial to other social groups
of what confers honor stifles the sense of honor.

In recent times other reasons have been sought and asserted: the
exclusive possession by the nobility of presidential positions is a
holdover from the polity of estates and represents the position of
these estates; and the nobility must remain in possession of the officer
positions in order to provide for its more needy members. It is ob-

vious that the first reason is a specious one; survival from the past is
no reason for sparing an institution. Any one disposed to reflect more
or less clearly on human activity will feel that it is extremely harmful
to concede support to a significant status group making no effort—
not to mention that officers' posts furnish a meagre livelihood—especially if sinecures are not to be created out of certain positions.

Inheritance of positions of honor necessarily means that the true
concept of honor will be lost. It becomes anchored in purely for-
tuitous events rather than in true merit. Those who are excluded from
the possession of such positions and who cannot gain them by merit—
or at least only with difficulty and usually only by chance—acquire a
feeling of inferiority ruinous to their powers, or one of hate and
disdain which poisons every right attitude on their part.

If the aristocracy is not to be a burden, we must renounce this
antiquated method of ownership. The nobleman who acquires possession irrespective of birth will be all the more honored. His prestige will rise, and on the other hand the other groups will be relieved
of the pressure under which they have been suffering. A number of
forces will gain free play, to the advantage of the state, which thereby
is sure to gain in strength.

(2) EXCLUSIVE OWNERSHIP OF ESTATES

Formerly the nobility had almost exclusive ownership of the
knight's estate. Such an advantage could only be burdensome to the
whole body social. It put agriculture especially into the hands of a
class of citizens not qualified by any of their other relationships to
cultivate the soil. Owners of capital, which particularly could accomplish something significant, were excluded from acquiring such estates. An effort was made to lessen the pressure by means of exceptions and dispensations; but the exceptions resulted from arbitrariness and so made the pressure upon and the prejudice to the interests
of the whole still more striking.

As a basis for maintaining exclusive ownership nothing more was
adduced than that the estates must not be allowed to be the object
of commercial transaction—a phrase which, often as it has been used,
has no meaning at all, at least in our time. Perhaps formerly there

was a reason for assigning little value to the desire for profit and for regarding estates merely as a basis for the main purpose of their existence, that of enabling the owner to perform military service. This reason no longer is valid, and increasing speculation will benefit the entire nation. Another argument has even less basis, that we must provide for certain families through possession of estates. If ownership of these estates provides those families with means to gain privileges for themselves, one should not overlook the question of why one should force them to do so, particularly in view of the risk of their making no use of the means and of preventing others from using them.

The commonwealth, culture, patriotism—everything suffers because of this favoritism, even the nobility as owners of the estates. Lack of competition lowers the value of estates. Individuals are forced to lead a wretched existence because they are unable advantageously to be rid of estates which they cannot maintain. With their property they are unable to undertake what their talents demand. The nobility as a result of being favored in this way is especially excluded from bourgeois enterprises, leases of the crown lands, etc. Thus there is nothing to do but to abolish all privileges and restrictions.

(3) COLLECTIVE VOICE OF THE NOBILITY

Even if the nobility as such has had no special voice in affairs of state, it had one as exclusive owners of estates to which such power adhered.

This power disappears as soon as the advantage described in (2) is abolished. The voice is then that of those who have the requisites for owning an estate, as a rule those who have known how to acquire or maintain an estate.

(4) FREEDOM FROM TAXATION OF THE NOBILITY

The nobility has exemption from many state taxes, especially from the land tax. Formerly there was a reason for this; the nobility did something in return. This reason has disappeared now that the nobility as such no longer does special service for the state. It must give up this privilege, a privilege that weakens the state and arouses envy and opposition. In order for the present nobility not to suffer too much as estate owners, the change must occur everywhere, and this can best be achieved by means of a new tax register. By following a simple principle, this can easily be drawn up. Then any reason for complaints about the burden will be obviated. The tax will at the same time cover an important part of the increased needs of the state. It will accrue to the honor of the nobility to make the sacrifice of a significant right. The value of its estates will suffer by the tax payment, but not so much as seems the case at first, if the reform is general and the competition of buyers is increased by means of other suggested measures and the estate owner gains freedom to use his land as he sees fit, unhampered by pointless state regulations.

(5) PRIVILEGED JUDICIAL POSITION AND JURISDICTION

The nobility has up to the present time possessed the advantage of a privileged judicial position and of patrimonial jurisdiction. It loses the latter with the exclusive ownership of the estates. There is no doubt that this jurisdiction no longer conforms to our age and results in a great deal of harm. In the meantime, abolition of these jurisdictional rights belongs to another investigation.

The privileged judicial position of the nobility is of no especial harm. It is often burdensome to the nobles themselves because of higher costs; however, an external advantage in public prestige attaches to it, and such advantage ought not to be touched so long as it does not injure society as a whole, and so long as the nobility is not completely abolished.

(6) PRIVILEGES OF THE OLD NOBILITY IN FOUNDATIONS, ORDERS, ETC.

The old nobility possesses here and there special privileges in foundations, orders, etc. These may be family foundations, which deserve some consideration. The spirit of our age is not favorable to orders, endowments, etc., gained incidentally by chance. If these are the result of chance, the nobility can no longer claim them without disadvantage to itself. We shall discuss further below what should be done with these endowments for the good of the whole. The difference between old and new nobility is no longer appropriate to the true concept of aristocracy.

In accordance with the foregoing proposals, by means of a new constitution most of the exclusive privileges would be withdrawn from the nobility.

The nobility in the future would designate merely a status group upon which the state would make special demands that it distinguish itself. This trust placed by the state in the nobility is honor enough to insure it great general confidence and hence to make it much easier for each member of the group to achieve distinction. Thus the nobility will be elevated and, by the abolition of all pressure, the other social groups will be raised as well; the state hereby gains strength.

The state would leave the nobility the privileged position inherent in its title and traditional forms. It would give the nobility honor and increased prestige in that it recognized by ennoblement only outstanding merit on the part of other social groups and never conferred nobility without outstanding merit. Conferring of this honor would be a public recognition of the merit of whoever received the patent of nobility and would be regarded as an incentive to his successors. On the other hand, the state would never again regard mere possession of noble title as a merit, or grant preference to a nobleman merely as nobleman. Merit must be open to those without title of nobility in all positions of distinction, and noble title should be given only for distinguished service. Each dishonorable action, especially one noticeably harmful to the state, must entail loss of noble title, and this loss must extend to all descendants. The stricter the state becomes in giving and withholding noble title, the more respect the nobility will gain. At least the constitution will take a great step forward, and one can wait for further change until the *Zeitgeist* demands it. If the nobility cannot immediately become as beneficial as it once was, the blame lies not so much in the constitution as in the changing times. At least it will not be a burden and, even if it be only a prejudice, it will be as useful as possible.

b. The Burgher Class

The townspeople *[Bürgerstand]* in Prussia have disproportionately fewer privileges than the nobility. By means of expected reforms in the nobility they will obtain a much larger field of activity for their abilities. They must renounce all that they have previously possessed exclusively and allow the nobility middle-class means of support, leases of crown lands, etc. By means of privileges the townsmen oppress the rural population. This is especially the case because of their monopoly of trade and commerce. This onerous right must cease. One must destroy within this entire social group the idea that an individual, because by chance he belongs to the group, can demand sacrifice from other groups in order to spare himself exertion. The forces of the oppressed groups and of the townsmen themselves in this way will be freed for the good of the state.

Peasantry

Of all status groups the peasantry is the one which has possessed no privileges at all, the one upon which all burdens have been placed, and the one which for the most part has lacked personal freedom.

One can hardly believe that in a state like Prussia such survivals of the crudest barbarism as serfdom have endured.

This personal slavery which makes things out of human beings, the difficulties of owning property, the hindrances to moving from one social group to another have brought endless harm to the state and prevented the development of the nation. The very group which is physically strongest, which especially needs more humane training, and which has furnished the chief strength of the state has been thereby most shamefully stunted. The slave has no interest in the state. The destruction of his lord seems the best thing that can happen to him. Glowing hatred of his lord and the lord's social group is better than complete apathy. Only an especially good lord—an unpredictable phenomenon—can make bearable the position of the serf and keep him good and human. The state can never count on this. It is unbelievable that we have not seen this long ago and acted vigorously. Only the small hope which the Emperor Napoleon himself could have had of pressing forward rapidly into the regions where serfdom is still more oppressive may have prevented him from exploiting the feeling which this condition must arouse. In Courland he spread propaganda among the oppressed peasants, so that they declared that they were sure that he came only to free them from their lords.

One cannot adduce a single valid reason for maintaining this shameful blot upon the constitution. That the oppression is insignificant, as is argued, is not true and is only another reason for destroying the shameful idea that it can exist. The excuse that the serfs themselves do not want abolition is too weak to deserve further mention. No one who knows the regions where emancipation has taken place believes that there is any danger to be feared from the freed peasants. The harm that the lord may suffer, even if harm could be proved, deserves no notice when it is a matter of exercising justice and restoring natural freedom. The lord who has made moderate use of his rights will not suffer, and one who has been cruel and harsh deserves punishment. Once they are free, those peasants who cannot easily leave the country or can go only to distant parts will seek out the better lords, who can thereby be all the more effective agriculturalists.

Undoubtedly the most important matter at hand is immediately to abolish serfdom and all that goes with it. The more simply this is done, the more easily it will proceed. Formerly those who wanted to prevent emancipation used the artifice of coupling it with a mass of other matters completely unrelated to it.

The acquisition of property, a simpler list of feudal services, etc., will all come of themselves according to need as soon as human beings are free to have an interest in them. The state wins all of these persons who are released from serfdom; formerly they belonged not to the state but to the lord.

Union of the Nation with the Administration of the State

If through the constitution a nation rather than a mere collection of opposing social groups is to be made possible, it is important that we bind this nation more closely to the state administration—if the state expects to use and lead the forces of the nation.

Originally the status groups supposedly constituted this bond. Estates sufficed as long as internal and external relations were simple. Little education, almost nothing but common sense, experience, and uprightness, sufficed to furnish the state administration with advice and action; but as soon as affairs of state grew complicated, the situation changed. The estates could no longer compass the whole and soon formed a burdensome opposition. The rulers sought to exclude them from all affairs, and they allowed themselves to be excluded if their own interests were not disturbed. For this purpose each status group tried always to maintain a voice for itself. Thus administration fell entirely into the hands of paid servants, and the nation heard little or nothing more of the condition of affairs.

The situation discussed above resulted. Lack of participation, opposition, and a false view of things inevitably weakened the social forces and public confidence.

It would be quite wrong to try to restore the estates in their old form, and not all the estates had the right of representation. They are moved by a feeling of caste, if they still have any energy, and are not suited to be a bond between government and nation. They do not have sufficient education and experience in the very complicated affairs of state administration to be able to advise and act in these matters and to grasp their spirit. It would make the whole too unwieldy if one tried to instruct them about everything.

In order to give the nation more participation in administration, and so to rescue this administration from the death which is sooner or later inevitable if it is left entirely in the hands of paid servants, there is no other way but to incorporate some kind of national representation into the constitution. We can give here only a few of the main lines of the plan; for a draft would be too detailed.

It seems advisable to let the constitution begin from below. For this purpose:

a. Community affairs should be freed from the interference of state officials. In recent times the communities for the most part have held only the shadow of power over their own affairs. If more were left to them and care taken that they had an appropriate constitution, they would assume responsibility for many public matters which now burden the state administration and are badly executed or directed by paid officials. Many general matters of the provincial administration would gain hereby.

b. If this step is taken, it will be easy to elect representatives of these communities to be attached to the administering agencies. Wherever a division occurs according to counties, it will be useful to attach such representatives to the agency presiding over the county. From them the representatives to the provincial government can be chosen, and, finally, from the representatives attached to the several provincial boards, representatives can be chosen to aid the highest council attached to the king.

c. The choice should not be by estates, since this method would preserve caste feeling. These representatives are not to represent the interests of their electors but their share in the entire state administration. This is their essential difference from the provincial estates.

d. The representatives would receive from their electors not instructions but merely authority. Not the more limited view of the voters on the lower level must be effective in administration, but the wider outlook of the more distinguished elected persons with a higher standpoint from which they can overlook the whole.

e. The state should determine exactly the qualifications of the electors. These representatives should not be mistrained in long activity but have merely the education required for the position in which they are placed. A county representative does not need a wide knowledge of state economy; in the case of provincial representatives, this is more important, and in the case of the higher representatives, it is still more indispensable.

One need not be anxious about the evidence of qualification. Once the matter is under way, the necessary knowledge will be more widespread and a good choice will be possible. The very interests of the voters demand conscientiousness, and the royal officials, once they have comprehended the matter, will influence the elections.

f. The business should be transacted by the elected without pay. This must be a matter of honor or it will become a subject of common speculation. Provision for public distinction for these representatives is not inconsequential, but it is not difficult. So that no one can refuse the position and always takes care to deserve the confidence placed in him, it will be advisable to have them newly elected to their positions after a few years, perhaps every five or six years.

g. The number of representatives should be determined by the size of the provinces. It must not be too large to make the whole body unwieldy but not so small as to make it weak.

h. The purpose and task of the representatives would be twofold:

(1) to advise the board with which they work, to be exactly informed about the ideas of the administration, and in case of need, to be able to speak out with and alongside the paid officials;

(2) to inform those whom they represent about the ideas of the administration, to lead opinion when necessary, and to promote execution; also to lead in community affairs in accordance with the superior insight into things which they have gained.

The main gain remains that of linking the nation with the administration and thus assuring the latter its full strength. If this constitution is chosen, we can advance more forcefully against the caste spirit, which will soon perish of itself.

It is to be hoped that when this matter is undertaken it will be undertaken in a large way. The needs of the state should be determined in an annual budget, this truthfully compared with the foregoing year's accounts, and the provinces, counties, and communities must then be left to decide what they wish to raise toward meeting local expenses, in which everything should be included incidental to the special welfare of each. The state would take only general notice of this and lend a hand with advice. Then one or more representatives, depending upon need as determined by the constitution, must be drawn into affairs at the royal level. The benefit from this entire reform would be very great and would arouse confidence at home and abroad, certainly doubling the strength of the state. Especially would this innovation be important at the present moment. The idea should be made known as soon as possible, and at the same time a suitable provision be made for the first action, if need be, through choice by the king. All this could be easily effected.

Freest Possible Use of the Powers of Subjects of All Classes

Up to now a number of restrictions have existed hindering subjects of all classes in Prussia in the freest possible use of their powers. Hardly a state limits industry and the advance of national welfare more than does the Prussian state. Not only are the barriers which arose everywhere in the past maintained; but their number has greatly increased by means of an artificial system resting on an entirely false basis. The harm done the state, hampered in this way in reaching its full power, is difficult to estimate. Now when the state must double its strength, if it wishes to act resolutely again and preserve its independence, it is doubly important to reform this harmful condition. Much belongs to and must be accomplished through the administration; in part, however, the measures affect the constitution itself; in part, it is advisable to give them more weight by raising them to the status of basic law. If suddenly unreason were again to secure control, administrative measures could be more easily disregarded than such laws.

We must make a general constitutional law and publicly announce:

a. SIMPLIFIED OWNERSHIP AND USE OF LAND

This measure will provide that every citizen of the state may be able without restriction to acquire ownership of any piece of land and to have free use of it so long as it does not injure a third party, and that to this end all restrictions on free use not expressly confirmed may be regarded as abolished.

It is clear that anyone who wishes to buy land must assume all the obligations resting upon it. In case of doubt a judge must determine how far the rights of a third party may be injured by free use.

The measure will evoke endless activity, especially in agriculture. Anyone who has the means and special desire for and love of it will buy land, instead of as now when one person has an estate, another the capital and knowledge, or one of the two, but no land. All the undesirable results attributed to such complete freedom are largely fantasies, conceived by narrow-minded administration or by officials trying to make themselves important. Possible disadvantages would be compensated for by far greater advantages.

More widespread distribution of landed property and better use of it would be the first benefits. Anxiety lest undesirable speculation cause confusion is completely unfounded, since the balance corrects itself. The example of individuals successful in their speculations will lead to imitation. Fear that in case of absolutely free competition production of one or another commodity, wood, for example, would be inadequate can be supported neither by experience nor by scientific law, once one regards the matter in the large and reckons as gain only what makes most profit and does not consider as loss the failure of a productive enterprise or manufacture which is unprofitable.

If it should appear dangerous to pass from a condition of extreme control to one of extreme freedom all at once—a matter which ultimately is to be regarded according to the rules of politics—still the principle should be recognized at once. But actually no real disadvantage is to be expected if freedom is allowed all at once without any let or hindrance. The competition of those who wish to use it limits the possibility of too great speed. Each restriction is dubious, and the entire purpose will be missed if one cannot count on the officials' having the correct point of view.

The present moment is superbly suited to establishing basic principles. In view of the greater competition among purchasers of land and the possibility of exploiting land to a better advantage, opportunity will be given those harmed by the war to recover from the damage in various ways, and our economy will not be retarded by lack of persons and capital.

b. Free Use of Personal Abilities

Just as important and perhaps more important is that everyone gain the freest possible use of his personal forces—his capital, his hands, and his head—insofar as it does not harm a third party.

Up to now we have proceeded with incredible anxiety in this regard, and it will be difficult to put the principle into practice at once without reservation. If the principle is to be made effective in its entirety, many monopolies, the entire guild system, all compulsory services of individuals, and various establishments in the state must first be abolished. But in the meantime the announcement of the principle will gain much. We must state especially that:

(1) Anyone may operate a non-guild or non-monopoly business and may operate more than one at the same time. Often one business supports the other and supplements the time or ability that the other leaves unused. The timid differentiation between town and country must cease and to this end tax equality be introduced.

(2) All rates of payment and day-wage arrangements must be abolished, insofar as the work is not left to a guild. Competition decides the price as soon as it is not determined by monopolies, guilds, etc., and competition alone can determine that no unremunerative labor is performed. Excessive rates and wages can cause work to be unprofitable and also waste energy, thus harming the general welfare.

(3) No more monopolies should be granted, with the exception of the use of a new invention for a period of years. All existing monopolies must be held to the strictest observance of their obligations. If this is seriously done, owners will voluntarily renounce their monopolies. If they do not, their claim to compensation, in case of monopoly is to be abolished with compensation, will be much decreased in accordance with the above procedure. Each owner of a monopoly should lose it if another undertakes to perform the work and to do so without the right of a monopoly.

(4) We must abolish the entire guild system as harmful to industry and the state. . . .

Guilds are harmful. They no longer belong in our age. Once they were necessary to our entire social structure, when in view of the weak protection by the state private associations were needed to operate a trade in safety. But they are now harmful in every respect. In order to pursue a trade everyone must sacrifice more time and capital than are actually demanded. This makes labor expensive. The entire guild system is disadvantageous to the training of the worker because he is taught according to old routines. By preventing division of labor, limiting the number of helpers, and complicating the transition from an unprofitable trade to a more profitable one, the guild makes work more difficult than need be. The clever worker is held down and the less clever one favored, because no one can dismiss his own men. These are only some of the arguments against guilds. A closer investigation only shows everything against them and nothing in their favor. Experience indicates that they can be dispensed with; everywhere it is regarded as the greatest gain when labor is used in the factory way; that is, free of guilds.

One cannot deny that even if we keep guilds various measures can be taken to do away with many of the disadvantages; but still this is only a half-measure. If a significant step is to be taken toward giving the nation the most advantageous free use of its forces, the guild system must be abolished. A special edict must define details. Here are only a few provisions:

(1) All guilds must be abolished as soon as possible, no new guild be formed, and every guild be allowed to dissolve itself and to work in freedom. Those which wish to remain must gradually expire; no new masters will be created; instead, free workers must be taken on. Taking on of apprentices must cease, and that of journeymen cease with the death of the masters.

(2) Immediately all regulations in the guild system must be abolished which originate with the government and which would be eliminated without the guild's so far having had any right of opposition.

(3) The state must preserve the right, in case the guild members demand some compensation for abolition of a guild, to proceed to dissolution against their consent. In many cases the consequence of freeing these will be compensated without sacrifice of the state through increased income.

Finally,

(4) The state would have to announce the principle that compulsory services can be bought off, and in fact as soon as the owner received compensation for the provable latest return from the compulsory services due him.

Everything further can be easily worked out. The present moment is favorable for stating these principles. Many persons have lost their usual livelihood. They lack capital to begin anew. It will benefit them to be able easily to undertake another trade. By means of the entire system, labor, which has been unfree, will be replaced by free labor.

Suppression of All Inducements to Laziness and Abolition of the Outmoded

The foregoing proposals will largely do away with injurious means that encourage laziness. This includes everything which assures the preservation of a good life for the individual in idleness. We have already referred to exclusive ownership of property, forced labor, guilds, and monopolies.

Abolition or reorganization of foundations should be included. These and the knightly orders no longer are appropriate to our age. Without injustice toward the present incumbents the state will, by compensation, be able to dispose of them so that they receive recompense for services or it will become a refuge and boarding place for those who deserve it. At this moment when the state has so great need of many resources, not only for creating new power but for reducing misery, this matter deserves close attention. It is enough at first to accept and proclaim the principle.

MEANS OF BUILDING A NATION

All the foregoing proposals aim toward forming a nation in the Prussian state. In the proposals themselves lie the best means of realizing the aim. The following measures can help:

a. We should not attempt to erase provincial character but retain it and give it a direction beneficial to society as a whole; especially let us preserve the characteristics of each province, the result of its position and cultural history, not try to force the province suited to trade into being a manufacturing nation, etc. A struggle against national character is usually a vain waste of strength, resulting merely in a harmful veneer. This was the mistake in South Prussia, and in other provinces too there has been too much indifference about this matter. In the Litau region much could have been done by careful consideration of national character. When one leaves the national character untouched and only refines it, he preserves the entire force intact and can employ it for the general good. Just now when South Prussia and New East Prussia are gone, this matter is not so important; but the occasion can recur, and it deserves attention in the case of the remaining provinces.

b. National festivals and so on could be effective. We cannot try to imitate the miserable amusements used to entertain the Parisians and other mobs. National festivals will grow of themselves and assume the correct character once popular representation is introduced. Elections, public accountability, the formation of corps of burghers and peasants will bring many people together. These assemblies are important. Things thus harmonize more fully, and provincial and local jealousies decrease. It will be easy to choose days on which a religious festival can be celebrated at the same time, thus lending the assembly solemnity, dignity, and decorum.

Less important means will occur of themselves with a more detailed execution of the plan.

The foregoing will suffice temporarily to build a nation and to guide its united strength for the good of the state. Unless this is the case and absolutely the case, nothing will function well, and a miserable existence at best can be continued. Not to effect the highest good of the state because of prejudice, inertia, or restrictions, but to retain the old means, will bring about the decline of the state, no matter how one cloaks the limited tendency. Not to act vigorously without delay is in effect to ignore the matter entirely. It is foolish to make the excuse that the state is lacking in manpower for the task. Men will be found as soon as the idea is correctly grasped, and no sacrifice will be too great to put it into effect.

2. The Defense of the Old Régime

Friedrich August von der Marwitz: *The Last Resolution of the Estates of the County of Lebus to the King, to Which the Counties of Beeskow and Storkow Assented* (May 9, 1811)[*]

The resolution of the estates of the three counties of Prussia was drafted by the Junker army officer, estate-owner, and member of a large and influential family, Friedrich August von der Marwitz. Marwitz denounced the reforms that in an effort to revive the country after defeat by Napoleon at Jena in 1806 were being advocated and even executed in Prussia. One of the main objects of his indictment was peasant emancipation, which he thought threatened to undermine the Old Régime. The reader should note the many assumptions made by Marwitz about conditions, assumptions which the reformers refused to accept, as well as the problems evoked by Prussia's defeat but ignored by him. Marwitz argued in a way that he hoped would best defend the Old Régime against critics; in fact he sought to enhance the power of the nobility at the expense of the absolute monarch, and thereby to return to conditions of over a century and a half earlier. The point of view and the kind of argument that he employed were to be used throughout the century by conservatives in every crisis and in every country, in order to oppose institutional change.

The criticism by Chancellor von Hardenberg expresses the reactions of the most influential of the Prussian reformers to the Junkers' protest.

---

[*] Friedrich Meusel, ed., *Friedrich August von der Marwitz* (Berlin: Ernst Siegfried Mittler und Sohn, 1913), II, 2, 3-22.

Most Serene and Mighty King, Most Gracious King and Lord!

In deep distress we the undersigned estates of the counties of Lebus, Storkow, and Beeskow once again approach the throne of Your Royal Majesty to implore a gracious hearing.

We had a constitution which was suited to the times which had shaped it; we had a succession of wise and benevolent rulers during a series of years of happiness and prosperity. We gave ourselves to their wise and benevolent leadership with unlimited trust; and there was no occasion for the forms of our constitution to assume prominence, for the reason that nobody needed them for the preservation of his happiness and prosperity as a citizen. Indeed, they probably would have been entirely forgotten had not these rulers themselves — inclined far more by their own well-meaning motives than by our voice—had they not taken them into consideration on all occasions where measures were to be taken that affected our privileges. This happened in particular recently with the change in collecting the beer tax in the cities, with the introduction of the credit system for the nobles, with criticism of the universal civil code, and with

Perhaps to those times of past centuries, but not to those of the present, which are so very different—not to the times of the Prussian Kingdom!

For more than a century the Prussian rulers would also not have permitted this revival of antiquated, outmoded forms.

This has absolutely no basis in fact. Although the estates were asked for their opinion when the rulers thought it proper in connection with new laws and arrangements, this certainly did not happen in the most important instances, especially in the case of taxation. Were they consulted by King Frederick II when he introduced the system of *accise* taxes? Were they consulted by the kings who were his predecessors and successors, in many other circumstances? Even now the opinion of the estates and of judicious men still is requested where it is useful and necessary.

This is true of few of the undersigned and is out of place here.

It was bad enough.

That is, now unjust and unwise?

the regulation of the affairs of the country's poor.

But even in regard to these arrangements, no significant discussions could take place, since they were just and wise. We acquiesced each time with pleasure in the proposals of the government, and lived thus quietly under a benevolent guardianship. Suddenly we were released from this guardianship.

In the most unholy of all wars, when our province first came into the hands of the enemy and when the administrative authorities of Your Royal Majesty no longer could function, responsibility for satisfying the demands of the enemy fell upon *us*.

While we were thus assembled, either in person or through our sons and brothers, under the banner of Your Royal Majesty in the farthest province, we were obligated to carry on the affairs of all of us here. It is no wonder that under these circumstances and considering that this was our first public action (comparable to the precipitous actions of a minor suddenly deprived of tutelage) we did not act with the greatest possible success. Nevertheless we can claim that at the sacrifice of our possessions we preserved the property of Your Royal Majesty. We rejected the proposal of the

What? At the sacrifice of your possessions? You suffered from the war and suffer still from the burden of the times. You involved the province in great indebtedness, but when did you sacrifice your property? That which was paid by you in the levy, and in which the so-called contributive estate did not escape, was not so large. The sacrifices of Prussia and Silesia were quite different.

Who then is now paying the contribution? The estates of the Kurmark? Is it not taken from the royal domains, from ecclesiastical properties? Not from taxes, which affect everybody?

The governmental officials assert the opposite.

enemy for the mortgage and sale of the royal domains and instead transferred the burden to the contribution.[1] Indeed, not once did we take advantage of the proposals of the Royal Personal Commission to mortgage the royal lands by loans, after the example of Silesia.

The province was plunged into enormous indebtedness through payments which for the most part, as we long ago demonstrated, are merely advances for the state and for the other provinces; we did not however, contract the payments on our own initiative but did so through the authority of the Kurmark[2] administration, which assured our plenipotentiaries that all extraordinary demands would be deducted from the contribution to France, that accordingly by means of approval of them and acceptance of contracts, which we had rejected up to then, money would remain in the country.

This promise was *not* kept: *thence* stems the burden of debt of the Kurmark.

Following the evacuation of the land and the happy return of Your Royal Majesty, the emergency necessitated recognition of our consti-

[1] The contribution was a tax for military purposes paid by some nobles but mainly by the peasants.

[2] The word "Kurmark" refers to the Electorate of the Mark or administrative district Brandenburg.

This guarantee, about which so much noise is made, is no sacrifice at all, since domains have been made redeemable in return for it; and the estates of the Kurmark in particular have distinguished themselves by causing difficulty and continue to distinguish themselves in this manner.

Where are these sacrifices? Where is this renunciation? If the undersigned were convinced of both, this bombastic remonstrance would have been left unmade.

tution. We were brought together in an assembly to assume a guarantee of twelve millions in mortgages and obligations and to annul the old Kurmark statute (Landtag Declaration of 1602, Article 25, and the Compact of 1653, Article 15) concerning inalienability of the royal domains. We did so with pleasure, and later reported *also* on *our* need and asked for help. We have continued doing· so for two years but have received only occasional promises and often no answer whatsoever. Only during the past year has our committee received some temporary help, which we thankfully acknowledge; the settlement of the whole affair is still remote, although new needs on the part of the state are continually made known to us.

We have borne everything at the sacrifice of our property and with the renunciation of our vested rights, in the hope finally of receiving satisfaction through Your Royal Majesty's love of justice and in the conviction that during these times pecuniary sacrifices are unavoidable, that, however, nothing is lost as long as the laws of the land, its particular characteristics, and the sanctity of contracts are preserved. In this hope and conviction we were strengthened when during the past

You have striven precisely against this tendency. The administration cannot work wonders.

The true source of evil then supposedly lies in the fact that ancient prejudices and exemptions of a small number of citizens have not been honored.

The comparison with England is not at all relevant. England remained sound by quite different means. How foolish it is to assert that the prosperity of Prussia could have been assured by a constitution which several proud and prejudice-filled country Junkers wished to call out of antiquity.

How wrong that Austria has survived on this account. And is the financial condition of Austria to be envied?

How does this apply to us?

summer with the change in the ministry it was made known that henceforth all existing evils were to be thoroughly remedied.

The distress that we had experienced and that we saw in neighboring provinces had called our attention to the true source of this evil, and we believe that we know it. We did not doubt that the cure would go to the root of the evil.

We had observed that it is not temporary conquest which annihilates states but the acceptance of foreign laws and customs. We had seen that among all the states of Europe only one resisted the current, the one which most faithfully kept itself aloof from foreign influence. Even the often-defeated Austria always recovered because it remained true to its own customs and did not dissolve the ties uniting its princes with the people. We had also observed, however, that those states which were forced to assume the yoke of foreign laws, thus abandoning their own point of view and that of each individual toward his own situation in order to enter into a foreign one, were completely annihilated and sank into a vast, fermenting mass of ruin. From this moment on they were no longer Germans but Frenchmen. *We* were almost the only ones whom this bitter cup passed by. We called ourselves fortunate; the state of external co- ercion was past, and still no one *vol- untarily* had drunk this cup. We be- lieve that the real difference of the foreign point of view, hence the idea from which foreign laws pro- ceed, from that of our province [*Land*] must lie *in this:* that for- eigners always consider only *the present moment,* and since they re- gard neither the past nor the future, they always find ample means with which to achieve immediate ends. If then some old law stands in their way, it is overthrown and for the situation in question a new one is created, and within a short time this one must give way to another. If any local constitution is a hindrance to them, forthwith a new one is cre- ated, only in its turn to share the same fate. Since nothing is more of a hindrance to them than the loyal- ty of the people *to their laws and constitutions,* it is quite natural that their foremost aim is to destroy this loyalty.

For their success in this nothing is better than to have the rulers, laws, and constitutions in the sub- jugated territories [*Länder*] *changed as often as possible.* There- by they destroy all attachment to the king and his writ and selfishly leave the people with the conviction

Precisely because the govern- ment dare not consider merely the present moment but must take notice of the past and the future, it is necessary to correct the defects of the past and to construct an edifice for the fu- ture.

Do the great majority of the people inquire whether they are devoted to the previous consti- tution of the estates, whether they see in it their salvation?— Much less to that which you are attempting to derive from an- tiquity and completely altered circumstances.

that they must in every case submit to *the immediate authority.* This kind of practice accordingly is devised strictly for the convenience of the rulers; the well-being of the ruled is not considered. In order to maintain it continuously, however, it is necessary that the subjects tremble before the power of the actual rulers, for since love is out of the question, it follows naturally that should fear once forsake them, they will no longer obey but will destroy the state.

In our fortunate country the point of view animating the laws and the will of our princes was entirely different. In addition to the present it always took into consideration the past and future—i.e., changes in the existing conditions were undertaken *only by legal procedure* and established thereby in such a way that *our descendants* could live just as happily under our institutions *as we* did under those of our ancestors.

In this form our state was comparable to a large family; the father enjoyed the fullest trust of all members of the family, and everybody strove to establish as well the prosperity of the house for his descendants. Those states [which abandon their laws and customs], on the other hand, appear to us to be *simi-*

lar to an Indian plantation where the slaves are driven to work and *where the master, despite his great power, cannot sleep for a moment in peace.*[3]

We called ourselves fortunate that foreign principles had found no entrance into our country and believed that under other conditions the loss of external power and greatness would be easily replaced as long as we remained true only to *our* principles and strengthened ourselves further in them.

It seemed to us, furthermore, that the financial need which oppressed us, as already mentioned, for the most part arose out of our ignorance of public affairs, that the local officials suddenly left us to ourselves at the most difficult moment; that the *moral deficiency* — we cannot deny it — which oppressed our estate, namely the lack of patriotism and self-denial evident in many individuals, was to be attributed solely to the divorce of the individual from the state. It seemed to us as if the state had not revealed itself sufficiently to its citizens and, although the government was conducted wisely and in conformity with the law, as if it were not made sufficiently clear to the citizen that the state and he were one and the same

---

The comparison with an Indian plantation is more applicable to many lords of the manor and their hereditary serfs.

It is not foreign principles which have made headway with us, but those which are better, more just, by which the welfare of all citizens, not merely of one social group, is intended; and through whose constant observance the loss of power and greatness can under changed conditions alone be replaced.

This admission of ignorance and lack of patriotism and self-denial unfortunately applies also to the present all too well. And yet you want to be co-rulers with your King!

When has the state revealed itself most to its citizens? During the times which you prize or now? Where this has not taken place completely, political obstacles have stood in the way.

---

[3] The words in this sentence were underscored by Frederick William III.

thing. It was rather as if he were merely confronted with the state, or as if the state were to him an alien thing to which he had only to pay money and which thereafter took care of itself.

We hoped, therefore, that the promised cure for our ills would effect that:

1. The state and its citizens would be more closely connected, and the image of the large family be expressed more completely.

2. The financial need would be permanently remedied.

We felt obligated to cooperate toward these great ends insofar as we could; and, since a slavish maintenance of the existing constitution could endanger the first, and a literal insistence upon our freedom from taxation as sanctioned by sacred contracts the second one, we seized every opportunity open to us to declare:

that we were ready to make the necessary sacrifice of our personal as well as our property rights for the sake of the state.

We held ourselves all the more obligated to make this declaration of our views in that we assumed that the more deeply the government was convinced of the truth of the above principles the more doubts it would have about disturb-

But who are the citizens of the state? Certainly not merely the landed nobility?

This is the government's entire objective, and you are working against it.

If these are not merely empty words, then trust your King and obey his ordinances, which you so bitterly censure.

ing the fundamental laws of the state fortified by the most sacred contracts and *by the royal pledge of our monarchs;* that the more it should be recognized,

that without the foreknowledge of the Estates of the country and our advice and consent in affairs concerning the prosperity or ruin of the land nothing shall be concluded or undertaken:[4]

it should be all the more agreeable for the government to learn that we were ready to acquiesce beforehand in every necessary arrangement and change—that consequently it would be easy for it to place the stamp of legality upon all these arrangements, and thereby to make its work just as secure against future harm as it was safe in the past up to now.

What kind of interpretation then should be given to this position, and what will be the consequences? Certainly none other than that which it received under the Great Elector, during whose reign it arose, and maintained under all his successors? In which cases did all of these rulers restrict their decisions and measures to the foreknowledge, advice, and consent of the estates?

We learned from the Edict of October 28[5] that all this was only a dream and that henceforth the state would be governed by those foreign principles, that in fact the old Brandenburg-Prussian state was to be dissolved, since:

1. The ancient constitution of the estates was in effect discarded with the disregarding of their right to give advice and consent, hence robbing the countryside and the towns

This disrespectful utterance regarding ordinances of Your Majesty the King deserves the sharpest reprimand.

---

[4] From the *Landtags-Rezess* of 1653, Par. 14.
[5] The Peasant Emancipation Edict of 1807.

This was not a reproach against them in the Edict, but was only a reference to the fact that people make this reproach against them; and can this in fact be denied?

That no useful purpose could be achieved with the existing provincial estates and through individual discussions with them undoubtedly is apparent to every reasonable person. Think only of provincial egoism, of the jealousy of one province toward the others, etc.

Therein lies the reason for abolishing exemptions and privileges! Here the above-lauded patriotism, here the extolled self-denial should be applied! Moreover, the changes in legislation and taxation should prevent the very revolution which might arise with continued oppression of the masses and exemption of a few privileged persons.

of their former and consequently of their legitimate representation.—Indeed, the nobility, notwithstanding the praiseworthy recognition in the introduction of the Edict of the help given in assuring the contribution [to the French], was even publicly reproached in the course of the Edict with having avoided public burdens at the expense of their fellow subjects. Later it was declared by the state chancellor during a festive occasion and published in all the newspapers: "A conference with the existing provincial estates could serve no useful purpose." We must regretfully add that hereby seeds of mistrust and dissension have been sown by the Throne instead of the bond of union that we had hoped to gain.

2. Through this Edict all exemptions and privileges, not merely those presented as gifts but *original contractual* ones *sanctioned by the royal pledge,* and with them the existing fundamental laws of the state, the sanctity of contracts and of the royal pledge, consequently the basic principles by which we have hitherto lived and been ruled, all have been destroyed with one stroke of the pen; and precisely in this way those foreign principles of despotism and ruin have been introduced into this land, and

have begun to revolutionize it.

For although we could expect from the generous and fatherly intentions of Your Royal Majesty the greatest possible alleviation of the present financial distress and the greatest possible consideration respecting *the application* of these principles, it is the principles themselves which are important. Once the laws have been violated and the *dangerous* excuse that *the pressure of the moment justifies everything* has been allowed, then the successors of Your Royal Majesty and their ministers will make the same appeal and will sanction thereby every encroachment upon property, until finally popular respect for the law will likewise disappear, and the people will wield power as quickly as they are able to acquire it.

Although, furthermore, a new representation has been promised to the people as a substitute for that which has been lost, even this cannot help; for the important thing is not representation in general but representation *according to the law*.

A representation by gift is no representation; for it can be *taken away* as it was given, and no one will believe himself represented by it.

It will likewise happen that once the door has been opened to such experiments in general, every new

---

In Upper Silesia we witnessed a short time ago a situation in which the people wielded power against oppression by the nobles. This will not take place against a government which justly considers and promotes the well-being of all.

That is, then, a representation as desired and proposed by the landed nobility?

These utterances are highly improper and punishable in a remonstrance to the King!

Such expressions!

It dare not be satisfactory.

This refers to the poor-relief treasury of the country. Was this then the property of the estates? The facts of the case have been laid before His Majesty the King.

minister or ruler will believe himself called upon to issue a new constitution *of his own,* in part to show that he understands as well or even more fully what his predecessors understood, in part to win favor with those who were dissatisfied with his predecessors and their innovations. And so there will come into vogue even with us that pernicious change of institutions and constitutions which will alienate from the state completely and absolutely the feelings of the people and make momentary possession the prime desideratum.

We have sought every legal means to check the introduction of these disastrous principles; we have been listened to occasionally but *never* received a satisfactory answer. In one special case, where *in accordance with the same*[6] we *were actually robbed of our property,*[7] we went directly to the sacred person of Your Royal Majesty. We received no satisfaction. Through our deputies we asked for a personal audience, in order to make clear our complaints and at the same time our willingness to adjust ourselves to exigencies. We did not gain admission.

The deputy of County Lebus laid

[6] Underscored by Marwitz.
[7] Underscored by the King.

How is this declaration to the Sovereign to be regarded?

The places underscored here are highly presumptuous and impudent. They insult in the minister the Highest Person of the King and attack it, since only from Him does each minister receive his authority, which must be preserved completely if it is to be effective.

This was Major Marwitz, who, however, could be regarded in no way as deputy and who set himself up as such in an entirely unauthorized manner.

And that with good reason! He deserved even greater punishment.

Where did this happen? Acceptance was denied because of improper justifications, which would have stirred up dissensions and damaged confidence.

without effect at the feet of Your Royal Majesty the document in which Your Royal Majesty earlier during the most solemn occasion of Your Life had confirmed our rights, along with the explanation that we did not wish to interpret it literally but would be ready not to insist upon its *otherwise absolutely clear meaning*. Although we were not heeded, all the official newspapers were and are filled with slanderous articles against our estate, whereas our justification, even though ever so temperate, is denied acceptance. Nothing remains for us but to yield to pressure, which Your Royal Majesty has sanctioned. But we are obligated to Your Royal Majesty, to this country, to ourselves, and to our descendants to declare:

that we are giving in *only* to this pressure, that we have *not* given up our duly acquired and firmly established privileges, but regard them as still in existence until it shall please Your Royal Majesty to conclude contracts with us concerning those parts which might seem to run counter to the general well-being, and to annul them thus *in a manner conforming to law;* that we absolve ourselves from the consequences which the introduction of the foreign principles of despotism and force must of necessity have for this ruling family, in that *we* have perceived them, yet have not been heeded in our warnings.

We are convinced that not only the principles according to which the new decrees are drawn up but that even their tendency is directed entirely toward bringing evil and ruin to our country. We cannot sufficiently deplore the fact that *before carrying out* these decrees, instead of turning for advice to natives familiar with the land and its residents, and hence of necessity devoted to them, young foreigners, who influence the ministers of Your Royal Majesty, are allowed to experiment with their new-fangled theories *directly in our fatherland,* when certainly any other country would be just as convenient to them. These theories, which *are used solely to acquire money and to promote their personal welfare,*[8] stifle, however, the sentiments of the people, upon which the state rests more firmly than upon money. Yet these sentiments were very easy to preserve and money was easy to acquire, since nobody in the land was discontented either with the constitution or with the existing taxes; and not only we but all other provinces as well *declared several times that we were prepared to meet the deficit if we had merely been*

Similar assertions of influence are, moreover, not new to me. I have experienced them often with regard to myself and to others. They are as untrue as they are unjust.

Easy to raise?!

These are nice phrases; but to be certain of meeting the deficit and yet with the least burden upon everybody — that is the problem which must be solved.

[8] Underscored by the King.

Have the estates not hitherto opposed all arrangements which have been considered? For example, the income tax? The present duties?

Thus it is all the more difficult to fix upon a suitable tax system.

I should think that the entire disposition of the government showed exactly the opposite, that vain striving toward mere money inspires its measures just as little as despotism and the necessity of the moment.

To be sure, leveling of all classes before the law and with respect to taxation is the right tendency. Who is depriving the nobleman of his nobility in other respects? Let him preserve it by superb culture, by patriotism, by noble deeds! Then he will always have enough preference. The intermediate estate described here as necessary will form by itself. It requires no exemptions for this purpose. Are these possessed by the nobility in England, which is cited above as a model? Am I less of a nobleman if I pay comparable taxes with my fellow citizens, if I am not allowed to exert harmful pressure upon them?

Will not landed property, then, continue to bind one closely to the state? Is it not saleable

told how much was needed. There seems then to have been no need at all to overthrow the existing order; and so likewise the much-praised freedom of trade *[Gewerbefreiheit]* will not alone conceal the resulting evil or procure the money which is so urgently needed. The two most important requisites for its success —a market and security from abroad —are lacking for this. The vain striving toward mere money here as always will bring its own punishment in self-destruction.

Just as *despotism and the necessity of the moment*[9] are the principles upon which these theories are constructed, so their tendency is:

1. Leveling of all classes. We believe, however, that a monarchy without an intermediate estate between king and people cannot exist, because this intermediate estate divides the masses,[10] hence facilitates their control and binds them more closely to the state. Dissatisfaction, be it in this intermediate estate or among the people, can cause no concern to the ruler. But if *only one* great undifferentiated mass confronts the Throne, let the Throne beware of stirring up discontent within it!

[9] Underscored by the King.

[10] Marwitz used the term of 'intermediate Estate' to refer to the landed aristocracy, not to the social groups between this aristocracy and the peasantry.

through indebtedness, through judicial sale, and so on? This is not the place to speak against the error of the principles here referred to.

That is, the royal ordinances are ordinances of those who serve the minister, and this they dare to say to the King in a remonstrance?!

If this is so, by all means an improper imitation.[11]

This whole tirade is as unjust as it is unbecoming.

2. Free saleability of landed property. Everything is to be bought and sold and become involved in trade and commerce. And yet it is precisely landed property which is bound most closely to the state, whereas the merchant is one who fares equally well in all states.

This double tendency is evident in all the decrees and writings of those who advise the ministers of Your Royal Majesty. Already they deny us and our possessions the name which belongs to us because they regard it as *too good* for us.

The draft of an edict communicated to us concerning peasant relationships speaks of the "large rural properties, *which usually are called* noble estates."[12]

The *Jews,* on the other hand (to cite an example), no longer are given their names either, but for the opposite reason, namely, because they are considered *not good enough for them.* In the decree in which they are permitted to acquire landed property they are called:

"The professors of the religion of Moses."

These Jews, if they really are true to their belief, are the necessary enemies of every state (if they are not

[11] This comment was made by the King.
[12] The edict of September 14, 1811, regulating relations on the estates with the peasants.

No comments are required on the highly improper assertions opposite.

Who are the uneducated? Could one not direct the accusation against the landed nobles, the authors of this remonstrance, that they see only themselves and the worth of their persons and of their colleagues!

is constantly trafficking with his property is torn loose from the state and hastens *toward wherever* more money is to be acquired; in this way everything becomes an object of speculation, and with the decay of agriculture there will come general lack of food.

The leveling of all classes makes the lower, uneducated classes defiant; they see only themselves and the worth of *their* person, with nobody over them, since the King is too far removed from them. In addition there is a necessary change of systems in the government, since nothing is any longer *maintained* by true to their belief, hypocrites); they have the bulk of ready money in their hands. As soon, then, as landed property has declined in value to the point that it is to their advantage to acquire it, it will immediately pass into their hands; as landed proprietors *they* will become the chief representatives of the state, and so our old and honorable Brandenburg-Prussia will become a new-fangled Jewish state.

We venture to say that if the principle of despotism, the leveling of estates, and the rendering saleable of landed property actually are carried out, there appears to us to be no salvation for this state and for the exalted house of Your Royal Majesty. The landed proprietor who

Precisely the change of systems is to be prevented.

What has been said already regarding several assertions in this memorandum applies to this.

This is real boasting, for though several might be relied upon in this struggle, like Herr von Marwitz, I submit, how applicable is this whole tirade to most of the undersigned?!

means of basic law, and the contrary *is not excluded*. All of this must of necessity engender such burgher egoism, such political irreverence that the people will regard the state as an institution of coercion and will seize the first occasion to tear themselves loose from it in order to wield power themselves rather than to submit to it. We have experienced the fearful example of such a time during our life-span. We reject all *participation* in the principles which likewise will bring about these conditions in this country!

May that time be as yet afar and Your Royal Majesty's family not experience it! We who foresee it will be those who will persevere with Your Royal Majesty and will fight by Your side to the end, as we already have for Your Majesty and as our fathers with more success have fought for the greatness of Your glorious ancestors. And if we fall in this struggle for Your Royal Majesty—for victory may be impossible—we nevertheless shall be happy in *the* consciousness of having remained true to our duty and of having deserved better treatment than we now experience.

We remain ever your most devoted, most humble, and most loyal estates of the counties of Lebus, Storkow, and Beeskow.

3. The Kind and Amount of Representation To Be Allowed

Friedrich von Gentz: *Concerning the Difference Between a Constitution Based upon Representation by Estates and One Based upon Individual Representation* (1819)*

The conservatives of the Restoration period after 1815 had to contend with the question of representation that the French Revolution had made acute. In the following memorandum Friedrich von Gentz, adviser and publicist for Prince Metternich, attempted to explain two main types of representation, with a view to defending the one and condemning the other. The distinction that he drew between the two types furnished standard criteria during the century for the ultraconservatives. Gentz preferred a polity based upon estates (or estates constitution), a system too radical to be accepted in practice in Metternich's Austria and anathema in a country as autocratic as Russia. His memorandum reveals the fundamental distinction between representation by estates associated with the Old Régime and that of a society with a developing bourgeoisie. It initiates the reader into the range of constitutional expression to be found in the changing social structure of the nineteenth century. Between the English parliamentary system and Russian autocracy appeared many differing forms of governmental organization. Gentz's idea, notable as a tentative step toward representative government, will reappear briefly at times during the century, especially in Central and Eastern Europe; but it always gives way before the other form, that established in France in the Restoration and subsequently found there and elsewhere in a number of variants determined by the nature of the suffrage law.

* "Ueber den Unterschied zwischen den land-ständischen und Representativ-Verfassungen," in *Wichtige Urkunden für den Rechtszustand der deutschen Nation, mit eigenhändigen Anmerkungen von Johann Ludwig Klüber, aus dessen Papieren mitgeteilt und erläutert von C. Welcker* (Mannheim, 1844), pp. 220-30.

The correct interpretation of Article 13[1] of the Act of Union was and still is a matter of first importance, even if many of the questions involved have already been factually and unilaterally decided.

It is a question of defining as precisely as possible the concept of constitutions based on diets or estates and the difference between these and what is currently called "representative" constitutions.

It is necessary first to define both constitutions and then to explain and complete the definitions by a more precise exposition of their fundamental characters, their origins, sphere of activity, the characteristics generally recognized as belonging to them, and finally their relationships to the general constitution of Germany.

I. DEFINITION

Estates constitutions are those in which members or delegates of corporate bodies existing in their own right exercise a right to participate in general or specific aspects of legislation, by joining in the discussion, by approving or by offering counterproposals, or by acting in accordance with any other form established by the constitution.

The term "estates constitution," as long as there have been a German language and a German history, has never had any other meaning, and thus Article 13 could have had no other meaning.

Representative constitutions, on the other hand, are those in which the persons designated for direct participation in legislation and in the most important work of the state administration are not supposed to represent the rights and interests of separate estates, or at least not exclusively, but those of the whole body of the people.

In a constitution based on representation by estates there is of course representation, and one could call it a constitution of representation, if it were not that in the most recent meaning of "representation" the word is no longer applicable to the constitution of estates. The difference appears only in this new meaning, or perhaps in the opposition between constitutions based on estates and those based on representation.

---

[1] Article 13 reads: "In all states of the Confederation an estates constitution [*landständische Verfassung*] shall be established.

II. Fundamental Character

Estates constitutions rest on the natural foundation of a well-ordered civil society in which the estates relationships and estates rights grow out of the special position of the classes and corporate bodies on which they are based; and they exist, legally modified in the course of time, without curtailment of the essential rights of the ruler.

Representative constitutions are always in the last analysis founded on the mistaken idea of the supreme sovereignty of the people and of necessity go back to this idea, however carefully it may be concealed.

Thus it is that all constitutions built upon estates are by nature favorable to the maintenance of all true positive rights and all true freedom possible in a state.

Representative constitutions by contrast have the constant tendency to put the phantom of so-called popular sovereignty (that is, of general arbitrariness) in place of civil order and subordination, and the delusion of general equality of rights, or, what is no better, equality before the law, in place of the ineradicable social and legal differences established by God.

III. Origins

Estates constitutions grow out of fundamental elements of the state existing in and of themselves and are not created by man; they evolve along with these elements, and in the same way in which they have evolved they can and must proceed to progressive completion without forcefully harming existing rights. Representative constitutions are the fruit of outside power or arbitrariness—power, if they have been made necessary by previous revolutions; arbitrary action, if they have been created without outside pressure but from a false understanding of state affairs.

The representative constitutions of England and France arose in the first way. Through a long series of civil wars or law-destroying usurpations the state was completely broken up. In a moment of such irretrievable ruin, if the wrath of the revolutionary elements is to be brought to some kind of halt, the only solution is to try to found a new order of things. This has to be done either by those who legally held power before the outbreak of the storm, or by those who in the course of events have come into possession of it in at least a semi-legal fashion. If they can act with justice and wisdom, conscientiously sparing existing relationships and, especially, adhering to the fundamentals and rights of the former order and preserving as much as can be rescued from the holocaust, a condition develops which not only may lead to calming everything and reconciling many conflicting claims but also may bring about considerable unity, high morale, and a feeling of general good will. The phenomenon is so similar to phenomena which the physical world often shows after terrible holocausts that it justifies no conclusion contrary to the laws of the civilized world. Only insanity or maliciousness would burn cities and villages in order to raise a graceful edifice on their ruins.

It must not be overlooked, however, that constitutions drawn up after such violent revolutions can never overcome their origin, and that, even in times of greatest flowering and harvest, the struggle with hostile forces which they appear to have conquered and the restless convulsive movement which they occasion never cease. Thus only very great and powerful states with governments strong enough to assert themselves against continuing opposition and with an ever-ready support in the upper classes bound to the existing order by property rights can live under constitutions of this kind.

Smaller states, lacking, as they do, one or the other of the necessary counterbalances and usually both, will inevitably come to ruin under the representative system. Wherever representative constitutions do not result from compelling circumstances, they arise out of arbitrary action. If the ruler, in order to avoid momentary embarrassment, or from fear of the arbitrary organs of wildly exploding public opinion, or even because of a mistaken idea of being a benefactor to his country, daringly decides to try to unite according to an arbitrary principle the existing political parts of the state—not created by him and not subject to his authority—and so to bring about what today is called a constitution, he implements the decision either by virtue of his own complete power or by a contract formally concluded with his subjects. In the latter case, in which the foolish principle of supreme sovereignty of the people is directly and explicity recognized, the constitution itself is stillborn, since no constitution is consonant with this principle; in the former case, appearance of life may be manifested for a time, because, as long as the rule of the dynasty continues, the memory of its former dignity and the shadow of the old order work more or less against the onset of dissolution.

The entire difference between the two forms of constitution-making is limited to origin. The essential defect of arbitrariness attaches itself to both kinds, and the original defective legal right of the constitutional lawgiver can neither be concealed nor corrected by the fictitious consent of the people.

The results are the same, even if they develop at varying rates of speed.

Popular suffrage, inseparable from the representative system however much it may be limited by purely arbitrary conditions of ability to vote or to be elected, is always—especially in small or disunited states—the first step toward demagoguery. Demagoguery leads to repeated crises in which sooner or later legal authority must succumb.

IV. Sphere of Activity

In estates constitutions the participation of the estates in law-making can be more or less extensive, both in the subject matter and in the form of participation. The degree of participation is determined in part by earlier legal relationships, in part by regular legislative measures, in part by the independent wisdom of the ruler. The range of authority of the estates can change with conditions; even the internal structure of an estates constitution, insofar as it takes place legally, can undergo changes and reforms in accordance with the changes of time and necessity. But never should the co-participation of the estates go so far that the ruler ceases to be the supreme lawgiver; and if a right of supervision over this or that branch of state administration is associated with the power of the estates in legislation, the exercise of this right must find its limit at that point where it might hinder the government in any of its essential functions.

In representative constitutions the legislative power appears to be split into separate and quite unequal parts. In like manner the unity of the administration is atomized, in part by means of the authority given the popular representatives which is subject to arbitrary interpretation, in part because of increasing demands and aggressions of such kind that it is often hard to decide who actually rules under such constitutions.

Theoretically the alleged principle of the separation of powers is supreme in the representative system. This principle left to itself always leads to complete destruction of all power and even to pure anarchy. Its influence upon large compact monarchies can only be avoided when the possessors and administrators of the so-called executive power know how by ingenious and not always innocent means to assemble in their hands the disparate parts of their rule.

It is of no importance to the fundamental concept of this system whether in addition the representation is divided into one or more chambers, whether it consists merely of elected or in part of hereditary or appointed members. This is true even if the theory is expanded to read that "each chamber and every member of each chamber, without any consideration of special interests or rights, shall be regarded only as representative of the whole." In its consequences the difference between one and two chambers can be of significance only where a balance against popular representation is still possible. In large monarchies which learn by continuous effort, skill, and luck to endure the representative system, the existence of two chambers does unquestionably give an important and effective guarantee.

In smaller states it is nothing but a temporary palliative; the chamber of peers is never powerful enough to serve as a support to the throne, and the superior power of the popular chamber means destruction of both throne and peers.

V. Attributes

Wherever the representative system has gained the upper hand, the double responsibility of the ministers—that is to the ruler and then to the people or their representatives—public deliberations, full freedom of the press and of petition, etc., have been regarded as necessary attributes; and there can be no doubt that they are closely connected with the underlying nature of the system entailing supremacy of the so-called popular will.

Likewise no great acumen is needed to grasp the incompatibility of such institutions with the basic conditions for a monarchy. Some of these rights are so dangerous that even in the strongest monarchies they sustain a continual ferment and cause the government more trouble than the most difficult of its positive tasks. Where are rulers of weaker states to find the means and resources needed to resist a never-ending internal war continually reappearing in open or concealed hostilities? For example, the public conduct of the deliberations of the popular chamber is a direct step toward the denigration of all authority and to the destruction of all public order when that conduct is carried to the point of daily publication of the contents of the debates. This is the more certain in that as long as this system prevails every other curb upon the restraint of the press is impossible or useless.

All these and similar trappings of representative constitutions are foreign to estates constitutions, or they are associated with them only by chance and with modifications.

VI. Relation to German Federal Unity

In the present situation of Germany, estates constitutions, however they may be formed, can never contradict the principle and the basic conditions of the German Confederation. In these constitutions, as has been pointed out above, the ruler does not cease to be supreme lawgiver and head of the entire state administration. Everything concerning external security of the state and negotiations with other states incidental to this security remains exclusively in the ruler's hands. When internal matters of individual states are negotiated in common in the *Bundestag*, nothing prevents the individual ruler from consulting his estates insofar as their agreement is constitutionally required. He alone, however, is the recognized organ of his state in the general assembly of German princes. Even if he must take care that what is proposed or concluded for the good of the whole in the German Confederation does not run counter to the special interest and the peculiar constitution of his own country, one cannot imagine a case in which a prince would not be authorized to approve that which he himself and his co-regents in the common council recognize as necessary or salutary.

The decisions once made in the central body must be regarded as valid and binding in all German states without the intervention of any other authority. In view of their origin they rank above all local laws, and every prince may legally assume that he will accept nothing in the *Bundestag* which cannot be reconciled with his position *vis à vis* his estates and with the welfare of his subjects.

The continuation of a German Confederation is possible only in this way. No true estates constitution may or will contain terms in actual or seeming contradiction to the existence of this supreme guarantee of peace and to the independence of Germany.

As soon as there are representative constitutions in Germany everything will change. The irreconcilability of the representative system in individual states with the rights and duties given the German *Bundestag* is clear. The most ardent supporters of popular representation have themselves given us decisively and frankly the stronger arguments for this fact and we are therewith indebted to them.

These arguments are completely to the point, logical, and, so far as their premises go, unanswerable. No one can bring into a confederation more right and power than he possesses independently. A prince who is declared by the constitution of his country or held explicitly or implicitly thereby to be a part of the legislative power and who must answer to popularly elected representative officials for each of his administrative acts cannot of course take part in decisions of a council of princes without the consent of these officials. What an individual ruler cannot do at home he cannot be allowed to do when he deliberates with other German princes in person or through regularly appointed ambassadors.

This point of popular teaching is destined to break the back of the federal assembly, even in the unlikely case that all German states adopt representative governments. Neither can the assembly exist if a part of its members rule with estates, another part with popular representation; a part rule according to monarchical, a part according to democratic principles; a part rule as constitutional princes and another part as constitutional machines.

Feeling the impossibility of this entire situation but at the same time determined to sacrifice to the idol of popular representation every other right, every other interest, previous treaty, and the peace and security of Germany and of Europe, various of the outspoken friends of the representative system have proposed to allow the Federal Assembly to be supplemented by a popular Chamber of Deputies. No one will heed such proposals unless he wants a general revolution or thinks it unavoidable. The truth is that we are standing on a brink with only one path of return. If the German princes do not now unite on a single interpretation and execution of Article 13 of the Act of Union consonant with the security of their rights and their crowns, with the true welfare of their peoples, and with the preservation of the German Confederation, if those who have missed in the drafting of their constitutions the only true and admissible sense of this article cannot be helped skillfully and honestly to return to the true sense, then there remains nothing for us to do but to renounce the Confederation. Once this has been said, all further remarks are superfluous.

4. The Means of Preventing Further Revolution

Friedrich von Gentz: *Introduction to the Carlsbad Measures* (1819)[*]

The justification of the Carlsbad Decrees that Friedrich von Gentz formulated in 1819 exemplifies the unity of conservative thinking about constitutional, social, and cultural aspects of life. Each aspect appeared to supplement the other, and each was considered as a political means to preserve a way of life. The conservative attitude toward freedom of thought and expression coincides with that toward political freedom. Gentz thought out the program of the Austrian emperor, of the German kings and princes, and of Metternich to prevent revolution in Germany. His statement—particularly useful for insight into intellectual history—reveals the prestige of various professions or occupations not merely in Germany and Austria but in all conservative society. The exposition by Gentz of the functioning of the German Confederation discloses the obstacles that nationalists will encounter in any country not yet united into a national state. At the same time such an exposition reveals the dilemma that the princes faced in trying to preserve their particularist power by means of a confederacy. It helps one to understand why Bismarck chose the method of unifying Germany that he did. It should point up the self-imposed difficulties of governing a polyglot empire and expose those of unifying Italy, an area where no sort of confederation existed. For our own century, it affords insight into the impact of war and its aftermath upon the exercise of individual liberty.

His Imperial Majesty believes that He expresses His own wish and that of all members of the Diet in demanding that before adjourning the Federal Assembly take cognizance of the unrest and ferment of

[*] Gustav Schlesier, ed., *Kleinere Schriften von Friedrich von Gentz* (Mannheim, 1839), Pt. II, pp. 158-78.

spirit prevailing in a large part of Germany. It must examine thoroughly the causes of this critical phenomenon, which has become more evident daily for some years, and which has finally revealed itself in unmistakable symptoms, in writings preaching rebellion, in widely distributed illegal organizations, and even in individual acts of terror. It must consider seriously the means whereby order and quiet, respect for law, confidence in the government, general contentment, and the undisturbed enjoyment of the benefits which the German nation under a lasting peace should enjoy at the hands of its princes can be assured and strengthened in the future.

The sources of the evil, whose further advance it is now the holiest duty of all German governments to arrest, lie in part in the conditions and circumstances of the time which no government can influence directly and immediately; but in part they are related to definite measures, mistakes, or misuses which can be remedied through proper understanding and maturely considered common action.

Among the subjects ultimately deserving the first and most careful consideration the following are especially noteworthy:

1. vagueness of the meaning and the consequent misunderstandings of Article 13 of the Federal Act;

2. false conceptions of the powers vested in the Federal Assembly, and insufficiency of the means whereby these powers can be made effective;

3. defects in the schools and universities;

4. misuse of the press, and especially the offenses committed by the newspapers, periodicals and pamphlets.

It is His Majesty's express wish that the Federal Assembly treat immediately these important subjects, and the President is hereby directed to report various measures for adoption both in regard to the above four points and for naming a central committee, the designation and work of which will be more evident in the course of this discussion. His Majesty is convinced that the members of the Confederation will find again in these proposals and in the remarks accompanying them the principles of justice and moderation which have always served His Highness as His rule of conduct. He is convinced that the well-intentioned people of all German lands will not misunderstand either the pure and benevolent purpose which has guided His Majesty in His proposals or the upright, heartfelt, and unchanging sympathy for the fate of all the Federal states united for similar advantages, duties, and efforts.

I. UNCERTAINTY OVER THE MEANING OF ARICLE 13 OF THE FEDERAL ACT AND MISCONSTRUCTION OF THE SAME

When the illustrious founders of the German Confederation at the time of the political rebirth of Germany decided to give their peoples a pledge of their love and confidence in the maintenance or re-creation of constitutions based on estates, and to this end signed Article 13 of the Federal Act, they foresaw that this article could not be executed in all states in the same degree and form. Great disparity prevailed at that time among the states of the Confederation, some of which had preserved the old estates society in part or entire, others of which had lost their constitutions, still others of which had never had such constitutions or had in earlier times lost them. Great difference in the treatment of this important subject was accordingly necessary, a difference which was enormously increased by the newly drawn frontiers, by the joining of lands with different constitutional structures into a unified state, by the amalgamation of areas in which estates constitutions were more or less unknown with provinces where they had long existed.

In view of this condition not only the founders of the Confederation but later also the princes were concerned during the initial period of negotiations in the existing Diet with following the desire expressed on many sides, and occasionally in the Diet itself, for a guiding principle in the drafting of the estates constitutions mentioned in Article 13. Although failure to fulfill this desire, a fact we can no longer conceal, has caused a great deal of harm in Germany, it would still be wrong to misjudge the motives underlying the present silence of the Federal Assembly on this important matter. These are, namely, respect for the inherent right of every state to order its own affairs as it understands them, and fear that strongly expressed general principles would embroil individual states in various embarrassments, perhaps in insoluble difficulties.

The founders of the German Confederation could never have fore-seen, however, that interpretations would be given Article 13 clearly contradicting its words, or that conclusions would be drawn from it canceling not only Article 13 but the entire text of the Federal Act's principal clauses, thus endangering the survival of the Confederation. They could never have foreseen that the unambiguous principle of estates representation, upon the strengthening of which they placed great value, would be mistaken for purely democratic principles and forms. They could never have imagined that claims would be based upon this misunderstanding which immediately or in a very short time would become obviously irreconcilable with the existence of monarchical states, which (with the unimportant exception of the free cities taken into this union) must be the only members of the Con-federation.

The concern seemed equally ill-founded that anywhere in Germany the idea of limiting the essential rights and attributes of the Confed-eration itself by means of the estates constitutions would gain ground, or, as has already been tried, the direct attempt would be made to dissolve the only bond by which one German state is presently linked with another and the whole of Germany with the European state system.

All these serious misunderstandings and errors have not only de-veloped during recent years but, through an unhappy chain of events, have so engrossed public opinion that we have almost entirely lost sight of the true meaning of Article 13. The daily-growing inclination toward fruitless or dangerous theories, the influence of writers who are either misled themselves or prone to flatter every popular delusion, the vain demand to introduce into Germany constitutions of foreign countries whose present political form is as unlike Germany's as their entire previous history is unlike ours—these and many other contrib-uting causes, in part still more deplorable, have produced general political confusion. This great and noble nation of ours, otherwise notable for its thoroughness and profound understanding, threatens to devour itself. In the eyes of many members of estates diets, these factors have even so confused the principle on which the diets were constitutionally erected and so twisted the limits of their rightful sphere of activity that the governments are disturbed and hindered in fulfilling even their essential duties.

The reasons which formerly decided the Federal Assembly to abstain from influencing directly the constitutional form of the individual states must now give way to higher considerations. If the German Confederation is not to disintegrate, if Germany is not to be sacrificed to all the horrors of internal division, arbitrariness, and irremediable disturbance of law and well-being, it must acquire a strong, universally accepted basis for the most important of its tasks, the building of its future constitutions.

One of the first and most pressing tasks of the Federal Assembly must therefore be to achieve a thorough explanation and exposition of Article 13, one applicable to all the federal states in whatever situation they may be now, one deduced from German concepts, German law, and German history rather than from general theories or foreign example, and above all one for maintaining the principle of monarchy, to which Germany can never be disloyal with impunity, and for maintaining the Confederation as the only support of its peaceful independence.

The introduction of estates constitutions into all of the federated states where they do not now firmly exist is urgent, and must be accomplished without more delay, indeed with redoubled energy. It is equally desirable, in order to prevent further misunderstanding and to expedite our final agreement over the execution of Article 13, not to make, in regard to the work now being introduced into many states relative to the estates constitutions, any decisions in any way contradictory to the views here expressed and to the interpretation of the Article expected in a short time from the Federal Assembly.

II. Powers of the Federal Diet and Means for Carrying Out the Same

It is inherent in the concept and nature of the German Confederation that its official representatives constitute the highest legislative authority in Germany in all that concerns the maintenance and essential purpose of the Confederation as described in Article 2 of the Federal Act.[1] It follows that decisions of the Diet, insofar as they pertain to the external and internal security of the whole, the independence and security of individual members of the Confederation, and the maintenance of the legally existing order which is indivisible from both, must be universally binding, and that no individual legislation and no separate measure shall oppose the execution of such decisions.

The existence and continuation of the Confederation depend absolutely upon a firm and strict adherence to this principle. The Confederation's further development as well as a definitive statement of the powers and attributes of the Diet in general must be reserved for the continuing discussions about the full extension and strengthening of the entire authority of the Confederation.

However the final result of the discussions may turn out, it is obvious to all that, if the Diet is not given the necessary disposition of the required means and resources, the supreme principle itself remains without force and the laws and decisions of the Confederation are assured of ineffectiveness. The drafting of an appropriate measure of implementation must therefore be one of the principal subjects of the intended discussions; and His Majesty believes that all His colleagues in the Confederation will be able to come to complete agreement over the pressing need for such a law.

In the meantime, however, the Diet should not lack the required means for making and implementing decisions and measures necessary to the internal security of Germany. The Imperial-Royal President is therefore authorized to present for immediate examination and discussion the plan for a provisional act of implementation with express reference to Article 2 of the Federal Act.

III. Defects in the Schools and Universities

The attention of the Diet and of individual German governments was long ago directed to this subject, the exceptional importance of

---

[1] Article 2 reads: "The purpose of the Confederation is: the preservation of the foreign and internal security of Germany and the independence and inviolability of the individual German states."

which has vividly impressed all Germany. A proper and wholesome leadership of the public educational system in general, but especially that of the higher institutions which prepare for direct entrance into practical life, is regarded in every state as one of the most urgent. A special duty and more than customary responsibility, however, rests on the German governments. This is so in the first place because in Germany education for public effectiveness and state service is left entirely to the upper schools; thus, because these upper schools are a main link in the chain of German unity, and as the benefit accruing from them is spread over the entire body of the nation, their defects are sure to be more or less felt; finally, because Germany owes a part of its reputation and therefore its place in the European community to its famous educational institutions, which up to now Germany has successfully maintained and in whose continued maintenance His Majesty will take the warmest and most active interest at all times.

It can hardly be doubted that the actual situation of the German universities, with some recognized worthy exceptions, in many respects no longer corresponds to the reputation gained in better times. For some time thoughtful and well-meaning leaders have noticed and complained that these institutions have departed in more than one respect from their original character and from the purposes intended by their illustrious founders and patrons. Swept along by the stream of an age which is undermining everything, a large part of the academic profession has misunderstood the true function of the universities and has substituted an arbitrary and often pernicious one. Instead of training the youth entrusted to it for civil service, which was its first duty, and awakening in them the feeling from which the fatherland could expect mature fruits, they have pursued the phantom of a so-called cosmopolitan education, which fills minds ready to receive truth and error alike with empty dreams and infuses in them, if not bitterness, at least disrespect for and opposition to the established order. From a perverted course of this kind there have gradually developed illusions of higher wisdom, a disdain for all positive values, and the claim of a right to re-create the social order according to their own untried systems, to the great disadvantage of both the common good and the next generation; and a considerable

number of the youth has transformed itself into teachers and reformers.

The dangerous deterioration of the upper schools has not escaped
the attention of the German governments; but in part the praiseworthy desire not to hinder freedom of instruction so long as it did
not directly and disturbingly affect civil relationships, and in part
the confusion and distress brought about by twenty years of war,
have prevented them from fighting the progress of the evil with thor-
oughgoing countermeasures.

Today, however, although we enjoy the beneficent influence of
restored external peace and the honest and active effort of many
German rulers to prepare for their peoples a happy future, and although we might expect the upper schools too to regain those limits
within which they previously functioned so well for the country and
for humanity, the strongest antagonism to the principles and measures upon which the present constitutions and the internal peace of
Germany rest has come from this quarter. Because of the culpable
cooperation or the unpardonable carelessness of the teachers, the
best talents and instincts of our youth have been abused and made
instruments of adventurous political plans and frivolous, even if unsuccessful, schemes. Since these dangerous byways have led to deeds
which stain the German name, further indulgence would deteriorate
into censurable weakness, and indifference to further misuse of such
mistaken academic freedom would make all German governments
responsible before the world and eternity.

Clearly, in this serious situation, the maintenance of public order
must precede every other consideration; but the governments of
the Confederation will not lose sight of the great question of how
to help in overcoming the internal and perhaps very deep-seated
defection of the schools from their original wholesome purpose. His
Majesty therefore maintains that the Diet is obligated to take up this
question, one so important to knowledge and public life, to family
welfare, and to the solidity of the states; and it should not desist from
the matter until its efforts shall have led to thorough and satisfactory
results.

First, however, we must meet the trouble directly threatening us and take measures so that thoughtless enthusiasts or declared enemies of the existing order, in the present ruptured condition of several German universities, will be prevented from finding either material for arousing feeling further and deluded instruments for promoting plans, subjects, or weapons against the personal security of the citizens of the state. His Imperial Majesty therefore has no hesitation, in consequence of the preliminary memorandum on this matter, in recommending the accompanying plan of provisional measures proposed to this Assembly for immediate consideration and further discussion.

IV. Misuse of the Press

The printing press, especially the branch of it which produces the daily newspaper, periodicals, and pamphlets, during recent years has exercised an almost unlimited freedom in the greater part of Germany. Even where governments had reserved the right to restrain it by preventive measures, the force of these measures was frequently weakened by pressure of circumstances, and consequently a wide field for excesses was opened. The countless evils which have been spread throughout Germany by the misuse of this freedom have significantly increased since in various states the deliberations of the estates were opened to the public and expanded to include subject matter never before issued from the sanctuary of the Senate to the public except in regular official form, and never meant to serve as the plaything of idle curiosity and unthinking criticism. This publicity has furnished material for the insolence of writers and has given every journalist a pretext for raising his voice in matters presenting uncertainty and difficulties to the most able statesmen. How far this harmful arrogance has spread, what confusion in ideas, what turbulence of spirit, what denigration of authority, what conflict of passions, what fanatical misconceptions, and what crimes have resulted from this need no further discussion. One can hardly imagine any difference of opinion among the well-disposed and truly enlightened part of the German nation over so notorious an evil.

The peculiarity of the relation in which the states of the Confederation stand to one another gives the dangers connected with the licentiousness of the press a form and direction which they could never assume in states where the supreme power is united in one and the same center. In addition it excludes the application of legal means in seeking to curb the abuse of the press. In a confederation like that which has been established in Germany with the sanction of all the European powers, those powerful balances are lacking which in absolute monarchies protect public order against the attacks of rash or evil-intentioned writers. In a confederation of this kind, peace, harmony, and confidence can be maintained only by the most careful mutual prevention of disturbances and offenses.

Every question in Germany connected with freedom of the press must be regarded from this supreme point of view, which has nothing in common with the legislation of other countries. Only in conditions of the most complete quiet could Germany, under her present federal constitution, endure unlimited freedom of the press, insofar as it can be harmonized at all with this constitution. The present time is less appropriate than any other for it: the business, now before so many governments, of founding the present and future welfare of their peoples by means of good constitutions cannot possibly thrive in the midst of an intemperate division of opinion, in a conflict renewed daily which convulses all principles and dissolves all truth in doubt and delusion.

In these pressing circumstances the measures to be taken against the misuse of the press should in no way be aimed at curtailing the activity of useful and worthy writers, at putting chains upon the natural progress of the human spirit, or at hindering communication and instruction of any kind, so long as they remain within the boundaries which no previous legislation has permitted them to trespass. The spirit manifested upon occasion by all German governments guarantees that supervision of periodical literature will not deteriorate into suppression, and the charge that these governments intend tyranny over the mind need be feared by no friend of truth and order. The need for such supervision cannot longer be doubted, and since His Majesty may expect all members of the Confederation to agree on this important subject, the President is instructed to present to the Diet for examination and discussion the draft of a provisional measure for preventing the misuse of the printing press in regard to newspapers, periodicals, and pamphlets.

V. MEANING OF A CENTRAL COMMITTEE OF INVESTIGATION

Along with the discussions and resolutions brought forward in the foregoing sections, another measure which His Majesty recommends to the Diet for immediate consideration is necessary both for the protection of the public order and for calming all well-disposed persons in Germany.

Discoveries made in various states at the same time have uncovered traces of an extensive organization active in several parts of Germany. This seems to consist of numerous branches, sometimes more and sometimes less developed, whose continuing effort is directed not only toward the greatest possible spread of fanatic, definitely revolutionary teaching dangerous to the state, but even to furthering and preparing the most atrocious plots.

Even if the extent and unity of this criminal activity could not be completely ascertained, the number of facts, documents, and proofs already assembled is so large that we can no longer doubt the existence of the evil. Although opinions may differ over the size of the danger, it is sufficient that such serious aberrations could gain headway in Germany, that a considerable number of individuals is actually gripped by them, and that even if the whole thing ought only to be regarded as a spiritual disease, any neglect of means to combat it could have only the most dangerous consequences.

We must therefore investigate the matter thoroughly. Investigation will lead to a wholesome outcome in that it will disarm the guilty and bring them to punishment if the suspicion resting on them is proved; it will open the eyes of those who have been misled to the precipice before them; and it will prevent Germany from being deluded about real dangers and lulled into false security, or disturbed and led astray by exaggerated fears.

But if this investigation is to produce results, it must proceed from the Diet as a common center and be conducted under its direct supervision. The activities and plans so far discovered are as much against the existence of the German Confederation as against individual German princes and states. Moreover the Diet is undoubtedly also entitled to act, and through Article 2 of the Federal Act expressly obligated to take cognizance of these activities. In addition a central official agency is more suitable than any appointed by individual governments to assemble the existing data and those to be collected, to examine them in their complete relevance to one another with justice and lack of prejudice, and to arrive at a comprehensive view of the entire matter.

Finally, by reason of the publication of the entire negotiations at the end of the investigation of this committee, we shall best dissipate the fear of having harmed the innocent and having spared the guilty. In any case a complete revelation of the matter will set at rest many doubts, fears, and restless activities.

These are the reasons why His Imperial Majesty finds Himself moved to propose the naming of a Central Investigating Committee exclusively for the subject above mentioned, and the President is thereby directed to lay before the Diet the draft of a resolution to this effect for its speedy consideration.

5. The Justification of Civil Rights

*Viscount Dubouchage Defends the Right of Association and
of Assembly* (1834)*

During the nineteenth century the issue of civil rights almost
continuously occupied the attention of every country. The arguments used for and against were always about the same,
irrespective of time or country. We have read a statement by
Gentz against freedom of teaching and freedom of the press.
The speech of 1834 by a liberal member of the French Chamber of Peers, Viscount Dubouchage, offers arguments in favor
of freedom of association and of assembly that go beyond
an eighteenth-century assertion of the abstract natural rights
of man to a discussion of the practical advantages, even necessities, of this freedom. The kind of legislation that the French
government sought prevailed at some time in every state of
Europe during part or all of the century, in some countries all
of the time. Not until the Third Republic did France receive
almost complete freedom in this respect, whereas the German
Empire after 1871 continued to assert over associations and
meetings police supervision of greater or less severity depending upon the nature of the groups involved, and in Russia governmental supervision remained strict up to 1917. The statement by Dubouchage, read in conjunction with that of Gentz,
elaborates one of the essential problems of his century and
ours.

. . . I come to the bill submitted to you today, for it is arbitrary
power that the Government is demanding of you. It wants to condemn everyone in France to an isolated life.

Let us first establish the facts; we can discuss them afterward. We
shall see then the nature of the circumstances and the absolute need

* *Moniteur universel, Chambre des Pairs,* April 8, 1834, pp. 823-6.

in whose name they are hoping to wrest from you a law which will permanently destroy several articles in the new Charter. It is a tyrannical law in its terms, and one which creates confusion among the several jurisdictional powers and turns these over to the discretion of the Government, a law essentially tyrannical in nature, enormously arbitrary in the penalties which it allows, and finally a law altogether of the character of an exceptional law, although its duration is not defined. Indeed it is the character of the law and not its time factor which makes it an exceptional law; the time has nothing to do with it, except that the duration makes the harshness even more dishonorable. We shall close by examining the means of safety to be used to prevent this *next revolution* talked about in the other Chamber, one which actually threatens us, which everyone dreads, and which we all would like to prevent. The Government, however, is blindly rushing toward revolution by forcing itself into arbitrary methods and so abandoning the natural constitutional process. In abandoning this latter road we are on the road to ruin . . .

The matters to be recalled are five, and an exposition of them will constitute a good beginning for the discussion: (1) the inalienable right of man to free speech, press, and assembly, so that he may communicate his thoughts; (2) the Charter of 1830, prejudiced or violated by the proposed ministerial bill in respect to several of its articles; (3) Articles 291 and 292 of the Penal Code; (4) the actual bill of 1834 for an exceptional law; (5) the exceptional law of 1833 on the *state of troubles* to replace the ordinance of 1832 on state of siege and councils of war, which died in this Chamber last year even though it was less severe, arbitrary, and extensive than the bill of 1834. Happy omen for France! I have full confidence that the Chamber of Peers will act now as it did in 1833, that it will show the public and the Government that it is an impregnable fortress of public liberties.

Let us discuss each point in order.

1. The most precious right of man, the expression of his thoughts, is a gift of nature. Without the use of words man cannot communicate effectively with his equals. Speech is a social bond. It exists to be used

but it can hardly be used without the right of association. How can man spread knowledge without meeting with his fellows? Freedom of the press is only an auxiliary right, but speech is a natural right. Thus man has the inalienable right of freedom of communication by means of both the *oral* and the *written* word.

2. The Charter of 1830 sanctions this natural right. Article 7 provides that Frenchmen have the right to express their opinions without let or hindrance, provided they conform to the law. This article is precise. Everyone may express his opinion whether orally or in writing and do so without previously arranged impediment. Consequently there can be no censorship whatever and no previous authorization. But a restrictive law will punish any aberrations or abuses made of the right.

Article 66 of the Charter states that all the rights sanctioned by the Charter remain entrusted to the courage and patriotism of the whole body of French citizens. This article could not be carried out, however, if the citizens lived in isolation from one another. Thus they must have the right of associating with one another in order to defend the rights recognized by the Charter.

What has given rise to these societies that we now have here? The abuse of power is the cause. When the home is constantly violated, we meet to find means to prevent this, that is to say to make justice prevail and to punish him who has abused his authority. When individual liberty is not respected, we meet, we assemble to defend this liberty. The man who has been illegally arrested finds in association help, protection, money, and talent for securing promptly that liberty for which he would otherwise wait a long time, and which will thereafter be more respected by authority. Who thought formerly of forming societies? No one.

When the suffrage right is always concentrated in a few hands, we associate to give the elections more force and effectiveness. If elections have the basis they ought to have in a state founded on national representation, who would think of meeting to complain? No one. What is the reason for this kind of association? The resistance of the Government to honoring the almost universal will.

Are these the associations it wants to forbid? Yes, a hundred times yes! Has it the right to do so? No, a hundred times no, according to the Charter, our codes of law, and custom.

Who initiated meetings during the Restoration? Perhaps those who today would like to extinguish them and are furiously persecuting them. I ask them if they thought that they were doing anything illegal or especially unconstitutional. I know their loyalty; they will say "no." Well, now that they have the power, why do they refuse something which they thought legal enough when they did not have power? I beg them to consider this idea fairly. Societies, they say, are annoying and inconvenient, opposing their wishes and embarrassing the exercise of their authority. I answer that it is in this very fact that individual rights and the general liberty are protected. Representative government was not invented so that ministers might remain at peace.

Article 69 of the Charter provides for use of the jury in all cases involving political offenses and those of the press. But the press is only the written word, the supplement and accessory to the spoken word. Thus if the accessory, that is the offense of the written word, is referred to a jury, then the principal, that is the abuse of the spoken word, should certainly be so referred.

Article 4 sanctions individual liberty.

Article 53 provides that everyone must have judgment by his peers.

Article 54 provides that there are to be no extraordinary tribunals, under any name whatever and under any pretext whatever.

When I come to discussion of my fourth factual point, the present ministerial bill, I shall indicate how this bill violates, harms, or distorts the above three articles of the Charter.

3. This point concerns Article 291 of the Penal Code, which reads as follows: "No association of more than twenty persons whose aim is to meet daily or on certain specified days in order to concern themselves with religious, literary, political, or other matters may be formed without permission from the government and under conditions imposed by public authority upon the society. Among the number of persons indicated in the present article those living on the premises where the gathering is to be held are not included."

Thus up to now any assembly of twenty to thirty persons could be held without any authorization, every day, and with any purpose, even a political one. There you have the inalienable, free right of association as recognized and sanctioned by the most despotic ruler of France since Louis XI or Louis XIV.

Article 292 provides that if there is a breach of right the association is to be dissolved without penalty (without penalty!) for the ordinary members; the leaders only are to receive a fine of sixteen to two hundred francs.

The Emperor[1] knew the French too well and had too much intelligence to deny them the most precious of their natural rights, that of association, or, what is worse, to distort it and make it illusory as the ministers would like to do now. He too disliked clubs, popular societies; to use his own words, they were the masses, and he had a horror of the *masses*. France likewise recalls with terror the times when she was groaning under the fury of clubs and popular societies. None of us wants these daily or nightly assemblies in which orators drunk with anarchy daily used to harangue an ignorant multitude in order to draw it into excesses and to rule with its help over national representation itself. No one has forgotten the dismal times when scandal and crime became civic virtues through these clubs, whose picture the minister has painted for us in such sombre colors. I have followed carefully the fourteen sittings of the other Chamber while it was discussing the bill that we are now debating, and I have been struck by the frequent use of the words "clubs," and "popular societies" of '93, '94, or '99, repeated by the ministers and their friends. But where are these clubs? Where are the rooms where they meet every evening? Where is their rostrum? Where are their speakers? Where are the people so eager to hear them? You have seized, you say, arms, papers, and up to 80,000 cartridges (80,000 cartridges—made as if by magic!). Where? In what club? Cease this fantasizing! You are speaking to men who have lived through these terrible times and who know the difference between a club and an association.

But [you say] there are illegal and conspiratory associations! What a remarkable discovery! Is it only since yesterday, since you have

[1] Napoleon I.

been in power, that they have existed? Did no one see them during
the Restoration? Under the Empire? Never under previous reigns?
Is it some marvel reserved for the years 1833 and 1834 that men come
together for crime or conspiracy? And because you have encountered
a Society of the Rights of Man, which you say (I do not know of it)
wants to substitute a republic for the July Monarchy, you want turned
over to your mercy and discretion the good right of man to communicate his thoughts and opinions, to pool his talents, knowledge, and
good will, and to come together in groups already limited to from
twenty to thirty persons!

What have these societies or any group whatever in common with
the clubs of '93 and '99, groups without meeting rooms, a speaker's
platform, set meeting times, and without any popular organ to print
the cruel or stupid words of the fanatics? The Society of the Rights
of Man is plotting and you have not yet attacked it? You allow anyone to conspire under your very eyes? You are to blame, for you are
armed and in a position to frustrate conspiracy. You see them and yet
have not turned them over to the courts? You are waiting for a law
for that, a law on association? Are you serious? You mean that the
state, under whatever form of government it may have been up to
now, has had no effective law for seizing and punishing conspirators?
The facts show that you are quite wrong. A good many conspirators
in the last forty years have fallen under the sword of the law! Yet
there was no law of association such as you want now for less than
twenty persons. There were some associations, but they were not in-
dicted *en masse* because some bad citizens (for the bad citizen is
the one who conspires against the established order) had abused
the name and associated for a criminal purpose. I do not know of any
plot at any time which did not involve some connections among the
members of the conspiracy. But what legislator has ever thought
for this reason of taking away the natural right of association?

I hear you protesting that associations are societies within the great
body social, states within a state, governments within a government.
Whom do you hope to persuade with such words? Surely not the men
of state who are now listening to me!

You call a welfare society or a charity organization, a literary or political discussion group, an association for individual liberty or for some right recognized by the Charter, all conforming to the law in regard to membership of twenty persons, a state within a state! If there are small governments acting against the established governments, you will not find them in these harmless ranks. Look for them among the *secret societies,* the real plague of our age, to which you are now going to supply new affiliates outraged by the insolence of your law. Your law is the reverse of our times, our customs, and liberty as we understand it in France, especially since the July days. Such laws only bring on the trouble, discontent, and disorder, in the midst of which conspiracies are born and *secret societies* flourish.

Notice the great distance between your system and that of the powerful intellect which sponsored the Code of 1810. He not only allowed meetings of twenty to thirty persons but did not want offenders punished. If a political association of more than twenty persons turned up, it was ordered dissolved and no more. Such was his respect for the right. The leaders alone were punished by a small fine. You say, I know: The Emperor was feared, and besides he had other means of punishing than the Penal Code. For repressing or punishing whom? Conspirators coming together to establish a government other than his, a small state within a vast empire? Yes, he had other means, means which you have too, as I have already said. Who is denying them? Who wants to deprive you of them without your knowledge? He had terrible laws against conspiracy; he did not take these laws to St. Helena, he did not take them with him to the grave; he left them to you, as you cannot deny, and you cannot deny either that you do not know how to use them; you dare not use them. Look at the famous Article 415 of the Penal Code, which remained powerless in your hands against the action of some classes of workers in Lyons two months ago, and it was not a secret case but an open and punishable one, as you yourselves admitted.

When you have exhausted the legal means at your disposal, you can complain and beg for some more efficacious ones. Until then, no. And we shall see in your complaints of powerlessness only the desire for an arbitrary power denied you by the Charter, refused by the national will, by the spirit of our age, and by the blood spilled in

July to abolish forever in France the vestiges of all arbitrary power. The Chamber of Peers, the guardian of public liberty, knows its duty. It will never grant you the arbitrary power you seek. Too wise and prudent for this, it will save you from yourselves.

Now we come to the fourth point, the ministerial bill on associations.

The title is not exact; it does not do what it promises. When the legislator designates something as a violation, misdemeanor, or a crime, he begins by defining very carefully the nature of the violation, misdemeanor, or new crime, stating just how it is to be recognized by both the simplest citizens and the most skilled jurists.

That is exactly what Napoleon did in 1810. He prohibited certain associations and described clearly how even the most unenlightened citizen would recognize the prohibition. There are three of these indications: the number, the purpose, and the regularity of the meeting. There you have both clarity and equity. There was despotism perhaps, but not arbitrariness; it was not motivated by the well-founded fear of the numerous societies given over to orators of disorder and anarchy. Article 291 was necessary, and it still is.

But what do you do? You destroy its justice by depriving it of the definite restrictions constituting the prohibition. You say that it is not restrictive enough. It satisfied an absolute despot and the Restoraton, but is not enough for the July Monarchy, which is supposed to have created a reign of liberty! For the moment I bow to your advice. In reading your law, I do not see the ways in which one is to recognize how far you intend to carry this restriction. The title of the law is already a false one, a derogation of all justice and equity. No one will know any longer whether he is acceptable in your eyes. Who can help daily finding himself in the company of other persons?

You say that you are not persecuting meetings. I then reread your bill and see that it makes no distinction between what you are pleased to call a meeting and an association. Article 291, which you say you want to make specific and which you confuse, was more forthright. According to it a meeting and an association were identical if the society had a literary, political, or other goal and assembled regularly with more than twenty persons.

Under your law it would be impossible to distinguish a simple meeting from an association. Let me give you irrefutable proof. As I followed the discussion of this bill in the other Chamber in order to understand the arguments of both sides, I was astounded when after eleven days of debate and after the three articles of the bill were passed, someone asked the minister to explain the words "*meeting*" and "*association*." This was in regard to the electoral meetings. Some said that the two words meant the same thing in the new law; others said the contrary. One minister rose and said that it is necessary on this point to rely upon the wisdom of the courts, which will understand and interpret.

They will interpret! I have heard this word spoken several times by this minister, and I wrote it down at the time for fear that later my good sense would accuse my memory of deceiving me. Is it true that under the Charter the liberty of a true Frenchman is to be submitted to the interpretation of any power whatsoever? Three judges (of course strongly recommended) relying on their intelligence are to be able to see or create an association where there was only an innocent meeting! A strange law indeed to submit to our approval! Thus one of your fellow citizens under preventive arrest and accused by an impassioned authority (for all political power is passionate) could undergo a two-year imprisonment, a fine of 2000 francs, a deportation of four years far from home, property, and business, and a forfeiture of his civil rights because of the sole fact that he was at an innocent meeting which three men in their wisdom considered to have been an association, or part of an association. This is appalling arbitrariness!

The characteristics of a forbidden association enumerated in the old Article 291 disappeared entirely with the new Article 1 of the ministerial bill. The association, purposely not defined in order to allow it to apply to all, can still be persecuted when it is broken down into sections of fewer than twenty persons. Agreed. But at least tell us how we can clearly recognize a *section*. Give us a single characterisitc, even one. This is not too much to ask in a matter touching the security and liberty of every one of us. Will it be a gathering of ten, six, four persons? You do not say, and your law too fails to specify.

It is the arbitrariness that you want! Any definition whatever might snatch some citizens from your future tyranny; you want them all to be subjugated and not one to escape. This is what the Government will like, what will please the police and the courts of misdemeanors.

And we are told that our liberty is not in constant danger! The bill is a Damocles' sword hanging over the head of each of us. Who will be safe from suspicion, from being informed on for having been connected with an association *section*!

Will the minister dare to repeat that the bill carries no threat for Article 4 of the Charter, guaranteeing individual liberty? Article 1 does so in outrageous fashion. "Individual liberty [says the Charter in Article 4] is equally guaranteed, no one being able to be prosecuted or arrested except in the cases *anticipated* in the law and in the *form* therein prescribed."

As to the *form*, it will be simply preventive arrest, of which I shall speak in a moment. We saw how the ministerial bill *defines* the *case* which will carry loss of liberty for the citzen. Can one trifle with so serious and so sacred an article? Little more is needed utterly to exasperate the country. In this way tempests are sown and revolutions reaped.

Article 2 provides that in case of simple violation, that is for a meeting of up to the number of twenty persons, or in a section of less than twenty (perhaps three or four persons), without purpose and without regular times of meeting (here it is more vague; the law is precise), all will be punished equally. Article 292 of the despotic code of 1810 provided for punishing only the leaders. But Article 2 of the 1834 bill, beside extending the penalty to everyone, carries a fine of 2000 francs and two-year imprisonment, followed by four years of exile far from one's department, family, property, and business, under the control of the police. The courts of misdemeanors will have the administration of this monstrous penalty, which horrifies everyone when we learn that it is to be imposed for a simple violation like having omitted to present the society for the police's approval, perhaps even for being at a meeting while supposing that this formality had been taken care of.

As to the political misdemeanors committed by the association or section thereof, the Government has taken care to say in Article 3 of the bill that they will continue in the domain of the jury and consequently, I think, under the control of the Penal Code's punishments. But since even without any political offense, the penalty will be 2000 francs for a simple violation, I hardly see what the jury will still have to do; authority will already have its satisfaction. Furthermore it might often happen that the penalty resulting from a well-proved offense would be much less than that for a simple violation under the exceptional law of 1834. Without the slightest doubt the scope of the power asked will account for the most anomalous things' being done. One can predict in advance that political offenses committed by the associations will not much occupy the juries. However, the courts of misdemeanors will be very busy under the ministerial bill, and thus the constitution will be eluded, the citizens separated from their natural judges. Article 53 of the Charter will thus be distorted.

As to criminal matters, they are reserved for you if the Government finds it proper. Surely you will not forget when deciding whether the case is appropriate for your consideration that you always retain your traditional right to judge your own competency. In this way the accused can be returned to their natural judges, and they will always be so returned.

The ministry will still have the right (which is not found in its law in formal terms but which has been explained in the other Chamber) to arrest preventively those whom it desires to bring before the courts of misdemeanors for simple violation. This is its reason. It cannot tell if the individual suspected by the police of having been part of an association or section of an association for charity, agriculture, literature, or politics has committed a political offense or even a political crime in such a society or with such societies. Because of its extreme respect for the Charter, it must prejudge nothing, but first arrest the suspect. Later and at its leisure several weeks or months hence, it can determine whether there was a political offense or a simple violation of the law such as omitting to be properly authorized by the police.

The ministers have other fine arguments. They say that they want no arbitrary power, nothing but preventive arrest, which they consider to have proved to the most criminal-minded to be indispensable. The tribunals are to interpret the violation or offense which your law does not define. It is true that in every free state the law alone defines and leaves no loophole for interpretation. The judge is charged only with its application. Let us change that; but it is for the good of the country. The judicial power alone will appraise, will decide whether there is or is not association, misdemeanor, simple violation, or political offense.

I understand. The judicial power will share with you and under your initiative the inconceivable arbitrariness which you request. But the court of misdemeanors is made up of judges who like you are men and so subject to error. Thus, under a law which does not define what an association is, what a section of one is, or what a meeting is, the court will be able to see and create a case where not even the least intention of wrong-doing existed.

What do the ministers say of the huge fine included in their bill for the simplest violation? Such large fines are unheard of in our law codes, where a simple violation of the law is punishable by only a few francs' fine. Depending on his sense of justice a judge could punish a case of simple violation either with a sixteen francs' fine without prison or with one of 1000 francs and a year's imprisonment. You may ask: On the leaders only? No, on the members too—I was about to say on the innocent members. And if there is a second offense, the judges can raise the penalty to 2000 francs, two years in prison, and four years of exile, with loss of civil and political rights. No one has ever seen such penalties for simple violation of the law.

You want to do all this in a free country, in the midst of the unchaining of party politics, to give so great an extension of power to inflict punishment to three judges, men whose intentions will no doubt be pure enough, but which unknowingly will be modified by their political opinions.

The ministers will say that we are wrong to be frightened. The 2000 francs' fine, the two years' imprisonment, the four years' exile are only there as a deterrent. No such punishment will be exacted for a mere violation. I am not so sure. Why do you want then to put such terms in your bill? I maintain that since this is the way your law reads, it is your plan and your hope to punish in this way those who offend you. All absolute power by nature corrupts, and I know this from personal experience. It is a question of political parties, of political resistance, and whether it is justified or not does not matter. What man who is armed and powerful, when he is tired of constantly recurring opposition will not abuse his power?

I should like to ask the ministers this question: Since France's earliest days have they never seen the courts even without their knowledge bow to the influence of an irritated and vindictive Government? In those distant times when the estimation of the crime and the extent of the punishment were left to the wisdom of the judge, how many innocent men suffered! How many were executed out of vengeance! Our history is full of examples for which the proudest on the day of their fall have paid the price; for the powerful fall too, often cut down by the very arbitrary power which they prepared for the adversaries who embarrassed or incommoded them.

Arbitrary power! But are we not in the fourth year only of the July Revolution? It is no small matter to the nation whether this despotism results from an ordinance or a law. It is even more unsightly in case of a law, for then it assumes the mask of hypocrisy, whereas in the ordinance it has the aspect of naked force, and France feels less humiliated under force than under hypocrisy. Whence have these famous ordinances which have aroused so implacable an anger drawn their strength? From an article in the Charter. They were thus more excusable; though they were illegal, they had the appearance of constitutionality. The government of that period was nevertheless overthrown, demolished, destroyed, annihilated, so greatly is despotism abhorred in France.

But you are the Government of July, improvised there on the paving stones out of hatred of despotism and to prevent any possible return of it. Yet you, this very Government, after the famous Article 14 was effaced and the Charter remade precisely to remove everything that might give rise to or be a pretext for any arbitrary act, for two years now have been tormented by your councilors with the need for despotism! What blindness! But you must prevent this fatal delirium on the part of the Government. You must reject an unconstitutional law which will lead the Government to ruin. You must recall to it the new Charter which it did not grant but which has been imposed upon it. This Government would not have come into existence if it had not accepted all the conditions and sworn to observe them, and the principal one of these was that arbitrary power should never again rule in France.

There is another ministerial argument: Inform us, submit, be authorized, let us censor you. If your purpose is innocent, what does your submission matter?

It matters to many people, who do not like any form of censorship.

I ask the ministers: If an association for the extension of electoral rights petitions them, will this association be recognized?

If a society for decreasing the tax on liquor and salt came to them, would this society be authorized?

If an association for the defense of individual liberty, of liberty of the press, of all other rights presented itself, would this association be authorized?

I could enumerate other groups founded on rights granted in the Charter.

I maintain, and you because you are honest will not contradict me, that none of these associations would find favor in your eyes. All would be censored, rejected, prohibited.

Thus your bill implicitly attacks all the rights sanctioned by the Charter, since it tends to prevent their defense as entrusted to the general citizenry under Article 66.

The truth is that you want only meetings favorable to you. You want no one to be able to meet in France except your friends. But this is not as France understands it. Then it is no longer the association which is persecuted but the sacred right to associate, the natural right recognized by the Charter. But there is no longer any right when its exercise depends upon the consent of authority. The bill seeks to limit his right, and here your caprice, arbitrariness, or pleasure is evident.

Doubtless the Government asks only a temporary power, a despotism of several weeks, several months at most, subject, of course, to reporting to the legislative powers. Not at all. It wants the law for good, and as for reporting to the legislature on the handling of such extralegal power—it has not even any idea of doing so.

What will be the means of carrying out such a law? Espionage, seizure of lists, informers—there can be others, for the law does not define the association as does Article 291 of the Penal Code, which will be forfeited in favor of ministerial arbitrariness. A moral law, one worthy of respect and in the national spirit, rather than one which entails espionage, house search to hunt lists of so-called members, and informers! These phenomena are the results of the July Revolution then! We are going to see more fine days of denunciation. The valet will be received by the police and be praised for selling his master and taking the price of his betrayal. We know that in the case of treason the Government is not parsimonious and extensively uses secret funds put at its disposal.

I should praise the honesty of the ministry in this matter. It is pleasant finally to be able to approve this ministry, to cease to criticize and blame it! I saw the following: Before the opening in the other Chamber of the discussion of the bill now being discussed here, at the moment when the first speaker was to be called on, the Minister of the Interior (it was the previous one) came to the rostrum and said naively and frankly that the Government needed a supplement of 1,500,000 francs for the secret funds—without giving any accounting of course—for the success of its future law on associations. He then laid before it a bill for this purpose.

The ministry did not want the Chamber to be involved lightly. It wanted it to know in advance the full import of the law which it was to pass. It is all very well to act without finesse or guile. We must be warned then that in the law on associations there is an entire system of espionage and informing. Who would not be exposed to it? The door is wide open both to individual vengeance and to weight of power. There will be premiums given and profits founded on the misfortune of one's fellow man. We know that it is not the most honest men of the kingdom who have the ignoble position of informer; thus these scoundrels, in their desire to get and to continue to get their pay, will often expose and forfeit the liberty of honest men by false and lying reports.

The ministers say with candor worthy of their bill: Have confidence; leave the handling of the law to our sense of impartiality. But how can I believe in it after so many acquittals have been pronounced in favor of those accused of political crimes. Daily they fill the prisons and daily the jury empties them. What a fine institution is that of the jury in the midst of politics. And how much the peers of the realm especially charged with the conservation of national institutions must watch that they not be deprived of a single political offense. What finally remains of this high impartiality of the ministers and their agents? Almost always the memory of a long, useless, painful detention in which several have lost their health and fortune.

To sum up: The bill offered by the July Government is a vast network which is capable of enveloping all France and which will make it possible for the Government to arrest anyone it wants to, when it wants to, and to inflict severe punishment on whomever it will.

Confiscatory of a right of nature respected by Article 291 of the Penal Code and sanctioned by the Charter; arbitrary and infringing upon individual liberty; despotic and violating jurisdictional powers; despotic in regard to punishment, arbitrary even in the word *association*—such is the bill that the ministry offers you. Here is the power which it has just asked you to give over forever.

[Some paragraphs dealing with point 5 are omitted here.]

The ministry has told us that it needs this law because of circumstances. I want to say that I think circumstances and need do not make the law inevitable. . . .

We are to examine the nature of these pressing circumstances, this relentless need which the ministry has been urging before us for two months. We shall prove to ourselves, to the ministry, to the Chamber, and to France, already disturbed by these imaginary fears, that society is not in a state requiring a *coup d'état*.

For the ministerial bill is really a *coup d'état*. It does not matter whether the blow struck the Charter is by way of an ordinance or a law. The result is the same whether one of the powers of society usurps on its own account or usurps with the help of the two other powers because they are weak enough to formulate its will in the shape of law. The 10 August, 31 May, 13 Vendémiaire, 18 Fructidor were likewise terrible *coups d'état*. They also created arbitrary power for the benefit of one of the constituted powers. How were they accomplished? With laws. I have demonstrated sufficiently that the ministerial bill creates arbitrary power for the advantage of the government. Thus it is a real *coup d'état*, in which it would like to make you accomplices in the name of *necessity* and *circumstances*.

The ministers tell us that it is impossible to govern if you do not give them this law. I think too that they are incapable of governing within the limits of our constitution. They have proved this point. But I ask in my turn what necessity forces them to keep their portfolios. I myself do not see this absolute necessity, and I am convinced that, in view of their powerlessness to govern without exceptional or arbitrary laws in the midst of these circumstances of which they speak, if they wished to resign their offices Louis Philippe would easily find talent to conduct the ship of state in constitutional waters and to extricate it from these terrible circumstances with which they are trying to frighten you.

Are these circumstances as real as you say? You yourselves, gentlemen of the ministry, are going to prove the contrary to us. A little more than three months ago, on December 23, you were telling us by means of the Crown's press organ: "The peace of France has not been disturbed since your last session. It has had order and peace. Everywhere industry and labor are reaping their reward. The population, occupied and quiet, counts on the stability of our institutions and on our faithfulness in protecting them, and the public security is the measure of our national prosperity."

That is what you were saying three months ago to France, of whose peace, quiet, tranquillity, and prosperity you were boasting. How does it happen then that already three months ago you had your bill on association drawn up? What is the good of such a law if all is tranquil and prosperous? Are we to believe your words at that time or today? And what are we to think of a law so harsh and arbitrary as to be an exceptional law for your country while you address the country in pleasing words; for you spoke then of the stability of our institutions and of your fidelity in preserving them.

For two months you have been telling us that the country is on a volcano, that the societies are working, burrowing in it, undermining it in every way. Is a single month enough to have covered France with societies ready to overthrow it? Let us be more frank; the evil, if it exists, does not lie in the associations but in a power which would like to govern outside the conditions of its existence. These societies or associations are resisting, and that is the cause of the struggle. But since the Charter does not offer you, thank God, any way to end the resistance in your favor, you ask of us frankly an extralegal measure, a *coup d'état*, to assure yourselves a criminal victory.

The Chamber refuses you this *coup d'état*; I do not hesitate to be its interpreter. But who is in the right? You who are trying to escape Article 291 of the Code? Or those who submit to it? You claim that those who submit to it are conspiring. I have already told you that the right of association has nothing to do with conspiracy. Prosecute the conspiracy if there is any; it is your duty to do so; but leave the associations in peace; they will not stop being peaceable if you do not claim for yourselves an unconstitutional right over them.

Do not disturb the admitted peace prevailing since the last session. The nation has proved that it clings to its rights. Look how protests against your bill already are pouring in from all over the kingdom urging that the Chamber of Peers have the foresight not to adopt it into law.

If you are unfortunate enough to obtain this law, then you really will be in serious *circumstances.* I call as my witness this July Revolution which has brought you into being, of which you are the creation and the children. What set off a war to the death, a war of great results, violent, and yet over in three days? An arbitrary measure, based however on Article 14 of the Charter at that time. Your *necessity* is only an Article 14; but that article is entirely unconstitutional; the conquerors of July have killed it forever, and the new Charter of 1830 was its grave. Govern then within constitutional limits and do not leave this path; otherwise you will perish by plunging us all into another revolution.

You would like more strength and power for the Crown. But consider that it does not depend upon you or us to change a compact imposed upon us in the name of the sovereign people, one which we have all sworn to this same people to preserve intact. To try to curb its right of association more than is done by Article 291 of the Penal Code would only irritate it. I for one fear its wrath. Remember that after its last victory the people went to the City Hall and there laid the foundation of the future government. What was it? You know it as well as I do (but you have forgotten it in your law of associations). The principle was that of a monarchy surrounded by republican institutions. Do not drive the people to defend—as they already threaten to do—the right that you want to deprive them of. You say that if there is a revolt, you will come out victors as in June. Charles X counted too on coming out as victor in July. . . . The chances of political battle always are uncertain; if you succumb (who knows?), republican institutions alone will remain.

Will you agree to risk the existence of your country in this way?

You want to know how you are to overcome the evil of associations. First of all associations are not evil, and they will be of great benefit if only you encourage their development instead of opposing them.

How forgetful is man when he is prosperous! Yes, you have already forgotten who the fighters of July were. Let me recall them to you; they were the workers. Victory came as a result of their strength and courage, and you have said so a hundred times.

You would like these same workers whom you have praised a hundred times not to associate in order to try to participate, legally of course, by working for the well-being which you let them anticipate as a result of change within our institutions. They would like to see their pay raised. If they use threats, the law and Article 415 are there to punish them. You should not let this article be a dead letter, as you did two months ago so that you could say that the laws are insufficient and ask for an exceptional law. You yourselves should organize some social and economic societies. By organizing each interest separately you can avoid having the workers join political associations. True liberty will exist only when each profession, social group, industry, and trade has associations in which the interests of all are understood and balanced, when each has a spokesman, its president or manager, to present its complaints, its needs, or an improvement in its condition to authority and the legislature. Isolation kills liberty. A poor, weak being without protection begins to think of the need he has to associate himself with others to resist injustice or to make his legitimate demands count. I say again: Organize those of the same social group, industry, etc.; you will cause authority to give its blessing instead of cursing and provoking revolts by wanting to restrain that right of association which as an absolute need has become part of our way of life.

If you propose a law on associations of this sort, we shall accept it quickly. France will bless you. The workers will see that the July Revolution is good for France too, and they will avoid the evil counsel, if counsel it is, which you say pursues them to arouse them and push them into insurrection.

You will thus remain within the desired conditions of your existence and will not leave your path. Not only will you not perish, but you will assure the existence of your country without its being *necessary* to have recourse to laws which the Charter forbids us to grant you.

Peers of the realm! In rejecting an imprudent and unconstitutional law, you will fulfill the principal purpose of your existence by restoring to the peerage the eminence and weight indispensable to our representative system; you will extricate France from the state of anxiety and agitation into which for two years the liberty-destroying attempts of the July Monarchy have plunged her.

6. The Transition from Guildsman to Factory Worker

Notes and Letters of Journeyman Johann Eberhard Dewald
(1836-1838) *

Journeyman Dewald in his diary reveals the contrast between two ways of life, that of the traditional handicraftsman
and that of the emerging factory worker. The handicraftsman
regarded himself as a member of the middle class; the worker
was rapidly becoming a class-conscious member of the proletariat. The difference in attitudes toward work and moral
responsibility with respect to oneself and society, the concern
for culture in the one case and the lack of it in the other, the
cheerfulness of the one point of view as against the pessimism
and incipient bitterness of the other—these and many other
points of comparison can be drawn from the pages covering
two years' experience of J. E. Dewald. In every country, although at different times, similar changes were occurring.
Many journeymen found a successful life as craftsmen in the
developing industrial economy and remained within the middle class. Many others became, as workers, members of the
industrial proletariat. Others seized the opportunities of the
industrial revolution to become members of the bourgeoisie
as entrepreneurs or managers and foremen. Some raised themselves into positions of intellectual and professional leadership.
As a social group the handicraftsmen had a wide range of activities in the changing life of the nineteenth century, and
Journeyman Dewald's account reveals many of them.

The next day, March 4, we got our visas for Constance. In a cut-
ting north wind and an increasingly heavy snowstorm we journeyed
through Eckertsweiler to Offenburg. The sharp snow silenced us, and

* Dr. W. Fischer, *Quellen zur Geschichte des deutschen Handwerks* (Göt-
tingen: Musterschmidt Verlag, 1957), XIII, 123-35.

I had plenty of time to think over my ill-fated travel plans. On the way we met a good-hearted countryman who for love of God took our packs on his wagon. You should try walking in such thick snow while carrying your pack. I should not like to see how the pleasure in it would fade. This was not the first time for us, and we were glad to be able to creep behind the warm stove in the inn at Lahr. We had hardly warmed ourselves, however, before we went outdoors again to look around for work. Outside the storm almost bowled us over. The master for certification had a vacancy, and since I had no desire to sign up, my traveling companion decided because of the bad roads and stormy weather to take service. He left his pack with the master and went with me again to the inn to speak to the journeymen and to hear what he could. One hears news in all kinds of ways, and so it was here. But not much that was favorable came out. The journeymen gave the master a bad name. They let their tongues flap, and what they said I do not like at all. He is a skinflint, a miser, who counts every spoonful the journeymen put in their mouths and can not complain enough about how dear food is, so that one almost would vomit it up if one were not afraid the mistress would make another meal out of it. She is his image and not a whit better. Besides, to him the best of the experienced journeymen is no more than a young apprentice.

We had our ears more than full of the gossip and my companion was disgusted with the thought of going into service there. He wanted to go on with me but did not do so; first he enjoyed the free food and lodging and then joined me early the next morning. We went on to Kippersheim. The behavior of my companion was too much for me, however, and I told him quite plainly that his manners were unworthy of an upright and honorable journeyman. The word of a traveling journeyman is also something, and no master can be blamed if he refuses to sign a journeyman who has done such a trick. My companion kept quiet. He saw for himself how badly he had acted. In any case he no longer boasted of his trick and went with me to the church, since the bell began to ring as we entered Kippersheim. May he have honestly repented here before his God!

As the day advanced the road thawed. Our boots were already clumps of mud. After we spent the night in Emmendingen we started out early the next morning. The roads were slick as ice, and it snowed on top of this, but not quietly and regularly as snow usually falls; rather it swirled and danced around us so that it would have been fun if we had not been so bitterly cold. A traveling jacket does not keep one warm enough, and to wear an overcoat may be all right for settled people but not for travelers. Thus we were glad to be in Freiburg about eleven o'clock, where we turned in at the first inn behind Martin's Gate to liven ourselves up with a hot grog.

We spent the afternoon at the guild house and about seven o'clock sought the inn, where we were to spend a gay evening with Antoine and the students. We got ourselves up in clean clothes, and my blue coat and silk hat would have let me pass as a gentleman, although I am proud of my calling and not at all inclined to deny that I am a journeyman tanner.

Still my traveling jacket would not have been well taken by the students and I wanted no one to think that I was not honoring him. At first all went well. The students conducted themselves like us and treated us to wine, Kaiserstühler they called it, so that soon there was general merriment. They wanted to hear of our journey, and when we told about the annoyances we had endured from the soldiers who everywhere stuck different orders under our noses the students denounced them vigorously, brought big songbooks out, and sang with real enthusiasm about them. They treated the princes in the same way, and there was laughter and shouting when they had polished one off.

Finally one student called for quiet and delivered a long speech from which I know only that all frontier barriers must be burned, those on the roads and others too which divide the people of the German land. Germany has only one language, and the students from Rostock are not less German than those from Freiburg or the handworkers from the Rhine. So he said, and he called us welcome as German brothers. I did not know what that meant. Then he began to speak of a united Germany, in which only the upright man was to be respected no matter what coat he wore. Then he struck the table with his sword, they all sprang up, and they sang a song that I did not know with such enthusiasm and so loudly that my ears rang.

They were just in fine fettle when outside there was a knocking at the shutters. The singing stopped in a trice. In seconds the students crept away like cats; they called us but we did not know what was the matter. Antoine too had disappeared. We travelers stood among the empty glasses like poor sinners and looked perplexedly at one another.

Three town police entered the room and took us prisoners. At the police station we were questioned minutely. But what we said they did not believe, and in the end they put chains on our hands as if we were the commonest street thieves. Then we lay in a musty cell and did not know in the least why we were there. We felt miserable when we thought of the wild cursing of the soldiers. I thought that my entire journey would end in prison. The two others soon went to sleep but I could not close an eye. I had often heard how prisoners who had sung forbidden songs were roughly handled. What would they think at home, my parents and Therese. This funster of an Antoine had done me a bad turn.

I thought that it would never be day again. With the first light, keys rattled and a soldier called us to come out. In the watch room Antoine was arguing vigorously with the soldiers. His master wanted us free, for we were traveling, honest craftsmen as our passports showed. We had only by chance fallen in with the pack and their rebellious songs. Why had we been arrested anyway? He ran on like a flax-dresser, spoke of the passports which he had brought from the inn, and told the soldiers that it was against the law to put orderly wandering journeymen in chains. The sergeant pointed to my clothes and said that they did not look like travel. He wanted to see the passports before he would believe a word, since Antoine was well known as a talker. Thus we stood by the overheated stove and the discussion went on endlessly.

Antoine flew away as if possessed and in a short time was back again; meanwhile the constables heaped the most honorable names upon us. When they saw our passports, however, they made faces longer than the day before St. John's day and asked us to show our travel money. In addition and as if for pleasure, we were thoroughly searched and had to appear naked before the men. This is always a concern to me because one is embarrassed to be naked. All this because we had sung a song with the students to united Germany! They do not make it easy to be proud of one's country, but nothing shall tear the love of country out of my heart!

When we could go I said a prayer of relief and poured it on to Antoine. He did not hear much that was pleasant but laughed as if it had been a killing joke. We then quickly fetched our packs and got out of the town as fast as our legs could carry us. Behind the gate we met the company of the evening before. They took us joyously in their midst, hung our packs on their backs, and after some talk began the same song whose melody had since the night sounded so bad in our ears. There seemed no end to it. I saw clearly why the soldiers had been so annoyed, for in it authority was not treated well and Germany was always referred to with a cut at the princes. In a tavern on the road the students treated us and set before us a good breakfast. They were, God knows, lusty fellows and did not intend anything evil in what they chattered along about. We couldn't be angry at them any longer because of the infamous night. With all their big talk they are not bad friends, and we had to hear once more thoroughly that the situation in Germany could not forever continue as it was. All we young people must stand together for German liberty.—The good wine which they poured for us did much of course; but we felt that the feeling came from something else rather than from drinking. The heartfelt friendliness of the students to us wandering journeymen made our blood warmer than all the wine in the world could. So we went on heartened, and from the distance we could still hear them concluding the song which they sang to us in farewell. Then we turned into the valley and the song was lost in the sighing of the huge firs which covered the steep cliffs beside the road.

LINDAU

It lies to some extent on an island and is connected with the shore only by a wooden bridge. Now we were in Bavaria, where a traveling journeyman was under suspicion such as I had already amply experienced. Even at the city gate we were festively received. Here I suddenly saw how right in many ways the students in Freiburg had been. These eternal boundary lines in Germany are actually an invention of the devil. The unending passage of road controls and the prying into passports by constables and soldiers of all kinds are a source of much annoyance and are burdensome enough for a real journeyman who wants nothing more than to look about in the world and learn his trade. Like a web in which the best of us can be captured, the tariff barriers run throughout the country, and one might argue like the Freiburgers if only that would accomplish anything. But idle talk alone changes nothing, and the nine-times wise have not advanced the world a yard.

Having begun with some wise chatter, I will do better to write of how in Lindau at the gate we had to give up our passport books and were sent without ceremony to the town hall, to which in addition a soldier accompanied us. He was a good fellow and as German as we, something one could easily enough forget in view of all the inconvenience which the uniforms cause one. Stark naked, we were searched at the town hall and forced to show our travel money. I was angry and showed the secretaries my full purse; their faces were so lean that they easily could have butted a goat between the horns. They had nothing against me and that was fine with me. Still I had reckoned wrongly. My traveling companion got into difficulty because he had only a few *kreuzer* with him. The secretaries were glad of the prospect of putting him into municipal labor where he could earn his ten *gulden*. They grimaced with satisfaction, but I opposed them. I told them that my companion had lent me ten *gulden* in Constance, where I had left my luggage for transport, so that I had retrieved my pack only when I got to Nonnbach. Thus what I had shown was not mine alone; he had a share in it too. Now they eagerly counted it, but there was a goodly surplus, so they had to let us go. The secretary had to remind us, however, that we were in Bavaria and not just anywhere in the world. I told him very modestly that we had immediately noted that at the city watch, they had such pretty uniforms. This the man took seriously and he let us go. Worse than the city guards were the roads we had to travel, and they would have done better to tend to them than to search journeymen to the skin. Judging from all the care which has been taken with my body, I must have been full of mange.

On a hill we rested and looked out over the beautiful region of the lake of Constance, which lies like a clear mirror between the height of the Hegäus reflected in it and the snow mountains of the Alps, with cheerful villages and towns on the shore. It looked just like a plaything made for the pleasure of man. Then we went landward and lost the lake from view.

On the next day the roads were frozen as hard as stone. Until about midday we got on well; then it began to thaw, and we had to wade through mud. Because of our tired legs, it was very agreeable to us to turn into a tavern which lay near the great Seltmann factory, whose workers at four o'clock came here for supper. We were eager to hear all we could about work in such a large place, if they would speak to us about it. But they did nothing of the kind; instead they looked us over through a window in the door and did not even know how to offer us greeting. They did not have honorable guild customs enough for even one of them to speak to us and to ask about our journey. They laughed outside at the bar as if we were the cause of their mirth and then went away without looking back at us. Such behavior I had never met, and even though after the long journey we were covered with mud, they could easily see that we were upright journeymen. If they were to go to school for a while to the students of Freiburg, the tanners of Seltmann would soon learn how to respect worthy people and how the heart stirs when anyone calls another brother, as it should be everywhere in Germany. When afterward we introduced ourselves to the foreman to have our papers stamped, he invited us to visit the factory. I exchanged greetings with every worker, for I should have been sorry to disregard the polite guild custom which my father enjoined on my soul of never offending without cause. From Nellenbrück we continued our journey on March 14, 1837, on foot.

Spring advanced cheerfully over the country. Hill after hill stood in the light of day, and the beautiful clarity of the air made the distance seem near. We sang as heartily as we could. A seldom-experienced gaiety made every step farther into the world an unexpected joy. During a rest in a forest of larches, a kind of tree which I had never seen at home, my companion cut my hair, which had grown too long, and then lay down on his stomach to write in his diary and to write a letter, something I do in an inn and preferably at night when everything is quiet. I blew a few little pieces on my flute, tunes which I remembered from the innkeeper's daughter. In between I listened to the birds practicing in the stillness of the forest and more and more loudly accompanying my flute. The sun fell straight through the light canopy; it was warmer than at any time this year. Oh, dear Lord, how much you have blessed our German land!

MUNICH

Easter came. I shall never forget the Resurrection celebration in the Church of the Holy Virgin, when after the quiet the triumphal hymn "Christ is Risen" filled the broad nave with joyous sound. How insignificant is man and yet how much he is through God the Father, who permits him to perform wonders such as astonish man himself. I always think that whoever does not feel this cannot be sincere and cannot be happy in his work.

After that until evening I noted in my diary everything which happened up to that time, and much became clear to me which I have lately experienced without thinking about it.—

In the evening a fellow countryman from Königsfeld came in who works here. We were soon in conversation. He poured me a bottle of Rhine wine and assured me that he would be glad to have me as a countryman here with him. I was agreeable enough. But when he inquired among the journeymen on hand, they only half-heartedly listened and scarcely answered. Guild customs seem to have died out here, where most work is in factories such as are being everywhere established, and there is no longer any feeling of unity among the journeymen. So I shall have to give up taking service in Munich.

In view of the wretched roads in Bavaria, it was a blessing that the transport people took pity on us, and thus almost without having to walk we came by way of Ebersberg and Wasserburg to Trabersheim. Then we went on by foot. It was a gloomy day, since I was alone; my companion was visiting an uncle and was to meet me by another road. With companionship things go more easily, for a happy word cheers one on and is the best walking stick. I was most gloomy and so was all the more happy to find traveling companions in Traunstein. We had hardly left the town when a carrier let us ride to Teisendorf, for which we sang him some songs in return. A graybeard of a wanderer especially excelled; in a voice that was not bad he sang us all sorts of songs from the Liberation War in which he had participated as a very young man. In this way he had lost the habit of staying in one place. He had drifted from East Prussia and through the years had traveled the roads, taking service where he liked and leaving when he could not overcome his desire to wander. Thereby he was as young as anyone although his hair was grey at the temples. With his storytelling we came unexpectedly to the Austrian boundary and still had not heard enough of what he had to tell of the wartime. All must have been of one heart and one mind to drive out Napoleon, who at that time was making free in the German land with his legions. I thought again of the night with the Freiburger students who called us all brothers and sang their song about German freedom. My heart lifted, and I understood well what they sang, for now I stood at the Austrian boundary, behind which lies as good German land as anywhere on my journey.

On April 3 I visited the palace park at Hellbrunn, which is provided with beautiful fountains and, near them, groups of marble statues which seem to have risen right out of the water and which seek coolness in the shadow of the trees, so brightly shines the spray on the white stone. After that Salzburg did not seem much to me, and we went on by way of Neumark to Schallheim and Linz, where I got a visa. From Grünfeld we came to Wels through which the new railroad passes to Linz. That was a completely unexpected experience, and I was eager to see it. But it did not run on this day, since it goes only three times a week. A coachman took us there for twelve *kreuzer*, and during the journey he denounced lustily the invention which he said the devil had devised. For every honest carrier has now completely lost his small wage; and already, in his case, he could no longer provide enough food for his wife and eight children. What in the name of heaven would develop out of this? The world was becoming a madhouse and everyone was crazy for novelty and for machines, and what once was proper and had for generations passed as honorable is now nothing and just to be laughed at. But still nothing comes of all this cleverness except that there is no longer enough to eat.

I have written down all this cursing because in this way farewell is always said to all to which we are accustomed; the new always seems bad, even though it has brought much gain for us.

This thought occurred to me especially when on another day we took the railroad from Sonnfeld, as many after us will do. It is a strange feeling to travel with such rushing speed and to go in minutes over a distance which would take half a day to cover by walking. It is of course not very refreshing to be covered with the smoke and soot from the engine which the wind drives into one's face. Luckily canvas covers were stretched over the wagons or we should not have looked like human beings, since the smoke was hardly bearable. Without any trouble we got to Linz at 9:30. There wasn't much to be seen that was attractive, so we got visas for Vienna and with two other journeymen boarded a raft which was to take us down the Danube.

PRAGUE

In the factory of Pollak, which was now my work place, to my delight I met a fellow countryman. It was a new experience for me not to live with the master. But it would have been a difficult undertaking to get the many workers of the factory into a common lodging, especially since many were married and had children. A factory like this is quite different from a master's house and there is no unity among the employees. Each goes his own way and pays little attention to the others. Guild-like conduct is lacking and there is no intercourse as among regular journeymen. Moreover I do not like the work; all day long one has to do the same thing and so loses all sense for the whole. Of course it has to be so in a factory, but I can't adjust to it and always feel as if I only half ply my trade.

If the work did not please me, much less did my contact with the Bohemians, who speak another language and in addition were as sly as one can imagine. Because of my work, which I performed vigorously, my co-workers laughed at me and talked as if it were all right to loaf as much as possible. Pollak is a rich man, they said, and pays badly. But I did not succumb to their talk and answered with spirit: a rich man has no fewer troubles, only they are of another kind; he must look out that his factory gets on and does not one of these days lack work so that the workers are no longer needed. Then they made a face. I know from my father's workshop how he spent many an evening calculating and showed me his figures; the leather should not be too dear, so that with the wages he paid he could still get a price which would give him a profit and good customers. The journeymen in the house enjoyed their evening and knew little of the cares which troubled my father. But what good is talk when no one will listen? It is effort wasted and things only become worse.

MILAN

The next morning I went to the capital and was glad to be able to slip into the guild house. It was the same old story with the journeymen that one finds everywhere in recent times. Most of the lodgers were not at all like regular journeymen, and seemed to me not to honor their calling and not to behave according to their craft. No question of what to do or what not to do, but a dreary spectacle of the most ordinary kind. The old handwork customs are here completely disappearing. No feeling of comradeship and the worst behavior. The guild house was more like a pothouse than a respectable lodging. When I noticed that as stakes in their game, the men gave their girls, many of whom were amusing themselves suggestively at a nearby table, I had had enough. I took my pack and sought shelter in another place. Then I went for a look at the town. But I was taken for a beggar, since there are no houses belonging to the guilds here and they thought I was asking alms. The custom has completely disappeared of a journeyman's right to his guild certificate, and if he asks for it, he appears to be a loafer. I gave it up, for I should rather go hungry than bear such disgrace. But I shall not have to do that yet; I have still some money in my pocket.

In the afternoon I wanted to get a visa for Switzerland, but no one would give it to me under any conditions. The police were even suspicious, and I was given to understand that I should not express this wish any longer or they would put me in prison for a goodly time as a revolutionary. Many times I was carefully searched, and finally another officer came and the whole thing began again. I protested that I was an honorable and peaceful journeyman, as my passport showed, and that I was on my way home. After extensive discussion I was believed. But Switzerland must be a dangerous part of the earth and I should never have thought it possible to meet so many difficulties.

In spite of all my unpleasant experiences in Como, I made still another effort to get a visa for Switzerland, but in vain. I went nonetheless to the Swiss border in the hope of finding a way in somehow. But I reckoned wrongly in that I had not thought of the frontier guard or the Italian insurgents. I acted, however, as if I had come this way by accident, but I was seized by a guard and in spite of my protests arrested, and was taken back to Como under escort of two frontier soldiers who held their muskets ready in order to guard me better. They debated vigorously whether to deliver me to Milan but were afraid to do so, since with time I had gained practice and relied upon my passport, which had proper visas. I was right, and after rude unpleasantness I was allowed to go on my way. Again I was under suspicion of conspiring with rebels, although I cannot find that I have anything rash about me. Gradually, however, I seemed to myself to be of great importance; but I should rather be without this fatal reputation, which takes more time than is good for me. But even if too many mischances have been my lot, I am not in the least inclined to be considered a brigand.

AGAIN IN GERMANY

In Wangen I looked about and again received a proper seal. In Germany this is still a guild custom and one is not considered a beggar if one makes use of his guild right. From Lampertsheim we walked on before the cocks crowed on the roost.

In Ulm I found an old guild custom still in use in that the journeymen received not only a master's seal but also a town seal, such as in many places still is given. My father found that to be the case everywhere; it was a regular custom which is not now carried on.

After passing through Leibfriem we reached on the same day the friendly little town of Günzburg. It was truly a picture of the little towns of my homeland. It lay hidden between hills and the smoke rose in the evening light over the roofs. It must be an unending pleasure to be able to enter a friendly house and know that one is at home. I think that I must travel night and day, for in foreign lands I was never so full of longing for home as now, since I am not far from home any more. Therefore I refused the work offered me and got a visa for going on at once. It was against all custom, which I had never unnecessarily broken.

In Roth and Schwabach we ran away from the masters and entered Nürnberg on July 12, 1838. If we were to catch the train to Fürth, we had little time left. We had to wait until the last minute for friend Schneider, who arrived in a rush to travel like us. But the train approached, and in the great noise that it made the latecomer shouted in vain to the engineer that the train should wait, that he must absolutely go along. The train did not wait, although Schneider grabbed our coattails to force it to do so. We all fell together into the mud, which could have been a bad accident, as we could tell from the cries of horror of those standing about; for there were many standing by, attracted by curiosity to watch the spectacle of the train's departure.

For this day there was no other train to take; but since I had gone to Nürnberg to try out the train which I had been fortunate enough once in my life that time in Linz to do, and since we could not linger here longer than twenty-four hours because we already had visas for Fürth, there was nothing to do but to walk there and to wait until the next midday in order to ride the other way, from Fürth to Nürnberg.

This plan succeeded, and we made the trip from Fürth to Nürnberg in barely eighteen minutes. The journey back lasted actually only ten minutes because of the sloping terrain, which the train could lay behind it more easily. We saw the Danube-Main-Ludwig Canal, which is being dug between these two cities. The train route is also called the Ludwig Railway after the Bavarian King. It was a pleasant journey in the open wagons which let in the wind from all sides, for the wagons were without cover. Some courageous women, who had dared to sit with us men in the train carriages, looked anxious as the train rocked badly and they clung to their escorts, who remained unmoved or at least appeared to be so. Fear of a fall was quite unnecessary, since we traveled as safely as on any good road. We had to pay twelve *kreuzer* for the trip, not exactly cheap. I must say however that I should hardly have traveled on foot to Belgrade and Dalmatia if there had been such steam trains everywhere. I might have missed much, though, which I learned to my benefit. But I should have spared my feet, also not a bad thing. But before trains go that far much water will flow down the Rhine and many hundreds of years will go by.

7. Railroads and Nationalism

Count C. Cavour: *Review of Railroads in Italy* (1846)[*]

This famous review article by Count Cavour, the future leader in the unification of Italy, analyzes the part that he expected the revolution in transportation and communication to play in the life of peoples and states. Cavour wrote about Italy; but his general remarks could have been applied to any state of the world beginning to build railroads. The effect of railroad construction upon national unification was felt in nations like Italy and Germany which had not yet achieved formal statehood, and in those like France which had been politically unified for centuries. In all countries alike, railroads and other instruments of modern industrialism helped to substitute a national society of interdependent parts for a society composed of partially or wholly self-dependent local or regional units. The course of events in Italy was to prove that Cavour expected too much from the connection between railroads and nationalism; the revolution of 1848 occurred two years later, and when Cavour did unify the country he found it necessary to employ both revolutionary forces and power politics. Nonetheless the essay contains a clear statement of the fact that basic material changes made possible basic institutional reforms in public life. Economics, technology, politics, and social and cultural movements in this century as in all centuries went hand in hand.

No one with common sense contests the utility or even the necessity of railroads today. A few years have been sufficient to bring about a complete revolution of public opinion in their favor. The doubts that they inspired among statesmen and the uncertainties even the boldest

[*] Comte de Cavour, "Des Chemins de Fer en Italie" (by Comte Petitti, Conseiller-d'Etat du Royaume de Sardaigne), *La Revue Nouvelle*, VIII (1846), 446-79.

of speculators felt about their financial success have been replaced by unlimited confidence. The public has gone directly from suspicion to such enthusiasm that there is hardly a place in Europe so poor or a group of interests so insignificant that it does not expect in time to participate directly in the benefits of this marvelous conquest of the nineteenth century.

Of course public impatience is not free from exaggeration. Influenced by the violent reaction which has taken place, we may delude ourselves as to the immediate effects of the railroads. Yet if we consider the future and deduce all the consequences the general adoption of railroads must accomplish, we shall agree that, though the hopes that they have stimulated may be premature, they are nevertheless conservative.

The steam engine is a discovery which may be compared for the importance of its consequences only with printing, or, better yet, with the discovery of the American continent. These great discoveries are already almost four centuries old, yet their potential is still far from realized. The same will be true of the conquest made in transforming steam into a power supply unlimited in its action and applications. It will be many generations before we can determine all of its significance. No one has yet tried to calculate completely the changes this new power should effect in the economy of civilized peoples.

The influence of railroads will extend all over the world. In the nations which have reached a high level of civilization they will furnish immense impetus to industry; their economic results will be impressive from the beginning, and they will accelerate progress. But the social results which should take place, greater to us than the material results, will be especially remarkable in those nations which have remained backward. For them the railroads will be more than a means of self enrichment; they will be a powerful ally, with whose help they will triumph over the forces holding them in a dismal state of industrial and political immaturity. We are convinced that the locomotive is destined to diminish, if not abolish altogether, the humiliating inferiority to which many branches of the great Christian family are reduced. Thus considered, it fills a providential role; perhaps this is why we see it triumph so easily and so quickly over obstacles which have long prevented it from penetrating into certain regions.

If this is true, no nation has more right than Italy to place great hope in the potential of the railroads. The extensive political and social consequences which should result from them will testify better in this beautiful country than elsewhere to the great role they will play in the world's future. We therefore believe it will be of interest to our readers to see treated in some detail the questions connected with the establishment of railroads in Italy.

Our task will be singularly facilitated by the work whose title appears at the head of this article. Its learned author, Count Petitti, after having contributed greatly as a statesman to the success of the cause of the railroads in his nation, has sought in his capacity of distinguished publicist to allow his fellow citizens to participate in the knowledge which he has acquired, thanks to long work and fruitful research. With this aim he has written a book in which he has brought together first of all the most exact and detailed ideas about all of the railroads which have been built in Italy, about those on which work has started, and even about those which are still in the planning stage; thereafter he has treated illuminatingly and profoundly the principal problems created by the laying of railroads. His work in a way is a complete manual for the use of Italian readers. It is also destined to render the greatest service in a nation where the major industrial questions are familiar to only a small number of readers.

Everyone interested in these questions, no matter of what nationality, will do well to read this remarkable work in its entirety. We shall limit ourselves here to the facts needed to clarify what the future system of railroads in Italy will be, and we shall introduce the documents necessary to justify our opinion of the magnitude of their social influence.

The full development of railroads in Italy is still restricted. There are just a few locomotives, moving on a few short isolated trunks. However, there has been interest in railroads for some time. By 1835 companies had already solicited the governments of the peninsula regarding concessions for several important lines.

But from the beginning these colossal enterprises inspired among capitalists a lack of confidence which the financial crisis resulting from the events of 1840 only aggravated. The meager success of several French railroads made matters worse, and these first efforts were ineffective. The roads from Naples to Castelmare and from Milan to Monza are the only ones whose construction we can attribute to this period of sterility.

Since then the growing success and fame of the railroads in England, Germany, Belgium, and France have greatly modified the Italian position. In Italy as elsewhere, demand arose for construction of the marvelous roads which conquer time and space. Heeding the wishes of the people, most of the Italian sovereigns declared themselves in support of railroads. Several governments undertook direct construction of the main lines, though they did not reject the help of private industry for the secondary lines; others limited themselves to encouraging formation of powerful companies to construct all the State's roads.

At the present time, excepting the Roman States and several secondary principalities, all of the Italian states have actively begun work. Construction has begun on several important lines, and a much larger number of projects have advanced to such a stage that we cannot doubt their eventual completion. A point has been reached from which one may determine at least approximately an outline of the large network of railroads destined in several years to join all points in Italy from the foot of the Alps to the Gulf of Taranto.

To clarify the picture, we are going to sketch rapidly the principal lines which make it up. This outline should be enough to indicate its immense importance.

Geographically, Italy can be divided into two large sections. In the north there is the Po Valley, connected with the plains of Romagna and the Marches as far as Ancona and Loreto. In the south are all the states separated by the Apennines, surrounded on three sides by the Adriatic and Mediterranean Seas. The first section, the Po Valley, tied politically and commercially to Liguria, offers an admirable situation for railroads. We thus believe this region is destined for the most extensive development. The Austrian and Piedmontese governments, possessing the largest part of it, realize this, and have firmly declared their intention of cooperating in every way to construct the network that the country demands.

The sagacious Turin cabinet has profited by the considerable resources at its disposal and decided that the line uniting political and economic interests will be constructed at state expense. For the secondary lines it has called upon private industry, which, we are happy to say, has not been deaf to its appeal.

There are three lines established by the government which we may consider as being under construction. With the strategic city of Alessandria at the point of common departure, these lines lead to Genoa, Turin, and Lago Maggiore. A quick glance at the map of Piedmont will prove that they may be considered the great arteries of the country. In fact, they unite its capital with the sea, Switzerland, and the rest of northern Italy.

For achieving this last result, however, a slight hiatus exists in the approved projects. Because of several difficulties raised by the Austrian government, it has not yet been possible to decide how to unite the lines of Piedmont with the lines of Lombardy. Such a gap cannot exist for long. Lombardy has too real and pressing an interest in the establishment of quick and easy communications with the Mediterranean and France for the Viennese cabinet to be serious in its refusal to construct, or allow industry to construct, the short, simple line from Milan to Tesin, in order to permit trains to traverse freely the whole length of the Po Valley. The projects of the Sardinian government are not limited to those we have just indicated. It has declared its intention of carrying out a much more important and extensive enterprise. It wishes to tie Savoy to Piedmont by a railroad which will pierce the Alps near their base by the Pass of Mont-Cenis, already made famous by the route still pointed out as one of the marvels of Napoleon's reign.

Studies have been made on this excellent project, and if no insurmountable difficulties arise—and they seem not anticipated by those most competent in the field—we shall soon see construction begun.

The railroad from Turin to Chambéry, across the highest mountains of Europe, will be the masterpiece of modern industry; it will be the most impressive triumph of the steam engine, the culmination of its glory. After subduing the swiftest of rivers and the stormy seas, it has only to master the eternal snows and glaciers which create insurmountable barriers between peoples. This road will be one of the wonders of the world; it will immortalize the name of King Charles-Albert, who will have had the courage to undertake it and the energy to carry it out. The incalculable benefits which should result from it will cause the memory of his already glorious reign to be cherished forever, not only by his own subjects but by all Italians.

We may be criticized for exaggerating the importance of this route, but when one reflects that it will abolish the distances separating Venice, Milan, Genoa, Turin, and all of the other principal Italian cities from the leading cities of Europe, one will have to agree that we have underestimated rather than overestimated the influence of the "Railroad of the Alps" upon the industrial and political future of Italy.

This line will make Turin, situated at the base of the Alps where the Italian plains terminate, a European city. It will be the junction point of north and south, where the peoples of the German and Latin races will exchange products and ideas—an exchange especially profitable to the Piedmontese state, which already shares the qualities of both races. This magnificent destiny Turin will owe to the enlightened policy of the kings whose faithful capital it has been for centuries.

Private industry is preparing to respond to the government's appeal and the expectations of the nation. Several companies have been organized, or are in the process of being organized, in order to request concessions for secondary lines to join all points to the principal lines. Requests have already been submitted to the government for the lines from Turin to Pinerolo, from Turin to Savigliono, and from Casale to Valence. It is probable that before the close of 1846 these industrial firms will begin active construction on several lines.

Among the railroads private industry is called upon to undertake is one outstanding in political and economic importance. This is the line between Turin and Milan, which follows the left bank of the Po, passing through Vercelli and Novara. If the Po Valley formed a single state—that is, if all the states between Venice and Turin recognized one sovereign—this would be the main line of northern Italy; it would be part of the great artery to which all of the secondary lines would be joined. So long as the banks of the Tesin are separated by a customs barrier, it cannot hope to play this leading role among the roads of Sardinia; it must cede political preeminence to the road from Turin to Genoa. Nevertheless this road is now the most important of those which may be undertaken by private industry. Without considering future aspirations, we predict that it will exercise great influence and economic benefit. Designed to unite Turin with the better-cultivated provinces—with the busy valleys of Aosta and Biella and those bordering on Lago Maggiore—it will immensely stimulate internal commerce. In addition it will greatly assist exterior commerce and transit for the Sardinian states, terminating as it does in Switzerland on the one end and Milan on the other.

The states of Lombardy-Venetia were the first in Italy in which railroads were seriously considered. As early as 1838 a company undertook, at its own risk, to construct the small line from Milan to Monza, and this line has been open to the public for six years. Another company obtained from the Austrian government the concession for the line from Milan to Venice, but difficulties from the beginning have delayed execution of this excellent project. Municipal and provincial rivalry—the primary cause of Italy's miseries—for several years prevented agreement on the route to follow, and the company was almost forced to dissolve. Once these first obstacles were surmounted, one might have expected that the project would be pushed vigorously, but the almost criminal apathy of the Milanese capitalists and the suspicion of foreign stockholders caused the enterprise to stagnate. Its cause was considered hopeless, when the powerful Austrian government generously intervened to save it from catastrophe. On this occasion the Viennese cabinet manifested toward its Italian subjects sentiments as enlightened as they were benevolent; in the development of this route we are indebted to Austria for changing procrastination to activity. Thanks to the more enterprising spirit of the Venetian stockholders, the gigantic bridge over the lagoon is already completed and the railroad line laid from Venice to Vienna. Vigorously pushed in the past year towards the

gates of Milan, in a few months the road will reach all points of the
route planned. Unless an unexpected obstacle arises, the fervent
hope of the people will thus be realized, and the rich capital of fertile Lombardy and the ancient queen of the Adriatic will be but a
few hours distant from each other.

The Lombardy-Venice line will be incomplete so long as it is not
joined to the Sardinian lines to form with them the great artery of the
Po Valley. The gap we mentioned in speaking of the Piedmontese
roads will soon be filled in—the force of circumstances will easily surmount petty political and economic rivalries. Milan has more interest
in this line than Genoa and Turin because it is through these cities
that the principal products of Lombardy, that is, cheeses and silks,
must pass in order to reach the consumer on the shores of the Mediterranean or in France and England, on the other side of the Alps.

The union of roads we have mentioned may operate in two ways:
by a line going directly to Turin, which would cut the line from
Genoa to Lago Maggiore at Vigevano, or by a road from Milan directly to Genoa, passing through Pavia. Each of these systems has
special merits. The first, conforming more to the topography of the
country, would be more suitable to the general interests of the Po
Valley; the second, bringing Milan closer to the sea in effect, for the
moment would be perhaps preferable under commercial conditions.
Whatever their relative merits may be, it is essential that one or the
other be constructed promptly. When the advantages of railroads are
fully appreciated and political and economic conditions in Italy have
improved, we do not doubt that these lines will both be constructed;
they will form with the Piedmontese lines a wonderful triangle of
roads, of which Turin, Genoa, and Milan will be the corners.

The Lombardy-Venice kingdom, like Piedmont, requires a large
number of secondary lines. The concession for the road from Milan
to Como has already been granted. The roads joining wealthy and
important cities such as Bergamo, Mantua, and Cremona to the main
line will soon materialize. When the interior lines are completed, it
will still be necessary to link the Lombardy-Venetian system to the
lines constructed in the provinces on the right bank of the Po on the
one hand, and, on the other, to the German network of which Trieste
is one of the terminals.

There are enormous technical, economic, and political difficulties involved in joining the two banks of the Po by means of railroads. It cannot take place for several years, until the other parts of the Italian network are completed. By then the cause of railroads will have made such progress that the public will not permit the governments to let pecuniary considerations or other material obstacles stop construction.

Such is not the case with the line from Trieste to Vienna, destined to link Germany with Italy. This route presents almost no difficulties and is too important to Austria for us to believe that its construction will be long delayed.

Of all the railroads mentioned, this is perhaps the only one whose utility for Italy might be questioned. Although there are evident economic advantages in facilitating the export of Italian products to Germany, the road might also increase the means by which Austria could keep Italy dependent. This objection is plausible but not well founded.

A happier destiny for a reunited Italy can result only from a reshaping of Europe or from one of those great upheavals which are unaffected by railroads. The period of conspiracies is past; the emancipation of peoples cannot follow a plot or coup but has become the necessary consequence of the progress of Christian civilization. The material resources at a government's disposition will be powerless to hold conquered nations in submission when the hour of their deliverance strikes. They will yield to moral forces which gain strength daily and will sooner or later effect a political upheaval in Europe from which Poland and Italy will profit more than all other countries.

The road which will bring Vienna and Milan within a few hours of each other will not prevent such great events.

That being the case, the road from Vienna to Trieste is one of those whose construction is most desirable. At present it is advantageous for Italian agriculture to have numerous outlets, but the railroad will render immense services to the nation in the future, when friendly relations between equals will have replaced those established by the conquest. It will facilitate those intellectual and social relations which we strongly hope to see established between somber, profound Germany and clever Italy.

The matter of railroads has been much less promoted on the right than on the left bank of the Po. The small size of the principalities which make up the area, their financial weakness, their imperfect administrative systems, and, finally, their deep-rooted prejudices make problematical the construction of railroads in the southern part of the Po Valley which is not part of the Sardinian states. However, the instability we have been forced to describe is only temporary. There is no doubt that in the near future the rich Parmesan and Milanese plains as well as the other regions of Northern Italy will be equipped with a network of railroads. Already a company considered most distinguished by Bologna and the cities of Romagna has requested permission to build the road from Ancona to Bologna at its own expense, with the intention of extending it later to Modena and Parma. The pontifical government, through excessive prudence easier to explain than to justify, up to now has refused its consent for this project. Nevertheless it appears that the entreaties of the company and repeated popular demand supported by the distinguished prelate who administers the Legations are about to overcome the reluctance of the court of Rome. We hope to see a decree from the pontifical sovereign appear at once, granting the line from Ancona to Bologna to the company of which we have spoken.

We strongly urge this happy change in Roman policy, not only because of the importance of the line in question but because the construction in Romagna of great public utilities would bring immediate relief to the bitterly agitated lower classes of this area. And it will nourish the patriotism and energy of the upper and middle classes, facilitating the policy of patience and hope which is the only reasonable one in Italy's present situation.

The line from Ancona to Bologna will inevitably entail one from Bologna to the Sardinian states, through Modena and Parma. The company owning the first will have such an interest in the construction of the second that it will submit to all the sacrifices the governments upon which it depends wish to impose. These governments, aided by a powerful company, will not long be able to resist the rightful wishes of their subjects.

It is thus hoped that work on the railroads will soon be begun with equal enthusiasm on both banks of the Po. Without undue optimism we can predict that within ten years the magnificent basin formed by this river will have its entire length crossed by two great lines, with Turin as the point of common departure and the Adriatic the common destination. One will terminate in Venice after crossing the fertile plains of Piedmont and Lombardy, and the other will reach Ancona after passing through the Sardinian states, the Duchies of Parma and Modena, the Legations, and the Marches.

To these two principal lines will be joined a multitude of secondary lines which will allow populations and goods to circulate in all directions. Finally, when to this network are joined the German roads through Trieste and the French and Swiss roads through the Alps —King Charles-Albert's admirable inspiration—northern Italy will be able to recapture the high level of prosperity and power to which she is entitled by virtue of her geographical position, the richness of her soil, and her natural resources. We like to think that this will be the finest achievement of the railroads.

Tuscany, which in a way composes central Italy as far as railroads are concerned, has not allowed itself to be outdistanced by any other state. The principal line of the region, from Leghorn to Florence, has for a long time been approved and contracted for. The financial crisis of 1840 and the discredit weighing upon the railroads have for some time delayed construction; however, in the past two years work has proceeded so rapidly that this line, of such vital importance for Tuscany, and already in use for a third of its length, that is from Leghorn to Pontedera, will be open to the public within two or three years.

The general infatuation with railroads which has seized Europe, together with the unexpected success of the road from Leghorn to Pisa, has resulted in the appearance of numerous companies in Tuscany wishing to construct a large number of lines. Two of these companies have obtained formal concessions and have already started construction. The first is building the road from Lucca to Pisa, which should soon be completed, and the second has undertaken an extended line (called the central Tuscan route) which will link Siena to Florence and Leghorn, joining at Empoli the route which will unite these two cities.

The principal routes not yet conceded, or at least on which no work has begun in earnest are as follows:

1. the route from Florence to Bologna;
2. the road from Florence to Forli;
3. the line from Florence to Lucca, which would have a common trunk with the Bologna road as far as Pistoia;
4. the road from Florence to Rome;
5. a line which would go from Leghorn toward the Roman states along the sea, crossing the Maremmas along their whole length.

Certainly among the railroads just mentioned, and perhaps even among those omitted, there are several which offer reasonable chances of financial success as well as great usefulness for the country. There is one especially which we do not hesitate to point out as having prime commercial and political importance—the road from Florence to Bologna. We are not considering the difficulties presented by passage through the Apennines—, but we believe that if money can surmount them it is the duty and concern of the Tuscan government to aid the company undertaking to join the Mediterranean with the Adriatic, placing Leghorn in direct contact with Romagna, the Venetian provinces, and the port of Trieste.

But even though the Tuscan lines are demanded by general interest and capable of repaying the capitalists' advances, there are others whose construction will impose on regions or companies undertaking them sacrifices out of proportion to the advantages expected. Thus we cannot imagine what should be expected of a road crossing the desolate marches separating Leghorn from Grossetto. If this were extended to Rome, as is exceedingly unlikely, many years, perhaps centuries, would pass before relations between Leghorn and Rome would provide sufficient business to support so extended a line whose intermediary points could provide no commerce worth mentioning.

Most of the projects put forth in Tuscany during the last eighteen months, arising when the industrial fever was at its height, are destined to perish in ministerial portfolios. Their only effect will be disastrous stock-market activity in Leghorn and several other commercial cities and the enrichment of industrial adventurers at the expense of a multitude of people as greedy as they are credulous.

Tuscany, as we have just seen, is the nation of Italy where construction of railroads is the most advanced. The neighboring region, the Papal States, is in a diametrically opposed position. Nothing has been done there; and with the exception of the line from Bologna to Ancona, so earnestly solicited by Romagna, little is contemplated.

This is unfortunate, although the importance of the unhappy antipathy railroads inspire in the Roman government must not be exaggerated. Reality always triumphs over delusions. We are convinced that the results of a single great line will be enough to modify the convictions of a good number of Roman prelates. Six months after the road from Leghorn to Florence is opened to the public, most of the members of the Sacred College will change their minds; we even hope that the cause of the railroads will be won sooner in Rome. We have seen such rapid conversions and the disappearance of so many deep-seated prejudices that it seems unlikely that the pontifical government will long remain the only one in Europe preventing the people from enjoying one of Providence's greatest favors.

When the Roman court has modified its present position, Rome will soon become the center of a vast network of railroads, joining that august city with the Mediterranean and Adriatic as well as Tuscany and the Kingdom of Naples. The physical difficulties involved in the construction of this system can be surmounted by modern industry, and Rome will be assured of a magnificent position. Centrally located for Italy and, in a way, for the countries surrounding the Mediterranean, her already considerable attraction will be greatly increased. On the road from the Orient to the Occident all peoples will crowd to her walls to salute the ancient mistress of the world and the modern Christian metropolis, still in spite of numberless vicissitudes the richest in precious memories and magnificent prospects.

Thank heaven we are no longer confined to hypotheses and conjectures after crossing the Roman frontier. In the Kingdom of Naples are roads already completed, roads being built, and many wisely planned projects which will soon be carried out.

Naples was one of the first Italian states to inaugurate a railroad. For the past two years locomotives have run from Naples to Castellamare, and, more recently, they have run from Naples to Capua. These roads still have only slight economic importance, their principal merit being the pleasure they bring the Neapolitans and numerous visitors. They provide admirable excursions through enchanting places, but they will shortly play a more important role, destined as they are to head the principal lines of the kingdom. Their extension is determined upon. The road from Capua will extend to the Roman frontier, and will thus become an important part of the line which will join the two largest cities of Italy, Rome and Naples. The southern line at Nocera will run eastward, reaching the Adriatic at a still undetermined point. The second project, less advanced than the first, is still being studied and will be put into execution before long.

Neapolitan railroads will not stop when they have reached the Adriatic; turning south, they will probably cross the rich provinces bordering that sea and extend to the end of the peninsula, forming the outermost link for communications between the European continent and the Oriental world.

It is impossible to predict exactly when the Neapolitan network will be finished. It will probably be preceded by the system being constructed in the Po Valley. Nevertheless, the commercial advantages of railroads in so populated a nation as the Kingdom of Naples and the well-known sentiments of her king lead us to hope that southern as well as northern Italy will soon have new roads to influence the future of the beautiful Italian peninsula.

According to this account of developments in Italy we may predict a great future for railroads in this country. In a few years the Po basin will be crossed in all directions by a vast railroad system, uniting all the major points of the country; reaching France through Savoy and Germany through Trieste, it will place Italy in constant communication with the European continent. One or two routes will tie this system to the Tuscan network (destined to be greatly extended). Finally, in the Kingdom of Naples a complete system radiating from the capital will allow locomotives to cross from sea to sea, and extending as far as Taranto or Otranto will put Italy in communication with the Orient.

Judging the future by the present, we must acknowledge that the picture is obscured by the blank which the Roman States present. But this unfortunate blot will also disappear. Like so many others, the pontifical government will yield to facts and the unremitting demands of its subjects. Then railroads will extend uninterruptedly from the Alps to Sicily and obliterate the obstacles and distances separating the inhabitants of Italy and preventing them from forming one great nation.

Having discussed Italy's prospective railroad system, we must now determine its probable effects and justify the hopes we want to share with our compatriots.

Economically the railroads will render great service to Italy. They are as useful to rich agricultural countries as they are to manufacturing countries. This opinion may appear paradoxical at first but is founded on solid fact. Agricultural commodities and fertilizers are very different to handle from the raw materials and products of industry. Canals are preferable to railroads for agricultural transportation, but where no canals exist or where their construction is difficult because of topography or it is better to use water for irrigation rather than for canals, the railroads can render a very important service to agriculture.

What is true for the transportation of merchandise is also true where persons are concerned. Within a certain radius the population of rich agricultural regions circulates more frequently than an industrial population would. Where property is highly subdivided and farms are small, one cannot imagine the numerous trips farmers must take. The smallest transaction or the most unimportant contract can force the farmer to go to several markets. The sale or purchase of a pair of oxen often causes more traveling about than does the provisioning necessary to run a large Manchester textile mill for a month.

And this is not all; for where agriculture is extremely diversified, as in Northern Italy, the rural population must continually move from one place to another to satisfy the needs of the various agricultural operations. In the spring the mountaineers from the Apennines come down to the plains to pick mulberries. Later they are joined in other localities by people from a greater distance who reap wheat and mow the meadows. In the autumn the hill dwellers come to help the plainsmen and are later helped in their turn during the vintage.

This incessant movement, indispensable for the proper cultivation of a country as diversified as Italy, is much greater than that which takes place among the workers in the large industrial centers.

The developments in England substantiate this opinion. The line known as the Great Western, which relative to its state of development carries the greatest number of passengers, goes from London to Bristol through almost exclusively rural areas. Its superiority over the London-Birmingham road is all the more remarkable since the latter connects London with Scotland and Ireland as well as with the most populated section of England.

Moreover, the circumstances in Northern Italy make railroads especially advantageous for its agriculture. We know this region produces much raw material which not only has great value in relation to its weight but is essentially perishable, such as cocoons and milk products. Locomotives can cross great distances rapidly, permitting these products to arrive at manufacturing and consumption centers without fear of damage. When the farmers of the Po Valley can dispatch their fresh butter to the arid shores of the Mediterranean, to Liguria and Provence, they will have an almost unlimited market for the rich products of their irrigated prairies.

But Italy can count on the railroad as a powerful instrument of material progress where more than agriculture is concerned. Although this country has concentrated primarily on cultivating her fertile soil, she has not ignored the industrial movement which has spread so widely in Europe since the peace. She already has numerous factories, vast mills, and large workshops; in Piedmont, Lombardy, and Tuscany cotton, wool, and especially silk are processed successfully. By facilitating communication, reducing transportation costs, and encouraging the spirit of enterprise with which Italy abounds, a complete railroad system would contribute enormously to Italian industrial development. It would be unfortunate if special privileges and excessive protective tariffs inimical to the general interest were used to bring about such a vast development. Italy already possesses abundant natural resources—the almost unlimited power source furnished by the Alpine glaciers; a large variety of products of the soil; mineral wealth, particularly in certain parts of

Piedmont and Tuscany; and a sober, intelligent, hard-working population. Encouraged by equitable laws and provided with capable, well-educated leaders, her industry can reach a high level of prosperity by itself once she achieves the communication system we have described.

Commercially Italy can place great hopes in the railroads. By making internal communications swift, economical, and safe and in a way eliminating the Alpine barrier which separates her from the rest of Europe and is so difficult to cross for part of the year, the railroads will greatly increase the number of foreigners who visit Italy every year. When the trip from Turin, Milan, Florence, Rome, and Naples takes less time and trouble than a tour of a Swiss lake, an incalculable number of persons will seek these attractive provinces for reasons of health, sentiment or distraction. The profits Italy will reap from her sun, her cloudless sky, her artistic wealth, and her memories bequeathed by the past will increase considerably. This will be an undisputed benefit from railroads; but we believe that it is the least important one of the many we can expect, though it may strike the popular imagination more. The presence of many foreigners in our midst is a sure source of profit, but it is not free from disadvantages. Contact with rich, idle persons who in a way exploit in order to live scarcely favors the development of industrious, moral habits; it engenders a spirit of cunning and servility fatal to the national character. We put a nation's consciousness of its own dignity first and are unimpressed by the profits to be derived from insolence and arrogance. We do not wish to stop the progressive movement impelling foreigners to Italy; yet we cannot consider it as truly to her advantage until, thanks to the progress of her industry, she is able to dispense with them and can treat them with perfect equality.

When the railroad network is complete Italy will enjoy considerable transit commerce. The lines uniting the ports of Genoa, Leghorn, and Naples with Trieste, Venice, Ancona, and the east coast of the Kingdom of Naples will transport across Italy much merchandise and many travelers coming and going from the Mediterranean to the Adriatic. Moreover, if the Alps are crossed, as we have every reason to believe they will be, between Turin and Chambéry, between Lake Maggiore and Lake Constance, and between Trieste and Vienna, the Italian ports will join those of the Atlantic and the North Sea in provisioning central Europe with exotic products.

Finally, if the Neapolitan lines are extended to the end of the kingdom, Italian commerce will reach new heights. Italy's central position in the Mediterranean, like an immense promontory linking Europe with Africa, will give her the shortest, easiest path from the Orient to the Occident once the railroad covers her entire length. When one can embark at Taranto or Brindisi, the sea route to Africa and Asia from England, France, and Germany will be cut in half. It is thus unquestionable that the great Italian lines can then transport most of the travelers and some of the most precious merchandise circulating between these vast regions. Italy will also furnish the fastest route from England to India and China—another abundant source of new profits. Thus it is obvious that the railroads will open magnificent economic prospects for Italy and should give her the means of recapturing the brilliant commercial position she occupied during the Middle Ages.

Yet no matter how great the material benefits that the railroads will bring Italy, the psychological effects which they should produce will be still greater.

A few brief considerations will suffice to justify this assertion for those who know Italy.

Italy's misfortunes are of long standing. We will not try to set forth their historical background. Such a task would be out of place here as well as beyond our capabilities. But it is certainly true that they must be attributed primarily to the political influence exercised among us for centuries by foreigners. The principal obstacles to our freeing ourselves from this distressing influence are the internal divisions, the rivalries, even hostility among the members of the great Italian family. Next comes the distrust between the national princes and the most energetic segment of the population. This segment has a desire for progress, which is often too great, a lively national spirit, and a strong patriotism—all of which makes it, if not the pricipal instrument, the indispensable auxiliary of all efforts for emancipation.

If the railroads should reduce these obstacles—perhaps even make them disappear—they will be among the factors most favorable to the spirit of Italian nationalism. A communication system permitting the constant movement of persons in all directions must necessarily connect populations once strangers to each other and should contribute much to the destruction of petty municipal rivalries born of ignorance and prejudice—already disappearing through the efforts of enlightened Italians. This deduction is too obvious to be denied.

The primary psychological effect of the establishment of railroads on the Italian peninsula is so great that it should be enough to justify the enthusiasm railroads arouse among all true friends of Italy.

The second psychological effect expected has still more importance, although it will be harder to appreciate its significance at first.

The division of Italy at the time of the Congress of Vienna was as arbitrary as it was imperfect. This august assemblage, acting solely on the basis of "might makes right," raised a political edifice without moral foundation. Their act was based not on any guiding principle, or on legality, which was violated in the case of Genoa and Venice, or on national interest or popular will; they recognized neither geographical situations nor the general and particular interests created by twenty years of revolution.

Only bitter fruit could come from such an act. Despite the benevolent conduct of several national princes, the discontent provoked by the new development grew rapidly during the years following the Restoration, and a storm threatened to break out in the near future. The fiery agitators and innovators, exploiting the bellicose passions developed by the Empire and finding support among liberal sentiments affronted by the decrees of the Congress of Vienna, fomented the unfortunate movements of 1820 and 1821.

These revolutionary efforts were easily repressed because the upper classes were divided and the masses took but little part in them, but their consequences were nonetheless deplorable for Italy. Although the attempts did not make the governments of the region tyrannical, they aroused in them a strong distrust of all nationalist ideas and stopped the development of the natural progressive tendencies already manifest. Weakened, discouraged, deeply divided, for a long time after that Italy could not hope to ameliorate her lot.

Time was beginning to erase the traces of the melancholy events of 1821, when the July Revolution shook the social structure of Europe to its foundations. This great popular movement had a considerable impact on Italy. The people's victory over the guilty though legal government excited democratic passions, if not among the masses at least among the bold spirits who aspired to dominate them. The possibility of a moral war involving all Europe awakened hopes in those who dreamed of the complete emancipation of the peninsula with the help of a social revolution. The movements organized after 1830 (with the exception of one in a province with unusual administrative conditions) were easily repressed before they could break out. It had to be thus; for these movements relied solely on republican ideas and demagogic passions and could not have had serious significance. In Italy a democratic revolution has no chance of success. To prove this we need only to analyze the elements composing the party favoring political innovations. This party receives no support from the masses, who with the exception of a few rare urban groups are generally strongly attached to the old institutions of the country. Instead, the strength of this party is derived almost exclusively from the middle classes and a part of the upper class. Both of these have very conservative interests to defend. Property in Italy is the exclusive privilege of no class. Even where the remains of a feudal nobility exist, it shares land ownership with the third estate.

The revolutionary doctrines of young Italy have little appeal to classes so strongly interested in the maintenance of the social order. Except for a few youthful spirits whose schoolboy ardor is not yet dampened by experience, there are in Italy only a small number of persons seriously disposed to practice the exalted principles of a sect embittered by misfortune. We believe that a good number of very determined opponents and extreme republicans would appear in the front ranks of the conservative party if the social order were truly menaced and the great principles on which it rests were in real danger.

The revolutionary agitation following the events of 1830 had consequences as disastrous as the military insurrections of 1820 and 1821. Violently attacked, the governments thought only of defending themselves; setting aside all notions of progress and Italian emancipation, they occupied themselves solely with averting the dangers menacing them, dangers falsely magnified by the reactionary party. Although we do not wish to justify the repressive measures used in those unfortunate times, we cannot properly reproach the governments for their sentiments. Governments as well as individuals have the right to self-preservation, and the most rigorous moralist cannot define the limits of this right without exposing himself to gross contradictions or absurd consequences contrary to common sense.

Thank heaven the stormy passions of the July Revolution have subsided and their traces have almost disappeared. Events are resuming their natural course in Italy, and the shaken confidence of the national princes is gradually being reëstablished; already the people are feeling the salutary effects of this happy turn of events, and everything points to a better future for us.

This future for which we yearn is the achievement of national independence. Italy can gain this supreme goal only through the united efforts of all her children. Without this she cannot hope for any real and lasting amelioration of her political condition, nor can she walk firmly on the road to progress. In uniting our weak voice with the eloquent one of our friend M. de Balbo, we describe no mere dream resulting from lack of reflection or a fanatical imagination, but a manifest truth.

All history proves that no people can attain a high degree of intelligence and morality unless its spirit of nationalism is strongly developed. This remarkable fact is a necessary consequence of the laws governing human nature. The intellectual life of the masses moves within a highly restricted circle of ideas. Of those which they can acquire, the most noble and elevating other than religious ones are the concepts of patriotism and nationality. If the political circumstances of a country prevent these concepts from being manifest or give them false direction, the masses are plunged into a state of deplorable inferiority. But that is not all; if a people cannot be proud of nationality a feeling of personal dignity exists only incidentally among a few privileged individuals. The majority, occupying the humblest social positions, need a feeling of national greatness to acquire a consciousness of their own dignity. At the risk of shocking hidebound political writers, we might even say that this consciousness is an essential element of morality for the people as well as for individuals.

For the sake of the great issue of emancipation for Italy, all issues dividing us must vanish and all special interests fall silent; this must be accomplished so that our country can achieve not only power and glory but a level of intellectual and moral development equal to that of the most civilized nations.

Unless there is a disastrous upheaval in Europe—and this seems less probable every day, thank heaven—it is obvious to us that our precious nationality can be achieved only through the combined action of all the vital forces of the country, that is, by the national princes openly supported by all the parties. The history of the past thirty years as well as an analysis of the elements composing Italian society clearly demonstrates of how little importance among us are military or democratic revolutions. The nation's sincere friends must cast aside these useless, powerless methods; they must realize that they can contribute to the true welfare of their homeland only by rallying about the thrones deeply rooted in the national soil and patiently supporting the progressive inclinations of the Italian governments. This conduct conforms to the wise counsel of the patriotic and sagacious M. de Balbo in his remarkable book *The Aspirations of Italy*. It will unite the members of the Italian family and enable the nation to profit from the favorable political climate of the future so that she may free herself from foreign domination.

This union we advocate so zealously is not so difficult to achieve as one might suppose if one were to judge society from external appearances or dwell too much on our unfortune disunity. A feeling of nationalism has become general; it is increasing daily and is already strong enough to unite all the parties in Italy despite their differences. It no longer belongs exclusively to one sect or to fanatics. We thus believe that M. de Balbo's recent appeal to all Italians will move more than one state dignitary and awaken more than an echo among those who are faithful to their ancestral traditions and base their political beliefs on the rule of law.

To a certain degree all the social classes may cooperate in this important work. Everyone with some education and influence in Italy can fulfill a mission, from distinguished writers such as M. de Balbo and Count Petitti, who devote themselves to educating and enlightening their fellow citizens, to humble individuals who within the narrow circles in which they move can elevate the intelligence and moral character of those around them.

It is true that all these individual efforts would be fruitless without the concurrence of the national governments. But this cooperation will not be lacking. The suspicions aroused by the events of 1830, long maintained by a party weak in numbers but powerful in its machinations, are almost entirely dissipated. With renewed confidence our sovereigns follow their natural inclinations and present daily evidence of their benevolent and progressive dispositions.

In this regard we need only cite what is happening in Piedmont. The growth of primary education, the establishment of several chairs in social and political science, the encouragement given the corporate spirit in the arts as well as industry, and several other measures in addition to the railroads suffice to show that this distinguished and brilliant monarch has decided to maintain the glorious statecraft which has made his family the leading Italian dynasty in the past and should carry it to yet higher destinies in the future.

But more than any other administrative reform, and as much as large political concessions, the construction of railroads will contribute to consolidating that mutual confidence between governments and peoples which is the foundation of our hopes for the future. In giving these powerful instruments of progress to the nations whose destinies they rule, the governments only demonstrate their benevolence and feeling of security. Grateful for so great a benefaction, the people on their part will come to have complete faith in their sovereigns; tractable—though full of enthusiasm—they will permit their leaders to guide them to national independence.

If these arguments have some foundation, we must be justified in placing the moral achievements of the railroads in Italy above their material achievements and hailing their introduction among us as the harbinger of a better future. This is why, borrowing the vigorous language of M. de Balbo, we like to include them among the principal "aspirations" of our homeland.

8. National Unification and Constitution-Making

Frankfurt Parliament: *The Minority Report Regarding the Part of the Constitutional Proposal about the Empire and Imperial Power* (1848)*

Whether or not German Austria remained a part of a unified German nation-state, a constitution had to be devised appropriate for a country whose member states had different political forms. The minority report of the constitutional committee of the Frankfurt Parliament concentrated upon the fundamental issue of federal power versus states rights, and therein it sought to solve some of the problems that had caused Gentz's proposal for the German Confederation to fail and that the future unifier of Germany had to face. The comparison between German political conditions and those in the United States should illuminate the matter of why, in contrast to the American continent, power politics predominated in Europe.

The section of a proposal of a constitution for Germany which the Constitutional Committee now lays before the National Assembly pertains to one of the most important parts of the constitution, the relationship of the individual German states to the unitary state, the limits of subordination of the first, and the extent of the powers of the second. The committee has started with the view that the form of the federal state and not that of the former league of states is most suited to the present relationships and conditions in Germany. The undersigned minority of the committee in general shares this view of the majority; nevertheless it differs essentially from the majority in the execution of the principles of the federal union.

The concept of a federal union is not a definite and limited one;

* *Stenographischer Bericht über die Verhandlungen der deutschen constituirenden Nationalversammlung zu Frankfurt am Main*, October 19, 1848, ed. Franz Wigard (Frankfurt, 1848), IV, 2742 ff.

rather it oscillates between two outer limits, that of a league of states on the one hand, and of a centralized empire (*Reich*) on the other hand, so that the federal union can approach the one at one time and the other at another period according to whether the unifying bond is more or less loose or the central power more or less strong. In view of Germany's present situation, it seems necessary in respect to some of the most important rights of sovereignty to set up a greater unity and to weight the balance in favor of central power more than the majority has decided to do. The minority in no way wishes centralization of such a kind as to suppress the autonomous life of the several parts of Germany, to hinder the development of the individuality of separate German folk elements, or to regulate everything from above and deprive individual parts, persons, communities and single states of self-government in their internal and particular concerns. On the other hand we feel it necessary to have in external affairs and in power relationships a strong, firm, and indestructible unity.

We find the basis for this need not only in the fact that Germany is surrounded by powerful and unified neighbors with whom it constantly is in close contact and at any moment may come into serious conflict, in which case it must have its forces united in one hand—a circumstance which for the United States of America does not come into such serious consideration because of its isolated position—but principally in the following two points peculiar to Germany's situation and which make Germany quite different from the United States. One point is that Germany is overwhelmingly (with few exceptions) made up of monarchical states and not of republics like the United States; the second point is the great inequality in size and power relations among the several German states.

As to the first point: It appears almost natural that in the event of union among a number of monarchies only the form of a league of states or something closely resembling it is suitable, whereas the federal union is more appropriate for a group of republics. It seems to be in the nature of hereditary monarchy that the monarch and with him the state government, insofar as it is dependent on him, has a double and lasting interest, namely an interest in the welfare of the state and in the welfare and power of the ruling family. In many respects these interests of course coincide, and the welfare of the people assures the welfare of the monarch; in other respects, especially in regard to political power, the welfare of the ruling dynasty is often opposed to the welfare or the wishes of the people. In a republic it can easily happen, too, that the incumbent possessor of power follows selfish ends, but at least it does not here lead to a continuing family policy; it is something temporary and soon to be discarded. It is quite another matter in the traditional family politics of a hereditary monarchy.

In an independent and more isolated monarchical state with a free constitution and a politically educated public spirit, the interests of the ruling dynasty, though perchance in opposition to the welfare of the state, will not be very dangerous to the state; publicity and the love of freedom of the people will weigh so powerfully in the balance that the dynastic interests cannot preponderate. Concern for self-preservation in itself will keep the monarch of such a state from constantly opposing the welfare and will of the people.

It is quite otherwise and much more disadvantageous to popular freedom in the case of closely allied monarchical states, that is, in the case of a union of monarchies. The interests of the dynasties are here essentially united, since the continuation of the federation and the conduct of common matters lie in their hands and in those of the officials chosen by them and more or less dependent upon them. Only the head of state and not the people has a direct influence on the decisions of state, even if only through the choice of the delegates. Thus the power of the princes is united, and they will easily agree on the measures by which the princely power and interests are to be furthered; they will readily help and support one another when it is necessary to suppress the efforts for freedom of the people in one or another of the allied states. Each of the allied princes has in the others a support against his people; but the individual peoples are separated when it comes to opposing the united force of the princes; they are not organically bound into a whole, and the weal and woe of the one are not directly felt as the weal and woe of the others. The spirit of unity and of belonging together does not permeate the divided peoples; one of them can easily let itself be used as a policeman against the other; consciousness of the strength and power built on unity is lacking, and it is thereby easy for the united strength of the princes to cripple or even completely to destroy the freedom of the divided peoples. The union appears to be a mutual guarantee of the princely power against popular freedom.

Whereas on this point the allied monarchs will easily agree, they are all the more stubborn and reserved about making sacrifices for the whole and about submitting their own power to the power and prestige of the community, and especially in foreign affairs. It will be only too easy for each dynasty to try to increase its own power at the expense of the whole or by neglecting the interests of the whole. Each dynasty will be jealous lest it sacrifice more than another, lest another gain from the union more advantages, more power and prestige than it does. Thus monarchies are too obstinate and too stubborn for federal union; by nature they are too ambitious, too jealous, too self-centered—especially in their leadership—to succeed in making a truly organic union with one another. Support of one another in police measures against the striving toward freedom of their "subjects" will always predominate in their federation. It is quite otherwise in a federation of republics, in which the people are directly and not through princes alone bound together; the peoples then find their power and well-being only in the closest unity.

It is useless to say that the princes do not rule directly but through responsible ministers, that these latter by their responsibility must protect the interests of the people, that they can eventually, in states where the constitutional system is an actuality, depend only upon the majority in the chamber and are as dependent upon this as upon the prince. In a free and separate monarchy, all this may well be the case, but it is not applicable in the case of federated princes against divided peoples. In a monarchy, especially if the prince has outside support, an administration is easily formed parallel to that of the official ministers, and this administration is one principally for external and federal affairs, because in these matters it can function most easily, as well as most harmfully. Likewise, under these circumstances ministerial responsibility usually takes effect too late, when the harm has already been done. It is frequently far too easy for a ruler who has strong support in his brother rulers to thwart the results of ministerial responsibility, whether by legal chicanery or by force.

In addition to these considerations in regard to a monarchical federation for Germany, there is the second point mentioned above, the great inequality in power relationships among the several German states. This point is closely connected with the first, and this inequality is dangerous in the case of a federation of monarchs because of the greater isolation and the looseness of the union embracing them. Not only will the larger and more powerful states be tempted to go their own way and to follow their own interests, perhaps only the interests of the dynasty, and to increase their own power, even at the expense of the whole, but the smaller states naturally will become dependent on the larger and will have to follow the policy of the larger states even if this policy is harmful to their own interests. The fate of the smaller states will be indirectly decided in the larger states without the citizens of the small states and their interests being represented in the government of the larger. Then they will be oppressed by a feeling of subjection, of dependence upon a state to which they do not belong, a feeling which will never let them breathe freely.

This pressure upon the small states is all the more unbearable the less it rests on legality and the more it is merely a result of actual power relations, and the more the name and hypocritical appearance of sovereignty and freedom are left them. They have duties equal to those of the large states but cannot make an equal use of their rights and privileges. Such a federation rests on the supremacy of the larger states, on the inferiority of the smaller ones; one group rules, the other serves, if not legally at least in fact; and thereby arises dissatisfaction with the larger federated states on the part of the smaller ones, and a certain inclination to escape from their influence by looking about for support abroad.

In both of the points discussed the evils were principally to be found in the conditions which have rested so heavily on Germany; these evils have called forth the March revolution, and it is the task of the National Assembly to do away with them as much as possible. It is not enough to rely on the good intentions of the princes alone, for the person of the prince changes and the evils are too deeply imbedded in the nature of the situation. They lie too deeply in the nature of power, which drives its possessors to increase their power still more. But since the German states are monarchies and are to remain so in accordance with the desire of their populations, these evils can be eradicated only when the individual German states no longer appear as great states at home or abroad, but each state hands over to the community of the whole, or the central government those attributes of power which lend to it the character of a great state.

These attributes are primarily those of international, diplomatic intercourse, including the right of political treaty-making, of war and peace, and of military force. These rights must be completely given up by the individual states and handed over to the central power, if the task of the new unitary constitution is to be carried out even partially.

In regard to diplomatic intercourse, the negotiations of the central power will only be made more difficult, be frustrated, or be blocked if ambassadors, even only extraordinary ones, of individual states are permitted alongside ambassadors of the central power. Even ambassadors extraordinary, if they have a political or diplomatic character, would represent opposition to unity, would characterize the sending state as a power, and would afford opportunity for harmful separate political treaties, as in fact peace treaties negotiated by plenipotentiaries extraordinary usually are.

As to military affairs, there should be only one supreme command to which the duty and loyalty of the soldiers would be given, not two commands perhaps in disagreement. It must not be left to the good will of the government of each of the more powerful individual states as to whether it wishes to order its soldiers in a specific case to obey, or perhaps not to obey. The officers should not have to expect their promotion, their weal and woe from the princes of the individual states and so be bound to them, but should depend on the central power; otherwise the germ of dissolution and separation of the *Reich* is planted in the constitution. Although we consider it necessary to deprive the individual states of all power over the army, it cannot be our intention to make the army an abject tool of the central power; rather, once the army is reorganized on a popular basis, the imperial districts, from whom no misuse is to be expected, must be given greater independence, and the first levy of troops should be used to suppress domestic strife only at the command of the local civilian officials, and then only if the militia is inadequate.

Only in this way can the central power, as opposed to the individual governments, be strong and all the German folk groups be represented in accordance with the size of their populations, and only so can Germany gain a unity which is based on freedom and on the equal right of all. But if the separate states remain as powers, unity can be based only on supremacy, that is on domination by one and subservience of the others.

Incidentally, the central executive power must be based on democratic principles as long as the individual states are monarchies, for a hereditary monarchy tied in with dynastic interests as head of the federation would be too tempted to conspire with the territorial dynasties against popular freedom, and no constitutional forms would protect it against their combined, mutually supporting power. It would be the old Diet with a police chief at the head. That can be ignored only by the statesmen who are of the naive opinion that they have met and solved the problem of our special needs with theoretical proof of the excellence of constitutional monarchy.

In general this is our view regarding the political unification of Germany as it is possible today without too much disturbance and confusion. It will be said that our proposals cannot be carried out and that the greater German states will not renounce such important rights. We feel that the National Assembly will obtain what it considers necessary far more surely with public support if it expresses itself clearly than it will by half measures and efforts at compromise. Through these it will only estrange public opinion and give opportunity for diplomatic skill to wrench everything from its hands. The record of the National Assembly is not lacking in examples of this. . . .

9. The Formation of a Nation-State in an Old Imperial Region

Heinrich von Gagern: *Speech on the Issue* Grossdeutsch vs. Kleindeutsch (1848)*

The unification of the German people proved to be the most complicated question of political reorganization that Europe faced in the nineteenth century, and the question has not yet been settled. The problems involved had significance not merely for the German people; the constitution-makers of international organizations in our own period have had to try to overcome many of the same difficulties.

Heinrich von Gagern, a liberal, proposed the solution that was accepted in its essentials by the Frankfurt Parliament and later by Bismarck. Gagern, who was fully acquainted with the complications that the membership of Austria in the German Confederation caused in the effort to unify the German nation, in a speech at Frankfurt posed the issue that faced the German people in Germany proper and in Austria as well, and defended the idea of the German nation's cultural mission in Eastern and Southeastern Europe. He makes evident the intimate relation between liberalism and nationalism, and that between these and power politics. An estate-owner and former official and political leader in Hesse, at the time of his speech Gagern served as president of the Frankfurt Parliament and spoke as one of its most influential members. The reader should compare his proposal with the recommendation of Gentz with respect to the Carlsbad Decrees.

The German nation has been bowed in humiliation and we are seeking the means of its revival. Insurance against another catastro-

* *Stenographischer Bericht über die Verhandlungen der deutschen constituirenden Nationalversammlung zu Frankfurt am Main,* October 26, 1848, ed. Franz Wigard (Frankfurt, 1848), IV, 2896-2900.

phe requires that we formulate these means into principles of the future constitution. It is natural that we should first ask ourselves what were the principal reasons for our humiliation in our previous situation. What were the obstacles which prevented our nation from achieving the power it deserves? Foremost among these reasons ranks the relationship of the several states, a relationship in which German and non-German states under a monarchy were united into a federation. An effective change in this relationship is the first great difficulty to be encountered in discussing the constitution for which the nation is waiting.

In respect to mixed states created by the Federal Act, there is an essential difference between those states in which the area of German nationality is the dependent part and is united with a major part of non-German nationality, and those in which the German part is the major part and the non-German areas are dependencies. The former relationship is one which has proved most unfortunate for Germany; for it was one under which a national policy could not exist, much less be achieved harmoniously. It was this relationship which caused us to be despised even by lesser powers and to see our interests harmed. That was the relation of Luxembourg and Limburg to Holland and that of Holstein to Denmark. This situation must be abolished. No national existence can be maintained under such scrambled conditions. Whether Paragraphs 2 and 3[1] will directly resolve these conditions I doubt, since, as rightly pointed out here today, there are

---

[1] Committee Report on the German Imperial Constitution, *Ibid.*, pp. 2717 ff. The wording of the paragraphs referred to is as follows:

Par. 2. No part of the German Empire may be united with non-German territories of a state.

Minority-opinion Addition: In so far as the special relationships of Austria do not permit the execution of this Paragraph 2 and of the paragraphs regarding the same arising therefrom, the intended unity and power of Germany shall be sought through the most intimate connection possible of Austria and Germany by means of international alliance between the imperial power and the Austrian government.

Par. 3. If a German territory has the same head of state as a non-German territory, the relationship between the two is to be ordered according to the principles of a purely personal union.

Par. 4. The head of state of a German territory which has a personal union with a non-German territory must either reside in his German territory or place in the same a regency to which only Germans may be named.

international legal conditions which must first be taken into account.

Other conditions of irregularity existed and still exist in Germany, such as the connections of non-German territories with a dominant German state. Prussia has abolished one of these relationships by uniting with the German Confederation those significant parts of its monarchy which under the German Federal Act did not belong to the Confederation. Even if Prussia did not pursue a separate policy for these provinces, which were as German as any other, the national relationship was greatly simplified by uniting them, and one can say that they have been merged. Austria is another anomalous situation. There may be doubt as to which is the principal nationality within the Austrian complex of territories; but there is no doubt that the German element, although in the minority so far as population is concerned, is the most influential in the monarchy and must become more so. Therefore I cannot agree with the view that pressure should be used to separate Austria from the territories which up to now have been united with her, thus dissolving the monarchy.

In implementing Paragraphs 2 and 3, there is no doubt that German Austria would be separated from non-German Austria; that is, the monarchy would be dissolved, however one may attempt to veil this fact. For I consider it avoidance of the issue when I hear it said often, even here: "We do not want dissolution, we want Austria held together; but we want it by means of a personal union; the personal union is enough to hold it together." I had thought this matter settled; but since the arguments already so decisively developed have been so little heeded, since even men experienced in politics maintain that the personal union can assure a lasting connection, and since they have asked why a dissolution would result, I feel that I must reply. They seem not to have considered the interrelated effect of Paragraphs 2 and 3 of the constitutional proposal. Paragraph 2 forbids a common state existence; it orders the separation of German and non-German elements formerly united into a state, leaving the non-German to itself as an independent political body or group of nationalities. In the event of such an independent political body, however, it is obvious that continuing agreement on an accepted political goal between two constitutional states by means of a personal union is only a matter of chance. It is obviously possible that the executive powers in the states united only through personal union could be forced by the political majorities to take different directions, and could even assume hostile policies.

Let us look at the results which would ensue for Austria if Paragraphs 2 and 3 were carried out there, for I must immediately call your attention to this alternative. It is not enough to say: We want to set up 2 and 3 here as law and then leave it to events to see whether they will be carried out. When we assert that something should or should not be, that we consider it in the interests of the fatherland that it should be thus and not otherwise, then we must agree in advance as to the means for making it effective; that is, we should not leave the decision in doubt. We have the task of giving the nation a constitution, one for the entire German people. We have the task of giving the nation unity. But we also have the responsibility of considering the conditions and the facts, if we wish to create a workable constitution. What would be the results for Austria of implementing Paragraphs 2 and 3? We draw the German-Austrian provinces into the German federal state; we separate them from the non-German lands and provinces of Austria. These other parts of Austria, however, will not remain a unified state; rather, in the nature of things, they will fall apart when the common center provided by the German hereditary lands is removed. That point is sufficiently developed by other speakers; I can continue with further points. There would then be made an independent organization of Galicia, of Hungary (as has already been initiated in the constitution of that country), perhaps also the lands bordering on Hungary, and Italy. If we vote paragraphs which lead to such results, do they fit the situation which must be considered? Are they consonant with our natural obligations and not, as has been said today, drawn rather for an imaginary situation? It seems to me that at the moment when civil war occurs in a federal union, when the fire is smoldering, it is our obligation not to throw on more fuel. We act in a cooperative spirit when we help to put out the fire, when we do not act as if the existence of the unitary monarchy is in question but manifest the conviction that the Austrian monarchy, whose continuation as a political unit is in the interests of the entire fatherland, should endure as a mighty empire, strengthened by freedom and closely joined with Germany for the great national task. We must act in this sense or we shall not act responsibly as a good neighbor, much less as a national ally.

If we take Paragraphs 2 and 3 without reservation, and if we could force Austria to accept them, we should tear asunder a great empire and set adrift its non-German parts, not knowing what would follow, not knowing what role these parts would play in the relations of the family of European peoples, or what influence would gain ascendancy over them. Other nations would consider it their first duty in constitution-making to make sure of the possession of every single village. Are we casually to estrange an entire future state and a rich prospect of future national development from its previous connections and sacrifice it to chance? That cannot be our intent or our task. But that would be the result if we were to apply Paragraphs 2 and 4 [sic] to Austria and force the dynasty into a mere personal union with individual parts. That would be only a dynastic union, which was the complaint wrongly made against the Pragmatic Sanction, although this is something else entirely. When states can have nothing in common but a personal union, it is better to have nothing in common; each should go its own way, and that is something felt even by those who advocate this personal union and actually intend complete separation. Sweden and Norway were mentioned; but for a long time they have been busy creating something to make the bond between the two nations more useful, something similar to the Pragmatic Sanction for Austria. Either this effort will succeed or future separation will become more probable; the situation cannot remain as it is. The idea of personal union as applied to Austria would give us in the future four Austrian ambassadors, four Austrian armies, everything fourfold. We should thrust a chaotic situation upon Europe, already so undermined, thus sinning against the duty of a great nation in the family of European nations, at a time when this nation claims its proper rank therein following a change with unpredictable effects and a rearrangement of its vital relationships.

Our first duty is not to disappoint the hope and right of peoples to peace with freedom, by sowing the seeds of new revolutions inherent in chaotic situations. That would be true for the non-German provinces of Austria which have not yet claimed status as independent states, as is the case with Dalmatia and the coast, Croatia, and even Galicia. It has indeed been said that all these provinces are held to Austria only by bayonets, but proof of this assertion has not yet been supplied. The opinion of many that it is not possible otherwise, that every nation and group must consider its government as its enemy and must always bear within itself the drive toward revolution and dissolution, is only the exaggerated opinion of a few. Many of these provinces, content with their position, have not yet thought at all of political or even national independence. With the application of Paragraphs 2 and 3 to the Austrian states and their inevitable effects upon these states, we violate our first duty in relation to Europe; we offer no guarantee for the preservation of friendly relations; rather we destroy hope of it and would thereby embark upon an activity detrimental to international law and injurious to international conditions.

I ask further whether in the national interest we can so act. Can we leave the non-German provinces of Austria to themselves and to chance for the future? I have interpreted the calling of the German people to be one of the magnitude of a world power. One may laugh at this, cynically denying such a calling. I believe in it and would lose the pride of belonging to my nation if I had to renounce belief in a higher mission such as this. Our task must not be defined as one of creating a constitution aimed only toward the narrow limits of our present political conditions, one incorporating in the constitution a principle of unity which separates us from that which the unifying force depends upon, one which condemns us, as long as our neighbors leave us in peace and freedom, to warm ourselves at the hearth undisturbed while other nations are expanding in power and influence. What have we to strive for in unity? That we can devote ourselves to the mission which exists for us in the East. That we can draw into our planetary system like satellites those nations along the Danube which have neither call nor claim to independence.

We speak of the right of nationality. I concede fully this right where it exists, for example in Italy. For that reason it is my belief that in the general interest of the nation the disturbance in Italy can come to end only when Austria withdraws from Lombardy. To keep open a right of way to the Adriatic is the task which is important there to our national development. We must try with the entire strength of our national unity to secure the necessary frontiers for that, and in doing this and in limiting ourselves to this, we do not encroach upon the right of nationality. The Italians may then arrange their affairs; they can unite like us, and we can applaud when this Italian federation is concluded; with the guarantee of independence a guarantee of peaceful relations for the future is offered. A veil is drawn over the Polish situation and therewith over the future of Galicia. We shall not raise the claim to include Galicia in our national development. But the moment has not come to leave it to itself; we must try to keep it within united Austria. In view of the hostile position which the peasants have taken against the nobility, it would be possible for Galicia in case of independence to become the center of revolution, which would give occasion for war with Russia. We shall carry on any war which seems a political necessity with the entire effort of our revived national strength; but we do not want to invoke it capriciously. This would happen if an independent organization of Galicia should be formed now. A situation would then arise similar to but even more dangerous than that which led to the destruction of the free state of Cracow. Hungary enjoys constitutionally her independence of Austria, and whatever question has arisen there on one side or the other by reason of the recent disturbances will be worked out in the old spirit of brotherly affection, if the Magyars themselves do not infringe too much on the right of nationality.

In the other non-German provinces of Austria there exists neither the right of, nor the condition for, nor the claim to independent national development. The separation of the southern provinces probably would only play into the hands of foreign influence and power, to our own immeasurable disadvantage. Although for different reasons, two groups are pressing for the acceptance of Paragraphs 2 and 3. One group wants the dissolution of the Austrian monarchy into its parts. I have developed the reasons why I do not want this dissolution and believe that it is against German interests. The other group says:

We do not approve of this dissolution; it will not take place, for the personal union suffices to hold it together. That argument too has been answered. The dissolution of the unity of the state is in fact complete dissolution. Austria dares not give up the unity of the German and non-German provinces. We must not make the unreasonable demand of her of committing a crime against her provinces, which by constitution are entitled to retain the advantages offered them by unity of the state. Every constitutional state has the responsibility of self-preservation. With the dissolution of state unity in respect to the provinces which have not yet begun to think about a possible future for themselves separate from the monarchy as a whole, the Austrian government would fail in its first duties to itself. We must seek a way in which Austria does not have to separate her German from her non-German provinces but still is in intimate union with Germany. The question is this: Is it in Germany's interest that all Germany be so constituted and form so loose a union that Austria, without being forced to separate her German from her non-German provinces, can belong to the *Reich* under the same conditions as the other German states? Or is it in the national interest, both of Austria and of Germany as well, that at least the rest of Germany draw closer together, even if Austria because of her non-German provinces cannot enter this narrower federation under the same conditions, and that nevertheless a close union between Austria and the rest of Germany be maintained?

The concepts of federal state in the one case and confederation in the other are indefinite. Federal relationships can be conceived which lie between the two and create a bridge between them. Why did closer unity not develop previously in the union which the Federal Act created in Germany? Because no common interests existed; because these interests were consciously kept apart and particularism was encouraged to the extreme. Since when did the need for and the understanding of unity in Germany begin to develop in greater measure? From the moment when common national interests united a great part of Germany, excluding the possibility of a separate policy among these closely allied states; that is, from the beginning of the development of the Zollverein. Let us keep in mind the material interests and the possibility of uniting those of Austria and the rest of

Germany. In this way we can join Austria to us without being required to separate her German provinces from the non-German (even if we could so separate them). In this way unions are possible which lie somewhere between a federal union and a confederation.

But once again, are we in a position to force the separation of Austria, that is, the separation of the German from the non-German provinces? And if we cannot do this, can we conceive of Austria entirely out of, separate from, the rest of Germany? We cannot and do not want the former and must not have the latter. Whatever may be said on the other side about the feeling of the Austrians in regard to this question, I think that the majority of the Austrians want the continuation of the unity of their empire, as the Tyroleans have just said in their proclamation. There can be various opinions about this matter, based on various points of view. Each will form his opinion about it from the experiences and sources of knowledge which are at hand. The Austrians want to be with Germany but also want to keep Austria intact and make both unions possible. We must thereby, however, not neglect the task, so essential for the rest of Germany, of unification into a federal state, while Austria will maintain her world position with and beside us.

It is said that when German Austria is united with Germany into a federal union, non-German Austria will be left to an uncertain future, and then the united German people could fulfill with so much the more effect its mission in the East. I cannot follow this reasoning. When we loosen the political union that exists between the German and non-German peoples, new bonds with federated Germany will not soon be forged. The close relations which for centuries have existed among the Austrian provinces and between the dynasty and the non-German provinces will not soon be replaced if once broken. The means will not be at hand for a unified government of Germany —for the more distant imperial power—to operate in an equally beneficial way, to exert influence as the Austrian government does by its actual unity and by custom. Decades would go by before the imperial power could assimilate this heritage under such changed conditions, and we cannot spare for so long a time the influence in the East now exercised by Austria's world position.

The Eastern question, for whose solution Austria's position—and, through Austria, Germany's—can be and must be of such great influence, momentarily stands in the background. As the internal state situation of the European powers is put in order, it will soon return to the fore. Germany will not be stronger if it is more closely united with the German provinces of Austria but has been separated from the non-German ones and from their numerous connections with the South Danubian lands. We can emerge strong and powerful for the solving of this question if Austria, separated from Italy, has united political interests with Germany. It has been said, and in fact from this side [the Right], that Germany must pursue a national policy and thereby renounce Austria, if Austria will not separate herself from her non-German provinces. I ask in reply: What national policy can Germany have if it does not assume Austria's mission, the spread of German culture, language, and customs along the Danube to the Black Sea, into the thinly populated, varied national areas in these promising lands, whose entire civilization is accustomed to depend upon the Germans, and which long for German-Austrian protection and increased influence and would open a rich market to German initiative? Every prospect is opened up when the united power of Austria, which is called upon first to give the mighty impetus, is backed by the other united Germany pressing like a wedge with its interests and its power! The emigrants who now go westward will turn toward this region. Freedom too will be and already is there. Why should the person eager to emigrate not establish his dwelling on the shores of the nearby Danube rather than in America, and make work and capital useful among peoples friendly to us and for centuries acquainted with German customs and language, as soon as the roads are opened, the acquisition of free property made easy, and German protection, progress, and influence assured? German culture would then spread more quickly and help us to assume and maintain the position among European nations which we deserve.

If we renounce the mission of bearing German culture along the Danube—and we do that when we undermine the political relations of German Austria to the Danubian countries, or even entertain the fear that with the preservation of the united monarchy in Austria the Slav element might gain the upper hand—if we do not accept this mission in partnership with Austria for Germany, then others will accept it. If we do not strengthen our influence along the Danube, that of the Russians is known to be organized; and they will have outstripped us, until we come to our senses and leave Austria the freedom to maintain and to cultivate her previous political and neighborly relations with the Danubian countries.

Proceeding from such considerations, I urge that there be no delay in deciding the relationship between Austria and the rest of Germany. I think that we must immediately decide the matter and recognize that Austria cannot now enter the close federal union wanted by the rest of Germany, on the one hand because the majority of the Austrians do not want the condition of this entrance, the political separation of the German provinces from the non-German ones; and on the other hand because this separation and the dissolution of the Austrian monarchy and the decline of her world historical role, to be fulfilled in close alliance with Germany, is likewise not in the German national interest. I have therefore formulated a proposal corresponding to this view, and I have the honor of communicating it to this honored assembly:

> In consideration of her constitutional connection with non-German lands and provinces Austria remains with the rest of Germany in existing and indissoluble union.
> The organic conditions for this federal relation which changed conditions make necessary will be the subject of a special federal law.

I shall allow myself a few words in support of this resolution. As it is formulated, it should be placed after Paragraph 1, inserted between Paragraphs 1 and 2. I am of the opinion that the clauses following Paragraph 2 are in part not applicable to Austria, while nonetheless I want to see these clauses maintained for the federal union to be formed for the rest of Germany. It has been said that it is contrary to our mandate to found or to allow a double federal arrangement. We are called together to create unity so far as it is useful in the existing circumstances; our task cannot extend farther. But if we accept paragraphs which we foresee will not satisfy Austria, so that Austria would be forced by them to separate from Germany and could not belong any longer to the German Empire, then we have not created unity but destroyed it, and I oppose this destruction of unity. The question of the future position of Austria in and with respect to Germany has been coupled with that of the future head, of the possesor of the future imperial power. Months ago I publicly expressed my views about this matter; but I should consider it premature and inappropriate if I should read what I said about it at the beginning of our revolution. I have not wanted in any way to prejudice with my amendment the decision of this question. I am of course of the opinion that at the head of the federal union there should be a unitary sovereign, which excludes the idea of a Prussian hegemony. But for the leadership of all Germany, Austria included, a further arrangement must be created, and this would of course be a very important and different question, to be solved in the future. We should have to create an organism in which there would be a central control of the common interests of all Germany with the cooperation of its united representatives.

I have not discussed in my proposal whether the organic conditions for the wider federal relationship, which would have to be new, are to be put into the constitution. I want them to be a part of the constitution. But since these conditions previously lay outside the committee's range, I did not want by my proposal, even in case it should find approval, to prejudice the view of the committee in this respect. The more closely Austria can be united with the rest of Germany without destroying the political unity of her provinces, the more room thereby is left for the non-German provinces to enter into a closer political relationship with Germany, and then all the more completely will we have solved our problem. The federal state remains our goal; for this transitions are needed. We cannot avoid them without destroying, without doing the opposite of what we should do: creating the unity of interests for which the unity-formula in the constitution must be only the outward expression, the means to the end, not the end itself. Since we have been called upon to create this unity, we must take care not to choose too narrow a formula, not to force national interests into a straitjacket against their nature. Let us rather open the door wide so that we do not make difficult an entrance into the German family and into its great and hospitable house.

10. Political Theology and the Fear of Revolution

Donoso Cortés (Marques de Valdegamas): *Address on Dictatorship* (1849)*

This defense of dictatorship in the name of Christian religion exemplifies the extreme rightist plan for preventing revolution. The speaker expressed ideas that in greater or lesser degree were shared by many prominent persons in many countries, including Slavophiles in Russia, and that Pope Pius IX incorporated into the *Syllabus of Errors* (1864). Donoso Cortés, Marques de Valdegamas (1809-53), member of an old and prominent Spanish family, was a statesman and writer of philosophic works of history. A native Estremaduran, he studied law, then as a very young man turned to literature and became a professor. After 1832 he threw himself into Spanish politics, at first as a moderate liberal and rationalist. By the end of the 1830's he had become a defender of absolutism and the Church, and he expressed his views in speeches as member of the Cortes and in publications that gained for him a large Catholic following in Spain, France, and elsewhere. He was an intimate adviser to the Spanish royal family and was acquainted with the Orleanists and the high society of Romance Europe. In 1848 he sat as a member of the Spanish Crown Council, and he later served as ambassador to Berlin and Paris. Already in 1847 he had become disillusioned with the world and had concentrated his thoughts upon religion. The revolution of 1848 shocked him into writing, among other studies, the address, delivered January 4, 1849, given below. In it we are offered not the fantasies of a Kierkegaard or a Dostoievsky but the conclusions of a successful and thoughtful man of affairs, recipient of the Grand Cross of the Order of Isabelle the Catholic and a Grand Officer of the French Legion of Honor.

* Juan Donoso Cortés, Marques de Valdegamas, *Obras*, ed. Don Gabino Tejado (Madrid, 1853-1854), III, 253-274. (Trans. Lenore M. Berslin.)

Gentlemen, the long address that Señor Cortina delivered yesterday and which I am going to answer, considering it from a limited point of view in spite of its lengthy dimensions, was only an epilogue, the epilogue of the errors of the progressive party, which in their turn are only another epilogue, the epilogue of all the errors which have been committed within the last three centuries and which today have disturbed almost all human societies.

At the beginning of his address Señor Cortina, with the good faith which distinguishes His Lordship and so enhances his talent, showed that he himself sometimes has come to wonder if his principles are false, if his ideas are unfortunate; for he saw that they never were held by the party in power and always by the opposition. I shall tell His Lordship that if he would reflect a bit his doubt would become certainty. His ideas are not those of the party in power and are of the opposition precisely because they are the ideas of the opposition and because they are not the ideas of the Government. Gentlemen, they are barren, sterile, and disastrous ideas which must be combatted until they are buried here in their natural cemetery, under these arches at the foot of this rostrum. [General applause from the seats of the majority party.]

Following the traditions of the party which he heads and represents, following, I say, the traditions of this party from the February revolution, Señor Cortina has delivered an address divided into what I shall call three inevitable parts. First, a eulogy of the party based on an enumeration of its merits; second, a summary of its present indignities; third, a program or rather an enumeration of its future merits.

Gentlemen of the majority: I have come here to defend your principles but do not expect any eulogy from me. You are the victors, and nothing is so becoming to the brow of a victor as a crown of modesty. ["Good! Good!"]

Do not expect me, gentlemen, to speak of your indignities. You have no personal indignities to avenge; you have only the indignities inflicted upon society and the Throne by the traitors to their Queen and their fatherland. I shall not speak of your enumeration of merits.

What is the use of speaking of them? In order that the nation learn of them? The nation knows them by heart. [Laughter.]

Señor Cortina divided his address into two parts, both within the comprehension of the honorable deputies. His Lordship discussed the external policy of the Government, designating as external policy, important for Spain, the events which occurred in Paris, London, and Rome. I too shall touch on these subjects.

Later His Lordship turned to domestic policy, and domestic policy as treated by Señor Cortina is divided into two parts. First come the principles and then the question of facts; first the system and then the question of conduct. The minister has already answered the question of facts and that of conduct, as was his duty, since he has the data for an answer from the ministers of state and government, who have performed their part with their customary eloquence. The matter of principles is left almost entirely to me; I shall merely touch on it, but if the Congress [Cortes] permits I shall treat it more fully.

Gentlemen, what is the basic principle of Señor Cortina? Careful analysis of his address shows that the basic principle of His Lordship is the following: In domestic policy respect for law, everything for the established law, everything by lawfulness, lawfulness always, in all circumstances, on all occasions. And I who believe that laws have been made for societies and not societies for laws, ["Very good! Very good!"] I say: The social good, everything for society, society always, society in all circumstances, society on all occasions. ["Bravo! Bravo!"]

When respect for law suffices to save society, then let us have legality; when it does not suffice, let us have dictatorship. This awe-inspiring word—for it is awe-inspiring, although not so much so as the word "revolution," which is the most terrifying of all [Murmur] —I say that this awesome word has been uttered here by a man we all know. To be sure, this man is not made of the stuff of dictators. I was born to understand dictators, although I was not born to imitate them. Two things are impossible for me, to condemn dictatorship, and to practice it. For this reason I am incompetent to govern. I cannot accept office in good conscience; I could not accept it without bringing half of myself into war with the other half, without bringing my instinct into war with my reason, without bringing my reason into war with my instinct. ["Very good! Very good!"]

Therefore, gentlemen, no one can testify either here or elsewhere that he has encountered me on the crowded road of ambition. [Applause.] But all will meet me, all have met me on the modest road of the good citizen. Only thus, gentlemen, at the end of my days shall I descend to my grave without the remorse of having left society undefended from a barbarous attack, and without the bitter and unendurable grief of having harmed any man.

I repeat, gentlemen, that dictatorship in certain circumstances like the present is a legitimate government, a good government, an advantageous government, and one like any other government. It is a rational government that can be defended in theory as in practice. And if not, gentlemen, consider the nature of social life.

Social life like human life is composed of action and reaction, of the ebb and flow of certain invading forces and of other resisting forces.

This is social life just as this is also human life. The invading forces, called sickness in the human body and by another name in the social body but essentially the same thing, have two states. There is one state in which they are scattered throughout all society, in which they are represented by individuals only; there is another highly acute state of illness in which they are more concentrated and are represented by political associations. I maintain that if there are no resisting forces, whether in the human body or in the social body, they have to be supplied, if only to repel the invading forces. When the invading forces are scattered, the resisting forces are also scattered. They are scattered in the government, in the administration, in short throughout all the social body. But when the invading forces are concentrated in political associations, then necessarily, without anyone's being able to prevent it, without anyone's having the right to prevent it, the forces of resistance are concentrated automatically in one hand. This is the clear, luminous, indestructible theory of dictatorship.

And this theory, gentlemen, a truism in the rational order, is a constant fear in the historical order. Cite me a single society that has not had a dictatorship. If there was not one, see what happened in democratic Athens, what happened in aristocratic Rome. In Athens power was in the hands of the people and was called ostracism; in Rome that omnipotent power was in the hands of the Senate, which delegated it to a consul, and was called, as it is among us, a dictatorship. ["Good! Good!"] Look at modern societies; look at France in all its vicissitudes. I shall not speak of the first Republic, which was a gigantic, endless, bloody dictatorship full of horrors. I speak of a later period. In the Charter of the Restoration, dictatorship had sought refuge or asylum in Article 14; in the Charter of 1830 it was found in the Preamble. And in the present republic? Let us say nothing of that. What is it except a dictatorship with the nickname of republic? [Noisy applause.]

Here Señor Galvez has cited inopportunely the English constitution. Gentlemen, so wise are the English that their constitution is precisely the only one in the world in which dictatorship is not by exceptional but by common right. And the matter is clear. On all occasions, in all periods, the Parliament has dictatorial power when it wishes, since it has no limits except those set by the human powers of prudence. It has all authority, and this constitutes the dictatorial power of doing everything except to make a man of a woman or a woman of a man, as their jurists say. [Laughter.] It has the power to suspend *habeas corpus,* to proscribe by means of bill of attainder. It can change the constitution, it can even change the dynasty, and not only the dynasty, but it can even change religion and oppress conscience. In a word, it can do anything. Who has seen, gentlemen, a more monstrous dictatorship? ["Good! Good!"]

I have proved that dictatorship is a reality in theory and a fact in history. Now I am going to say something more: If propriety allows, it can be said that dictatorship is a fact in the divine order.

Gentlemen, up to a certain point God has allowed men the government of human society and has reserved for Himself alone the government of the universe. The universe is governed by God and governed constitutionally, if parliamentary language may be applied to such lofty things. [Loud laughter from the Left.] And, gentlemen, the matter seems to me to be extremely clear and most obvious. It is governed by certain precise, indispensable laws which are called secondary causes. What are those laws except laws analogous to those which are called fundamental with respect to human society?

Well, gentlemen, if with respect to the physical world God is the legislator, as are legislators with respect to human society, although in a different manner, does God himself always govern with these same laws which He imposed upon Himself in His eternal wisdom and to which He subjected all of us? No, gentlemen. Sometimes directly, clearly, and explicitly He manifests His sovereign will by breaking those laws which He Himself imposed and by twisting the natural course of things. When He acts thus, could it not be said, if human language might be applied to divine things, that He acts dictatorially? [More laughter from the Left.]

This proves, gentlemen, how great is the delirium of a party that thinks it can govern with lesser means than God, depriving itself of the sometimes necessary means of dictatorship. Gentlemen, this being the case, reduced to its real terms the question is no longer one of ascertaining if dictatorship is defensible, if in certain situations it is good. The question is one of learning whether Spain has arrived at this situation or passed beyond it. This is the most important point, and I am going to restrict myself to this point. To do so I shall have to glance—and in this I shall merely follow the lead of all the orators who have preceded me—at Europe, and take another glance at Spain. [Profound attention.]

Gentlemen, the February revolution came as death comes, unexpectedly. [Great applause.] God, gentlemen, had condemned the French monarchy. This institution transformed itself profoundly to adapt to circumstances and to the times, but in vain; the change accomplished nothing. Its condemnation and loss were unavoidable. Monarchy by divine right ended with Louis XVI on the scaffold; the monarchy of glory ended with Napoleon on an island; hereditary monarchy ended with Charles X in exile; and the last of all possible monarchies has ended with Louis Philippe, the monarchy of prudence. ["Bravo! Bravo!"] A venerable, ancient, glorious institution to which neither divine right, legitimacy, prudence, nor glory is of any avail, is a sad, lamentable spectacle. [Applause.]

Gentlemen, when the news of this great revolution came to Spain, all were distressed and astonished. Nothing was comparable to our surprise and consternation except the consternation and surprise of the vanquished monarchy. I am inaccurate. There was a greater surprise, a greater consternation than that of the vanquished monarchy; it was that of the victorious Republic, ["Good! Good!"] even right now ten months after its triumph. Ask the Republic how it triumphed, ask it why it conquered, ask it with what powers it conquered, and it will be incapable of answering. This is because of the fact that the Republic did not conquer: the Republic was the instrument of victory of a higher power. [Great astonishment.]

This power, gentlemen, once its work is begun, just as it was strong enough to destroy the monarchy with an insignificant republic, will be strong enough if it becomes necessary and suitable to its ends, to overthrow the Republic with an insignificant empire or with an insignificant monarchy. The causes and effects of this revolution have been the subject of much comment by all Europe, including Spain. I have often been surprised at the lamentable levity with which the deeper causes of revolutions are treated. Gentlemen, here as elsewhere revolutions are attributed only to the defects of governments. When catastrophes are universal, unforeseen, simultaneous, they are always considered providential because, gentlemen, these are characteristics that distinguish the works of God from the works of men. [Noisy applause from the seats of the majority.]

When revolutions present these symptoms, it is certain that they come from Heaven and that they come from the guilt and exist for the punishment of all. Do you wish, gentlemen, to know the whole truth concerning the causes of the last French revolution? The truth is that in February the day came for all classes of society to make their final settlement of accounts with Providence, and all were found bankrupt. On that day there came the settlement with Providence, and, I repeat, in that settlement all were found bankrupt. Not only that, but the Republic itself on the day of its victory declared itself bankrupt. The Republic had said of itself that it came to establish the dominion of liberty, equality, fraternity, those three principles which are not of the Republic but of Calvary itself. ["Good! Good!"]

What has it done since? In the name of liberty it has necessitated, proclaimed, and accepted dictatorship. In the name of equality, with the title of republicans of yesterday, republicans of tomorrow, republicans by birth, it has invented a kind of aristocratic democracy and a ridiculous heraldry. In short, gentlemen, in the name of fraternity it has restored pagan fraternity, the fraternity of Eteocles and Polynices, and brothers have devoured each other in the streets of Paris in the most gigantic battle that has been seen in the course of centuries within the walls of a city. I give the lie to this Republic which called itself that of the three truths. It is the Republic of the three blasphemies; it is the Republic of the three lies. ["Bravo! Bravo!"]

Coming now to the causes of this revolution, the progressive party ascribes the same causes to everything. Señor Cortina told us yesterday that there are revolutions because there are inequalities and because invariably and spontaneously peoples instinctively rise against tyrants. Previously Señor Ordax Avecilla had told us: "Do you want to avoid revolutions? Feed the hungry!" Behold then the theory of the progressive party in its full scope: The causes of revolution are on the one hand destitution, on the other tyranny. Gentlemen, this theory is totally contrary to history. I ask you to cite me one example of a revolution made and carried out by enslaved or hungry peoples. Revolutions are a sickness of rich peoples; revolutions are a sickness of free peoples. The ancient world was a world in which slaves composed the greater part of the human species; cite me a revolution that was made by those slaves. [From the Left: "The Spartacus revolution."]

The most that they could accomplish was to stir up some slave insurrections; but great revolutions were always made by very rich aristocrats. No, gentlemen, it is not in slavery, it is not in poverty that one finds the germ of revolutions. The germ of revolution is found in the overexcited desires of the multitude stimulated by the tribunes who exploit it and profit from it. ["Good! Good!"] *And you will be like the rich:* that is the formula of socialist revolutions against the middle classes. *And you will be like the nobles:* that is the formula of the revolutions of the middle classes against the nobles. *And you will be like kings:* that is the formula of the nobles against the kings. Finally, gentlemen, *and you will be like gods:* that is the formula of the first rebellion of the first man against God. From Adam, the first rebel, to Proudhon, the last infidel, this is the formula of all revolutions. ["Very good! Very good!"]

The Spanish government, as was its duty, did not want this formula to be applied in Spain. It was all the less desirous because the internal situation was not the most auspicious, and it was necessary to be on guard against both internal and external eventualities. Not to have done so would have meant ignoring completely the power of those magnetic forces which arise from the center of revolutionary infection and go through the world infecting everything.

In brief, this was the internal situation: The political question was not, has never been, is not completely solved. Political questions are not so easily solved in societies quickly roused by passions. The dynastic question was not settled because—although it is true that here we are the victors—we did not have the submission of the conquered, the complement of victory. ["Bravo!"] The religious question was in a very bad state. The marriage question, as you know, was bitter. Since, as I have already proved, dictatorship may be legitimate and advantageous under given circumstances, were we or were we not in such circumstances? What more dangerous circumstances have appeared in the world? Experience proved that the calculations of the Government and the foresight of this Chamber had not been un founded. You all know it, gentlemen. I shall speak of it only in passing because I detest anything that stirs up passions; I was not born for that. Everyone knows that the Republic was proclaimed through the streets of Madrid by bursts of gunfire; everyone knows that without the energetic, active resistance of the Government, all of Spain, from the Pillars of Hercules to the Pyrenees, from sea to sea, would have been a lake of blood. And not only Spain. Do you know what misfortunes would have been spread throughout the world if the revolution had triumphed? Ah, gentlemen! To think of such things is to exclaim that the ministry that was able to resist and to triumph deserves praise from the fatherland. ["Very good! Very good!"]

This question became complicated with the English question. Before entering into it—and I hasten to announce that I shall treat it lightly as it is fitting and proper to do—the Congress will permit me to express some general ideas which seem fitting to me.

Gentlemen, I have always believed that blindness in men, in governments, and in nations is a sign of perdition. I have believed that God always begins by blinding those whom He wishes to destroy; I have believed that in order that they should not see the abyss that He puts at their feet He begins by disturbing their reason. Applying this idea to the general policy followed for the last few years by England and France, gentlemen, I have predicted for a long time great misfortune and catastrophe. A historic fact, an ascertained fact, an indisputable fact is that the providential mission of France is to be the instrument of Providence in the propagation of new political, social, and religious ideas.

In modern times three great ideas have invaded Europe: the Catholic idea, the philosophical idea, the revolutionary idea. In these three periods France has always become an agent to propagate these ideas. Charlemagne was France personified in order to propagate the Catholic idea; Voltaire was France personified to propagate the philosophical idea; Napoleon has been France personified to propagate the revolutionary idea. [General applause.] In the same manner I believe that the providential mission of England is to maintain the just moral balance of the world and so to offer a perpetual contrast with France. France represents the rising tide and England the ebb tide. ["Very good! Very good!"]

Suppose for a moment a rising tide without the ebb tide; the sea would cover the continents. Imagine an ebb tide without the rising tide; the sea would disappear from the earth. Imagine France without England; the world would move only amid convulsions. Each day would have a new constitution, each hour a new form of government. Imagine England without France; the world would vegetate forever under the venerable King John's charter, the prototype of all British constitutions. What is the significance, gentlemen, of the coexistence of these two powerful nations? It signifies progress limited by stability, stability enlivened by progress. ["Good! Good!"]

I call upon contemporary history and your memories, gentlemen, to attest that for some years these two great nations have lost the memory of their deeds and of their providential mission in the world. Instead of spreading new ideas throughout the world, France preached everywhere the *status quo:* the *status quo* in France, in Spain, in Italy, in the Orient. Instead of preaching stability England preached revolution everywhere: in Spain, in Portugal, in France, in Italy, and in Greece. And what resulted from this? What inevitably must result: that the two nations in playing a role that had never been their own have played it very badly. France tried to convert herself from a devil into a preacher and England from a preacher into a devil. [Great general laughter accompanied by equal applause from all parties.]

This, gentlemen, is contemporary history. But speaking only of England, because it is of her that I propose to speak briefly, I entreat Heaven that she shall not suffer as has France the catastrophes that she deserves for her errors; because nothing is comparable to the error of England in supporting revolutionary parties everywhere. Unfortunate country! She does not know that should danger arise these parties will instinctively turn their backs upon her. Has this not happened already? It must necessarily happen because all revolutionaries in the world know that when revolutions are in earnest, that when clouds gather, when horizons turn dark, and when waves dash high, the ship of revolution has no other pilot than France. [Loud and prolonged applause.]

Gentlemen, this was the policy followed by England, or rather by its government and its agents during the last epoch. Prompted by important considerations I have said and I say again that I do not wish to discuss this question. My first consideration is that of the public welfare, because I must declare here solemnly that I wish the most intimate alliance, the most complete union between the Spanish and English nations. I admire and respect England as perhaps the freest and strongest nation on earth and the most worthy of being so. Thus I should not like to exacerbate this question; nor should I like to impair or hinder subsequent negotiations. There is another consideration which moves me to refrain from speaking of this matter. In order to speak of it I should have to speak of a man who was my friend, more of a friend than Señor Cortina; but I cannot help him so much as Señor Cortina helped him. Honor allows me no other aid than silence. [The name of Bulwer is repeated among the deputies of the majority party.]

In discussing this question (allow me to speak frankly), Señor Cortina suffered a sort of vertigo and forgot who he was, where he was, and who we are. His Lordship believed that he was a lawyer, and he was not a lawyer, for he was an orator of the Congress. His Lordship thought that he was speaking to judges and he was speaking to deputies. His Lordship thought that he was speaking in a tribunal and he was speaking in a deliberative assembly. He thought that he was speaking of a lawsuit, and he was speaking of a great national political matter, for if it were a lawsuit it was a lawsuit between two nations. Well, gentlemen, did it behoove Señor Cortina to be the lawyer of the party contrary to the Spanish nation? [Applause from the majority party.] Is that patriotism, by chance? Is that being patriotic? No. Do you know what it means to be patriotic? To be patriotic, gentlemen, means to love, to abhor—to feel what our fatherland loves or abhors. ["Bravo! Bravo!"]

I said, gentlemen, that I would pass very lightly over this question, and so I have treated it. . . .

But neither serious internal circumstances nor the complicated and dangerous external circumstances are sufficient to weaken the opinion of the gentlemen who are seated on those benches. And liberty, they say to us. Well what of it? Is not liberty above all else? And liberty, at least individual liberty, has it not been sacrificed? Liberty, gentlemen! Do those who utter this sacred word understand the principle that they are proclaiming and the word that they are uttering? Do they understand the times in which they are living? Has not the rumble of the latest catastrophes reached your ears? What! Do you not know that at this hour liberty has come to an end? Have you not observed, as I have observed with the eyes of my soul, its painful suffering? Have you not seen it scorned, ridiculed, treacherously wounded by all the demagogues of the world? Have you not seen it endure its anguish in the Swiss mountains, along the banks of the Seine, on the shores of the Rhine and Danube, on the edge of the

Tiber? Have you not seen it invade the Quirinal, which has been its Calvary? [Noisy applause.]

Gentlemen, the word is frightening, but we must not shrink from uttering frightening words if they tell the truth, and I am determined to tell it. Liberty has ended! [Great amazement.] It will not be resurrected in three days, in three years, or perhaps in three centuries. Are you frightened, gentlemen, by the tyranny that we suffer? You are easily frightened; you will see worse things. And now I beg of you, gentlemen, that you remember the words that I am going to say, because the events that I am going to announce will be carried out to the letter in a near, or more remote but still not too distant, future. [Rapt attention.]

The basis of all your errors, gentlemen [addressing the seats of the leftist party], consists in not knowing the direction of civilization and of the world. You believe that civilization and the world are receding when civilization and the world are returning. The world, gentlemen, is moving with very rapid steps toward the formation of a despotism, the most gigantic and devastating in the memory of man. Civilization and the world are traveling in that direction. I need not be a prophet to announce these things. It suffices to consider the frightening aggregate of human events from the only true vantage point, that of the Catholic.

Gentlemen, there are only two possible kinds of repression, one internal and the other external, the religious and the political. These are of such a nature that when the religious thermometer is high, the thermometer of repression is low, and when the religious thermometer is low, the political thermometer, political repression, tyranny, is high. This is the law of humanity, a law of history. And if you do not think so, consider how the world was, consider how society was before the time of the Cross; tell me how it was when there was no inner repression, when there was no religious repression. That was a society of tyranny and of slaves. Name me a single people of that period that did not have slaves and one without tyranny. This is an incontrovertible fact, this is an indisputable fact, this is an obvious fact. Liberty, true liberty, liberty for all and by all, came to the world only with the Savior of the world. ["Very good! Very good!"] This is also an incontrovertible fact; it is a fact recognized even by the socialists themselves, who confess it. The socialists call Jesus a divine man, and the socialists do more, they call themselves His followers. His followers, great heavens! They, the men of blood and vengeance, followers of Him who lived only to do good, of Him who spoke only to bless, of Him who performed miracles only to free the sinner from his sin, to free the dead from death; of One who in the space of three years brought about the greatest revolution that the centuries have witnessed, and He brought it about without having shed any blood except His own. [Cheers, and general applause.]

Gentlemen, I beg you to heed me. I am going to make you aware of the most marvelous parallelism that history offers. You have seen that in the ancient world, when religious repression could sink no lower because none existed, political repression rose to the utmost heights because it rose to the height of tyranny. With Jesus Christ, with whom religious repression is born, political repression disappears completely. This is so true that when Christ established a society with His disciples it was the only society that has existed without a government. Between Jesus and His disciples there was no other government than the love of the Master for His disciples and the love of the disciples for the Master. That is to say that when inner repression was complete liberty was absolute.

Let us continue the parallel. We come to apostolic times, which because it suits my purpose I shall consider to extend from apostolic times strictly speaking up to the ascent of Christianity into the temple of Jupiter at the time of Constantine the Great. At this time, gentlemen, Christian religion, that is to say, inner religious repression, was at its apogee; but although it was at its apogee, there happened what happens in all societies composed of men: A germ, a mere germ of license and religious liberty began to develop. Observe the parallelism: As the religious thermometer begins to fall, there is a corresponding rise in the political thermometer. As yet there is no government, government is not necessary, but a germ of government is necessary. Thus in Christian society at that time there were no real magistrates, only arbitrating judges and referees, who are the embryo of government. Really there was no more than that. The Christians of apostolic times did not have lawsuits, they did not go to court; they settled their disputes by means of arbiters. Observe, gentlemen, how government increases with corruption.

We come to the feudal period, and religion is still in its apogee but to a certain extent vitiated by human passions. What is going on at this time in the political world? A real and effective government already is necessary, but the weakest of all suffices, and thus the feudal monarchy is established, the weakest of all monarchies.

Continue observing the parallelism. We come to the sixteenth century. In this century with the great Lutheran reform, with this great political and social as well as religious scandal, with this act of intellectual and moral emancipation of the people, the following institutions coincide: In the first place monarchies change from feudal to absolute. You undoubtedly believe that a monarchy can be no more than absolute; can a government be more than absolute? But the thermometer of political repression had to rise higher because the religious thermometer continued falling; and as a matter of fact it did rise. And what new institution was created? That of standing armies. And do you know, gentlemen, what standing armies are? To know that, one needs only to know what a soldier is: A soldier is a slave in uniform. Thus you see that at the moment when religious repression falls, political repression rises to absolutism and goes beyond it. Governments were not content to be absolute; they asked for and obtained the privilege of being absolute and of having a million arms.

In spite of this, gentlemen, it was necessary for the political thermometer to rise higher because the religious thermometer continued to fall; and it did rise higher. What new institution was then created? Governments said: "We have a million arms, but they do not suffice. We need more; we need a million eyes." And they had the police with a million eyes. In spite of this the political thermometer and repression had to rise because in spite of everything the religious thermometer continued to fall.

Governments were not satisfied with having a million eyes; they wanted to have a million ears, and they had them with administrative centralization, through which all demands and complaints converged upon the government.

Well, gentlemen, this did not suffice. Because the religious thermometer continued to fall, it was necessary for the political thermometer to rise higher—how far, gentlemen? Well, it rose higher.

Governments said: "A million arms are not enough for repression; I need more than a million eyes for repression; I need more than a million ears for repression. We need more: We need to have the privilege of being everywhere at the same time." And they had it. The telegraph was invented. [Great applause.]

Gentlemen, such was the state of Europe and of the world when the first outburst of the last revolution came to announce to all of us that there still was not enough despotism in the world because the religious thermometer had dropped to zero. Well now, gentlemen, one of two things—

I promised, and I shall keep my word to speak with complete candor. [Attention is redoubled.]

Either religious reaction comes or it does not. If there is religious reaction, you will see, gentlemen, how when the religious thermometer rises the political thermometer begins to fall naturally, spontaneously, with no effort on the part of the common people or of governments or of men until it registers the fair day of the liberty of the common people. ["Bravo!"] But if on the contrary, gentlemen, (and this is serious; it is not customary to call the attention of deliberating assemblies to the questions toward which I have turned today; but the gravity of events in the world will excuse me, and I believe that your benevolence will also pardon me)—I say that if the religious thermometer continues falling, I do not know where we shall stop. I do not know, gentlemen, and I tremble when I think of it. Consider the analogies which I have presented, and if no government was necessary when religious repression was in its apogee, no kind of government will suffice when religious repression no longer exists. All despotisms will be inadequate. [Great astonishment.]

Gentlemen, we are putting our finger on the open sore; that is the question of Spain, the question of Europe, the question of humanity, the question of the world. ["True! True!"]

Consider one thing, gentlemen. In the ancient world tyranny was fierce and destructive, and, nevertheless, that tyranny was limited physically because all states were small and because international relations were absolutely impossible. Consequently in the ancient world there could be no tyrannies on a grand scale with one single exception: that of Rome. But now, gentlemen, how things have changed! The way is prepared for a gigantic, colossal, universal, immense tyranny; everything is prepared for it. Gentlemen, consider it carefully. There is no more physical or moral resistance. There is no physical resistance because with steamboats and railroads there are no frontiers; with the telegraph there is no distance; and there is no moral resistance because all minds are divided and all patriotism is dead. Tell me, then, whether or not I am right when I worry about the immediate future of the world; tell me whether in discussing this question I am not discussing the essential question. [Astonishment.]

Only one thing can prevent the catastrophe; one and only one. It cannot be prevented by giving more liberty, more guaranties, new constitutions. It can be prevented if everyone tries to the limits of his strength to arouse a healthy religious reaction. Well, gentlemen, is this reaction possible? It is possible, but is it probable? Gentlemen, I now speak with the deepest sadness. I do not believe it is probable. I have seen, gentlemen, and known many individuals who have left the Faith and have returned to it; unfortunately I have never seen any people who have recovered their faith after having lost it.

If I still had any hope left, recent events in Rome would have dispelled it; and here I am going to say a few words about this question, also treated by Señor Cortina.

Gentlemen, the happenings in Rome beggar description. What would you call them, gentlemen? Would you call them deplorable? All the events that I have cited are deplorable; these are much more so. Would you call them horrible? Gentlemen, those events are beyond all horror.

There was and is no longer in Rome upon the most eminent throne

the most just, most saintly man on earth. What has Rome done to
this saintly man, to this just man ? What has this city done, the city
in which heroes, Caesars, and pontiffs have reigned? It has exchanged
the throne of the pontiffs for the throne of the demagogues. Rebellious
toward God, it has fallen into the idolatry of the dagger. That is what
it has done. The dagger, gentlemen, the demagogic, the bloody dagger, that is today the idol of Rome. That is the idol that has overthrown Pius IX. That is the idol which troops of savages are carrying
through the streets. Did I say savages? I was wrong, for savages are
fierce, but savages are not ungrateful. [Noisy applause.]

Gentlemen, I have proposed to speak with complete frankness, and
I shall so speak. I say that it is necessary for the ruler of Rome to return
to Rome or else, even though it may distress Señor Cortina, one stone
will not be left upon another. [From the majority section: "Very good!
Very good!"]

The Catholic world cannot consent and will not consent to the virtual destruction of Christianity with the surrender of a single city to
the frenzy of madness. Civilized Europe cannot consent and will not
consent to the toppling of the dome of the edifice of European civilization. The world, gentlemen, cannot consent and will not consent to
the ascension to the throne in Rome, the holy city, of a new and
strange dynasty, the dynasty of crime. ["Bravo!"] And let it not be
said, as Señor Cortina says, as they say in newspapers and in the addresses of the gentlemen who are seated in that section (addressing
the Left) that there are two questions here, one temporal and the
other spiritual, and that the question has been between a temporal
ruler and his people; for the Pontiff still exists. A few words on this
question: a few words, gentlemen, will explain everything.

Without any doubt the spiritual power is the principal attribute of
the Pope. The temporal is merely an accessory, but this accessory is
necessary. The Catholic world has the right to demand that the in-
fallible oracle of its dogmas be free and independent. The Catholic
world cannot be certain that he is independent and free except when
he is sovereign, because only the sovereign depends upon no one.
["Very good! Very good!"] Consequently, gentlemen, the question
of sovereignty, which is a political question everywhere, is in Rome

in addition a religious question. The people who can be sovereign everywhere cannot be so in Rome. Constituent assemblies that can exist everywhere cannot exist in Rome. In Rome there can be no constituent power other than the established power. Rome, gentlemen, the Pontifical States, do not belong to Rome; they do not belong to the Pope. The Pontifical States belong to the Catholic world; the Catholic world has entrusted them to the Pope so that he might be free and independent, and the Pope himself cannot divest himself of this sovereignty, of this independence. [General applause.]

I am going to conclude, gentlemen. . . .

After discussing the three external matters that Señor Cortina discussed, I shall turn in conclusion to an internal matter. Gentlemen, from the beginning of the world until now it has been a debatable question whether a system of resistance or a system of concessions was a better means of avoiding revolutions and upheavals. But fortunately, gentlemen, what has been a question since the first year of creation until the year '48, the year of our Lord '48, is no longer a question of any sort because the matter is settled. If the discomfort in my mouth would permit, gentlemen, I should review all the events from February until now that prove this assertion. But I shall content myself with recalling two: first that of France, gentlemen. There the monarchy did not resist and was overcome by the republic which scarcely had the strength to move. The republic which scarcely had the strength to move overcame socialism because it did resist.

In Rome, the other example which I wish to cite, what has happened? Was not your model there? Tell me, if you were painters and wished to paint a model ruler, would you find a better original than Pius IX? Gentlemen, Pius IX wished to be like his Master, admirable and liberal. He found exiles in his country and he extended his hand to them, returning them to their fatherland. There were reformers, gentlemen, and he gave them reforms; there were liberals, and he gave them liberty. Each of his words was a benefaction. And now, gentlemen, do not his indignities equal if not exceed his benefactions? And in view of this, gentlemen, is not the policy of concessions at an end? ["Very good! Very good!"]

Gentlemen, if one should try here to choose between liberty on the one hand and dictatorship on the other, there would be no disagreement; because if one can embrace liberty, who would fall on his knees before a dictatorship? But this is not the question. Liberty does not really exist in Europe. The constitutional governments which represented it years ago are almost everywhere now only a framework, a lifeless skeleton. Remember imperial Rome. In imperial Rome all the republican institutions exist: the omnipotent dictators exist, the eminent consuls exist. Of all this only one thing is lacking: one man excels, and the republic falls. ["Very good! Very good!"]

That, gentlemen, is the nature of constitutional governments in nearly all of Europe. Unintentionally, without realizing it, Señor Cortina demonstrated that to us the other day. Did His Lordship not tell us, and rightly so, that he prefers what history says to what the theorists say?

I appeal to history. What has become of those governments, Señor Cortina, with their legitimate majorities always overcome by turbulent minorities; with their responsible ministers who are responsible for nothing; with their inviolable kings who are always violated? Thus, gentlemen, as I have previously said, the choice is not between liberty and dictatorship. If it were between liberty and dictatorship, I should vote for liberty, as would all of those who are seated here. The question is this: One must choose between the dictatorship of insurrection and the dictatorship of government. Placed in this position, I choose the dictatorship of government as less oppressive and less ignominious. [Applause from the majority section.]

One must choose between the dictatorship that comes from below and that from above. I choose that from above because it comes from cleaner and more serene regions. One must choose between the dictatorship of the dagger and that of the sword. I choose that of the sword because it is more noble. ["Bravo! Bravo!"] Gentlemen, as we vote we shall be divided on this question. We shall be consistent with our own policies. You, gentlemen, will vote as usual for what is most popular. We, gentlemen, shall vote as always for what is most beneficial. [Great excitement follows this address. The orator receives the congratulations of almost all the deputies of the Congress.]

11. Church Control of Education

Count Montalembert: *Speech in Support of the Falloux Law* (1850)*

In the following address Deputy Montalembert defended the bill that was to become known as the Falloux Law. One of the great conflicts of the century both in Catholic countries and in those containing a large percentage of Catholics came over the issue of whether education should be controlled by the state and be of a secular, that is, nonreligious, character, or whether it should be kept in the hands of the Catholic Church. Napoleon had set up a system of education centralized in and dominated by the state; but after his fall in 1815 the Church had established schools, usually conducted by religious orders. The existence of these orders was well known to the government, although they were not officially approved. In their demands for liberty of education the extremist Catholics implied freedom for the Church to conduct schools without state permission or supervision. Deputy Montalembert and his friends took a moderate position, seeking in the bill under discussion the right of the Church freely to carry out its educational work under a minimum of public supervision. In their bill they tried, however, in the name of freedom of instruction, to extend the Church's influence over state education itself. The defenders of wholly secular state education on the one extreme and the ultra Catholics on the other both opposed the bill; but in the end a majority of the deputies approved it into law. Montalembert's speech illustrates the close connections between religion and politics, the Church and society, and the extent to which religion and the Church were used as bulwarks of order. The controversy between Church and state over control of education has not yet been everywhere resolved, nor is it

* *Moniteur universel,* January 17, 1850, pp. 197-200.

likely to be. Later among these documents there is a speech from 1879, the time of another phase of this same struggle in France, in which the Republican deputy Paul Bert sought to justify a state monopoly of education to the exclusion of the influence of the Church.

The previous speaker has criticized the law before you for not saying all that it means; he has referred us to His Majesty the Emperor of All the Russias for lessons in plain speaking as exemplified by his ukases. I consider this reproach unjust; but even if it were just, it will vanish, I hope, after you have done me the honor of listening to me, for I am going to make you recognize all the law means, or at least all that I think that it ought to say.

For twenty years I have been fighting the official teaching, apology for which you have heard today, and for a year I have been negotiating a treaty of peace with the former defenders of this teaching, a treaty now submitted to you for your ratification. I need to justify to you both the war and the peace; that is to say, to explain to you the nature of the evil and the nature of the remedy.

First the evil.

Let me invoke your classical memories in order to summarize my thoughts on this subject.

Like me all of you probably have expounded Livy and like me have forgotten it. But the other day in rereading him I found a historical fact which seemed to me to sum up the recent role of public education in France. You remember the siege of Falerii by the Roman army under Camillus? While the town was besieged by the Romans the teacher in charge of the elite of the Faliscan youth led them gradually to the advance posts of the enemy camp and turned them over to the besiegers.

I am not afraid to say that that is what public education (the monopoly held by public education) has done in France.

I am not speaking of any individuals, and I make allowance for exceptions; I know many honorable ones. I speak only of the general spirit of the institution, and I say that this great institution has delivered the youth of France into the hands of the enemy besieging French society.

Under the Restoration the monopoly of public education turned out what were called at that time liberals and revolutionaries; under the July régime it made republicans; and under the Republic it is turning out socialists.

Our president was telling us the other day that it was very difficult to define Socialism. I am going to try to define it, or at least I shall try to explain what I understand by Socialism.

I understand by Socialism in practice the party which the day after the February revolution wanted to substitute the red flag for the tricolor; the party which on May 15 broke into this chamber, put us out of it, and proclaimed a capital levy of a billion francs; the party which on June 24, 1848, gave battle to society and cost us more generals than the defeat of Beresina or Waterloo; the party which last June 13 put us beyond the law, and which today until something better turns up proclaims the abolition of taxes and capital; finally, the party which every day makes new recruits among those of discontented ambition, wounded vanity, ruined careers, all eager to seize the first occasion to get control of society by surprise attack. That is what I call Socialism in practice.

Alongside it there is Socialism in theory; that is to say the spirit which is never satisfied with anything, which makes every reform a pretext or an occasion for revolution, which the day after 1789 wanted 1792 or 1793, which the day after the July Revolution wanted a republic, and the day after the democratic, constitutional republic announces the social republic, that is, the dissolution of society. That is what I call Socialism in theory. [On the Right: "Good!"]

I know that this is called the spirit of progress and life. But I call it the spirit of death and destruction and, to give it its true name, the spirit of revolution.

Be assured that by revolutionary spirit I do not mean the spirit which is attached to the defense of this or that conquest of modern revolutions, this or that result of modern revolutions acceptable to and accepted by everyone; the spirit that I mean, far from accepting these results, compromises them, threatens them, disgusts the people with them, and tries to lead them violently back to despotism. This is what I call the revolutionary spirit.

I consider that we have been sent here as a majority—and without wishing in the least to be lacking in respect for the minority, I may say that today I do not expect to address myself to this minority—to combat Socialism, to fight the revolutionary spirit, to fight it by law and with ideas.

Gentlemen, since I have been in this Chamber, as you will bear me witness, I have supported all the measures proposed and taken against Socialism. Even before the explosion of June 24, I mounted this tribune for the first time to oppose the initial appearance of Socialism in the bill to take over the railroads. The other day I voted with you again for a law which did not inspire me with full confidence, the law against primary teachers. I have supported all the proposed remedies against the inroads of Socialism. I have supported all the obstacles which have been erected against it. I had to do so because this was the mandate I had received from my constituency. But I have always said and thought that these remedies would be insufficient and ineffective unless we were to add to them or superimpose upon them a remedy of another kind, one going to the root of the evil, to the source of things. We believe that we are bringing this remedy to you today, at least in part, and it consists of giving back to the country religious education, in returning religion to education through liberty.

This is what we have attempted in our law, and this is what we regard as the first and most important of remedies for the evil which I have just pointed out.

I do not expect to show this evil to those who deny it; but I want to describe it to those who admit its presence but perhaps do not fully take it into account. This evil exists, and since the February revolution it should be evident to all. It is not merely the fact of the February revolution of which I speak, but the social state revealed to us by the revolution of February and existing since that time. These symptoms prove that the experience of a state monopoly in teaching has not succeeded. It cannot be denied that our youth is brought up to be against society and against us. Public education as given in

France foments ambition, vanity, and greed, and the pressure of these is crushing our society. It develops artificial needs which cannot be satisfied. It divides most of those whom it trains into two categories— the mediocre and the discontented—and it creates a group of pupils who belong to both at the same time. [General hilarity.] It creates a core of aspirants who are ready for everything and good for nothing. And this not only is true of primary instruction but is equally and perhaps even more true of secondary instruction. I ask permission to cite a passage on the subject from a remarkable work recently published by the son of one of our most illustrious colleagues, M. de Broglie. This is what he says of the B.A. degree: "The bachelor's degree is a letter of exchange underwritten by society and sooner or later to be paid for in public office; if it is not paid when due, we have this bodily constraint called revolution." [On the Right: "It is very true!"]

In fact, this is so true that there is not a government in our century which has been able to resist the pressure of the generation which it has itself trained. It has barely ceased training one generation in the space of fifteen or twenty years before this generation rises and over-turns it. Is this the fault alone of the school system? I think not.

This state of society is not the fault of the system alone. In large part it is the fault of the blindness of fathers who change the positions of their children by the unnatural education they try to give them. [Ironical laughter on the Left.]

In large part it is the fault of our entire society, of the atmosphere which it breathes, and, as I was just saying, of the blindness and ambition of the fathers who educate their children—for what? In order to launch them into public service, that is to say to throw them upon the budget as upon a prey. That is what we see every day. [Lively approval on the Right.]

Finally, the result is what I have just said: Each government raises up generations which overthrow it when they come to maturity.

Whence comes this cruel weakness of our time? Through our public education we kill respect for authority, above all respect for the authority of God. We do not act intentionally; but the result is that in public education we destroy respect for God, for the father of the family, and finally for the power of the state.

We teach our young people knowledge but not duty; we teach them reason but also pride. We kill that humility which forms the basis of all public and private virtue, and by freeing this reason or rather this pride, we have arrived at the condition which we sense and at a problem which we find insoluble even before stating it; namely, how to achieve the means of maintaining social authority along with the general freeing of pride disguised as reason.

We are proposing a remedy for this state of affairs, and the remedy is to return religion to education through liberty, to return it not in order to kill reason but to regulate, to discipline, to enlighten, and to purify it. [Exclamations on the Left; assent on the Right.]

Where today is to be found the defense of the social and even of the material order? Do you want me to tell you? For a long time we believed that the maintenance of society and of French civilization rested on two pillars: unlimited distribution of property and elementary education.

As to the unlimited distribution of property, it has certainly done a great deal to help in the defense of the social order. But I am not sure that this obstacle to evil will last for long. As to elementary education, I think that after the debates of the other day regarding the law against primary teachers, after the revelations from this tribune made by the head of public instruction and by men competent in this matter, there is no longer any way of counting seriously on this means as an obstacle to the progress of the barbarism which threatens us.

Who defends property and order in the country? Is it the teacher so long cherished and petted by the people of property, the bourgeoisie, as we say now? No. One must say no, always allowing for exceptions, a very large allowance, as large as you wish.

Who defends order, often involuntarily and instinctively, forcefully and with admirable perseverance? It is the curé! [Ironical laughter on the Left.]

. . . .

. . . Today the curé, the clergy in general, and especially the clergy in rural areas, who have the care of souls, represent order, even for those who are unbelievers, who do not enjoy the Church, as was said under the Restoration. They represent at the same time both the moral order and the political and material order.

There are two armies in France, each with 30,000 to 40,000 men, the army of teachers and the army of the curés. I ask you once more whether the army of primary teachers supports order. Some of these teachers are excellent; but there are many more who are mediocre, and as a group I think that they are today condemned.

. . . .

. . . Among the 30,000 to 40,000 rural curés, some are bad ones . . .

There are some, as I must admit and as we all know, who are infected with what is called democratic and social Catholicism, something which is still worse, if that is possible, than the democratic and social republic. There are many who are mediocre. I do not say that all are saints or angels; far from it. But I say that as a whole the group is excellent, that it functions admirably in its social mission, admirably in the interests of society, and I ask every enlightened dweller in the rural areas if it is not the safeguard of society in our country? [On the Right: "It is true!"]

Here we have a conclusive fact in regard to primary instruction. But it would be a big mistake to believe that the evil is limited to public instruction. It looms just as large in secondary education, and that is why we have been attacking it continuously. Socialism is not yet taught there; but what I consider the same thing is taught, skepticism and rationalism; for what is called skepticism and rationalism at the upper level is called Socialism below. Professors are too often in the towns what elementary teachers are in the villages. To translate this remark into fact I wish only to remind you of the twenty or thirty professors of the teaching body, not of the body of primary teachers, but of what we call the University body, who were more or less compromised by participation in the various ramifications of the June 13 affair. I have had proof too in the recent circular, available to all, from the Minister of Public Instruction to the rectors, in which he points out the evil in secondary instruction and indicates the power of repression accorded to him by law in regard to primary teaching.

Let me speak freely on this subject. After having spoken against the "reds," as they are called, let me say something against the "whites," as we say. It is with the condition, however, that the whites and the reds will not unite against me. [Hilarity.]

In the popular sense of the word, "whites" is almost synonymous with "bourgeois." [M. Charamaule: "That means legitimist."]

Well, let us lay aside these colorful epithets and take the common, popular term "bourgeois."

This is what I mean: By bourgeois I mean all of us, especially the class from which this Assembly comes. It seems to me that essentially we are a bourgeois assembly.

So far I have not seen in this Assembly any serious proletarians, these eloquent proletarians who would appear, we were told, as a result of universal suffrage, any more than I have seen feudal lords or knights in armor. I see only that here we are all bourgeois, in the usual modern sense of the word.

I say that we all have contributed to the evil which frightens us now; for all of us have by our attitude, example, and teachings more or less spread rationalism and the skepticism which with a change of atmosphere and scene have become Socialism.

But here is what I add for the consolation of the French bourgeoisie: I say that by special grace from on high it has been given the means of correcting the evil which it has done. It can still correct the evil, and seldom in this world can one retrieve a wrong done in the field of politics.

The bourgeoisie can do so on two conditions, by curing itself, and by taking the evil into account. To do so ought not to be too difficult after the cruel warning which it received in February and continues to receive every day.

In fact, let us never forget that this society, so disdainful of all spiritual help, so proud of itself, this society which began in 1789, which is so sure of its future, of its grandeur, of its prosperity, is being undermined, disturbed, threatened, invaded, conquered, in a day, in the twinkling of an eye, and by men whom it did not even do the honor of fearing. [Commotion.]

Who menaces this civilized and intelligent society today? Who threatens it? Who inspires in it the terror translated into almost all the measures on which we have to vote? Who threatens it? Are they austere and pure men like the martyrs of old who changed the face of the pagan world by the introduction of Christianity? Certainly not. Are they even scoundrels on a grand scale such as overturned the French society of the Old Régime and created the Republic of 1793? [On the Right: "Yes, rascals and not great ones!" On the Left: "The rascals are the men of 1815." M. le Président: "They have changed color." On the Left: "The rascals are the Jesuits."]

Not at all. Society is threatened by conspirators of the lowest level and by horrid little orators whose mediocrity is as incontestable as it is powerful. Society is turned upside down by men whose success and influence in the eyes of history will be the most incomprehensible phenomenon of our century. And what then? What is this society defending against these horrid little orators? Must I tell you?

. . . .

. . . Is it perchance some refinement of civilization, some vague perfection of constitutional or political liberty? No, No. You all know that it is the ABC of social life, that is, property and the family. That is what for two years by every possible means of force and reason France has been condemned to defend. To this cause the Honorable M. Thiers devoted his whole mind, and M. Charles Dupin all his statistical resources. And the Academy of Moral Sciences has been convoked by the head of the executive power to answer these men on elementary questions, on matters such as savages barely emerged from barbarism affirm and maintain! That is what France, arrived we are told at the apogee of civilization and progress, in the midst of the nineteenth century, has been obliged and is still obliged every day to defend!

If this is not a lesson for the French bourgeoisie and for entire French society, and if society does not profit from the lesson, then I do not know when or where or how it will find one more useful!

I am far from wanting to pursue to the utmost or to denounce here what I have just called skepticism and rationalism. Nothing is farther from my thought. When at times I find myself in the presence of souls dominated by these ideas, I bow my head in compassion and even with a kind of respect—I do not know if that is quite the right word—such as a great misfortune or great poverty arouses.

It is not God's will that I should come here today to seek out and denounce this great vice of thought. But I do pursue the propagation of this vice as justly described by a man whom I have long fought, a former minister of public instruction, M. de Salvandy, who spoke of it to the elite of French youth in the distribution of prizes as "the proselytizing of disbelief and the cruel courage of denying to the young those beliefs which fortify and console without having anything to put in their place." That is what I am persecuting and denouncing, and what I do not fear to point to as the principal cause of the deplorable condition which, if there is still time, you are called upon to heal. What M. de Salvandy says of the youth, I say of the many or of what we used to call the masses, that is to say, the laboring and indigent classes. There is a pitiless cruelty in wanting to take from them, and as has been done, in taking from them the beliefs which comfort them, without putting anything in their place.

. . . .

And when I say "without putting anything in their place," I am mistaken; for you will see what has been put in their place. We thought that in encouraging, spreading, supporting all the immoral novels, all those culpable journals, all those literary figures and dramatists that have depraved the taste and soiled the soul of France we were destroying only religious faith; yet without meaning to we have destroyed social faith. Yes, it is true, only too true! And do you know the result? Unintentionally, we have given Socialism to the people for a religion, because a religion is necesasry to the masses; you all say that. Well, when the former religion has been taken away, when the faith in God Who made Man according to the Gospel has been taken away, do you know what is substituted? The Faith in man, who according to Socialism created God, is substituted.

For in the end what is Socialism? It is man believing himself God, in the sense that he believes himself able to destroy evil and suffering.

Doubtless it would have been more comfortable to stop, satisfied with skepticism and rationalism. This food suits the proud and refined minds which used to be called strong minds. But it is not a food for the masses; they cannot and do not wish to stop there; they immediately upset the frail structure of a negativistic reason and throw themselves from the heights of truth to the very depths of error. Thus they have not wanted to stay within the no man's land offered them and have run to Socialism. Their old faith in God is destroyed; but they have immediately found another, faith in man, or Socialism.

There is something more absurd than Socialism, and that is the pretense of maintaining a society without dogma, without faith, without supernatural or spiritual beliefs. Many enlightened and powerful men in all classes of the country have sought to do so. That is even more absurd and ridiculous than Socialism, and that is what has brought about the existing condition.

The Honorable M. Pierre Leroux told us one day from this tribune that there was no middle way, that we had to choose in point of doctrine between Socialism and Jesuitism. I accept this alternative, with an amendment however; in place of Jesuitism I propose a term which everyone will understand and accept. I say with M. Leroux that there is no middle road between Socialism and the Catechism. Not Jesuitism but the Catechism is what I propose.

. . . .

The Catechism is certainly not all of society, but without it there is no society and there is Socialism. Those are the two poles between which, on the advice of your friends and your enemies, you the majority must choose. Do you know what great service the Church will render the French people through education if it can resume its appropriate role through education and the Catechism? Do you know the great service it can render us all? It will not flatter us! It will not extol all our evil propensities; it will not deify our greed; it will not search into every forbidden theology and absurd philosophy for justification of all the evil passions of humanity. This the Church will never do; it will never flatter the evil at the bottom of all our hearts which is so relentlessly flattered today. [Long applause from the Right.]

On the contrary, it will say every day to those in all ranks of society who so much need it: You are dust, and your entire life must be a series of sufferings and struggles whose reward is not here below. It will tell man that he comes from nothing, that he must defy his weaknesses and restrain them. This it will say to society, to the people, and this is the greatest service to be rendered to modern society. [Lively approval from the Majority benches.]

It does still more for the people; it deposits within the conscience of each of us the foundation of all government. It makes the soul of each of us the true type of government, that is, the image of a society ordered like itself. This is the role of the Church in education. It creates in the human soul the model of all government. It teaches man to reconcile the divine liberty on the one hand which he has received with life, the liberty to choose between good and evil, with the authority on the other hand to which he is obliged to submit the exercise of this liberty.

There you have the services which the Church will render to education and through education to each member of society. Then you will be able to have a governable people, and surely under a republic as under a despotism the first social need is a governable people; today, it is ungovernable.

That is why an illustrious contemporary, M. Guizot, said that Catholicism "is the greatest school of respect which exists here below."

I ask you, is not the first need of our modern society respect for the law, respect for power, for society and property? Is there a better founded, less indisputable need than that? [A voice: "And respect for oneself."]

You are a thousand times right—respect for oneself. Go to a school where you can learn this respect, the school of the Church. There you have a definition of the remedy. Listen now to a definition of the evil as given by a man who was once your colleague, the Honorable M. Proudhon.

I grant that I am fond of this writer. [Laughter.] . . . And this is why—he holds a torch in his hand which lights up the walls of the shadowy cavern where we have been for two years.

Here is what he says of democracy. You know this writer equated democracy with Socialism. When he speaks of democracy, he speaks of Socialism, and reciprocally.

Here is how he defined democracy: "Democracy is the destruction of all temporal and spiritual power." [Excitement.]

I know that this definition cannot be acknowledged in this Chamber. It must be denied, and one is right to reject it. But it is a great misfortune that the French people are so logical; for it is a misfortune to be too logical in politics; it is a misfortune to push to logical extremes the consequences of stated principles.

We must fear that the people may see in the democracy which is preached to them every day a realization of the definition which M. Proudhon has given us.

Another of our colleagues, M. Pierre Leroux, said from this same tribune that the goal of Socialism, which he too confounds with democracy, is the destruction of the very idea of authority. He said that each man ought to be *his own priest and his own emperor*. [Laughter.] At least that is what M. Proudhon imputes to him. How are you to govern a people among whom these ideas are popular and daily spread about? These ideas, in a form not so clear or so crude as that which I have just given them, but more moderately expressed without being less dangerous, are spread among us by the ministers of the official instructional system, that is to say on one hand by the primary teachers and on the other by too many of the University body.

I repeat here what I said regarding these two categories: What the primary teachers are for the peasants, the professors of the colleges are for the upper classes. The one group spreads Socialism, the other leads toward Socialism and sometimes even ends in Socialism.

Listen to this advice given by one of the editors of a review just cited, if I am not mistaken, *Freedom of Thought [La Liberté de penser.]* This magazine is edited by the flower of the University, the professors of the most advanced classes, the most distinguished pupils of the Normal School, and the most famous professors of the colleges of Paris.

This is what the editor-in-chief of the review wrote to a colleague, in a paper which is called *Republican Education [L'éducation républicaine].* This I think is openly socialist: but here is what the editor-in-chief of *Freedom of Thought* writes: "We are neither flatterers nor men of ambition [he says of himself and his colleagues], neither Catholics nor defenders of eclecticism; we are democratic republicans, even a little tainted by Socialism." So much for the identity of the two levels of teaching.

That is enough about the evil; now I must speak of the remedy which we think we can apply.

The remedy consists in religious education. And notice that there are fundamentally only two kinds of education, religious education and irreligious education; there are not three kinds. All education which is not religious is irreligious and cannot be anything else.

How will you make public education religious in France? The law as I interpret it indicates two means: first and foremost, by liberty, and then by the reform of the official system of teaching. It is difficult to undertake these two tasks at the same time, and we have done so in a spirit of unity, conciliation, and peace, which I shall presently explain. Why do we want liberty? First of all, because the constitution demands it. Secondly, because, although we do not believe in the infallibility of freedom of teaching, we believe nevertheless that, through this freedom, religious teaching will resume its rights and will exercise a legitimate preponderance in the training of French youth. It will do so even without the reform of the official system of teaching, but rather by means of competition with this teaching. That is what we believe and what we hope. We believe further that the exercise of this liberty [of teaching] presents a great deal less danger than the exercise of other liberties, and it does so because its exercise is based upon two conditions, namely vocation and devotion—both conditions which, unfortunately, no other liberty demands of its devotees.

We shall say next that we want liberty because the contrary experience has not succeeded, and that even if there should not be the promise of liberty in the constitution, the evil of monopoly would constitute a sufficient reason for us to try out liberty, and, for the general security, to call upon all the systems and all the methods which good people can approve; the law does not admit of others.

Do we give this liberty in our law? Or is it true that we refuse liberty in a law drawn up to give freedom of teaching? . . .

Yes, we give liberty within the conditions required by the constitution; for the constitution is opposed to unlimited liberty, to liberty as it is in Belgium, or like that which I demanded here from this tribune at the time of the Constituent Assembly. The constitution opposes such liberty, thanks to the vote of members who are our adversaries today. The constitution requires certain conditions for liberty and certain limits to it. We have respected these; but in doing so, we are convinced that we have given such liberty as is likely to satisfy all reasonable requirements. I shall explain how very briefly.

The three restrictions of the constitution are morality, ability, and supervision by the state. Those who have taken the trouble to read the law will not find that we have been too exacting with respect to morality; nor will they find that we have been too harsh as to ability. . . .

We have set the most moderate limits in regard to ability, in order that liberty may be respected and hence that liberty may be sincere and complete. We can silence all those who boldly accuse us of recanting or not living up to our previous convictions by recalling that our law demands less than has ever been proposed in any other law on this matter.

We have demanded only one term of probation—the usefulness of which everyone recognizes from a moral point of view—and a bachelor's diploma. And we require these two conditions of whom? Only of those who wish to set up or direct a secondary school, without asking anything from the professors or superintendents. This alone is enough to create a great difference, to the advantage of liberty, between our bill and all former proposals.

This liberty, I repeat, is complete and sincere, and it will be exercised not only to the profit of religion but also to that of philosophy, whenever philosophy wants it. Whenever philosophy is embarrassed or misunderstood in other schools, it will have this liberty which we have invoked and won for it as for ourselves.

That is the liberty which we have given you, and to which, I do not hesitate to say, we have added the implicit repeal of measures of proscription contained in the former laws and bills against those religious orders which the Church uses principally for education. By their omission we have dropped all such measures in order to pay homage to the common law, liberty, and religion.

That is what we have done both for your liberty and for ours.

Now there are in the law some restrictions on the use of this liberty. There are some, I think, which the constitution does not require. They are: organization of a special inspection, of a special jurisdiction, and then maintenance of the status quo for the conferring of degrees. This question has been reserved for another bill which we were not appointed to draft. Thus in our law we have not had to deal with this serious question.

. . . .

. . . I say with the experience and conviction of twenty years of conflict that the conditions of our bill are such that if they had been proposed under the last Government in 1844, at the time when we were discussing this same question in the Chamber of Peers, we . . . should not have hesitated an instant in accepting them and in accepting them gratefully. I say without hesitation that at this time they suffice to assure the benefits of liberty to teaching in general and to Catholic teaching in particular. I strongly desire that the men who may wish to devote themselves to religious teaching realize this fact; for I am sure that this militant party of Catholicism—which has for so long counted me in its ranks—should now change its attitude and substitute for polemics and the criticism that have already lasted for twenty years the action that we need. This is my conviction, and this is why I declare the actual bill completely sufficient for the needs of the cause. I even fear that after voting this law, the Catholics may be wanting in liberty rather than that liberty may be lacking to Catholics.

This is the avowal of a man who, as you see, is not a flatterer of his cause or of his party, but one who is its soldier and devoted, sincere friend.

So much for liberty.

I come to the second part of our work, the reform of the official teaching system. And here I am obliged to declare that I regard official teaching itself, that is the teaching given by the state, as a mistake, a danger, an evil; I think that the modern state in itself does not have the mission to teach.

I must say this in passing because I have not changed my way of looking at principles. I have two very simple reasons for this conviction. I think that the modern state, stripped as it is of all religion, does not have the moral authority necessary for teaching. Moreover, I think that the state already has too much responsibility; I do not want to add to it the immense weight of a national official teaching system. But still we have a national institution in the system. This is a basic fact; there is a prejudice in its favor, a habit deeply rooted in the heart and will of the majority of the French people. I believe firmly that the French people want to keep the official system. This is a wish which I am bound to respect even while censuring it. But in respecting this great institution we all have the responsibility of its improvement. We have undertaken the task in complete sincerity, with the intention of making this teaching as good, as lasting, and as solid as possible.

How are we to achieve this? While respecting the institution, we have had to recognize that it has given the expected results. The institution appeared good to its supporters and possibly to the majority of the French people, but its results have not been satisfactory from the social and political point of view.

This being so, we wanted to change it in this way: first, to change the authorities hitherto directing it by replacing the council of the University[1] with the higher council of public instruction, whose composition I shall not go into now; to replace the existing academies with the administration of public instruction by departmental academic councils which we have organized in the departments; to call upon all the great social forces, the religious, judicial, political and elected authorities to sit on these councils, and thus to control public

---

[1] Napoleon I organized all levels of education under a State-controlled body to which he gave the name "University." Montalembert uses the term "University" in this sense.

teaching while watching over free teaching; finally, to substitute for the existing and inadequate direction of primary instruction the authority exercised by the same academic councils and often by the cantonal delegates, the mayors, and the curés.

These are the great changes which we have introduced into the control of official teaching. Alongside these changes, which do not destroy but transform, we have introduced competition—competition through liberty—and this we regard as rendering a great service to the official system of national education.

In the third place, we have invoked one of the principles most appealed to today even in the interests of official education—decentralization. For this reason we have added to the academic councils which we have created some general councilors equal in number to all the other members.

And finally—and here we think we have done most for the official system—we have called upon religion, represented by the ministers of various sects and especially by the episcopate, to intervene regularly, solemnly, and efficaciously in the control of education given by the state.

That is what we have done for the reform and transformation of public instruction, with the sincere hope that its results from now on will be more beneficial than formerly.

You will perhaps say: Through this last measure you are only renewing a work which has already failed, which has been tried unsuccessfully under the Restoration by the Bishop of Hermopolis.

I say: No, we are not returning to the work of the Bishop of Hermopolis. His work differs completely from ours. We in no way intend to impose religion on public teaching in the name of a political principle or a more or less popular government. It is the nation itself, represented by its delegates here in the National Assembly and by its other delegates in the General Councils, which we call upon to introduce, as it wishes and to the degree that it wishes, a religious influence into its teaching system.

That is a first difference. Another which one could point out is the difference of times and events, the possible difference between the general state of mind in our time, after the lessons that we have had and the experiences that we have undergone, and the state of mind under the Restoration.

The third and most considerable of the differences is that at the time of the Bishop of Hermopolis the monopoly was placed partially in the hands of the clergy; there was no liberty under a monopoly, and those who did not desire the intervention of religion into public teaching could say rightly that they were condemned to hypocrisy or exclusion. Today there is nothing similar; alongside national teaching, if it becomes religious, there will be this liberty of teaching which we have gained, one in which religion will be able to find a refuge if it feels itself compromised by alliance with the state, but also one in which philosophy will be able to erect its citadel if it finds itself oppressed or injured in the State system.

Such is the immense difference between our work and that of the Bishop of Hermopolis. Our work honors liberty of teaching, competition of private teaching and, if one wishes, philosophical teaching alongside private Catholic teaching and the official teaching of the state. We wish religion to play a role worthy of it and worthy of our country.

In a word, we want to substitute the action of the entire society, as represented by the magistrates, the priests, and the elected delegates, for the action in the government of an independent corporation, one which in the words spoken here by the minister of public instruction depends only on itself, on this corporation called the University, which up to the present has presided over public instruction in our country. We have tried to transform public instruction by substituting society for the University but not for the state.

That is what we have tried to do. Whether we shall succeed or not, I cannot tell; but even if we founder, we shall have proved our spirit of unity and our devotion to the social cause and to national intelligence and morality.

This work which arouses in you in this room strong opposition, causing you to describe the bill as ultrareligious, ultramontane, Jesuitical, has also encountered opposition of quite another kind. I regret for my part that this opposition has not been expressed here, because you could have judged it better than you will be able to do from my account. But this opposition is too serious a fact and too essential an element of the discussion for me not to acquaint you with it in some detail.

Yes, gentlemen, it is important for you to know that this work has encountered the violent opposition of a very considerable portion of the Catholic press and even from what has been called here the Catholic party. These are our own soldiers, and they have turned' against us, who formerly fought with them for this same liberty, and have pursued us constantly for six months with their criticisms, accusations, and recriminations.

They have wanted to respect our intentions but at the same time have attacked and condemned our acts and our ideas. They have given us, old and tried champions of the liberty of teaching, the choice of passing in the eyes of the religious public as traitors or imbeciles.

.   .   .   .

And not only journalists have treated us in this way, but priests and perhaps even bishops. A case of conscience has been made against us with huge publicity.

.   .   .   .

Yes, it is unhappily true and this by the fulminations of the religious press. We have been denounced to the Catholic world, we the oldest defenders of freedom of teaching. M. de Fallous, author of the bill, M. de Melun, M. Beugnot, and I have been denounced as having betrayed the cause of liberty of teaching and the interests of religion, and we have been denounced every day for six months. Is it a fact or not? Let him deny it who can.

We have been reproached first of all for not having given absolute liberty. As if we could do this in the face of the constitution whose provisions I have just explained; as if M. de Falloux and I had not urged it in the Constituent Assembly; and as if, once the constitution was voted, those who today are so exacting had complained about it! You know that no one either here or outside this room has urged it once the terms were voted into the constitution.

We have been blamed for compromising with the state teaching system, for not having left it to itself. They accuse us of making an alliance in which we are dupes and victims, of concluding an honorable peace in place of perpetuating the struggle, and after guaranteeing liberty for ourselves and others, of accepting for religion a serious part in public instruction. In a word, we are blamed for having substituted alliance for conflict.

Well, I have made war and loved it, I have done so longer, as well as, and perhaps better than, the majority of those who now accuse me of ending it.

But I did not consider war to be the primary need of the country. On the contrary, I thought that in the presence of the common danger, of circumstances so serious and so menacing, and in the face of attitudes which I found in men whom we used to consider as adversaries, the first of our duties was to respond to the new tendencies. For the past year I have consecrated all my activity and devotion to this worthy idea.

I do not pretend to have been more important than any other in this patriotic and religious work. I do not pretend any more than my collaborators and friends do that we have found a sovereign and perfect solution; I am as modest as possible in my appreciation of our efforts and work.

Nor do we pretend that we have converted our former adversaries; we do not pretend that we have subdued them; we have encountered diverse natures among them; we do not claim to have produced any effect whatever upon some intractable natures, on what I shall call the implacable pride of false philosophy. No, we have had no effect on them. Neither we, nor the circumstances, nor events, nor the history of the modern world could enlighten them.

But we have met others upon whom the lesson of events has not been lost any more than upon ourselves; for everyone has had to learn, to profit. We have found men, adversaries of yesterday, who stretched out their hands to us the day after what we all thought an unforeseen catastrophe. Should we reject this help? No. It would be the greatest regret of my life if I had done so.

Of course, these men do not believe all we believe; they do not want all that we want. I award them neither this praise nor this blame (as it would be in certain eyes); but they believe today in the peril which they formerly denied and which we are pointing out in advance; like us they want a remedy for this peril: they wish the safety of society and have asked us to work with them to this end.

We have accepted the invitation with the eagerness of people devoted to country and society.

Gentlemen, peace is made the day after a victory and the day after a defeat, and it is made especially, I think, the day after a shipwreck. [Excitement.]

The Honorable M. Thiers may allow me to say that we have had a shipwreck, he and I, in February; when we were sailing together, when we were riding on the good ship Constitutional Monarchy. Yes, when we were sailing on this ship which for thirty-four years has so honorably borne the destinies of France, when we were traveling together not knowing or barely knowing each other, we could and we had to disagree on the direction of the ship. But the tempest came, the pilot has been thrown overboard, the ship has foundered; we should have perished if Providence had not allowed us to find one another, on the raft—I call the present government a raft. I do not know toward what shore this raft is taking us; but I must say that while regretting the ship, I bless the raft.

We found ourselves together the day after the shipwreck on this frail plank which barely separates us from the abyss. Did we need to resume the old struggle? Were we to reject the hand which quite naturally we were led to offer one another? Were we to revive all the old recriminations and resentments, even if they were legitimate ones? I did not think of doing so, I did not wish to do so, and I have not done it.

. . . .

That is why I dare to say that the work we have placed before you, despite its imperfections, despite its complexity, which we are the first to recognize and deplore—that is why I dare to tell you that this work, which may perhaps be sterile, is a sacred work consecrated by the spirit which has dictated it, by the spirit of unity, peace, and reconciliation as well as by the patriotism which inspired it. We have been working on it for a year; we have entered upon this work with the memory of our former conflicts; but we have kept this memory only to encourage us through the boredom, the difficulties, the contradictions, and the bitterness inseparable from an undertaking of this kind. We have sacrificed to it no affection, no conviction; rather we have added to these the conviction of the need for union in the face of the common enemy, and an ardent and sincere love for the peace of this society which is so constantly menaced. We have sacrificed neither truth nor justice but only the spirit of contention, bitterness, and exaggeration, unfortunately all inseparable from every prolonged legitimate struggle.

That is why I am not afraid to maintain from this tribune and to apply to this law the word "concordat" which I risked in the committee discussion. . . . I saw the army which I had built up during twenty years of struggle. I saw the men whom I had guided and led in the battle for twenty years turn against me at the very moment when I thought the conflict was ending; I saw them shed tears, as they say in their press, at what they call my suicide.

. . . .

I do not here indict the intentions of the men of whom I am speaking. On the contrary, I accept this test, the greatest of my political life. I know not whether I have at other times misunderstood the intentions of my adversaries; I think that I never have; it is no act of contrition which I have just repeated on this platform; I have already made one which I uphold and which is sufficient. But if ever I have unknowingly misconstrued the laws of justice in respect to my former adversaries, I am expiating my sin! I know what it is to be misunderstood not only by enemies but by friends. But if, on the contrary, I have nothing to expiate, as I truly believe, I again accept this test as a last homage and a last service to the cause of the liberty of the Church.

I have given my life to this cause—my courage, and twenty years of perseverance and devotion. I offer to it again today as a last act of homage the harvest of ingratitude, unpopularity, and injustice which this law has caused me to reap within my own party.

Moreover I am convinced that I have acted completely in accord with the spirit of the Church. Believe me, I have not spoken here as a bishop from outside, as I was accused yesterday of doing, for I do not pretend to be a successor of Most Christian kings.

I speak as a layman, or, if you like, as a simple Jesuit.

I say that the work which we have undertaken, or at least the thought which has suggested it to us, conforms in every point with the spirit of the Church, not only regarding the motives discussed here so eloquently and forcefully the day before yesterday by the Bishop of Langres; not only because for the Church there is here an occasion for self-sacrifice and that, as he said so well, wherever good is to be done the Church hastens forward; not only for this reason, but also because the Church in being inflexible in the struggle against pride always at the moment when peace has come surpasses its adversaries and rivals in the spirit of conciliation. When one takes a step toward her, she takes two steps toward you. That is the role of the Church as I have studied and appreciated her history. Inflexible against what I have just called the incorrigible pride of false philosophy, the Church is full of gentleness, sympathy, and tenderness for men who take a step toward her. She does all that she can to encourage them to take a second step and goes to meet them. The Church never wishes to humiliate anyone before her but humiliates only before God. The Church never says the two expressions which we hear every day in the sphere of politics—*All or nothing* and *It is too late*. She never says *All or nothing*, for it is a term of pride, of human passion, which wishes to enjoy and conquer today because it must die tomorrow. As has so often been said, the Church is patient because she is eternal, and that is why she never says *All or nothing*. Nor does she say *It is too late*, because it is never too late to save a soul, and it is never too late to save a society which consents to be saved.

We are told that we are playing the dupe and that we shall be dupes in what is improperly called a "bargain." It is not a bargain but a conciliation, and at the same time it is an experience that we shall judge by its fruits. . . . I consent in advance to being a dupe of my good faith, of my confidence, patriotism and devotion to the true interests of society and France. [Lively approval on the Right.]

I know well that in our age it is easy and safe to speculate on ship-wrecks, checkmate, or bankruptcy even of the best enterprises and the best ideas. That is easy and one has the odds on one's side. In spite of the odds, I prefer to speculate on something else, on good faith, and on the blessings of God, who never refused these to works inspired by devotion, disinterestedness, and reconciliation. I prefer to ruin myself with this speculation rather than to make my fortune in the other way.

I conclude and summarize with one last consideration.

For sixty years the spirit which I shall not characterize too severely if I call it a spirit of negativism has dominated the world.

This negativism has produced, or at least allowed the birth of, some good things about which no one was in disagreement two years ago, namely political liberty and liberty of conscience. I recognize them, and I submit that no one failed to do so even two years ago; but I submit as well that in continuing indefinitely and immoderately its work the spirit of negativism compromises precisely those good things so precious to us all; and if it should continue this work without being stopped by us in time, we should be led again with a sword at our backs through anarchy into intellectual and material despotism.

What opposition are you to make to this spirit of negativism which I described just recently as the revolutionary spirit? The material opposition of military force has of course rendered good service. I honor it, I have always given homage to the sword of France, which was recently in the hands of General Cavaignac and today in those of General Changarnier. It is well placed thus against the enemies of society. But I am sure that the intelligent and courageous men who hold this sword know better than anyone the insufficiency of the force at their disposal for struggling against universal anarchy. Who will battle if it is not the religious element, if it is not the Church?

I am convinced that it is not the only barrier, though the principal and most indestructible of all. But it is necessary to disengage the Church from obstacles in order to allow her to fight and to reestablish equilibrium between good and evil.

It is impossible not to recognize that we are advancing toward anarchy. As under the July régime we were advancing toward the

Republic without doubting the advance, so under the Republic, we are advancing toward anarchy without being or wanting to be in doubt of the fact. I remember that in the first days after the Revolution of July an eloquent voice never forgotten by those who heard it, the voice of M. Laine, was heard one day in the Chamber of Peers saying: "The kings are departing!" And you know how right this prediction was. I say to you with sadness, judging by the symptoms on all sides, if M. Laine were living today and could use his prophetic voice to denounce our evils, he would say today: "France is decaying, society is decaying, modern Europe is decaying!" [Violent exclamations on the Left.]

You know the American river which rolls on through deserts, towns, lakes, and forests and then with one blow throws itself with irresistible force and from a frightful height to form the most formidable cataract in the world, Niagara Falls.

Woe to those embarked on this river who do not stop themselves in time—they are engulfed.

Woe to us, gentlemen, for we are embarked on a similar river, and it is not necesary to lend a very attentive ear to hear in the distance the rumbling of the cataract which will engulf us.

We shall be engulfed, if we do not reach the bank or with vigorous strokes turn back from demagoguery up the stream of rationalism.

But you can only turn back with the help of the Church. Be sure that the Church as such is disinterested in the question; she is sure of herself, not only by virtue of her divine and super belief but by reason of the very phenomena of our age, which are all in her favor. All revolutions end in something of value profitable to her.

In 1830 the revolution in France gave the Church an independent and proud attitude very different from that which the Bishop of Langres spoke of yesterday. In Belgium the revolution brought complete liberty. The Revolution of 1848 in Germany emancipated the Church in the most unexpected way. For the Church, revolutions are not to be feared; they are to be feared only for society. And especially because of her love of society the Church repels and fights against revolutions. Whatever you may do, the Church will issue victorious from all our trials. Her emancipation, her liberty is the invisible axis of all revolutions. Everything will be stopped when she is free, free to do good as she wishes, as she is able; then we shall recover our tranquillity.

It is then in the interest of society that I proclaim for the Church the liberty of doing good, and that I ask you to destroy through this law the hindrances which up to now have encumbered her in the noble field of teaching. Be sure that if I were a Catholic only, like the Church I should be disinterested, and I should try to isolate myself from the contemplation of the evils of the country to console myself with the certain triumph of the Church. But I am French also, and so are all the Catholics associated in our recent struggles. We passionately love the grandeur, glory, and the prosperity of our country. That is why we desire ardently that society of itself come to free the Church, to deliver it from the bonds which hinder its activity and fertility.

That is what I have to say in recommending to you the work of conciliation, peace, and patriotism which we bring you. I like to think that after hearing me you will at least not accuse me of having misrepresented either the import of the law or the motives which have guided us. [Prolonged applause from the benches of the Majority.]

12. The Decay of Autocratic Society

Alexander Herzen: *An Open Letter to Jules Michelet* (1852)*

Alexander Herzen, Russian nobleman, estate owner, and radical author, left Russia forever in 1847 and ultimately settled in England. His essay, a reply to one by the French historian Jules Michelet, offers an answer to one of two questions that engrossed Russian intellectuals of the century: What is the matter with Russia? He has less to say (except in a negative sense) about the other question: What should be done to improve conditions? He states what he does not wish for his people; he does not prescribe a remedy. His analysis of the evils of Russian government and society makes clear that serfdom and autocracy produce a morality of sycophancy, corruption, brutality, despair, suffering and heroism. These are revealed in art and literature as in government and social relations. Herzen tends to idealize the Russian peasant, but he leaves a vivid impression of essential characteristics of the members of this class. He also makes the reader aware by indirection of the impact that emancipation of the serfs will have upon all classes and institutions of society, irrespective of nation or country.

The Russian peasant who has, as you have rightly observed, a strong aversion to every form of landed property, who is improvident and indolent by temperament, has gradually and imperceptibly found himself caught up in the tentacles of the German bureaucracy and the feudal power. He has submitted to this degrading yoke with, I

* Alexander Herzen, *From the Other Shore*, translated from the Russian by Moura Budberg; and *The Russian People and Socialism: An Open Letter to Jules Michelet*, translated from the French by Richard Wollheim, with an introduction by Isaiah Berlin (New York: George Braziller, Inc., 1956), pp. 180-201.

agree, the passivity of despair, but he has never believed either in the authority of his lord, or in the justice of the courts, or in the equity of the administration. For almost two hundred years, his whole life has been one long, dumb, passive opposition to the existing order of things: he has endured oppression, he has groaned under it; but he has never accepted anything that goes on outside the life of the rural commune.

The idea of the Tsar still enjoys some considerable prestige in the mind of the peasant. But it is not the actual Tsar Nicholas whom he adores, it is rather an abstract idea, a myth, a kind of Providence, an Avenger of evils, an embodiment of justice in the popular imagination.

Apart from the Tsar, only the Clergy are capable of having any moral influence on Orthodox Russia. The higher clergy are the sole representatives of ancient Russia within the administration. The clergy have never shaved off their beards, and through this very fact have remained on the side of the people. The people have complete faith in anything they are told by a monk. However, the monks and the higher clergy, for all their talk about being dedicated to matters not of this world, are almost entirely indifferent to the people. The village priest has lost all influence on account of his greed, his drunkenness, and his close association with the police. Here again, it is not the man but the idea that the people respect.

As for the Dissenters, they hate both the Tsar and the village priest, both the man and the idea.

Apart from the Tsar and the Clergy, all the other elements within society and the administration are utterly alien and ultimately hostile to the people. The peasant is, quite literally, outside the law: the law contrives to offer him absolutely no protection whatsoever, and his only share in the existing order of things is confined to the payment of the double tribute which grinds him down: the tribute of blood and the tribute of sweat. So, spurned on all sides, he comes to feel that the government is not for him but against him, that the single aim of the administration and the nobility is to extort from him as much work and as much money as possible. Realizing this and blessed with a certain shrewd, cunning intelligence he manages to deceive all of them all the time. Nor could he very well do anything else, because if he told them the truth, that would be an admission, an acceptance on his part of their power: if he didn't steal from them (and notice that he is accused of stealing when he conceals any part of the produce of his own labour), if he didn't steal from them, then this would be a recognition on his part—and a quite fatal one—of the propriety of these exactions, of the rights of the landowners and of the fairness of his judges.

In order to appreciate the real position of the Russian peasant, you need to see him before one of these courts of law: you have only to see for yourself the sad, frightened eyes, the sullen set of the jaw, the anxious searching look he turns on all around him, to realize that his position is no better than that of a captured rebel brought before a court martial, or that of a traveller facing a gang of brigands. From the first glance, it is quite clear that the victim has no trust in these cruel, hostile, implacable creatures who interrogate him and torture him and finally mulct him dry. He knows that if he has any money, then he will be acquitted, and if he hasn't, he will be condemned without mercy.

When he speaks, he uses a somewhat antiquated Russian: whereas the judge and his clerks use the modern bureaucratic language which is so garbled an affair as to be barely intelligible. First they fill whole folios with the ungrammatical solecisms, and then they reel it off at the peasant in a high nasal twang as fast as they can go. What he hears is an undifferentiated flux of noise, of which he must, if he is to preserve his skin, make such sense as he can. He is fully aware of what is at issue, and is on his guard. He is sparing in his use of words, tries hard to cover up his nervousness, and the result is that he stands there with an asinine look on his face, like a great booby, like someone who has lost the power of speech.

He leaves the court in the same wretched state whether he has been condemned or whether he has been acquitted. The difference between the two verdicts seems to him a matter of mere chance or luck.

In much the same way, when he is summoned as a witness, he insists on perjuring himself, on knowing nothing, on denying everything, even when the evidence on the other side is overwhelming. In the eyes of the Russian people, there is no stigma attached to a man merely because he has been found guilty in a court of law. Convicts and those who are sentenced to transportation are in popular parlance called '*unfortunates*'.

The Russian peasant has no real knowledge of any form of life but that of the village commune: he understands about rights and duties only when these are tied to the commune and its members. Outside the commune, there are no obligations for him—there is simply violence. The fatal element in his character is that he submits to the violence, not that, in his own way, he denies it and tries to protect himself by guile. It is far more honest to lie before a judge whom one doesn't acknowledge, than to make some show of respect for a jury packed by the police, whose monstrous corruption is as clear as daylight. The peasant respects his institutions only in so far as he finds embodied there his own notions of Right and Justice.

There is one fact that has never been denied by anyone who has any real first-hand knowledge of the Russian people. And that is that they very rarely cheat one another. An almost boundless good faith prevails amongst them: contracts and written agreements are quite unheard of.

Problems connected with surveying are necessarily extremely complicated on account of the perpetual subdivision of the land according to the number of people working on it.[1] And yet the peace of the Russian countryside is never disturbed by any complaints or litigation. The government and the landowners ask for nothing better than some pretext for interference, but none is ever afforded them. The petty differences that arise are quickly settled either by the elders or by the commune: everyone abides by such decisions without reservation. The same thing happens in the nomadic communes of artisans (the *artel*). There are a number of such *artels*—builders, carpenters and other sorts of artisans—each consisting of several hundred people drawn from different communes, who come together for a given period of time, for a year for instance, and so form a group. When the year is up, the workers share out the produce on the basis of the work they have done, in each case abiding by the general decision. The

[1] And not according to the number of children.—A. H.

police have not so far had the satisfaction of being able to interfere in these arrangements. The association, I must emphasize, generally holds itself responsible for all the workers who comprise it.

The bonds between peasants of the same commune are much closer when the commune is not Orthodox but Dissenter. From time to time the government organizes a savage raid on one of these Dissenting communes. The whole population is imprisoned and then deported, without any preconceived plan, without any repercussions, without any provocation, without any necessity, merely in compliance with the instructions of the clergy or the depositions of the police. It is in the course of these persecutions of Dissenters, that one can see the Russian peasant as he really is and observe the solidarity that ties him to his fellows. One can see him on such occasions tricking the police, rescuing his fellow believers, hiding the holy books and vessels, undergoing the most appalling tortures without uttering a word. I challenge anyone to produce a single example of a Dissenting commune that has been betrayed by a peasant, even an Orthodox.

This trait in the ordinary Russian makes all police inquiries extremely difficult to carry out. And I heartily congratulate him on it. The Russian peasant has no other morality than that which flows quite instinctively and naturally from his communal life: it is profoundly national in character and the little that he knows about the Gospels fortifies him in it: the shocking corruption of the government and of the landlords binds him ever more closely to his traditional customs and to his commune.[1] The commune has preserved

[1] The peasants on one of the communes belonging to Prince Kozlovsky, bought their freedom at a price agreed upon with the landowner. The land was then divided up between the peasants in accordance with the amount of money that each had contributed to the fund that had bought them their liberty. This arrangement seemed to be one that was as fair as it was natural. However, the peasants found it so awkward and so little in accord with their ordinary way of life, that they decided to make themselves jointly responsible for the purchase money and regard it simply as a debt incurred by the commune as a whole, and to proceed with the division of the land on what was for them the normal system. The authority for this is Haxthausen who recounts it in his *Études sur la vie populaire en Russie*. The author visited the commune in question personally.

M. Tengoborski, a member of the Russian Council of State, in a book recently published in Paris and bearing a dedication to the Emperor Nicholas, says that the system of land-division seems to him unfavourable to agricultural development (as though agriculture had to be favourable to agricultural development!),

the Russian people from Mongol barbarism, from Imperial civilization, from Europeanized landowners and from the German bureaucracy: the organic life of the commune has persisted despite all
the attempts made on it by authority, badly mauled though it has
been at times. By good fortune it has survived right into the period
that witnesses the rise of Socialism in Europe.

For Russia this has been a most happy providence.

The Russian aristocracy is entering on a new phase of its existence.
Born of an anti-national revolution, it has accomplished its appointed
task. It has brought into being a vast empire, a large army, and a
centralized government. Devoid of all principles and traditions, it
has nothing further to do. It has, it is true, arrogated to itself another
task, that of importing Western civilization into Russia, and it had
some measure of success in doing this so long as it played the part of
being a civilized governing class.

This part it has now abandoned.

The government which originally cut itself off from the people in

---

but he adds: 'It would be very difficult to obviate these disadvantages, because
the system of land division is bound up with the organization of the communes
which *it would be dangerous to touch:* it rests on the fundamental notion of the
unity of the commune and the equal right of every member of it to a share in the
communal land. In this way, it reinforces and strengthens the communal spirit
which is one of the stablest elements in the social organization. It is at the same
time one of the best bulwarks against the increase of the proletariat and communist ideas.' (It is easy to realize that a people already enjoying the practice of
the commune has nothing to fear from communist ideas.)

'What is remarkable is the good sense and the efficiency with which the
peasants, generally without any external assistance, modify the inconvenient features of the system to suit local conditions, and the readiness with which they
make adjustments to offset any inequality of distribution arising out of the
quality of the soil itself, and the confidence with which they submit to adjudica-
tion by the elders of the commune. One might easily imagine that these land
allocations, which have to be frequently revised, would give rise to innumerable
disputes, and yet the parties involved seldom appeal to established authority.
This fact, which is surprising in itself, can admit of only one explanation, and
that is that the system, for all its potential defects, has become so much identified
with the way of life and habits of the people that they put up with its drawbacks without a murmur.'

'The notion of association'—says the same author—'is as natural to the Russian
peasant and as integral to all aspects of his life, as the notion of corporation, the
municipal idea, which is central to the bourgeoisie of the West, is in conflict with
his habits and outlook.' *Études sur les forces productives de la Russie*, by M.
Tengoborski, vol. I, p. 331 and p. 142—A. H.

the name of civilization, has now, a hundred years later, hurriedly cut itself off from civilization in the name of absolutism.

This happened as soon as it detected the tricolour of liberalism dimly visible, like a spectre, through the tendencies of civilization. It then tried to fall back on the idea of nationalism and on the people. But this was impossible: there was by now no common ground between the people and the government—the people had grown completely away from the government, and the government in turn seemed to see in the masses something even more terrifying than anything it knew—the Red Spectre. All things considered, liberalism seemed to be less dangerous than the prospect of a new Pugachev.[2] But the horror and the disgust in which all liberal ideas were held had now become such that the government could no longer make its peace with civilization.

From then onwards, the sole aim of Tsarism has been Tsarism, ruling for ruling's sake. Immense new forces have been called into being, each one of them at once supplementing and neutralizing all the others, so that in this way a quite artificial stability has been attained.

But autocracy for autocracy's sake is ultimately an impossibility; it is too pointless, too sterile.

This has now been realized, and so some sort of outlet has been looked for in Europe. Russian diplomacy is feverishly active: there is a constant despatch of notes, agents, suggestions, threats, promises, spies. The Emperor sees himself as the natural protector of all German princes. He dabbles in every petty intrigue in every petty court. He settles all their little differences, bestowing on one a reprimand, on another a Grand Duchess. But even this doesn't exhaust his energy. He has become the policeman of the whole world, the prop of all forms of reaction and all forms of barbarism. He sets himself up as the supreme representative of the monarchical principle in Europe, giving himself the airs of an aristocrat, as though he were a Bourbon or a Tudor and had for his courtiers Devonshires, or, at the very lowest, Montmorencys.

The sad part of this is that there really is nothing in common be-

[2] Leader of a cossack peasant revolt in the 18th century.

tween feudal monarchy with its avowed principles, its roots in the past, its social and religious ideology, and the Napoleonic despotism of St. Petersburg, which has no principles behind it, and is based entirely on grim historic necessity and some passing need that it satisfies.

And gradually the Winter Palace, like a mountain peak at the end of the warm season, becomes covered over with layer upon layer of snow and ice. The sap, which was artificially induced to rise into these elevated social reaches, now slowly recedes from them, so that all they can now command is a certain brute strength, a mere physical hardness like that of a rock good for a while longer against the waves of revolution which break idly at its base.

Surrounded by his generals and his ministers and his officers and his bureaucrats, Nicholas defies his isolation, but visibly he grows gloomier: he becomes morose, preoccupied. He realizes that no one has any affection for him, he senses the gloomy silence that surrounds him, through which he can hear only too well the distant rumblings that seem to draw closer. The Tsar tries to forget all this, and announces to the world that his sole concern is the aggrandizement of the Imperial power.

Such declarations are nothing new: for the last twenty-five years he has toiled unremittingly, without respite, for this cause and this alone: in pursuit of it he has spared nothing, neither tears nor blood.

Everything that he has undertaken has prospered: he has crushed Polish nationalism, and in Russia he has extinguished liberalism.

What more can he want? Why is he so depressed?

The Emperor knows that Poland is not really dead. And in place of the liberalism that he has persecuted with such gratuitous savagery, for that exotic flower could never have taken root in Russian soil, being quite alien to the national character—he now sees another problem lowering like a storm cloud.

The people are beginning to murmur and grow restless under the yoke of the nobility: small revolts break out all the time: you yourself, Sir, have referred to one terrible instance of this.

The party of movement, of progress, demands the emancipation of the peasants; and its members are ready to set an example by sacrificing their own rights. The Tsar is in a state of permanent indecision, and has lost the power of all real thought: he wants emancipation, and yet does all he can to prevent it.

He has come to see that the emancipation of the peasant is tantamount to the emancipation of the land: and that the emancipation of the land would in turn usher in a social revolution and would make rural communism sacrosanct. To evade this question of emancipation is certainly impossible: to postpone it until the reign of his successor would be easier but cowardly, and the time gained would really be no better than time spent in a wretched posting-station waiting for fresh horses.

From all this you can see what a blessing it is for Russia that the rural commune has never been broken up, that private ownership has never replaced the property of the commune: how fortunate it is for the Russian people that they have remained outside all political movements, and, for that matter, outside European civilization, which would undoubtedly have sapped the life of the commune, and which to-day in Socialism has achieved its own negation.

Europe, as I have pointed out elsewhere, has never solved the antimony of the State and the individual, but it has stated the problem. Russia approaches the same problem from a quite different direction, but it has had no greater success in finding a solution to it. It is then in the shadow of this problem that we find the source of our equality.

Europe, now on the point of taking the first step forward in a social revolution, is confronted by a country that can provide an actual instance of an attempt—a crude, barbaric attempt perhaps, but still an attempt of a sort—in the direction of the division of the land amongst those who work it. And observe that this lesson is provided not by civilized Russia but by the people themselves in their daily lives. We Russians who have absorbed European civilization cannot hope to be more than a means to an end—the yeast in the leavening—a bridge between the Russian people and revolutionary Europe. The future of Russia lies with the *moujik*, just as the regeneration of France lies with the worker.

But if this is so, then surely the Russian people have some claim on your indulgence? Surely, Sir, this is so.

Poor peasant! So intelligent, so simple in his habits, so easily satisfied, he has been seized on as the butt of every vicious attack. The Emperor decimates his number by conscription: the landowner steals every third day of his working week: the *tchinovnik*[3] worms out of him his last rouble. The peasant suffers all in silence, but without despair. He holds hard to his commune. If someone tears a limb off it, it heals over, it comes together all the more. The fate of the poor peasant surely deserves pity, and yet he receives none; instead of commiseration, he is showered with abuse.

You, Sir, deny the last refuge that is open to him, the one place left where he can still feel himself to be a man, where he can know love and not fear. For you say that 'his commune is not really a commune, his family is not really a family, his wife is not really his wife: before she belongs to him, she belongs to his lord; his children are not really his children, and who knows who is their father?'

In this style you hold up this unfortunate people not to scientific scrutiny but to the scorn of the whole world, which will read and accept and admire all these fine stories that you give them.

It is then my duty to say something on the subject.

The family is something very highly developed amongst all the Slav races: it is possibly here that we have the source of their conservatism, the limit of their negative tendency.

The prototype of the commune is the family owning all things in common.

Amongst these rural families, there is no desire to split up into different households, and so one often finds three or four generations living together under one roof and ruled over in a patriarchal manner either by the grandfather or by a great-uncle. Women, for the most part, lead a rather oppressed life, as is generally the case in an agricultural community, but in Russia they are treated with respect when their sons come of age and even more so if they are the widows of family chiefs.

[3] i.e. the government official.

It is by no means uncommon to find the conduct of affairs entirely in the hands of a grey-haired grandmother. Can it, then, really be said that the family doesn't exist in Russia?

Now let us turn to the relations that exist between the landowner and his serf families.

But if we are to have a clear picture of the situation, we must first distinguish between the law and the abuses of the law, between what is permitted and what is criminal.

The *droit du seigneur* has never existed among the Slav peoples.

The landowner has no legal right to demand either the first joys of marriage or any subsequent infidelity. If the law were properly enforced in Russia, then the seduction of a serf would be punished in exactly the same way as an offense against a free woman: That is to say, it would make the offender liable either to penal servitude or to exile in Siberia according to the gravity of the actual offence. So much for the law: now let us look at the facts.

It is undeniable that with the social position that the aristocracy are allowed by the Government, it is very easy for them to seduce the wives and daughters of their serfs. The landowner, with his powers of confiscation and punishment, can always find husbands willing to hand over their wives, and fathers ready to dispose of their daughters —rather like that splendid French nobleman in the middle of the eighteenth century who, according to Peuchot's *Memoires,* begged for the special privilege of being allowed to install his daughter in the Parc-aux-Cerfs.

It is scarcely surprising that honest fathers and husbands can obtain no redress against the nobility, thanks to the excellent judiciary in Russia. They find themselves in a position much like that of Monsieur Tiercelin whose daughter of eleven was abducted by Berryer with the connivance of Louis XV. I do not deny that such disgusting abuses are perfectly possible—indeed one has only to think of the crude and depraved habits of one section of the Russian nobility to realize it. But this does not mean that the peasants are indifferent spectators of their masters' debauchery: far from it.

Let me produce some evidence for this.

Half the landowners who are murdered by their peasants—and

statistics show that the total is between sixty and seventy a year—are killed in revenge for their erotic exploits. The peasant very seldom brings an action against his master because he knows that the court will completely disregard his grievances. But he has his axe, in the use of which he is a real master, and he knows it.

So much for the peasantry: and now, Sir, I beg you to bear with me for a little in what I have to say about civilized Russia.

Our intellectual movement has fared no better at your hands than our national character: with a single stroke of the pen you dismissed everything that we have ever done, all the work of our fettered hands.

One of Shakespeare's characters, at a loss for some way to humiliate an opponent he despises, exclaims: 'I even doubt your existence.' You have gone further, Sir: you don't doubt the non-existence of Russian literature.

I quote your very words:

'I cannot attach any real importance to the efforts of a few clever people in St. Petersburg, who have experimented a little with the Russian language rather as if it were a learned language and have deceived Europe with a wan travesty of a national literature. If it were not for my deep respect for Mickiewicz and his saintly aberrations, I really should blame him for the charity, one might almost say the indulgence, with which he speaks of this frippery.'

I am quite unable, Sir, to find any reason for the scornful way in which you receive the first agonized cry of a people awakening in its prison-house, a movement which the gaoler tries to stifle at birth.

Why have you been so unwilling to listen to the heart-rending accents of our sad poetry, of our songs which are merely tears given tongue? What is it that has warped your understanding of the nervous, hysterical laughter in our literature, of the unfailing irony which conceals the deep wound in our heart, and which is, in the last analysis, the terrible confession of our utter impotence?

How I wish I could translate for you adequately some of the lyrical poems of Pushkin, or Lermontov, or some of Koltsov's ballads! Then you would welcome us with open arms, you would be the very first to beg us to forget everything you had said before.

Apart from the communal life of the *moujik,* there is nothing so characteristic of Russia, nothing that bodes so well for her future as her literary movement.

Between the peasant and literature there looms up the ghastly figure of official Russia, of 'the Russian lie, of the Russian cholera'— as you have so well named it.

This Russia starts with the Emperor and you can follow it right down from soldier to soldier, from clerk to clerk, until you come to the humblest official in a police-station in the farthest district of the Empire. In this way it ramifies indefinitely and at every stage—like the *'bolgi'* of Dante—it gains a new power for evil, it becomes even more depraved and tyrannical. So we have this living pyramid of crimes, abuses, impositions, floggings, the work of inhuman German officials everlastingly on the make, of illiterate judges everlastingly drunk, of aristocrats everlastingly toadying: the whole thing welded together by ties of common gain and common guilt, and in the last resort upheld by six hundred thousand automata armed with bayonets.

The peasant never defiles himself by any contact with the world of cynical officialdom: he suffers—that is the extent of his guilt.

The opposition to official Russia consists of a handful of desperate men who spend their lives in denouncing it, attacking it, unmasking it, sapping its strength.

From time to time one of these lone champions is dragged off to prison, tortured, deported to Siberia, but his place does not stay empty for long: fresh champions step into the breach. Such is our tradition, our inalienable inheritance.

The ghastly consequences that attend the spoken word in Russia inevitably increase its effectiveness. The voice of the free man is listened to with love and veneration, because in our country, it is raised only when there is something serious to say. The decision to put one's thoughts on paper is one not lightly made when at the foot of every page there looms up the prospect of a policeman, a *troika,* a *kibitka,* and in the distance Tobolsk or Irkoutsk.

In my last pamphlet, I wrote enough about Russian literature: here I shall only add a few general observations.

Sadness, skepticism, irony—these are the three strings of the Russian lyre.

When Pushkin begins one of his finest poems with these restrained, melancholy words:

'There is no justice on earth—nor any above us either.
That is as clear to me as a simple musical scale.'[4]

doesn't this chill your heart, don't you seem to see behind the apparent tranquillity a broken life, don't you detect a man who has become inured to suffering?

Lermontov, barely 30 years of age, filled with disgust at the society in which he finds himself, addresses one of his contemporaries in these words:

'I look on my generation with grief: its future is blank and grim: it will grow old in inaction, it will sink under the weight of doubt and barren science.

'Life exhausts us like a journey without a destination.

'We are like those ratheripes which are sometimes found, strange orphans amongst the blossom: they delight neither the eye nor the palate: they fall as they ripen. . . .

'We hurry towards the tomb, without happiness, without glory, and before we die we cast a look of bitter scorn over our past.

'We shall pass through this world unnoticed, a pensive, silent, soon forgotten company.

'We shall leave nothing to our descendants, no fruitful idea, no work of genius, and they will insult our remains with some contemptuous verse or with the sarcasm a destitute son might use to his spendthrift father.'

I know of only one other modern poet who has sounded the sombre notes of the human heart with the same intensity. He, too, was a poet born in slavery, and he likewise died before the rebirth of his native country. I mean that apologist of death, the famous Leopardi, he

[4] *Mozart and Salieri*. The poem has been quite perfectly translated into German, by M. Bornstaedt, in a little volume of translations from Pushkin and Lermontov.—A. H.

who saw the world as a vast league of criminals ruthlessly warring against a few virtuous madmen.

Russia has produced only one painter who is widely known: Brullov.[5] Where did this artist look for his inspiration? What is the subject of his masterpiece which won him something of a reputation in Italy?

Look at this strange work.

Across an enormous canvas you see groups of terrified and bewildered people. Despite their efforts to escape, many are dying, the victims of an earthquake, of a volcanic eruption, of a truly cataclysmic storm. They are overwhelmed by some savage, senseless, evil force against which all struggle is unavailing. Such is the kind of inspiration that can be drawn from the atmosphere of Petersburg.

The Russian novel is entirely a study in pathological anatomy. It is one long diagnosis of the evil that consumes us, one sustained work of self-accusation, pitiless, inexorable accusation. What we never hear is that gentle voice which comes down from Heaven, the voice that announced to Faust the forgiveness of the young, sinful girl. We must not look here for consolation, the only voices to be heard are those of doubt and damnation. And yet if Russia is to achieve salvation, it will be on account of this profound awareness that we have of our predicament, and the scant trouble we take to conceal it from the world.

He who frankly admits his failings, feels that he has something within him that will survive and overcome any disaster: he knows that he can redeem the past, and not only hold his head high but, that

---

[5] Karl Brullov (1799-1852), the first Russian painter to win an international reputation, was born in Italy, of Huguenot extraction and came to Russia as a child. He studied in Rome, and his reputation was made entirely on the strength of *The Destruction of Pompeii* (1828-30). This picture was inspired by a visit to the ruins and influenced by Pliny's descriptions and Pacini's opera *L'ultimi giorni di Pompei* (1825). The enormous vogue that it enjoyed was due partly to its vast scale, partly to its eclectic combination of melodramatic lighting and reminiscences of Italian masters. Sir Walter Scott is said to have stood in front of it for an hour and declared it to be not a picture but an epic. It directly inspired Bulwer Lytton's novel. On his return to Russia, Brullov never repeated his early success, although some of his portraits are interesting studies. *The Destruction of Pompeii* now hangs in the Russian Museum, Leningrad.

as in Byron's tragedy, he can turn from being 'Sardanapalus the profligate to Sardanapalus the hero.'

The Russian people do not read. Nor, of course, were Voltaire and Diderot read by villagers; they were read by the aristocracy and the Third Estate. In Russia the enlightened section of the Third Estate is part of the aristocracy, for the aristocracy nowadays includes everyone who is above the level of the people: it even includes an aristocratic proletariat which at one end merges into the people, and it includes a proletariat of freed men who work their way up the social scale and then become noble. This process of movement, this continual flux, gives the Russian aristocracy a character which you find nowhere else amongst the privileged classes of Europe. In short, all Russian history since Peter I is entirely the history of the aristocracy, and of the influence of European civilization upon it. Here I must mention that the size of the aristocracy in Russia is at least half that of the total number of electors in France, since the law of May 31st.[6]

During the eighteenth century, the most important theme in neo-Russian literature was the development of that rich, sonorous and magnificent language that we use to-day: a language which is at once supple and powerful, capable of expressing the most abstract notions of German metaphysics, and also the light, witty, sparkling phrases of French conversation. This literature, called into being by the genius of Peter the Great, bears, it is true, a sort of governmental imprint—but in those days being on the side of government meant being on the side of reform, almost on the side of revolution.

The Imperial throne was, right up to the great revolution of '89, majestically draped in the grandest robes of European civilization and philosophy. It was fitting that Catherine II should be entertained with villages[7] made out of cardboard and with wooden palaces with the distemper still fresh upon them: no one knew better than she the

[6] French electoral law of May 31, 1850, abolishing universal male suffrage and reducing register of voters from 10 million to 7 million.

[7] Herzen is here referring to the famous Tauric expedition of Catherine II, January-June 1787, when the Empress made a ceremonial progress down the Dnieper to the Crimea: en route she was joined by Joseph II. Potemkin is said to have decorated the river banks with cardboard villages.

art of *mise-en-scène*. At the Hermitage Voltaire and Montesquieu and Beccaria vied with one another in displaying their talents. You know, Sir, the reverse of the medal.

Meanwhile, a strange, unexpected note began to break in on the triumphal choruses of pindaric odes to which the Court was given over. It was a note in which sarcastic irony, a tendency towards criticism and skepticism were apparent, and it was, I must say, the one truly national note to be heard, the only note sounded that had any real vitality in it, that gave any promise for the future. The others, transitory and exotic affairs, were doomed to perish.

The true character of Russian thought, whether in poetry or in speculation, emerges only in a fully developed, vital form after the accession of Nicholas. The distinctive traits of this movement, are a new and tragic sense of right and wrong, an implacable spirit of negation, a bitter irony, a tortured self-questioning. Sometimes a note of wild laughter accompanies it, but it is laughter without gaiety.

Living under these truly oppressive conditions, the Russian, who possesses an unclouded intelligence and a ruthlessly logical mind, soon emancipated himself from religion and traditional morality.

The emancipated Russian is the most independent creature in the world. And what indeed could there be to restrain him? A sense of the past? . . . But then isn't the starting point of modern Russia just the denial of tradition and national sentiment?

Or a sense of the past indefinite, the Petersburg period? But that surely lays no obligation on us: 'this fifth act of a blood-stained drama, set in a brothel'[8] freed us from our old beliefs, but committed us to no new ones.

Your history, on the other hand, the history of the West, provides us with certain lessons, but no more: we do not consider ourselves the legal executors of your past.

We can share your skepticism—it is your faith that leaves us cold. You are too religious for us. We can share your animosities—it is your attachment to the legacy of the past that is incomprehensible to us. We are too oppressed, too wretched to make do with a mere half-

[8] As it has been admirably described by a writer in *Il Progresso*, in the course of an article on Russia, August 1st, 1851.—A. H.

liberty. You have your commitments to consider, your scruples to restrain you—but we have none of this, no commitments and no scruples
—it is merely that for the moment we are powerless.

Here, Sir, is the source of that irony, of that rage that drives us to
desperate measures, that takes possession of us and forces us on and
on until it brings us to Siberia and the rack, to exile and early death.
We have dedicated ourselves to a cause but without hope, in disgust
and boredom. There is something truly irrational about our lives, but
nothing that is either banal or stagnant or bourgeois.

Do not accuse us of being immoral merely because we do not respect the things that you respect. Would you condemn a foundling
for having no respect for his parents? We are free agents, because
we are self-made. The only element of tradition that we accept is
that involved in our organic, our national way of life: and that is
inherent in our very being: it is in our blood, it acts upon us more
like an instinct than like some external authority to which we feel we
must bend our wills. We are independent, because we possess nothing. There are literally no demands upon our affections. All our memories are tinged with bitterness and resentment. The fruits of civilization and learning were offered us at the end of the knout.

What obligation, then, have we, the younger sons, the castaways
of the family, to acknowledge any of your traditional duties? And
how could we in all honesty accept this threadbare morality of yours,
a morality which is neither humane nor Christian, which has no existence outside a few rhetorical exercises and speeches for the prose-
cution? How can you expect us to have any respect for the praetorium
in which you administer your Barbaro-Roman justice, for those
gloomy, oppressive vaults, where no light or air ever penetrates, rebuilt in the Middle Ages and then patched up by the enfranchised
Third Estate? What goes on in them is possibly better than the rob-
bery that goes on in the Russian courts, but could anyone maintain
that it had anything to do with justice?

It is quite clear that any difference there may be between your
laws and our Ukases lies almost entirely in the wording of their pre-
ambles. Ukases start with a painful truth—'The Tsar commands . . .'—
whereas your laws start with an insulting lie, the triple Republican

motto, the ironical invocation in the name of the French people. The *Code Nicholas* is intended to be unreservedly against mankind and in favour of authority. The *Code Napoléon* seems really no different. There are already enough impositions that we are forced to endure, without our making the position worse by imposing new ones on ourselves of our own free will. In this respect our situation is exactly like that of the peasantry. We bow to brute force: we are slaves because we have no way of freeing ourselves: but whatever happens, we shall accept nothing from the enemy camp.

Russia will never be Protestant.

Russia will never be *juste-milieu*.

Russia will never stage a revolution with the sole aim of ridding herself of Tsar Nicholas only to replace him by a multitude of other Tsars—Tsar-deputies, Tsar-tribunals, Tsar-policemen, Tsar-laws.

Possibly we ask too much, and shall achieve nothing. That may be so, but we shall not despair. Before 1848, Russia neither should nor could have embarked on a career of revolution. At that time she had still much to learn—and she is learning it. Even the Tsar himself sees this: and this is the reason why he has made himself the scourge of the universities, of all speculation, of all learning. He is struggling hard to isolate Russia from the rest of the world and to stamp out all civilization: He is true to his profession—*il fait son métier*.

Will he succeed?

I have said elsewhere one must not put blind faith in the future; every foetus has the right to develop, but for all that not every foetus does develop. The future of Russia does not depend on herself alone: it is bound up with the future of Europe as a whole. Who can foretell what lies in store for the Slav world, should Reaction and Absolutism triumph over the European Revolution?

Perhaps it will perish—who knows?

But then Europe also will perish. . . .

And history will continue in America. . . .

13. The Corporation as a Social Institution

Corporations from the Standpoint of Economics and Politics (1856)*

During the nineteenth century the corporation became one of the characteristic institutions of modern society. Although developed as an economic form in the later medieval period, it first gained a position of pervading power with the development of the industrial economy. The impact of the new institution upon every aspect of society was so profound that it aroused vigorous discussion, especially during the third quarter of the century.

The lengthy selection which follows is taken from an article published anonymously in 1856 in a German periodical. The issues discussed by the author were relevant both to Germany and to all other countries as they became industrialized and adopted the corporative form of business enterprise. The writer based his article upon English and French experience with the new form, as well as upon that of Germany and Austria. The reader should compare the rather pessimistic inclination of this judgment with the optimistic opinion of Schmoller given in Volume II. Then on the basis of a knowledge of subsequent developments he may discuss which critic proved to be more accurate in his judgment.

* * * * * * * * * * *

If one inquires in the first place what essential characteristics are to be observed in corporations, i.e., by what peculiar manifestation they are to be distinguished from other associations or from individual persons, remarkable economic as well as political and social circumstances are to be found.

* "Die Aktiengesellschaften, Volkswirtschaftlich und politisch betrachtet," *Deutsche Vierteljahrsschrift* (1856), No. 76, pp. 29-64.

In an economic sense one has first to distinguish between those characteristics inherent in the nature of all corporations and those belonging exclusively to one of the two major kinds. Among the first, several characteristics appear on the whole as advantageous.

Corporations naturally take greater risks than do individuals under the same circumstances. In part the manager himself has only a relatively modest interest in the venture; in part the individual participants in the company, who in like manner do not risk everything on the venture, raise no objection when one would be justified. Naturally under these circumstances things occasionally turn out badly. But the frequent gain always encourages the formation of new plans, and as a matter of fact these can be undertaken more easily and yield considerably more profit in that competition rarely occurs in the case of risky and ambitious undertakings. Over and against the unsuccessful mining company in Mexico, the unfortunate colonization attempts in Texas, on the Mosquito Coast, and elsewhere, the blunder with the huge restaurant at the Louvre, the relatively few unprofitable railroads and the like, are the many completed and in part highly lucrative railway lines, the sugar refineries, the joint-stock spinning mills, the water utilities, the life, fire, and flood insurance—and perhaps the digging of the Suez Canal can be added. Would even the richest capitalist recruit armies and wage war in order to engage or extend his business or his dominions into the East Indies as these anonymous associations have done without hesitation and with amazing success?

A second very significant economic characteristic of corporations is that those who actually undertake and draft the plans for them as well as those who carry them out—all these may be designated as technicians—are different from those who provide the capital. There arises in this way a division of labor, which seldom takes place in the same manner and only on a small scale in other situations, and has very great consequences. In view of the considerable sums which are brought together by corporations, and in view of the great scale of their operations and hence of their gross income, it is possible for them to offer unusual salaries and other advantages to directors and officials, thereby acquiring excellent businessmen who never would have gone into the service of single individuals, and who as a rule would not have possessed the means for pursuing similar undertakings on their own. Since, moreover, the limited partnership in principle restricts the influence upon the management of a business of the individual partner—as the share corporation restricts it in practice—with the result that narrowmindedness, a traditional approach, and timidity may do less harm, the device of partnership—or corporation—can only be conducive to the success of the business. It gives, in any case, the character of determination and good judgment to the entire conduct of business by the companies.

. . . .

Of course corporations also have economic characteristics less desirable than those mentioned above.

One must not forget that the exclusive aim of such organizations is to make as large and as quick a profit as possible. Their sole objective is to realize a return on the investment. They exist only for this reason; the stockholders are concerned only with this; and hence the directors and officials direct their attention only toward this end. The size of the return has a double advantage for the stockholder, partly because the dividends will be increased thereby, partly because the sale value of the stock is measured accordingly. It would therefore be completely foolish to expect anything different and to hope for a way of operating which no one intends, and from which those most directly concerned, namely the directors and officials of the company, are restrained by important interests. The method of operating described above can be useful economically, although it has harmful aspects.

First of all, any higher and general benefit like that which an able individual citizen or a conscientious state official may pursue is completely alien to the nature of a corporation aiming at profit. The corporation is not founded to make sacrifices for the common cause and consequently is not guided and administered in this way. It is basically egoistic and shows this openly in its entire behavior. It would be more than foolish to be misled by some individual gifts which a wealthy corporation occasionally makes for the construction of a church, upon the birth of an heir to the throne, or the like, whether it is an act of courtly service or a gesture to make among the masses a good name for itself which may be used to advantage at some future occasion. This egoistic and exclusive search for profit, however, is the more conspicuous in that it is necessarily precipitous and short-sighted. The stockholders demand speedy and significant dividends; and actually they are not in the position, insofar as they frequently are small capitalists, to make long-term advances in order to obtain a larger and more lasting profit in the future. It is thus inherent in the nature of the matter that the whole conduct of the business must be directed, at least in the main, toward immediate profit, an action that obviously by no means always coincides with the achievement of the highest and most lasting advantages possible.

Furthermore, it is part of the relationship that the individual director and official cannot be permitted to give way to any one pressure or to a special preference for some plan of improvement. Such action costs money, delays assured income, and takes up time engaged to achieve other things. The individual may undertake endeavors of this kind in his private business and at his personal risk; or opportunity and means may be given perhaps by a wise and well-meaning government to a capable official; but in keeping with their whole nature corporations can make or permit at most only such attempts at improvement as are directly useful to themselves. Indeed, the history of human civilization and especially of technical inventions shows that the great advances of human welfare are produced only through unselfish love of the cause itself and through a passion for improvement irrespective of profit. From the tremendous resources of corporations we might of course expect striking applications of inventions which already have been perfected, multiplication and acceleration of commerce, utilization of ever more powerful machines, and possibly improvement of the establishments required by them. The general welfare may also be promoted indirectly through an undertaking aimed chiefly at the selfish advantage of the company, for example agricultural or commercial establishments benefiting from the proximity of a railroad. But these accumulations of private resources, the greatest ever seen in history, have as yet furnished no new ideals, have been devoted to no improvement of the menacing social situation, have never used their colossal power for improvements which were not at the time definitely of advantage to themselves. And we may expect nothing of this kind from them in the future.

A further manifestation of the same basic situation is the effort of corporations to reach the lowest possible level of administrative costs in order to increase dividends. Only in the case of high executives and perhaps one or two indispensable officials are exceptions made, partly as a result of calculated interest, or partly from the impotence of the general body of stockholders as against well-initiated or cunningly concealed plans. Although naturally there is nothing objectionable in general about economy in administrative costs, there are nevertheless cases in which parsimony applied in the wrong place certainly does not diminish the income of the company (otherwise it would be discontinued), but very likely is contrary to the legitimate interests of a third party. For example, the significant number of accidents on the English and even more so on American railroads is to be attributed solely to a detrimental economy in supervisory personnel and an excessive use of rolling stock and tracks. The companies involved increase their dividends at the cost of the lives and limbs of hundreds of their fellow citizens. Individuals as employers would have more sensitive consciences or they could be intimidated by public opinion, whereas state-owned enterprises are directed according to quite different principles.

Finally, the selfish bent of corporations towards profit shows itself quite maliciously in that they are not at all squeamish in selecting the means to achieve their ends. The general observation that a corporation feels no shame, and that it commits acts which no member singly and for himself would commit, is also proved here, and is even necessarily true because the existence of these corporations is based solely upon profit, and hence evil means to this end are available on the one hand, and on the other hand their utilization appears natural.

A second and likewise derogatory characteristic of corporations— and especially of those based upon the sale of shares—is that the members have no personal attachment to the enterprises of the company;

individuals are not responsible for the same; and accordingly no particular zeal arising from the growing together of the person and the enterprise is felt in times of difficulty. The stockholders, especially when many and complicated enterprises are pursued, are slightly or not at all acquainted with the undertakings in particular, are told on the occasion of the annual accounting only as much as the directors and officials think advisable, and have generally only the size of the dividend in mind. Through the fact that the shares pass easily from hand to hand, that they are in part themselves the object of speculation, that the stockholders are constantly changing and that the deciding and controlling board can be changed at will, any strong attachment to the undertaking and any marked character in the management of the same are impossible. Consequently one may not expect persistence in case of misfortune and perseverance based upon principle and a sense of honor. To be sure, a wealthy company is better able to withstand a sudden shock than an individual; but if the difficulty lasts long, the stockholders will pull out. And even among the motley crowd which comes and goes in response to the stock-exchange list, a panicky fear might spread, perhaps leading to a blind dumping of shares and endangering the stability of the whole. A share corporation is a multitude of forces regulated more or less by fate. It is not a true organism, having neither the mechanical nor moral characteristics of one.

A third undesirable characteristic of a corporation is that those at the head (board members or officials) seek above all to derive the greatest possible personal advantage from their situation and influence. To be sure, the prosperity of the company is doubly in the interest of all in that (1) they themselves are share owners, and (2) a good dividend more than anything else insures their places. But the advantage which they derive directly from the exploitation of their position through high salaries and secret benefits as a rule is far more significant than the higher dividends they would receive as owners of company shares in the event of greater limitation of their personal claims. And if the latter is on the whole satisfactory, perhaps also if those who profit thereby are cautious not to express their personal income in actual figures but hide the same behind accounting procedures, then they scarcely need be anxious about criticism or dismissal by the annual general assembly. There is no essential difference in this respect between a limited partnership and a share corporation; only the forms of exploitation by the company leadership, but not the inclination or the effects, are different.

One should not object, however, that a general accusation of this kind is invalid, and that one by no means always has the same experience with state officials or with those who manage capital not their own. Where a relationship rests upon a moral foundation, and where personal connections exist between the one who gives orders and the one who carries them out, personal advantage will not always be ignored, but selfishness will at least be limited by an ideal connection and by personal relations. *Vis-à-vis* a company, a huge firm of changing and unknown shareowners, or *vis-à-vis* a juridical fiction one feels no gratitude, reverence, or personal respect. Sacrifice for a community of this kind which only aims at and pursues profit does not make sense; the universal example corrupts. Thus we see in actuality that almost without exception all corporations make unquestionably the greatest demands for stewardship and service—in part to an incredible extent—upon those who are influential.

So much for the economic characteristics inherent in the nature of corporations and therefore occurring more or less in all of them. There are in addition, however, some significant characteristics of each of the major kinds to note. That they are if not exclusively at least predominantly harmful is not to be denied.

Among corporations which have a single, fixed purpose, a tendency toward routine is not unusually noticeable once the undertaking has begun and it has assured the stockholders of a satisfactory return eventually. In such cases the convenience and the mutual indulgence of the managers and officials come into conflict with the raising of profits through renewed and voluntary zeal and the consequent obtaining of further benefits for the holders of the company's shares. In the absence of an inner moral principle in the situation, however, egoistic considerations easily win out. There is slight prospect of censure and of proposals for improvement from the stockholders if glaring mistakes or negligence is avoided. The power of inertia and lack of understanding keep even the majority of them in hand. Moreover, especially among share corporations, a single annual assembly is a very inadequate means for pushing through proposals which executive board, directors, and officials have a common interest in opposing. In this regard state establishments are in a far more favorable position, although undeniably they too generally are in danger of acting according to habit. Occasionally there may appear among them a zealous or restless superior clothed with sufficient power for improvement, or an assembly of interested groups may expose the wrongs, or finally an aroused public opinion may take up the cause.

Among corporations without a specific purpose, however, both of the following characteristics undoubtedly are basic to their natures.

First, they develop a restless activity which constantly reaches beyond itself, urging them into new undertakings and changes in existing business conditions, and for more than one reason. All their capital must be kept constantly in circulation if it is to yield ample return. When, as often happens, one or another of the undertakings is concluded, or perhaps even sold to advantage, new opportunities must be found. Then the consent of the partners is required. A major gain for such undertakings consists in raising the dividends of the business by starting a new business in the expectation of larger profits. If the partners are accustomed to income of this kind or to the increase of their capital, they naturally demand progress at the same rate and constantly demand new ventures. This restless and consuming activity undoubtedly has advantages; but often it has ruinous effects, especially upon a third party, as will be explained in detail further on.

A second attribute of these companies with indefinite purposes is that they like to pursue ways peculiar to their undertakings. The necessity of distributing large dividends drives them forward. And since the maintenance of existing business procedures scarcely offers the prospect of extraordinary advantage, either entirely new ideas or new ways of implementation must be devised, or it is at least necessary to centralize businesses which are small and operating individually, giving them a new and profitable organization. Obviously, here, too, good and bad are mixed.

The nature of corporations is less sharply expressed in social and political relations.

Unquestionably corporations which possess much or even immense capital, and which carry on significant and often gigantic undertakings that affect the entire life of the people, are powers with which even the state must reckon as of commanding influence upon the social situation. The exercise of their power in political and social spheres however is uncertain and more accidental; for action in this direction is not one of their basic objectives. In any case their capacities in this direction are of a more negative kind.

Many corporations have no national and still less a patriotic character. The company shares may belong to foreigners, and many corporations principally do business abroad. A bank, for example, may conduct its transactions principally with foreign countries, may especially concern itself with foreign countries and foreign shares on the stock exchange, and participate in foreign businesses. The new banks and *Crédits mobiliers* have quickly expanded the field of their operations beyond the borders of the country of origin. The *Crédit mobilier* of Paris purchases the Austrian railroads, constructs others in Switzerland; the Dessauer Bank founds a bank in Moldavia; Cologne bankers obtain official permission to do business in Darmstadt or Luxembourg, and they construct sugar refineries in Galicia, etc. One might say of these establishments that they require from the state only a point on which to stand, after which they certainly look out for themselves. What local character and what close political connection do the banks of Meiningen and Dessau and Gera and Hesse-Homburg and Waldeck have? What virtue in a patriotic sense and in regard to distinctively local character can these states expect of them?

A second social and political characteristic of a large bank is that it does not assume a definite position in state and society; it belongs to no distinct party, no particular class, no special nationality. Therefore the influence which it may exert cannot be predicted on the basis of realistic probability. Its course in political affairs—and this, according to circumstances, can be of great significance—will ultimately depend solely upon which people happen to possess a great many shares or have other decisive influence. These decisive persons may belong to every possible social situation and tendency, and they can quickly change. A new and indeterminate factor has entered into the probabilities of statecraft. It may be assumed that in general the large financial establishments cannot favor revolution and insurrection; yet this implies nothing about their opinions in constitutional and international questions. Obviously the state of affairs has grown definitely worse in comparison with the former preponderance of several great debtors or, in this case, creditors. The competition of financial establishments has already had the effect essentially of breaking the exclusive influence of individual financiers upon European politics. Old Amschel Rothschild no longer could say: "There will be no war because Rothschild wants none." Yet this is in no way identical with the disappearance of all influence of financial power upon states; it is merely that other less calculable powers have arisen.

One should not diminish the significance of the situation by attributing no desire and no capacity for political influence to these companies which are purely commercial and aim solely at profit. This would be empty solace in view of the accessibility of such associations to everybody. It can easily happen that those who are politically or socially ambitious can influence decisively a powerful financial establishment, and that on occasion they vigorously and wilfully exploit their influence. One should remember that noble families participate in many corporations, particularly in the newest and most powerful and that they may occupy leading positions. The *auri sacra fames* may induce them to do so; nonetheless these families have acquired significant new power through such participation, and nobody will undertake to say definitely in what way, in what connection, and with what limitations this influence will and can be expressed in state and society.

It is further significant for state and society that a share corporation certainly can be a real power as long as for some reason it exists, but it splinters into atoms as soon as it ends. When the term of its existence granted by the state is past, when it is dissolved by some strong power or must liquidate, it leaves no trace behind for state and society. Naturally its material creations do not necessarily cease with it; they may be taken over by any legal successors, perhaps purchasers or creditors, and to that extent its influence for good or ill can be felt for a long time. Yet it disappears completely when legal death has overtaken it and does not even leave social forms to recall its significance and perhaps continue its political influence. The only exception may be provided by one or two directors or officials who have used the connection more or less honorably to become wealthy. Even this happens seldom and accidentally, since earnings generally are divided among a thousand stockholders; and in any case only property remains and not a particular position and a specific interest.

In one way such a condition is convenient in that the epigones of earlier power situations present no difficulties; but it is disadvantageous in that our atomized social conditions thus acquire no basis and no organization.

Finally, still another negative peculiarity of large corporations is that they diminish the significance of the individual person for the state. What is the wealthiest and most enterprising person in comparison with such a mighty corporation driven irresistibly into activity and equipped if it wants with efficient and intangible powers? Since the state by founding new companies and by prolonging existing ones may call forth such significant and efficient powers almost at will, it is for the future less dependent in the execution of numerous and important matters upon the accident of personalities. This allows it in many respects to make more permanent arrangements; on the other hand this also makes it less needful of the good will of certain people and consequently may induce it to neglect duties and ultimately its own advantage.

Individual Consequences of Corporations

In the foregoing discussion of the characteristics of corporations, reference has been made to the consequences related to their nature. This still has not provided a view of their entire effectiveness. It goes without saying that such powerful companies devoted exclusively to business and profit have far-reaching consequences, some only distantly though not less actually connected with them, others shown to be connected only after close investigation. The exposition of them is requisite to complete judgment of the entire situation and forms the basis for needed measures by the state. After what has been said above it can surprise no one that these consequences are partly advantageous, partly damaging to the general public.

1. *Useful Consequences*

Among the useful consequences of corporations we may distinguish those which are economic and those which are political or social.

First the economic:

Here it is obvious that companies of various kinds have put a great deal of capital to use which otherwise would have lain dormant, or at least in its isolation and insignificance would have brought the owners and the entire economy little or no advantage. Naturally this is far from the case for all invested amounts; on the contrary a large part of them, as will be discussed in more detail below, is drawn from previous investments. We are neither so well off nor so foolish as to have had lying idle the hundreds and thousands of millions of marks which are currently invested or to be invested. Yet it is pure gain if the corporations attract amounts lying idle, or induce greater savings. They operate in this way like savings banks, however dissimilar they may be in other respects. The amounts thus attracted for the production of goods naturally cannot be as exactly estimated as can be done with savings banks, or even be calculated with some degree of probability. Yet with the spread of shares among all classes of society and into all levels of property, the total result must be significant.

Still more striking is the fact that corporations create enterprises which otherwise could never have come into existence, and in a twofold respect.

In part, of course, they make advances to private individuals or to small companies, thus enabling them to establish industrial undertakings or pursue them more vigorously. Whether this be in the form of loans or through formal entry into the business is immaterial. That corporations exert significant influence in this regard is daily experience. Banks as well as credit establishments in a restricted sense participate, as is known, in railroad undertakings, spinning mills, mining, machine works, and so forth. Naturally they are paid for their assistance, and indeed—since they must pay big dividends—as well as possible; but a capable entrepreneur receives the necessary larger amount from one source. Or a business which needs further capital gains a wealthy associate who offers the means for the desired expansion. In part the corporations operate industries directly and under their own management that never would have been brought into existence by individuals or by states with public means. A significant number of the marvels of our present material culture already have been executed by corporations and are maintained and continued by them. Associations of women and children, of shopkeepers and clerks, are bringing enterprises into existence which outdo anything created by Oriental despotism or theocracy. By far the greatest part of the railroads in all parts of the world are constructed by corporations. All the gigantic steamships regularly and quickly carrying the stream of traders or immigrants to the United States, the gold coast of California and Australia, the East Indies and La Plata, belong to corporations. One corporation owns the seventy steamers of Lloyd's, other corporations own the fleets of floating palaces or powerful tugboats on all the major rivers of Europe, America, and gradually Asia as well. Such companies have spanned our rivers with bridges surpassing the work of the Romans. They have constructed the docks where hundreds of ships and great riches lie in safety; most canals are their work. Share corporations have constructed and maintained in production enormous factories of every kind. Mines, insofar as they do not belong to states, are scarcely ever operated except with invested capital; especially the coal mines, upon whose existence a large part of all industry and prosperity now depends, are almost exclusively in the possession of limited partnerships or share corporations. Such companies illuminate our cities, supply our water, build entire urban sections for rich and poor. They provide us with transportation; they produce newspapers for us. They establish institutions for intellectual and social entertainment; they welcome travelers in fine caravansaries. And these amazing achievements, from all indications, will fade beside the undertakings planned by new and better companies. Perhaps railroads will traverse North America, run from Moscow to the Amur, from the North Sea through Europe, and from the Near East to India; tunnels may pierce the Alps and run under the British Channel; cables may span the Atlantic Ocean. The opening of Hungary, Galicia, the principalities of the Danube to civilization and abundance is still of course distant and appears merely the result of idle imagination. Yet even though some things may fail, unbelievably great things will in all probability come to pass as the world is transformed intellectually and economically. . . .

A third useful consequence follows from the fact that the corporations operate with great amounts of capital. This makes it possible for them to plan their undertakings on an unusual scale and hence to effect savings in general administrative costs. Machines are now practicable on a wide scale for such extensive operations, and their purchase is not too costly for corporate resources. Partly through these, partly because of the size of the undertakings, an extensive division of labor and the combination of various parts of work are practicable. Financial resources allow quantity purchase of raw materials at the most opportune time, and, if it seems advantageous, from the producer. Finally, such wealthy undertakings may make the most advantageous arrangements for the sale of their products or other utilization of their output. They are able to grant long-term credit, establish their own agents, erect warehouses, etc. In a word, large companies have not only the advantage of factories over small producers, but they even stand in relation to ordinary factories as factories do to the hand-worker, in regard to both quality and cost.

A fourth and final economic advantage of corporations is that they are able to combine many services and transactions usually performed by many individuals . . . into large, unified organized undertakings, being thereby able to operate in accordance with supply and demand. For example, it is an obvious advantage when a large company buys up or in some other way unites a number of small railroads which are under different managements and run according to different plans, interests, and ideas. It is an advantage when such a company combines a steamship service with its railroad. It is advantageous when one company acquires all the water supplies of a large city, meeting all previous needs with a well-considered plan and perhaps fulfilling many additional and previously neglected requirements. When a large company takes over a transportation establishment—for example a freight system, a shipping line, or a tug-boat service, etc.—it may arrange a well-organized and nicely interrelated network of connections within its natural region, thereby securing the advantage of through service and avoiding inconvenient and expensive loss of time. . . .

Thus economic advantages which corporations produce are many and great, and apart from their indirect benefits in advancing industry and the national welfare they directly afford considerable advantages in a social and political sense.

They relieve the state through their undertakings of various difficult tasks. Nobody will deny that one of the great difficulties of contemporary political life consists in the ever-expanding and often unforeseeable demands which are made upon the body politic and social in consequence of the growth of civilization and of the ever more diverse intellectual and economic activity. Even with the best intentions the means of the state are not sufficient to lend assistance in all cases properly needing its help. Although a disinterested third party might absolve the government of responsibility in a necessary refusal of this kind, nevertheless anyone disappointed in his justifiable expectations encounters ill will or indifference all too often and is embittered. And this is not all. Even in case of the granting of aid, either the need for revenue or the indebtedness of the state is increased, both undesirable conditions. When therefore corporations are able by the sizeable means which they have assembled to take over enterprises that are public utilities, they may free the state from a greater or lesser burden. That they gain or wish to gain from such investment does not alter the beneficial result.

Another at least occasional advantage consists in the fact that often such companies buy unprofitable property from the state. They need the property for their operations, or they hope to make a greater profit than the state was able to make. Objects of this kind are both buildings or estates and great affairs like transatlantic communications, mines, and entire railroad systems. It may be that some of these sales are censurable because of the low purchase price or even on general principles, and that it would have been desirable had the state not been required to sell. However if there is need or desire to sell, it is a decided advantage to find a wealthy competent buyer. For example, it may have been desirable for Austria not to have had to sell its railroads because of its finances; but it cannot be denied that once it was forced into selling it could have found a buyer quickly only in a corporation with an enormous amount of capital at its disposal.

Since we are speaking of states whose finances are in difficulty, a further advantage may be noted in passing, namely that share corporations frequently must purchase permission for their incorporation or their extension with significant payments to the public treasury or are induced to participate in government loans.

It may be recognized as an undoubted if indirect advantage for the state and social relations that the aristocracy, through its very noticeable and ever-increasing participation in large capitalistic corporations, is beginning to assume a more appropriate attitude toward contemporary society. A major reason for the strident discord of our public life is undoubtedly the stubborn adherence of the nobility to traditional pretensions and the ensuing ill-feeling between it and the educated and prosperous middle class. The aristocracy is profoundly embittered that its privileges, uncontested for centuries, no longer are conceded. It complains, and partly with justice, of powerful encroachments upon duly-acquired rights. It feels uneasy because it stands apart from the real and powerful current of civilization, and it conceals this detachment and lack of influence only artificially by shutting itself into a narrow and haughty circle, whereby it poisons relations still more. In a word, it recognizes clearly, or at least it has the strong feeling, that while remaining a special caste, it is not a genuine aristocracy, that is, it no longer stands at the top of the active organization of society and is not the center of the prevailing interests. In regrettable delusion it has sought to protect, perhaps to avenge itself, by retarding and turning back the natural course of events, and to this end it has used fully the remainder of its formal rights, heedless of the fact that it thereby dammed up the flood waters and ultimately created danger to itself and the monarchy as well, and perhaps in the long run to public order and higher civilization. An unexpected and welcome means of adjusting this strained and, in the long run, unendurable situation is to have our distinguished families participate financially in the new companies and to have many of their proudest names appear at the head of them. This of course may have its drawbacks, not merely because it is still unusual and to many does not seem honorable for princes and lords to appear and make money in company with Jews and partners of Jews, but also for more profound and serious reasons which are to be discussed below. But at least it is possible that a better relationship of the aristocracy with the reality of life and with the forces which control it is being formed. To be sure the aristocracy is attaching itself primarily to material interests; but much is gained when it no longer opposes the majority. In addition a transformation may be anticipated from the shift in the center of its aspirations and as a logical and necessary consequence of changing relationships and its new position. This interpretation of the situation perhaps may not be appetizing to pure democrats, who find satisfaction only in complete leveling of classes. But he who recognizes the validity of historical conditions and considers social structure unavoidable and useful will think otherwise. This view at least poses the possibility of a peaceful solution, where formerly an ever-threatening civil war of extermination appeared certain.

Not of comparable importance, but of merit and significance as it becomes certain, is the fact that numerous members of the influential educated class are more favorably inclined toward industry and commerce than formerly as they acquire shares in great enterprises. The capital that they are able to contribute is not large, but the public profits in various ways when out of self-interest they are occupied with economic affairs. . . .

2. *Harmful Consequences*

Unfortunately the advantages which an impartial observer of corporations must acknowledge are offset by numerous disadvantages. These are present both in the economic and in the political and social spheres.

As to the economic disadvantages, the formation of large combinations of capital unfortunately is possible for the most part only through withdrawal of a corresponding amount of capital from other investments. The millions of marks required by companies shooting up like mushrooms—and for whose provision the subscribers of partnership agreements or the purchasers of shares pledge themselves—are not conjured up by magic or created merely by signing a paper. The companies seek help insofar as this is practicable through permission to issue bank notes; but only a small part of the deficiency can be created in this manner. At the most, individual banks receive permission to issue notes, and though the matter may be carelessly managed, the entire amount of notes put in circulation does not increase the circulating capital because the banks are required by law to keep an equivalent amount of cash in the vaults. The great majority of corporations do not obtain the right to issue notes, but must obtain their entire capital through cash payments from shares purchasers. Since the latter have only a small part of their means lying idle, they must call in their outstanding investments in order to cover the payments as they gradually become due. They are compelled to do so because as a rule failure to meet payment dates results in forfeiture of what already has been paid and all claim upon the company. In this way money loaned to agriculture and small industry as well as to the state is withdrawn with the force of an air pump, thus causing the greater hardship because the general demand for money makes it almost impossible for the debtor to obtain new loans. This is worst for the private entrepreneur. Some of those required to repay go bankrupt, and through the depreciation of land and buildings, a necessary consequence of the coincidence of numerous offers to sell and disinclination toward new investment in such properties, more or less money is lost to the proprietor as well as to the more poorly secured creditors. But even those not forced directly into bankruptcy are circumscribed in their business, or in case they succeed in borrowing new capital, they are forced to pay a harmful interest rate. They cannot soon obtain inexpensive sums for improving and expanding business, and favorable opportunities and new improvements are fruitless since the prerequisites are lacking. The rejoinder made to allay this apprehension, that corporations put the contributed capital back into the money market and thereby quickly fill the gap again, is gross sophistry. Naturally the money is reinvested but in other branches of the economy, and this is the issue. Since large banks lend nothing to peasants and small businesses, extensive credit shortages must face these classes because of payments into corporations. This is one of the greatest economic evils. One cannot hope or expect that this situation will soon improve by the reinvesting of large corporate dividends in previous forms of investment. These sums would in any case fill the gap very slowly. Capitalists become accustomed to high returns and will not wish to return to the low interest rates of traditional loans, applying their savings instead to the acquisition of corporation shares. Added to this, as experience shows, is the easy opportunity for such investment, partly because new companies constantly appear, partly because existing ones attempt to expand their business and their capital, and to this end seek to encourage their current partners by offering new shares at a favorable price.

Both private parties and states and their creditors suffer from this need for money to pay into corporations. Although the pressure for capital to be used elsewhere is not directly destructive to states and to their credit, because loans cannot be withdrawn arbitrarily from them, nevertheless the matter is important since new loans may be necessary. The exchange rate of state bonds naturally sinks, since money is withdrawn from public funds in order to buy corporation shares; and when a new bond issue is necessary . . . it cannot be placed under favorable conditions, since the exchange rate of state bonds is depressed by corporate shares and new loans are dependent upon the existing rate of exchange. As far as the individual creditor of the state is concerned, he loses nothing directly so long as no change takes place in ownership. But when he or his legal successor must sell the bonds or transfer them by inheritance to another, the individual loses money.

These disadvantages are all the more deplorable because the business made possible by the new large investments is not advantageous in all respects.

The new corporations create an oppressive competition for small and medium-sized business. Although the powerful new enterprises may bring direct advantage to the stockholders and the economy in general, as is the case with all factory businesses, an evil exists in that growing numbers of businesses supporting an independent and well-to-do middle class are done away with. However much economic theory may extol the consolidation of business activity into large establishments because the latter favor the most advantageous purchase of raw materials, the use of machinery, the division of labor, efficient marketing—nevertheless this is not all there is to be said in evaluating these conditions. A higher general consideration of the human and political situation shows that reduction of large masses of workers to dependent day laborers, the constantly increasing difficulty of maintaining a modest business adequate for a family of the lower middle class, in short the ever greater division of society into a wealthy minority and an overwhelming proletarian majority are not desirable and fortunate circumstances. The best possible situation is not the presence of a multiplicity of cheap and perhaps also good commodities, but an organization of the national wealth and human occupation in which there is a large number of independent, modestly well-to-do burghers satisfied with their lot and favorable to intellectual and moral betterment. Since the entire trend of recent economy is toward mastery by capital and machinery and toward repression of persons of flesh and blood, the sudden irresistible increase in this trend is regrettable. What is to become of the peoples of Europe once they are nothing but a great factory, headed by a few omnipotent and extremely wealthy leaders, while all the others are merely dependent, well-nigh dispensable and consequently little esteemed appurtenances of a well-ordered whole of machines of capital? One speaks scornfully of England's "cotton textile lords." The Quaker and non-Quaker owners of the cotton mills and frequenters of the stock exchanges are vastly different in their appearance, behavior, and life work from the iron barons of the Middle Ages, and the difference between the two kinds of aristocrats lends itself to satire. But the matter is serious. An extensive system has arisen of individual masters and a defenseless mass of tenants and serfs of industry. And the comparison may be pushed further. Whereas in the Middle Ages the petty burgher in the towns had to defend life and property with the utmost effort against feudal princes and knights, now the small business man must struggle with all his might to preserve his livelihood and independence. Unfortunately the outcome is quite different. During the Middle Ages freedom and education were established by the gradual victory of townspeople over the military caste. Today large capital resources seem more and more to dominate human personality. Whatever contributes to this result to a special degree is for the statesman and humanitarian an evil, however fine the beet sugar or the yarn, or efficient the steam engine. The concentration of capital in corporations and the large industries thereby founded are contributing mightily to the victory.

One needs no more than the most common economic theory to fear the disadvantages of business enterprises of banks and *Crédits mobiliers*. Without going beyond the realm of mere bookkeeping considerations, one becomes convinced of the destructiveness of monopoly. It lies in the nature of great financial powers to form monopolies. In this way the highest possible profit is assured; for monopolies possess in abundance the means of stifling competition. . . . We anticipate a situation in which many of the necessities of life will be monopolies of corporations, that is, supplied by them alone. And there is not the least basis to assume that all the consequences of monopoly will not soon show themselves, namely, high prices along with poor work, stagnation, laziness, and lack of consideration of needs. This point of view is the less consoling since, as already noted, a restless acquisitiveness lies in the nature of a corporation. . . .

But, one objects, corporative undertakings will not always succeed. Undoubtedly not. Experience with earlier stock swindles shows that once sound undertakings have been acquired, the restless spirit of the profit motive throws itself, consciously or unconsciously, into the most absurd plans offering not the remotest chance of success. Although sponsors in these instances generally know how to save themselves from ruin without injury and perhaps even with profit, the great mass of deluded stockholders remains in the sinking ship. In this way much slowly accumulated capital is lost, which, if sensibly invested, could have served to stimulate legitimate and wise activity. The bursting of numerous stock bubbles spread unspeakable distress in England during the twenties. The failure of undertakings is no consolation; rather it is a further unnecessary but probable curse associated with the entire process.

The center of this process is the amazing increase in playing the stock market on the part of corporations. The latter contribute toward this in several ways.

For one thing, the mere presence of such a vast number of securities so easily exchanged is a stimulus to activity on the stock market. Through its rise and fall money can be earned by brokers, bankers, and all financiers; consequently they too are kept in movement. This can happen more easily in that the plans of the companies are ambitious, changing, and incalculable. They give full scope to hope and fear and even complete insanity.

The intentional manipulations of the corporations contribute to the frantic activity in stocks even more than these causes which are natural, so to speak. Among those corporations which have a serious purpose, for example the building of a railroad, it has occurred that, not so much the future profit from this undertaking as rather the immediate advantage of an anticipated rise in the sale value of stocks immediately upon the founding, even before the actual founding, has become the major reason for participation. This occurs as much among the entrepreneurs as among those who subscribe to shares. The founding of the new corporation is initiated by well-paid announcement in the newspapers. There appears a prospectus offering glittering prospects in nebulous phrases; and where possible a name of a person is placed at the head which either promises acquaintance with all the tricks and dodges of indiscriminate profit or impresses by its historic fame and its aristocratic ring—doubly effective, of course, if both characteristics are united in one fortunate person. Finally, a subscription of shares exceeding the need is provided, perhaps a hundred times over, so that the unpleasant duty devolves upon the entrepreneurs of restricting their friends to thousands of shares rather than the hundreds of thousands they had hoped for. Now the stage is set for the farce on the stock market. Before anything at all has been done and often before any kind of payment beyond a guarantee has been made, the shares are placed on the market at a high premium; and through all kinds of expedients and by means of accomplices the price is maintained at an artificial level and is pushed ever higher. The credulous public walks into the trap, crowding to receive in return for a high entrance price some of the rain of gold. Thus the play is continued, either to catastrophe or the gradual realization of genuine profits. Of course the instigators and whoever else is in on the secret are not affected by a subsequent decline in the fraudulently inflated exchange rate. They have sold secretly at the right time, and in any case have preserved this profit. Indeed, as the thermometer of morality now stands, they may be commended for special virtue if they do not cause the lowest possible decline of the exchange rate when they sell their original shares. This enables them to buy from terrified stockholders at low prices and then to drive the exchange rate suddenly upward again until new profits may be achieved through resale. The farce of the stock market plays on, driven by its instigators to the heights of frenzy.

Finally, the corporations contribute powerfully to the mad game of chance in that they themselves use accumulated capital for speculation on the stock market with other favored shares. With the enormous amounts which stand at their disposal, they can do this on a huge scale. The fact that the purpose of the corporation is fundamentally different, that the capital was accumulated for quite other uses does not impose the slightest restraint. The stockholders are completely satisfied with a large dividend since they are concerned with this and not with the execution of the declared plans of the corporation; and in view of the height of the profit, unattainable in other ways, they easily overlook the possibility of a loss in playing the stock market. Where did a participant in the Parisian *Crédit mobilier* complain that in the year 1855 forty per cent of his capital was swindled away? If, however, a self-appointed trouble-maker complains about the delay in executing the handsome plans that were pressed so urgently and censures the use of capital in playing the stock market, he is indulgently told by experienced and exalted businessmen that such a large undertaking requires longer preparation, that they cannot permit so much money to lie idle in their coffers, and that temporarily they have invested it in trustworthy state bonds and other interest-bearing bonds. Then hired newspapers overwhelm the critic with ridicule for his stupid conscientiousness; and finally, as though this were the most conclusive refutation, the mischief continues even more shamelessly than before. At times the managers spare themselves the hypocrisy altogether and designate in the plans of the new corporation that a considerable part of the total capital will be used for undertakings on the stock market.

To set forth the disadvantages of the stock-market farce in greater particular is completely superfluous. For purely economic reasons it is obvious that employment of capital for a turnover which merely transfers money from the pocket of the imprudent or uninformed into that of the more lucky or cunning, without producing at the same time any new value or creating anything useful, and that an activity in which the gain of one comes from the loss of another is completely unproductive and detrimental. Add to this the spreading conviction that acquiring wealth and rising to higher social circles may be reached far more quickly and with less effort through sly deception of others and through blind risks and wagers than through diligence, usefulness, dependability, thrift—in short through moral and intellectual effort. The stock market brings the dregs of the population into contact on the same basis with all classes and dulls the moral sense for merit and honor. Widespread playing of the stock market is among unreliable groups the cause and the consequence of bad civil and moral circumstances, a sign of corruption and a breeding place of the same. A wilder play of the stock market than the one just now evoked and even perpetuated by corporations hardly ever has been witnessed. And when finally the entire apparatus is inevitably shattered in consequence of some sudden calamity or through its own excess, when finally the more impecunious gamblers are reduced to poverty, the wealthier, bolder, and shrewder ones have at least been able to survive the general ruin with a remnant of fraudulently accumulated riches, of course it is true that generally speaking the material wealth of the nation will not for the most part have suffered actual injury. But the dream of fabulous riches will give way to a horrible awakening, and actual wealth will be in quite different hands from those anticipated. Yet for all this the economic damage is the more frightful because the moral fitness of the people and consequently their productive capacity will be shattered for a long time.

Mention must be made of the evil consequences of the surplus of banks mushrooming as a result of the stock swindle. It is incredible that the repeated troubles of England and especially of North America remain so completely unheeded. One cannot sufficiently blame both the irresponsible ignorance and indifference and the thoughtless and unscrupulous selfishness. The mass of these establishments . . . must necessarily in the near future plunge Germany into distress. For upon what reasonable basis can it be assumed that among us the desire, not to mention the necessity, of drawing high yields from bank capital, of irresponsible loans, of support of nebulous projects will not shortly lead to the promotion of all kinds of frauds? Then there will be no honest and trustworthy businesses, to which the hundred of millions of marks assembled by new banks can be loaned. A short period of apparent business prosperity will be followed by one of those frightful financial crises with privation and ruin on all sides and thousands reduced to poverty. Stormy demands upon the public treasury will then be made in Germany to limit the evil through generous interference, that is, at the expense of industrious burghers and peasants whose taxes must be correspondingly raised to save some people from well-deserved ruin and protect the ill-gotten wealth of others. These consequences will appear all the more since banks as a rule are granted the right to issue bank notes; that is, there is a possibility of doubling or tripling fraudulent undertakings. In a country where such highly dangerous undertakings may come into existence in some thirty different places and without any common supervision and moderation, one can contemplate the future only with grave apprehension. Small states frequently confront overpowering financial groups, and a significant quantity of state paper money, sometimes already far in excess of every need, exists alongside the notes of banks, probably to be swept along with these into the abyss. Only great thoughtlessness or intolerable ignorance can look upon this as a chimera.

One could still accept this state of affairs if it did not portend, or had not already given rise to, serious social and political disadvantages.

No impartial observer will deny that the extensive diffusion of corporations throughout all classes, and the interest of many highly placed persons in them foretells corruption of the point of view of our influential classes. When princes and princely persons, state officials and members of the estates are deeply involved in these undertakings, often far beyond their means, they unavoidably assume a wrong stand on public affairs. Whereas only disinterested persons are fit to render honest and impartial evaluation of many questions on legislation, administration, and control, in the future the influence of those who are highly interested personally is to be feared, not necessarily from bribery or other intentional and positive forms of baseness. Even without offers of gifts, genuine zeal for the public welfare, impartial judgment, personal independence in relation to great financial powers will not always be present when poverty or riches depend upon a judgment, a proposal, a vote, an approval—and this in the knotty questions where a soothing of the conscience through sophistry is so probable. It has been rightfully praised as a salutary aspect of the constitutional order that civil officials keep the personal financial interest of princes entirely separate from their administrative activity. There are laws in all states which prohibit officials down to the village mayor and the warehouse keeper from pursuing businesses through which they become subject to compromising situations and can be misled into selfish neglect of their duties. No one may participate in a judicial decision in which he or a relative has the slightest personal interest. All of these precautionary measures become ineffectual—they are strong means against relatively small evils —when participation in corporation and stock-market affairs is spread among high and low state officials. The longer one lives in the world the more he realizes that much more depends upon an honorable conviction and a genuinely honest intention than upon knowledge and understanding. A spreading of situations in which the strict and scrupulous sense of duty among those in power is placed in constant conflict with profit and luxury must lead to the worst general consequences. Once the purity of conviction is tarnished, it is never possible to determine to what extent and where the effects will appear.

These half involuntary wrongs inherent in the situation are not all; the danger of crude and flagrant corruption is great. The number and kind of cases which a large corporation may utilize contrary to law and public advantage is incalculable and inexhaustible. The possibility begins with the granting of a license when wisdom and honor counsel denial. Omitting or changing a point of law entirely overlooked by one who is uninformed may be of the utmost importance for the corporation. It may wish the state to guarantee payment of interest, or want the cession of state property at low prices, or the assumption of a part of the capital stock by the state treasury. It can be a question of monopoly, or of the nonenforcement of a means of control, or the neglect of a duty to the stockholders or to the public. The extension of the duration of a profitable undertaking is naturally desired. Perhaps it is a question of the right to issue or accept notes by the state treasury. These wishes are expressed by extremely wealthy corporations, and satisfaction may depend entirely or partially upon impecunious officials condemned, in fulfilling their duty, to lifelong restraint and enforced frugality. When amounts equal to a fortune are offered and perhaps offered for a mere omission or for an opinion whose substance imposes no legal responsibility; when the bribery is not done clumsily in the form of a gift but through an offer of participation, likewise not legally assailable, in the corporation; when not the official himself, but a representative, a son-in-law, a loved one is favored, will virtue in these cases always be the winner? Protection against bribery in small amounts is afforded by a passable salary and by fear of severe punishment. The situation is fundamentally different when hundreds of thousands of marks may be gained without fear of punishment. One should consider two points. First, at the

present time the almost universal principle of admitting every qualified person to all offices may bring men without means into the most
influential and even highest positions, whereas a misguided frugality,
particularly of many state diets, contributes to an offensive and unfavorable disparity between position and income. It is no slander
against the leaders of large corporations if one does not credit many
of them with excessive prudishness in money affairs. This is part of
the nature of their business. Whoever set out every day to exploit on
the stock exchange his astuteness and knowledge acquired by chance
and even by violation of duty—that is, in a manner to cause others to
lose their fortunes—cannot possibly remain fastidious in financial
matters. Therefore attempts at bribery will not be lacking. Western
Europeans have witnessed with horror the widespread venality of
Russian officials; but at least the beginnings are already visible in
France and perhaps elsewhere.

Once corporations develop to their full strength, it is to be feared
that the will of the state can no longer prevent injury. Possession of
such huge sums of money is a significant power. He who holds power
wants to use it, especially for his own advantage. It is easy to foresee
that capitalists will want to influence and will be able to influence the
filling of official positions and the direction of legislation and administration in tariff matters, in financial questions, and in matters of
public debt. They will seek to control elections to state diets. Sometimes they will wish to win, sometimes to intimidate. In a diet election, for example, an investment bank is in a position to hold out the
prospect of granting or denying a sum to a factory, participation in a
network of railroads, and so on irrespective of how much or how
little the government will be reproached. One need not indulge in
fantasy to see in these powerful associations with unlimited leadership a new element in state and society with which the present order
of things cannot contend and whose influence cannot be calculated.
It is certain that this influence does not benefit the entire society,
since a corporation of this kind aims not at the common advantage but
exclusively at its own economic gain. Corporative power is all the
greater in that it confronts relatively small states. It should not be

forgotten that the influence of corporations may be exercised in behalf of foreign interests, be they governments or businesses. Not only may the seat of the establishment lie abroad, but if this is not the case, influential members from other countries may belong to the corporation and act from a foreign point of view.

14. Constitutionality and Authoritarian Rule

The documents below concern the constitutional conflict in Prussia and form a unity. The Address to the King (A) by the majority of the Lower House of the Landtag states the liberal interpretation of the constitution, one that was in harmony with Western European thinking as most clearly practiced in Great Britain. Bismarck's reply (B) sustains the gap theory of a constitution that was upheld successfully in other states, the most notable example at the time being that of Denmark. The speech exemplifies the manner in which numerous persons of power have, in the course of the nineteenth century and the twentieth as well, interpreted a constitution to suit their own views. Most constitutions have gone through this authoritarian stage. Some have developed into instruments of parliamentary government; others have never advanced so far. The correspondence between the two distinguished German liberal historians, Heinrich von Sybel and Hermann Baumgarten (C), over how to resolve the conflict reveals the dilemma of all liberals in 1848, in 1863, and at other times, and in all countries, that of how to achieve political power without revolution. The Prussians did not follow the English example of the seventeenth century; they succumbed to authoritarian rule.

A. *Petition of the Liberal Majority of the Prussian Lower House to the King* (1863)*

Most August, All Powerful, All Gracious King and Sovereign!

1. Your Majesty has again called into session the two houses of the Royal Landtag. The House of Representatives has answered the call,

---

* *Stenographische Berichte über die Adress-Debatte des Preussischen Abgeordnetenhauses am 27., 28. und 29. Januar 1863.* (Berlin: W. Moeser Verlag, 1863), pp. 284-5.

full of the earnest will to display anew unswerving loyalty to the Crown, the most conscientious concern for the preservation of the constitution. It does not conceal from itself the fact that it begins its work under somber auspices. But because of this fact it feels all the more its duty to represent to Your Majesty openly and respectfully the condition of the country.

2. The last session was closed before the budget law for the year 1862 provided for by the constitution was passed. The budget bill for 1863, which should have been agreed upon before the close of the previous year, was withdrawn. The request to Your Majesty's Government to present this budget again at an early date remained unheeded.

3. Since then the ministers appointed by Your Majesty have conducted the administration unconstitutionally without a legal budget and thus, in opposition to a special declaration of the House of Representatives, have ordered expenditures which were definitely and expressly refused by decisions of the House.

4. The supreme right of popular representation, that of authorizing expenditures, was thereby violated—a right which is absolutely the foundation of constitutional government, which all existing constitutions therefore guarantee, and which up to this time was exercised by the Prussian popular assembly with full recognition by the Government. The country with horror saw the entire gains of our previous political development placed in jeopardy. It supported its representatives.

5. Only a small minority, long estranged from the nation and supported by the ministers of Your Majesty, has carried the grossest defamations against one branch of the legislative power to the very steps of the Throne and has not hesitated to confuse the judgment as to the extent and meaning of clear constitutional rights.

6. At the same time a manifold misuse of governmental power has appeared, such as occurred in the troubled years before the beginning of Your Majesty's rule. Officials loyal to the constitution, chiefly those who were likewise representatives, have been afflicted with crushing measures. The press has been persecuted for defending the law. An effort has been made to prevent the exercise of undoubted

civil rights on the part of men of the nonmobilized military reserve by inadmissible orders of military superiors outside the chain of command.

Most Gracious King and Sovereign!

7. Your Royal Majesty has recently declared that no one may doubt Your will to maintain and protect the Constitution which You have sworn to support. In fact no one dares to raise such a doubt. However—and allow this, Your Majesty, to be said openly—the constitution is already violated by the ministers. Article 99 no longer has any validity. Our country suffers the grave wrong of a government without a budget. And the new session has begun without any expectation that we shall succeed in returning to the legal handling of finances and the reestablishment of military affairs on a legal basis.

8. Foreign countries behold with astonishment the lengthening conflict, which daily diminishes the respect for the name of Prussia, and which threatens to deprive of its best resources the voice of the Government in the council of nations. They know well that duty and conscience force the popular representatives of Prussia to observe the right which the constitution gives them, without exceeding their authority but also without allowing their power to erode on all sides. They know that the expectation of external involvement is no means for settling our internal disputes. They know that Prussia can regain her influence in Germany and thereby her strength only when she reestablishes constitutional order and calls upon the German people and its representatives to participate in the political unification of the great fatherland.

9. In the midst of this crisis the Prussian people, which has been tested in many dangers, which is surpassed by none in loyalty and steadfastness, does not give up hope that Your Majesty in Your wisdom will distinguish the loyal voices of Your legal representatives from the advice of those who in the party conflict try to cover and to support their efforts, powerless in themselves, with the illustrious name of Your Majesty.

10. Your Royal Majesty, our position as representatives of the country gives us the categorical duty to declare solemnly that in-

ternal peace and strength abroad can be restored only by a return to constitutional conditions.

B. Otto von Bismarck: *Speech on the Gap in the Constitution* (January 27, 1863)*

The draft submitted to you by your committee performs an undeniable service in clarifying our mutual relationships. Less than a year ago (if I am not mistaken it was during the elections), the contention that the Landtag was disputing with the King over domination in Prussia was emphatically rejected. After you have accepted the Address now before you, this repudiation will no longer be possible. In this Address rights are claimed for the Lower House which the House does not at all or does not alone possess. If you, gentlemen, had the exclusive right finally to determine the total amount and the particulars of the budget, if you had the right to demand of His Majesty the King the dismissal of those ministers who do not retain your confidence, if you had the right through your resolutions concerning the budget to determine the strength and organization of the army, if you had the right—as constitutionally you do not have, although you claim it in the Address—to control the relationship of the executive power of the government to its officials, then you would in fact possess the complete governmental power in this country (Prussia). Your Address is based upon these claims, if it has any basis at all. I believe, therefore, that its practical significance can be characterized in a few words: "Through this Address the Royal House of Hohenzollern is requested to transfer its constitutional governing rights to the majority of this House."

You clothe the demand in the form of a declaration that the constitution is violated insofar as the Crown and the Upper House do not bow to your will. You direct the accusation of violation of the constitution against the ministry, not against the Crown, whose loy-

---

* *Stenographische Berichte über die Adress-Debatte des Preussischen Abgeordnetenhauses am. 27., 28. und 29. Januar 1863.* (Berlin: Verlag von W. Moeser, 1863), pp. 58-64.

alty to the constitution you place beyond all doubt. You know as well as anyone in Prussia that the ministry acts in Prussia in the name of and on behalf of His Majesty the King, and that in this sense it has executed those acts in which you see a violation of the constitution. You know that in this connection a Prussian ministry has a different position from that of the English. An English ministry, call it what you will, is a parliamentary one, a ministry of the parliamentary majority; but we are ministers of His Majesty the King. I do not reject the separation of the ministers from the Crown which is assumed in the Address in order, as was suggested earlier from the tribune, to make of the Crown a shield behind which the ministry could be protected. We do not need this protection; we stand firmly on the ground of our good right. I repudiate the separation because thereby you are concealing the fact that you are in conflict with the Crown and not with the ministry for control of the country. You find the constitutional violation specifically in Article 99. Article 99 reads, if I remember the words correctly: "All income and expenditure of the state must be estimated each year in advance and brought together into a state budget."

If the article continued that "the latter will be fixed annually by the Lower House," then you would be completely justified in your complaints in the Address, for the constitution would be violated. But the text of Article 99 continues that the latter, the state household budget, will be fixed annually by law. Now, Article 62 states with complete clarity how a law is passed. It says that for the passage of a law, including a budget law, agreement of the Crown and of both Houses is necessary. That the Upper House is justified in rejecting a budget approved by the Lower House but not acceptable to the Upper House is, moreover, emphasized in the article.

Each of these three concurrent rights is in theory unlimited, one as much as the other. If agreement among the three powers is not reached, the constitution is lacking in any stipulation about which one must give way. In earlier discussions this difficulty was passed over easily; according to analogy with other countries, whose constitutions and laws, however, are not published in Prussia and have no validity here, it was assumed that the difficulty can be settled by the two other parties yielding to the Lower House, that if agreement over the budget is not reached between the Crown and the Lower House, the Crown not only submits to the Lower House and dismisses the ministers who do not have the confidence of the Lower House, but that in case of disagreement with the Lower House the Crown also forces the Upper House by mass appointments to agree with the Lower House. In this way, to be sure, the sovereign and exclusive rule of the Lower House would be established; but such exclusive rule is not constitutional in Prussia. The constitution upholds the balance of the three legislative powers on all questions, including the budget. None of these powers can force the others to give way. The constitution therefore points to understanding by way of compromise. A statesman of constitutional experience has said that all constitutional life is at all times a series of compromises. If the compromise is thwarted by one of the participating parties wishing to enforce its views with doctrinaire absolutism, the series of compromises will be interrupted and in its place will occur conflicts. And since the life of a state cannot remain stationary, conflicts become questions of power. Whoever holds the power prevails, for the life of a state cannot remain immobile even for a moment. You may say that according to this theory the Crown can prevent the passage of a budget as the result of every insignificant difference of opinion. In theory that is indisputable, just as in theory it is indisputable that the deputies can reject the entire budget, in order thereby to cause the discharge of the army or the dissolution of all government agencies. But in practice this does not happen. Such misuse of the undoubted theoretical right of the Crown has not occurred in all these fourteen years [of constitutional government]. In the present situation, we shall hardly agree on who is to blame for not having reached a compromise. I recall, however, that following the dissolution of the preceding Lower House the Crown voluntarily offered substantial concessions. The budget was reduced by several millions; the surtax of twenty-five per cent was voluntarily dropped.

Consideration was given your wish for an itemization of the budget, the execution of which is not without difficulty for the government. Your response to these attempts at understanding was that in September you passed a resolution, an act about which I do not scruple completely to return the charge of misuse of power made by you against us in the tenor of your Address. You used your right of consent in the determination of the budget to pass a resolution impossible of execution unless we make Prussia defenseless, and unless we are not to count all previous expenditure for military reorganization as useless. I do not know how many millions it would take to begin the reorganization anew next year. You asked of His Majesty the King, provided you wanted at all that your resolution be executed—and that you could have passed a resolution without wanting it to be carried out is to me incomprehensible for an assembly such as this—you asked dismissal of one-half of the infantry, one-third of the cavalry, 119 battalions—I do not know how many regiments. The resolution was thus completely impracticable, for it pertained to something already past.

As stated previously, I wish to engage in no further recriminations concerning the past than historical narration requires. With this radical resolution you have wandered into a blind alley from which you will with difficulty find an exit consistent with your wishes. But in response to it the Government came to you with an offer of agreement: It declared itself ready to agree to the provisions of the amendment presented by Freiherr von Vincke. If you had responded to this step with the expected approval—[Protests from the Left.]

I remember that, at the time when I rejected the Vincke amendment, you gave the same signs of disapproval which I have noticed several times today; but there is no agreeing over motives. I have attended many decision-making assemblies, but I have never heard that there is agreement about motives. . . . The Lower House should have accepted the overture, I think. It would have led last year to settlement of the controversy over the budget of 1862 and to a resumption of consideration last year of the budget of 1863, reconsideration of which was intended by Deputy von Vincke in his amendment. One of the greatest sources of controversy would thereby have been eliminated; but you [the deputies] replied to our attempt at agreement with a resolution which destroyed all hope of achieving understanding.

We closed the session in the hope that you would return in a more conciliatory frame of mind than that in which you left us. You expect the Crown to give in; we expect you to do so. The Government is convinced that it is your turn to make concessions, and unless you do so, we shall hardly resolve the conflict. The Upper House rejected, and the Royal Government thinks justifiably so, the budget law which you voted as insufficient for the needs of the state. We actually confronted a situation in which no budget came into being, a situation considered impossible. The fact belied the assertion of impossibility. What has occurred unquestionably can be repeated. If the constitutional stipulation that the Crown and the Upper House share equally the right of consent to every law including the budget is not to be completely illusory, then the situation can be repeated. That a gap exists at this point in the constitution is not at all a new discovery. I myself at that time (and I believe that an assertion of mine from this period was cited during my absence) attended the discussions concerning revision of the constitution. For several days we thoroughly examined this possibility, which now for the first time after eighteen [sic] years has become an actuality. It occurred to no one at the time that it was impossible, but we were unable to agree upon the means by which to avert such a situation. I must absolutely and most decidedly reject the assertion that we have acted unconstitutionally, that we have violated the constitution—and I repeat what I said in the committee: Gentlemen, we take our oath and vow to the constitution just as seriously as you do yours. Learn to respect the sincerity of your opponents' convictions and do not be too generous with accusations of constitutional violation and the oath-breaking which that involves. Theories about what is lawful when no budget is passed have been advanced, and I do not intend to evaluate them here. Some say that if no budget is passed the budget of the previous year continues of itself. Others state that in consequence of the *horror vacui* contained in the law, the gap in all cases not covered by the most recent law is filled by supplementing with long-established law, just as we revert to the Joachima[1]) when statute law does not suffice,

---

[1] A legal code by which the Elector Joachim I in 1527 introduced Roman law into Brandenburg.

or to customary law and ancient royal ordinances where the Royal Code does not apply. Consequently, the authority of absolute power would again apply if the budget law fails. I do not wish to pursue these theories further. It is sufficient for me to recognize the necessity of state and not pessimstically allow to come to pass a situation in which the treasury is closed. Necessity alone is decisive, and we have taken this necessity into account. You will not demand that we suspend paying interest and salaries of officials. I repudiate absolutely, as I have always done, the idea that the resultant state of affairs is unconstitutional. I also believe that this view [that the government acted unconstitutionally] is shared by no one among the thousands of officials who have sworn allegiance to the constitution. None of the officials has refused to cooperate with the government; none has declared that from the first of January he does not wish to receive his salary. I make no accusations; I merely conclude that the charge of having acted unconstitutionally is not so unassailable; otherwise at least one among the thousands of officials would have had a troubled conscience and would have refused to work under this government.

The situation, moreover, in which we find ourselves is in no way more unconstitutional than the situation which for fourteen years existed during the first four to six months of each year when we were without a budget. You say that the present situation is worsened by your explicit rejection of certain parts of the budget. Pardon my remarking that your resolutions in themselves, as long as they stand alone, carry no force of law whatsoever. Through your individual resolutions you can neither authorize us to make any kind of expenditure, nor in the absence of a budget law can you set a limit for satisfying state needs. It is always necessary to secure the consent of the Upper House and the approval of the Crown in order to make your action legal. As long as this is not the case the law does not exist and the government is not empowered to do anything by your vote alone. I shall not concern myself with reciprocal accusations and recriminations; but from my words I think you will understand our firm conviction that we are not in conflict with the constitution and thereby our resolve to resist strongly and energetically, as long as we retain the confidence of His Majesty, any pressure for an extension of your competence beyond the limits which the constitution approves. Those rights which the constitution grants you shall be completely yours. Any demands beyond this we shall reject, and we shall steadfastly protect the rights of the Crown against your claims.

It is a peculiar coincidence that the discussion of this manifesto which you propose to present to our Royal Master falls exactly on the birthday today of the youngest heir presumptive to the Throne. In this coincidence, gentlemen, we see a double challenge to stand fast for the rights of the monarchy, to stand fast for the rights of the successors to His Majesty. The Prussian monarchy has not yet fulfilled its mission; it is not yet ripe for becoming a purely ornamental decoration of your constitutional edifice, not yet ready to be integrated like a lifeless mechanical part into the mechanism of a parliamentary regime.

C. *How to Defeat Bismarck and the Hohenzollerns and Make Prussia Liberal* (1863)°

Heinrich von Sybel to Hermann Baumgarten

Berlin, May 9, 1863

You say that if we do not hasten to overthrow Bismarck it would be a great misfortune. True, but tell me, how would you do it? What means would you find to do it? The release of an Address to the King was advised by me in order to speak again about foreign policy. The party turned it down, on the ground that I could not deny that such a step would not discredit the minister with the King, but would strengthen his position, and it brought forward as proof the interpellation in regard to Inowrazlaw, where we sufficiently blasted the minister. That we neglected to pursue the ministers with attacks cannot be proved—ministerial responsibility, education, budget, Polish questions followed one another—but show me any parliament in the world that is able every day to deliver a great, brilliant debate to

° Julius Heyderhoff, ed., *Die Sturmjahre der Preussisch-Deutschen Einigung, 1859-1870: Politische Briefe aus dem Nachlass liberaler Parteiführer.* (Bonn, 1925), I, 149-53.

resound throughout Germany and the world. As you know, we have no procedure for impeaching the ministers, but they have money and soldiers and an old bureaucratic machine stuffed full of reactionary powers. And since we have absolutely no material power, we are simply not in a position to realize a quick victory. We are fighting to preserve moral superiority; in Prussia up to now we have done so successfully. If we are not brilliant enough for you others, I am very sorry; we do what we can, and as I said, it is not correct that we have left the ministers in peace.

Hermann Baumgarten to Heinrich von Sybel

Karlsruhe, May 22, 1863

The outlook for Prussia's future is bad if her fate remains tied to the judgment and will of the Hohenzollerns, if the people cannot take their affairs into their own hands. We must compel narrow-minded men as well as conceited ones to be understanding or get rid of them entirely. I naturally prefer the former and in view of experience elsewhere do not doubt success also in this case. But we must act in bitter seriousness and arouse in the persons affected the very definite feeling that everything is at stake for them if they do not soon come to reason. For this purpose the speeches of the Lower House appear to me not sufficient; the entire country must rise up and speak its will decisively. To me and to us here the battle in Prussia up to now seems to have been carried on too tamely. Men who, like bad boys, despise the constitution, reasonableness, and law we must make tremble. We must arouse in them the lively fear that one day they will be killed like mad dogs. We must oppose them with passion, ardent and determined if need be to go to all lengths. Such a way of fighting is certainly not to the taste of cultivated people. But it is not a matter of taste but of necessity. Let Bismarck even temporarily succeed and revolution seems to me unavoidable. If Prussia endures permanently such a régime, her position in Germany and in Europe would be at an end. One asks how we can prevent such fearful dangers. Let righteous anger be fully and energetically expressed! Bring deputations to Berlin from all the cities and counties! Let these, accompanied by thousands of respectable citizens, go to the Palace and there speak with seriousness and determination! You will only be doing what the English did in 1770 against the North ministry. It is possible that you will convulse the peace. But on the other side is the certainty of a terrible revolution or a profound humiliation.

Believe me, I do not write this lightly. For months we have followed every step taken in Berlin with the most intense attention. The affair is not in our opinion becoming too long, but it leaves us full of doubts. An enormous amount is at stake, our entire future. One cannot negotiate with these men; one can only attack them, and every week the attack needs to be stronger. If the attack of the representatives is not enough, the entire country must go into action, and from time to time signals must be given with the reckless energy of a Junius. I repeat these views because experience strengthens me in them every day and because you in Berlin are deciding ours as well as your own fate.

Heinrich von Sybel to Hermann Baumgarten

Berlin, May 26, 1863

. . . The plan for a mass demonstration, which you suggest, has often been discussed here since December; I have always supported it because I too think that in case it succeeded a real impression would have been made in high places. But the leaders of the Progressive party always thought that it would be difficult to set people in motion exactly for this purpose; to petition in the presence of this man again would be most unpopular. And it would be a great defeat if the demonstration should turn out to be thin. But if it succeeded, the gain would be less than you seem to think. If 40,000 delegates came in one day—they would get a polite refusal and would go home. There would be another chapter in the agitation and anger of the people, true, but I can assure you that there is already a surfeit of these things in Prussia. I cannot really contradict that calculation of chances by the Progressives. Our rulers have long ago ceased to tremble at addresses to the Throne, deputations, and popular feeling; they know well how categorically they are considered by the latter.

Their only question is—Have we money and reliable soldiers? They tremble before every junior officer who reads the *Volkszeitung*,[2] before every word in Parliament which could attract the soldiers, but not before anything else. You are right in your view that as long as the army remains loyal, the people cannot make use of any material power. Their régime will last until the army declares for the constitution or until it is broken in a foreign war—provided we had the good fortune, as in England in 1688 with the Prince of Orange, of a split occurring in the higher circles, and, for example, the Crown Prince himself declaring for the constitution. This situation is cruelly clear to us, and I must therefore defend the Prussian people against your remark that it would be doomed to being rightly despised in Germany by a longer duration of this régime. If Germany condemns us for this reason, then I think that it would pass a very hasty judgment. Where a disciplined army of 200,000 men still holds obediently together, a people has never accomplished anything by force. In 1789 the army mutinied with the people; in 1830 Charles X had hardly 12,000 men in Paris under the weakest leadership; in 1848 half the Government was for the revolt and a large part of the officer corps too. Whether a *coup de main*, as in 1848 here, would be possible today is doubtful alike to all intelligent persons and to the agitators; I am not practiced in these matters, but I can assure you that I have heard a different judgment from no one, and I know very well that Bismarck longs for a riot even more eagerly than Napoleon did on December 2.

[2] A democratic newspaper published in Berlin.

15. Society and the Proletariat

Manifesto of the Sixty (February 17, 1864)[*]

The Manifesto given below was drafted by sixty French labor leaders to support labor candidates running in Paris in the by-elections of 1864 for the Legislative Assembly. Labor had also put up candidates in the general election of the previous year; but, partly for the reason explained in the Manifesto, the results had been disappointing. The workers had voted overwhelmingly for the liberal candidates rather than for those of labor.

In the Manifesto, the Sixty stress the identity of bourgeois and working-class interests, and the interdependence of their fates in the common struggle against authoritarianism. In France authoritarianism took the form of Napoleon III's political and social order. In most of the rest of Europe it expressed the will of absolute monarchy and the nobility, that is of the persisting forces of the Old Régime. Although the workers were becoming class-conscious wherever modern industrialism expanded, they also were aware of the fact that the new capitalists were not their only enemy, and not necessarily their major one. At a certain stage in the evolution of labor-capitalist relations, class conflict became acute in fact; but to a greater or lesser degree, depending upon circumstances, workers of the new industrialism shared for decades, often up to 1914, the essential ideas of the Sixty about democracy.

The theories of the Manifesto are non-Marxian in origin. Some of them derive from Proudhon. Others, for example the one emphasizing the right to organize, were borrowed from English experience. Most striking is the continuing power of the ideals of the French Revolution. Workers not merely in France, but also in the other countries that had felt the effects of the Revolution, quickly drew the implications of liberal and

[*] Albert Thomas, *Le Second Empire (1852-1870) in Histoire Socialiste, 1789-1900*, ed., Jean Jaurès. (Paris: Publications Jules Rouff et Cie., 1907), X, 215-22.

democratic thought for the improvement of their own condition. In the light of the ideas in the Manifesto the usual concentration upon the study of Marxism for understanding the
labor movement of the nineteenth century is not in accord
with history. Emphasis upon Marxism needs to be moderated
after an investigation of the role of other socialist theories and
of liberal and democratic ideals and practices in the development of the working class.

On May 31, 1863 the workers of Paris, more concerned with the
triumph of the opposition than with their own interests, without hesitation and without haggling over their support voted for the list published in the newspapers. Inspired by their devotion to liberty, they
furnished a strikingly new and irrefutable proof of this devotion. In
this way the victory of the opposition was not only as complete as
was ardently desired, but even more impressive than many had dared
to hope.

Workers' candidates were admitted, it is true; but they were supported with a moderation that everyone had to admire. In upholding
their candidacy only secondary considerations were advanced, and in
view of the exceptional situation which gave the general elections a
particular character, the supporters intentionally abstained from pos-
ing the problem of poverty. In regard to propaganda and argument,
the proletariat, this evil of modern society as slavery and serfdom
were of the ancient and medieval societies, attempted to express itself with true reserve. Those who acted had foreseen their defeat, but
they thought it a good idea to take a first step. This candidacy seemed
necessary to them to affirm the profoundly democratic spirit of the
great city.

In the next elections conditions will no longer be the same. By
electing nine deputies the liberal opposition in Paris has secured
great satisfaction. Whoever they might be, the newly elected, chosen
under the same conditions, would add nothing to the importance of
the vote of May 31; whatever might be their eloquence, it would
scarcely add to the brilliance of the orators of the opposition. There is

not a point in the democratic program which like them we would not want to implement. Let us say once and for all that we are using this word 'democracy' in the purest and most radical sense.

But if we are in agreement politically, are we in agreement socio-economically? Are the reforms we desire and the institutions we want the liberty to erect acceptable to all those who represent the liberal party in the legislative body? The question is the Gordian knot of the situation.

One fact illustrates bluntly and sadly the difficulties of the workers' position.

In a country whose constitution rests upon universal suffrage, and where everyone invokes and extols the principles of 1789, we are obliged to justify workers' candidates, to tell minutely and at length *how* and *why*, to avoid not only the unjust accusations of the timid and reactionary but the fears and dislikes of our friends. Universal suffrage has made us of age *politically*, but we still have to be emancipated *socially*. The liberty won so energetically and patiently by the middle class must be extended to all the citizens of a democratic country like France. *Equal political rights necessarily imply equal social rights.*

It has been repeated endlessly that there are no more classes, that since 1789 all Frenchmen are equal before the law. Yet we who have no other property than our hands, we who must submit every day to the legitimate or arbitrary conditions of capital; we who live under exceptional laws[1] such as the law of associations and Article 1781, which prejudice our interests as well as our dignity, find it difficult to believe that equality exists here.

We who in a country where we have the right to select deputies have not always the means of learning to read, who for lack of the power to assemble or to organize freely are powerless to institute vocational training, and who see this precious instrument of industrial progress become the privilege of capital, cannot help feeling disillusioned.

[1] These were laws passed with the purpose of curbing socialist and trade-union activities.

We whose children often spend their young years in the demoralizing and unwholesome atmosphere of the factory or in an apprenticeship even now little short of domestic service; we whose wives, in a move contrary to their nature and destructive to the family, leave the home for excessively hard work; we who have not the right to agree among ourselves to defend peaceably our wages, to assure ourselves against unemployment—*we declare that the equality inscribed into law is not so written into practice and still has to be realized in fact.* Men who are deprived of education and capital cannot combat selfish and oppressive demands through liberty and solidarity. They must submit inevitably to control by capital, and their interests remain subordinated to other interests.

We know that interests do not regulate themselves, that they avoid the law, that they can be reconciled only by means of particular agreements as mobile and changing as the interests themselves. Without liberty for all conciliation is impossible. We advance to the conquest of our rights peaceably and loyally, but energetically and persistently. Our liberation would soon show real progress in the morale of the workers, that huge multitude vegetating in what is called the *proletariat* and which, to use a more exact expression, we shall call the wage-earners *(salariat)*.

We say, to those who imagine that we shall organize resistance in the form of the strike as soon as we acquire liberty, that they do not know the workers; they pursue a greater and more fruitful course than that of exhausting themselves in daily struggles, from which the two sides would emerge in the end only to face ruin for the one and misery for the other. The Third Estate used to say: What is the Third Estate? Nothing. What should it be? Everything. We say to ourselves that the bourgeoisie, our elder in emancipation, in 1789 knew how to absorb the nobility and destroy unjust privilege; for us it is not a matter of destroying the rights which the middle class justly enjoys but of winning for ourselves the same freedom of action. In France as the democratic country *par excellence a few cannot be allowed to monopolize* the privilege of all political rights, all social reform, and every instrument of progress. In the nature of things the nation in which the spirit of equality is inborn tends irresistibly to make this the heritage of all.

Every means of progress which cannot be extended and popularized in such a way as to contribute to the general welfare down to the lowest layer of society is not completely democratic, since the withholding of this means constitutes a privilege. The law should be broad enough to allow each man, individually or collectively, to develop his abilities, to use his strength, talents, and intelligence without any limitation except respect for the freedom of his neighbor.

Let no one accuse us of longing for agrarian laws, an unreal equality which would put everyone on the Procrustean bed, [laws providing for] equal division of property, maximum, forced tax, etc. It is high time to make an end of these lying rumors spread by our enemies and taken up by the ignorant. Liberty to work, to be trusted, to have mutual responsibility constitutes our dreams. The day when these come true for the glory and prosperity of a country dear to us, there will be neither bourgeois nor working class, neither owners nor workers; but all citizens will be alike in the rights they hold.

It is said to us that the elected deputies can ask for all these reforms we need and can do so better than we can; for they are the representatives of all and chosen by all.

We shall answer that we are not represented, and this is why we raise the question of workers' candidacies. We know that one does not speak of industrial candidacies, commercial candidacies, military candidacies, journalist candidacies, etc.; *but the thing is there even if the word is not.* Is not a very great part of the legislative body made up of large landowners, industrialists, business men, generals, journalists, etc., who vote quietly, or who speak only in their offices and only on questions of their specialties?

A very few speak on general matters. Of course we think that elected workers should and could defend the general interests of the democracy; but even if they should confine themselves to supporting the special interests of the most numerous class—what a specialty! They would fill a hole in a legislative body lacking in representation of manual labor. We who have at our service no fortune, contacts, public offices, or publicity are forced to give our candidacy a clear and meaningful title, and to call things as much as we can by their rightful names.

We are not at all represented, for in a recent meeting of the legislature there was a unanimous expression of sympathy in favor of the working class, but no voice was raised to formulate as we understand them, moderately but firmly, our aspirations, desires, and rights.

We who refuse to believe that misery is a divine institution have no representation. Charity, a Christian virtue, has recognized its own impotence as a social institution. Doubtless in the good old days of divine right, when the king and nobles considered themselves as fathers and elders of the people and when happiness and equality were confined to heaven, charity had to be a social institution.

In the days of universal suffrage and popular sovereignty, it is and can no longer be more than a private virtue. The vices and weaknesses of human nature will always leave a wide enough field in which brotherhood can be practiced; but *undeserved* misery such as that in the form of sickness, insufficient wages, or unemployment encloses the vast majority of workers of good will in an iron ring—such misery we solemnly declare can be made to disappear and will disappear. Why has no one made the distinction? *We do not want to be either dependents or charity cases; we do want to become equals; we renounce alms; we wish justice.*

No, we are not represented; for no one has said that the spirit of antagonism is abating daily in the popular classes. Enlightened by experience, *we do not hate men, but we want to change things.* No one has said that the law of association is only a scarecrow which instead of destroying the evil increases it by closing the exit for whoever believes himself oppressed.

No, we are not represented; for in the matter of labor chambers a strange confusion has grown up in the minds of those who used to recommend them. According to them the labor chamber [*chambre syndicale*] would be composed of owners and workers in the manner of professional trustees, referees chosen to decide from day to day questions which may arise. But what we ask for is a chamber made up entirely of workers elected by universal suffrage, a *Chamber of*

Labor analogous to the Chamber of Commerce, whereas a kind of court is offered us.

No, we are not represented; for no one has mentioned the considerable movement within the working classes to organize their credit. Who knows that now thirty-five mutual-credit societies are functioning in Paris? They contain the germ; but for their complete flowering they would need sun and liberty.

On principle few democrats of intelligence contest the justice of our demands and no one denies us the right to make them prevail.

The opportunity, the ability of the candidates, the probable obscurity of their names at the time of the choice, since they will be chosen from among the workers practicing their trades, are the questions raised in concluding that our plan is not practicable and that besides we should lack publicity.

First, we assert that after twelve years of patience the opportune moment has come; we should not admit that we must wait for the next general elections six years away. In this way eighteen years would be needed before a workers' election could be opportune—twenty-one years after 1848! What better districts could one choose than the first and fifth! There more than anywhere else should be elements of success.

The vote of May 31 has decisively settled in Paris the great question of liberty. The country is calm. Is it not wise politically to test the power of free institutions *which can facilitate the transition from the old society* founded on wages to the future society to be built on common right? Is there not danger in waiting for a crisis, when passions are aroused by general distress?

Would not the success of the workers' candidates have a great moral effect? It would prove that our ideas are understood, our conciliatory feelings appreciated, and that no one is afraid to practice what he recognizes theoretically as just.

Would it be true that the workers' candidates must possess the qualities of orators and publicists? We think not. It would suffice if they know how to appeal to justice by explaining clearly the reforms we ask for. Would the vote given them not give their words a greater authority than the best orator would have? Coming from the midst of the masses, the meaning of these elections would be all the more striking in that the successful candidates would have been heretofore obscure and unknown. And has in fact the gift of eloquence or universal reputation been demanded up to now as a necessary condition of the chosen deputies?

In 1848 the election of workers made political equality a fact; in 1864 their election would mean social equality.

Unless one denies the evidence, one has to agree that a special class of citizens having need of direct representation does exist, since the chamber of the legislature is the ONLY spot where the workers would be able *worthily and freely to express their views and claim for themselves a share in the rights which other citizens enjoy.*

Let us examine the actual situation without any bitterness or prejudice. What does the democratic bourgeoisie want that we do not want with equal longing? Universal suffrage without any hindrance? We want that! Freedom of the press, of assembly, rule of common law? We want these. Complete separation of church and state, a balanced budget, municipal franchises? We want all those.

Without our help the bourgeoisie will hardly obtain or keep these rights and liberties, the essence of a democratic society.

What do we wish even more than it, or at least more energetically because we are more directly interested in it? *Free compulsory primary education and the freedom to work.*

Education develops and strengthens the feeling of human dignity, that is to say the knowledge of human rights and duties. He who is enlightened appeals to reason and not to force to realize his obligations.

If freedom of labor does not serve as a counterweight to commercial freedom, we shall see a financial aristocracy. The lower middle class, like the workers, will soon be no more than its servants. Is it not apparent that today, instead of being widespread, credit is being concentrated in a few hands? Does not the Bank of France exemplify the flagrant contradiction of all economic principles? It enjoys both the monopoly of issue of paper money and the unlimited right to raise the interest rate!

*Without us, we repeat, the bourgeoisie can build nothing solid;
without its help our liberation can be delayed a long time still.*

Let us then unite for a common goal—the triumph of true democracy.

Publicized by us and supported by the bourgeoisie, the workers'
candidacies would be the living proof of the serious and lasting union of democrats, without distinction of class or position. Shall we be
abandoned? Shall we be forced to pursue in isolation the realization
of our ideas? For the good of all let us hope not.

To avoid all misunderstanding, let us summarize:

The essential political meaning of workers' candidacies would be
this:

To fortify by completing the activity of the liberal opposition. In
the most modest terms it has asked for the necessary liberties; the
workers' deputies would ask for the needed economic reforms.

EUROPE IN THE
NINETEENTH CENTURY

VOLUME II

EUROPE IN THE NINETEENTH CENTURY

A Documentary Analysis of Change and Conflict

VOLUME II

1870-1914

By

EUGENE N. ANDERSON
STANLEY J. PINCETL, JR.
DONALD J. ZIEGLER

THE **BOBBS-MERRILL** COMPANY, INC.
A SUBSIDIARY OF HOWARD W. SAMS & CO., INC.
1720 EAST 38TH STREET · INDIANAPOLIS 6, INDIANA

Preface

The two volumes presented here contain contemporary documents chosen to discuss changes during the nineteenth century in the institutional structure of European life. The first volume offers sources relating to the period from about 1815 to 1870, the second volume from 1870 to 1914. The documents analyze basic issues treated in every standard textbook and have been selected to elucidate the matters of what was at stake and why an event had historical importance.

The criteria for including the materials may reveal the nature of the objective toward which the editors have aimed. (1) The documents illustrate major developments in all important aspects of society. (2) Each document illustrates a fundamental development in more than one country. (3) Each reveals the significance of the subject for other aspects of social life than that with which it is directly concerned. (4) In the case of foreign relations only documents are used which discuss the issues in connection with internal affairs as well. Questions of diplomatic policy alone are excluded as too restricted in scope. (5) Since basic changes during the century occurred to a greater extent in France and Germany than elsewhere, a larger number of documents relates to the history of each of these two countries than to that of any other country. (6) Each document is selected from the history of a state closely involved in the issue under discussion. (7) The documents are written by persons active in affairs rather than by men of pure theory. The authors of documents include representatives of royalty, the nobility, the bourgeoisie, several professions, handworkers, and industrial workers. The only major group not represented is that of the peasantry, for this social group has left few first-hand records of its reactions. (8) Since the reader has easy access to many sources relating to British history, documents pertaining directly to the life of England have been excluded. Wherever relevant and practicable, materials have been selected that compare conditions in the continental countries with those of Great Britain and, at times, of the United States. (9) Since the documents have to do with changes in the structure of European life, they discuss ideas in relation to institutional change and may be read as intellectual history. (10) They are spread chronologically over the century so that except for the 1820's every decade is represented. (11) Approximately an equal amount of material is offered about social and economic aspects and about political and constitutional life. (12) Each selection is interesting in itself.

The length of any one of the sources brought together in these volumes is determined by the needs of its writer. Some subjects are treated in much briefer compass than others. In a number of instances the editors have omitted the parts of a document which seemed irrelevant or unimportant for understanding the whole.

Many more documents were rejected than were approved for inclusion in this publication. Suitable materials proved difficult to find, and, when they were on occasion abundant, lack of space compelled the editors to reproduce only one or two points of view. The pleasure of imagining for himself other attitudes and comments is usually left to the reader.

The documents are arranged in chronological order for the sake of convenience and because of the difficulty of finding any other organization that would not mislead the reader. Since the documents are few in number the reader should be able to relate any one to the relevant topic of study. Yet each is so rich in content that it may be related to several subjects within its chronological period. The impact of the selections upon the reader's thinking is and should be cumulative; thus arrangement of the documents under general headings has been avoided lest the reader be confused or discouraged from using each item as variously as it should be used.

Most of the documents are translated for the first time. Translations from the French and German languages are the work of the editors and Pauline R. Anderson. Stanley J. Pincetl has assumed general responsibility for translations from the French, Donald J. Ziegler for those from the German; but each of the translations has been checked for accuracy by two other persons. Professor Lenore M. Breslin translated the selection by Donoso Cortes and Paul Sonnino the essay by Baron Sonnino. Mrs. Jean Hanchett and Mrs. Stanley Pincetl have aided in translating a number of the French documents. Professor Harold Lionetti has advised in the selection of Italian and Spanish materials, and Neal Brogden placed his special knowledge at our disposal in the choice of documents relating to French military reform. To all of them the editors express cordial thanks.

The editors hope that use of the materials will justify the unexpected amount of time and energy which they have devoted to the preparation of these volumes.

EUGENE N. ANDERSON
University of California, Los Angeles
STANLEY J. PINCETL, JR.
San Diego State College
DONALD J. ZIEGLER
Carroll College (Wisconsin)

Contents

EUROPE IN THE
NINETEENTH CENTURY

VOLUME II

Introduction

The nineteenth century of European history lies between two long periods of war and revolution. Much of the character of the century derives from the continued reaction of society to the French Revolution and the Napoleonic expansion and from the complications leading to the wars and revolutions of the present century. Since the conflicts of 1789 to 1815 had affected all aspects of life, the way to reorganize society continued to be argued, especially before 1870, within the framework of the ideals and practices of the French Revolution and its opponents. At about the same time that Germany and Italy completed their political unification and the Balkan peoples asserted their national independence, the industrial revolution began to expand on the continent, modifying and often aggravating older sources of controversy, creating new bonds of social unity, engendering profound problems. Change and resistance to change in the internal affairs of each country characterize the century. The brief continental wars were as much civil wars as international conflicts; social reform was often both cause and effect.

I. The Period from 1815 to 1870

The issues provoked by the French Revolution dominated European society before 1870, and even after the events associated with 1870 their influence persisted. The servile peasantry demanded emancipation and in this period, legally speaking, gained its freedom (Readings 1, 12, and 13). Many landed aristocrats struggled to preserve the way of life of the Old Regime, including serfdom and privilege (Reading 2). Royalty, many nobles, and members of other social groups endeavored to maintain the status quo by preventing further revolution (Readings 3 and 4). To achieve their end they compelled the services of the bureaucracy, the church, and the educational system, thereby rendering crucial to all reformers the issue of civil rights (Reading 5). Many conservatives gravely doubted the wisdom of permitting widespread change in industrial production, transportation, and communication. Although desirous of the material benefits flowing from change, they feared the effects upon their own political and social status. On the other hand most of the bourgeoisie and many aristocrats welcomed material change as likely to improve their own role in society, and they saw it as an exponent of emerging liberalism and nationalism (Readings 1 and 7). Handicraftsmen and others whose world seemed disappearing found themselves constrained to adjust to a society in rapid transition (Reading 6). Some members of the passing order sank into the proletariat; others rose to be successful members of the bourgeoisie; still others formed a new lower middle class or status group for skilled services. Liberals and nationalists, forced to search for new institutions and procedures for carrying out their ideals and ambitions, were experimenting with constitutional forms (Readings 1, 8, and 9) and with economic forms (Reading 14). As pressure for reform increased decade by decade, conservatives sought ways of preserving what they called orderly society (Readings 10 and 11). Some of them recognized the need for concessions and devised means of preserving authoritarian government and society behind a liberal, national, constitutional façade (Reading 15 B), thereby frustrating the liberals (Reading 15 C).

By 1870 Europe sustained a greater variety of ways of life, standards of living, forms of government, and social organizations than ever before in its history, even though common trends appeared to a greater or lesser extent in all countries. The Old Régime, still strong in most of Europe, had clearly weakened, its leading forces everywhere fighting a rearguard action. The peasantry slowly awakened to a sense of its social importance. The industrial proletariat, newly conscious of its numerical power, began to form a class or social group of its own (Reading 16). The bourgeoisie, aided by some of the nobility and, in varying forms, by other social groups, in some countries took the lead in experiments with social, economic, and political institutions; in countries where the social power of the bourgeoisie was still weak its intellectuals by their writings stimulated the demand for change. European society, transformed at varying speeds according to country and area, evolved organizations hitherto unimagined.

II. The Period from 1870 to 1914

Many of the forces and sources of friction which had dominated prior decades continued after 1870 to characterize European life. Two additional factors appeared that basically affected the course of society, namely the expansion of industrialism and the greatly augmented significance of power politics and the power state.

Europe now harbored a larger number of power states than this small continent had ever beheld. Spreading competition in internal and international affairs imposed responsibilities upon government which were comparable in nature to those under absolute monarchy but different in that they had a popular basis. Awareness of governmental responsibility in the several states varied with the level of culture. The level of culture in turn depended to a major extent upon the expansion and social maturity of modern industrialism, although —significant of the complicated life of the century—the prestige in international affairs of a power state was not yet entirely correlated with the degree of industrialization within its borders. A country of large geographic expanse and numerous population like Russia enjoyed respect from a preceding age which by material and social standards this empire did not then merit.

In 1914 standards for judging conditions appeared as confused as they had been at the beginning of the nineteenth century, so that control of internal and international affairs suffered from the inconsistency of criteria. The varied cultural stages of Europe's nations or regions resembled a Dadaist collage; yet all nations shared in the effort to industrialize and to impose upon government a burden of social responsibility, for which few governments were prepared. A close correlation existed as well between stability in government and society on the one hand and industrialization on the other, which entailed increased economic opportunities and a rising standard of living. Or conversely, where industrialism largely or entirely failed to develop, where opportunities for material improvement had not increased and the condition of the masses had improved but little, government employed physical coercion most. Autocracies (Reading 11) or countries of inefficient authoritarianism employing extreme means of protection evoked radical countermeasures (Reading 6). A spectrum analysis would show that a majority of countries possessed conditions somewhere between Russian autocracy and British liberalism.

In the period after 1870 certain problems resembled those of previous decades; thus the examples found in succeeding pages may be applied to many earlier situations. First, nationalistic issues, involving the use of native language (Reading 5), or concerning the total reform of society (Reading 13), recall similar ones in Germany and Italy before these countries were unified. In the later period, however, these issues affected the life of empires and the aspirations of small states which considered themselves torsos. Second, the forces of the Old Régime continued the effort to retain their positions of political and social leadership in the new industrial culture, in some cases—irrespective of country—by adjusting to new conditions and accepting the bourgeoisie as allies, in others by refusing to adjust and deploying the physical force of government in their defense (Reading 11). Third, the power state continued to require the acceptance of at least the new sources of strength created by industrialism and the ideal of popular participation in a minimum of public affairs (Readings 1 A and B). Here one sees an age-old process in a new stage, the power state imposing its demands upon the groups of the Old Régime (Reading 3) and upon those of industrialism, although doing so nationally with different degrees of awareness and response. Military service (Readings 1 A and B) and education (Reading 4) came especially into question, as did also the kind of economic and social structure most conducive to the creation of state power (Reading 9).

Industrialism, already emergent in the previous period, began to transform the structure of society. Should the industrial working class become a proletariat or a lower middle-class group? At first neither lower nor upper classes knew where the new mass fitted into the social structure, and professors (Reading 2), trade union leaders (Reading 8), socialists (Reading 6), and bourgeois politicians (Reading 12) debated the problem and sought a practical solution. It became evident likewise that political unification alone did not satisfy popular demand in respect to the efforts of the nation state. Popular constitutional government, insofar as it failed to improve the social and economic life of the people, became of doubtful value (Reading 7), and on the eve of World War I authoritarian constitutional monarchy supplied the prevailing form of government and society. Germany furnished the model, Russia offered a caricature, Baron Sonnino chose constitutional monarchism for Italy; France alone among the powers held to the popular republic. Where local government was corrupt (Reading 10) the central government, no matter how ostensibly parliamentary, could not escape contamination.

By 1914 Europe had scarcely begun to achieve the new society made possible under industrialism. The documents from the years after 1870, like those of the preceding period, exemplify the range of problems discussed and of solutions proposed; but nowhere is it certain that the author of a document has found a solution, and often he does not even pose what subsequently proved to be the essential question. Reading the documents may make the American student reared in the tradition of the eighteenth-century Enlightenment aware of the great variety of beliefs and ways of life possible at any one time in the life of a continent with three thousand years of history. It may lead him to consider whether this Europe should have dared to risk its civilization in a world war, whether the kind of society that Europe experienced in the nineteenth century did not bear within it the explosive forces of the twentieth century.

1. Military Organization and National Power

The French Revolution compelled each power state of Europe to maintain its competitive position by military reform. During the Revolution France developed the national conscript army; but the Bourbon kings later established a system partly conscript and partly mercenary that persisted to 1870. On the other hand, in 1814 Prussia introduced reforms that proved able to pave the way for the victories of the German wars of unification. German success forced the French to reconsider their system of recruitment. The conflict of views seen in the speeches of Deputy Raudot and of Thiers, president of the Republic, may be regarded as typical of the ways that leaders in all continental states, including Prussia, differed in times of crisis over the question of defense. The professional military, the rulers, and other conservatives frequently advocated a long term of service and a relatively small, thoroughly drilled army with unquestioned loyalty to the régime. The liberals stood for a nation in arms, in which every able-bodied male served for a short time, at most two years, and in which universal military service and universal male suffrage complemented each other in a liberal state and society. Each side saw the close connection between military organization and social organization. Each side believed that its plan would afford the nation its maximum strength. It is one of the extraordinary manifestations of European history that under the stress of national defeat French liberal republicans should consider the Prussian military organization an ideal worthy of imitation. Thiers, on the other hand, remained one of the last statesman of a major European nation to defy power politics by rejecting the urge to adopt a military organization and methods similar to the German and to favor instead a solution along purely French lines. The French parliament in the main followed his advice, and France found herself again unprepared to withstand a German advance in 1914.

A. Deputy Raudot: *Speech Advocating the Introduction into France of the Prussian Military System* (1872)[*]

Gentlemen, the French are usually accustomed in all questions to rely on specialists. On so grave a question as this we are very handicapped; the experts are completely divided. We hear a famous general recommend three years of service; we hear another famous general recommend five years' service; and I rank among the famous generals the President of the Republic [i.e., Thiers; there is general hilarity in the Assembly], who, certainly, would like to obtain not five years but seven or nine years of service.

Gentlemen, the majority of us are neither generals, colonels, nor captains, and yet we must decide on a matter of extreme gravity. For that purpose, it seems to me that we should have recourse to the lessons of contemporary history and to common sense, and with permission I shall give you the result of my study and reflections. . . .

The choice of service is now between three and five years.

The committee wants five years. But we stated in the first part of the law that service would be personal, compulsory, and universal. What would happen upon the application of this principle? Five years of service? If we decided that all the eligible men should serve in the army for this length of time, you would have an army so big that financially you would be completely ruined; you would have more than 800,000 men under arms. It would be impossible for you to tolerate this situation because, under the pretext of increasing the military forces, you would destroy your financial strength and the means of reproducing your wealth, and in the end France would see its strength diminished instead of increased.

With a five-year system it would be necessary to divide the levy into two classes, one group serving for six months or a year, and the other serving for five years.

What now becomes of the great principle that you have put at the

[*] *Annales de l'Assemblée nationale,* June 7, 1872, pp. 188-95.

beginning of your law? ["Very good! Very good!" from several benches.]

This great principle is three-quarters destroyed, and things remain about as they are today. . . .

You are therefore going to put a part of the soldiers into the army for five years; the other part will serve only six months or a year. Following that, the men will return to their homes and be in the reserve.

The five-year soldiers will also enter the reserve at the end of that time.

How many men will that make in the reserve with an organization such as the committee proposed? About 800,000, and the regular army will be composed of about 425,000 men, not including the gendarmes.

But, gentlemen, if a major war breaks out, what will we do? We would call up the reserves; and I maintain that we would have to recall all the reserves. The pressure of public opinion, in case of a great war, will force you to call all the reserves. But if you have 800,-000 reserves and an army of 425,000 men, what will happen? The reserves, much more numerous than your regular army, will, as it were, drown your army; for every man in the army you will have two men in the reserves.

Will these reserves be real soldiers? Here are men who have been in a regiment for six months, a year; but after that you send them back home. Here are men who have served for five years or four years, and you send them back home. But what will these reserves do in the regiments when they are recalled? That is what I am wondering.

They will do exactly what the reserves did during the last war. Then also you had reserves who had been trained for six months; you had reserves which were made up of veterans. What became of all them during the last war?

You had masses of men wandering the roads and railroads, trying to rejoin their regiments, and three-quarters of the time they did not succeed. As for those who succeeded in finding their regiments, they knew neither their officers nor noncommissioned officers, and no one knew them. In short in this great war, and war is now carried on with unbelievable rapidity, these reserves which should have doubled the strength of our regiments were useless. I am afraid that the reserves organized according to your law will give exactly the same results.

What should be done? I will tell you one thing which may ruffle national pride but which nevertheless seems to me dictated by simple common sense.

We must do what our enemies have done. We must adopt their system. The Prussians, although not so wealthy as we were, created a system which has allowed them in peacetime to assemble a modest number of men. This did not overburden their finances, and in case of war they could throw against the enemy almost an infinite power. We must do the same thing. The Prussians have a three-year service. Let us adopt a three-year law to allow all men to serve with the colors.

M. Marquis de Castellane: They do not serve three years in Prussia!

M. Raudot: Almost all of them do, and the *Landwehr* has not only all the veterans but also men who have not served in the active army, whereas your territorial army, made up exclusively of men thirty to forty years of age, will be composed only of men who are not capable of making war.

Several members: Why not?

M. Raudot: Why not! Because men of thirty to forty years of age will say that there are 1,800,000 young men of twenty to thirty years, in their prime, the majority of them unmarried; men of thirty to forty who are almost all married will not leave before them.

You want to form a territorial army made up of men from thirty to forty years old. That is not the way it should be done; as in Prussia, you should have taken men from twenty-seven to thirty-seven years old.

The Chairman: And even up to forty-three years of age.

M. Raudot: I repeat: How can you form a real army capable of making war, capable of resistance, when the men of twenty to thirty years have not been organized? They are the ones who are the strength of France and must be organized.

From the Government Bench: That is what we are doing.

M. Raudot: You are doing it! Well, I shall show you how you are doing it.

According to the report, you have 1,215,000 men in the first nine classes, not including the exemptions and the men provisionally exempted, whom you declare that you will call in time of war, and who will number at least 450,000. These 1,215,000 men include more than 800,000 men from the reserves.

I say that the 1,200,000 men cannot be officered in the present army. . . .

I suppose you to have at present 150 regiments of infantry. I am told that we will have 153. Good. There will be 70 cavalry regiments and 36 artillery regiments. I agree to all that. But how many men can the officers of these regiments command? I maintain that your reserves and your army cannot be staffed in the regiments of which I have been speaking, and that if you are to have a number of regiments capable of staffing 1,200,000 men permanently, you will ruin yourselves financially. [Various movements.]

What did the Prussians do? They created two armies; they organized an active army and a territorial army. Everything is territorial in Prussia, and that is what makes its army superior. I will prove it to you if you wish. The Prussians have two armies with their complete cadres, and these two armies conduct annual exercises, yearly carrying out big maneuvers. This is how Prussia can have a very considerable number of men always ready to make war.

With your army composed of the regiments just referred to you will never be able to staff the reserves. 1,200,000 men are going to be called into the army which you expect to form! But the army will be harmed by the enormous number of reserves arriving at the outbreak of war, for whom, I repeat, you will not be able to provide officers.

What happened when the last war started? The Minister of War sent orders to all the recruits to rejoin. What happened to these recruits? Were they able to rejoin their regiments? Were they able to serve usefully? No, gentlemen. Why? Because you had not adopted a system of prompt mobilization; because afterward the men called up did not know their officers or their noncommissioned officers and were not known themselves. For example, in a regiment of 1,200 men, you pour in 20,000 men. So far as I can see, the regiment was lost from that very instant. It would have taken three months for the newcomers to be able to amalgamate with the veterans.

Let me recall facts of great importance.

The war of 1870 was declared toward the middle of July. On the 15th of July, the order was sent from Berlin to all the army corps of Prussia, the active army and the *Landwehr,* to mobilize; eleven days later all the army corps were ready.

On July 15, as I was saying, came the order of mobilization; on August 4, unless I am wrong, the battle of Wissenbourg; on August 6, Reischoffen. There were already almost 500,000 Germans in France, while you had an army of not more than 240,000 men. Several days later, August 14, came the battle of Borny, August 16 that of Gravelotte, August 18 that of St. Privat; that is, twenty-four days after the order of mobilization the Prussians had brought into France enough men to pursue the remains of MacMahon's army, surround the army of 200,000 Frenchmen, and force it to retreat into Metz.

At this time there were at least 600,000 Germans in France, and when we speak of the degeneration of the French army, I am completely of the opinion of General Ducrot. The French army still had all its qualities; but it was facing an enemy infinitely superior in numbers and organization. It is doubtless true that encircling movements could have caused some disaster to the Prussians, if we had had distinguished generals at our head, but we should have had in addition to generals of genius a sufficient number of troops. When we were one against three or four, the encircling movements of the Germans were always sure of success, and in fact that is what happened at Metz, Sedan, and everywhere.

Why, I repeat, did the Germans succeed? Because they were always at least two against one.

All the wars of the future will be conducted as the Germans conducted this one. It is no doubt a question of organization; but it is especially a question of numbers and mobility. Mobilization must be extremely rapid, or nothing worth while will be achieved.

Under your bill you have not the officers necessary to staff your reserves, and you do not have a suitable organization to carry out rapid mobilization.

M. Marquis de Vogué: The organizational law has not been presented.

M. Raudot: M. de Vogué, permit me to tell you that in Article 37 all matters of organization are compromised—the thing is as clear as day. When you decide how many years should be spent in the active army, in the reserve, in the territorial army, you decide everything. When you announce that the territorial army will be made up of men of thirty to forty years of age, you decide everything in advance. Your territorial army is not at its post. . . .

We have just been told: "But we are going into an immense unknown; do not throw yourself into the unknown!"

I am moved by this observation in general, but it implies that the test has not been made here. It was made, and unfortunately at our expense. [Various interruptions.]

It was made when you saw Prussia, which then had only 19,500,000 inhabitants, declare war on Austria, vanquish not only Austria and its veteran troops, but Hanover, Württemberg, Bavaria. When you saw this small nation of only 19,500,000 perform such prodigies, did you not recognize that the reason for its success was its energetic and intelligent organization?

This is not the only test which was made. A second was made at our expense in 1870. But do you refuse to admit that we were vanquished, not because we were completely degenerate—although I am among those who maintain that there were many reasons for decadence in France, I do not pretend that our troops were not composed of valiant soldiers—but because against us we had numbers and so intelligent and powerful an organization that we could not resist? That is what makes me insist on our adoption of the Prussian system in its entirety.

We seem to believe that in adopting three-year service as in Prussia, we will be completely freed from further duty once we have done these three years. That is not correct. In Prussia men are three years with the colors; but for seven years they are at the disposition of the government; and furthermore every year the army corps are mobilized completely and carry out maneuvers. In short, the army is always ready to march.

I was reading again yesterday about the composition of the effective forces of the German army. At this time it has on active duty slightly fewer men than we have; but that would not prevent it from sending 1,200,000 men to France if we had the misfortune to be at war with Germany tomorrow.

If you want to provide for something efficient, adopt its system. It was tested, it will be as feasible in France as in Prussia. It will be even more effective. Is not our population as energetic, as suitable for military service as the German population? Certainly.

We should not overlook the fact that there are two great schools of thought on this question, whose arguments should be weighed and examined.

There is the school of those who pretend that with a middle-sized army we can vanquish armies much more numerous. This is the old system.

I know very well that on this point I have the illustrious President of the French Republic against me. I have read his speech of 1868, when the proposal was made to organize mobile battalions, and here is what M. Thiers said, amid the applause of a crowd, in answer to Marshal Niel, who had spoken of the 1,300,000 men which Germany could put under arms:

We should not trust this fantastic figure which is bandied about all over Europe today. There is a fatal impulse to exaggerate armaments, and I deplore it, as you do; but nevertheless we should not have figures which are altogether fantastic presented as real. If these figures were true, we should ultimately have to despair of the future of France. Italy would have 900,000 men to oppose us, Prussia would have 1,300,000; that would make 2,200,000 men under arms between the two powers. These are fables which have no reality. And I may say it because we should reassure our country. We need not persuade her that she is in such frightful perils.

When we see that the army with which we might confront the enemy would be, depots deducted, 540,000 men with seven years of service, 600,000 with eight years, and 680,000 with nine years, I say that France would have time to breathe behind so powerful an army, and I have confidence myself that this army would allow time for the militia national guard to organize.

Is it so difficult a thing to organize the militia national guard?

You have too little faith in our nation, much less than you should. The principle on which the laws of 1831 and 1851 were based was this: When war breaks out, thanks to the nature of our nation, there will be an immediate outburst of patriotic fervor such as I found in 1840—when war was very improbable—and I am convinced that in this state of mind you would find a highly useful zeal. I am going to cite you an example:

Apparently France is as military as Italy. Well, did you not see Italy organize with extreme rapidity twenty or thirty battalions of the national guard, which were embarked at Genoa and sent into the south of the peninsula? Did they take longer than what I am asking of you now? Do you not always have two or three months, that is to say more time than is needed, to organize the militia national guard?

If it will cost you 20 or 30 millions for the militia national guard that you intend to organize, would it not be better to apply this money to the regular army so as to render it more capable, better supplied with everything and, thanks to a larger peacetime force, better prepared rapidly to enter the campaign?

There is only one way, I repeat, of making war, and it is to advance on the enemy as fast and as directly as possible. We do not carry out a defensive war when we can conduct an offensive. War should be made by an active army; therefore, it is the regular army that should be our first concern and on which we must concentrate all our efforts. As for the national guard, I believe that what was written in the laws of 1831 and 1851 will suffice.

M. Thiers, President of the Republic: Will you permit me to interrupt you since you quote me?

M. Raudot: Please go ahead.

M. Thiers: I claim the right to interrupt you about the quotation from my speech.

At the time of which you are speaking, I constantly said to Marshal Niel that everything we were doing to organize the reserves was just about useless because these reserves would arrive too late, and that the strength of a nation resides principally in an army vigorously organized on a peacetime footing.

I told Marshal Niel that all we would spend for the militia national guard, if we wished to staff it, would cost much more than the twenty millions of which they were talking and that all that money could be applied much more advantageously to the regular army in order to bring it up to 500,000 combatants. And if you had such an army around Metz, surely the misfortunes which we suffered would have been spared us.

As for myself, the long study which I have made of the issues has taught me that at the beginning of a war it is only the peacetime force which wages the first and decisive battles. In 1868, I constantly demanded that the sums which we wanted to spend to maintain the reserves, which would arrive only too late, should be assigned to the active force; and I say that again today we should be invincible, if all that we desired to spend on this system were assigned to having an active army of 700,000 to 750,000 men, because if 500,000 men with vigorous military training can take part in the first encounters, striking results will be obtained.

It is against the impracticable ideas that I protested and that I am protesting. You speak of an invasion of 1,300,000 men. I shall prove to you that this is an exaggeration, that Prussia did not move this number of soldiers, that she would not be able to; she mobilized 900,000 men.

M. Raudot: Gentlemen, I thank the President of the Republic for having interrupted me to confirm the ideas which he stated in 1868.

The President of the Republic believes that a strong army of 500,-000 to 600,000 men is sufficient to meet all the dangers which France may run.

There are the two systems face to face—that of the President of the Republic; that of those who believe that in case of war with Germany an army of 500,000 men, even if excellently organized and well commanded, would be insufficient.

Now the question is sharply defined. It is not only a matter of knowing if the length of service should be for five or for three years, but of knowing if we can have a large and good army at the same time, or if we should restrict ourselves to an army of 500,000 or 600,-000 men.

The President of the Republic: I did not say 500,000 or 600,000 men.

M. Raudot: Let us say 700,000, if you wish.

The Chairman: Article 37, which is at this moment under discussion, concerns only the length of service; the committee proposes five years, and several amendments demand that this length be reduced to three years. This is the only question for the moment.

M. Raudot: Gentlemen, do not try to diminish the importance of the debate.

After the two terrible experiences which we have seen with our own eyes, the war of 1866 and that of 1870, I think it is completely wrong to believe that a perfectly organized but relatively small army is sufficient.

We must not overlook the fact that the German army is the German nation in arms.

The President of the Republic: Not at all!

M. Raudot: Everything we have said about the excellence of the armies commanded by great generals was perfectly true before the two experiences of which I have spoken. But in face of the organization of the German army—for it is a matter not of the Prussian army but the German army, which is unfortunately still greater because of our disasters—we must remember what has just taken place; we have been told that if we had 250,000 more men in the line we should have been victorious. That is possible; but experience has shown that the German troops, even though their service is not five, six, or seven years, form a formidable, perfectly organized army which fights well. If you have against you an army of 1,300,000 men, what would you do with your 500,000 men? You could have some success, perhaps, but if the war were prolonged it would be the large battalions which would come out on top.

Note still another thing. Your organization does not permit the rapid mobilization of your limited army.

You have spoken of a territorial army organized by regions; but the regular army will not be made up by regions; the army corps will be recruited by administrative divisions. . . .

I know that you tell me that you are going to organize the army by administrative divisions and that the regiments will be formed not of men recruited in the region but of Frenchmen from all the departments.

How will you go about calling up the reserves so important to your system? You say that we will put them in the nearest regiments. But your recruits will not know their officers, and the officers will not know their soldiers. This will not make for homogeneous corps, ready to face the enemy. A certain length of time is needed for that; and you will not have the time. That is the important point.

Note that Prussia in the space of twenty-three days threw 500,000 men into France.

While you will be sending the reserves to their regiments and trying to absorb them, the enemy will invade the country; it will win battles against your inadequate armies, and all your recruits, your reserves, will be useless, as in the last war.

If you want to do something efficient, the Prussian system must be used as it is in Prussia. With the exception of the royal guard, which is recruited from the entire kingdom, all the territorial corps, the active army, and the *Landwehr* are recruited by administrative districts and by region.

The immense advantage of this system is that every year you may subject all the organized corps to maneuvers not ruinous to the treasury.

The entire army, soldiers and reserves, maintains a military *esprit*. And when war breaks out and orders are sent to the men of the region, within six or seven days all will have been mobilized; they know their officers and their noncommisioned officers, and they are known. They form compact regiments, while yours will not.

This is extremely rapid mobilization; you must equal it, or else you are sure to be vanquished.

Since the creation of the railroads, which allow an army of 100,000 men to be transported in two or three days, there has been a complete tactical change.

What Napoleon and all the great leaders have done previously can no longer occur. We must change with the times and take new conditions into account.

With this rapid mobilization of armies, war may be ended in a very short time; and he who is ready first is sure to be the victor.

I am told that we do not want to do as Prussia does because we would have army corps made up of the people of the same locality, and that may be dangerous. If you have army corps of Bretons, Burgundians, Provençals, or Languedocians, they would fight against each other. [Lively denials.] . . .

If you introduce the Prussian organization into France, you will have an army as easily mobilized, as well recruited, and as perfectly organized as the Prussian. You will have men who will know each other, who will be used to one another, who will touch elbows, who will be bound to each other. With the system which you recommend, you will have men who are strangers.

. . . .

It is said that this question of corps presents difficulties or dangers in France. But Prussia, which is composed of states, of conquered nations, for that reason should never have adopted it. But she did not fear having a territorial army corps in the Grand Duchy of Posen; she was not afraid of forming one in Hanover, which she had just annexed; and at this moment she is forming one in Alsace-Lorraine itself, despite the fact that she knows very well the hostile temper of the population. Why does she do this? Because she finds it so highly advantageous that she does not want to change anything in an organization of whose strength she is sure. She says to herself: "Yes, we shall have a hostile army corps there, but at the beginning of the war we shall send it far outside the territory and it will not be dangerous there but useful." And she is going to form the Alsatians into army corps.

M. Keller: No! No! Never, M. Raudot!

M. Raudot: Very well, I shall not speak of Alsace, despite the fact that it is true; but you, gentlemen, know that Prussia has no fear of establishing the territorial system even in the countries which she has just conquered, because it has so many advantages that it overcomes all disadvantages. If the territorial system of army corps is established in France, you will not have the drawbacks which are found in Prussia. You will find the promptness with which you can mobilize the men an advantage of primary importance, especially in case of war and especially in an offensive war; you would give heart to all those who have lost courage and make France invincible.

Gentlemen, what did we do to organize the French army in a modern fashion? We set out to crush all the ideas prevalent in all the different parts of France and we scattered all the men from these different areas among all the regiments.

The President of the Republic: And we did well!

M. Raudot: I do not deny that we did well toward destroying the former *esprit*. But we maintained regiments by conscription, and we wanted to make a family and an *esprit de corps* in the regiment.

Gentlemen, it is very difficult to give *esprit* to a conscript.

In regiments there are brave men in great numbers, but there are others who are not brave. In a campaign, in a battle there are men who give way, who are cowards, who get to the rear of the army, who pretend sickness, who become stragglers; they are the scourge of armies. Suppose that the battalion is composed of men of the same area. These men would be dishonored forever on return to their homes; whereas now when they have saved their skin, they return to their homes with no one knowing anything of their disgraceful conduct.

When you have men belonging to the same area in a corps and beside them in another corps men from another area, there is competition between them. One does not want to be inferior to his neighbor. If you would, for example, place Bretons beside Burgundians, there would be competition as to who is better. ["Yes! Yes! Very good! Very good!" from the Right.]

And I say the same of all the areas of France. But there is one thing which is still more important.

When it has lost battles at the center because of its organization, France is lost, vanquished, annihilated. For myself, I wish all parts of France to live! If we establish complete territorial army corps with their own generals, matériel, and organization, France will be invincible. In the provinces of unhappy France, after the battles which she has had the misfortune to lose, we have seen that there was nothing left. If there had been territorial army corps organized for a long time as I said, a different *esprit* would have animated all parts of France. Everywhere resistance would have appeared. I remain faithful to my lifelong ideas, and as a result of long meditation on many things I say that it is excessive centralization which has killed France! [Approval from various benches. Objection from others.]

Let us see to it that we have vitality everywhere, resistance everywhere, and that an order from the office of the Minister of War to attack the enemy is not needed. Then you will have security because the enemy will know that there is no way to break down a nation in which resistance is vigorously organized throughout. ["Very good! Very good!" from several benches.]

B. President Thiers: *Speech Advocating Adherence to the French Military Tradition* (June 7-8, 1872)[*]

Gentlemen, today's question is of the greatest interest to the nation, and if we make a mistake, I do not say that the future of France would be destroyed—it cannot be—but I say that it would be gravely compromised. It is this feeling of gravity that has kept me at work on this subject, and I now bring you the fruit of long reflection. . . .

Article 37 determines the length of service; it is on this essential subject that I came to an understanding with the committee.

We started from very different points of view. However, as was said several days ago in strong terms, it is the duty of good citizens to sacrifice all secondary considerations but not to sacrifice basic convictions. The committee has loyally done what it could to establish compulsory service—which from my point of view would be the least dangerous. In my opinion they have met the greatest objections in agreeing to a long-term service. I thank them very much! . . .

Now, gentlemen, I come to the subject itself. You will pardon me for speaking here with the utmost frankness and without deviating from the essentials of the discussion. No, I admit to my country that I do not share the prevailing opinion on this subject; I greatly distrust the current supposedly irresistible ideas in our country, and without being contentious I made it a point of honor and duty to resist them.

We are seeing today what took place in the eighteenth century, when after the battle of Rossbach we were concerned only with military exercises. All the military scientists of the period discussed the thin-order and deep-order drill; after the celebrated battle of Lützen, the oblique formation. Frederick the Great, that very powerful, intelligent, individual mind, made fun of us. He knew very well that it was not this or that military system, this or that fashion of lining up on the battlefield which had brought our misfortune and his glory; he knew that it was the genius of the man who was in command on that day. . . .

[*] *Annales de l'Assemblée nationale,* June 8, 1872, pp. 200-15.

What, gentlemen, was the cause of our misfortune [in 1870-71]? For my part, four great faults were committed which explain everything: a political fault, and three great military faults. . . .

The great political fault is that there is no other example in history of a war's being announced, declared, started in eight days. Louvois was the first organizer of our army; he was our greatest minister of war, and yet I would have challenged him to be ready in eight days when we started with absolutely no preparation, with infantry regiments of eleven, twelve, or thirteen hundred at the most!

The Prussian system offers an extraordinarily remarkable degree of speed of mobilization. The Prussians were in considerable force at Trèves. It is said that they wished to make war against us. That is false. What is true is that they were expecting war; they were ready, and yet they so much dreaded the test that they drew back publicly before France, which had taken so unexpected a stand regarding them. We who were not ready, we braved war. [Sensation; numerous voices: "That is true!"] . . .

The essential merit of the present Prussian organization lies in its ability to be ready first. The Prussians took more than twenty days to come in reach of the mouths of our cannons.

And we! To be ready in six days! We cannot imagine such blindness. Our misfortunes resulted from that and from several obvious military faults that I am going to point out to you.

How could you expect to be ready in eight days? As a matter of fact it took more than twenty days. I must admit that we displayed great activity. We were able to muster 250,000 men. But when no order of mobilization is given and from one end of the country to the other we must muster 250,000 men, great activity is needed.

We did not lack dispatch the day war was declared, but we had extreme trouble in mobilizing even 250,000 men.

That is not all; matériel was needed. We have spoken of that here. Guns were not only sufficient in quantity but excellent; the breech-loading rifle, except for the ammunition, which all nations of Europe were trying to improve, is recognized as excellent. Except for guns, the rest of the matériel was not sufficient. You have been told, and it is true, that there were 21,000 pieces of artillery.

I have not contested it. There were 12,000 pieces of siege artillery, 9,000 campaign pieces. All these pieces existed, and except for those which the enemy took from us, all of these are still in our arsenals. Of these 9,000 campaign pieces, there were 5,000 which we could not put in the line because they were pieces of smooth bore. There were only 4,000 grooved pieces which could be put in the line. But were these 4,000 artillery pieces utilized? That is the question. Do you know how many of the personnel we had mustered could man these artillery pieces? There were 930. This means there would have been enough, in the proportion at present generally adopted, for an army of 250,000 men.

Thus all the resources of France at the time provided only 250,000 men. Was this the fault of the law of 1832? Certainly not, for if we had had a month, a month and a half—such as one can always procure during negotiation—the law of 1832, modified by that of 1868, could have yielded a million men. The misfortune is that we counted on a million men being furnished by the existing law to enter the ranks, while at least a month or a month and a half or two months were needed to bring them in.

Another great misfortune that had a considerable influence on the war is that our fortresses were not in a state of defense. The most important fort around which we were to pivot all the operations, the fortress of Metz, was not in a state of defense. Its works were not finished; there was not a cannon on the ramparts, and there were scarcely any provisions. I admit that there was only what we could bring together at the last minute.

It is in this situation that we met the Prussian army. This was not an army of 1,200,000 men. As I pointed out to you yesterday, it was not one even of 1,000,000 or 900,000 men. During the first days there were about 400,000 men confronting us.

In the presence of the enemy, what did we do? I do not want to discuss campaign plans here. I want to speak briefly of accomplished facts.

We remained in a position which all the world recognizes as anything but military. There were 250,000 men spread over a line of one hundred and twenty-five miles from Thionville to the banks of the

Rhine. We had our right beyond the Vosges and in a position where we could scarcely come to its aid. We remained twenty days in this situation facing 400,000 men. What took place? Everybody could have foreseen the results. Our right, placed beyond the Vosges, beyond the principal strength of our army, was wiped out. It resisted heroically. Nothing in the most glorious days of our history was greater than the engagement of Reischoffen and those engagements which preceded and followed it; we fought one against three. ["That is true! Very good!"]

After the egregious error of having declared war in eight days, a political error which resulted in the administrative mistakes that followed and ruined us, we committed the military mistake of remaining in the presence of the enemy twenty days without taking what we can call a military position, and our right was exposed and destroyed.

. . . .

We are asked why France was not able to revive despite the patriotism she displayed, despite the 800,000 militia, who were not all regular soldiers but all of whom, or almost all, had manly French hearts!

Why, despite all this, did we not recover? It was because we did not have the staff. ["That is true! Very good!"]

I saw companies on the Loire—and these were much larger than our companies usually are—companies of as many as one hundred men with a second lieutenant and one or two noncommissioned officers to lead them. The real cause of our misfortunes, epitomizing and explaining all our disasters, is that lacking organization at Metz and Sedan we were obliged to send all our regiments to the Rhine in a single day. At one blow all our military effective force was lost. That is the true cause of our misfortunes; we err in seeking others. Our army was as brave as ever; everybody admits this, and foreigners themselves recognize it—with pride of course, for they would not have wanted a victory over a degenerate France. ["Very good!"]

Thus our inertia in the face of the enemy made us remain twenty days on a line one hundred and twenty-five miles long, completely compromising our right. The reason for our calamity was that after the misfortune we did not immediately move to the rear so as not to be surrounded. After having lost twenty-five days in forming a reserve army, we were surrounded; then when there was no longer time we attempted a breakthrough. From these misfortunes the complete loss of all our staff and of everything that formed the base of our military force resulted. That is why France succumbed.

Do not tell us that the Prussian system vanquished France. It was not the Prussian system which vanquished the French system. I shall tell you what defeated France. In Berlin there was a great government. This government had broad diplomatic aims, men of war who might be called organizers of victory, energetic army generals, and a clever king who did not resent the fame of men placed around him but took their glory for his. He united them as one man, managing, as it were, to give back to Prussia a Frederick the Great. [Prolonged agitation.]

It was this and not the Prussian system vanquishing the French system; it was the Prussian government vanquishing the French government. [Signs of agreement.]

. . . .

What I am trying to realize with your cooperation and with the funds which you have requested are 150 regiments of infantry, which with respect to the staff is a more effective force than we have ever had. There will be 30 regiments of artillery with 64 regiments of cavalry. We have 60 today. The necessity of completing the number of dragoons will oblige us to create four more regiments with three regiments of engineers, and a fourth will be necessary. With the number of regiments which I have indicated you can just staff 864,000 men.

By using all the support which you will grant the army for the peacetime effectives, by retaining as many as we can of these men designated to serve eight years, and by retaining six classes, that is those designated to serve six years, we would have the most solid army imaginable.

I regard as mad any French policy attempting to make war without allies. . . . With allies and an army of 800,000 men, with 550,000 to 600,000 combat troops, we should have nothing to fear from anyone and should possess a solid army. In addition we should not have the great disadvantage in a position such as ours of carrying out an experiment of doubtful outcome.

There is no law in need of more support from a country than the military law. Sixty years were necessary to accustom France to conscription. We shall need much more time to become accustomed to the new military law. I should prefer not to make the experiment, but we are obliged to do so. . . .

Now let us form a correct idea of what we mean by the Prussian system. The fundamental principle of this system, according to what we are told, is the armed nation. Everyone serves and we do not see what is usually called flagrant injustice, that is to say, the possibility of putting a man who is a professional soldier in one's place by paying for it. In future the injustice of having to do military service for money, benefiting the timid or one strongly attracted to his business, will disappear from our laws; everyone will serve. Then we shall not lack men but have an armed nation, so to speak. Doubtless there will be a great number of men. Moreover, the application of that principle will inculcate into the souls of all Frenchmen the spirit of civic duty. We shall at the same time regenerate the nation and the army and obtain that rapid mobilization which the honorable M. Raudot extolled, a commendable result but one that can be given France by other means.

There are many illusions in this proposal. Unfortunately, we love to talk. The nation armed! But when will there be a nation armed? . . . It is always a portion of the nation which we put under arms. Do you know what the peacetime effectives of the Prussians are, including all Germany? They are 400,000 men.

Thus there is in no way an armed nation; only a portion of the nation is chosen, designated by different means, but only a part of the nation. And like all nations wanting victories and not defeats, the most energetic portion is chosen as often as possible. If it is too early for persons to enter the ranks, they are made as fit as possible by vigorous drilling and almost unendurable hardships. They are exposed to the enemy as often as possible. The law, the true law, is that a portion of the nation be well chosen, well drilled, and accustomed to danger by the constant sight of war. That is the truth; let us not have any illusions. . . .

The Prussian service does not have what we call a substitute. It has its own special character, which in my opinion does not have everything desirable in the way of military results.

In every society vocations should be recognized. For certain men obstacles making it impossible to serve in the army should be acknowledged. With one it is health; with another his interests. The Prussian law recognized this but did not compensate for it by substitutes. Instead it counterbalanced the effect with the expenditure which the committee proposes to imitate. A man may not by individual contract procure a substitute. The government takes care of this, declaring who will be excused from armed service for a certain length of time.

That is the entire difference in this matter.

But I acknowledge another considerable difference in the Prussian system, the regional army. The regional army has unquestionably great advantages.

I trust that you know what is meant by this phrase "regional army," for often we employ words without understanding them well. [Smiles.] Here is what the regional army is: Each province of the nation furnishes an army corps; all the men who make up the army corps are born in the area and belong to it. The regiment may represent a canton, the brigade an arrondissement, and the army a department. I use French administrative language. There is clear advantage in this system. It greatly facilitates and shortens the time of the procurement of officers and noncommissioned officers. . . . But I should question the Hon. M. Raudot. I know him very well and give him credit for being a true liberal. I know also that he is a liberal especially when it concerns economy. [Laughter.] But I define him as a liberal of pre-'89 times, a liberal of Brittany, and I will say to him, "Yes, you have an independent mind and heart, but would you, liberal as you are, return to before '89?" We should blame the French Revolution for its crimes, those of party strife. But overlooking the worst of its excesses, do you want to annul the great social advantages of the Revolution? Would you exchange the departments for the provinces? [Interruptions from the Right.] Would you want to do so? No, you certainly would not want to do so!

. . . .

Would you want to put only the Provençals or the Bretons, only men of Dauphiné or Burgundy in the regiments? You say that this has no disadvantage, but you had scarcely touched the subject when you stopped. You did well, and I shall stop too. You spoke of foreign nations' knowing how to sustain this condition; you have told us that Prussia did not hesitate to use this regional organization in the Duchy of Posen. Do you know what they did in the Duchy of Posen? With a remarkably clever policy, through the good offices of the King—father of the present Emperor—who had assigned to the purpose a part of his finances, Prussia implanted in the Duchy a whole German population. If they had to make war on the frontier of Poland, do you think that they would send an army corps formed in the Duchy of Posen? Of course not! Do you suppose that Austria would use Italian soldiers in a war with Italy? No, they would use Galician or Hungarian soldiers.

On the contrary, we can use French regiments everywhere. In case of great military necessity we do not fear the sacrifice of a regiment or an army corps as happened at Eylau; the corps of Augereau was entirely lost. No, we are not so fearful of the consequences of such a sacrifice. Do you know why? Because the misfortune, the loss was spread over all the nation. With the regional system when a regiment is destroyed, an entire population, an entire province will be destroyed by the misfortunes of war. [Prolonged agitation.]

Thanks to the unity in our regiments, which is the greater in that the faults are neutralized and virtues spread, I dare say that our regiments today are the most exemplary part of the population. They do not deserve what was said of them here; for they are admirable schools. Today, thanks to the diligence of our officers and noncommissioned officers, do you know what is happening? After four or five months all classes of the army know how to read and write, and they learned in the regiment. We have been carrying out the experiment for fifteen months; there are colonels who write me: "Of all the men who have been in the regiments four or five months there is not one who does not know how to read and write. [Lively expressions of satisfaction.]

Moreover, our officers have taken the trouble to educate themselves. We are only concerned with teaching, and a colonel wrote me these fine words: "It is not the fever for promotion that consumes us; it is the fever for rehabilitation!" And he meant rehabilitation: not foolishness, but the great aim of returning France to her former position—a position many vainly desire to deprive her of after misfortunes that we hope are only passing ones. . . .

Do you believe that there would be no provincial spirit if you had a regional army? Do you believe that you could say what I say here, that the army has no political opinion? No, the army would have the opinion of the provinces to which its members belonged; the unity, the obedience would be compromised. Gentlemen, let us keep what we have; if we have had the misfortunes of the French Revolution, let us keep its great achievements, the unity that our kings began.

I repeat that we must know what we want. When we do not want the regional army, we should not claim all the advantages of the regional army. We should not pretend to form noncommissioned officers in two years; we should not pretend to have two armies, an active army and a reserve army; and especially we should not pretend to have the rapid mobilization of the Prussian army. Is it, moreover, impossible to achieve it? Here under the walls of Paris we are carrying out a brilliant experiment, though it has not been without disadvantages and difficulties. We were told of the danger of having an army of more than 100,000 men mustered, submitted to encampment in the most severe season. I was frightened by these difficulties. But there was no complaint in the army. [Rumblings from several benches.]

.   .   .   .

What was our situation before this great experiment? When the war was finished, all the army corps disintegrated; only regiments remained organized in France. Do you know what the difficulties are for prompt mobilization of the army? With the existence of railroads today there is no difficulty in bringing soldiers from Bayonne, Toulon, or Dunkirk. A few days are enough. But what is difficult is to mobilize two regiments into a battalion of foot soldiers to make up the brigade, two brigades to make the division, three divisions to make the army corps, several army corps to make the grand army.

For all this, personnel must be chosen, and time is needed to make the choice. Then it is necessary for the generals to find aides-de-camp, horses, and war equipment, and to make the acquaintance of their soldiers and subordinates. Is a month or two enough for this? No.

Then there is the question of war, now grown to immense proportions. Instead of two pieces of artillery for 1,000 men, four are needed. A great amount of time is necessary to gather this matériel. Even while blaming them I must give credit to those who mustered 250,000 men at Metz in twenty days; it was an extraordinary feat.

Take for example the practice of permanent formations which will not be very expensive—of having two or three armies always organized. During the winter season these armies will send a part of their force back to their homes, but they will always remain organized. Their central armories and artillery horses will remain with the peasants in the area, and the men will know their officers, their general of brigade, and their general-in-chief.

This system of permanent formation is not very expensive. We have just tried it. With it you will have Prussia's rapid mobilization without changing our way of life. ["Very good."] . . .

But there is something which you will not obtain, for no one has ever obtained it; it is the creation in two years of a real army, that is to say the creation of a good staff of officers and especially noncommissioned officers. The staff is not all; in addition it is necessary to have a number of veterans, indispensable to the completion of the staff and without whom the staff could not lead 150 men under fire. I speak of the company staff. There is the difficulty. If you do not have five years of service, the creation of the staff, a good staff, is completely impossible. It is this consideration which makes me fully support the system of the committee; it had the courage, the loyalty, and the good sense on the basis of experience to declare for the five years.

In this respect the Prussians can do what we cannot yet do. Permit me on this subject to give you detail. . . .

Do you know on what the Prussian nation bases the creation of a good staff? It has a submissive, docile people. . . [Rumblings from several benches on the Left. From various benches, "Yes! Yes! That is true!"] composed of vigorous men, and beside this people there is, pardon the word, and certainly the word has no need of pardon, there is the nobility. We have a nobility in France, but it is no longer numerous, nor does it have the position of the Prussian nobility. They have a very numerous territorial nobility, usually of modest fortune, very brave and enlightened. One must not deny that Protestant peoples are highly educated—having the taste for and pride in arms and a passion for national greatness. Below this nobility is a very intelligent bourgeoisie, receiving its tone from this same nobility and wanting to equal it.

Do you know what the proportion of the nobility in the Prussian army is? It makes up about half of the staff. Of 16,000 officers, it supplies from 7,000 to 8,000 of them. Is that the situation in France? This aristocracy in Prussia is accepted, it gives the tone to all the rest; it lives on its lands, surrounded so to speak—the word is quite proper; they are very liberal in Prussia—by vassals. Thus things impossible here are possible in Prussia.

In France we have the principle of equality. I wish that we had to the same degree that of liberty. [From a large number of benches, "Very good! Very good!"] . . .

In France we know only one thing, proved merit.

How do we develop officers? In schools first of all.

Each system has its advantages; ours has great ones. I observe our nation, and its faults cause me much sorrow; but I also know its superior qualities, and I take profound joy in them. ["Very good! Very good!"] You can easily appreciate the advantages of this system, and you are aware of the studies demanded at Saint-Cyr. There you will see together the sons of the nobility, the bourgeoisie, and the peasants of some fortune. You will see these young men applying themselves for long hours to the rigorous infantry drill, which after an entire year makes the students of our military schools the most highly trained in Europe. You will see these same young men, for another year, applying themselves to artillery drill, despite the fact that all or almost all are destined for the infantry. No part of the art of war is neglected by them. And that is not all; not only are they foot soldiers, not only are they gunners; they must also be familiar with cavalry exercises. It is thus that we see them dash at an almost untamed horse, seize it by the mane, vault into the saddle, fall, get up, often at the risk of being stamped upon.

Daily in addition to these various drills do you know what they do? Half worn out from fatigue they return to their classes and listen to learned professors. They are instructed in the history of war, that is to say what Napoleon so justly called the real school of war. Thus their days pass, completely filled by this work and these studies through which they learn to be worthy of command by first scrupulously obeying their chiefs.

After the young men have done all these things for two years, are they officers? Not at all. Once they have acquired the knowledge of the schools, they go into the regiments where their characters are formed; and it is only after several years passed in the military family that they are truly officers.

This is how we develop our officers.

As for the noncommissioned officers, are they developed in the schools? No. Do you know where they are formed? In the regiments and only in the regiments.

The noncommissioned officers are developed in the regiments and by the regiments. Later, when the noncommissioned officers have become real men of war, when among them are men worthy of reaching higher rank, then there is a school where they enter to learn what others more favored by fortune have learned before at the schools of Saint-Cyr, Metz, or Saumur, that is to say. all the things which constitute the education, the real education and instruction of officers. . . .

. . . . General Trochu told us the other day that the perfect soldier is the three-year man. Nevertheless the perfect three-year soldier should be given preliminary training.

And where, I asked him! In the lycées?. . . Perhaps for a very small part of the population. There among children of the enlightened classes, I recall, I who was a student in the imperial lycée—the soul takes fire very quickly. When the poor young people taking instruction in mathematics, Latin, or Greek were told the hour of the day when there would be military exercises, they all rejoiced. That is a preliminary training that I understand.

As for the man from the country, where will you give him basic preliminary training? Will it be by sending him to the regimental depot, at least twenty, thirty, fifty leagues from his village? And for how long? If so, be careful, for it is really a year more of service; for when you place this man for basic training for five months, four months, three months or less, he will have lost the year. You can not say any more that three years are necessary; you need four, of which one, that of preliminary training, does not count.

This is not reasonable. You will admit that three years are needed to make a good soldier. The first year he spends his time getting over his apprehensions, receiving the disagreeable treatment necessary to make a man a brave man. That is not so widespread as has been said, nor so long; but for this man to become acclimated, a year is necessary. The second year he is at ease and the third year he is happy; then he is your favored soldier; but right away you make him leave. [Hilarity from several benches.]

You want the noncommissioned officer to command men, to command his comrades, and the first year the new soldier is all upset; it is certainly not in the first year that you will make him a corporal; the second, he starts to become used to the situation; the third, he barely starts to take shape as a soldier. I ask you at what point will you have him made corporal, sergeant, sergeant-major? . . .

One of our generals, a man uniting vigor as a man of action with a reflective mind, told me openly and wittily: "Yes, we take three years to make our noncommissioned officers, but when we have taken three years to make them, leave them with us at least two years so we can enjoy them." [Laughter of approval.]

This was a profound truth in a simple and witty form. But the regiment must be formed, and time is necessary to give birth to the fine phenomenon which we call military *esprit, esprit de corps;* that is not done in a day. . . .

You take from our countryside uneducated men not brought up on or familiar with the works of Turenne, Condé, Vauban, Caesar, Hannibal and say to one of these men: "Do not think about your well-being in peacetime. Society is obliged to feed you. It is obliged to make you run unnecessary dangers. Here is your life, and peace is but an accident in your existence. When necessary, you will bear cold or heat, you will throw yourself into the icy Beresina, and almost against hopeless odds you will die to save the army; you will bear the burning heat of Africa, and your honor, your glory, is death beneath the flag!"

Is that the usual life of an honest man? No, it is a special life, the life of a soldier. The institution supports certain men and finally makes soldiers of them. It is by means of it that the soldier is formed. To know how to suffer, suffer unbearable hardships; to have always before one's eyes the idea of death; to be almost happy when the moment of danger approaches and one may place himself beside his chiefs and behind the flag; and to be joyous, joyous as with a personal happiness when one is victorious, triumphant: this is the life of the soldier.

And you believe that all this is assured in learning geometry and topography? This is derived by living a long time in the same society with men who live by these ideas; in this way soldiers are formed, and you do not reach this extraordinary result in three years. You grant us five years, and I accept them with gratitude. If I were master of the destinies of my nation, I should ask six years, eight years. We cannot have too much time to make a good soldier. . . .

And now permit me in concluding to read to you two pages from an admirable man, Marshal Bugeaud, who is one of the most distinguished minds that I have known.

The basis of your system [he said to the committee], the fundamental idea, is to bring many men under the flag in order to teach them military exercises. . . .

I admit that you give military training to those whom you call up, and I know, as you do, that three years are enough to instruct a soldier in what he should know, if this time is judiciously employed. This time is enough also to form *esprit de corps* when the soldier knows that he still has three or four years to serve under the flag; but when he knows that at the end of the three years he will be sent home, he does not trouble himself to become—permit the expression, gentlemen—a real soldier, and he will not conditon his mind to a profession he is going to quit. ["That is true! That is true!" from several benches.] . . .

The Committee has lost sight of the basic ideas of my system. These ideas are:

1. That mechanical or physical or material instruction of the soldier is infinitely less important than the love of country, *esprit de corps,* military honor and discipline.

2. That because of the political and especially the geographic situation of France, a well-formed army and essentially mobile reserve is needed.

3. That since the first battles are ordinarily decisive, owing to the topography of northern France and to our poor fortifications system, it is necessary above all to have an excellent permanent army which can guarantee initial success. . . .

With us quality must replace quantity, for we are exposed to enemies who may deploy forces more numerous than ours. I declare with the greatest conviction that I should rather go into battle against 100,000 enemies with 60,000 men who have served six years with the colors than with 100,000 men such as your present system will give us. It is only after the figures reach 50,000 to 60,000 men that quality is more influential than numbers.

That is the basis of my system; I want above all to have an excellent active army, ready for the first battles. After that, let us have the least mediocre reserve possible, but do not sacrifice the active army to it as you are doing now.

Why does the recruiting law impose seven years of service? Because the legislators judged that time is necessary to have a good and sufficiently numerous army. You have made a three-year law in order to bring many men into the army, with the sterile advantage of superficial and incomplete education, a little practical instruction everywhere, great morale nowhere.

Gentlemen, after such words from so great a master, I can add no more that is useful.

2. The Social Optimism of a Bourgeois Intellectual

Gustav Schmoller: *Social Relations and Social Progress* (1875)°

Gustav Schmoller, for many years a professor of economics at the University of Berlin (d. 1917), in his essay interprets the character of the decades prior to World War I. The essay originally appeared in 1875 during a controversy about the working class and socialism between Schmoller and the historian and publicist Heinrich von Treitschke. Schmoller approved its reprinting some twenty years later in unchanged form. Although the prose is cumbersome, Schmoller's social ideals stand out as the expression of an optimistic member of the German intellectual élite. For half a century Schmoller participated vigorously in the public discussion of social and economic problems, and, to some extent, of the basic political ones. He had wide contacts among official and business circles, and he was esteemed as one of the intellectual leaders of the time. He and other professors who held similar views were called "Socialists of the Chair" because of their advocacy of reforms by governmental initiative. Many business men and political leaders condemned their ideals; however these professors offered one of the most practical and concrete programs of action that the developing bourgeois society of industrialism was to produce, and they influenced legislation. A comparison of Schmoller's statement with that of Donoso Cortés or Montalembert or that of the socialists will once more stamp nineteenth-century society as one having a great variety of standards and objectives. A national society from which emerged a prominent public individual able to put forward seriously the views that Schmoller did in this essay and in the work of the Association for Social Policy

---

° Gustav Schmoller, *Ueber einige Grundfragen des Rechts und der Volkswirtschaft: Ein offenes Sendschreiben an Herrn Professor Dr. Heinrich von Treitschke* (Jena: Verlag von Friedrich Mauke, 1875), pp. 98-128. Translated and printed by permission of Duncker & Humblot, Berlin, West Germany.

49

must be classed with that of England as one of the most advanced in Europe at the time. The essay can be used in judging the social situation in the latter part of the century not merely in Germany but in other countries as well.

In his admirable remarks about the philosophy of history while discussing the education of mankind, Lotze makes the objection that it is only an infinitely small minority which is educated to higher spiritual culture and which represents progress through its culture, whereas alongside this minority an overwhelming majority always remains essentially the same. What you [von Treitschke] regard as a natural result of the aristocratic social system leads Lotze to the painful question of how, under such conditions, one can speak at all of a history of mankind.

I am convinced that Lotze is deceived if he thinks that the lower classes of the present are on no higher a level than those of the past. I believe, as I often mentioned, that the goal of history is to attract successively larger numbers of persons to the higher benefits of culture, successively to raise the level on which the lowest and most miserable members of society must abide. History does not reach this goal by any simple road. I concede that for a long time historical development seemed to tend rather toward the opposite. Inequality of wealth and division of labor produce an increasing differentiation of mankind, and, when it goes too far, this differentiation ends with the destruction or the crippling of individual groups of society. Thus this differentiation exposes the immoral character of the naked natural process. At this point the contrary cultural process begins to assert itself all the more strongly, seeking to maintain the mechanism of division of labor as far as it is necessary to produce great technical achievements, but also seeking to place the same laborers, formerly totally exhausted by the divison of labor and exploitive class rule, under cultural conditions suitable to keep them human beings. The principle of equal justice begins to protest against economic and social injustice; more humane forms of economic organization begin to fight their way through; the idea of cooperation and of raising the lower classes is taking root. More recent centuries show fewer differences in wealth and education; that new cultural world appearing on the stage of history begins with social institutions which no longer allow a proletariat and the immoderate wealth of a few to be so easily and so quickly built up. Even if inequality of education and income occasionally arises, and this natural process appears to be occasionally and temporarily necessary to raise and equip individuals or classes so that certain cultural advances can be made by them, perhaps at first one-sidedly, and be represented in them, the essential trend of history will remain the reverse, directed to the moral cultural end. Above all, the present, if it is to remain true to the great reforming ideals of the eighteenth century, liberalism and humanity, should not lose sight of this goal.

If, with all the reserve that I implied in the previous section, I am to outline how my historical imagination pictures the social advances of the near future, I must first repeat that all these advances, if they are to endure, must be both moral and psychological ones. That means that men must not only become other than they are in order to confront one another in a different way in the relationship of lord and serf, owner and laborer, *rentier* and beggar; but their thinking and acting must so affect the quantitative relations of the economy, that is the supply of labor and capital, that these relationships under a nobler arrangement of our social system do not come into opposition. We must come to a more just and normal division of wealth without coercing either supply or demand. The interests of social classes must be clarified; but furthermore the classes must maintain through the progress of the economic organization such relation to one another that conflicts will be fewer and more easily overcome. Harmony of interests is one of the ideals which we are nearing with each advance of history, even if we never reach it completely any more than we do the summoning of all to share the higher benefits of culture.

A mere fiat of law would be able only with difficulty and probably only temporarily to create a higher income for the lower classes. It is a matter of bringing the income from capital investment into a more normal relationship to income from labor, and in connection with this more and more of endeavoring to see that even the greatest wealth does not cease to produce some labor—as custom and law in Germany at least are already essentially tending—and that likewise the least amount of labor leads to some wealth.

The superiority of wealth as such over labor, the possibility of amassing immoderate wealth from the surplus income of capital investment, will diminish to the extent that in the competitive struggle labor secures a more favorable position in respect to capital. Without that, no reform of law and custom and no socialistically inclined social organization will help for any length of time. If the population grows too fast without having an outlet in emigration, and if land and capital are lacking, social misery will always set in again.

For the future I hope for an international system of law, for an increase in the means of communication, for a closer connection of the American and Australian colonial life with our countries which are culturally older, for activity such as is already exercised in England by the trade unions in regard to emigration, in brief for easy emigration of superfluous labor such as we do not know today. Up to now the spread of culture to new lands and large-scale, far-reaching emigration have taken place only when great social misery has been prevalent somewhere beforehand. The future must change this erratic movement, so often bound up with crises, into a constant one led consciously and without crises. The expansive force of the population seeks successively to carry higher civilization to all parts of the world; but it does not need to be so irregular, so acute; it can be constant and without violent movement.

Moreover, superiority of wealth is to be lessened in that the workers and lower classes learn in marriage, in the procreation of children, and in the leading of children into an occupation, not to follow instinct and chance alone but to use consideration, foresight, self-control, such as often appear today in the middle class and in the upper classes and in these classes only maintain the standard of living. With the first-mentioned factor are bound up great moral dangers of many kinds which can be overcome with time. Distribution of the rising generation into the various occupations perhaps can be planned only when we have new statistical methods suitable in the future for use by conscious and far-seeing leadership, whether that of individuals or of the state. Today this distribution is largely left to chance. In any case the kind of laborer who thinks and who is technically and humanly better educated will have quite a different attitude toward capital from that of the present working class. The education of the lower classes to political economy is one goal about which the optimistic free-traders and academic socialists *(Katheder-sozialisten)* agree. And this goal will be reached all the more easily the higher wages are and the more the worker has a little property such as a house of his own. Today thoughtlessness and lack of thrift are occasioned by the worker's saying to himself, "It's all no use."

I believe that the future will never create state industries, corporations, or production associations only; but I hope that a time will come when state and community can take over without danger much which they cannot yet assume, or not entirely, and do so without harming the independence of the individual and the integrity of our administration. The economist Roscher says, with regard to the increasing activity of the state, the community, the corporation, and associations in the modern civilized state: "In fact one can assert that we have come closer to a community of goods than anyone could have dreamed a century ago. And indeed the institutions under discussion are largely those in which the characteristic power and efficiency of our age shine forth." The more state or community undertakings of this kind grow, the more they are able to do so without falling prey to red tape, idle patronage, and spineless status-seeking. Likewise the more large corporations analogous to the state and community employ hundreds and thousands of workers, the more the cultural nature of the occupation, that is of a livelihood involving numerous legal and moral duties, will replace the mere wage relationship which considers money profit alone and evokes little or no responsibility for the labor done. Then a nobler, more moral conception of earning one's daily bread, such as obtains in the case of a profession, will gain acceptance. I consider an increase in production cooperatives possible to the degree that the economic education of the worker improves; the great increase in the number of simple partnerships today is a forerunner of this change.

Sharing by the workers in the profits of an undertaking already exists for all highly trained workers, that is for directors, chemists, etc., and, as I have already explained, will increase as the working class raises itself and as the direction of enterprises no longer rests in the hands of the capital owner himself. Where the latter condition exists, the entrepreneur's profit already today appears in a form which no reasonable person questions—as a higher reward for the talent of the manager and his greater effort and achievement. Every comparable form of labor deserves similar reward, a similar share in the profit. Common manual labor, however, is to be protected from a relapse into a lower standard of living and therewith to low wages by factory laws, a humane development of the labor contract, by unions and their activity, and by arousing a new, healthy corporative spirit among the laborers. The principle of insurance will take effect in quite other ways than now, and provide for the sick and for old age as it does not now. In the future insurance will supplant our still indispensable charity in its naked form, with its dubious psychological and material results. Eventually a kind of constitutional organization of big industry will assure workers an influence upon factory routine and a share in the execution of disciplinary power. Without this discipline, factory and large-scale agricultural enterprise cannot function; but as it now exists it represents a misuse of power similar to that of the immunity and the manorial law of the Middle Ages, practices which undermined the former German state organization.

If we were only as far along as I have described, society and the economy would have an entirely different appearance from that which they have today. My hopes, however, go even farther, but in doing so they project into a still more distant future. I hope that the time will come when the interest rate will sink permanently to one and one-half or two and one-half per cent, and I hope that just as the lowering of the rate from fifteen or twenty per cent to four to six per cent greatly reduced the power of the propertied classes and diminished the possibility of their exploiting the non-possessing class, a further sinking of the interest rate will effect a similar improvement. I hope for a democratizing of credit, for a more vigorous extension of personal credit, which again diminishes the advantage of the possessing group over the propertyless one. I do not doubt that progressive income taxes and progressive inheritance taxes will be possible in the future without crippling the acquisitive instinct. I hope that a more equal division of income will change the entire direction of our industry, will abolish the unnatural condition which increases the demand for certain luxury goods more than that for the necessities of life for the masses, when the masses are not properly clothed, fed, and housed. I hope that the great moral dangers concealed today by our wealth and urban life will be diminished.

I could continue in this vein. But for certain readers, too much rather than too little has been said. I wanted only to suggest how I think social advance is possible without losing connection with the present. Nothing of what I have mentioned belongs to the realm of the impossible. Everything moves in channels which in part have been open for centuries, and in any case are now open. Whether these goals will be reached in decades or in centuries, what would then come to the fore, how the forms of economic life will look in detail, how custom and law will take shape—those are questions which I leave entirely unanswered.

I seek faithfully and without exaggeration to advance against your social theory, my theory of social progress and the changing of economic forms of organization.

You hold that history begins with the rightful power of the stronger and cleverer; you derive all social structures from this idea; you have only praise without blame for the caste and slave systems. You seem to accept Haller's theory of the state which recognized only the ruler-and-ruled relationship. Civil society is to you simply the essence of the relationship of mutual dependence. Progress in history is achieved only by the replacement of old relations of dependency by new relationships of dependency. Thereby nothing is changed in the aristocratic social organization. You regard an abiding and always increasing inequality of goods and income and a growing difference in education and classes as something normal, even necessary and desirable. You declare that higher culture, large-scale industry, and the flowering of art are not possible without even greater differences than we now have. We must have more great fortunes, you think. We need them for those virtuosos of enjoyment who are also virtuosos of the spirit, for those sybarites and gourmets like Wilhelm von Humboldt, Gentz, and Heine, who could develop their powers only in the atmosphere of refined sensuous existence. It appears normal to you that the workers and lower classes have no Muse, since they could do nothing intelligent with it and would only fall prey to vice and poisonous demagoguery. Their breeding and way of thinking always remain about the same. You think that it is normal that the lower classes have a different belief, other ideals, another way of life, in fact another moral order than do the upper classes. You who yourself once complained of the unholy division which today separates the educated and uneducated of our people say nothing about the dangers inherent in these circumstances, and about the fact that this kind of division of labor does not create a unified nation but rather classes, castes, social status groups, or whatever one wants to call them. You allow the idea of equality to arise only after centuries, and after more centuries only a few timid demands to appear. Up to the present a reasonable equality should demand only five things: recognition of every individual as equal before the law; freedom of thought and belief; free use of physical and intellectual talent, in order to rise within the given social system as far as individual ability and good fortune permit; the duty of the state to give every person the education consonant with the accepted standard necessary for the development of his personal ability; and finally support of the poor in case of abject misery.

I am neither satisfied nor in agreement with these ideas. They rest on your premise that no essential progress can be made in changing the social structure. At the least they contain great exaggeration of fundamentally sound ideas. Most of your arguments could be used with equal right by the privileged of any age against every effort to raise the lower classes. You openly confess your preference for that high aristocratic society which in your view alone was able to embrace the world of ideals while heaping all its cares upon the patient shoulders of its slaves. I find it fairer for the upper classes to stand fast on the ground of reality rather than to be moving in clouds of the ideal and to take part in the work and worry of the world, and I should like the lower classes to have some part in the world of the ideal and not exist like pariahs.

I consider your historical starting point not quite tenable. Very early in history, at least in the case of peoples most advanced culturally, we see something more than relationships of power and domination. Very near the beginning of their history we find the free contract alongside force, partnership along with rulership, the ideal of equality along with class rule; and these ideas never become entirely extinguished. For thousands of years people have shared soil allotments and war booty equally; the French king could take no part of the booty from the least of his warriors; the first centuries of the flourishing of German industry rested upon an organization whose guiding idea was the equality of every member.

It is of course true that beside or in front of these pictures occur others of an opposite nature. You are enthusiastic about the Indian castes "as the model of the caste articulation of all Indo-Germanic peoples." So far as I know from recent research, the Indo-Germanic peoples before their division were far from having the actual immoral caste system, so-called, which we found in India, and so it cannot have been a model for us. You see in slavery an act of saving civilization: the tragedies of Sophocles and the Zeus of Phidias are in your view not too dearly bought at the price of wretched slavery for millions. In others one would call that frivolity. No one who knows you would accuse you of this fault; but everyone would urge you not to look at one side only. Slavery was needed for some centuries, perhaps for millenia; it was an advance because it was technically necessary to function as the great school of the masses of workers. For those who gained thereby it was justified not because every use of force was at that time legitimate and healthy, as you picture it, but because it was less an act of force to let the conquered work for the victors than to kill them; it was an advance because it put some moral limits to the use of power by the conquerors. Much greater was the further advance, however—and you in your praise of slavery do not even mention it—which forbade the conqueror to treat the prisoners as slaves and ordered him to impose on them only specific burdens as his serfs. This advance was the greater in that it increased the difficulty of using force unfairly by limiting the possible injustice and by moderating class rule.

Modern times go farther in that they forbid every hereditary labor contract, every tying to the soil, because it is hoped to bring the "have-nots" into a better position in relation to the "haves." But we have not yet given the labor contract a form which assures the have-nots against sinking to a lower level than they occupy.

In spite of the formally more favorable law which the modern age gave to the worker, and in spite of many benefits with which he has been provided, the system did not prevent mass misery in England into the 1840's and with us into the 1860's. The present rise in wages is likewise no guarantee that the working class will permanently raise itself and that a sound middle class will grow out of the better elements of the workers.

That is the basic question of our time. Quite apart from the question of whether we can bring about a social advance is the question of whether we are not retrogressing (of course temporarily) in that we are losing a part of our middle class, which is being changed into a part of the propertyless and uncultured proletariat. That is the fundamental social question of our time, and let us keep it firmly in mind. Modern big industry with its unhealthy buildings and activities, with its upsets and crises, with its labor of women and children, with its economic education, with the mentality and morals which it has more or less imposed upon the workers, has had the same lamentable results wherever particularly imaginative personalities or especially favorable circumstances have not counteracted the effects. Our large-scale agriculture, where it dominates exclusively and is not interspersed with small farms, where masses of have-not day laborers stand opposed to a few aristocratic property owners, exhibits in part even more unfortunate social results. Here we encounter a working class neglected morally and economically in every respect, one which has improved its lot somewhat in the nineteenth century, but even then achieving just that level of self-consciousness sufficient to drive great numbers to America. Here we witness the final effects of feudal misdeeds, of feudal class rule of the seventeenth and eighteenth centuries. In addition we have the chronic crisis of the craftsmen, the distress of the lower-school teachers and of the pastors, of the lower and the trained bureaucrats, the question of how long the peasants can resist being bought out by large-scale landowners. In the latter respect the results as shown in the province of Saxony differ markedly from and appear less favorable than those both on the Rhine and in East Prussia.

You evade the issue when you exemplify the present social conflicts with the begging mother, contrasting her with the race horse strengthened by a bottle of wine. Such accidental individual cases always appear. Rather it is a question of whether the average conditions under which entire classes live are normal, whether the separation of different social classes by ever deeper and broader abysses is desirable.

You evade the issue further when, as I suggested above, you treat the interests of culture and of large property ownership as identical. If it were certain, as you apparently assume, that with every rising inequality of wealth the lower classes do not retrogress in their economic position and in their cultural condition and that the upper classes correspondingly increase in spiritual and material power, the social question of today would be quite different. But it seems truer that the lack of education and culture increases both in the proletariat and in the social classes that acquire wealth most quickly and that the social classes which represent true culture and morality, the middle class in the widest sense of the word, are in important segments at least partially weakened economically and lose influence in state and society. A prosperous, open-minded, and sensitive, well-educated middle class is also my ideal, and I hope that in time and in spite of the present dangers we shall have one. I am always ready to do battle for privileges of culture but not for those of money and birth. I am an aristocrat in the Aristotelian sense of the word. What today is called by that name, that is political control by wealth and birth, Aristotle always calls oligarchy. According to him oligarchy is, like democracy, a degenerate form of constitution. Between the degenerate forms of tyranny, oligarchy and democracy, however, democracy seems to him the more endurable.

I shall now consider the individual arguments which you adduce for your theory: (1) the question of whether the present increase of inequality of wealth is normal and must continue in the future; (2) the question of whether inequality in division of wealth is necessary to the flowering of culture and industry; (3) the parallels of our present democratic and social movments with those of ancient Greece; (4) the question of whether great wealth and education on the one side, hard labor without education on the other, are necessary corollaries; (5) the happiness and the rights which you are willing to grant the working class. When I have discussed these points it will be necessary to proceed to the measure of common morality and ideals which I consider the absolute presupposition for every normal condition of the state.

It is true that up to now within the same people the great advances of technology, trade and commerce, and production have been accompanied as a rule by rising social conflicts. What was the cause of this? To a certain extent it came about through the greater complexity of the economic process, in which greater talent and chance acquired somewhat greater scope than they would have had in simple relationships. The increasing inequality of wealth is thus justified, insofar as it is determined by difference in talent. But this difference explains much more why in recent years Banker X made only one million and Banker Y made twenty millions, why Worker A as foreman made 600 thaler annually but Worker B remained a handyman at 200-300 thaler. Correspondingly, at least for the situation of the economic classes, a much more important factor played a role. In times of rapid transition to new economic forms, in times of a general change in the value of money, the economically stronger are able to grow rich more easily at the cost of the masses than in times of a quieter economic period proceeding according to fixed laws and customs. Similarly, we cannot now avoid the influence exerted upon this division of wealth by irresponsible promotion and by all the factors incidental to this phenomenon, nor can we prevent quick and easy profits in certain of the new industrial and commercial enterprises where quality is not demanded by the customers or the workers. As to the credit system, a small number of people, as Lasker so rightly demonstrated in one of his speeches, possesses the secret of using the forms of modern credit which are more or less unknown to the masses so that these few may gain princely wealth in the shortest possible time at the expense of the rest of a more or less deluded society.

Is that normal? Or are the many chance events which today with the changing location of industry, with the building of new streets and lines of communication, suddenly make Property-owner X or Y into a millionaire and transform a number of hardworking peasants into idle *rentiers,* as Hanssen once said—are these fortunate occurrences? Certainly not. We cannot prevent them or forbid them with the means which we now possess, and we can never entirely do away with such chance happenings and such profiteering. But we should praise them even less as a normal, fortunate development. We should not assert that big industry and the birth of culture are impossible without increasing inequality of wealth.

Our big industry in any case must follow the line of association in obtaining its capital in small amounts; in this regard a sound system of industrial stocks is democratic, as Schäffle showed years ago. But today the really big business seldom remains in the hands of a few entrepreneurs; state, community, associations, stock companies, co-operatives, etc., have replaced them and will do so more and more. Our art, the art of all time, what of it? The highest point of Greek art came in Pericles' day when the state had unheard-of riches to use; all the artistic treasures of the Acropolis represent the victory of the idea of the new democratic state and were called into life by the state and not by the princely wealth of individuals. The greatest German writers came together in Weimar a hundred years ago, and the most talented German painters and architects of our time have assembled in impecunious Bavaria, in Munich, where assuredly no private person yet possessed a million marks. Let us ask our artists. All noble natures are incensed over the lack of taste with which the parvenus of the stock exchange, those too-quickly-grown-rich industrialists, buy pictures by the yard according to vanity and the size of the nudes portrayed. The state, the church, and the community always give art its great stimulus. The blossoming of Italian art was determined by that cult which sought to make the churches the favorite meeting place of the entire community, of the poor as well as of the rich.

The flourishing of art and of knowledge, high culture, a refined way of life are bound up with a certain well-being, even with a certain wealth, but not with the highest possible inequality of property ownership; this cultural flowering arises from the same social and political and moral causes as the rising standard of living itself. Great inequality in the division of property has up to now more often led to their decay. Every people which history has so far described endured longer insofar as the inequality of wealth was postponed or retarded. Thus I say that our culture remains all the sounder the less inequality increases, the more all social classes take part equally in progress, and the more the lower classes can successfully be raised to a position somewhat nearer that of the upper classes.

If that does not succeed, if we continue in the elemental whirlpool of a growing inequality of property, the downfall of our culture will bring new political and social institutions based on the reforms which are beginning today, just as our current culture evolved out of the reforms which Christianity, Stoic philosophy, classical Roman jurisprudence, and the democratic spirit of the Germans built into the Roman culture without achieving its salvation.

The essential objection which you have against my conception is your theory of the deficient capacity of the lower classes for culture and good manners and of the need for maintaining an uneducated working class if culture for the upper classes is not to be impossible. Hard, menial labor, a limited economic condition, and brutal feelings on the one hand seem to you the indisputable correlative of high breeding on the other. And so that this outlook may not seem too dreary, you assign to the lower classes the honor of being exclusive or principal bearers of the religious life and the life of feeling.

Your entire argument appears to me to lean here too exclusively on the cultural conditions of ancient Greece. All the examples from which you argue are taken from Greek history. All your fears are concentrated on a decline of aristocratic culture by means of mob rule as in Greece. The average cultural level of the working classes is supposed to have been correctly indicated by Aristotle for the entire future. You cite him, although this is the weakest point of his thought.

He says that the masses live like slaves, like cattle, always given over to desire and enjoyment. He does not believe that slavery can ever be abolished. Your idea that technology will never progress so far as to make of the present laborers something essentially different rests on the same principle.

In addition to your reference to Aristotle you base your assertion about the continuing morality of the lower classes upon the sentence: "Whoever daily lives from hard labor, whose thoughts seldom rise above the level of his personal interests, is held prisoner by economic life." I reply that above all it depends upon the school and other cultural influences to which the person in question may submit. In any case your assertion holds true for merchants and industrialists as well as for workers. Both, however, have changed in two thousand years. How can it be right to compare our workers, who in spite of all their mistakes are accustomed to industrious economic activity and are led by quite other ideas of culture, with the mob which stood behind Cleon? However, I should like to attack on quite other grounds the comparison of our times with the victory of democracy in Greece. The entire theory of the fall of Greek culture because of wicked mob rule is today often regarded as a legend which anxious philologists thought out at the time of the French Revolution and of the Carlsbad decrees, and more and more since Droysen's and Grote's researches it has been considered antiquated. According to the modern view this much at least is sure: The later democratic period, the period of the supposed mob rule, was a necessary phase of development; it was not a time of actual decline and was not without both culture and art. The sins of the mob, that is of the democratic party, were the necessary results of those things which their opponents the oligarchs perpetrated. "Oligarchical tendencies and these alone have directly brought about the fall of Athens," says Droysen in the introduction to the *Knights* of Aristophanes.

In any case the parallel is doubtful; the conclusion drawn about our lower classes from the democracy of Greece, which existed under totally different conditions, is very dubious because so much was different at that time. That fact is clearest when one compares Berlin and Athens, which you do in order to show that there is no essential social progress. You say that in Athens' golden age as large a part of the population, perhaps even a larger part than in present-day Berlin, could live for the ideal purposes of the state, for art and knowledge and for the Muses. This comparison speaks in my favor and not in yours, if one looks at it more closely. The difference between Athens and Berlin lies in the fact that those who ruled in Athens and lived for the Muses, and who had come to share the rule after a hard and violent struggle with a still smaller number of aristrocrats and rich men, were constantly inactive economically, pleasure-loving, ambitious citizens, who let themselves be paid for their appearance in the assembly, who went to the theatre at the cost of the government, who indeed took care of certain state duties in Athens but exploited all the rest of Greece for it, lived at the cost of the state, and united with their proletarian mind a high spiritual and low moral culture; it was a social class for which we have no analogy today, unless that of the aristocratic roués who have run through their property and then sell themselves at any price in order to be able to continue a life of pleasure. This democracy was always a minority and stood opposed to an army of slaves overburdened with work, brutally treated, and shut off from all higher culture. The educated Berliner, also the property-owner—generally, at least—is accustomed to work in spite of education and material comfort, and the middle and lower classes on the other hand are not excluded from all culture; they do not live like cattle, given over to desire and pleasure like slaves; they read the same newspapers, they attend the same theatres as the educated, in part even the same or similar schools, they serve in the same regiments; the minority no longer rules the majority as in Athens; they cannot exploit and mishandle them as was done there; the chasm between the upper and lower classes has become much less. That is the cultural advance which I value and which you deny, or seem to deny.

"The millions must hoe, forge, and hew so that a few thousands can pursue knowledge, paint, and govern," you say, and a certain section of the press jubilantly echoes your statement. I answer, however, that this is not the question at all; no one has ever denied that. The question is what education and position in life the farmers, smiths, and carpenters are to have, and what share of the property and income the researchers, artists, and rulers are to enjoy. All that differs today from the situation in Greece which you have in mind. Fortunately, with us the rulers have not been exclusively or even principally the men of property; the penniless intellectuals in sharp conflict with the former possessing class made Prussia great. Our bureaucracy and our officer group, a true aristocracy—that is an aristocracy of education and culture—have been recruited essentially from the possessing class, but they have not received their ways of thinking and acting from property and the economic, egoistic interests of the latter; rather, royalty and the bureaucracy and the penniless intellectuals and the handworkers' sons like Kant and Fichte have imprinted their stamp on these classes and thereby made them able to govern.

The political theory of Gneist, the results of which have penetrated deep into our political life, can be summed up in the simple sentence: We cannot exclude our wealthy citizens from influence on the state, but, if they and their interests are left in control, they will ruin it by class rule. We must therefore educate them by local self-administration, by unpaid service in the community and county, so that they will take a statesmanlike view and not look upon government merely as something through which to fill their pockets.

This thought is undoubtedly right, but alone it is not enough. The soundness of the modern state and society rests on a principle opposing that of antiquity and in part that of the Middle Ages as well. This principle is that, alongside those of property whose wealth is able to give them an invaluable independence of state power but who therefore easily succumb to dependence on their special selfish interests, a broad and influential social class appeared, one which lacked material independence but was more idealistic in outlook and psychologically independent of egoistic class interests. Our present religious leaders, teachers, state and municipal officials, officers, physicians, lawyers, writers and artists are in the main people who, without property or large wealth, have access to the highest culture. Dependent upon a modest income corresponding at least in general to their service, they yet maintain their social position from generation to generation through the education of their children rather than because of property. Less directly involved in everyday economic life, they act upon the life of the state from higher motives than mere desire for gain. But even in older periods the great ages of our culture—and it seems to me that we all have too often overlooked this fact up to now—were closely connected with analogous social influences.

During the Middle Ages, when state service first threatened to degenerate through feudalism into group rule by large landowners, the Ottos transferred the administration of the towns to the bishops, that is to royal, nonhereditary officials who were not expected to work primarily for their own enjoyment. When the conflict with the Church broke out and the bishops, like the princes, began as vassals to conspire against the emperor and the empire, the Hohenstaufens created in the ministerials the first real bureaucracy, which mastered, mainly without wealth, the misdeeds of the feudal lords, the property-owners of that time, and which after centuries brought Germany to a high point of her power, economic development, and humanistic and artistic culture. The ministerials were not alone responsible for these fruits; the knights and upper bourgeoisie also contributed; but both remained healthy only as long as the ministerials held the balance for them. With the incorporation of the ministerials into the feudal system, that is into the possessing class, the Hohenstaufen state and the political institutions of the empire suffered a death blow; society began to rule the state instead of the other way around. The possessing classes now comfortably established themselves in town and country and plundered the state power in order to enrich themselves, until ultimately the Prussian kingdom and its bureaucracy under a system of enlightened despotism brought changes.

Even in England, where the wealthy were preserved from the unlimited egoism of France and Germany by training in self-government, the very parliamentarism of the eighteenth century, as Gneist, Noorden, and Bucher have shown us, was not free from the sins of egoistic misdeeds. Only people like the younger Pitt, who after he had ruled a world empire did not leave behind enough to bury him, held a bar against selfish economic class interests by the strength of their great and pure character and raised the much-vaunted parliamentarism above the level of class rule.

Your sentence that the rulers must necessarily be rich, or that a good government is only possible with great inequality in the distribution of wealth, is indefensible. Nor must the scholar and artist be rich people or come from the capitalist classes, at least not in Germany. They are the men of talent, not the wealthy of the nation, and therefore we have really great artists and scholars, whereas in countries with oligarchical constitutions there is only a group of rich men who dabble in painting and writing.

Conversely, hard manual labor is no longer unworthy of an educated man, as it once was in ancient Greece. The great advance of our age lies in the recognition of the dignity of labor. Governing and the arts and scholarship are no longer all that is worthy of a respectable man, and manual labor and education are no longer regarded as mutually exclusive. The East Prussian peasant, the rich Hanoverian farmer, and the owner of a knight's estate all farm their land; the factory worker, the foreman, the son of the owner all forge and plane, as did the Württenberg craftsmen who spoke to me in Latin in my father's house and with whose sons I sat on the same Latin school bench. Hundreds of miners, chemists, engineers, as well as thousands of agriculturists, ship's captains, pilots, sailors, one-year volunteers, soldiers, officers who today belong to the company of the educated, do hard menial labor. It is a matter merely of whether they do so exclusively, as slaves did, whether their education is a correspondingly higher one, whether they have leisure and how they use their leisure hours. Your assertion that the factory worker should have no Muse because only he who knows the speech of the Muses understands how to use them is clever alliteration but is refuted on every page of the English factory inspector's reports. "The masses," says one of these reports, "have shown themselves worthy of the gift which has been given them; they have not misused it." Much can be said about what the factory workers have undertaken with their leisure hours, how they have attended evening schools, how various organizations for mutual aid have risen in prestige, how the Easter and Whitsuntide holidays have been spent in more intelligent pleasure than before, how intelligence, obedience to law, the general tone and attitude of the workers have kept pace with the progress of the times. Another report says: "The active and flourishing institutes for intellectual development, the lectures, the musical evenings, the suburban gardens, and all the other sources of enjoyment and profit which are found not only in the towns but in almost every hamlet of the factory districts date from the possession of the privilege which less work has made possible for the workers. I am referring to the Saturday afternoon, in itself one of the greatest blessings which has been bestowed. And it arises from knowing exactly when the employer's time is over and their own time begins." As the pious Huber has often shown us, this progress in England does not go hand in hand with the church loyalty of the workers concerned. What is the purpose of your bitter and seemingly insulting conclusion that the present-day workers need no leisure, that long hard labor and religious piety suit them, if you still want a duplication of this friendly English factory legislation which only makes sense if it creates leisure and seeks to make something out of the workers?

The farmer, carpenter, or smith of today differs from the slave of ancient times because he co-governs and should co-govern in the community and county, because the school of today and universal military service elevate him, because he takes part in political and other organizations and exercises his right to vote, because he must constantly learn to think and judge; he reads newspapers, and takes part in cultural pleasures in the towns without being deeply unhappy thereby, as you think he is. You wish to assure the workers of their happiness by excluding them from higher education. You say that human happiness must be sought in that which is attainable by all, in the inner life, the comfort of religion, a happy family life. I shall come back to the religious question. What about the others? Certainly a deeper inner life and more family happiness even in modest conditions of existence are imaginable. I have emphasized this point from the first in my social-political works and in the lecture you attacked. But the prerequisite for such happiness is a certain education, a certain property and income, and indeed enough so that they are not below the average level of the time. It is simply laughable to comfort the worker by telling him that his forefathers lived in caves and subsisted on acorns. It is pharisaical egoism to say to the lower classes that one can be happy with any income. You close your remarks with a reference to Fritz Reuter's idyls in order to show how false it is to ask too much for the lower classes. As if Uncle Bräsig and the honest Havermann were hungry proletarians! As if all of Reuter's poetry did not revolve about middle-class, well-off farmers and leaseholders, village mayors, and members of the lower middle class—all threatened by modern progress!

Everyone compares himself and his situation with the average conditions of his time. He can feel happy if, insofar as he does his duty and no especially unfavorable events befall him, he amasses a small property for a secure old age, if he has the possibility of advancing a little, of bringing up his children so that progress is possible and the chance of their remaining on the same social level is greater than that of their falling to a lower one. Can we say this possibility is the case today for the lower half of our middle class and working class? In this regard were the peasant and handicraft workers of earlier times not in a somewhat better position, although they did not know many pleasures and, for example, were undoubtedly more poorly clothed than our contemporary working class?

You admit that state and society are responsible for a certain level below which the lower classes must not be allowed to sink. The five formal rights of equality which you concede as the outcome of a reasonable equality make sense only if their result is a material one, if they have definite consequences for the psychological and material life of the lower classes. And historically speaking there can be no doubt that your demands go further than we went a century ago, and that they therefore do not express for all time what the principle of equality demands and what can eventually occur that will assist in raising the lower classes.

Already in some respects the state offers more than you demand; the principles of tax equality and universal military service are not contained in your five principles; the duty of raising the suffering, stunted classes from whose activity the Prussian state became great cannot be included under the rubric of "right of the poor" which you use. Two of your demands are absolutely indefinite, namely that every man shall be able to exercise his talents in order to rise as high as ability and good luck permit, and that every man shall have an education in accordance with the general cultural level. This involves a great deal, or, depending upon circumstances, less than we already have now. Ease of rising in society for the gifted depends on social and political arrangements of the most varied kind. It is a question as to how these are implemented in detail, and whether they promote the rise of talent or not. Moreover, what is the indispensable amount of education? In the previous century it was held that the peasants would refuse all obedience once they were enlightened. It seemed dangerous to teach a girl to write; an old schoolmaster wrote in 1772 that "for young girls writing is merely a vehicle for a disorderly life." Even Justus Möser thought that as a man of the people he could not marry a woman who could read and write. You protest similarly against too much education for the lower classes; you assert that it is dangerous when a majority oversteps a certain degree of education, and you oppose state continuation schools and obligatory attendance. You do this in a time when our craftsmen and peasants are absorbed by large-scale enterprises everywhere, not because big industry can accomplish more but because business and technical education in small business has lagged too far behind; a time when every manufacturer and master craftsman complains of the lack of schooling, and only a minute fraction of our workers have the technical and humane education necessary to care for the machines and attend to the simplest correspondence or written regulations. An organization for employing women in Berlin declared that only nine per cent of the women and girls among the hundreds making application had the ability in reading and writing needed for a special task. I have often been told the same by manufacturers from the province of Saxony. One of the latest writers on social questions, Ludwig Felix, who otherwise sympathizes in many ways with your views, closes his discussion of this subject with the words: "And still narrow-minded people struggle against the spread of enlightenment from fear that the result would be a lack of workers for the heaviest labor and lowest jobs."

You see too that the five rights which you represent as the consequence of reasonable equality have no definite limits; one could speak with comparable validity of six or seven demands of equality. No one of these single rights contains a controlling principle, as, for example, does that phrase of Schleiermacher which might serve as the cornerstone of modern ethics: "No man should be only a means for the purposes of another; each must, even if he functions as an auxiliary member of society for other purposes, at the same time be recognized as an end in himself, as a monad and as something holy in itself." With your theory, however, that the ordinary should serve the noble, that the common man earns the right to survival only through this service—with the application of this theory to a ruling, enjoying, and possessing minority and an obedient, praying, and working majority, you not only deny the Schleiermacher idea, but you support the presumption that every possessing aristocracy is the noble part of a people and the lower classes are vulgar. History teaches us about many able, ambitious aristocrats but also about just as many idle and degenerate ones. It teaches us that every aristocracy of wealth changes with time from an exemplary leader of the people to a pleasure-loving and parasitic drone possessing rights but recognizing no duties. I assert therefore that as often as the vulgar served the noble, the noblest was forced to serve the vulgar. Out of the resistance to this have come all great political and social reforms, first of all the monarchy itself, whose only ideal legal right lies in the protection of the weak and abused against class domination.

If I speak of the monarchy in this way, I mean its common vocation in world history; I do not mean that it always finds it necessary to restrain and control the wealthy class, as did the Roman Caesars, the Tudors, the French Cardinals Mazarin and Richelieu, and the great French and Hohenzollern kings between 1640 and 1840. A free state demands a balance between monarchy and aristocracy and between upper and lower classes. It demands likewise, however, in still greater degree than does the form of the normal state, whatever its constitution, a certain unity of feeling and culture.

Unity of culture is possible only if the division of wealth is not too unequal and if the class differences are not too great, and when the educational facilities and the technical and humane training of the various classes are not too different. This unity of culture of the ruling concepts and ideas seems to me so important that I should like to say that in comparison inequality of income and wealth is unimportant. I regret the latter especially because it appears to threaten the cultural foundation of a free state. If this foundation is lacking, the beginning of the end is already here; the various classes cease to understand one another. If they can no longer communicate, conflict takes the place of understanding and revolution that of reform.

Every people and every state, at least every free state, comprises a moral community, where it is demanded that in the hour of danger the individual sacrifice his life for the commonweal. It is a demand which can be made only when the people feels itself a moral entity and has common ideals which are placed above individual values. In the great days of the Roman state, the religious feeling for the state was the bond uniting all; in the Middle Ages Christian faith was the chief unifying element; among the Moslems it was a fanatical hope of Paradise. The essential point about modern conditions is the freeing of the state and also broad classes of society from the Church, from the moral community of its faith. One may regret this development, but it it a fact to be reckoned with; it is a fact which is necessarily connected with the development of the modern spirit. Modern philosophy, toleration of all religions and confessions, the best part of modern knowledge—these are conceivable only in a state freed from Church and in a sociey where humane education and pure human ability and integrity provide as good a right to existence as adherence to the Catholic Church or the Augsburg Confession. The further consequence is that the Church and belief in the Church no longer control the masses, especially the lower classes, and cannot control them as they did earlier, and that the belief in and hope of a better hereafter as consolation for the injustices and burdens of this life cannot prevail to the same degree as they did earlier.

At this point you begin your criticism: you urge with passionate pathos that we must not rob the poor of their faith. But you completely forget that a man who does not himself believe in this faith any more has no right to say this; you forget what an insult to human dignity lies in demanding for an educated minority all the pleasures of culture under the protective roof of philosophical free thought, but at the same time offering the masses for their labor and a life of privation only religious faith and a hope for the next life, things that the majority of the possessing class, especially those pleasure-seekers of fashion and luxury for whom you demand large properties, openly admit that they no longer accept. That is a dose of aristocratic philosophy which our age simply will no longer swallow.

I am convinced that the situation is thus. Perhaps we are approaching a great reform of our church life, a reform going more deeply than the Lutheran and offering a purified creed to which the majority of the educated can subscribe and which will reconcile Catholics and Protestants into a national church. In this case we shall again have as the foundation of our culture the democratic unity and equality that we now lack. Then we who are cultured will have a right to admonish the people to hold fast to the faith of our fathers.

If this change does not come about, as seems likely, then we have to leave religious and philosophical movements to themselves and their own power, which will be so less than before, and for political and social life adopt entirely the standpoint of the state. Then the modern state more than before must assume particular functions which earlier fell to the Church. Through its schools it must provide homogeneous, humane and cultural education, at least in certain fundamentals; it has to arrange its institutions and division of property in such a way that each one, the man without property, the worker, no matter to what faith or cultural level he may belong, can be content with his lot. The Middle Ages could do without the living feeling for the state because it had its ethical churchly foundation. Modern society cannot manage without intense patriotism and feeling for the state; but this state loyalty is not possible without a higher social justice on the part of the state and without the state's acting on behalf of those on whom the burdens of the state, the taxes and universal military service, press most severely. You admit that thousands of harmless, stunted people had the feeling, unfortunately justified, that the state and the wealthy classes took their plight far too little to heart. In the same breath you are angry about the unpatriotic feeling of the Social Democrats and demand that religion reconcile the workers with their lot.

You say that it is not possible that the lower classes will come to understand the laws of communication sufficiently to judge what is due them and what could be done for them. I do not know whether that is as difficult as you think. In any case it is merely a matter of restoring belief in the good will of the ruling circles in regard to reform of social conditions and of maintaining that belief where it exists. We must show the lower classes that the possessing class does not confront them with a narrow-minded feeling of superiority and pharisaical conceit, that a feeling of responsibility still exists in the upper classes and that we are ready to discuss with them any reasonable reform.

One thing more! The upper classes must not merely boast about their knowledge and education; they must also preserve feeling and religion, that is they must remain human. I cannot agree with your theory that the highest spiritual functions of mankind are divided—culture and knowledge for the upper classes, feeling and religion for the lower. This is the implication of your theory. I consider this theory false in tendency and wrong in fact.

The life of feeling and emotion is not more developed among the lower classes. Feeling and religious emotion need cultivation, of which the educated are more capable and likely to partake. Education and wealth do not entirely coincide, perhaps not even for the most part. There are those of wealth from whom vanity, luxury, and boredom take away feeling; offspring of those many marriages based on money and fashion easily grow, as every doctor knows, into cold, tired, spiritless people who are a curse to their parents and a shame to mankind. In individual cases the life of feeling in the lowest social group seems deeper than that in the upper classes because the simple feeling is concentrated on far fewer objects and is capable of more elementary outbursts of nature. In general, however, the highest feeling, like the highest spiritual life, flourishes in the conditions of the golden mean, which is found essentially above the level of today's factory and farm workers. It is only a seeming comfort which you extend to the workers when you so praise and emphasize the spiritual and religious life of the little man. Our reformers and teachers, as well as many of our best officials and ablest big industrialists, have come from the middle class rather than the proletariat.

Just as the upper classes should retain their spirituality and religious sense, one may not and should not do as you do and deny the lower classes all knowledge. Self-conscious definite purpose is everywhere an advance over the merely traditional. You grow so excited about the shamelessness of half-education that you overlook the fact that the way to education lies through half-education. Anyone who, like you, wants to reserve all education for the upper classes must first attack our entire elementary school system. One of our mutual friends, one of the best Prussian patriots, said to me once that there are only two intelligent kinds of schoolmasters, the old Prussian noncommissioned officers of the previous century who taught only discipline and order and the schoolmaster who has studied at the university and so is truly educated and able to teach peasant lads. I agree entirely; but the road from noncommissioned officer to university-trained teacher will require a couple of centuries; we are in a transitional period and either must allow for the dark side or openly and honorably attack the elementary school, do away with it entirely, and make the lower classes again governable by means of Metternichean school principles, or at least by the Stiehl school law.

You demand an improvement of our elementary schools; you defend yourself against the fact that your concept of the working class is identical with the cynical view of the eighteenth century of "the classes decreed by fate to serve" or with the poisonous new French hate of the *classes dangereuses*. Anyone who knows you intimately will think that you are serious; but he who only has read your essays on the patrons of socialism will tell you that the consequence of your protest against the higher education of the lower classes and of your theory of an economic as well as a spiritual and emotional division of labor only leads to socialism and is in opposition to the best achievements of our age.

Schiller and Hölderlin, and all the idealists of the eighteenth and nineteenth centuries, tell us that we shall be ruined by division of labor. Man as such must again be more highly regarded than his particular achievement. Justus Möser has already preached that every intellectual should learn a trade. Instead of a professional army we have introduced universal military service; it is a step backward in division of labor, but it contributes to the physical and spiritual health of our people; and everywhere this solution is continued; alongside minister and councilor, that is the technician and specialist, we introduce the house of representatives or laymen, along with the judge the jury, along with the city council the municipal representatives, alongside the pastor a church council—laymen alongside specialists. These innovations are all sins against the division of labor, but in the interest of humanity, in the interest of a many-sided education, a balance of forces.

At such a time is it wrong to protest against a division of labor which would make cogs out of the workers of our factories? Is it wrong to ask for them participation in the benefits of our culture, in the pleasures of our art, in the blessings of knowledge, in political rights? Is a teaching utterly foolish which finds in the calling of an increasing number of people to the benefits of culture the meaning of history?

You are angry over universal suffrage. Of course it has its disadvantages; but are these not less than those under other systems of voting? Is not this system more in accordance with our ideas and views and more healthy for our development than a property qualification? Is there not in this system of voting a sounder means of educating the lower classes and a sturdy hold against the egoism of the upper classes? Is it not a necessary complement to the principle of universal military service, as Gneist always emphatically maintained?

Universal military service is much more democratic than universal suffrage and is thus thoroughly hated by the full-blooded aristocrats of the old type. Is the most cultivated, for whose education thousands were expended, to serve as cannon fodder like the stupidest peasant boy? This practice means the thorough democratization of the state;

everything else is less important than life, than the question of the sacrifice of individual existence. "The state which to the individual says, 'Give me your blood because I am in danger,' is at another time to say, 'Die of hunger for I do not know you.' That state which forces the primer upon the young child is not willing to stand by the father in seeking bread. And there is a principle which forbids this? Insanity, senselessness, contradiction!" This is what Ludwig Bamberger wrote in 1868; he was then somewhat nearer his prime than now. But he is perfectly right when he deduces from the universal blood tax that the state cannot evade democratic institutions and measures for raising the lower classes.

Thus to me the goal of social development is more democratic than to you; it was my starting point. I count any country happy which has a healthy aristocracy, which along with persons of small wealth has those of medium and great property; but I want the inequality to decrease rather than increase, and I believe that in times like ours it is increasing immoderately and that therefore we must consciously endeavor to bring about the opposite.

The difference between us in this regard lies in the fact that you have an aristocratic, even oligarchical point of view and I have a more democratic one. Which of us departs from the legal standpoint of today is still a question. The aristocratic-oligarchical tendencies seem to me to be much more anti-monarchical than the democratic ones. Whoever is enthusiastic over parliamentary ministers is already a republican. I am so little among these that even for the United States I expect the introduction of monarchy, as in France I expect the return of the empire, because I expect class rule, now of the wealthy, now of the lower classes, wherever there does not exist a monarch as head with an able bureaucracy. Therefore I am a radical Tory or a Tory radical and not, like you, an oligarchical aristocrat.

3. Society and the Nobility

Crown Prince Rudolph: *The Austrian Nobility and Its Constitutional Vocation: A Warning to Aristocratic Youth* (1878)*

Except through novels, we know little about the social history of the nobility in the nineteenth century. That it had dominated the Old Régime, that it suffered severely once the ideals of the French Revolution came into practice in Europe, that its superior position in society was being steadily undermined by industrialism and the rise of the bourgeoisie, that it found the task of ruling peasants far easier than that of controlling a proletariat and modern nationalists—these general facts are well known. In many areas it continued as a group in a position of power, however, and the forms and extent of its adjustment to changed conditions need investigation.

The "Warning to Aristocratic Youth" has special significance because of the identity of its co-author, Archduke Rudolph of Austria-Hungary. His condemnation of the nobility was not entirely deserved by all its members in every country—for example not in most of Germany. But from what we know at present, the picture we have here is true in general of the reaction of the group to the changing opportunities and demands of the century. The "warning" should aid in understanding why in the present century the European nobility suffered almost wholesale destruction, at least as a group.

THE AUSTRIAN NOBILITY AND STATE SERVICE

The value of a status group [*Stand*] to the social body lies in the service which it performs for this body. A social or status group which

* *Der Oesterreichische Adel und sein constitutioneller Beruf:* Mahnruf an die *aristokratische Jugend von einem Oesterreicher* (Munich, 1878). (The Austrian economist Karl Menger was co-author.)

78

does not have the ambition to excel others, at least in some respect, cannot in the long run claim for itself a prominent place in state affairs. One of the most significant symptoms of political incompetence in a group may be seen when the majority of its members avoid the opportunities for entry into the higher professions that serve the general welfare. Such a symptom is evident in the fact that only a very few wealthy Austrian aristocrats seriously devote themselves today to public service.

The unprejudiced observer will be surprised at the extent to which the Austrian civil service is neglected by the members of the landed aristocracy. Especially is it astonishing to see the heirs of the old military nobility of Austria turning away more and more from a military career, whereas at all times the aristocracy has claimed for itself the right to be the favored bearer of the knightly way of life, and the military actually has been the gathering place for the youth of the nobility. The explanation of the regrettable present state of affairs lies in circumstances which are in no way a source of pride for our contemporary nobility.

It is known that as the result of bitter experience our army has undergone a complete reform during the last decade. I have no intention here of indulging in any recriminations; but we all remember that the period which proved so injurious to our army and which had such fateful consequences for us, and from which the reforms I mention sprang, was that period in which the nobility filled the majority of the high-ranking positions in the army and held a dominating position in it. A complete lack of serious military knowledge and of any effort to distinguish itself through intelligence at that time characterized almost the entire military nobility. It excelled in horsemanship, in loving care of the prized knightly spirit, and in extraordinary courage in the face of the enemy. In cavalry attacks those nobles in the lower ranks rushed into enemy fire in defiance of death. Later, in their old age, as noble officers with high commands, they took their places in the front ranks of their brigades, in order, by a display of personal courage, to avoid responsibility for the leadership to which they did not feel equal and which they anxiously shunned. In this way many of the nobility fell on the Austrian battlefields, while brigades, divisions, and even entire army corps were left to the inadequate and often not respected guidance of general-staff officers, and so were defeated.

In time of peace the situation was still worse. During wartime the aristocrats awed us with their truly heroic courage. But in time of peace, when work should be done in the army, the troops exercised in difficult maneuvers, and the officer corps technically trained in military science, almost nothing was done in any of these respects; the upper commands provided no impetus. On the contrary they tried to preserve the untenable *status quo* by derisive remarks about any and every act of progress. The entire thinking and endeavor of the noble higher officers aimed only at maintaining in the officer corps a light, gallant tone and at training outstanding riders. All reforms in organization were anxiously avoided, and it was self-confidently believed that the army, composed of old soldiers, would remain invincible by reason of its great courage and the daring of its leaders.

The bravest of Austria's sons died on the Bohemian battlefields, a sacrifice to this blindness.

The bitter experience which Austria drew from these fateful defeats bore good fruit, however, and the army too began to introduce progress. The organization, weapons, and training of the army underwent energetic reform; a vigorous system of examination gradually purged all ranks of their untrained elements; universal compulsory service called all classes to the colors; and now after more than ten years of really remarkable effort the Austro-Hungarian army stands forth as a military model.

With this reorganization, however, most of the aristocracy slipped out of the ranks of the army. The older men had become useless, partly in the last war and partly during the years of reorganization; it was understandable that they should go. But the younger nobility discontentedly withdrew from military service, and the present aristocratic youth seeks in all too many cases to get through the year of service as quickly as possible, as if it were a burdensome interruption, and believes that with this service it has done enough for the fatherland. Not a few are delighted when for some small defect they are declared unfit, sometimes to everyone's astonishment; for one can see the strongest noble youths galloping through the Prater avenues, quite unashamed of being known as unfit for the service of their country. Only relatively few young aristocrats—honorable exceptions!—dedicate themselves to the difficult task of being modern professional soldiers.

Excuses for this way of acting certainly exist. The aristocrats gladly emphasize the argument that the modern army is not the right place for the nobility; for, since the law places the nobility on a basis of full equality with the other classes, the nobility cannot serve joyfully, etc. Actually, the reason for their unpatriotic abstention lies in quite other directions, especially in the boundless indolence of most of the young aristocrats and in their faint-heartedness toward any kind of serious study. The series of severe tests which bars the way of the indolent and frivolous to the higher military positions, along with the strenuous work with the troops as well as with the general staff, frightens the young nobleman. Even the cavalry has long ceased to be a privileged do-nothing career and is no longer the gathering place of aristocratic youth. These are the true reasons why our young noblemen avoid the army.

What a profound lack of true sense of honor lies behind the above excuse. It is considered a sufficient reason for withdrawing from military service that ability rather than birth determines the Austrian military career! To outdo the middle-class through serious effort and distinguished performance is unthinkable! In the main our young aristocrats only smile at the idea of gaining an advantage over the middle class by cultivation of the military spirit and by military training in the aristocratic families and the consequent attainment of military prestige in an honorable and valid way. The above excuse is a true disgrace for those who hope to use it to quiet the stirrings of conscience warning them that military service is an old and imprescriptible responsibility of the well-to-do nobility.

What is one to say of the attitude of those aristocrats, grown gray in the army, who proudly emphasize their military ways on every occasion but do not have the patriotism to raise their sons to be able officers? Often these old gentlemen constantly return to the thought that entrance into the army has been made impossible for the nobility by the reforms of the last decade.

Do not answer what we have said by arguing that in the moment of danger the young aristocrat will hasten to the colors just as he once did; this is no longer a matter of merit but a compulsory universal duty. And if it were an act of merit, a patriotic sacrifice, of what value for an army setting out against an enemy is a number of inadequately trained and at the same time highly arrogant officers? They are as often an embarrassment as a help to the army command.

No less sad is the case in regard to the participation of the aristocracy in the civil service. I do not want to be bitter toward anyone; but everyone knows how hard it is to fill posts with representatives of the upper aristocracy who are technically well prepared for their profession, even though the nobility is otherwise especially suited to the civil service. Who can deny that here too the nobility does not satisfactorily fulfill its duty to the country?

THE AUSTRIAN ARISTOCRACY AND ITS PARLIAMENTARY VOCATION

A variety of remarks may be made about the position which the Austrain aristocracy occupies in our parliamentary life; but there can be no disagreement on one point, namely that the position assigned to the nobility by the constitution in parliamentary life is as outstanding legally as it is insignificant in practice.

Under our constitution the heads of noble families with land holdings constitute the core of the Austrian upper house [*Herrenhaus*], and consequently they control the decisions of one of the three factors of our legislative process. That the landed nobility is assured likewise a significant influence over the lower house and in the provincial assemblies strengthens in no small measure the weight of the above-mentioned parliamentary power position.

If we inquire, however, about the actual influence of our nobility upon legislation, we meet a situation scarcely more favorable than that described above.

A not insignificant part of our aristocracy holds itself aloof from our constitutional life and rejects the legislative influence which is assured it under the constitution. Another part remains completely indifferent to constitutional life; whether it does so because of lack of understanding of the importance of the parliamentary task assigned to the nobility under the constitution, or because it is conscious of its small ability for the task need not be decided. The fact is that part of the hereditary membership of the upper house makes little or no use of its right to take part in the sessions. Only a relatively small number of the heads of our noble families called to the upper house under the constitution regularly and actively participates in the work of the *Herrenhaus*. Everyone who follows the work of the upper house with even moderate attention knows that this latter number is furthermore not the most outstanding part, and that the parliamentary burden of the upper house in general is not borne by the hereditary, aristocratic members of the *Herrenhaus*.

The informed scarcely need to be told that such a state of affairs is far from gratifying for our public life. The constitution did not assign to the aristocracy so important a position in constitutional life without a plan and purpose in mind; the aristocracy was not given such participation in the legislative process of the empire and its constituent parts just to increase the glory of a certain number of noble families by the hereditary title of *Reichsrat*. The aristocracy, along with the grant of so unprecedented a parliamentary power in our reformed constitutional state, was also given a public mission, the fulfillment of which is both a right and a duty. This mission is to represent in our legislation the conservative point of view.

When a part of our Austrian aristocracy rejects its entrusted parliamentary task out of antagonism to our constitutional institutions, and another part performs its task in a highly inadequate way out of indifference to parliamentarism and even more frequently out of incapacity, the conservative point of view rests in incompetent hands. Continual vacillation in parliamentary affairs, the innumerable difficulties which every Austrian government encounters, and especially the impossibility of a free development of our liberal parties result from the above disturbance in the balance of constitutional forces. Our entire constitutional life is diseased because of the lack of an informed conservative party which with an eye to the needs of the present and of the future might unite a feeling for the importance of the existing and of the traditional. Our nobility, if not entirely at least in the first instance, must bear the blame for this disease.

I am certainly not inclined to criticize personally the present heads of the Austrian noble families, especially in cases where insufficient capacity for serving the conservative cause is to blame for the above evil. Whoever knows to some extent the situation of our nobility knows that the present holders of the title of hereditary *Reichsrat* in the upper house have largely spent their youth with other matters than preparation for political affairs. When the Austrian constitution appeared, no one at all acquainted with conditions could avoid the feeling that the Austrian nobility by and large is merely a bearer of conservative interests. No one could actually think that it was at the time capable of adequately representing these interests.

What could have been expected and what must be expected as a basic tenet of our constitutional life was the gradual growth of a well-informed conservative party within the ranks of our nobility. It could have been expected that the aristocracy—the older members by active participation in parliamentary life, the younger ones through serious study—would energetically seek to prepare themselves for their important role in our national public life.

This did not occur. Neither by comprehensive participation in parliamentary activity nor, so far as one can see, by serious intellectual effort has our aristocracy sought to prepare itself for the task assigned it by the constitution and by the very nature of things. Almost nothing has occurred in this respect. After more than fifteen years under the constitution, not even the beginning step of building a well-informed conservative party has been taken. This is a reproach which even its warmest friends cannot spare the Austrian aristocracy.

The Way of Life and the Social Habits of Our Aristocracy

In judging a status group, the public achievements of its members are not the only decisive criterion; its social customs are almost as important. Significant achievements on the part of individual members of a group are often symptomatic of the spirit which in general animates the group, but still they are the work of single individuals. Social customs, on the other hand, are the true expression of the whole of a social class, or at least of its dominant majority.

I should therefore be giving a very incomplete picture of the present condition of our aristocracy if I did not go into this matter of social customs, so important for judging them. I shall thus try first to describe the apparently uniform way of life of our aristocracy as objectively and dispassionately as I can.

In the spring after the last horse races, mostly at the end of May, the married members of the nobility go to the country to while away the beginning of the season in hunting, riding, and visiting in the neighborhood. This diversion lasts until the middle of the summer, when a large number travel to Switzerland, to the sea coast, or in the Austrian mountains, where in the greatest boredom they await the end of the summer. Shortly before the onset of autumn the hunting for big game begins, and the gentlemen, some of whom are owners of hunting properties but most of whom are members of hunting societies in the mountains, can fill their time with mountain-goat hunting. In the meantime the ladies visit their parents and other relatives in the country, where they pass the time in making plans for next winter's balls and other festivities and in carrying on unbelievably trivial conversation. Once back in his manor house in autumn, the noble begins to hunt small game; the neighbors gather 'round along with the young bachelors, who come to take part in the pleasures of the hunt. In the evening there is a big tea and sometimes even amateur theatricals—of course in French. In this season too the ladies plan and arrange marriages, and these affairs furnish the subject of endless conversation.

In late autumn many gentlemen and some of the ladies go to the hunt in Pardubitz, the center of the sport. The coursing with hounds, which takes place there in good weather, is regarded by a part of the nobility as the more serious part of life. If the weather turns out unfavorable for hunting, they soon all go back to the country, where December is spent amid hunting and other pleasures.

After Christmas they journey to Vienna, and the most important part of the year begins. The events of this period consist of balls, evening parties of many sorts, now and again amateur theatricals, theatre-going, riding, drives in the Prater, skating, and horse-racing, all activities which are carried on with the greatest seriousness and about which the conversation turns from midday, when skating begins in the Schwarzenberg Gardens, until far into the night in the smoking rooms. Between times, gentlemen and ladies find time to take part in the other pleasures of city life insofar as these appeal to individual taste.

Year after year this program fills with few exceptions the life of our aristocrats; it absorbs their every thought to such a degree that most of them scarcely ever imagine the efforts, struggles, and achievements of the other parts of society! And if this group is disturbed for a moment by a more significant event, it only sinks back the next minute into the old ways, conscious again that it is leading a meaningful life as "society."

If only this program—so shallow and so far from the great goals of today—were at least carried out with elegance and grace! In this respect, too, in recent years the observer finds very unpleasant manifestations. The Austrian nobility in general and Viennese society especially were famous everywhere a short time ago for their gentility and for the refined tone which pervaded their circles. The nobility of the old school, of whom we still see a few like relics of another age wandering about, were for the most part superficial, uneducated, often frivolous people; but they had a certain nobility of bearing which distinguished them. We cannot say even this of the present aristocrats, especially of the younger generation. They have renounced as uncomfortable many old customs, a thousand considerations which earlier characterized class and family, and have put in their place nothing of excellence. The unprejudiced observer will be astonished to see that some of the younger generation of noblemen have a bearing which can be described in no other way than as completely uncouth, and that obviously they cultivate this kind of behavior with the greatest care and try to develop it to a certain point of virtuosity.

The ideal for this is the so-called cabby fashion or sporting manner, which consists essentially of nothing more than boundless rudeness and disdain for every social form, and whose only merit is to surmount the difficulties of social life without intellect and education. Thanks to the great effort which many young men expend on the study of these manners, they are seldom surpassed in them by stable boys or jockeys.

Strangely enough, this coarsening of manners has spread not only among the young men, but to no small degree it has won over some of the ladies too. In Vienna there are smoking rooms for aristocratic women whose conversations, carried on until late into the night, recall in tone those of the low-class theatre and the art world, and indeed not in the best sense. A foreign prince, on leaving Vienna recently, made this exaggerated although in certain cases not entirely untrue statement: "I amused myself excellently with the ladies of the Viennese aristocracy, but I couldn't find a 'lady' among them." I repeat that this is a gross exaggeration; for many aristocratic circles, however, it may be a good description in few words. In any case it can be taken as a telling symptom of the fact that the famous elegance of the Viennese aristocracy has greatly declined.

A perfect proof of this, in case such is still needed for anyone who knows the situation, was an event which came into the open from within the inner circle of aristocratic society and thus directly challenged public criticism. I speak of the theatre production given by the aristocrats for the benefit of the flood victims in the spring of 1870. The purpose was worthy enough, but the means could not be ennobled even by the most sterling purposes.

Some antagonism is always aroused in a city where there is truly no lack of theatres, when persons who are not professional actors appear on the stage of a public theatre and present themselves as objects for approval or rejection, of amusement or displeasure. This is especially strange in the case of persons who exhibit great pride in dealing with their fellow men and mostly think of themselves as better than these. However, as we have said, the project had a humane purpose and intrinsically nothing can be said against it. But when for this noble purpose trivial and even worse than trivial means are used, every unprejudiced person asks in surprise whether such a thing could have been undertaken by an aristocratic group. This question was on everyone's lips on the evening of the production.

The play chosen and the manner of its production had nothing in the least uplifting; they did not even have the light frivolous character which usually dominates our stage and contributes at least to the amusement of the less-educated public. The pieces and acting were heavy and indescribably ignoble.

If patriotic tableaux from Austrian history had sufficed and the other productions deemed necessary had been left to professional actors, and if only a right choice of pieces had been supervised, no one could have had occasion to censure. But what an impression these pieces and this acting created!

The gentlemen played badly and awkwardly; but some of the ladies achieved the most astonishing effect imaginable as they came before the audience with affected ease and self-possession and spoke and sang the most licentious words and songs. The unaccustomed situation made their movements awkward and clumsy, and the presentation hereby lost the light tone which saves such pieces, even if they are trivial, when they are performed by able artists. It was a pitiful performance. The evening did great harm to the reputation of aristocratic Viennese society, for everyone saw what taste they had, what they thought interesting, and with what they amused themselves.

These facts, which indicate the shallowness of the social existence of our aristocracy, are not matched by even a few which would indicate a general interest on the part of our nobility in the intellectual endeavors of our time. How isolated among our aristocrats are those whom not only the servile flatterer but also the judgment of the informed could designate as promoters of our national intellectual efforts!

About the Present Education of Our Aristocratic Youth

In the above sections I have pointed out the position which the Austrian nobility occupies in our public and social life and how little this corresponds to its great tradition. I have indicated its diminishing role in the Austrian civil and military service, in our parliamentary life, and even in social life. I have in no way concealed the fact that the above evils are to be traced by and large to the limited interest in education of our aristocracy and to its aversion to serious consistent work. It will now be my task to picture the present situation of education in aristocratic circles, in order to be able on this foundation to present to the public my proposals for improving present conditions.

A rather large part of the aristocratic youth, especially the sons of religiously disposed nobles, are sent at the age of between eight and nine years to the Jesuit *gymnasium* at Kalksburg, where the young gentlemen remain for eight years. As to the method of instruction there—it has often been discussed publicly, so that I can dispense with any further discussion of it here. As to the line of instruction, it is no secret that in this establishment the young receive an education which is in no way friendly to the modern age. Instead of being filled with understanding and respect for the great cultural efforts of our time and with love for their revived nation and its institutions and instead of being prepared for public effectiveness in the modern state, these young aristocrats learn here to misunderstand the cultural institutions and currents of our age, perhaps even to loathe them, then to embark into active life as strangers, not filled with conservative ideas and with love of the traditional but with aversion to the existing legal institutions and to every cultural advance.

The young noblemen go from Kalksburg largely to the University of Innsbruck. Here amid the Tyrolean people, influenced by the ultramontane views of the social circles in which they move, they develop the stubbornness which unfortunately employs their character and will in ways antagonistic to culture.

This part of our nobility is as good as lost to the modern state. It has only resentment against the state and no understanding of its nature and its needs. It is therefore completely unable to take its place as a useful part of the organism: it is only a hindrance to every natural development of our public institutions.

The other and less clerically influenced part of our nobility has its sons follow much the same road. The young boys, after they have had their elementary schooling at home, are sent to a public *gymnasium,* mostly with the intent to bring them into contact with young people from other classes and to arouse their ambition, and their instruction always begins here under the most hopeful circumstances. Strangely and almost without exception, they all leave these public schools in a very short time. It is usually said that the society of the others was not suitable, that the young gentlemen might be ruined, and this becomes the excuse to take them home and return them to the house tutor. In fact this is only an excuse, and the real reason why the young noblemen leave their studies so regularly after a short time is quite another one.

In recent times in the Austrian *gymnasia* great demands have been made upon the effort and talent of the students. If the young people are to follow lectures intelligently, they need to follow the custom of passing the day in the classrooms, the morning and evening hours in study. Today the *gymnasium* demands much of even gifted pupils and absolutely requires a quiet life of few diversions.

The young noblemen are absolutely deterred by the social customs of their families from such a way of life. They must incessantly go home or be present at time-consuming festivities at relatives' houses; they must visit the theatre with their parents or attend dances especially arranged in carnival time for the young, pay visits to cousins and friends, help with tableaux and theatres, etc. It is understandable under such conditions that their studies finally suffer and that the young gentlemen have to endure in public the teachers' unpleasant warnings and the mockery of the middle-class pupils. Deeply offended, they complain to their parents, who are themselves largely without any understanding of the conditions for a successful education and naturally take the part of their sons.

In addition the school holidays in summer are inconvenient for the parents. Because of the boys they have to come back from the country earlier; they must leave the hot city later than is pleasant. Mostly they lack the spirit to sacrifice convenience and enjoyment for the education of their children.

It is understandable that under such circumstances the first opportunity is seized of some excuse to take the boys, who of course feel most uncomfortable on the school bench, out of school and to entrust them to the house tutor. Actually this step is brought about by their poor progress, caused by the lack of effort of the young people and their helter-skelter way of life, and by their parents' unwillingness to sacrifice.

The entire effort of their further instruction is then directed toward getting the boys through their examinations in some *gymnasium* or other. The method of accomplishing this is to have the young man memorize the necessary material, thereby of course completely losing the whole point of the school training, the formal education of the mind for the difficult problems of further education.

Once the examination has been passed the young men go to a university, that of Vienna, Prague, or Bonn, where they register for the law, mostly without bothering to attend lectures, which they are quite unable to grasp because of their inadequate preparation. This goes on until they come up against their first state examination, usually at the end of the fourth semester, when they are convinced that the law is too boring and that the study of agronomy is much more important to them. The study of agriculture is then pursued with about the same energy as was law and is likewise dropped before the first examination, and the entire business usually ends with "private lessons in agronomy."

Such is the course of education of the sons of those aristocratic families which are less influenced by ultramontanism; and those are not the least able of these young men, since the others do not go to the university at all. Cases in which wealthy young aristocrats finish their law studies in the normal way and gain academic degrees are praiseworthy but not very frequent exceptions.

One hardly needs to mention that an education such as we have described is completely worthless for the life and especially for the practical effectiveness of our young noblemen. There can be no doubt that it exerts a ruinous influence upon the mind and character of these young people. Already in youth it accustoms the nobility not to take responsibilities seriously, to regard them as inferior to social considerations, and to see no disgrace in lagging behind others in application and energy. They early learn all sorts of ways of slighting duties. They grow accustomed to pursuing their studies only up to the examination stage and consequently to pursuing other duties also only to the decisive point. Hence they lack the knowledge derived from serious study and the training of mind and character which a carefully executed education imparts for life to those who have gone through it.

Thus it is this lack of education on the part of our young aristocrats which comes to light so clearly in their later public activity—if it does not entirely exclude them from this life. Our young aristocrats do not lack talent, but they have no intellectual training which would make their talent of value; they lack that fund of positive knowledge which is necessary for taking an effective part in today's public affairs. Especially do they lack the seriousness, persistence, and consistency of will which alone can lead to significant success in public life. The deficient education of our aristocratic young people is the basic reason for the insignificant role which the nobility plays in public life. Thus here is the point from which any effort for improvement of the above conditions must proceed.

How the Sons of the Nobility Should Be Educated

In the foregoing section I have discussed the evils of the educational system used with our young aristocrats and its harmful consequences upon the public effectiveness of the nobility. In the following section I shall discuss the means for improving the situation and describe the education which should be undertaken to train the aristocratic youth for the public calling of the nobility.

I consider that in general the question of whether elementary education should begin in public schools or with private instruction is of little importance. Both ways have their own advantages and disadvantages, and the superiority of the one over the other is largely dependent upon the special circumstances under which instruction takes place.

Teachers for the most part adequate and sufficiently prepared exist for private instruction in elementary subjects, and the boys who receive private teaching escape many harmful physical and psychological influences; indeed, energetically conducted private instruction in elementary subjects by and large leads to more intensive results than attendance at the public schools. Moreover, it imposes less sacrifice upon the convenience of the family, as it is not so tied up as public education with definite times of the day and year. The disadvantages of private instruction in the first period of schooling— i.e., the lack of competition with the boys of the same age, the lack of severe discipline, etc.—are undoubtedly noteworthy; but they can easily be circumvented by clever pedagogy. In cases where the tutors have enough authority and the parents enough understanding and good will to keep the children consistently away from all influences disruptive of the purposes of teaching during the time devoted to instruction, where a family regards the instruction as an important factor in the future of the boys, to which all other considerations must be secondary, carefully chosen private teachers will certainly succeed in obtaining satisfactory results in elementary education. Where such is not the case and the instruction from the beginning is looked upon as secondary, public school instruction will prove useless likewise.

It is otherwise with private study at the level of the *gymnasium* and similar intermediate schools. At this level private study is thoroughly reprehensible, apart from a few exceptions discussed below.

In the first place, suitable personnel for such teaching is nonexistent. Where can a private tutor be found who would be competent in all branches of secondary instruction? The fact that such universal ability does not exist has led in all countries with advanced methods of teaching to the so-called subject-teacher system in the secondary schools, under which every secondary-school teacher is responsible for one field, or at most two related fields. It has long been recognized that one teacher cannot give successful instruction in all the *gymnasium* subjects. The idea is simply absurd that a house tutor—usually a man who has failed as a secondary-school teacher or one preparing for this career—could achieve the necessary results.

Instruction in the disciplines of the *gymnasium*, as private scholars receive it from their house tutors, is therefore on the whole the most wretched imaginable. As a rule the pupils are trained with some thoroughness only in the special field of the tutor, insofar as he has one; in all other fields the training is confined to the most superficial memorizing of the material presented, which is often insufficiently understood by the teacher. The entire intellectual effort of specialized teachers in the public *gymnasium*, with its profound influence upon the educational process of the pupil, is in the case of the private student entirely lost. At most the private students memorize enough to get through the examinations, but the real educational effort, the mastery of the intellectual content of the discipline, remains alien to them. Private study is from the first a renunciation of the most essential part of the educational results intended by the *gymnasium* and could at best be regarded as desirable only in a few isolated cases, those in which the instruction is given by a number of competent specialized teachers directed by a tutor. With this very occasional exception, almost impossible because of the lack of teachers and the high cost, private instruction at the secondary-school level is thoroughly undesirable.

In addition there is the fact that private study, as it is usually carried on by our young aristocrats, is highly injurious to both the seriousness and the consistency of their education. *Gymnasium* training and the training of youth in general are not intended, as aristocratic circles so frequently imagine, to fill the young people with information. This is only one of their many purposes and by no means the most important. The essential aim of the education of young people consists of the training and development of their abilities and character. The individual branches and the entire system of knowledge are only means to this end. Private study may at best give the pupils such knowledge as will suffice for the examinations; but the intellectual training and rigorous discipline of the will which result from competition of young minds led by specialists and from the seriousness of public teaching can never be achieved by means of private instruction. It is for this reason that I consider private study in gymnasial subjects pernicious in the highest degree. If all our nobility were to send their sons to well-known public *gymnasia,* I think that a very important step would be taken toward the improvement of education in our aristocratic circles.

Of course not everything would be achieved with this move. In order for the young nobles to play a worthy role in the public schools they must be able to fulfill their duties there. In the same spirit of sacrifice and with the same understanding of the middle-class families, the older members of the aristocracy would have to see that all disturbance in the course of education is avoided. They would have to exercise their right of control and their authority toward the actual and complete achievement of the goals set by the course of study at the *gymnasium,* whereas at present unfortunately just the opposite is frequently the case. I come here to a point which

I must discuss at length, in view of the incredibly slight understanding in aristocratic families of the purpose of study in general and especially of gymnasial training.

Nowhere is there more inclination than in the noble family to ask about the usefulness of a subject. History, geography, the principles of mathematics, natural science, literature, and a few others are excepted from their objections. But why Latin? Why the more complicated problems of mathematics, never used in real life? Why the laborious study of Greek? There are certainly few aristocratic families in which the parents themselves do not divide the disciplines of the *gymnasium* into those which are useful, or in any case useful at some future time, and those which are quite useless, directed only at making the young suffer. There are few who would not support their sons in the opinion that a large part, and indeed the most difficult part, of academic study is worthless for life and purely the hobby of pedantic professors.

Those who share these views seem not to know that the plan of study of the *gymnasia* and especially the number of hours assigned to each subject is set not by the teachers of the *gymnasium* but by the highest of our educational officials. That these latter have accepted the study of ancient languages, including Greek, into the secondary-school plan of study, in agreement with the legislative bodies of all civilized nations, is explained by their correct understanding of the purposes of these schools. The secondary school is supposed, as already mentioned, to provide the young people who attend it with positive and useful knowledge for their lives; but this is not its only purpose. Much more—indeed above all—its purpose is to assure young minds a formal education and to train them for the difficult tasks of their further education. The experience of past centuries has taught us that for this educational purpose no study has shown itself more effective than that of ancient languages, just because of their incomparable difficulty and the variety of the intellectual powers of the young which their study sets in motion. The study of ancient languages in the man who has completely overcome their difficulties leaves as fruit of his effort a training of the mind to handle the most varied and abstruse problems of science and practical life.

The study of ancient languages, of complicated mathematical prob-

lems, etc., is therefore of decisive importance for the further education of young people, and, in the final analysis, for the effectiveness
of these young people in practical life.

Of course neither training in ability to think nor the study of
ancient languages is necessary for moving about gracefully in the
ballroom, for flushing a mountain cock, or calling out an encouraging "tirez-haut" to a neighbor on a pheasant shoot, or for similar
situations of practical life. But to pursue successfully the study of
law and political science [*Staatswissenschaft*], in order as a member
of a legislative body or as a statesman to solve the difficult problems
of legislation and administration which demand formal training of
the mind in the highest degree, in order in the midst of the conflicting
considerations of practical life to be able to hold fast to mankind's
highest goals, one needs intellectual training and a feeling for the
ideal, for which all specialists in the field agree there is no better
preparation than the study of ancient languages and of those excellent works written in them.

As long as our aristocracy lacks this point of view and makes the
usual difference between useful and useless subjects in the gymnasial
course of study, as long as young men find support on the part of
their families for their easily understandable effort to avoid the most
difficult fields of study, their secondary-school training will necessarily be highly inadequate and their preparation for university
study and for their professions completely insufficient. Only when
their parents send the aristocratic young men to public schools, and
demand of them a rigid fulfillment of their responsibilities in the
same way as middle-class fathers demand it of their sons, will the
young men of the nobility be equal to the university and, later, to
the difficult tasks which they must confront in practical life.

I believe that likewise the young men of the nobility who dedicate
themselves to the military should go through the foregoing course
of study with the same seriousness; the loss of more years in service
would be more than counterbalanced by their higher competence.
Also those who intend to turn to agriculture, without the study of law
or political science, can before they enter a higher school of agricultural training find no better preparation for it, and no better oppor-

tunity for acquiring an all-around education, than by attending a good public *gymnasium*. But the young aristocrats who aim at parliamentary life or intend to devote themselves to the civil service will have to choose this road and afterward go to the university in order to obtain from the legal and political-science faculties the technical training they need for their future professions.

At the university the nature of the training is so much freer that a strict, detailed supervision of it by the parents or by a tutor is hardly possible without great disadvantage to the efforts of the young men. The simplest and most appropriate course of action here is to allow the young as much freedom as possible in the choice of means and use of their time, but to demand from them that they take the examinations absolutely on time.

The young men must realize that they are to expect the worst at home if they return without taking the state tests. The known difficulty of these will of itself lead the young noblemen to use their time at the university wisely, once they know the full seriousness of the situation. An examination well passed is on the whole a sign that time at the university has been well spent, whereas withdrawal from law studies just before the test under the excuse that legal study is useless, etc., can well be taken as the best proof that the young men have wasted their time. This is not to say that unusually talented young people will not try to go beyond what is required to pass the examinations; I only mean to affirm that the passing of the examinations is the very least the parents can demand from their sons who go to the university, even in case of modest ability, and every effort on the part of the young men to avoid these rocks is nothing more than empty pretext. It can be demanded from the more talented, without danger of overburdening them, that in accordance with their ability they take some general historical and philosophical courses along with their professional courses.

If I demand here that the young aristocrats follow exactly at the university the course of study laid down by law and controlled by examination, it is because I think that under present circumstances this is the best way to keep them from completely wasting their time at the university. In no way do I fail to recognize that our law and political-science faculties no longer fully meet present conditions, and especially not the needs of our aristocratic youth.

Those young aristocrats who intend to dedicate themselves neither to the army nor exclusively to agriculture expect to acquire by going to the university the necessary knowledge of law and political science to fit them for their future professions as members of parliament or as state bureaucrats. In addition, most of them may want to acquire at least a little knowledge in the various branches of agronomy in order to be able to oversee the administration of their estates with some understanding. The fact that agricultural subjects are not taught in our universities means that they must give up this wish or visit a higher institution of agriculture after they have finished their university studies. Usually the result is that they do not finish either their legal or their agricultural studies, since only a very few can be expected to attend two higher institutions of learning one after the other. But even those young noblemen who renounce the training in the main branches of agriculture which is so necessary to them, and try for a thorough education in law and political science, find themselves in more than one respect disappointed with the present arrangements in our higher institutions.

The neglect of political science in our universities has so often been pointed out as to make mention of this bad situation superfluous. It is known that even in our most distinguished universities no chair exists for a number of the most important disciplines in political science, and the time allowed the study of the subject in general is most insufficient. It is entirely impossible at an Austrian university to acquire completely the training in political science necessary for an official or a member of parliament. The universities decidedly offer much too little, in many respects practically nothing, for anyone seeking to prepare himself for a political career of any kind.

In addition they burden a future man of politics with historical legal study far beyond any real need.

The future official, diplomat, or parliamentarian has to take historical law exclusively for four full semesters, that is for half the university course. He has two semesters of history and institutions of Roman law, two semesters of the Pandects and Roman civil law, three semesters of German law and its history, and finally two semesters of canon law.

It seems questionable to many whether so extensive a course in historical law is necessary for those who want to train themselves as jurists, that is for our future judges and advocates. However, it is beyond all doubt that so much historical law is entirely useless; indeed it is absurd for all those who intend to go into a political career, and this is notably true of the youth of the nobility.

Every well-informed person knows that the man of politics cannot succeed without a knowledge of law, and that he should be well versed in the law of his own country. The reform movement of recent times is not directed against the study of indigenous law or against such historical studies as are needed to grasp this law. Public opinion is with ever-increasing vigor critical of the system which requires the students in the faculties of law and political science to fill half of a four-year course with the study of historical law, irrespective of whether they intend to go into a legal or into a political career. The public is opposed to this requirement, not in the sense that the amount of historical law taught in our universities today is of no use at all, even for our future political figures. What public opinion advocates is the obvious fact that the future political figure could well pursue during the first two years of the university a much more useful course than is now the case. Let him occupy himself with the study of the historical law as much as appears necessary for grasping the law of his own country; but for the rest of the time let him pursue the special historical and theoretical subjects which his special political profession demands.

Let no one think that our educational system as described here continues in its present condition without a profound influence upon the education of those groups of young men of which I am especially speaking. The young nobleman knows very well that two years of historical law are ahead of him at the university. He knows that at the end of the second year of his four-year course he must show by examination the results of these studies, that accordingly he must take the study of historical law seriously and for four semesters devote his full powers to it, if he is to take in the regular way the work in the faculties. He knows very well that he does not need these studies to the extent to which he must take them and that consequently he is doing without more important and useful courses. He knows too that no small part of what he needs to know is not taught at the university. The consequences of these considerations is that young noblemen are actually frightened away from regular study at the university.

If the study of law and political science in our universities were so reformed as to open an independent course of study corresponding to the needs of those students who intend to take up a political career, the youth of our aristocracy would make use to a much greater degree than is now the case of the opportunity which would be offered them to prepare themselves for their future calling, especially if likewise the main fields of agriculture were to be introduced into the new course of study, at least as optional subjects.

It would then be fairly unimportant for the purpose whether or not this reform were to be expressed in the division of the existing law and political-science faculty into two separate faculties. If only those going into a political career were offered the opportunity, by means of the new arrangement in legal and political-science studies, to acquire all-around knowledge in all branches of political science, in the main aspects of agriculture, and in as much law as is needed for a political career, it would be of less importance whether the division now called for in many quarters for separate law and political-science faculties were carried out or not. I even think that, because of the close connection of law and political science, the complete separation sought by many would prove unnatural. The separation of the two faculties in any case is not necessarily in any way connected with the purpose of the reform—unburdening the future statesman of excessive historical legal studies and developing the offerings in political science in our universities.

If the above-suggested reform of our legal and political-science faculties, on the details of which experts could easily agree, were demanded only by the specific needs of the young nobles, I do not doubt that such a reform would find only moderate support of public opinion because of its being largely in the interest of only one group

in the population. The reform is, however, one which has been requested for decades by the most enlightened proponents of a rational
organization of our higher education in the interest of legal and
political studies, and the fact that it would at the same time correspond especially to the needs of the young nobility can be seen only
as a further reason for bringing it about. It is clear that the present direction of our legal and political-science studies not only does not
correspond with the needs of the young aristocrats who want to
prepare at the universities for their future calling, but, as I have
already indicated, it does not help the other students who intend to
go into the bureaucracy or into some form of political activity.

Until these reforms are carried out—I repeat, the regular course of
study in our faculties of law and political science will be the best
means of training for young noblemen who intend to go into the
civil service or who aim at a parliamentary career.

4. State Control of Education

Paul Bert: *Speech in Behalf of Secular Education* (1879)*

In contrast to the views of Donoso Cortés and Montalembert, M. Paul Bert uses arguments common among the many opponents of the Roman Catholic Church. These opponents became increasingly numerous and vocal as the century progressed, and they included among their number positivists and rationalists, scientists, liberals and nationalists, and others such as a man like Bismarck of the *Kulturkampf*, who belongs in none of these categories. On a greater or lesser scale a *Kulturkampf* occurred in every state in which a considerable number of Catholics was to be found, not only in Germany and France, but in Switzerland and Austria, and even to some degree in Italy, Spain, and elsewhere. Control of education usually constituted the decisive issue; but in countries like Germany, where the state already controlled popular education, other aspects of the relations between church and state appeared in the foreground. M. Paul Bert did not speak for all the multifarious opponents of the Church; yet his speech shows the conflict between an old institution based on revealed dogma and the beliefs of an age of change occurring in every fundamental institution of public life.

M. Bert: I think that it would be superfluous to call the attention of the Chamber to the importance and gravity of the questions submitted to it by the Government's bill. Perhaps it is advisable to bring the debate back within more realistic limits. A storm has arisen inside the country over these bills. Oppression and martyrdom have been complained of, and even in the speech which opened the discussion these preoccupations were evident. It appears that the very

* *Journal Officiel, Chambre des Deputés*, June 22, 1879, IV, 5490-8.

foundations of society have crumbled, that everything has become uncertain.

Apparently at issue is the freedom to teach, legally allowed since 1833 for primary instruction, since 1850 for secondary instruction, and since 1875 for upper schools. It seems that liberty of conscience is itself threatened by us, the sons of the Revolution which proclaimed this liberty, of the Revolution which every one blames for proclaiming . . . Well, I think that there is nothing in this criticism. The question, in spite of its real importance, is not one touching upon these great principles.

I feel, and the committee which has done me the honor of naming me its president feels, that the law submitted to you is one neither of doctrine nor of organization. It is simply a law for the protection of society. It is not a doctrinal law, for it does not meddle with the principle of freedom of teaching. It proclaims this principle; more exactly, the law imparts to the principle its true meaning and true sphere of action; it removes from earlier laws the drastic arrangements which have restricted true freedom of teaching, that is to say liberty of teaching for each individual citizen. It makes some new conditions, or it creates, if you like, a new qualification for a class of citizens.

It is not an organizational law, for it alters nothing in the conditions set by the law which was voted by the Assembly in 1875 for opening, founding, and maintaining upper schools.

It only deprives these schools of a title which actually they have usurped. . . .

It is a law of social protection for two reasons. It puts the state back in full possession of an undeniable prerogative . . . , that of choosing freely the members of the boards of examinations which grant the degree necessary either for obtaining certain state positions or for entering certain professions.

Secondly the law requests that the right to teach at any level, primary, secondary, or upper, be taken from a group of those considered —wrongly or rightly we shall not discuss now—ineligible to use this right either to oppose our liberties or to attack the foundations of our civil, democratic, lay society.

And it is not only for reasons of doctrine that the law relieves the members of this group of the right to teach which is permitted them by previously existing laws; it is also because these men aspire to live in the bosom of our society in secret associations without presenting their organizational statutes for state approval.

. . . .

Among these associations there is one whose name is so celebrated, whose activities are so well known, and which here and in many other countries has so often been brought into court and been proscribed by governments that it seems as if the law were directed only against it. Indeed, in the public mind and national opinion and in the views of our constituents, the law proposed to you aims at depriving the Jesuits of the right to teach French youth. Thus to vote for or against this law appears equivalent to voting for or against the existence and the recognized right to teach of the Society of Jesus.

. . . .

For this reason your committee, with a unanimity marred only by the dissent of M. Gaslonde, has rejected the amendments submitted to it previous to the presentation of the report and has discouraged the submission of new ones by its members. For this reason its president has withdrawn voluntarily a bill which he offered on the same subject for which he had a paternal regard. Likewise we have refused to attempt anything additional or better and have been unwilling to amend the bill of the Government. Except for a few unimportant details we present it to you exactly as it was submitted to us. At a time when the Government chosen by the Assembly of the 363 was assuming its position and was advancing against the enemy, we thought it inopportune to carry on a parliamentary flirtation and to differ on points of detail.

On the Right: What do you call the enemy? You have no right to treat us as enemies. One cannot treat the French as enemies!

One member of the Left: They are not Frenchmen!

M. Bert: It has been used . . . .

M. Huon de Penanster: The president would have called us to order long ago if we had used such a word.

M. Bert: It has been used eloquently from this tribune, and you know that it is in consequence of this word that you have been driven from the Chamber.

M. Huon de Penanster: But we are still in this Chamber!

M. Bert: Clericalism is the enemy!

M. Baudry-d'Asson: As for me, I say that the republican majority is the leprosy devouring society.

The President: M. de Baudry-d'Asson, I call you to order.

M. de la Rochefoucauld: Is it permissible to say that we are enemies?

The President: To mention the Jesuits is not to speak of the members of the Chamber.

M. de la Bassetière: There you have the law of liberty and of appeasement!

M. Bert: For this reason we reached unanimity, and we hope that the Chamber by an immense majority will now support the Government in depriving the party of counterrevolution of the most recent and, one might say, the most audacious and one of its most important conquests. This Government wants to deprive those who have made themselves adversaries of society . . . . [Vigorous protests from the floor.]

M. Bert: Your protests do not surprise me. They prove that much confusion hovers over this discussion; there exists an ambiguity not cleared up either in 1850 or in 1875, and it is time to get rid of this ambiguity and to speak frankly. We are using the same words but they do not have the same meaning for us both.

M. de Baudry-d'Asson: You should have spoken this way before the elections. If you had, you would not be here!

M. Bert: We do not speak the same language, we the sons of the Revolution and on the other side the representatives, the champions and defenders of the Catholic Church, which alone is at stake in the debate.

When we speak of liberty we can neither hear nor understand one another. Thus we need to define it.

Liberty for us—but I shall not make of it something metaphysical;

I do not mean to speak of anything but freedom of teaching—freedom of instruction for us is the practical realization of a personal liberty.

It is a particular case of that precious liberty consecrated by the first Declaration of Rights of 1791: liberty for every citizen to express his thoughts in any form and under all possible circumstances under the watchful eye of the law. It is this liberty which for us is freedom of teaching. For us who believe in progress and perfectibility, to hand down, to teach to others like us what we have learned—that is our right and our duty.

I am proud of having written some time ago these words: "We speak of the right to teach! We should speak of the duty to teach. No one can keep a part of the truth to himself without being a culpable egoist." This liberty, when put into action, like all others knows only one restraint—again defined by the Declaration of Rights—and that is the liberty of others; it stops only at the point where it tramples on the liberty of other citizens.

Is it the same liberty as that meant by the Catholic Church?

That cannot be. We start with human rights, whereas the Catholic Church proceeds from divine right. It has received its investiture from on high; it has received a sacred institution; it has received the order to teach. It has been told: "Go and teach!"

. . . .

The Catholic Church asserts that it has a divine mission to teach truth, that it alone is the depository of this truth, of the truth about the earth beneath and the heavens above, that no one can contradict it in these things, that it has the holy sign, that light does not struggle and does not deign to struggle against obscurity, that error must disappear before truth. It possesses the absolute truth, immutable, eternal, supreme; thus it is intolerant, and this is its right.

The sole fact that it draws its investiture from regions into which we have not penetrated means that its liberty is not, like ours, only the right to speak the truth, to teach its principles. The Church feels its liberty violated by the sole fact that someone says and teaches something contrary to its doctrine.

This liberty cannot endure competition; it must not, and it refuses to do so.

M. le comte de Maillé: Competition! But that is what it asks for!

M. Bert: Beware of heresy, if you want that! For it is written that no one can limit the rights of the Catholic Church, that the Church should have the right to direct and watch over all instruction; that when the pestilential schools—those which are not exclusively Catholic—stand up before the Church, it is an outrage to the Church's liberty.

Your silence proves that you accept this doctrine.

A member of the Right: Not at all. The Church has never said that.

M. Bert: Since you do not accept my reasoning and think that I translate badly—and that does not surprise me—the thought of the Catholic Church and its doctrines, permit me to adduce more competent authorities.

I was saying that the Church needs not only liberty but monopoly, which it wants and exacts. I say that it is right, for tolerance is one of the marks of certainty, and in religious matters intolerance is one of the forms of skepticism. The Church demands monopoly and demands as well that governments come to its help and relieve it of what offends, wounds, or abuses it. Listen, since you do not believe me:

The duty of the state is to aid the Church . . . in the work of education and public instruction. . . . It has the right to set up and found public schools and chairs for all faculties and branches of instruction; it may entrust the teaching to all manner of persons, to laymen as well as religious and ecclesiastics; but always on condition that the Church, the sole depository of faith and of the interests of Christ and of souls, watch over the instruction, prevent error from slipping in under the pretext of science or literature or history, and find in its teachers assistants in the great work with which God has charged it.

Such in all its fullness, is the thesis of freedom of teaching.

We are happy when we truly enjoy this miserable equality between the lie and truth, heresy and faith, which in the modern style is called freedom to teach. For us it is indeed liberty although not complete and entire liberty. For others, for the rationalist teachers, Protestants, free thinkers, it is only license. When they demand liberty to teach, they ask not for liberty of instruction but for license in teaching. They ask for and receive not the noble right to make use of teaching but the disastrous privilege of abusing it. In our poor France this is the case with public teaching.

That is the doctrine.

On the Right: Who is the author of these lines?

M. Bert: I am quite ready to tell you. The author is an ecclesiastical worthy both distinguished and well known, Monseigneur de Ségur, and the book from which I quote is approved by a papal brief.

M. le comte de Maillé: You always confuse the question of dogma with the practical question.

M. Bert: M. de Maillé is right and I thank him for his interruption, not that I do confuse the theoretical with the practical, but I am going to speak of the one before the other.

Some schools run by Protestants or, so it appears, by free-thinkers have been opened this year in Rome. It is not Mgr. de Ségur now who speaks but the Pope himself. It is not theory but fact which matters. What does the Pope say?

We cannot remain silent when foreign impudence has gone so far as to open anti-Catholic schools at the very gates of the Vatican. . . . The resulting situation is such that we are compelled to see error raise its head in our city without being allowed to impose silence upon it.

There you have the practical question, I think. And if you do not understand this text, you have only to turn to the Middle Ages to read this sentence by the light of the pyres of Vanini, Campanella, Giordano Bruno.

Such is the thesis. To whoever laughingly protests I quote:

Anathema.

Anathema to him who says: All direction of the public schools in which the youth of a Christian state is raised, excepting in a certain measure the episcopal seminaries, can and must be returned to the hands of the civil authority, in such a way that no other authority is recognized as having the right to interfere in the discipline of the schools, in the direction of studies, in the conferring of degrees, in the choice or approval of teachers.

Anathema to him who says: Catholics can approve a system of education which is outside the Catholic faith and the authority of the Church and which aims only at knowledge of purely natural things and at an interest in the social life of this earth.[1]

There you have the truth and the situation.

Am I right in saying that when you say "liberty" we cannot understand one another? Am I right in saying that when you say "liberty" what you hear and what we understand is "monopoly"?

I know that the times are hard, that sometimes we are obliged to compromise with the spirit of the century and must then be content with half-liberties.

Mgr. de Ségur says:

The Church may find itself face to face with inimical influences, indifference, or friendly forces. It says to the first: Why do you strike me? I have a right to live, to speak, to fulfill my divine mission of benevolence; you are wrong to do me evil, not to leave me free. It says to the second: He who is not with me is against me. Why do you remain indifferent to the cause of your God? Why do you regard the lie as truth, evil as good, Satan as Jesus Christ? You have no right to remain indifferent. It says to the third: You walk in truth and do the will of God; do all you can to make Christ reign and through him justice, peace, goodness; help me to make disappear as completely as possible all which is contrary to the holy will of God and to the true goodness of man.

Such is the language of the Church in the midst of the world; basically it asks only one thing, namely liberty of the good, the only true liberty.

I hold that when you say "liberty" you mean "monopoly." And I can say that when we make a law of the kind brought to you in this Chamber, you can perhaps in the name of the logic of our principles attack us and say: "You contradict your principles, you violate them, you are not logical, and we shall prove it." It is your right; it is part of the discussion. But there is one thing which you have

---

[1] These are quotations from the *Syllabus of Errors* (1864) of Pope Pius IX.

no right to do and that is to be angry, because this anger reacts against your own principles. The proof of this statement is found in the history of the freedom to teach in our country.

Was there any question of freedom of teaching before the Revolution? There was then a flourishing university, that of Paris, a number of other small universities, most of them in decay, and some even practically closed. No other school could be opened without the consent of the king. And these universities were giving degrees only by direct delegation of secular power. There was no question of freedom to teach. Here and there some congregations opened colleges; they were forbidden the granting of degrees, sometimes even all preparation for degrees, and they opened only after receiving licenses from the king.

It was a monopoly. And why did the Church support it so patiently? Because it was mistress of them; because these universities received canonical instruction, because nothing could be taught, absolutely nothing, which smelled of heresy. It is because the composition of the teaching body, as well as its supervision by the bishops and by the king himself, guaranteed the orthodoxy of the doctrines, because in the last century the fires of the Sorbonne, although benign enough since they no longer burned, were like the books taught there an effective protection. In addition the king, conservator, protector, defender of the Catholic Church—those are, I believe the words of Domat—the king who used to swear on his honor to exterminate heretics, sufficiently protected teaching against all dangerous frivolity. Who then would have dared to demand freedom of teaching?

The *philosophes* were reduced to using secret or Dutch presses; and as to the Protestants, in 1787 they were still asking civil status for their children.

M. de la Bassetière: Louis XVI gave it to them.

M. Bert: Yes, Louis XVI gave it to them; but almost unanimously the *cahiers* of the clergy of 1789 protested against this measure.

The thesis and doctrine of the freedom of teaching appeared during the Revolution. It is implicitly contained in the Declaration of

Rights of 1791; it was formally inscribed into legislation by the decree of 29 Frimaire Year II, the first article of which reads: "Teaching is free."

But at the same time conditions were imposed upon those who wanted to teach, and that is the real point.

Freedom to teach as a natural right, as the Revolution understood it and as we understand it, consists in expressing one's thoughts freely. Then all liberty should be given, all facilities should be allowed by law to him who publicly addresses himself to citizens like himself, to ripe, mature minds, who gives them certain doctrines, certain theories, and seeks to enlist them in certain scientific, historical, literary or doctrinal groups.

But when children and not adults are involved; when it is a matter of speaking in a class or school and not in public, of holding young minds under privately chartered associations, of keeping them from all outside contact, of having them under a single influence, often isolated even from the control of the family; when it is a matter at this tender age of imprinting on this malleable wax a mark which will always remain, then the legislator intervenes. He intervened after Frimaire Year II, and he laid down certain conditions in respect to capacity and worth, without which schools could not be opened. Once a school was opened, certain precautions were taken to watch over its operation.

The legislature introduced inspectors to see that nothing in the schools constituted a danger to peace and public morality. There you have the true thesis as it was proclaimed by the Revolution.

You still protest against what I am saying. I know that today these protests have no great force. But whoever has followed the struggle over the laws of primary and secondary teaching which began in 1830 to end only in 1850, knows in what terms this doctrine was opposed. It was said that it undermined the rights of fathers—as is said today—by preventing them from choosing the teachers to whom they wish to entrust their children in primary schools, and by forcing these children and the professors designated by the fathers of families to undergo certain inspection. It was said that the state, in substituting itself for the fathers of families, had pretensions of which it was unworthy, for it did not have the doctrine and could not have the authority to teach.

I found a trace of this thought again in the speech of M. Boyer, when he said that the state has no doctrine and no moral philosophy. I was astonished by such a remark on the part of so wise a man and one so highly regarded in the Chamber and in the country. To say that the state has no moral philosophy! What are our law codes, then, and what is the body of our legislation?

Could you not put above our codes of law "Commandments of the State," just as you would write at the beginning of other books the words "Commandments of God and the Church"?

The state, then, does have a doctrine and a moral philosophy. What you could say, what should have been said in place of using the celebrated phrase of Royer-Collard on state teaching, is that the state has no religion or metaphysics.

It was claimed that the preliminary conditions and the supervision violated paternal rights. *We* have the right to invoke these paternal rights; but we ask how they of the other side dare to call upon them. They have eloquently expressed the passion and grief of the father obliged to send his children to a school where they will be taught doctrines which offend his conscience, which in his eyes compromise their eternal safety and earthly morals. All this has been said and rightly so; but those who were angry must consider themselves fortunate to be speaking in the nineteenth century and to be Catholics, for if they had happened to live in 1686 and to be Protestants, they would have undergone the effects of the edict of Louis XIV which took away Protestant children at the age of five and sent them forcibly to Catholic schools.

M. Bourgeois: That proves that we want to be of our own age!

M. Bert: Do you want to make a covenant with progress and modern civilization?

M. Bourgeois and several members of the Right: Yes! Yes!

M. Bourgeois: There is a place for both God and science in the world.

A member of the Left: The Pope says "no."

M. Clémenceau (ironically): Science is heresy.

M. le comte de Maillé: Liberty of conscience was given for the first time in 1814, by the Charter, and I defy anyone to tell me and to prove the contrary.

M. Bert: We are told that things will change, that there are new doctrines, that we are of our own times, that we can make terms with liberty and progress, that there is a Catholic liberalism. I do not want to send you back to *l'Univers* or the *Civiltà Catholica,* but listen to the last anathema of the *Syllabus* of 1864: "Anathema to whoever shall say: The Roman pontiff can and should be reconciled to and place himself in harmony with progress, liberalism, and modern civilization."

M. Bourgeois: We should not cite this without explanation.

M. Bert: You have not the right to expound it.

M. Bourgeois: I shall explain it.

M. Bert: The Pope in a brief of 1869 declared that no one should expound or interpret these words, that they should be applied to the letter.

. . . .

Can an unrecognized right of the state be placed in doubt? No. As I was saying, the state has no scientific doctrines. It allows the Church to have an astronomy, a geology, a physics, a history of its own; it has no scientific doctrines; but it has the moral doctrines of social conservation.

In this field it is sovereign. It must scrupulously examine whether the men to whom it confides or allows to be entrusted the teaching of young people are worthy of this confidence; it has the right to see whether their ideas are dangerous to the public peace and social order; it has the right to see that in turning over these young people to them it is not preparing for civil war in the more-or-less near future.

M. de la Biliais and M. Ernest de la Rochette: It is an insult! We have been raised in these schools. We protest!

. . . .

M. Bert: . . . We are in the area of the general doctrine—which obtained in the kingdom before the Republic succeeded it—that the state, in an absolute manner, or rather in an abstract manner, has the right to concern itself with the consequences of the doctrines which are taught young minds. This fact cannot be questioned.

I should understand your protests if there was a monarchy to deal with. You might not make them then, but I should understand them. Then there would be the single, supreme will of a man come to power by the accident of heredity or by usurpation.

I speak of pure doctrine, and I swear that I do not understand your protests. I can see storms ahead for the time when I come to the realm of facts.

I say that one might fear that, if put into the hands of a monarchy, this state power would have disastrous consequences, that it might degenerate into tyranny—we know examples of this—but how can you have this distrust, which may be justified under the authority of one man, in a democratic republic? Who is the master if not the nation? Who promulgates the laws and imposes its conditions if not the whole body of citizens consulted through one or several chambers? Who then will be sovereign in the nation if not the nation? Who will be judge of the nation if not the nation? Do you say that it is the Church?

Admit then that you will return to your belief in absolutism, but do not speak to me of the freedom to teach.

The public system of education followed the proclamation of liberty by the Revolution.

There you have a concept of some grandeur; it has shown and still shows it. But this school system had a weakness within it—monopoly. And the monopoly consisted in saying not as the republicans did: You will have liberty to teach on condition that you previously have fulfilled certain formalities and have received certain certificates of capacity and morality, but in saying: Even if you have certificates of capacity and morality, you will open schools only with my authorization.

That is monopoly.

Nevertheless, the instruction given by the schools of the state was so wise and moderate, and so in harmony with the moral needs of the majority of the nation, that liberals did not object. With unparalleled vigor and intolerance the Church alone protested.

Today the theme has been softened. Another direction has been taken. They say voluntarily that they respect the public system; they are honored to have been a pupil in it, of counting some friends among its teachers. That is fine; but formerly it was not like this when they were making a frontal attack against it. At that time the public system was a pestilential school, the great bazaar of public instruction. It was spoken of as "the negation, the annihilation of all conception of good and evil, of all divine and human laws, of all true sanctions, the support of fatalism, suicide, crimes of all kinds, the destruction of all morality." (*Le monopole universitaire.* Paris, 1843.)

This is one example out of thousands.

The bishops in their insults were guilty of maligning authority.

Then the Church alone protested against the monopoly of public education. And why did it protest when it so willingly accepted the monopoly of the old régime? Quite simply because it formerly had dominated the teaching and because now the university, without excluding it from guidance, had not left it in absolute control of curriculum, teaching, or personnel.

Even then, the legislators of 1818 wrote above the constitution of the public system of education: "Teaching will be in accord with the doctrines of the Catholic religion." In 1814 the Catholic Church again became the state church and its principles once more became entrenched.

But no matter. Time had passed and the Revolution had done its work. The idea of liberty of conscience had become a habit. Though the general dogma of the Church was treated with respect, the teaching of religion was given a separate place in the public teaching system. It did not dominate. Out of that separation arose this dispute, this hoisting of shields in the name of liberty, the campaigns of 1831, 1844, finally the triumphant campaign of 1850.

If the Church had dared then to formulate its claims in the terms which I indicated at the outset, no doubt they would have been rejected by the good sense and wisdom of the country. But people hid behind paternal liberty, this sacred liberty the least harm to which offends what is most intimate, most sensitive in us. This liberty served to shield those who came to ask for churchly monopoly, and who if they had been masters would have returned to the declaration of 1686, which meant suppression of paternal liberty.

. . . .

The bill under discussion provides for true freedom to teach, which it gives to all those who can meet certain conditions for proving their capacity and moral integrity. It does not return to monopoly, since it does not return to the previous authorization; regarding the freedom of groups and associations, it allows what actually exists to continue, but it reestablishes this freedom on the true foundation of individual liberty.

What is new? What is Article 7? For, since it arouses so much anger, we shall have to come to it. It adds a new condition to those already required. It creates a particular disqualification which will weigh upon one category of citizens. . . . The question is whether this humiliating condition is justified—whether the state was right in creating this disqualification, this incapacity. That is the whole question.

. . . .

The principle of liberty is not touched; there is established a new condition of unworthiness—whether justified or not justified we shall examine later.

Is it justified? That question opens discussion which will take time, which will require that a good many documents be brought to this tribune, and prevents me because of its very importance from considering it at present. We shall see when we come to the special discussion of the article whether the non-authorized congregations really deserve the disqualification which is here in question.

It is the Jesuits especially who are meant in Article 7, and next the non-authorized congregations.

. . . .

We on the committee found ourselves faced with an amendment which will no doubt provoke considerable debate in this Chamber. We were asked what we fear from the teaching of religious congregations. What is it that we want to oppose by Article 7 of the bill, we were asked. We were told: You want to combat the doctrines taught by the congregations because you consider them dangerous. Rightly or wrongly you think that there exist, in this society based on national sovereignty, associations which teach distrust of this national sovereignty. You think that in a country such as ours, with universal suffrage and a republican form of government, there exist associations teaching distrust of universal suffrage and the republican form of government.

You fear a social danger inherent in these doctrines of the Jesuits, so many times proscribed and so universally rejected, at least in the last century.

And you say that because of these doctrines we must prohibit Jesuit teaching. But be careful! These doctrines were simply Jesuit doctrines in the last century; they are no longer so; they have become the very doctrines of the Catholic Church. Every parish, and even more all the members of the secular clergy, all those who receive Catholic investiture are obliged by their conscience to teach Jesuit doctrines. The Catholic Church, so to speak, has crystallized around the Jesuits.

If it is, then, because of doctrine that you want to forbid the unauthorized sects to teach in public and private schools, be logical, extend the prohibition to the recognized congregations and to the secular clergy itself, for teaching will be just as dangerous in their hands as in those of the Jesuits. There you have the argument which has been given and which will probably be supported from the tribune by our eloquent colleague M. Madier de Montjau. The committee has refused to follow this line of thought for two reasons. The first is that if the Government thought that it ought to make a distinction between these two orders of persons, comparable from the point of view of doctrine, doubtless it had reasons for thinking that what are certain dangers in the one case do not exist in the other case. Perhaps through information accessible to it from inside the country and especially from beyond our borders it has reason to think that some change is being prepared. Perhaps it senses some symptoms of change being called for by serious minds, even sincere

Catholics, who may be able to restore harmony between the Church and progress, liberalism, and modern civilization.

Moreover, as we said, logic is not for this world, and if the Government asks us to draw a line between non-authorized and authorized associations it has its reasons for doing so.

We have taken refuge behind an axiom of St. Augustine, who said something like this:

God who is all-powerful allows in the world a little of the evil that He could prevent, probably from fear that greater goods might be suppressed and greater evils provoked.

So with governments, which often tolerate a certain evil from fear of preventing a great good or of allowing a still greater evil to occur.

There you have our first reason. I have done what I could to clothe it with an authority capable of making it acceptable to everyone.

Here is our second reason. It is that in fact there is a great distance between the secular clergy and religious congregations; and there is also a distance between recognized sects and non-recognized ones.

M. de la Bassetière: Not as doctrine; they have proved the contrary.

M. Bert: Doubtless not; I am not speaking from the point of view of doctrine. I am saying that there is a great distance between religious congregations and the secular clergy named by the bishops and invested and paid by the state.

The clergy has and ought to have our confidence; we cannot prevent it from teaching privately. Congregations, whether authorized or not, are alike in their doctrines. For the lay state, however, there is a big difference between two types. On the one hand, there are associations which submit to the conditions imposed by the laws, which bring their statutes to the state and modify them at its demand as such brotherhoods did at the beginning of the century, and which seek the assistance of the state and recognize the rights of the state; on the other hand, there are those groups which organize outside the law and the state, refuse to show their statutes, refuse to submit to civil society and to recognize its rights and its supremacy.

A member of the Right: It is an error.

M. Bert: Why do they not ask for recognition of their statutes?

M. Plichon: They recognize the civil society and all its laws.

M. Blachère: If they violate the laws, charge them with the violation.

M. Bert: In general, those who circumvent the laws are the very ones who know them best. I do not deny that they know them. What is certain is that they do not wish to submit to the state and do not recognize the nation as sovereign. It is certain that they violate Chancellor Pasquier's principle of the law positively prohibiting that any society whatever be formed within a state without the approval of the full power of the nation.

I say that they declare war upon the state, injure the state; I say that the state has a right to say to them: You did not wish to recognize me, and I do not wish to give you who despise my rights the permission to teach the youth.

. . . .

I repeat that between these unrecognized congregations and the legal ones is the immense distance separating those who submit to the laws of the state and those who do not wish to recognize them. That is why we have accepted Article 7, with the distinction it provides between recognized and non-recognized congregations.

Another objection is made as to form. We are told: Article 7 is out of place; it deals with religious congregations. It does not belong in a teaching law. Also: The article concerns primary and secondary teaching; it is too general to be placed in a special law about upper-school teaching.

The minister of public instruction will answer this line of argument convincingly. The committee has not wanted to oppose the Government at the moment when it was acting with vigor and to refuse to vote for an article which we approved, under pretext of its being perhaps out of place. Why have we not wanted to? Because the real reason for our decision would not have been recognized. It is the right of political parties to interpret the actions of their opponents.

No one would have said that we rejected this article for formal reasons but rather that we rejected it on principle. We did not want to give our adversaries the satisfaction of making this explanation.

Those are the reasons which decided us to vote for Article 7, the most important, considerable, and novel part of the law.

Another arrangement seems out-of-date in the second draft, so much so that the anger it aroused seems only an echo of that of former times. This is the article which gives the state the right to confer degrees.

. . . .

It is said that the conferring of degrees does not affect these questions of principle, that nothing fundamental or vital is involved, that the Government is only seeking a measure to disturb and kill off the Catholic universities.

On the contrary I believe, and in 1876 the Chamber indicated the same opinion by an immense majority, that this is a right which cannot be taken from the state. The reason is very simple. In every country and at all times the state has demanded of its officials certain guarantees of ability, and these guarantees can be given only through those delegated by the state to act for it.

Whenever the choice of entering certain professions is involved, a choice which the state rightly or wrongly has considered as potentially dangerous to soundness of mind or public security if left entirely free, the state has required that proofs of ability be given. It was evident that such proofs could be made only before representatives of the state.

Thus it is quite clear that the state should be absolutely free in the choice of its delegated officials. But what does the law of 1875 do? It takes away this freedom. It forces the state to associate with certain auxiliary bodies which it really does not recognize, over whose recruitment it has no control, and over which it has only a very vague right of inspection. It forces the state to draw some of the members of the examining jury from these bodies, when it should be absolutely free and sovereign in its choices.

There is something potentially attractive about the idea of a special state board of examiners, a point which will certainly be made from this tribune and which your committee has not failed to consider. Your committee has likewise not failed to consider the solution, recently adopted in Belgium, which consists in giving the free [i.e., non-state] universities the right to confer their own degrees, by means of a direct and special delegation of power to them by the state. Moreover, one of our colleagues, M. le duc de Feltre, has taken up the idea in his plan.

In the case of the Belgium universities the principles of which I have just spoken may conceivably have been violated. These universities are old, have already certain guarantees, and have won the appreciation of the public and the state. It is impossible to discuss whether the state must relinquish the conferring of degrees solely because a faculty of four or five professors is to be established. Thus we have rejected the proposal made by M. le duc de Feltre as inadequate, dangerous and premature.

There remains the idea of a state board of examination. How would you create such a board?

No one has considered depriving the state professors of the right to give degrees to their own pupils. . . . It would be necessary consequently to create a board for the free universities. That would make two sources for the same degree, the most foolish and illogical thing imaginable. We have rejected this system.

We have found that the teaching and examining body of the state faculties already constitutes the proper state examining board. That is the reason why we have passed the article which gives to the state the conferring of degrees.

But, we are told, this article is destructive and ruinous; it will cause the closing of the universities. And dishonor accompanies the destruction, for here you deprive them of rights which they have had since the thirteenth century. Since the thirteenth century, it is said; for by a special miracle of genealogy, universities founded three years ago invoke the memory of ancient faculties and are considered as their heirs.

. . . .

I have been much surprised to find this thesis developed in one of our more important reviews by a writer who bears a name respected in the university. This writer protests that things did not happen in the same way in 1850, that the same harm was not then done to the secondary schools, that they were not refused the right to bear the title of lycées and colleges.

I do not know whether this idea was thought of in 1850; it is certain that no one imposed this prohibition. But it is likewise certain that under the Empire a decree of 1860 restricted the title of college or lycée exclusively to state schools. It imposed the limitation for the reason that these titles are state titles, that they are a possession of the state, that their usurpation constituted a true violation of ownership. At the same time a question of loyalty was involved.

. . . .

I think that the act of taking from the upper schools their titles of faculties, of universities, and this other act of restoring the conferring of degrees to a state board cannot endanger the existence of these schools. I dare to think that even those schools which protest with so much violence neither intend to close their establishments nor fear that they will remain idle.

We can offer some examples.

A school which has some prestige, which is becoming famous even abroad, the school of political science established some years ago in Paris, is prosperous; it has numerous pupils. It does not call itself a faculty, awards no degree; or at least the certificates of ability which it grants have no official value.

The same is true of a more recent school but one which will no less come to fame, the school of anthropology.

. . . .

No, you have nothing to fear. If you do what you say you should do, if you want to fill certain needs, to provide certain courses neglected by the state or only to improve the teaching in the state schools, if you really want to work for the progress of knowledge, for the betterment of upper-school teaching, your institutions will prosper.

. . . .

I have not favored the creation of this freedom for advanced teaching. Not that I am opposed to it in principle, but I distrust the consequences.

I have explained myself previously on this point from the tribune of the National Assembly, and I ask your permission to repeat the theory that I outlined at that time.

I said, speaking first of the régime of monopoly: Here are two children born in the same village, sons of two friends; they will go together to the village school, from there to the royal college; from there to the state faculty. They will sit on the same bench, follow the same course of study; yet they will not be cast in the same mold, as has been said, and will not be replicas of the same imprint—as is amply proved by the differences among us who were educated in this manner. But at least the two boys will have learned to know and like one another. Among their professors, among their older colleagues, they will have encountered the expression of different feelings, opinions, doctrines; they will have compared them with what was taught in the bosom of the family; and they will gain a belief, a conviction from this process. It may be a wrong one, but it will at least be held in the spirit of tolerance, which is the fruit of sincere contradiction.

There you have the result of monopoly. It has its drawbacks, as I have said, but it also has its utility and its grandeur.

In the actual state of things what happens? One of the children follows the course I have just described: he goes to a lay school, to the state lycée, to the state faculty; and in his course he receives this instruction to which I have just alluded, education in toleration. . . .

Yes, and it is precisely because the child is imbued with tolerance, because he is inimical to fanaticism, that fanatics have claimed that his character was being weakened.

The other child will go to the parochial school, to the Jesuit college, finally to the Catholic faculty, without seeing his friend for many years. And what kind of instruction will he have received? I do not speak of scientific teaching; that does not interest the Chamber much, although I cannot refrain from recalling this maxim of a man whose spirit will have dominated his entire education, the most celebrated and eloquent of the scholars, who if he were living today would defend the Catholic universities, Joseph de Maistre: "Ignorance is better than knowledge (science), for knowledge comes from men and ignorance comes from God." [Laughter and applause on Left and in the Center.]

M. de la Biliais: He did not put this teaching into practice.

M. Bert: There are some things one puts into practice with respect to others—for example, those whom one wants to control and of whom one wants to make instruments of power.

.   .   .   .

If you do not want me to cite De Maistre I can give you facts which I know from my own experience. I can tell you of pupils coming up for the baccalaureate and putting some water from Lourdres in their inkwells for the purpose of being passed. . . .

There you have science and moral philosophy; but we are a political assembly; let us see what the child will have learned from the political point of view.

He will have learned that the Church should be sovereign mistress and should control lay governments from above. These governments have only duties toward the Church, whereas it has all the rights; for it is queen or it is nothing, as M. de Montalembert used to say.

If he has been at the law school at Lyon he will have learned that "even in questions of simple social utility, the government is able to do nothing without the consent of the Church."

He will have learned that "the law as practiced since the Revolution is a deception of Satan, more dangerous than all forms of violence."

He will have learned—these are sacred words—that "there is anathema against whosoever claims that the civil power has the right to decide what are the rights of the Church and within what limits the Church can exercise them."

He will have learned from the mouth of Gregory XVI that liberty of conscience is an absurdity.

He will have learned from the last Pope that universal suffrage is a universal lie; that it is insanity to claim that the citizens have a right to free expression of their opinions. He will have learned, in a word, distrust—and from there it is only a step to hate—of all the principles upon which our society is built, upon which our state and

political world rest. And he is fortunate if he has escaped, for example, being in the diocese of Toulouse and being regimented into
the papal militia, if he has not been told in fiery orders of the day
that the hour has struck, that the trumpet has sounded, that the flag
has been unfurled, and that it is time for the new Maccabees to draw
their swords and march to victory or martyrdom.

I ask you how a boy who has undergone this kind of instruction will
regard his friend when he rejoins him. What provisions will you have
made for the public peace? I said to you, and I repeat, that you will
have prepared a spiritual civil war! May God grant that national
feeling and the common sense of the public may prevent this civil
war from going further!

And we are told that it is the effect of liberty!

M. de Baudry-d'Asson: But we have two ministers who have been
raised by the Jesuits.

M. Bourgeois: Those who have applauded you put their sons with
Jesuits. They are very illogical.

M. Bert: I ask you whether the authoritative and even sacred quotations I have used are no longer taught by the congregations? Is it not
true that Count Albert de Mun, a man whom I regret not to see here,
for he was not one to conceal his thought. . . . [Interruptions.]

You know what he used to say from this tribune; you will recall the
statement which was published in the teachings given in the Catholic
faculties, notably at Lyon: "It is not possible for you, the government,
to say where the Catholic Church begins and ends. Its authority
extends over all."

They tell us that these are the results of freedom. I do not believe
it; I think that one could have liberty under other conditions; I think
that one could organize liberty even in state schools.

I have envisaged it quite otherwise. I have dreamed of liberty in
full daylight, with full right of opposition. I thought that we would
be able to open great centers of education in which all doctrines
would be taught, all theories, all opinions would come into the light.
I had no fear of contradiction. One of my colleagues said to me just
yesterday: "You would not be worthy of the name of a man of science

if you feared contradiction." I have no fear of it on one condition—
that it be carried on with fairness and in the light of day.

M. Anisson-Duperron: You did not have to exclude your adversaries.

M. Bert: This is not what they wanted; they wanted to hold minds
under a private corporation; they mounted guard around them; they
wanted no opposition to reach them because this was the most certain
means of preparing some men for future eventualities.

They are not especially devious about it. This is, however, not
perhaps so much the case in political gatherings, where they are
more prudent; but in certain books they say: "Our duty to all is to
profit from the poor choked liberties we still have, in order to provide
a core of Christian generations deeply steeped in the faith, ardent in
the cause of the Church, knowing the true liberty, so that the future
at least may be better than the present and that a fine spring may
succeed our interminable winter."

Alas! Poor children, poor youth! How many are the lost souls
because of the false liberty of teaching!

. . . .

It can be summed up in a word: They have taken refuge behind
liberty in order to prepare for slavery.

When such doctrines are taught, and taught in secret, can you as
a political assembly afford to deprive the state of its poor and inadequate right of investigation, which empowers it to question the
students as to whether these doctrines have not prevented them from
acquiring at the least some positive truths?

When certain men have refused to submit themselves to the laws
of the state and to bring their statutes to obtain its authorization. . . .

Voice on the Right: They have not been asked to do so! They have
not refused.

M. Bert: Do you imagine then that it is the Government's responsibility to ask for the statutes of a secret society? That is a strange idea!
Can you deny to government the right of refusing, to those who propose to teach the young, the possibility of doing what I have just
described?

What you want is a deaf and dumb government, a government without power, and that is governmental nihilism, the abdication of government. We cannot subscribe to this abdication, and so long as a breath of life remains we shall fight for the nation to be sovereign in its own house and to receive orders from no one.

M. de Baudry-d'Asson: You will not be fighting alone, M. Paul Bert. I reply to you that there is a Catholic France behind you. Do not forget it!

M. Bert: These gentlemen claim, I believe, an homage which I am entirely disposed to grant them. I know that when the tocsin sounds on the frontiers, when the foot of the enemy is on the soil of our country, you will be on hand.

Voice on the Right: Yes! Yes!

M. Bert: And if I had forgotten it, you have often enough repeated it for me to remember.

M. Viette: They are not the only ones who have defended the country. Everyone has taken part in this defense.

M. Bert: But you have not done it alone. . . .

In conclusion I have shown that you should restore to the state a prerogative which belongs to it and whose return will arouse no legitimate surprise. I have shown that there are dangerous doctrines which you have the right to prohibit from being inculcated into the minds of the nation's youth. That is the whole intention of the law. Now will you allow me before leaving the tribune to give a warning? I shall not say advice, for you would not like that. I made so bold as to give this warning during the discussion of the law presented by M. Waddington. It was not heeded. I said then to many among its opponents that it would be wise to accept this law.

If it is accepted, I told them, one could consider it as a compromise. . . . If it is voted, I said then, this law will constitute a kind of middle ground which can be retained. What you call freedom to teach in the upper schools will be protected by this law voted by republican chambers. If you reject it, your triumph will not last long. Soon new elections will come; soon senatorial elections will reestablish harmony between the two chambers, and this time perhaps it will be a matter not alone of the conferring of degrees. You may lose much by not knowing how to give a little.

A member of the Right: We may also gain a great deal.

M. Bert: No one listened to me then. They will not listen to me if I repeat the same warning in almost the same terms, for this entire law can be summed up by a formula given by the famous Leibnitz when he said, "Liberty is not a right owed those who wish to use it only to teach how to hate and to overturn all liberty."

There you have the sense of the bill itself.

I say to you now: Take care! For if the bill is rejected, if the intolerance of the sects, if the Jesuit and ultramontane machinations continue to arouse public feeling, some day, somewhere bolder men surely, doubtless less prudent, less wise, I think. . . .

M. Bourgeois: More logical!

M. Bert: . . . but more logical, as is suggested to me, may demand that we translate into legislative and administrative language the conclusion of the formula of a great philosopher: "Tolerance itself is not owed to the intolerant."

5. Empire and Language

Czech Deputy Dr. Gregr: *Speech in Behalf of the Czech Language* (1884)°

The right to use one's language freely, the right to have it accepted on a basis of equality with other languages, is a prerequisite to the assertion and development of a national cultural personality. Thus the language question provides occasion for a conflict of nationalities within an empire. The issue arose in almost every country in Europe in the nineteenth century. Solved in Switzerland by the recognition of three major languages, and having only slight significance in a one-language country like France or Italy, it appeared as an acute problem in Germany, in Russia, and especially in Austria-Hungary, where during the latter part of the century it dominated events. The Czech Deputy Dr. Gregr, during one of the many debates on the subject in the Austrian parliament, stated the standard arguments presented by such minority groups as the Czechs of Bohemia. The reader should imagine for himself the main lines of argument offered in reply by the German Austrians—not a difficult feat—and then he should consider whether any solution would have been feasible. This exercise in language and nationality problems will aid the student in understanding the background of the League of Nations and the United Nations, and it may lead to some reflection on the history of our own country, at once the most multilingual and yet monolingual of all countries.

Honored House! I begin my speech with the open and frank admission that my fondest wish is to see realized that part of the

° *Stenographische Protokolle über die Sitzungen des Hauses der Abgeordneten des österreichischen Reichsrathes,* IX. Session, XI. Band (Vienna, 1884), pp. 11, 182-93.

Wurmbrandt bill which seeks a language law for the solution of our language differences.

I do not want to go into the details in regard to the form and manner in which this might take place, and I do not want to discuss the competence of the legislative bodies, that is, what role is to be assigned to the *Reichsrath,* what to the *Landtag* in drafting and promulgating a language law. I am an autonomist, and I agree in this respect with everything that was said yesterday by several speakers from this side [the Right]. I simply wish to confirm the fact that the Bohemian nation has for years felt the need of a language law, and it is well known that the Bohemian *Landtag* as early as 1871 even attempted to begin the drafting of a nationality or language law. Even though this effort came to grief through the opposition of the Constitutional party [Hear! Hear!" from the Right], nobody will deny that the Bohemian *Landtag* at least utilized the short span of time in which it was permitted freedom of action, in order to achieve what the first part of the Wurmbrandt bill attempts. The Constitutional party, on the other hand, during the entire series of years when it was at the rudder and in possession of power and authority, did not even consider transforming Article XIX (of the constitution) into flesh and blood through a language law or through a law of implementation.

It did not have the need to do so at that time, since it is understandable that the party in power interprets and utilizes Article XIX precisely according to its taste and inclination—I will not say arbitrarily. The non-German peoples of Austria felt at that time all the more, however, the pressing need to shelter their language under the aegis of a just, reasonable, and universally satisfactory language law. But it is my conviction that it is not so easy to produce a just and universally satisfactory language law. If the honorable speaker preceding me attributed, as it were, a superficial disposition to those men called to work out such a language law, permit me in a certain sense to agree with him. I am likewise convinced that the man called to produce a just and universally acceptable language law—for it is in universal satisfaction through this law that its guarantee of longevity lies—must not only be motivated by the higher, I should like to say pure, sense of justice which recognizes no other criterion than the principle of equal justice for all, not only for all citizens but above all for all peoples and nationalities of this empire. Those responsible for such a law must also feel a burning desire to bring about peace among the contending peoples of the state. They must above all slough off the dross of national prejudice, of national arrogance, and they must above all be free of the unfortunate prejudice which holds there are some nationalities in Austria predestined to mastery and others to servitude. ["Quite right! That is so!" from the Right.] They must proceed from the standpoint characterized by the very honorable deputy on that side [the Left] from Bohemia, Dr. Russ, in his fine words to an assembly of voters in Tetschen: "Refrain from all comparisons with the other nationalities of the empire which could be drawn from the history of cultural development and from the present cultural situation. Yes, place all peoples on the same high level as the German nation; regard all the peoples of Austria as brothers." ["Hear! Hear!" from the Right.]

That is the true, genuine Austrian standpoint; and nothing is lacking for the achievement of peace among the peoples of Austria but for the gentlemen of that side [the Left] to take these fine words as a guide not only for noble speeches but also for noble deeds. . . .

It is not easy for a party government to create a good and acceptable language law satisfactory to everyone; for a purely party government is too subservient to the influence of the party. I must therefore state openly and candidly that I am surprised by a certain action of a party which never tires of reproaching the existing Government, at every opportune and inopportune moment, for fostering non-German languages and nationalities at the cost of the German nationality and the German language, and which also reproaches it for proceeding from partisan considerations at the expense of the German nationality; I am surprised that such a party actually comes to this Government—so often accused, *horribile dictu,* of being a Czech Government—with the wish that it issue a language law for the protection of the German language and nationality. [Laughter and "Very good!" from the Right.] I must confess that I cannot place so great a trust in the present Government with regard to my national language. ["Quite right!" from the Right.]

But you certainly have cause to place your trust in the present

Government. I am convinced that among the long series of Governments and ministries with which Austria has been blessed since the year 1861, there probably has been scarcely one which has done such abundant service for the German language and the German nationality as the present one. ["Very good!" and laughter from the Right. Scornful laughter from the Left.] You laugh about it, gentlemen; allow me to prove it to you.

Imagine a Government which is German to the utmost, composed for example of the president of the school association and Herr Ritter von Schönerer. I think that one can hardly imagine a more German ministry. Do you believe that under such a Government, for example, the man here on this side [the Right], who has stood and fought during his entire life at the forefront among our national champions, would have spoken the fateful words: "Every educated Bohemian must understand German"? Do you believe that Bohemian professors at the Bohemian university would have sponsored under another Government the well-known examination ordinance pertaining to the law faculty, whereby the national, the linguistic part of the university actually was transformed into something ridiculous? Do you believe that under such a Government, which is German to the utmost, deputies of the Bohemian nationality would have voted for Paragraph 17 of the school law ["Very good!" from the Right], whereby in the public schools of Bohemia the German language not only maintained the advantage of a state language but even was recognized as a preferred language of the country.

If you wish a more striking illustration of how the present government thinks with regard to the German language, take any banknote of the state and observe that under the present Government, except for German and Magyar, all other languages of the peoples of this empire—language which under a Metternich and a Bach at least found a modest little corner on our banknotes—finally have been excluded; and this with the assistance of a finance minister of Slavic ancestry.

And still another quite recent illustration concerning the University of Bohemia:

The professors of the Bohemian University in Prague sent their communications to their German colleagues in Prague in the Bohemian language, which certainly was quite natural. The Germans in Prague were so kind as to return one of these communications, with the notation that they did not understand the foreign idiom, that is, a language which is spoken by two-thirds of the population of the country and four-fifths of the population of Prague. The Bohemian professors naturally were not content and complained to the ministry, which decided in its wisdom that it was indeed permissible for the professors of the university of Bohemia to compose their communications in the Bohemian language—how kind, gentlemen—but that they must send this communication to the governor's office in Prague for translation into German and transmission to the German university. This is an illustration of how pleasant our situation is in Prague.

But is that not a recognition, a preference, accorded the German language even in Bohemia, a preference which, I am convinced, the Wurmbrandt bill does not intend in this degree?

I have said this only to refute the accusation made from that side [the Left] yesterday and again today that under the present Government the area of the German language is being continually narrowed and diminished. Indeed, on the contrary, it is being continually extended.

I should like to refer to a merit of the present Government called to my attention by the very honored speaker from that side [the Left] who spoke first, Deputy Dr. Tomaszczuk, reminding us of the time when masses of materials for Russian language instruction were being spread among the people of Bohemia. That was really the case. I no longer recall the year, but I recall very well that it took place under a Government of your party, and that this remarkable occurrence was the consequence of the pressure at that time on the Bohemian people and the Bohemian language from your Government. ["Quite right!" from the Right.]

That was the effect of your Government, and if these Russian grammars have disappeared today among the Bohemian population, that is to the credit of the present Government. ["Very good!" from the Right.]

I do not say this in order perhaps to earn a benevolent glance from His Excellency the Minister President. [Laughter from the Right.] My political and national views are so diametrically opposed to the political and national views of His Excellency that I probably have no hope ever of being accepted among his political friends. [Laughter.] But I say this in justice to the truth and in order to prove to you on that side [the Left] of this honorable house, that it is sheer black ingratitude of you not to have accepted long ago His Excellency the Minister President Count Taaffe among your national saints. [Uproarious laughter.]

Gladly as I should like to see the creation of a language law which is just and universally acceptable, as found in one part of the bill of Deputy Count Wurmbrandt, I must speak out just as decisively against the second part of the same. I object to the sentence which, to be sure, has slipped in, yet which certainly is basic—namely I object to the promotion of a language, I do not wish to say the German, but in general any language, to the status of an official language. I speak against it forcefully for the reason that this second part actually negates the first part of the Wurmbrandt proposal. For if liberation of the nationalities would be accomplished by the first part, precisely the opposite must arise from the second part.

I acknowledge quite readily that the official state bodies which negotiate with one another must also understand one another. I grant gladly that when the state is viewed, as by one honorable speaker, as an abstract personality, this personality should not be mute. But it by no means follows that the state must speak only one language. Indeed I believe that the state, if personified, will be less mute the more languages it knows. ["Quite right!" from the Right.] If one, then, does not wish that this person of the Austrian state, allegorically regarded, be mute toward those with whom it has the duty to speak, toward its peoples, then it follows logically that even this person, like every private person, must understand the language of those with whom it associates. Therefore the implication of this figurative view would be exactly the opposite, and it would follow logically that the Austrian government should understand all of the languages of its peoples.

I gladly grant and acknowledge that it is a real convenience when certain political bodies are not required to understand several languages, and that it is a considerable relief in certain spheres of political life and political procedure when they need to use only one language and when this is the German language.

That I gladly grant. But this relief which lies in the use by certain political bodies only of the German language actually exists. And the minority recounts a whole series of cases in which the German language alone is employed. That consideration indeed was already emphasized here even from this side [the Right], and I am of the opinion that what the Wurmbrandt bill attempts already exists. It exists without the introduction of a special imperative law or decree. It exists because it has evolved from practical life, according to the strongest of all laws, the law of necessity, and such creations which have evolved from practical experience according to the law of necessity appear to me to have more capacity to endure than creations formed by law.

Although what the Wurmbrandt bill proposes partly exists in fact, although to my knowledge no attack has been made or is planned upon the actual position of the German language in Austria, the motives behind the Wurmbrandt bill were, I must frankly admit, unclear to me; and I sought the motives in order to get at the heart of the projected law, to find the actual stimulus for it. It is quite understandable that I sought these motives first in the speech of justification by the gentleman who proposed the bill and then in the justifying report of the minority. Permit me to turn as briefly as possible to these motives and to criticize them as objectively as possible.

I begin first with the motives of the gentleman who introduced the bill. I shall be done quickly, since they are scattered rather sparingly throughout his lengthy opening speech. The first motive I find is this: "We wish an Austria which is permanent, unified, and strong; we do not want an empire which is idealistically national, which is torn from within, an Austria based upon chimerical concepts; we want our old Austria, based upon the concepts by which it has been created." "Bravo!" it says here in the stenographic report. I do not know, gentlemen, whether this "Bravo!" also resounded from this side [the Right] of the House. I should join in this "Bravo!" with all my heart, for we on this side wish an Austria which is permanent, strong, and unified just as much as the gentlemen on the Left side. And as to what is involved in these long-established concepts by which Austria has been created and through which it has arisen, there can exist no difference between our points of view and those of the honorable gentleman who introduced the bill. Certainly one can read in every textbook of Austrian history how Austria came into being; and this origin has already been alluded to yesterday by a very distinguished speaker from this side [the Right] of the House. We know that after the fall of Ludwig, King of Bohemia and Hungary, in the battle at Mohacz, the estates of Bohemia and Hungary elevated Ferdinand I, Archduke of Austria, to the throne and thereby laid the basis of Austria as a great power.

You know that at that time these territories *[Länder]* were loosely bound to one another and that the Pragmatic Sanction under Charles VI first succeeded in tying them more closely together. You know, furthermore, that the Pragmatic Sanction at that time left intact the autonomous character of the kingdoms and the territories. You know that the Pragmatic Sanction was recognized by all the governments as the basic law of the state and that this fundamental law was clearly recognized by His Majesty our reigning emperor in the October Diploma. These are the long-established concepts according to which Austria was formed; and if the honorable gentleman who introduced the bill wishes that Austria continue to be maintained according to these long-established concepts, certainly he will nowhere find greater and more sincere consent than precisely from this side of the house. [Acclaim from the Right.] When the gentleman says on this point that he is conservative with regard to these long-established concepts, I am surprised at one thing, namely how with this conservatism he could have gone astray and joined that side [the Left] of the House. ["Very good!" and laughter from the Right.]

But how the German language as the language of the state supposedly results from these autonomous bases of Austria is to me inconceivable.

The gentleman cited a second motive, that all great powers possess an official language. This simply is not true; indeed, on the contrary, there is not a single great power which has a legally established official language.

There are, in a linguistic sense, in general only two categories of states. One category consists of states which are populated by single-language nations—France, Italy, Spain, etc.—and it plainly would be not only superfluous but also ludicrous if it were legally determined that in France Frenchmen should speak French and that in Italy Italians should speak Italian.

Of course, one could cite an example of a great power in which a state language has been legally established. That is in Prussia in respect to Posen. In Prussia the German language has been established by law as the state language for the grand duchy of Posen. But even this example is for us repulsive, and I believe that it cannot demonstrate to us *ad oculos* the benefit of a state language in Austria as well. ["Quite right!" from the Right.]

Regarding the second category of countries and particularly Russia, a matter discussed yesterday by the gentleman who moved the bill, I must confess that it does not seem to me valid to compare absolute, I should like to say despotic, states with constitutional states in this respect. They are so heterogeneous that they do not easily admit comparison; and also the circumstances are rather unclear to us, despite the points which the gentleman who moved the bill presented from the brochure regarding the growth of the Finnish nationality.

But there is another category of states, that is, those which are populated by a multilingual people, such as Switzerland, Belgium, and, if you wish, also Hungary. With regard to Switzerland, the pertinent article of the Constitution of the Confederation, Article 109, simply reads as follows: "The three principal languages of Switzerland, German, French, and Italian, are national languages of the country." ["Hear! Hear!" from the Right.] Here you have three official languages defined by law. It is not true that a state, considered as a person, must have only one language. Here we have the kind of abominable personality which converses quite well in three languages; and we could congratulate ourselves in Austria, if we were to maintain a situation like that which exists in this trilingual Switzerland.

In regard to Belgium, where as you know two languages are customary, namely Flemish and French, the relevant Article 23 of the Constitution of 1831 states: "The use of the languages which are customary in Belgium is optional." ["Hear! Hear!" from the Right.] It is thus immaterial whether a person in Belgium uses the French or Flemish language. It is well known to me that in Belgium the French language has achieved an extraordinary preponderance over the Flemish and that French is actually recognized as the principal language of the country. But such recognition has not taken place on account of statutory regulation; it has developed just like the situation here regarding the relation of the German language to the others. The Flemish people have voluntarily and uncomplainingly recognized the preponderance of the French language. But the way in which the Flemish people regard this matter demonstrates something which is unfamiliar to you, gentlemen. In Belgium it happens that attorneys, in representing before French courts a case involving Flemish persons, at the beginning of the trial set forth for the record the express declaration that they are legally entitled to employ the Flemish language even for the entirety of the trial, that they however do not choose to make use of this right. This procedure takes place for the purpose of maintaining the rights of the Flemish language, in order to keep it from becoming obsolete or losing out on the basis of precedents. Here we have, then, the second state in which a population with two languages exists, where there is no question of one official language but where both languages are statutory languages of the country.

Several speakers from that side [the Left] referred to Hungary, and it was asserted that indeed in that state, which is our neighbor, state, the Hungarian language has been established as the state language. The gentleman who reported on the bill even stated that the other nationalities there depend upon toleration. Now I thank the reporter for the gracious prospect which he has accorded us, that our nationality likewise shall be tolerated in Austria. But surely if we want to draw a parallel between Cisleithania and Transleithania, then I ask you at least not to compare long-established, powerful, and illustrious nations which in the course of centuries have formed their own sovereign states—for example the Polish, the Bohemian, in part also the Slovenian nation—with mere splinters of peoples which never have possessed independent political form, as for example the Slovaks in northern Hungary or the Germans in the Zips. If you want to draw a parallel at all between the lands of the Hungarian crown and Cisleithania, this would be perhaps more valid if you compared Hungary and Croatia on the one hand with Bohemia or Galicia and Austria on the other. ["Bravo! Bravo!" from the Right.] And if you want to create for us a language law which contains the same stipulations as the Hungarian-Croatian Compromise, I believe that all the deputies of this side [the Right] would be grateful for it.

Permit me in this connection to present to you the relevant and very brief paragraphs of the Hungarian-Croatian Compromise.

Paragraph 56 reads: "In the entire area of the Kingdom of Croatia and Slovenia the official language is the Croatian, both in legislation and in the courts and in administration." Paragraph 57 states: "For the organs of common administration the Croatian language is likewise fixed as the official language within the borders of this kingdom" ["Hear! Hear!" from the Right]; and Paragraph 58 states: "The proposals and addresses drawn up in the Croatian language and submitted from the Kingdom of Croatia and Slovenia to the common ministry are to be accepted by this ministry, and the answers to them are to be published in the same language." Paragraph 59 determines that the deputies of the Kingdom of Croatia are fully entitled to use the Croatian language in the common *Reichstag* and in the delegations ["Hear! Hear!" from the Right]; and finally Paragraph 60 says: "The laws passed by the common *Reichstag* and signed by His Royal Imperial Apostolic Majesty shall be published for the Kingdom of Croatia and Slovenia in the Croatian original and transmitted to the *Landtag* of this Kingdom." ["Hear! Hear!" from the Right.]

Such is the language question in wicked Hungary, which you, gentlemen, have brought up as an illustration. And as we stated, we most certainly would be content with these stipulations. ["Very good!" from the Right.]

I refer further to how the Croatians regard linguistic equality in practice, and all of you are acquainted with the most recent conflict in Croatia concerning the Magyar inscriptions on the official sign-boards. If we in Bohemia were to be so scrupulous [laughter from the Right], then truly we should have many conflicts and much to do.

I have finished with the motives of the gentleman who introduced the bill; I find no more. I leave it to the judgment of all impartial men of this honorable House whether these motives are sound or not, whether they explain or justify the proposal for the promulgation of a law concerning a state language.

I believe that the minority report is no more fortunate in its motives. I was curious to learn them, first because such distinguished men and sagacious jurists are to be found on that side [the Left], and secondly because the minority states directly at the beginning of the report that it is a quite incontestable proposition that the German language must be preserved as the official language in Austria.

On what grounds is this considered incontestable? First of all, says the minority, it is recognized that the German language already has existed in law and practice in Austria for a century. If that is true, then I really do not know what more the gentlemen want; if what the minority says is true—and it says expressly that the German language has existed for a century in law and practice in Austria as the state language, —then in fact the Wurmbrandt proposal is un-necessary. The gentlemen want to introduce in law and practice what exists in law and practice. But I do not wish to dwell further upon this motive.

A second motive offered by the minority, and a very important one, is the assertion that under the present government for the last four years the Germans have been suppressed; they are defense-less, and the like. [Laughter from the Right.] That is a serious accusa-tion; but if what the minority says were true, that the German nationality and the German language are suppressed, then it would be the duty not only of that side [the Left] of the honorable House to stand firm against this oppression but the duty as well of this side [the Right], which has this inscription upon its banner: "Equal rights for all nationalities!" ["Bravo!" from the Right.] And it would be above all the duty of every liberal person, regardless of the nationality to which he belongs. For the highest and most noble attribute of freedom is the allocation of equal rights to all peoples and nationalities. But it is not true that the Germans in Austria are suppressed. When one expresses such a serious accusation in an assembly like this honorable House, one should at least make good his accusation with factual proof. Take the minority report, however, and search for the proof of this harsh utterance and you will read: "The minority of the Committee refrains from entering further at this point into the particulars of the inexhaustible and intolerable range of weapons of cunning and violence, of proscription, denunciation, and of terrorism to which the Germans in such lands [that is, the Slavic lands] have already been exposed without protection for more than three years." That is all. I beg to ask—I appeal especially to the gentlemen of this House educated in the law—can a judge, can a just man condemn anyone upon accusations which are so general and so hastily made without the slightest factual proof? The minority has produced no factual proof because it has none. ["Quite right!" from the Right; "Oho!" from the Left.] I am not acquainted with the situation in other provinces *[Länder]*. I believe, however, it is certainly not the case that in purely German provinces—Salzburg, Tirol, Vorarlberg—the wicked Czechs suppress the Germans. I am acquainted with the situation in my fatherland Bohemia; it is indeed against us Bohemians that this accusation is aimed, and I reject this accusation with indignation and anger, for it is without any basis.

The minority adds one fact in proof of the suppression of the Germans, and that is that the state has established a Bohemian university. Now it is true that after long struggles and after difficult, even proportionally quite great, sacrifices we have finally succeeded in acquiring a Bohemian university.

I do not wish to proceed further into how this university is constituted and into its deficiencies.

But I appeal to the sense of justice among all the Germans of this House when I ask: Is it an injustice that, although the long-established, splendidly endowed, luxuriously equipped university has been left completely intact for the Germans in Bohemia ["Quite right!" from the Right], alongside the same a paltry Bohemian university has been established? Is an injustice committed against the German nation when another nation receives its due? Is it a suppression of the Germans when other nationalities are not suppressed? ["Quite right! Bravo!" from the Right.] The university situation is factual proof of the "suppression" of the Germans in Bohemia.

Another assertion of the minority is that all discussions and decisions of this House are influenced and dominated by the nationality and language question. That is a statement with which the speaker who immediately preceded me began his speech. I grant this assertion. It is actually true that our entire public life, and in part our private life as well, has been unmistakably poisoned by the distressing nationality and language question. And nobody wishes more ardently than I that this question finally might be brought to a happy solution. But the Wurmbrandt proposal is not the oil which can calm the dashing waves of the nationality struggle. It is the oil which will be poured upon blazing flames. ["Quite right!" from the Right.] Have you considered what effects, what results this Wurmbrandt bill, taken in its various consequences, must have upon the non-German populations and nationalities of this empire? The effects and results of the Wurmbrandt bill above all would be that the non-German nationalities of this empire would necessarily feel bitterness against the German language itself, bitterness at having a language forced upon them.

There are arrangements in political life which, although they involve injustice, nevertheless are borne quietly and without murmur; however, they immediately arouse opposition as soon as they are incorporated into a law. The feelings of a just person are aroused at the idea that an injustice is becoming legalized. A chain which one carries voluntarily is no chain, but when this chain is forced upon one, it becomes an unbearable yoke of slavery. ["Quite right!" from the Right.]

If you want an even more striking illustration of the results of the Wurmbrandt bill, you need merely call to mind the so-called language ordinance which comes next on the agenda. You say that the language ordinance, which in and of itself is nothing but a refurbishing of existing legal institutions, has caused the greatest disturbance among the German people.

How much greater would be the disturbance among non-German peoples if Article XIX were to be turned directly into an illusion by the bill of Count Wurmbrandt. ["Quite right!" from the Right.] Would a wise government try to calm a part of the population in such a way as to cause unrest among a much larger part? Would it be intelligent to extinguish the conflagration in one part of the house and set fire to a greater part? ["Quite right!" from the Right.]

I find no further motives in the minority report of any importance other than the one involved in the observation that Austria is becoming federalized, that the territories *[Länder]* of the Bohemian crown will form independent units unless the German language is advanced as soon as possible to official status. Yet this really is not seriously meant; for if it ever should be written in the book of fate that the territories of the Bohemian crown were again to become independent, this mighty process could not be restrained by such petty means as the Wurmbrandt proposal.

What this Wurmbrandt bill could achieve would be actually the revival, the strengthening, of the longing among the Bohemian population for an independent grouping of the territories of the Bohemian crown—precisely the opposite of that intended by the proposal. ["Quite right!" from the Right.]

Since I found so few arguments in the opening speech and in the reports in favor of the bill, I was interested to hear whether new and stronger motives and bases of proof would be offered by the honorable speakers from that side [the Left]. I must confess that I have found and heard nothing new; the most that I can do is to reply to several remarks which were dropped.

I wish to emphasize what the first honored speaker mentioned from that side [the Left], Professor Tomaszczuk, in that he called upon us, especially us Bohemians, to learn German, since otherwise we should lag behind in our cultural development. It is very nice of the honorable Professor Tomaszczuk to have such concern for our cultural development. But I can assure the Professor that the way to cultural heights was known to the Bohemian people at a time when Austria did not even exist. We can show periods in the history of our fatherland when the Bohemian people achieved a cultural height above the achievements of all neighboring countries without the Ger-

man language and without the gracious advice of Professor Tomaszczuk. Several speakers from that side [the Left]—and not only
here but also in other places—have reproached us in a most friendly
manner for our low cultural position in order to represent us as
dwarfs in comparison with the immense achievement of German
civilization. I have the highest regard for German education and
culture. Nobody can esteem the products of the intellectual life of
the great German nation more than I do, and I know that the intellectual achievement of that nation has created a hall of fame for
itself which towers over that of other peoples. But how much the
Germans of Bukovina have contributed to this German hall of fame
[uproarious laughter from the Right] I have not found in any cultural
history, and how much my German-Bohemian countrymen have
contributed to this hall of fame—this we Bohemians know quite well.
You should not boast as if you had produced a Goethe, a Schiller, a
Humboldt. When you call upon the great German nation and its high
culture and its intellectual achievement, I am always reminded of
poor relatives calling upon their rich uncle. [Uproarious and continual laughter from the Right.]

I have now finished with all the reasoning and remarks that I have
to produce, and certainly the reflection that the discerning and ingenious parliamentarians and jurists on that side [the Left] were not
successful in producing more important arguments awakened in me
the suspicion that quite other motives must be concealed behind the
proposal of Count Wurmbrandt. It is really the case that the reasons
adduced are in fact more or less specious ones. [Acclaim from the
Right.] It is not a question of preserving the domain which the German language now controls, but one of extending this domain in
breadth and depth, one of raising the German language over all
other languages of this empire, one of lowering the non-German
peoples of the empire to an inferior level, one of decreeing superiority
and inferiority for different nationalities [acclaim from the Right],
and, as a logical consequence, one of inevitable Germanization of
the non-German peoples of the empire. [Acclaim from the Right.]
That, according to the conviction of the whole Bohemian population,
is the gist and the keystone of the Wurmbrandt proposal. ["That is
so!" from the Right.]

One hesitates of course to declare such a purpose openly, and for this reason it was not at all possible for the gentlemen to propose a definition of a state language. Indeed it was quite difficult for them to define something that they did not want to say. They did not wish to call the child by the right name, and for this reason they clothed it with an indefinable concept, namely the concept of "state language." It is called "state language," but it means Germanization. ["Bravo!" from the Right.] That this, however, is the real meaning of the measure, and that I would not make such a statement without being able to prove it—that is revealed already by what was mentioned yesterday. That is to say, voices are being raised on that side [the Left] and among wide circles outside this House to propose the exclusion of Galicia and Dalmatia from the sphere of the projected state language. And today even the honorable speaker who preceded me expressed the same point of view. ["Quite right!" from the Right.]

Now to whom actually is this German state language supposed to apply? Not to Hungary, not to Croatia, not to the Germans of inner Austria—for that would be superfluous. Galicia and Dalmatia are to be excluded. There remain only the Bohemian and Slovenian territories *[Länder]*, and is that then the state of Austria? That is a small part of the state of Austria, and this separation, this parceling of the state, aims at piecemeal Germanization, only in order to facilitate complete Germanization. [Acclaim from the Right.]

Even from the assertions of the minority it is entirely clear that the real kernel of the Wurmbrandt bill is none other than the Germanizing of the Slavic peoples of this empire. The minority states among other things, on page 11: "The state has the duty to effect the compulsory learning of the German language in the entire empire." Since, however, this assertion of the learning of the German language as compulsory is in open contradiction with the clear wording of Article XIX, the minority has escaped from this awkward difficulty by the remarkable discovery of the "state language," in fact by opposing the "state language" to the provincial language *[Landessprache]*. We now are fortunate in having three kinds of language. We have a vernacular language, the provincial language *[Landessprache]*, and now finally we shall have a "state language." [Call from the Right: "Official language!"] They put forward sometimes the one, sometimes the other category as it is needed to evade Article XIX. If we in Bohemia for example say: "The Bohemian language is to be established as a language of the province *[Land]* entitled to equal rights throughout Bohemia in office, school, and public life," the gentlemen say: "Bohemian is not the vernacular language among us in Brüx, Komotau; we shall not introduce it."

"Fine," we say! In Pisek, Czaslau, Tabor neither is the German language a vernacular language; we shall not, therefore, in these purely Bohemian districts introduce it in official and public life." "No!" the gentlemen say, "That is another matter; the German language is the language *[Landessprache]* throughout the entire kingdom and is entitled to equal rights throughout the entire kingdom, hence also in Bohemian districts [laughter from the Right], and must therefore be established in official and public life.

If we, however, demand that both the German and the Bohemian provincial languages be learned as required subjects in all intermediate schools and state institutions throughout the entire kingdom, the gentlemen say: "Ah, that surely contradicts Article XIX, which says that nobody can be compelled to learn a second language *[Landessprache]*." "All right," we say, "you have a point. Therefore neither can we be compelled to learn the German language." Ah, that again is another matter. [Laughter from the Right.] The German language is the official state language, excluded from the regulations of Article XIX, and for this reason the state can demand the compulsory learning of the German language. ["Bravo!" from the Right.]

From this you can see what a game one can play with the concept of language. These juristic arguments, I must confess, at first absolutely dumbfounded me, not because I marveled at the juristic ingenuity—it is a well-known and ancient maxim that ultimately one can make a farce out of any law—but because then I was still of the opinion that one ought to treat the basic laws of the state somewhat seriously. [Approval from the Right.]

We Bohemians can give you the best information as to what the compulsory learning of the German language means. I still recall the time very well when in all of our schools, from the primary school up to the university, no other language was heard but German, although the children understood nothing of it. I remember that documents drafted in the German language required the signatures of Bohemian peasants, even though the peasants had no idea what was in the document. Officials were placed in Bohemian districts who understood not one word of the language of the people. Indeed, Slavic peasants were compelled to take the oath in court in the German language, even though they did not understand it. ["Hear! Hear!" from the Right.] And the death sentence was read to the criminal in the German language, although he did not know what it was. Those were the golden times of the compulsory learning of the German language among us, and because we have this experience behind us, we shrink from every act which could have similar results.

We fear every attempt such as this as the burned child does the fire, and we are guided by the wise maxim: *principiis obsta*. That, however, the return of such circumstances as I have just described actually is the objective of a certain party, one finds again proven with indisputable clarity in the minority report itself. The minority report recalls with a melancholy sigh, for example, the charter edict of Emperor Joseph, and yesterday the gentleman who introduced the bill read to us here the wording of these decrees by which Emperor Joseph established the German language as the universal language of the empire. The minority thus wishes something similar. The results which the Germanizing attempt of Emperor Joseph eventually produced and their particulars were already discussed yesterday by a very distinguished authority, and I do not wish to speak further about it. All of you are acquainted with the famous revocation of January 29, 1790, in which Emperor Joseph expressly withdrew what he had done in this direction and established once again those conditions which had existed before his accession. The noble, the great monarch terminated his life amidst the wreckage of his work, and as Emperor Joseph lay on his deathbed the Hungarian nobles brought home the crown of their country amid the unending jubilation of their people. I say this not to offend the memory of the great Emperor. One could scarcely find anybody who would be more enthusiastic than I am over the liberal and humanitarian intentions of that noble monarch. But it is my conviction that if Emperor

Joseph were living today, he himself would recognize his Germanizing and leveling attempts as the greatest mistake of his system of government. [Approval from the Right.] And yet these Germanizing measures of Emperor Joseph were not only explainable but were also excusable, for at the time of Emperor Joseph the national consciousness not only of the non-German but also of the German people had subsided and sunk into lethargy. Emperor Joseph believed that it was no injustice when he did away with something which in his view no longer existed. But if the national consciousness at the time of Emperor Joseph had been only half as awake as it is today, the noble friend of man would have turned in revulsion from measures which would have appeared to him as a crime against the inalienable rights of man. [Applause and acclaim from the Right.] If one thus uses the name of the great Emperor in such a way as to celebrate him as a Germanizer, then this is nothing other than an abuse of the memory of the great Emperor. [Acclaim from the Right.]

What, however, could not be carried out by an Emperor Joseph through hard absolutism—that you intend to achieve with your laws?

You intend to achieve in a time of national enthusiasm what you could not carry out during a time of national unconsciousness? You will sow hatred and dissension among the peoples of Austria. You will make the national struggle permanent, cripple the state, and convulse its foundations; but you will never strip peoples who are coming of age of their nationality, of their individuality, of the language of their fathers! [Acclaim and applause from the Right.]

There were periods in the history of this empire in which it was to some extent conceivable and understandable that one might wish to invest the state of Austria with a German mask. I say a German mask since it is understandable that a state of which scarcely one-fifth is populated by a German people is by nature no German state. I say, therefore, that to some extent a certain political rationale existed for investing the state of Austria with a German cloak.

At the time of Holy Roman Empire, when the crown of the German emperor was placed on a succession of heads of the House of Hapsburg, it was on the whole quite conceivable that the statesmen to some extent wished to assimilate the smaller into the larger and thereby to bind the whole together by means of the German people. But since the year 1806, when Emperor Francis laid down the crown of the Holy Roman Empire, when Germany went its own way and Austria went its way, this reason of state has had no further justification.

Likewise it is understandable that at the time when, under the pressure of the French war, the German Confederation came into being and Austria was forced into it, the statesmen of Austria wished to put a German cloak on the empire; for Austria, which had given Germany such a succession of excellent rulers, did not wish to be a secondary power in the Confederation. It wished to justify, as it were, its primary position in the German Conferedation directly by means of its German character in order the more easily to withstand the competition of its purely German rival. ["Quite right!" from the Right.]

This was at that time a reason of state; but since the events of the year 1866, when this rival forced Austria out of Germany, this political rationale has lost all justification and all meaning. Today Austria is dependent upon itself and its peoples and is no longer tied to Germany. As the situation stands today the transformation of Austria into a purely German state would, I am convinced, be dangerous in the highest degree to the vital interest, I should like to say to the existence, of Austria. ["Bravo!" from the Right.] It certainly is quite natural, during a time when the nationality principle has become a state-building factor, that the great and powerful national states should exert an irresistible attraction upon their smaller and weaker neighbors of the same nationality. I am convinced that there would sooner or later emerge from this process, in a completely Germanized Austria, certain centrifugal forces against which even the distinguished and recognized patriotism of the honorable gentlemen from that side [the Left] could scarcely maintain the balance for long. But the best means and the best bulwark against these possible centrifugal movements lie precisely in standing up for the vigor of the national diversity of this empire. For the non-German nationalities of this empire are guided, as it were by their instinct of self-preservation, into participation in maintaining the vigor and power of Austria. It is therefore clear that a completely Germanized Austria would not guarantee the sovereignty of the empire so well as the non-German nationalities—failing as they do to comprehend the familiar metaphor of the leaden birds and the magnetic mountain [Laughter from the Right.]

You also say that the Germans are the cement of the empire which holds the peoples together. The honorable Deputy Dr. Beer compared Austria with a magnificent edifice. This is a very appropriate comparison. Austria is a huge and magnificent edifice composed of large blocks, and these huge blocks are the peoples of the empire; and the cement which holds these blocks together is the feeling of justice, the feeling of protection which these nationalities find within this magnificent edifice regarding their individuality, regarding their nationality, regarding their language. ["Bravo! Bravo!" from the Right.] Do not tamper with this feeling, for then you loosen the real cement of the empire.

I therefore see as the purpose of the entire Wurmbrandt proposal, as I have said, Germanization, although this purpose is cloaked in official state language; but still another reason is basic to the Wurmbrandt bill. The bill is to serve as a battering ram for breaking through the iron ring of this side [the Right]. The deputies on that side [the Left] know very well that with their liberal fifes [laughter from the Right] they cannot lure the gentlemen of the Tyrol and Salzburg into their bowers, and they thus seize upon a national shawm. [Renewed laughter from the Right.] And even though you believe that you will not influence the gentlemen sitting here with your siren song, you nevertheless believe that you can influence their voters. [Very good!" from the Right.]

The Wurmbrandt bill is meant to trip gentlemen in the next elections. The desired results are the destruction of the present majority, the suppression of political opponents, and the recovery of the lost hegemony and power of that party—this seems to me to be the basic consideration from which the proposal proceeds. But you shall not achieve power in this way. It is a dead-end street that you have entered, the way of the exclusive idea of nationality. I do not know what you consider to be the reasons for your loss of leading position and power. But allow me to speak my opinion openly and clearly without bitterness. I believe that the causes of your loss of power lie in the fact not that you have been too little inclined toward German nationalism, but that you have come to be untrue to the standard of freedom. Yes, you entered upon the new arena of our public and political life as the liberal party, as men of progress, as men of true constitutionalism, and the liberal elements of this empire looked upon you with trust. This was the reason why you acquired power. How have you justified this trust? I do not wish to engage in recriminations, for the list of offenses which you have committed against freedom is a long one. But I shall permit myself to choose a few illustrations at random.

Let us take the election law. This certainly is your work. It was brought into being by men of your party, fostered by you and brought to fruition by you. Is this a liberal election system, when the worker is without rights, when the peasant has a hundred times fewer rights than the city dweller, the city dweller a hundred times fewer rights than the large landowner, when political rights are divided according to the tax returns and the genealogical tree? ["Very good!" from the Right.] And the honorable Deputy Professor Beer proved yesterday [laughter from the Right] that things have not yet been improved in this respect, when to my horror he leveled the accusation against this side [the Right] of the honorable House that the clerical and conservative party wishes to allow even the masses to vote. [Laughter from the Right.]

I am no conservative and still less a clerical; but this is what I want to do too, and if it is true that the clericals and conservatives want universal suffrage, then they indeed are liberal and not you. This certainly is the first paragraph in the liberal catechism, namely universal suffrage.

Let us now take, for example, the press law, which is likewise your brain child. In what liberal textbook have you found a press law which exposes every public expression of opinion to the sheer discretion of the state and police authorities, to the district attorney? Let us take Article XII, which guarantees to citizens the right of assembly and the right of association.

Has not this article of your constitution actually become a caricature, when each—even the smallest—assembly and association is dependent upon the benevolent sanction of the police authorities? And
let us finally take Article XIX of the constitution. The only means
which can reconcile the non-German nationality in any way to the
constitution is equal language rights. Now you are about to append
to this article an enabling law which can only turn this article into a
sheer illusion.

This is how it stands with respect to the freedom which you
brought to the people of Austria. And with regard to freedom in the
economy, the way to this goal, as it has evolved under your leadership, is still moist today from the tears of the widows and orphans
who have lost all their property from the so-called economic upswing.
You have sinned grievously against freedom. You have sacrificed
freedom to power, and so it has turned out that everything finally
has been lost—freedom and power. You have also lost thereby the
right to level against this [the Right] side of the House the accusation of retrogression. You have lost the right to assume in the future
the directing role and leadership of the liberal elements of Austria.
[Enthusiastic approval from the Right.]

The noble count who introduced the bill concluded his speech of
yesterday with the mournful confession that formerly, at the beginning of our parliamentary activity, he had thought that the liberal
elements would form the liberal parties of this House without regard
to national differences. And he admitted that he had already given
up this hope.

Now I close with the same thought, only with the difference that
I have not given up this hope. The day will come, and it must come
to the advantage of the people of Austria, when the directing role and
leadership will be placed again in the hands of the liberal party. But
this party will be composed of other men, and it will be oriented
toward other principles than the present liberal party. It will consist
of men of all nationalities and all tongues, who will inscribe on their
coat of arms the motto: "Equal rights for all peoples." It will consist
of men who will hold aloft the nationality principle, but a nationality
principle in the noble, in the lofty, sense of the word; a nationality

principle which desires the welfare of its people without plunging another people into distress; a nationality principle which teaches its people to love without hating another; a nationality principle which strives for the freedom of its people without wishing to place another in servitude. [Continued acclaim from the Right.] And this nationality principle—this is the basic idea, this is the true political idea of this empire. And because this proposal is not the motivating idea of the Wurmbrandt bill, because the way taken by this bill will lead not to the peace and welfare of the empire, but to everlasting conflict and to the destruction of the state, for this reason I vote against it. [Spirited and continued acclaim and applause from the Right. The speaker is congratulated from many sides.]

6. The Question: Has Self-Government Failed?

Baron Sonnino: *Let Us Go Back to the Constitution* (1897)°

Baron Sonnino, the author of the article reprinted here, was one of the most prominent Italian political leaders, a deputy in the Parliament, and at times a minister of state. The experience that he analyzes was characteristic not merely of Italy but also of Spain, of the Balkan countries, and to a lesser degree of France and Central Europe. Wherever parliamentary institutions had been established on the Continent, by the end of the century they were being subjected to criticism. The outcome of the Constitutional conflict in Prussia, discussed in Number 7, had assured to Germany a form of government resembling that advocated by Baron Sonnino. The German élite believed that their country had the most progressive and the most stable government and society in Europe, a form designated by German political philosophers as constitutional monarchism. Although Baron Sonnino repudiated any thought of dictatorship, the reader aware of the experience of Fascism can see the Fascist form of government as another possible answer to the problems that the author describes.

The fiftieth anniversary of the granting of the *Statuto* [Constitution], that is, of the legal and historical basis of our representative institutions, will be celebrated within a year in Turin with a solemn national exposition.

It is time to pause to reflect calmly on the road which has been traversed during half a century of parliamentary history.

With what feelings does the nation today regard parliamentary institutions?

° "Torniamo allo Statuto," *Nuova Antologia*, Fourth Series, LXVII (Rome, 1897). (Trans. Paul Sonnino.)

Must our undeniable disillusionment about the value and future of these institutions really be attributed to defects inherent in the *Statuto* and in its fundamental principles? Or should it be attributed to the accompanying doctrines gradually used to interpret and explain these principles while altering and falsifying, little by little, their underlying motives?

Undoubtedly the parliamentary system, as it operates in Italy, is sick. We must study its symptoms and prepare the remedies if we do not want to see it wasting away before us, undermined by the indifference and scorn of the nation.

Moreover, it is not only in Italy that this process is taking place. Parliamentary government is being questioned throughout the entire European continent, wherever this term is taken to mean government by parliament.

It is a fundamental truth, increasingly clear to everyone, that the simple bringing together of particular interests, even when these are represented by a great number of single territorial groupings [electoral districts], does not give us the sincere expression of the general interest of the nation. In fact, such a system does not provide us with the means of protecting this national interest.

The most substantial adverse criticism of the parliamentary system, about which so much has been written and said in these last years, may be summarized in a few comprehensive and almost self-evident statements.

The general interest of the state is not identical, day by day, with the sum of all particular interests, individually and subjectively considered; much less is it identical with the sum of a varying combination of those interests, capable only of attaining a temporary majority of one more than half of the votes cast by their political representatives.

In a government based almost entirely on elections, representation of the collective general interest is missing from top-level direction of public affairs. In case after case combinations of personal or local interests predominate.

Nor is it at all possible to base every governmental action solely on the principle of pleasing immediately those for whom it is taken, or of obtaining for it, in advance or concurrently, the support of the interested party.

Therefore, the elective element seems better adapted to determine the general course of legislation and to control the action of the government than it is to govern, either directly or through its delegates.

The so-called parliamentary system is currently experiencing the same thing which befell absolute government during the period when it still existed, although general opinion in Europe was already contesting its legitimacy and its usefulness. The parliamentary system too could suddenly be overthrown, and no one would raise a finger to defend it, or would bemoan its passing.

This situation represents a grave danger to the future of our civilization, because, although the parliamentary system has been fully discredited, there is no generally accepted body of doctrine which suggests a specific and positive evolution toward another system, toward another basis for liberal, orderly government. Meanwhile, socialism is organizing menacingly on one side; clericalism, with theocratic intentions, on the other; both despotisms, one just as stifling as the other to every civil and moral liberty.

On the one hand, whether from fear of the growth of subversive elements or from a desire for a firm restoration of order and discipline, a conservative, almost reactionary movement is emerging. This movement increasingly favors the ecclesiastical hierarchy as the representative and spokesman of a divine law of social morality opposed to individualistic utilitarianism.

From the other side a socialist movement is rising. Gathering force from dissatisfaction, from the friction produced by intensive individual competition, and from feelings caused as much by desire for equality or by democratic envy as by humanitarian sympathy, this movement is striving to idealize and intensify the concept of the state. The socialists hold that the state is the supreme representative of the collective whole, and as such must impose the iron law of its own collective utility upon every individual liberty and desire.

We cannot ignore these two tendencies. Increasingly they are dividing the nation into two great extremist parties and consequently are threatening every moral, intellectual, political, and civil liberty.

The moderate liberal element, in its desire for a proper balance between state power and individualism, is paralyzed. It is aware of the failure of the chief doctrines which it has been preaching and praising; and it is further rendered helpless by the complete discredit cast upon some of its slogans, which it no longer believes itself although it lacks the courage to repudiate them.

"And yet I hope," said the honorable Di Rudini in his Palermo speech of spring, 1895, on the eve of the elections which brought the present Chamber into being, "I strongly hope that enlightened public opinion, directed by our statesmen, may become convinced that we must neither impair nor suppress our representative institutions. *Rather, we must recall them to their original principles,* limiting the Chamber and the Government to their respective powers and, above all, taking away from the Government the means of exerting illegitimate pressure and undue influence on the elected and on the voters."

I am in complete agreement with the honorable Di Rudini that there is a need to recall our institutions to their principles, but I consider his remedy insufficient and incomplete. He makes it consist entirely of restricting the powers of the Government and of the Chamber and of reducing the duties of the state by delegating some of its functions to local bodies and authorities. He fails to envisage as equally necessary and urgent the restoration of the executive power to the person of the Prince, and to recognize that the Government is not just the ministry considered alone, but the ministry as the organ responsible for the acts of the Prince.

There are actually two questions rather than one, although they are intimately connected. The progressive usurpation of the executive power by the elected Chamber has resulted in confusion between the functions of the Government and those of the Parliament, particularly the Chamber of Deputies, and in the deplorable interference by the Government in elections; it has also resulted in the ministry's virtual usurpation of powers belonging exclusively to the Prince. The Prince's authority is relegated to a negative and inactive part, and the executive power is considered as legally and actually belonging to the ministry rather than to the Prince.

The fact that the elected Chamber has exceeded its functions and has invaded the powers of the Crown is explicitly due to the doctrine which transformed the ministers of the Prince into ministers of the Chamber, thus submitting them to direct dependence on changing parliamentary majorities.

In a country like ours, where the activity of the state is so great and where there is constant demand for its increase, we cannot at present successfully deprive the Chamber of its usurped powers and repair the entire functioning of the parliamentary machinery. We must first free the ministers to some extent from direct dependence on the Chamber, truly restoring their former character as ministers of the Prince.

In some countries, because of the substantial development of local life and also because of the activity and independence of the individual, the action of the central government and of the state in general is reduced to a minimum. In such countries numerous powerful historical organisms act as checks and guides to the functioning of democratic institutions. Thus the formal dependence of the ministry upon the elected Chamber does not necessarily have grave consequences; it does not corrupt the parliamentary atmosphere or force the ministry, in its own defense, to use every means to make the Chamber subservient. Where, however, as among us, in the midst of inertia and widespread indolence the functions of the state increase daily, and where everything is asked and expected of the central government, departure from the standards of the *Statuto* results in disaster and is fatal to the operation of representative institutions.

Let us also do whatever we can to reactivate local life. If we delegate to the local bodies as many additional functions of state as can successfully be taken away from the central government without endangering the total health of the national organism, much will be gained. But whatever we do, we shall not succeed today in Italy in reducing government solely to the functions dreamed of by the followers of Herbert Spencer.

The very ministries and ministers who from morning till night preach the need for decentralization have been traversing the entire country to promise piers, streets, schools, land reclamation, aqueducts, and stations to every city and region.

The very law which granted even to the minor communes the right to elect their own mayor left the Government full and unrestricted powers to dissolve the communal councils.

The state is called upon from every side to favor infant industries, to protect all those already in operation, even when these may be solid and flourishing, and to aid those in need.

These same standard-bearers of the liberal school have currently told us at Montecitorio [The Parliament building] that the state must now contribute to the national old-age fund.

The best-known liberals claim that the state must direct internal colonization and must force proprietors to farm their lands, expropriating the inept, the incapable, and the slothful.

A self-styled liberal ministry has declared that the state must even guarantee the basic shares of shaky private institutions and the interest on loans owed by insolvent communes.

However this may be, and without going to such dangerous extremes, even those who are most worried by the defects of centralization must admit that in many cases when functions properly belonging to the state are delegated to a local authority rather than to the central government, the result is not the promotion of liberty and the development of the individual personality. Rather, given our social conditions, the risk is sometimes run of facilitating and aggravating the tyrannies of local cliques and the oppression of one class by another, thus barring social authority from its most important duty.

In any case, as long as conditions in Italy make the extensive activity of the central power unavoidable for the maintenance of security and even individual liberty, for public works, education, etc. (and none of us living today will see the end of it, not even those who will reach the hundredth anniversary of the *Statuto*), every direct and immediate dependence on the elected Chamber by the executive power personified in the ministers will be converted into a continued attempt by the ministries to coerce the Chamber. This will be done through multiple acts of the Government in the individual electoral districts, that is, through promises of favors or threats of reprisals and harmful acts.

The ministry (and I am not speaking of this or that cabinet but of the institution considered abstractly), having made itself almost independent of the sovereign and having assumed the real and actual functions of government in the name of the elected representatives of the people, would now like to make itself independent of the Chamber by taking away from the latter all power over the executive. In other words, the cabinet, which has made use of the Chamber to dispossess the Prince of his basic powers, would now, instead, like to find a way to free itself from the Chamber and its bothersome demands, relying on the principle of separation of powers and the rights of the Crown, that is, the rights of the executive power which the *Statuto* would reserve to the Prince.

It is neither practically nor logically possible to reach the happy medium which the honorable Di Rudini as well as all liberal conservatives desire, unless we return to the principles of the *Statuto*. This document establishes that the ministers, that is, those persons elevated to the direction of the great administrative branches of the state, are neither collectively nor individually ministers of the Chamber and even less ministers in their own right, but are simply the ministers responsible for the actions of the Prince. Such a return to the principles of the *Statuto* is a necessary basis for a renewed vigor in our parliamentary life. Then the deputies will be liberated from pressures by their constituents, who seek daily interference in the administration of public affairs on behalf of their personal interests, and the ministers will be freed of the illicit pressure and interference of the Parliament.

If we reinvest the Sovereign with his rights, we shall easily succeed in restricting the powers of the elected Chamber, in reinvigorating those of the life-appointed Senate and, what is more, in reactivating both by returning their true functions to them.

The Chamber has nullified its own power by its attempts to impose itself too much. It has wanted not only to legislate almost independently but also to govern; and now it is in the control of any man who can appropriate power for himself by organizing a local clique, by uniting around himself the deputation of a single great region, by manipulating public disturbances, or by any other means or expedient. There is no desire that the Prince, because of his integrity and high vantage point, should be authorized to resist and to point the way personally, subject only to the free examination and open public judgment of the acts of his government by Parliament.

The interests of the Crown are far broader and more permanent than those of the politicians who succeed one another in the ministries. The return to the Crown of the powers and offices entrusted to it by the *Statuto* would mark the liberation and rehabilitation of the Chamber and of Parliament in general. For the Senate too, if it were truly and not just formally appointed by the Prince, would have much greater prestige and authority than it does at present. It consists today only of progressive layers of different colors, corresponding to the succession of various factions and groups in the Government and to the inconsistent vicissitudes of parliamentary alchemy.

The elected Chamber will be more independent and will resume its legislative function and its exercise of financial control with greater seriousness and efficiency as soon as it gives up its claim that the ministers are its creatures and are in practice to be designated by it. It must consider them as ministers of the Prince, that is, as organs responsible for the will and action of the Sovereign, to be chosen and appointed by him alone.

This may perhaps weaken somewhat the so-called cabinet type of government, but it will establish a real separation of powers between the different levels of representative government, and it will give to public opinion and to the national will a greater freedom of movement and of action in determining the course of legislation and in controlling the acts of the Government.

Nowadays the Chamber is often obliged, because of the political "question of confidence" which is raised on every occasion, to stand blindly by and allow the passage of legislative measures to which it morally objects.

With the elimination of the direct dependence of the ministry on the uninterrupted support of the majority of the Chamber, the latter becomes freer from extraneous concerns and able to express its objective judgment both on individual legislative proposals and on individual acts of the Government; for every disapproval or admonition by the Chamber would no longer necessarily signal the political death of a minister or of a cabinet, nor would it signify the withdrawal of confidence by the Chamber. As it is now, the constant concern with politics and the fear of endangering the fate of the cabinet or the general equilibrium of parties and parliamentary groups over one special question too often move the Chamber to neglect the conscientious discharge of its legislative function.

The majority of the deputies, whose primary interest and consequently primary concern lies in the safety of *its* ministry, currently shows itself all too frequently disposed to permit tampering with the rights and prerogatives of Parliament rather than to endanger the life of the cabinet, and thus its own predominance in the Government, by a negative vote. This explains the great docility with which majorities have been seen to submit repeatedly to laws by decree, even when these, in normal times and circumstances, compromise questions of great constitutional, economic, and financial importance.

With the activity of the Chamber brought back within legitimate boundaries, the majority no less than the minority will always show itself jealous to maintain inviolate the collective rights of the institution to which it belongs.

My thesis is not that the fate of the ministry or of individual ministers must not and can in no way depend upon the votes of the Chamber, as long as these votes stem from a true, considered, and constant purpose and reveal a serious movement of public opinion. Even today, when such dependence is declared to be fatal and inevitable, it has not always worked out disadvantageously in practice. I am not even saying that the provisions of our *Statuto* exclude every influence of the elected national representatives on the life of the ministry or of the ministers. Such action, however, is not to be considered as *a priori* always equally and constitutionally necessary.

It is understood that no law can ever be authorized without the prior approval of the Chamber; nor is the power of the Parliament denied to make its will felt against a given ministry or minister by means of the vote on the budget, in which case there is a real and constant divergence of purpose.

The monarchical representative system, like every other form of government, functions neither automatically nor mechanically. It demands from its organs a careful and continuing consideration of the state of affairs under which they operate.

To carry out this reform neither an amendment to the *Statuto* nor any law is needed, nor for that matter spectacular or energetic action; it is enough for the public conscience to become convinced. As things now stand the defect is not in the law but stems from a violation of the fundamental law of the state.

The phenomenon which has been unfolding in the kingdom of Italy, particularly during the last quarter century, is truly strange.

Little by little a new institution, in no way envisaged by the *Statuto*, has emerged and developed; and every day it tends more toward making itself into an autonomous, extra-legal power, feeding and fattening on all the functions of which it is openly or secretly despoiling the other constitutional powers. This new, hybrid institution, which tends increasingly to threaten all the other powers, is the ministry taken as a whole; however, it is especially represented in the person of the president of the Council of Ministers.

I am not referring here to the old question of chancellor-ministers, cardinal-ministers, and grand viziers, that is to the matter of the internal organization of the ministry and the opportunity of concentrating the collective representation to a greater or lesser extent or in one or more persons. I refer to the position of the ministry considered as an institution in itself, in relation to the Sovereign on the one hand and to the Parliament on the other.

In every ministerial crisis, however it originates, all those who individually or collectively are centers of some political influence exert every effort to seize power by securing a commission from the Sovereign to form a cabinet.

It is generally agreed that, among the various leaders of parliamentary factions, whoever somehow manages to get the first call to form a cabinet will surely get the majority of votes in the Chamber, if he is careful and imaginative, and above all if he is not so naive as to appear too consistent in his principles or too scrupulous in his actions. Thus in moments of crisis every instrument, every pressure, and every bit of cunning is put into operation so that one's own candidate, that is, the one from whom the greatest advantages can be expected, will get the call. All means are fair. Open and secret threats are even made to the Sovereign to the effect that if his choice should fall on others, disorders and disturbances will ensue. Thus use is made of that mysterious terror which, like a memory of the Jacobins, permeates all Italy in the face of every mob movement.

Once the coveted commission is received, the whole trick is to act fast and put together, without regard to their political views, about ten ministers whose adherents add up to a substantial number of deputies. It does not even matter whether this number constitutes a majority of the Chamber; for what is lacking will be obtained along the way. No one bothers about a program. Doing differently from one's predecessors, inspiring widespread fears and hopes—that is all there is to it!

Having taken possession of the central fortress of the government, the new ministry turns threateningly against all those who do not support it. Secure in its possession of power, it is ready to defy both the Chamber and the Senate and if necessary the Sovereign himself in order to maintain its position. It represents an almost autonomous constitutional authority, separate from both Crown and Parliament and having its own rights and legal foundation.

If the Crown manifests the least sign of a will of its own in governmental affairs, the ministry is aroused and questions the Crown's right to independence. On the theory that the Prince reigns but does not govern, the ministry holds that it is against both the letter and the spirit of the *Statuto* for the Prince to have, much less manifest, any desire opposed to that of the ministry. This view obtains especially if the ministry can muster a majority in the Chamber, even if the majority is one of only a single vote, or one obtained by questionable means.

In the face of a Chamber which shows an inclination to rebel, the threat is made of dissolution, with general elections to be held under high governmental pressure. It is scarcely ever admitted any more that, in case of disagreement between the ministry and the Chamber, the Sovereign could refuse the demand of the ministry that the Chamber be dissolved. On every occasion friends of the ministers secretly spread the word that, in case of an unfavorable vote, the ministry *will not* resign. In the corridors of Montecitorio are whispered the supposedly confidential statements of the president of the Council: "No matter what happens, I am not leaving. The life of the Chamber depends on its future conduct. If I receive an unfavorable vote, I remain at my post and I am not resigning. If the Sovereign does not want me, he will have to dismiss me by his own decree and on his own initiative." And it is sometimes added, "I am ready to use any means. I am even ready to go down into the public square, etc."

Meanwhile work is begun (without ever admitting that either the Sovereign or anyone else could take part in it or observe it) on the so-called preparation for the general elections. Prefects and officials on every level are changed. Those who are believed to be loyal to former ministers are dismissed. Others are intimidated, especially the administrators of communes, charities, credit institutions, etc. The attempt to get political instruments ready everywhere is made with the thought in mind, "We should like to see somebody try to pull all this work down quickly when the crisis comes." And so, one by one, the deputies are intimidated, each seeing in his own electoral district the entire Government machine lying in wait for the elections, either to support him or, if he is an opponent, to fight him.

As to the Senate, the technique is simpler. Some forty or perhaps eighty friendly senators are nominated, and again, contrary to the *Statuto*, it is of course not admitted that the Prince should have any voice.

And as for the press, supposedly the fourth power, it is taken care of with state money or with threats and inducements to the politicians and financiers who hold the strings.

It is the story of the so-called Old Man of the Sea in *The Thousand and One Nights*. Having jumped on the neck of Sinbad the Sailor, the old man makes a slave out of him by threatening to strangle him at any sign of rebellion; Sinbad cannot get rid of him until one day the old man gets drunk. The same thing is true of the ministers. Parliament succeeds in getting them off its back only when they are drunk with power.

Under this system there is no longer anyone to be concerned with the continuity of governmental action, the conservation of good administrative traditions, and consistency in policies.

The new ministers have to get themselves talked about, so each one has to have some new technique and to make drastic changes in what his predecessors have done, whether there is urgency and need for reforms or not. Above all it is imperative to appoint new employees, change organization, etc.

The bureaucracy remains the only guardian of the traditions of the government and of the continuity of its acts, insofar as it is not also overcome or upset by the political current; contrary to the provisions of the *Statuto*, it too no longer finds any protection through the action of the Sovereign, whose right to refuse changes in personnel, dismissals, appointments, transfers, and so forth is scarcely admitted. If it is conceded that in practice the ministers should have some regard for and not oppose too strongly any single wish of the Sovereign, the concession is made out of consideration for the great dignity of the Sovereign's position or from fear of pushing things too far, and not because it is granted that he could or should regularly interfere in administrative questions, even in the case of the highest officials.

Now all this is in direct contradiction to what the *Statuto* prescribes. The latter expressly makes the following provisions regarding the powers of the Prince:

Executive power belongs to the Prince *alone*. He is supreme head of the state, *commands all land and sea forces*, declares war, makes treaties of peace, alliance, etc. (Article 5)

The Prince *appoints to all offices of the state*. (Article 6)

The Prince *alone* sanctions and promulgates laws. (Article 7)

The Prince may issue pardons and commute sentences. (Article 8)

The proposing of laws shall belong to the Prince and to each of the two chambers, etc. (Article 9)

The Prince *appoints* and *dismisses* his ministers. (Article 65)

Justice emanates from the Prince and is administered in his name by judges whom *he* appoints. (Article 68)

Legislative power shall be collectively exercised by the Prince and the two Chambers: the Senate and the Chamber of Deputies. (Article 3)

The Senate is made up of members appointed for life by the Prince, numbering, etc. (Article 33)

If a proposed law has been rejected by one of the *three* legislative powers, it cannot be, etc. (Article 56)

As to the ministers, it must be noted that the *Statuto*, although it refers on several occasions to the ministers of the Prince, makes no mention of a ministry, or cabinet, or Council of Ministers.[1] As to their functions, in addition to the article previously cited which attributes their nomination and dismissal to the Prince and to another which prescribes that ministers who are deputies or Senators can vote only in their own Chamber and that they can enter and speak in both (Article 66), we have *only* the two following articles in the *Statuto*:

Ministers are responsible. The laws and acts of the government have effect only when accompanied by the signature of a minister. (Article 7)

The Chamber of Deputies has the right to make charges against the ministers *of the Prince* and to bring them before the high court of justice (Article 47), that is before the Senate convoked by royal decree. (Article 36)

The Prince then, according to the *Statuto*, personifies the state in its most necessary and normal attributes, and he has an active, not passive, function in safeguarding these attributes. It is he who represents the tradition of government, the continuity of policy in the state, and the stability of its laws; in a word, he stands for the general interest of the fatherland, both in the present and in the future. And he is the only institution to which these functions are entrusted under our laws.

Under our constitution the dynastic Prince represents the continuous, permanent element in the complex organism of the state, in contrast to the elected elements, which are temporary, changing, and subject to time and place.

To the Sovereign, therefore, according to the precise letter of

[1] Even in Article 15, where, speaking of the convocation of the Chambers to name a regent when the Prince is a minor and there is neither a mother nor a male relative, it is necessary to refer to the ministers collectively, the *Statuto* says, "the Chambers, convoked within ten days *by the ministers*."

the *Statuto,* belongs: (1) executive power; and (2) a role not inferior to that of Parliament in the legislative power, since he shares equally with it the right to propose laws, and the right of sanctioning them is reserved to him alone.

Nor can the spirit of the *Statuto* be separated from the literal provisions of its text.

The executive branch in governing must keep itself aloof from parties, must not favor the interests of the majority rather than of the minority, or of the voters rather than the non-voters, but must consider all citizens equally, keeping in view only the general interest of the state. Consequently, it must be independent from those who cannot always identify themselves with this general interest, and it could never be entrusted to an institution dependent upon a majority and upon one party.

If the Government, personified in the ministers, were to depend directly on the parliamentary majority even for its membership, the entire legislative power would—in obvious contradiction to the spirit of the *Statuto*—be absorbed by the elected Chamber alone, in fact, by the majority of its members. In such a case, laws would first of all be proposed by the ministers, direct representatives of the majority (the royal decree authorizing the presentation of projected laws being reduced to an empty formality); then they would be discussed and modified at Montecitorio by the majority of the deputies in rebuttal of their own delegates; and lastly the laws would be reexamined, if only for polishing and finishing touches, at the Palazzo Madama [The King's residence]. Thus the decision would be in the power of the ministers, that is, of the organs and direct representatives of the elected majority, and the legislative powers would actually be reduced to one instead of three as the *Statuto* stipulates.

The power of the Prince must be brought to bear especially on matters outside partisan politics. Matters bearing on the following are more fittingly his concern:

1. the defense of the state and the conservation of the morale and spirit of its military forces;

2. foreign policy;

3. justice, not only civilian and criminal but also administrative justice, along with social justice as well, which concerns social relations between different classes or orders of citizens and the protection of the weak;

4. high-level administration of the state.

I hasten to conclude this discussion with a brief review of the ideas advanced thus far.

Two great social and political forces are arising and organizing themselves in Italy, both with revolutionary tendencies and aspirations in regard to the liberal representative monarchy.

On the one hand, socialism wants to suppress every individual liberty in the name of equality. Because free competition, as exaggerated by the doctrinaire exponents of the laissez-faire school of economics, can actually impede the development of the human personality and of the individual liberty of the mass, the socialists suppress every individual liberty outright by organizing the state as the sole owner of the means of production and sole distributor of the fruits of labor. They tend in actuality toward bureaucratic despotism and toward the tyranny of a mandarinate.

On the other hand, in the name of the highest ideals of mankind as well as in the name of order and of the conservation of past social traditions, the clerical organization is making gigantic leaps. Enemy as it is of freedom of thought and of conscience, it tends in reality toward the most tolerant obscurantism and toward the suppression of disorder by means of the suppression of progress and of every movement of the human spirit.

In the face of these rising dangers the liberal state is carelessly demolishing its own defenses, more completely every day.

Parliament is despoiled of all credit and prestige when all its activity must be based on a continual conflict of local and personal interests and when dissension and struggle are the conditions for life and action in the administration of public affairs.

At the same time the prestige of the office of Prince is diminished, when it should form the backbone of the political structure, should embody the concept of the state as the defender of liberty and not as the oppressor, and should promote the general welfare for the sake of individual development. Instead, our doctrinaire thinkers would like to make of the Prince a semi-hypnotized being, who is to accept everything and submit to everything, with no will or opinion of his own, but who is simply to designate in moments of crisis, like an automatic manometer, a president of the Council who can be expected *per fas ac nefas* to obtain a majority of the votes of the deputies. One cannot expect the public to accept this incongruity in the Prince's position: on ninety-nine days out of a hundred he is to be an inactive element, with no opinions or feelings concerning public affairs, but with a benign attitude toward any cabinet which manages to extract the consent of the Chamber; then on the hundredth day, in moments of greatest difficulty and passionate crisis, the Prince, up to then ignored and without real functions, is to instantly become respected and venerated by all as being the great moderating force in the state, as having a clear and certain consciousness of what line to follow in putting power into new hands, and as deserving blind faith and universal consent.

Everything depends today on the will of the majority of the representatives of the voters; therefore every consideration and every effort of those politicians who actually have the government in their hands is centered on getting control of the organs of state and all political institutions which might depend on these organs. Their purposes in this effort are to lure or force the voters to follow them and at the same time, by personal inducements and threats, to gain control of a majority in the Chamber in order to insure that the entire battery of official and governmental influence will be arrayed against every single deputy in his own district.

And on the other hand, every scheme, every effort of the individual deputies centers around assuring themselves of reelection, that is, around satisfying then and there and in any way possible the greatest number of interests and desires of individual voters.

The result is the contempt of the voter for the deputy, of whom he makes use and by whom he is used, and the contempt of the nation for the government and for the very institutions of which the government is the visible product.

All idealization of the state is lacking, every tradition of the government is interrupted, the principle of authority loses all prestige, and the nation becomes ever more disenchanted with the agreements upon which it is based, condemning them all together—individuals, institutions, and principles.

Mixed governments, being complex and made up of various autonomous institutions, each with its own proper and distinct functions, presuppose for their normal functioning that each power and each institution will watch over the conservation of its own rights and the integrity of the functions entrusted to it.

In Italy instead, I repeat, a new power has emerged, parasitical, hybrid, and not contemplated by the *Statuto*. By making itself the instrument and sounding board of the dogmatic demands and rising usurpations of the Chamber of Deputies, which would like to appropriate the sole right of speaking as the interpreter of the will of the nation, and by declaring itself the legitimate and authorized outgrowth of the national representation, it has progressively usurped nearly all of the normal functions of the Crown, and has tended to push the Prince ever more into the shadows. At the same time, on the other hand, it has perverted or destroyed the proper functions of the elected Chamber. The Chamber, having wanted to extend its governing functions to a realm not its own, has come instead to lose in practice even the free exercise of legislative functions, which the *Statuto* attributes to it. It finds itself increasingly a tool of the ministry.

Meanwhile the great mass of people, worried and mistrustful, puts itself more and more into the hands of revolutionaries, of dreamers who promise miraculous cures, and of loud talkers who promise an age of gold, or else of the clericals, who offer the reign of God through the government of his ministers.

Strengthened by the letter and spirit of the *Statuto*, the nation turns to the Sovereign and says to him, "Your Majesty, be on your guard to maintain unimpaired the functions which are entrusted to you and which successive ministries have allowed to be usurped or have attempted to seize from you. Executive power belongs to you alone. To you alone belongs the appointment and dismissal of the ministers who must countersign and answer for your governmental acts. The nation looks to you and trusts you, certain, on the one hand, that you will not tamper with a single liberty and that you will not withdraw a single right which your glorious ancestors have granted or delegated to others, and no less desirous, on the other hand, that you conserve alive and unimpaired our mother institution, which represents to us the defense of the general interest of the fatherland. Awake, Sire! Your interest is preeminently our interest, everyone's interest, Italy's interest."

No less than socialism, the liberal monarchy possesses a lofty and dominating concept of the state, distinct from any class preferences.

And in the face of the invading Church it represents, aside from a stout defense of social morality, freedom of conscience and thought; it guarantees the rights of all religions and opinions, and the right of each citizen to make full use of his individual faculties in all basic functions of civil life; and it assures the protection of material interests as well as the civil progress of the nation.

Our liberal monarchy, in opposition to mob socialism and obscurantist clericalism, identifies itself with the idea of the national fatherland and at the same time personifies the principle of individual liberty. Thus it sets up an ideal for itself well worthy of being a rallying point; it is a nucleus around which to gather in the midst of the quick turnover of men and groups in power and of the whirling of their transient passions and grudges.

Do we want a clerical, moderate-liberal, or radical-socialist Italy?

Soon we shall have to choose among the three.

The moderate-liberal elements, their credo too individualistic for the day-to-day struggle, find themselves in the position of volunteers facing the standing armies of the extreme parties. These parties, whether through the ecclesiastical organization, which extends all the way down to the parishes and makes use of a thousand types of interconnected associations and brotherhoods, or whether through workers' mutual-assistance, consumption, and production societies, and unfortunately with the not infrequent aid of governmental and communal employees, always have their formations ready for war mobilization.

Thus we often see the mass armies of the moderate-liberal parties dispersed by the less numerous although compact and disciplined bands of their adversaries.

Under these conditions the moderate-liberal party is divided into two factions, which by perpetual strife virtually cancel each other out. Thus the party is powerless, not only to fight against the two other united groups, but even to be able to have a dominant voice in the agreements or transactions which it makes with either one.

Even alone we are strongest and most numerous, or to put it better, we should be if we knew how to stay united and organize ourselves, if we knew how to consider the reality of things and not just feed upon stereotyped theories taken from foreign books, if we knew how to put aside personal discord and rivalry and to close ranks firmly around the great civil and liberal ideas represented by the Italian monarchy of the House of Savoy, if we knew how to shake off the inertia which paralyzes our faith and moral fortitude, if we knew how to be sincere in expressing our will and manfully resolved in attaining it.

I wish that my voice could summon all men of good will who are at the same time liberal and conservative for the organization of a great party. This party, in order to fight socialism and clericalism effectively, would immediately set up a program for the establishment of limits upon the functions of the various powers of the state and upon the development of the functions of the Crown; at the same time the new party would advocate giving back to the state and the Crown the rights sanctioned by the fundamental pact ratified in the plebiscites which created the kingdom of Italy.

I do not mean to press at all for any kind of Caesarism or autocratic government without controls, or for any form of despotism or absolute government.

We want the liberal and representative monarchy of the *Statuto*, with the monarch as a real and active Prince who is not to be delivered in chains to a "mayor of the palace" called the president of the Council of Ministers.

The elected Chamber and the life-appointed Senate must cooperate actively in legislation and, moreover, must always control, discuss, and curb the acts and tendencies of the Government through their action on the responsible ministers as well as on the laws and budgets which these present. But they must not exercise, either directly or by means of one or more of their delegates, the executive power. This is exclusively under the jurisdiction of the Prince (himself, like every other power or person, subject to the law), who also concurs in the formation of this executive power through his right of proposing and approving legislation.

I have not intended in this essay to make allusions to or accusations against the present ministry any more than to make reproaches against past ones. I have merely intended to bring out and analyze a transformation which is occurring in our institutions and which, it seems to me, has been one of the principal causes of their progressive decline. It is a transformation which finds expression in the formula, "The Prince reigns but does not govern," and it is in direct contradiction to what the *Statuto* demands and the nation expects in order to conserve free institutions in Italy.

7. The Character of Underground Work

Madame Krupskaya: *In Petersburg, 1893-1898*[*]

The memoirs of Madame Krupskaya, wife of Lenin, reveal the nature of the underground work that subversive forces carried on not merely in Russia but in many countries at different times during the century. The motives for this underground activity differed according to the group. Russian liberals in 1825, members of Young Italy, Spanish anarchists, German socialists under Bismarck, Polish nationalists in Russia, to mention a few groups, had to work secretly under the constant threat of the police, just as did the communists about whom Krupskaya writes, and the methods used by both sides were similar in all cases. To illustrate the kind of life that the participants led, the following memoirs were chosen primarily because of the subsequent fame of the central figures. The reader can learn from them not merely about the remarkably petty nature of much of the subversive work, but also about the kind of persons who were active revolutionaries, their social relations, and the way in which they tried to make ideas into social reality.

Vladimir Ilyich arrived in St. Petersburg in the autumn of 1893. I did not get to know him at once, however. Some comrades told me that a certain learned Marxist had arrived from the Volga. Then they brought me an exercise-book containing a screed *On Markets*, which was being passed round for comrades to read in turn. The book contained the views both of our Petersburg Marxist (the technologist Hermann Krassin) and of the new-comer from the Volga. The pages were folded in half. On the one side, in a straggling

[*] Nadezhda K. Krupskaya, *Memories of Lenin*, trans. E. Verney (London: Martin Lawrence Press, 1930), pp. 1-24.

scrawl, with many crossings-out and insertions, were the opinions of Krassin. On the other side, carefully written, and without any altera- tions, were the notes and replies of our newly arrived friend.

At that time the problem of markets very much interested all us young Marxists. Among the Petersburg Marxist circles a special tendency was already beginning to be crystallized. To the repre- sentatives of this tendency the processes of social development ap- peared as something mechanical and schematic. Such an interpreta- tion of social development completely neglected the role of the masses, the role of the proletariat. The revolutionary dialectic of Marxism was stowed away somewhere, and only lifeless "phases of development" remained. Nowadays, of course, any Marxist would be able to refute this mechanical viewpoint. At that time, however, our St. Petersburg Marxist circles were very much concerned about this issue. We were still very poorly equipped. Many of us knew nothing of Marx's works save the first volume of *Capital,* and had not even seen the text of the *Communist Manifesto.* It was thus more from instinct that we felt this mechanicalness to be quite the opposite of live Marxism.

The question of markets was closely connected with this general problem of the interpretation of Marxism. The advocates of me- chanicalness generally approached the question very abstractly.

More than thirty years have passed since then and, unfortunately, the exercise-book I have referred to has not been preserved. I can therefore only speak of the impression it made upon us.

Our new Marxist friend treated this question of markets in a very concrete manner. It was linked up with the interests of the masses, and in the whole approach we sensed just that live Marxism that takes phenomena in their concrete surroundings and in their devel- opment.

One wanted to become more closely acquainted with this new- comer, to find out his views at closer range.

I did not actually see Vladimir Ilyich until Shrovetide, when it was decided to arrange for certain Petersburg comrades to confer with him. The conference was to take place at the home of the engineer Klasson,[1] a prominent St. Petersburg Marxist, who had been with me in the same study-circle two years before. To screen our conference, we organized it as a pancake party.

At that meeting, besides Vladimir Ilyich, there were present: Klasson, Y. P. Korobko, Serebrovsky, S. I. Radchenko, and others. Potressov and Struve were to have come, but, I believe, did not turn up. I remember one moment particularly well. We were discussing the lines that we ought to follow. There did not seem to be general agreement. Someone was saying—I think it was Shevlyagin—that what was very important was to work in the Committee for Illiteracy. Vladimir Ilyich laughed, and somehow his laughter sounded laconic. I never heard him laugh that way on any subsequent occasion.

"Well," he said, "if anyone wants to save the fatherland in the Committee for Illiteracy, we won't hinder him!"

I ought to say that our generation of young people still witnessed the skirmishes of the *Narodniki*[2] with Tsardom. We saw how the Liberals at first were "sympathetic" about everything, but after the breaking up of the "Narodnaya Volya"[3] Party, became cowed, feared every whisper, and started preaching "little things first."

One could quite understand Lenin's sarcastic remark. He had come to discuss how we could take up the struggle together, and in response was treated to an appeal to distribute the pamphlets of the Committee for Illiteracy!

Later, when we had become closely acquainted, Vladimir Ilyich once told me about the attitude of the Liberals toward the arrest of his elder brother. All acquaintances shunned the Ulyanov family. Even an aged teacher, who had formerly come every evening to play chess, left off calling. There was no railway at Simbirsk at that time,

[1] The meeting at R. Klasson's house took place during the Shrovetide of 1894. In the autumn of the same year, at Klasson's, Vladimir Ilyich read his article, "The Economic Content of Populism." The Lenin Institute was given this information by Klasson himself.

[2] Populists. Members of the parties "Zemlya Ivolya" and "Narodnaya Volya."

[3] "People's will." A Russian revolutionary Party pursuing terrorist tactics, and most active at the end of the 'seventies and beginning of the 'eighties of the last century. Considered to be the predecessors of the Socialist Revolutionary Party.

and Vladimir Ilyich's mother had to go on horseback to Syzran in order to go on to St. Petersburg, where her eldest son was imprisoned. Vladimir Ilyich was sent to seek a companion for the journey. But no one out wanted to travel with the mother of an arrested man.

Vladimir Ilyich told me that this widespread cowardice made a very profound impression upon him at that time.

This youthful experience undoubtedly did leave its imprint on Lenin's attitude towards the Liberals. It was early that he learned the value of all Liberal chatter.

In the autumn of that same year, 1894, Vladimir Ilyich, in his article *The Economic Content of Populism, and Its Criticism in Mr. Struve's Book,* wrote: "The bourgeoisie rules both in life in general and in Liberal society. It would seem, therefore, that it is necessary to turn away from this society and go to what is diametrically opposed to the bourgeoisie." [*Collected Works*, Vol. II, page 18, Russian Edition.]

And farther on:

"You (the Narodniki) attribute a desire to defend the bourgeoisie to anyone who demands that working-class ideologists break completely with these (Liberal) elements and serve exclusively those who are 'differentiated from the life' of bourgeois society." [*Ibid.*, page 54.]

But Vladimir Ilyich's views on the Liberals, his mistrust of them, his continual exposure of them . . . these are well known. I have merely given a few quotations relating to the same year that the meeting took place at Klasson's house.

At the "pancake party" no agreement was reached, of course. Vladimir Ilyich spoke little and was more occupied with contemplating those present. People who styled themselves Marxists became uncomfortable beneath his fixed glance.

I remember how, when we were returning home from the Okhta along the banks of the Neva, I was first told about Vladimir Ilyich's brother, Alexander. He was a member of the Narodnaya Volya, and took part in the attempt on the life of Alexander III in 1886. He perished at the hands of the Tsar's hangmen before he had even come of age.[4] He was very fond of Alexander. They had many common tastes, and both of them liked to remain alone for long periods in order to concentrate. They usually lived together, at one time in a special part of the house. And when any of their numerous boy or girl cousins called, the brothers had a favourite phrase: "Oblige us with your absence." Both brothers were tenacious workers, and both were of revolutionary dispositions. But the difference in age probably made itself felt. For Alexander Ilyich did not tell Vladimir about everything.

Vladimir Ilyich told me of his brother's activity as a naturalist. The last summer that he came home, he had been preparing a dissertation on worms and was working all the time at the microscope. In order to get as much light as possible, he rose at daybreak and immediately set to work. "No, my brother won't make a revolutionary, I thought then," Vladimir Ilyich recounted; "a revolutionary cannot devote so much time to the study of worms." He soon saw how he was mistaken.

The fate of his brother undoubtedly profoundly influenced Vladimir Ilyich. What in addition played an important part was the fact that by this time Vladimir Ilyich had already begun to think independently on many subjects, and had already come to his own decision as to the necessity of revolutionary struggle.

Had it been otherwise, probably his brother's fate would only have caused him profound grief, or at most awakened in him the resolve and aspiration to follow his brother's footsteps. In these circumstances his brother's fate whetted his brain, brought out in him an unusual sobriety of thought, the capacity to look truth straight in the face, not for one moment to be carried away by phrases or illusions. It developed in him an extremely honest approach to all problems.

In the autumn of 1894 Vladimir Ilyich read his work *The Friends of the People* to our circle. I remember how everybody scrambled for this book. It set out the aims of our struggle with remarkable

[4] Among the First of March Exiles, members of the Narodnaya Volya exiled in connection with the assassination of Tsar Alexander II on March 1, 1881, in which attempt Vladimir Ilyich's brother participated.

clarity. *The Friends of the People,* in duplicated form, afterwards passed from hand to hand under the alias of the *Little Yellow Books.* These were unsigned. They had a fairly wide circulation, and there can be no doubt but that they had a strong influence on the Marxist youth of those days. When in 1896 I was in Poltava, P. P. Rumyantsev, who at that time was an active social-democrat and had just been released from prison, characterised *The Friends of the People* as the best, the strongest, and the most complete exposition of the stand-point of revolutionary social-democracy.

By the winter of 1894-1895, I had already got to know Vladimir Ilyich fairly intimately. He was occupied with the workers' study-circles beyond the Nevsky Gate. I had already been working for years in that district as a teacher in the Smolensky Sunday Evening Adult School, and was already fairly well acquainted with local working-class life. Quite a number of the workmen in Vladimir Ilyich's circle were my pupils at the Sunday School: Babushkin, Borovkov, Gribakin, the Bodrovs—Arsenius and Phillip, Zhukov, and others. In those days the Sunday Evening Adult School was an excellent means for getting a thorough knowledge of the everyday life, the labour conditions, and the mood of the working masses. The Smolensky School had six hundred scholars, not counting the evening technical classes and the attached Women's and Obukhov Schools.

The workers displayed unlimited confidence in the "school-mistresses." Thus the gloomy watchman from the Gromov timberyards, with face beaming, told the teacher that he had been presented with a son; a consumptive textile-worker wanted her to teach her enterprising suitor to read and write; a Methodist workman who had spent his whole life seeking God wrote with satisfaction that only on Passion Sunday had he learned from Rudakov (another pupil) that there was no God at all. And how easy things had now become. For there was nothing worse than being a slave of God, as you couldn't do anything about it. But to be a human slave was much easier, as here a fight *was* possible. Then there was a tobacco-worker who used to drink every Sunday until he lost all human semblance. And he also seemed so saturated with the smell of tobacco, that one could not

bend over his exercise-book without one's head beginning to swim.
He wrote (using pot-hooks and hangers and leaving out the vowels)
to the effect that he had found a three-year-old kiddy in the street,
that she was living in their *artel*,[5] that they would have to hand her
over to the police, and it was a pity. Came a one-legged soldier and
said—"Mikhail, whom you taught to read and write last year, died at
work from exhaustion; while dying he remembered you, told me to
give you his compliments and wished you a long life." A textile-
worker who was a proud defender of the Tsar and priests uttered a
warning: "Beware of that dark chap there, as he's always prowling
about on the *Gorokhovaya*."[6] Then an elderly worker argued that he
could not possibly give up being a churchwarden "because it is
sickening to see how the priests gull the people, and they must be led
to see things clearly. But he is not at all attached to the church and
understands quite well about the phases of development," and so on
and so forth.

Workers belonging to our organisation went to the school in order
to observe the people and note who could be brought into the circles
or drawn into the movement. These workers did not regard all the
women teachers in the same light. They distinguished to what extent
the teachers were versed in the work of our circles. If they recognised
a schoolmistress to be "one of us," they would make themselves
known to her by some phrase or other. For instance, in discussing the
question of the handicraft industry, they might say: "a handicraft-
worker cannot compete against large-scale production." Or they
would intervene with a leading question, such as: "What is the difference between the Petersburg worker and the Archangel *mujik*?"
And after that they would give the teacher a meaning look, and nod
to her in a particular way—as much as to say: "One of ours—we
know."

They immediately related all that was doing on the highways and
by-ways, for they knew that the teachers would hand on the information to the Organisation.

It was a kind of silent conspiracy. We were actually able to talk

[5] A group working on a coöperative basis.
[6] The site of the Tsarist secret-police office in St. Petersburg.

about anything in the school, although there was rarely a class without a spy; one had only to refrain from using the terrible words "tsar," "strike," etc., and the most fundamental problems could be referred to. But, officially, it was forbidden to discuss anything at all: on one occasion they closed down the so-called recapitulatory group, because an inspector who had put in an unexpected appearance discovered that the ten-times table was being taught there, whereas, according to the syllabus, only the four rules of arithmetic were allowed to be taught.

I lived at that time on the old Nevsky, in a house with a through courtyard. On Sundays Vladimir Ilyich usually called to see me, on his way back from working with the circle. We used to start endless conversations. I was wedded to the school then, and would go without my food rather than miss a chance of talking about the pupils or about Semyannikov's, Thornton's, Maxwell's, and other factories around the Neva. Vladimir Ilyich was interested in the minutest detail describing the conditions and life of the workers. Taking the features separately he endeavored to grasp the life of the worker as a whole—he tried to find what one could seize upon in order better to approach the worker with revolutionary propaganda. Most of the intellectuals of those days badly understood the workers. An intellectual would come to a circle and read the workers a kind of lecture. For a long time a manuscript translation of Engel's booklet, *The Origin of the Family, Private Property and the State*, was passed round the circles. Vladimir Ilyich read with the workers from Marx's *Capital*, and explained it to them. The second half of the studies was devoted to the workers' questions about their work and labour conditions. He showed them how their life was linked up with the entire structure of society, and told them in what manner the existing order could be transformed. The combination of theory with practise was the particular feature of Vladimir Ilyich's work in the circles. Gradually other members of our circle also began to use this approach.

When the Vilna pamphlet *On Agitation* appeared the following year, the ground was already fully prepared for the conducting of agitation by leaflets. It was only necessary to start work. The method of agitation on the basis of the workers' everyday needs became rooted deeply in our Party work. I only fully understood how fruit-ful this method of work was some years later when, living as an *emigrée* in France, I observed how, during the tremendous postal strike in Paris, the French Socialist Party stood completely aside and did not intervene in the strike. It was the business of the Trade Unions, they said. They thought the work of the Party was simply the political struggle. They had not the remotest notion as to the necessity for connecting up the economic and political struggles.

Many of the comrades working then in Petersburg, seeing the effect of agitation by printed matter, were allured with this form of work, and forgot that it is one of the forms, but not the sole form, of work among the masses. It was they who took the path of "Economism."[7]

Vladimir Ilyich never forgot the other forms of work. In 1895 he wrote the pamphlet *The Law on Fines*. In this pamphlet he gave a brilliant example of how to approach the middle-grade workers of that time, and, on the basis of their needs, lead them step by step to the question of the necessity for political struggle. Many intellectuals thought this pamphlet long and dry, but the workers read it willingly, for it was clear to them and near to them. (It was printed at the Narodnaya Volya press, and distributed among the workers.) Vlad-imir Ilyich used to study the factory laws carefully. He reckoned that by explaining these laws it was particularly easy to enlighten the workers as to the connection between their position and the State. Traces of this study are visible in quite a number of articles and pamphlets written at that period for the workers, in the pamphlet *The New Factory Act*, and in *On Strikes, On Industrial Courts*, and other articles.

Going the round of the workers' circles, however, could not be done with impunity: police surveillance began to increase. Of all our group Vladimir Ilyich was the best equipped for conspiratorial work. He knew all the through courtyards, and was a skilled hand at giving police-spies the slip. He taught us how to write in books with in-

[7] Economism was the term used to denote the tendency among Social Demo-crats which believed Tsarism could be fought by economic means alone (strikes, etc.), and neglected the political struggle.

visible ink, or by the dot method; how to mark secret signs, and
thought out all manner of aliases. In general, one felt the benefit of
his good apprenticeship in the ways of the Narodnaya Volya Party.
It was not for nothing that he spoke with such esteem of the old
nihilist Mikhailov, who had earned the nickname "Dvornik" (the
watchman) by dint of his prowess at conspiracy.

The surveillance kept increasing, and Vladimir Ilyich insisted that
a "successor" should be appointed who was not being watched and
to whom he could transfer all the contacts. As I was the "cleanest" of
them all [i.e. least known to the police as an active revolutionist—
Trans.], it was decided to appoint me as the "inheritrix." On the first
day of Easter five or six of us went to "celebrate the festival" at
Tsarskoye Selo with one of the members of our group—Silvin, who
earned his living there at odd jobs. We travelled by train, pretending
not to know one another. We sat nearly the whole day discussing
which contacts should be preserved. Vladimir Ilyich showed us how
to use cipher, and we used up nearly half a book. Alas, I was afterwards unable to decode this first collective ciphering! One consolation, however, was that, by the time these records were required to
be deciphered, the majority of the "contacts" were no longer usable.

Vladimir Ilyich carefully collected such "contacts," and sought
everywhere for people who, in one way or another, could be useful
for revolutionary work. I remember how a conference was once arranged, on Vladimir Ilyich's initiative, between the representatives of
our group (Vladimir Ilyich and, I believe, Krzhizhanovsky) and a
group of women Sunday-school teachers. Nearly all of them became
Social Democrats afterwards. Among them was Lydia Mikhailovna
Knippovich, an old member of the Narodnaya Volya, who after a
certain time came over to the Social Democrats. Old Party workers
still remember her. She had tremendous revolutionary firmness of
character, was strict with herself and others. At the same time she
had the knack of understanding people, was a fine comrade and
showed her affection and concern for those with whom she worked.
Lydia immediately appreciated the revolutionary in Vladimir Ilyich.

Lydia Mikhailovna volunteered to maintain liaison with the Narodnaya Volya printing press. She used to make all the arrangements for
the printing, hand on the manuscripts, and receive from the press the

printed pamphlets. She carried these round in baskets to her friends and organised literature distribution to the workers. When she was arrested—on the information of a compositor at the press who turned traitor—twelve baskets full of illegal pamphlets were confiscated from various friends of Lydia's. The Narodnaya Volya press at that time printed masses of pamphlets for workers: *The Working Day, What Different People Live On,* Lenin's pamphlet *On Fines, King-Hunger,* and others. Two of the workers at that Press—Shapovalov and Katanskaya—are now in the ranks of the Communist Party. Lydia Mikhailovna is no longer among the living. She died in 1920, when the Crimea, where she lived in latter years, was under the Whites. On her death-bed, in a last delirium, she craved for her own folk, for the Communists, and died with the name of the Communist Party, so dear to her, on her lips.

From among those school-mistresses, I believe, were also P. F. Kudeli, A. I. Meshcheryakov (both now Party members) and others. Another teacher in the Nevsky Gate district was Alexandra Mikhailovna Kalmykova. She was a fine lecturer; I remember her lecture for workers on the State Budget. She then owned a bookshop on the Liteyny. Vladimir Ilyich became very closely acquainted with Alexandra Mikhailovna. One of her pupils was Struve, and Potressov, an old school-mate of Struve's, was always at her place. Later, Alexandra Mikhailovna subsidised with her own money the old *Iskra,* right up to the time of the Second Congress. She did not follow in the wake of Struve when he went over to the Liberals, but definitely associated herself with the *Iskra* organisation. Her alias was "Auntie." She got on very well with Vladimir Ilyich. Now she is dead, after having been bed-ridden for two years at a sanatorium at Detskoye Selo. She used to be visited sometimes by youngsters from the neighboring Children's Homes. She told them all about Ilyich.

Alexandra Mikhailovna wrote to me in the spring of 1924 that we ought to publish as a separate booklet Lenin's 1917 articles, filled as they were with his burning passion and his ardent appeals that had such effect on the masses. In 1922 Vladimir Ilyich had written Alexandra Mikhailovna a few lines of fervent greeting, such as only he could write.

Alexandra Mikhailovna had been closely connected with the

"Emancipation of Labour"[8] group. On one occasion (I believe in 1899), when Zassulich came to Russia, Alexandra Mikhailovna arranged for her illegal sojourn, and continually maintained contact with her. Under the influence of the workers' movement then beginning to grow, of the articles and books of the "Emancipation of Labour" group, and of the Petersburg Social Democrats, Potressov went "Left," as also did Struve for a time. After a number of preliminary meetings the ground began to be sounded for joint work. It was proposed to publish jointly a symposium: *Materials Characterising Our Economic Development*. Our group was represented on the Editorial Board by Vladimir Ilyich, Starkov, and Stepan Ivanovich Radchenko; theirs by Struve, Potressov and Klasson. The fate of that symposium is well known. It was burned by the Tsarist censor. In the spring of 1895, before going abroad, Vladimir Ilyich went more and more often to Ozerny Street, where Potressov lived, hastening to finish the work.

Vladimir Ilyich spent the summer of 1895 abroad, living part of the time in Berlin, where he attended workers' meetings, and partly in Switzerland, where he first saw Plekhanov, Alexrod and Zassulich. He came back full of impressions and brought from abroad a trunk with a double lining, the space between this and the trunk walls being crammed full of illegal literature.

No sooner had he returned when the police were hot on his trail. They followed him and they followed his trunk. At that time I had a cousin working at an address bureau. A couple of days after Vladimir Ilyich arrived she told me that the night she was on duty a detective came and turned over the index of addresses (the addresses at the bureau were classified in alphabetical order). He said boast-

---

[8] The group of revolutionary Social Democrats, most prominent of whom were George V. Plekhanov, Vera Zassulich, and P. B. Alexrod. Emigrating to avoid Tsarist persecution, they founded the group in Switzerland in 1883, for the propaganda of Marx's ideas in Russia and to combat the Narodniks, who denied that the working class was destined to lead the revolution. This group, together with Lenin's *League of Struggle for the Emancipation of the Working Class* (founded in 1895 in Petersburg) and other Social Democrat groups, combined in forming the Russian Social Democratic Labour Party (1898). After the Party split into Bolsheviks and Mensheviks (in 1903), Plekhanov's group joined the Mensheviks.

ingly: "Look, we've tracked down the important State criminal, Ulyanov—his brother was hanged—he's just come from abroad, but he won't escape us now." Knowing that I knew Vladimir Ilyich, my cousin made haste to inform me of this. I of course immediately warned him. The most extreme caution was necessary. But the work could not wait, and we got still busier. We divided the work up, according to districts. We began to draw up and distribute leaflets. I remember that Vladimir Ilyich drew up the first leaflet for the workers of the Semyannikov works. We had no technical facilities at all then. The leaflet was copied out by hand in printed letters and distributed by Babushkin. Out of the four copies two were picked up by the watchman, while two went round from hand to hand. Leaflets were also distributed in other districts. On Vassilievsky Ostrov, for example, a leaflet was got out for the women workers of the Laferme tobacco factory. A. A. Yakubova and Z. P. Nevzorova (Krzhizhanov-skaya) had recourse to the following method of distribution: they rolled up the leaflets into little tubes so that they could easily be taken one by one and arranged them in their aprons in a suitable manner. Then, immediately the hooter sounded, they walked briskly towards the women who were pouring out in throngs from the factory gates and, passing by almost at a trot, scattered the leaflets right into the hands of the perplexed workers.

It was further decided to publish—and for this we had to thank an illegal printing press—a popular journal, *The Workers' Cause.* Vladimir Ilyich assiduously prepared the material for this. Every line passed through his hands. I remember a meeting in my rooms when Zaporozhetz was telling us with great enthusiasm about the material he had succeeded in collecting at the boot factory near the Moscow Gate. "We are fined for everything," he said. "Shove a heel on a bit to one side and bang goes another fine!" Vladimir Ilyich said laughingly: "Well, if you put a heel on all askew, you deserve to be fined." Vladimir Ilyich very carefully collected and verified this material. I remember, for example, how the material about the Thornton factory was collected. It was decided that I should send for a pupil of mine named Krolikov, a sorter in that factory, who had previously been deported from Petersburg. I was to collect from him all information, according to a plan drawn up by Vladimir Ilyich. Krolikov arrived in a fine fur coat he had borrowed from someone, and brought a whole exercise-book full of information, which he further supplemented verbally. This data was very valuable. In fact Vladimir Ilyich fairly pounced on it. Afterwards I and Apollinaria Alexandrovna Yakubova put kerchiefs on our heads and made ourselves look like women factory-workers, and went personally to the Thornton factory-barracks, visiting both the single and the married quarters. Conditions were most appalling. It was solely on the basis of material gathered in this manner that Vladimir Ilyich wrote his letters and leaflets. Examine his leaflets addressed to the working men and women of the Thornton Factory. The detailed knowledge of the subject they deal with is at once apparent. And what a schooling this was for all the comrades working then! It was just then that we were learning attention to details. And how profoundly these details were engraved in our minds.

Our paper, *The Workers' Cause,* never saw the light. On December 8th a meeting was held in my rooms, at which the first number was finally revised for the press. There were two copies of the proofs. One was taken by Vaneyev for final examination, and the other remained with me. Next morning I went to Vaneyev for the corrected copy, but the maid told me that he had left the house. It had been previously arranged with Vladimir Ilyich that in case anything went wrong I should seek information about him from his friend Cherbotariev, who was also a colleague of mine at the head offices of the railway where I was then employed. Vladimir Ilyich used to dine at Cherbotariev's and went there every day. But Cherbotariev did not turn up at the office. I went to his house. Vladimir Ilyich had not been in to dinner. It was clear that he was arrested. I took the copy of *The Workers' Cause* that had remained with me to Nina Alexandrovna Gerd for safekeeping. She was an old school-friend and the future wife of Struve. In order to avoid any more of us being arrested, if was decided not to print *The Workers' Cause* for the time being.

This Petersburg period of Vladimir Ilyich's work was one of extreme importance, although the work was unobserved and not apparent in substance. He himself so described it. There were no external effects. We were not concerned with heroic moves, but with how to establish close contact with the masses, to become intimate with them, to learn to be the expression of their best aspirations, to learn how to make them understand us and follow our lead. But it was precisely during this period of work in St. Petersburg that Vladimir Ilyich became moulded as leader of the working masses.

When I went to the school for the first time after the arrest of our people, Babushkin called me into a corner beneath the staircase and handed me a leaflet written by the workers about the arrests. The leaflet was of a purely political nature. Babushkin asked me to get it reproduced, and to let them have the copies back for distribution. Up till that time I had never let him know directly that I was connected with the organisation. But I handed the leaflet on to our group. I remember that meeting—it was in S. I. Radchenko's apartment. All the remnants of the group were gathered there. Lyakhovsky read the leaflet, and exclaimed: "Do you think we can print this leaflet? Why, it is on a purely political theme." However, as the leaflet had undoubtedly been written by the workers on their own initiative, and as they had asked us to print it without fail, it was decided to do it.

Contact with Vladimir Ilyich was very quickly established. In those days prisoners under preliminary detention were allowed to have as many books sent them as they liked. These were subjected to a rather superficial examination, during which it was not possible to notice the minute dots placed inside various letters, or the hardly discernible change in the colour of the paper where inscriptions had been penned with milk. We rapidly perfected our technique at secret correspondence. Characteristic of Vladimir Ilyich was his concern for the other comrades in prison. Every letter he wrote to the outside world contained various commissions to be carried out on behalf of the prisoners. Thus, so-and-so has no visitors—you must find him a "sweetheart"; or tell such-and-such a fellow-prisoner, through his relatives when they next visit him, to look for a letter in such-and-such a book in the prison library; or bring so-and-so warm boots. . . . He corresponded with a great many of the comrades in prison, for whom his letters were of tremendous significance. Letters from

Vladimir Ilyich vibrated with courageous spirit, and spoke mainly of our work. Those who received them forgot they were in prison, and themselves settled down to work. I remember the impression from those letters (in August 1896 I also was in jail). Letters written in milk came through from outside on the day for sending books— Saturday. One would immediately look at the secret signs in the book and ascertain whether a letter was inside. At six o'clock they brought hot water for tea and the wardress led the criminals out to the church. By this time the "politicals" would have the letters torn into long strips. Then they would make their tea, and as soon as the wardress departed begin to drop the strips into the hot tea. Thus the letters would be "developed." (In prison it was not advisable to treat these letters by candle-flame, and it was Vladimir Ilyich who thought out the idea of developing them in hot water.) And what courage these letters breathed, how absorbingly interesting they were to read! Just as Vladimir Ilyich was the pivot of all our work outside, so in prison he was the center of contact with the outside world.

But apart from this, he did a great deal of work in prison. He prepared *The Development of Capitalism in Russia*. In his legal letters Vladimir Ilyich ordered necessary material and statistical works. "It is a pity they let us out so soon," he said jokingly. "I would have liked to do a little more work on the book. It will be difficult to obtain books in Siberia." Vladimir Ilyich wrote not only *The Development of Capitalism in Russia* in prison. He wrote leaflets, illegal pamphlets, and the draft programme for the First Congress (which did not take place until 1898, although it was to have been held earlier.) He also gave his opinion on questions discussed in the organisation. In order not to be discovered while writing with milk, he made little milk-"inkpots" out of bread. These he popped into his mouth immediately he heard a rattle at the grating. "Today I have eaten six inkpots," ran the postscript of one of his letters.

But no matter how much he mastered himself, no matter how much he set for himself a definite regime, even Vladimir Ilyich was affected by prison melancholy. In one of his letters he put forward this plan: When they were taken out for exercise, it was possible through one of the windows in the corridor to catch a momentary glimpse of a fragment of the Shpalernaya pavement. So he suggested that at a definite time I and Apollinaria Alexandrovna Yakubova should come and stand on this piece of pavement, and then he would see us. Apollinaria for some reason or other was unable to go. I went several days and stood a long while on that spot. Something went wrong with the plan, however, though I do not remember what.

While Vladimir Ilyich was in prison, the work outside still extended and the workers' movement grew. After the arrest of Martov, Lyakhovsky and others, the forces of our group were further diminished. It is true new comrades joined the group, but these were people with less theoretical training. There was no time for study, for the movement demanded active service and a tremendous amount of energy. Everything went in agitation. There was not time even to think of propaganda. Our printed agitation was very successful. The leaflets were often drawn up hurriedly without an adequate study of concrete conditions. The weavers' strike of 1896 took place under social-democratic influence. This turned the heads of many comrades. The basis arose for the growth of "Economism." I remember how once (I think at the beginning of August), at a meeting in the woods, Silvin read out aloud the draft for a leaflet. In one place a sentence had crept in which absolutely limited the workers' movement to the economic struggle alone. After reading this sentence out aloud, Silvin stopped short and said laughingly: "Why, I've tripped up myself. What could have prompted me to do it!" The offending sentence was deleted from the draft. In the summer of 1896 the Lakhtinsky printing press collapsed, and we were no longer able to print pamphlets. Our arrangements for the journal had to be postponed indefinitely.

During the 1896 strike we were joined by the Takhtariev group, who were known by the pseudonym "The Monkeys," and also Chernyshev's group, known as "The Cocks."[9] But while the Dekabrists[10] were in prison, and maintained contact with outside, the work still followed the old course. When Vladimir Ilyich was released,[11] I was still inside. In spite of the commotion which surrounded anyone

[9] On August 12th another crash came: nearly all the "old men" were caught, and the best elements of the "cocks."

[10] Nickname for those arrested in December 1895. The original "Dekabrists" (Decembrists) were, of course, the people concerned in the rising of December 1825.

[11] Vladimir Ilyich was released from prison on February 26th, 1897.

coming out of prison, Vladimir Ilyich, at a number of meetings, contrived nevertheless to write me a little note about what went on. My
mother told me he had even got fatter in prison, and was a terrible
weight.

I was released soon after the "Vetrova affair" (a woman prisoner
named Vetrova had burned herself alive in the fortress). The gendarmes then released a whole number of women prisoners, letting
them remain in Petersburg until their case was completed, but
putting on a couple of detectives to follow their every step. I found
the organisation in a most lamentable state. Out of the former active
members there remained only Stepan I. Radchenko and his wife.
He was not able himself to carry on the work under conditions of
secrecy, but continued to act as centre and maintained contact.

Contact was also kept up with Struve. He married Nina Alexandrovna Gerd shortly afterwards. She was a Social Democrat, and
at that time he was himself more or less a Social Democrat. He was
quite incapable of working in the organisation, and still more so of
illegal work, but it undoubtedly flattered him to be applied to for
advice. He even wrote a manifesto for the First Congress of the
Social Democratic Labour Party. In the winter of 1897-1898 I called
fairly often on Struve with commissions from Vladimir Ilyich. Struve
was then editor of the *Novoye Slovo* (New Word). Many things also
brought me in contact with Nina Alexandrova. I used to observe
Struve. He was a sincere Social Democrat at that time. Yet I was
astonished to see how bookish he was, and to note his complete lack
of interest in the "living tree of life," in which Vladimir Ilyich's
interest was so keen. Struve obtained translations for me and undertook to edit them. He was visibly wearied by this work and quickly
tired. (With Vladimir Ilyich we would sit for hours at the same
occupation. But he worked quite differently, putting his whole weight
into even such a job as translation.) For recreation Struve took to
reading Fet. Someone has written in his memoirs that Vladimir
Ilyich liked Fet. That is not so. Fet was an out-and-out feudalist and
not worth while even dipping into. But Struve really did like Fet. In
those days Struve was unquestionably on good terms with Vladimir
Ilyich.

I also knew Tugan-Baranovsky. I was at school with his wife, Lydia Karlovna Davydova (daughter of the woman publisher of *God's World*), and used to visit them. Lydia was a very good and clever woman, although weak-willed. She was more intelligent than her husband. In his conversations one always felt he was not one of us. Once I went to him with a collecting sheet for a strike (I think it was at Kostroma). I received something. I forget how much, but had to hear a dissertation on the theme: "I cannot understand why we must support strikes. A strike is not a sufficiently effective means of combatting the owners." I took the money and made haste to leave.

I wrote to Vladimir Ilyich about everything I managed to see and hear. But there was little to write about concerning the organisation. By the time of the Congress, only four of us were left in the group: S. I. Radchenko, his wife, Liubov Nikolaevna Sammer, and I. Our delegate was Stepan Ivanovich (Radchenko). But on returning from the Congress he told us practically nothing about what happened there. He extracted from the back of a book the "manifesto" written by Struve and adopted by the Congress, with which we were all well acquainted, and started grumbling: nearly all the delegates to the Congress—there were several—had been arrested.

I was given three years' exile in the Ufa Gubernia. I made a request to be transferred to the village of Shushenskoye, in the Minussinsk region, where Vladimir Ilyich was living. For this purpose I described myself as his "fiancée."

8. The Rights and Responsibilities of Trade Unions

Carl Legien: *The German Workers' Right to Organize, in Theory and Practice* (1899)°

This memorandum by the head of the central organization of German trade unions deals with the position of the industrial workers in the social complex—that is, with the advantage to society of having trade unions, with the struggle on the part of the trade unions for recognition, with hostility shown by government and employers to workers' associations, and with the improvement, in spite of antagonism, of the living and working conditions of the workers. Only sixty years earlier Journeyman Dewald had thought of himself not as a common worker but as a guildsman. His experience in comparison with that of Legien belongs to a distant and naive past. By 1900 workers had become definitely class-conscious, not entirely through their own desire, and they had developed the trade union as a form of labor organization suitable for mass bargaining on equal terms with employers. Legien rightly regards the trade union as an institution of both social and economic importance. In addition, because the union promoted in its own affairs the practice of self-government, it was out of step with the constitutional monarchism of the German government of the time. That Legien's analysis would apply to any society in transition from a simple to an industrial economy can be inferred from the national range of his quotations. It should be noted that just as industrialization had advanced further in Germany than in any other continental country, so the trade-union movement was stronger there than elsewhere.

° Carl Legien, *Das Koalitionsrecht in Theorie und Praxis* (Memorandum der Kommission der deutschen Gewerkschaften (Hamburg: General Commission of German Trade Unions, 1899).

THE VALUE AND SIGNIFICANCE OF TRADE UNIONS

Every book dealing with questions of political economy proves that modern methods of production have completely transformed the labor contract and abolished the patriarchal relation between employer and worker. Today the buyer and the seller of labor face each other as contractual parties without any personal relationship. They negotiate like buyers and sellers of any other commodity and handle labor like any other item. The seller of labor has the disadvantage, however, of being closely bound up with his wares, and so the buyer controls the means whereby the preservation of the commodity is made possible. Thus from the beginning the seller, as one party to the contract, finds himself in an unfavorable position, and insofar as he is dependent upon himself he is forced to accept the proffered terms. "Earlier both employer and worker had been under the authority of the law; now theoretically they were equal, but actually the worker was bound by the will of the employer in respect to the terms of sale of his wares. Standing alone, his only chance was acceptance of these or unemployment." (Brentano, *Arbeitergilden der Gegenwart*, II, 252.) He has to be satisfied with what wages the employer offers him as a means of living, and only so much time remains for his own use as the buyer of his labor is willing to allow him. Ultimately he falls into a personal dependency upon the man to whom he has sold his labor, and is thus in a position similar to serfdom. "This completely helpless situation of the isolated single worker before the powerful employers was and is a danger to present and future culture; it made possible and many times brought about the danger of an actually servile relationship of the workers to the power of capital, a state of affairs differing to their disadvantage from the corresponding legal relationship of ancient and medieval times because of the lack of any responsibility on the part of the wielders of power for the welfare of their dependents." (Löwenfeld, *Archiv für soziale Gesetzgebung*, III, 392.)

One would console himself falsely by telling himself that the entrepreneurs, in the fullness of their economic power, would grant the laborer an adequate wage from a feeling of humanitarianism.

In view of the complete separation of employer and worker which exists in modern large-scale industries, any possibility of personal interest is lacking, even if individual employers might be inclined toward it. But even such an inclination is extremely seldom encountered; on the contrary, the rule is to keep wages as low as possible and to hold down the compensation for work done as much as possible. Professor Kleinwächter devastatingly criticized the conduct of the German employer on the basis of the reports of the factory inspectors for 1890, writing in the *Jahrbücher für Nationalökonomie und Statistik*:

If one reads the reports of the factory inspectors deploring the inadequacies in the factories and discussing the innumerable larger and smaller conflicts arising from labor-management relationships; when one reads about the pitiful way in which ruthless employers conduct themselves toward their workers, what barbarities they allow themselves, how little they concern themselves with the health and life of the workers or protect them against the harmful influences or dangers of their work, even when the required protective measures would cost very little, how hard they try to keep wages as low as possible, how they do not shrink from petty subterfuges (payment in kind and the like) and even from direct dishonesty such as the use of false measures and weight in reckoning workers' wages, just to be able to deduct something from their already small pay—then one must conclude that these conscienceless employers and not the workers are the true source and propagators of the socialist movement which is today sweeping through the world.

This harsh but accurate judgment is all the more valuable in that it comes from a source other than the worker, with his endurance of hardship and the daily bitter feeling of hoping in vain for any change in his misery and indignity. The situation would be hopeless if there were not means to abolish it without having to count on the understanding and good will of the employers.

The workers themselves have the means of acting, by uniting their separate forces and cooperating to bring about a higher value and greater respect for labor and the workers. "Between the demand for labor and the supplying of it by isolated workers there enters a social factor, the uniting of the suppliers, who by curbing the supply can increase the difference between this and the demand. The allocation of wages and profits then results not from the economic situation alone, but likewise from the social activity of the interested parties." (von Walthershausen, *Die nordamerikanischen Gewerkschaften,* p. 200.)

By means of organization the worker gains control of the supply of his labor on the market; thus he is enabled to offer it under conditions and, by holding fast to the conditions of sale, to have a voice in the bargain made. He gains the independence which every other seller possesses, by gaining the freedom and the power to dispose of his person. He is then able to separate his person and his wares, which thus become a commodity like any other for sale. By means of organization, then, labor becomes a commodity and the worker a seller of goods. Whenever he needs protection he can immediately find it in accordance with his need. (Brentano, *op. cit.,* p. 21.)

Without the right of organization, under the modern system of production the working class would become depressed to the lowest imaginable level of material and spiritual existence, and thus a situation would be created which would endanger the entire culture. The opportunity exists, of course, to prevent such a situation by means of law; but for this the workers would need a greater influence upon legislation than they have, and especially they would need the good will of those who at present wield decisive influence. The workers, however, will gain the possibility of influencing legislation only when they have reached a higher level of existence, both material and spiritual; and the good will to assure this higher level to them does not exist among the factors decisive in forming legislation. In Germany this fact is most clearly revealed in the attitude of the government and the majority parties of the Reichstag toward the issue of the legal regulation of the working day and in the delay in preventing the exploitation of human labor, especially that of women and children in small handicrafts and in house industries. Thus the working class finds it necessary to organize in order to assure itself a continuing influence upon the wage scale and the length of the working day, and it can force through legislation to this end only when it has achieved through organization the physical power of resistance and spiritual alertness.

Organization will not be able to reach this goal directly or in the case of all categories of workers. The rise of trade unions, however, has its effect even upon those groups which, because of frightful misery and ruthless exploitation, do not feel within themselves the power to join. Especially does trade unionism make possible an adequate return for their labor for those workers whose ability to perform does not exceed the average and who would undoubtedly be defeated otherwise in the struggle for existence.

The need for and usefulness of the trade-union organization of the workers is recognized by all those who do not want the majority of our people to lead an existence hardly differing from that of animals, in order to create for a few élite in society an existence of pleasure and happiness.

Sensible persons must admit that such a condition, if left to itself, will lead only to the destruction of our culture. He who recognizes this will regard as self-evident the necessity for the two factors, the worker and the exploiter of labor, to be in competition for the larger share in the product of labor; he will consider this competition as something proceeding from the nature of the given circumstances. He will recognize that this struggle must assume the character of class warfare. "The greater intensity of class interest among the workers lies in the nature of the existing method of production. As long as the entrepreneur stood somewhat in the role of a lord in relation to the worker, class interest on the part of the workers could be held more easily in check. But this phase of economic development is already past and cannot be recalled." (Lexis, *Gewerkvereine und Unternehmerverbände in Frankreich,* p. 5.)

Anyone who fights trade unionism on the grounds that it tends to strengthen the workers' class consciousness has as little justice on his side as one who wages the struggle against it out of material interests. Wherever such material interests have not yet extinguished all feeling that each member of society should be accorded equal consideration, unions will be recognized as useful even by those against whom they are primarily aimed. One of the owners of a large machine factory in England, C. Browne, said in a speech on October 14, 1898 to an engineers' society in Newcastle: "Of course the friction between employers and workers is acute, but if we consider the large number of workers and the hardships with which they have to struggle, it is doubtful whether relations among men under similar circumstances are carried on anywhere more peaceably. The idea that trade unions are the cause of industrial strife is losing ground daily."

Disinterested parties who undertake a study of labor relations also emphasize the educational effect of the unions and especially their favorable influence upon the moral attitude of the workers. Brentano states this is his book *Die Arbeitergilden*:

A foreman in a machine shop who had been a member of the union for fourteen years and had left it six years before, and who, as I know personally, had not been on very good terms with it since then, wrote to the trade-union committee of the Social Science Association: "I am of the opinion that the unions help to augment the activity of the worker and to develop his skill. The workers are taught to care for one another; in discussion of issues of right and wrong in their meetings they learn from one another things which would otherwise remain unknown to them; since they vote on matters which affect the conscience, unions improve, so it seems to me, the workers' morals. Without the trade union the workers would have much less confidence in one another; competition would drive them apart and they would become a kind of rabble, without any mutual trust. As a rule I prefer the union members to the non-members. They are more independent, less servile, though of course they are harder to lead." (Pp. 54-55.)

The Massachusetts statistical bureau for labor relations sent out a questionnaire about the effect of the trade unions upon individual workers in this state, and received the uniform answer that the chief effects of the unions upon those questioned was the moral, intellectual, and social education the unions furnished and their influence for moderation.

What is said of the unions in England and America is equally true of German unions. The government factory inspectors may be considered unimpeachable witnesses of this assertion. These have, especially in recent years, expressed themselves in their annual reports in regard to labor organizations, and their judgment is entirely in favor of the unions. The inspector for Hesse II says in his report for 1896: "The educational influence of labor organizations should in no way be underestimated. They erect a useful counterweight to employers' groups, which must deal with them; for introducing regular conditions and for carrying out legislation and grasping the most important industrial questions, the labor organization usually will be beneficial."

The supervisory official for Baden emphasizes the favorable educational effect which the unions had upon their individual members. The leaders often intervened for the maintenance of order and good behavior on the part of the workers. More than formerly the workers concerned themselves with matters regarding their occupation. "It is, however, very desirable and in the interests of continuing development that those groups of the population outside the labor movement show more interest in and respect for the individual efforts of the workers to achieve positive goals than is on the whole yet the case."

The factory inspector for Hamburg writes: "The numerous strikes of the last year seem to lead to the conclusion that participation by the workers in labor organizations is again greater. If this were to result in fewer strikes in the future or in their being avoided entirely and in the settlement of labor-management disputes by peaceful means, as has repeatedly been the case in the book-printing industry to the satisfaction of both sides, then certainly it is in the interests of economic progress not to stand in the way of the growth of such organizations."

What is said in hundreds of articles in the labor press and almost daily in their meetings is here recognized without reservations as correct by the officials who come into contact with the workers and the workers' organizations.

And, in fact, trade unions help civilization not only in that they raise the living standard and thereby the education of the working class, but also in that they work directly to the advantage of the workers' intelligence. They train him to unity; and just as the propertied classes consider well-expressed self-consciousness and class consciousness to be spiritual progress, so the workers, borne up by a feeling of solidarity, raise themselves above the standpoint of crass and petty egoism, which is always synonymous with lack of education and knowledge.

The feeling of solidarity educates the unions not only in time of struggle but also in times of peace. The unions commit the workers, by means of their dues, to maintaining co-workers through unemployment, illness, or other misfortune. Thus they do away with the crude abuses of the struggle for existence, the striving toward personal advantage without thought for one's fellow men. They develop in the worker recognition of equality and the idea of securing his own advantage by protecting the interests of all instead of by sacrificing these. They smooth the way for the worker to rise to the highest level of culture, and in this respect they have accomplished more than any other institution in the state and community, whatever names these may bear or of whatever kind they may be.

The trade unions seek to lift the intellectual level of the workers by making reading material accessible to them. The establishment of libraries, reading rooms, and information bureaus, the presentation of lectures at their meetings—everything that the unions do for their members beyond carrying on the wage struggle and providing material help serves the spiritual growth of the workers and thereby the progress of our culture.

But if this effect of the unions is to be fully realized, freedom must be given them to develop their powers, and the unlimited right to organize must be assured them. Any limitation of this right hinders the worker in reaching the highest level of perfection.

The Right of the German Workers to Organize

The German workers secured the right to organize at a time when, in accordance with industrial development, some form of organization had to exist to assure an adequate wage and a normal working day.

The guarantee of the right to organize was given in Saxony in 1861, and a bill for this was put before the Prussian House of Representatives in the same year. In 1865 the Prussian House voted such a bill, and in 1866 the government proposed a bill to abolish the restrictions on organizing for all workers; but this bill was not passed.

The so-called emergency law on association, abolishing the restriction on the right of association, was not promulgated for the North German Confederation until 1867. Until then, in Prussia the following paragraphs of the industrial code of January 17, 1845, were in force:

Par. 182.

Apprentices, journeymen, or factory workers who seek to influence either the craftsmen or management in behalf of certain concessions by agreeing upon the stoppage of work or its obstruction with a few or a number of workers, or who incite others to such an agreement, shall be punished by imprisonment for up to a year. This rule is also to be applied to workers employed in mines or smelting plants, on roads, railroads, defense installations, and other public works.

Par. 183.

The organization of associations among factory workers, journeymen, helpers, or apprentices without police permission, insofar as no harder punishment is prescribed by law, is to be punishable with money payment by the inciters and leaders of up to fifty *thaler* or with four weeks' imprisonment, by the rest of the participants with up to twenty *thaler* in fines or up to fourteen days' imprisonment.

A final regulation of matters came first in the industrial code of 1869, which contained the following paragraph, still in force:

Par. 152.

All prohibitions and penalties with respect to craftsmen, helpers, journeymen, or factory workers because of their agreements and associations for the purpose of securing favorable wages and working conditions, especially by means of stoppage of work or dropping of workers, are abolished.

According to its wording this law gave the German workers an unlimited right to associate, but actually this right does not exist at all. In paragraph 152 of the industrial code it was not expressly stated that organizations created for the attainment of better wages and working conditions must not be subject to the laws of association of the individual states. These regulations, originating in the laws of the so-called period of reaction, are such as to abolish completely the rights which paragraph 152 of the industrial code gives the workers. And these legislative provisions are and will be used to the fullest extent against the trade unions. The Prussian supreme court decided on November 28, 1878, as follows: "The goal of the spiritual and material elevation of the working class is to be regarded as a public affair, if by this is meant elevating the working class as such, as a social institution, in relation to and with respect to other classes."

The later decisions of the court interpret the term "public affair" still more narrowly, and especially do they systematically avoid making the concept more precise, so that every police sergeant can interpret "public affair" as he sees fit.

Union activity, which of course seeks to raise the spiritual and material level of the working class and which is therefore approved by every friend of culture, is according to the court's decision a "public affair." Thus it comes under the state laws, which under these circumstances in some states forbid the unions outright, and in others impose conditions upon the unions which completely thwart their purpose.

In 1874 the state governments, relying upon these laws, began a war upon the unions which reached its peak in the Socialist Law of 1878 and ended with the ruin of the laboriously developed union organizations. Still, under the Socialist Law, although they were in constant danger of falling prey to this state action again, the workers rebuilt their unions, first locally and later centrally. In 1890 the Socialist Law was repealed, but the hindrances to union organization by no means disappeared. The spirit of the Socialist Law is still alive today in the application of the laws of association and in the measures of the officials against the unions.

The first condition for effective union activity is the associating of all the workers of one occupation in the entire country and eventually even beyond the frontiers of the nation. The Prussian law of association forbids those organizations which intend to discuss political subjects in their meetings to enter into union with other similar organizations and to enroll women as members. Once the effort succeeds of labeling the unions as "political organizations," the ground is cut from under them for any effective activity. No further discussion of the effect of this law of association is needed. Reference to the facts that production is for the world and not the local market, that with modern means of transportation masses of workers can be moved from one place to another in a few hours, and that in industry, trade, and commerce 1,378,585 women are employed, is enough to indicate that unions cannot be of a local nature but must extend over the entire country and that they cannot be limited in the acceptance of members.

The effort to impose upon the unions the label of political organization has succeeded. The Prussian supreme court went so far as to declare: " 'Political subjects' in the sense of the law of association include those which concern social policy, especially the *regulation of the hours of work.*"

With this decision the police gain the right to decide the fate of the unions. A union prepared for economic struggle can at the decisive moment be temporarily closed down, and its regulation of labor conditions by strike can be made impossible. Even if afterward it were established by the courts that the closing of the union was illegal, the laboriously erected structure would be destroyed for a long time, since heavy penalties threaten whoever continues to be a member of a closed union.

The Prussian workers therefore have not a right of association with legal guarantees, but one dependent upon the goodwill or in fact upon the grace of the police.

But if the unions are allowed, they still are subject to the police and, as associations which intend to discuss public questions, are under all of the rules applicable to these associations. The resulting obligations are not only burdensome for the unions, they are dangerous for the members. The membership list has to be turned in to the officials. It has been proved that officials have shown these lists to employers and that this action was approved by the head of the county government [Landrat]. One district official went still further, duplicating the lists sent him and distributing them to the employers. The result of such actions is the punishment of union members.

But a breech of official secrecy is not even necessary in order for employers to learn of the union membership of certain workers; social position brings the employers and officials together, even if not exactly as in Paruschowitz in Upper Silesia, where the manufacturer is officially head of the district at the same time and as a state official supervises the meetings of his workers.

The unions recognize the danger which threatens them, especially in small towns, when they hand in their membership lists. They try to avoid the danger by not organizing local unions but by establishing only a treasury handled by a reliable person.

Even so there arises, as in the case of the question as to whether unions are political associations or not, an interminable number of trials; one can indeed say that in these cases the state is put to no small expense, while for the workers all kinds of annoyances arise along with the costs. Even though the outcome of all these suits depends upon fortunate circumstances, and good fortune does often bless the workers' side, nonetheless suits arouse a feeling of insecurity about the organizations which makes it impossible for the unions to develop on a firm footing and to be able to exercise on their members the educational influence needed to moderate the social struggle.

The purpose of this activity against the unions is not only to create respect for law but also to make labor organizations difficult; this purpose is indicated in the attempts to apply legislation created for quite other purposes in such a way as to take from the unions their welfare arrangements and thus to undermine the unity of the membership. Certain paragraphs of the law, such as those in regard to gross misdemeanor, extortion, and coercion, are applied by the states' attorneys and courts to activities for which they were certainly not intended when the paragraphs were incorporated in the penal code. This practice has gone so far that the state court in Dresden condemned to six months' imprisonment and three years' loss of all civic rights a mason who threatened that if he did not receive his previous wage the contractor would be prevented from obtaining workers.

What cannot be accomplished by legal means is accomplished by the intervention and excesses of the police officials. In the case of a strike, a state of emergency for the workers is declared by special police decrees. If the police do not intervene ruthlessly in the interests of the employers, the latter complain that the police are lax in the matter.

A worker who, in the case of a strike, tries to influence his co-workers without making himself liable to a punishable crime, since on the basis of paragraph 360, line 11, of the Reich Criminal Code he would be accused of gross misdemeanor, is told by the judges in the verdict that "the conduct of the accused constitutes an attack on the existing social order, since the court saw it as the unworthy conduct of an agitator who keeps other honorable people from their work and causes them trouble." (p. 14.)

In all countries where the workers have full right of association, it is considered an obvious right of the strikers to explain about the strike to new workers called in by the employers and to set up "pickets" for this purpose. In the case of the strike of machine-tool workers in England in 1898, Brentano wrote: "Since 1875 the picket has been expressly allowed for the purpose of imparting information, and woe to the police official who oversteps the law by turning away the picket or by arresting him."

In Germany picketing is considered a gross misdemeanor and is punished with a much greater penalty than is usual for such acts. It has even happened that the police have declared a strike ended and forbidden the strike committee to engage in any further activity.

After these facts, all confirmed in detail by examples, what remains to the German workers of the right of organization guaranteed in paragraph 152 of the industrial code? A knife without handle or blade! Whatever is graciously left the worker by the officials and the courts is stolen from him by the employers. The weapon which was given the worker for defending his existence, his honor, and his human dignity is taken from him by the organized employers after he has already been weakened by his struggle with officials and courts, and he faces the employers completely disarmed and fully aware that his spiritual and physical powers are being destroyed by unlimited exploitation.

The employers quite openly demand of the workers that they give up their right to organize or be thrown into the street.

The present paragraph 153 of the industrial code cannot be applied to this mockery and violation of the law. If we are to assure the workers the right to organize, there must be a law providing that whoever hinders the worker in the exercise of this right will be punished just as much as whoever forces others to enter into such associations by violence, threat, or attack on their honor.

Far from providing the workers with any such protection, the officials do not even apply the relevant legal clauses to the employers and their organizations. Paragraph 8 of the Prussian law of association does not apply to the employers' associations. The Central Union of German Industrialists, a federation of forty-eight independent associations, concerns itself with political subjects in its meetings of delegates. Its central leadership does the same, as its report of 1895 shows: "A very important part of the business of the Central Organization since the last committee meeting related to questions of commercial policy."

Petitions are constantly being sent by the Central Organization to the government and to the Reichstag. In 1896 it sent in a petition "against the decision of the Reichstag Committee on the Civil Code regarding the legality of associations. According to this decision the legal power of the associations is to be greatly extended, an act which would have serious effects upon all workers' unions," and it is jubilantly stated in the report of the directors that "as you know, the Committee's decision has been changed by the Reichstag in accordance with our petition."

The Central Organization was not ashamed in 1893 to direct a petition to the chancellor demanding the limitation of the right to organize—of the workers, of course. According to this petition, industrial circles have become convinced that "it is necessary in the interests of the security and the steady development of the entire national economy to return to the clauses proposed by the federated governments for revising paragraph 153 of the industrial code."

It is the height of shamelessness to abolish all restrictions on the organization of employers and to see the workers even more tied down than they already are.

It is just the same with the other employer groups. A similar memorandum of the builders' association led to the issuance by the Secretary of the Interior of the well-known confidential circular according to which material was to be assembled for reconsidering "the revision of paragraph 153 of the industrial code proposed by the government in 1890 and the placing of a new bill before the Reichstag at its next session."

These are circumstances which make a mockery of those clauses of the Prussian constitution which state that all citizens are equal before the law. Matters have gone so far that former Minister of Commerce von Berlepsch has felt called upon to say:

It is absolutely inexcusable that the law can be used against one and not the other. It is absolutely inadmissible that when the same conditions exist, the state authorities prosecute one association because it considers it harmful and leaves the other unmolested because it considers it harmless or useful. Such action leads to arbitrariness —that is, injustice—and injustice breeds bitterness.

The foregoing legal inequality is, more than all other real or imagined reasons for complaint, likely to produce bitterness among the workers and to undermine or to weaken noticeably the effects of the best laws and institutions.

In addition there is the further complicating fact that the workers become entirely dependent upon the unions to represent their common interests, while laws give the employers organs that are not subject to the law of association. The agrarians in the agricultural chambers, the merchants and industrialists great and small in the chambers of commerce, the craftsmen in the guilds—all can discuss and plan what they like as long as they deal with the interests of their occupations. The workers have no such legal representative organs, and thus the way in which the clauses of the law of association are applied to their unions becomes more and more unjust. (*Soziale Praxis*, 8, 1897.)

The measures taken by the employers against the workers must be added to these official administrative attacks. The workers who use their right to organize and refuse to sacrifice their human dignity are secretly declared to be of bad repute; they are hounded from factory to factory and from place to place, even pursued beyond the frontier of the country. This is done by means of "black lists." These seldom fall into the hands of the workers, but their known number is still so great that one can assume that their use is a general practice of all the employers' organizations.

The workers try in vain to protect themselves against this oppression. The paragraph about gross misdemeanor, extortion, and compulsion is used against them on every imaginable occasion. The complaints lodged against the employers by those declared in bad repute are rejected by the courts. The black lists are used by state officials and therefore it is understandable that the workers cannot gain any protection against this wrong.

In this situation it is no wonder that the workers in Germany conduct economic warfare with bitterness. The unions and the right to organize are not to blame, but rather the exceptional situation created for the workers in spite of the prescribed right of association.

Even if the law were changed and there was no more threat of the dissolution of the unions if they came together as supposed political unions, things would not be much improved; other clauses of the law of association hinder union activity. That is evident in Saxony and Bavaria, where the former limitation has been abolished. Not the word of the law is decisive, but rather its application.

As long as the present police and court practices are employed, the German workers have no right to organize, and equality in making labor contracts does not exist. Where equality is lacking, actual discussions with the buyers of labor will be exceptions, and thus hatred and bitterness will and must be provoked.

The Tactics of the Workers and Employers in Economic Warfare

A favorite device of the opponents of trade unions is to picture them as organizations which try only to bring about strikes and thereby to disturb economic activity and to cripple it periodically. The simple facts deny this assertion and they cannot be unknown to those making it. The unions do not seek to bring about strikes but rather try to decrease the number. It is a known fact that in those districts where the workers are not organized strikes break out more easily and are carried on more bitterly than in those where unions have influence. We know this not only from remarks of students of the union movement abroad but likewise from officials who know the facts of economic life in Germany, namely the factory inspectors.

The inspector for Middle Franconia wrote in his report for 1897: "In view of the lively economic activity which prevailed during the past year in most branches of industry and might have enticed workers to seek better working conditions, the small number of strikes is remarkable. This is in part a result of the good discipline in the ranks of organized workers, whose leaders did not want a strike; but it is also due in part to the fact that both sides have learned to approach the solving of existing questions with more calm and understanding."

The official for Lower Franconia made the following observations: "Experience has also shown that the efforts of worker representatives from unions or similar organizations had decisive influence with the working masses for peaceful and speedy settlement of differences in the interests of industry."

What is borne out in these comments by officials is generally known, and those who deny these facts do so with the intention of taking from the workers the support which the unions offer them. But the latter do not reject conflict if it becomes unavoidable; experience has taught them that the buyers of labor show themselves ready to pay a higher price for labor in accordance with the pressure of power, and not with their own inclination. What does a temporary disturbance of economic activity in one industry or in one place mean in its effect upon the entire organism of the nation, when compared with the cultural progress which an improvement in the workers' standard of living brings? The most interesting observations made by an official on this subject are contained in the fifth annual report (1888) of the labor commissioner of New York. Only a few sentences are quoted from this report, as follows:

Strikes, their causes and effects, are the things which have for years aroused interest in the workers' movement. If the worker had remained passive and borne everything silently as he had for centuries with only an occasional outbreak, we should have walked in the footsteps of our forefathers. But the long strikes, the workers' organizations, the repeated disturbance of capitalistic installations for making money have aroused interest in the demands and wishes of the workers. In fact it must be a strong motive that can move a man to stop work and rob himself of all his wages. Such a man often makes mistakes but is always very serious. He shows this by self-sacrifice, the clearest proof of loyalty and principles, if not of judgment and wisdom. Strikes have helped to raise wages, to shorten working hours, to improve the condition not just of individual workers but of all mankind. A strike in a factory for reasonable causes often ends with a general improvement.

The strike is the last protest of the workers against the greed, exploitation, and ruthlessness of the employer.

Many similar expressions about the justice and influence of strikes could be given also.

That even employers' newspapers recognize the strike as justified is surprising but nonetheless a fact. In *Shoe and Leather* there was an article in 1896 by Dr. Bernet, in which he said in part: "The worker today is personally free; therefore the employer has to buy labor from him for a certain definite money wage. Accordingly the strike, regarded purely from the standpoint of economic theory, is nothing more than a struggle between buyer and seller—i.e., the purchaser of work and the seller of work potential—over the value of a commodity—i.e., human labor—such as can and does occur in the case of every other sale."

The Lord Chief Justice of England in November, 1898, made the following remark: "Strikes are undoubtedly an evil, but it is a comforting thought that they are a sign of the progress which labor has made, a sign that labor stands upon its own feet and is able to fight for its own rights."

These views can easily be multiplied; the above are enough to show that in all those circles which have no interest in slandering the struggles of the workers the justice and favorable effects of striking are recognized. In spite of this fact, unions use such means only when all others fail. They take precautions in their rules or in

special regulations against members' resorting to the strike hastily.
How far some of these prescriptions go is shown by some rules of
the Metal Workers' Union:

The leader of the decisive meeting is required to describe the
causes of the differences objectively to the members.

He is to refrain from any illusion-building in favor of a cessation
of work and to limit himself to the facts.

He should oppose all exaggeration of the facts, of the number of
the organized, and of the amount of support to be expected from
the union, and should do everything possible to allow the decision
to be made naturally through the vote of every individual member.

In every union the rules express the idea of peaceful settlement
of conflict, with stoppage of work only as the last resort.

The position of the employer and the employers' organizations is
quite different. The organized workers are punished; the representatives of the workers are turned away when they go to see the employers to discuss such disciplinary acts or to present the wishes of
the workers regarding regulation of working conditions. This rejection of the workers' representatives leads to the severest conflicts.

Often a strike occurs because the employers refuse to receive a
deputation which comes in the name of all the workers. This happens not only when a union official is a member of the deputation,
but even when the deputation is made up of members of their own
factory workshops. In fact, according to the uniform evidence of
workers and employers, the refusal to receive workers' deputations
and to deal with them has been much more the occasion of strikes
than the demands themselves made by either of the two parties. It
is a matter of recognizing the equality of the workers to negotiate
the terms of the labor contract. If this recognition is denied, a strike
results because of wounded pride. (Brentano, *op. cit.*, p. 254.)

If the employers do not receive the representatives of the workers
for discussion, or if they turn them away with hard words, small
differences which could be settled with a few words and a minimum
of concessions lead to strikes which last months and cause deep
bitterness. As the evidence shows, German employers especially
have done much to bring about dissatisfaction. The workers in the

construction industry often forward their demands in winter when building is only slightly active, so that contractors can make terms accordingly. Instead of acknowledging the good will of the workers the employers exploit the occasion, since the time is one in which the workers cannot strike successfully, to discipline and lock out the workers.

Noteworthy is the following remark which the contractors in Teterow made to the locked-out carpenters: "We [the employers] will strike now; by spring the journeymen will have lost their taste for striking."

The kind of good will the employers use toward the wage committees chosen by the workers is illustrated by the remark of a master carpenter in Arnswalde. The committee was told: "Carpenters from elsewhere will get 30 *pfennige* an hour [the demand of the journeymen], but those here will not; they'll come of themselves in winter when the lice begin to bite them."

Such remarks drive the workers to strikes, and one can see only too well how bitter those must be who have to work for such employers.

The workers prove that they prefer a peaceful solution of their conflicts to a strike in that they often negotiate for months and are not driven to a strike in spite of being repulsed repeatedly and openly put off by the employers. In Dresden the coopers negotiated no less than nine months with their employers without reaching an agreement, and when finally they resorted to a strike, their demands were granted. Negotiation is still regarded as the more peaceful way of settling differences. Often the employers take the point of view that they are giving something away if they negotiate with the workers, and even the workers' committee of the factory, set up in accordance with the industrial code, is turned away. It is eventually told: "I recognize no workers' committee; I am the workers' committee, and that's the end of it!"

If the workers call on the officials or the industrial court to mediate the strike, the employer only says that he has nothing to do with industrial courts and forbids any interference in his affairs.

If the workers have the misfortune to live in houses which belong to the employer, the latter exercises his power doubly. If the workers strike, they are brutally driven out of their houses without thought of whether they can find another place to live and without considering the time of year and the misery which must ensue if the workers are put out in winter. A letter is simply sent the workers saying: "You are hereby notified that on or before tomorrow night your house must be vacated, or other measures will be taken by us."

This makes it clear why the employers want to build such company houses and why in doing so they regard the welfare of the workers as the least of their considerations. When at length the employers want a strike so that their customers know of it, or declare that they prefer a strike to a peaceful settlement, anyone who looks at the matter objectively must see that the workers are not to blame for the strike.

Nor do the employers hesitate to break their word in order to drive the workers to strike. This happened in Torgelow, and the unhappy events of that strike, occasioned by the employers' perfidy, led to many workers' spending years in jail. The trial proceedings in this case in Stettin show that the strike was provoked by the employers. Factory owner Mentzel, as witness, replied to the following remark of the court:

Court: In the agreement (made before the industrial court in Uckermünde) it was stated that the employers should not be concerned about the existence of the union.
Witness: Yes.
Court: But you have demanded the signing of a counter-bill in which the workers are to pledge themselves not to enter the union.
Witness: Yes.
Court: But that was against the agreement.

Even when the intervention of a trade-union executive committee prevented a strike that the workers of the respective factory wanted to carry on, after the settlement of the cause of dispute employers provoked an uprising by demanding that the workers leave the organization which had prevented the strike.

In judging the proof of these statements, one must especially consider that in recent years the unions have grown, thus improving their position and giving the employers more occasion than formerly to negotiate with the workers. As the reports of the executive committees show, numerous differences have been settled in recent years through negotiations, and it is the strengthening of the unions and the attitude of the workers toward strikes which are responsible for this, not the good will of the employers. The executive committee of the printers' union is justifiably able to say in its report: "The fact can be affirmed that it is the strong union organization which is responsible for fewer and less harmful economic conflicts."

If the employers recognize labor unions as a rightful party to labor contracts and negotiate with union representatives, in most cases an agreement will be achieved without resort to the strike. The German employers seldom come to this intelligent view and are therefore usually the reason for the workers' resorting to the strike weapon. The consideration of the evidence produced by the representatives of the unions will lead anyone who is objective to the conclusion which the trade union committee of September 29, 1898, gave as follows:

The representatives of the executive committees of the approximately 420,000 members of the Central Association of Trade Unions, united in the trade-union committee, declare that in their long experience in trade-union affairs they have found that the responsibility for the outbreak of a strike lies in most cases with the employers. The organized workers have in all cases sought to bring about a peaceful agreement on their wages and working conditions before they resorted to a strike or called for a stoppage of work. With few exceptions and entirely in the spirit of the ruling tendency in German public life, the employers have ruthlessly refused to recognize trade unions as a legitimate party to labor contracts, have prevented peaceful understanding between employer and worker, and so have provoked the workers to strike.

9. Imperialism and Internal Affairs

Wilhelm von Blume, General of the Infantry Reserve: *Agriculture, Industry, and Commerce in Their Significance for the Armed Forces* (1900)[*]

Whether a predominantly agricultural or predominantly industrial economy is more advantageous for the total power of a modern state was disputed in every country at some time and to some extent during the nineteenth century. It became acute when a country began to pursue a policy of imperialism. The controversy raged in Germany with an intensity not achieved elsewhere, for about 1900 Germany was the most aggressive state and the most frustrated in the pursuit of *Weltpolitik;* generals as well as professors, not to mention lesser figures, discussed power as a product not merely of political will but of social and economic forces as well. In doing so they formulated standards by which one could gauge the relative importance of the states of Europe, not to speak of the rest of the world. Measured against General von Blume's criteria, few if any of the states would have deserved to be called sovereign. The intimate connection between domestic conditions and international policy shown in this essay may be regarded as a fact in any régime; it became especially apparent, even to the general public, as universal manhood suffrage, mass conscription, and the resources of an industrial society awakened in all individuals a personal interest in politics.

The influence which the modern economic development of Germany exerted upon the armed power of the country has been much

[*] Wilhelm von Blume, "Landwirtschaft, Industrie, und Handel in ihrer Bedeutung für die deutsche Wehrkraft," *Preussische Jahrbücher*, 101 (1900), pp. 1-29.

discussed in recent years. The occasion was given by a lecture, delivered in Munich in 1897 by professor Lujo Brentano and later published, which sought to disprove the view that the repressing of agriculture by the development of industry harms the armed power of the country. His exposition has been refuted from various quarters. In the *Preussische Jahrbücher* this task has been undertaken with complete success by Arthur Dix.[1] Brentano nevertheless maintains his view and seeks in a recent work published jointly with Robert Kuczynski, "The Present Basis of the German Armed Power,"[2] to prove it still more conclusively.

The great significance which the question has for the future of our land and people, especially in view of the important decisions to be made shortly in regard to Germany's tariff policy, will justify a second consideration of the Brentano view. We find this expressed most clearly in the following passages of the previously mentioned work:

The sooner countries make the transition from agriculture to industry and commerce, the wealthier and more powerful they become. Of the great empires England was first to make this transition after Holland, which on the same foundation rose to become a great power.

The most recent German occupational statistics of 1895 show that Germany is proceeding along the same course as England before it; indeed, this development is more rapid and energetic in Germany than in all other states of the European continent.[3]

It is true that Holland and England quickly attained wealth and power through the predominance of industry and commerce in their economic system, even if not through them alone. But in regard to Holland, its flowering was as transitory as that of a hothouse plant placed in cold air. This beautiful land still is wealthy even today, but its power is gone. Only by firm and continuous support from a greater whole could the gifted Dutch again achieve vigorous partici-

---

[1] *Preussische Jahrbücher,* 91, pp. 51 ff.; 28, pp. 154 ff.

[2] Published as article 35 of the *Münchener Volkswirtschaftlichen Studien* (Stuttgart, 1900).

[3] "The Present Basis of German Armed Power," *op. cit.,* p. 6.

pation in the civilizing tasks of mankind. It is doubtful whether the present inhabitants of Holland can equal in fighting power their poorer relatives in Africa, the heroic Boers, who live only by farming and cattle-breeding.

In England we have the type of a modern industrial and commercial state. Agriculture there has been sacrificed almost entirely to industrial interests. According to the report of the Royal Commission charged in the middle of the nineties with investigating the condition of agriculture in Great Britain, the capital value of land which was agriculturally profitable sank between 1875 and 1894 by approximately one billion pounds sterling, and more than half of the land still is used only as pasture land, although the livestock has diminished in number. Wide stretches lie untilled, numerous farms are deserted because their cultivation no longer pays. Brentano says:

While the population of England at the time of Louis XIV still subsisted up to 72.7% upon agriculture, the number of persons over ten years of age dependent upon agriculture amounted in 1891 only to 6.1% of the population. The wealth of England, however, rose during the same period from 650 million pounds sterling to 10 billion pounds.[4]

And England's power, like her wealth, increased. This fact has been little altered by the trying defeats which England recently incurred in the drive to conquer the Boers, who number scarcely one quarter of a million persons. In order to repair this damage and to pursue the war with the prospect of final victory, it was necessary for England not only to muster her entire land force and to send by far the largest part to Africa, but also to call upon her colonies. If, notwithstanding the indignation which British power politics has aroused almost everywhere, the security of that country has not been endangered and her power position has remained intact, the reason is that her security and political influence are based, not like Germany's primarily upon her army, but upon her commanding sea power and upon her position of being protected by the sea—especially the latter, as long as the English navy maintains its su-

[4] *Ibid.*

premacy. If Germany's land power should ever sink to the level of the British, her independence would be at an end even though her navy ruled the seas.

It is therefore beyond question that the power position of England rests ultimately upon her present economic system. Yet, since the conditions for existence of England and Germany differ so greatly, no conclusions can be drawn from the case of England applicable to that of Germany. Nor will any reference to Holland's passing glory attract anyone who considers the lasting power of the nation as more important than the wealth and renown of the present generation.

But Brentano has entered upon a detailed analysis of the question: "Does the development of Germany from a predominantly agrarian state to a predominantly industrial state endanger the capacity for defense of the German Empire?" He answers this question in the negative, in that he stresses the value of industry and commerce for the financial strength of the state and seeks to demonstrate that industry also offers more favorable conditions for military recruitment than does agriculture. The largest part of his work is devoted to this demonstration. If it could be considered successful and if Brentano's arguments exhausted the theme of "The Present Basis of German Armed Power," the transformation of Germany into a purely industrial and commercial state could not be promoted quickly or vigorously enough in the interest of the armed forces. But neither supposition is correct. Just as the cessation or even the decline of our industrial development would not be sound policy, so we cannot warn too strongly against any underestimation of the significance of agriculture for the nation's armed forces.

An impartial examination of all conditions bearing upon armed power leads to the conclusion that German economic policy is most beneficial when it has these effects:

1. that our industry is able to satisfy as fully as possible the needs of our country for industrial products, especially for war matériel;

2. that likewise the need for agricultural products is covered, insofar as at all possible, by home production;

3. that industry, over and above the demands under the first head-

ing, provides the means of exchange for desirable products of other countries not obtainable in our own country, that is, insofar as the means for them are not present at home in surplus natural resources, or cannot be created more advantageously through trade and commerce, capital investments abroad, etc.;

4. that as large a portion of the population be held to agricultural activity as can be fed without harming the demands upon industry stated under 1. and 3.;

5. that industry offer that portion of the expanding population which is dependent upon productive employment and which agriculture is not able to feed sufficient opportunity to make a living and, insofar as this aim requires, raise its production for the foreign market above the limit that the demand stated under 3. stipulates; it may be, then, that surplus productive power will find more advantageous employment in national colonies;

6. that trade and commerce correspond to the demands which follow from the preceding.

The following may serve to support the argument:

Clearly Brentano is correct in maintaining that flourishing industry and expanding commerce increase the wealth of a country more quickly than agriculture is able to do. I add to this that the advantage of a flourishing industry for the armed power of the country is not restricted to the financial gain which it yields; it makes us more independent of foreign countries in respect to our need for industrial production, particularly for war matériel. If we are dependent in considerable degree upon foreign countries, we are restricted in our freedom of action, not only toward them, but—since neutrals may not according to the principles of international law furnish belligerents war matériel—also toward other states. Freer and stronger is that state which is able to supply from within the country the ships, cannon, arms, munitions, and whatever else it requires in war matériel. An industry which is productive in this respect is of great value for the defense of the country; a heavily populated country is able only through it to employ effectively in case of war the full strength of the nation. The equipment of the million-men armies of our age and their maintenance in readiness for combat are unthinkable without efficient industry. Their speedy mobilization and effective employment assume a highly developed system of transportation such as can exist only in industrialized countries with vigorous commerce.

Sea power produces only a sea-faring people, whose navigation can of course prosper only through exchanging goods with other nations. The former sea power of Holland rested essentially upon this basis, and likewise the present commercial fleets of England and Norway serve, only to a smaller extent, the import and export needs of their own countries. But it is in the nature of the situation that brisk overseas commerce of a country requires a national fleet and entails the need as well as the capacity for sea power. And in like manner it lies in the nature of the situation that the rise of industry and the expansion of commerce go hand in hand.

Generally speaking, everything which serves to open up and expand the material resources of the country, to advance the standard of living of the people, to raise the intellectual level, and to arouse enterprise in the nation is in itself useful to the armed power of the country. Industry and commerce, especially commercial exchange with foreign peoples and foreign countries, contribute much to this process. Where they flourish they not only increase the material wealth of a country; they also stimulate the intellectual life of the nation.

Quickly expanding wealth certainly also conceals dangers for the moral health and vigor of the people. Pleasure-seeking, selfishness, and effeminacy appear only too often in its train and diminish the sensitivity for noble impulses, the self-sacrificing devotion to national concerns, the strength to resist distress, suffering, and danger. History instructs us about this decadence in numerous examples of the decline of peoples and states. Almost always it could be traced to the fact that greedy desires, nourished by economic prosperity, came to dominate and worked to disintegrate the life of the state and people. Though we have every cause to rejoice in the economic prosperity of our fatherland, we nonetheless have urgent need to combat forcibly the moral dangers which are bound up with it. One means to this end consists in preventing the depopulation of the countryside and in assuring the agrarian population an influential place in the life of the people. For if agriculture has indeed participated to a smaller degree than industry and commerce in the increase in material wealth of the country, the population belonging to it has been less exposed to the dangers involved. It forms a strong buttress against the disintegrating effects of modern economic life. I shall return to this point, but I should like first to take up several other considerations.

At least equally important to the country's independence of foreign industry is the ability to satisfy its need for raw materials, above all for foodstuffs, insofar as possible through domestic production. Certain foods and luxuries must be imported from abroad because their production in our own country is, climatically and otherwise, at least in part impossible and very unprofitable. At present, however, although not confronted by compelling circumstances, we have become dependent to a considerable degree upon foreign countries even for covering our requirements in grain and meat. During the years 1894-97 we imported from foreign countries approximately one-eighth of the rye, one-third of the wheat, over one-third of the barley, and one-twelfth of the oats that we needed, more than 600 million marks' worth of grain annually, in addition to a considerable number of cattle and a quantity of meat. If in case of war the importation of these indispensable foodstuffs were interrupted or merely made considerably more difficult and more expensive, a contingency which we must always have in view, especially in case of an unfavorable turn of the war, then the capacity of the country for resistance would suffer, in certain circumstances to a dangerous extent. Varying opinions also exist—quite apart from the danger of blockade—as to whether and under what circumstances foodstuffs are to be considered war contraband.

The means of exchange for the grain and meat we lack, as well as for the provision of all other foreign products, must be created in large part through the export industry, since the natural products of the country after serving our own requirements do not suffice to cover this additional need. The importation of grain and meat thus presupposes or makes necessary an increase of the export industry.

Industrial export production, however, is doubly dependent upon foreign countries—that is, both in marketing its wares and in obtaining the raw materials which it processes. The German soil contains a rich treasure of coal and iron; most of the other necessary raw materials needed for industrial purposes, however, we do not possess in the country in sufficient quantities to cover our own needs. Thus, by way of example, in the year 1898 the surplus value of exports over the value of imports amounted to 187 million marks in woolens, 150 in cottons, 127 in silks, 95 in leather goods, 51 in copper wares. In contrast, more raw materials and partially manufactured goods were imported than were exported, to the extent of 293 million marks in wool, 249 in cotton, 106 in silk, 109 in leather and hides, and 72 in copper.

What, then, if trade and commerce, importation and exportation come to a standstill, as they usually do in times of war? The industrial areas affected by extensive coal strikes have repeatedly experienced a small foretaste of the situation which would then arise. When an additional increase in the price of the most essential foodstuffs is added, the capacity and willingness for sacrifice is weakened among the people in districts dependent for livelihood upon industrial activity. When these people are very numerous and the resources of the state, the municipalities, and the propertied groups are absorbed to the utmost by the demands of war, so that little can be done from these quarters to alleviate the need, pressure arises from below which can require the conclusion of peace before the aims of the war have been achieved. This situation may be all the worse in that under some circumstances the morale of the army of a people may be influenced by an unfavorable popular mood.

Among the agricultural population, the means of earning a living is far less exposed to disruptions of the kind previously mentioned in case of war—outside the theatre of war itself. Because of the reduction of their work force they must let postponable work go, perhaps even suffer a temporary reduction of their herds, or leave this or that piece of land uncultivated. But they produce as before the necessities of life, and the salability of their products is little impaired.

From the point of view of the country's military defense, it is therefore not advisable to increase our export industry more than is necessary to provide exchange for the foreign goods we cannot otherwise obtain and to offer our population sufficient opportunities for a livelihood. Military defense, however, is promoted through increases in agricultural production and through intensive settlement of the rural areas.

Today there surely exists—the Prussian minister for agriculture just a short time ago expressed it in the Lower House without being disputed—the distinct physical possibility of producing within the country the necessary grain for the existing population in Germany and even for a still more numerous one. If this were to take place we should not need to import 600 million marks' worth of grain annually from foreign countries; we could decrease correspondingly the export of industrial manufactures as well as the import of raw materials for industrial purposes, and we should thus gain significantly in economic independence of foreign countries.

This program of course would not serve the interests of commerce. Commerce, however, is not an end in itself but a means to an end; it exists—insofar as it does not seek its gain in providing transportation among foreign countries—merely for the service of home production and consumption, and for these the interests of commerce are not decisive. We are not justified in making ourselves more dependent upon foreign countries for the advantage of commerce than is necessary for economic and cultural purposes.

We are compelled to accept the disadvantages and dangers of such dependence when and as long as we can not provide subsistence for our people in any way other than through increasing export industry. In view of the rapid increase of population and the limited resources which our land offers, it is probable that this situation sooner or later will be reached, unless it is obviated in time by the appropriate acquisition of land and the diversion to it of our excess population. For effecting both these measures we need stronger land and sea power, in the first case to hold the import and export lanes open, and in the other case to protect the colonies outside the mother land and our communication with them. And it is in keeping with prudent foresight to strengthen ourselves in due time for this, especially by increasing our sea power. Sufficient inducement, moreover, would not be lacking for this increase in strength even if our overseas trade were for some time to progress more slowly or even to diminish.

At present, however, there is no population surplus whose support would require the enormous increase of our industry, although such an increase is in fact taking place. Proof: the ever-louder complaints over the shortage of workers raised for some time by agriculture but also recently by industry; and the flooding of the country to the detriment of our nationality with foreign workers, mostly of inferior races.

How well founded the complaints of agriculture are over shortages of workers is shown by the statistics. While the total population of Germany rose between 1882 and 1895 from 45,222,000 to 51,770,000 people, the agrarian population (occupational division A: agriculture, gardening, stock-raising, forestry, and fishing) decreased during the same period by 724,000 people. Its share of the total population decreased from 42.51% to 34.74%. On the other hand, from 1882 to 1895 the industrial population (occupational division B: industry, construction, mining, and smelting) increased by 4,200,000 people, its share of the total population from 35.51% to 39.12%, and that of the population of trade and commerce (occupational division C) from 10.02% to 11.52% (by almost one and one-half million people).

If one takes into consideration only employed persons, divided according to sex, the following picture emerges:

			1882	1895
		Men	5,701,587	5,539,538
A.	Agriculture, etc.	Women	2,534,909	2,753,154
		Total	8,236,496	8,292,692
		Men	5,269,489	6,760,102
B.	Industry, etc.	Women	1,126,976	1,521,118
		Total	6,396,465	8,281,220
		Men	1,272,208	1,758,903
C.	Trade and	Women	298,110	579,608
	commerce	Total	1,570,318	2,338,511

Women therefore are much more numerous proportionally in the agricultural group than in either of the others. In the period from 1882 to 1895 the number of women employed in agriculture increased by 218,245, that of men, on the other hand, decreased by 162,149. The rest of the decline of the agricultural population concerns the children of agricultural laborers, who at a comparatively early age enter the classes of employed persons, overwhelmingly in industry, while the peasant proprietor seeks to keep his children on his farm where he needs them. One undesirable result of the rural depopulation, certainly, is that those pouring into the cities from the countryside are members of the proletariat almost exclusively.

Also very noteworthy are the age relationships of employed persons. While according to the occupational census of 1895 the number of employed persons of both sexes in agriculture, etc. (8,292,692), is almost exactly as large as in industry (8,281,220), in the former category the number of those who have passed the fiftieth year of age is almost twice as large as that in industry (2,103,357 *vs.* 1,193,-941). On the other hand, there also are more employed persons under eighteen years of age in agriculture than in industry (1,280,942 *vs.* 1,139,466). In particular the relationship of the male employed persons who are at the age of their greatest productivity and therefore also at the age of military service (from twenty to forty years of age) to the total number of employed persons appears as follows:

	Total Number		Those 20 to 40 years old	
Agriculture, etc.	5,539,538	33.5	2,065,427	28.0
Industry, etc.	6,760,102	40.9	3,354,391	45.3
Trade and commerce	1,758,903	10.6	873,127	11.8
Other occupations	1,447,939	8.8	991,014	13.4
Independent without occupation	1,027,259	6.2	119,644	1.5
Totals	16,533,741	100.0	7,403,603	100.0

Thus in 1895 these percentages were involved in the specified fields:

	Agriculture	Industry, trade, etc.
Total population	35.74%	50.64%
Employed persons of both sexes	36.19%	46.35%
Employed males	33.5%	51.5%
Employed males, 20 to 40 years old	28%	57.1%

From the above table it is clear that in the case of males from 20 to 40 years of age (those liable to military service) the number of those in industry already exceeds by more than twice the number of those in agriculture; that is, the ratio is 57.1: 28, rather than 50.64: 35.74, or 46.35: 36.19, which are the percentages for total population and for all employed persons.

In a politico-economic sense it follows from the figures cited that the shortage of workers in agriculture is not only a matter of diminished numbers and a higher representation of women here than among the employed persons of industry. It is even more obviously a matter of proportionally smaller numbers of those in the prime of life employed in agriculture than in industry.

The cause of this phenomenon is to be traced in part to the sudden flourishing recently of industry as well as of trade and commerce. The numerous factories which have of late arisen and expanded would perhaps often have seen an advantage in having available a considerable body of older and skilled workers. Since these were not present in the desired numbers, workers who were unskilled and yet in the best years of their life found ready acceptance to a correspondingly greater extent. Thus the transition of numerous younger men from agriculture to industry took place, helped along by the unfavorable situation of the agricultural worker. After the agricultural population, especially in the middle-age groups, was in this manner thinned out to the extreme, inevitably an ebbing of the flood of workers into industry occurred. Yet the founding of new industrial concerns and the expansion of existing ones continues on an accelerated scale. This situation will lead ultimately to catastrophe for industry itself and will have a sobering effect. But in the meantime no thought is given to more active colonization of rural areas; and the capital which is lost in industrial bankruptcies would have found better employment in the improvement of our agricultural production, which suffers from lack of capital as it does from the labor shortage. The future will show that the quickest possible advance of our economic development along the currently prevailing lines reacts adversely upon industry itself and upon the possessors of capital, and even more so upon the interests of the fatherland. Further substantiation of this view requires more intensive discussion of the question of the influence which industry and agriculture exert upon the military potential of the people.

Brentano approaches discussion of this question[5] "from the standpoint that the military potential of a country is always in proportion to the number of men fit for military service provided by the area to be defended." He proceeds then, meticulously and with the use of statistical material, "to prove that the areas of the German Empire which are engaged chiefly in industry and commerce provided a greater number of troops for every thousand square kilometers than those dependent chiefly upon agriculture," and he concludes that "the transition from a predominantly agrarian state to a predominantly industrial state therefore also strengthens rather than endangers the other basis of the armed forces of the German Empire, the troops."[6]

Neither premise will be disputed, even though the first considers only one of the numerous requisites for the military potential of the country, and even though the second is not valid without many qualifications. It is nevertheless beyond question and requires no further substantiation that an industrial city produces more recruits which are useful than a manor occupying the same amount of land. And when Brentano points out[7] that the kingdom of Saxony, with an area of 14,992 square kilometers, provided 44,058 recruits in three years, while the administrative district of Gumbinnen, on the other hand, comprising 15,877 square kilometers, furnished only 16,060 recruits during the same period, this is a proportion which would become painfully apparent to the administrative district of Gumbinnen in the event of war with Saxony. In regard to a war conducted by the German Empire, however, it makes no difference whether this or that part of the country furnishes more troops but only how strong the German military power is in its entirety.

With these reservations one can, as stated, grant the validity of both premises of the Brentano argument but not the conclusions which have been drawn from them. They would be correct only if a

[5] "The Present Basis of German Armed Power," *op. cit.*, p. 8.

[6] He previously designated finance as the first basis.

[7] "The Present Basis of German Armed Power," *op. cit.*, p. 33.

predominantly industrial population provided a greater birth surplus of men of undiminished robustness or delivered abler men to the army than a predominantly agrarian population was able to do under otherwise similar conditions.

It is true that when the industry of the fatherland guarantees an opportunity for sufficient livelihood to a part of the expanding population which cannot be supported by agriculture because of the limitation of land area, the situation is more advantageous to the armed forces of the country, in terms of the numerical strength of the army, than if that part of the population were forced to emigrate through lack of livelihood. This is indeed what Brentano had in mind in attributing superiority to the industrial state over the agrarian state in respect to the provision of troops. But he did not say it; rather he obscured the truth contained in the above statement by his square-kilometer theory, which overlooks the fact that population growth which industrial regions receive by internal migration is not synonymous with population increase.

The basic military potential of a people largely depends upon the number of its men who are militarily fit and efficient in armed service. A man is militarily qualified if he possesses the minimum characteristics demanded by war; greater ability, however, compensates within certain limitations for a smaller number.

The number of men increases naturally with the number of people, which is advancing rapidly in Germany. The increase here between 1890 and 1895 amounted annually to an average of 1.1%, in France to only 0.01%. The surplus of births over deaths in Germany, however, is not equally great everywhere; regional [Stamm] characteristics and influences of the most diverse nature—inherited conditions, health influences, social and moral conditions, etc.—produce differences in this respect which are often difficult to explain. Thus one must admit that some parts of the country with a predominantly agrarian character have a lower birth rate than some industrial areas. On the other hand, it has been proved statistically that on the whole the surplus of births in the countryside is considerably larger than in the cities, and that although the latter during the period from 1882 to 1895 somewhat improved through reform of health conditions, nevertheless the growth of the agricultural population was still greater. The birth surpluses in the kingdom of Prussia, per 1000 of population, were as follows:

Year	In the state	In the cities	In the country
1882	12.2	10.2	13.4
1883	11.5	9.0	12.9
1884	11.9	9.4	13.4
1885	12.4	10.1	13.6
1886	11.7	9.0	13.3
1887	13.9	11.5	15.4
1888	14.7	12.5	16.1
1889	14.0	11.6	15.5
1890	12.6	10.7	14.0
1891	15.0	12.6	16.5
1892	12.9	11.2	14.0
1893	13.7	10.5	15.2
1894	15.0	12.5	16.5
1895	15.2	12.0	17.3

This statistical result appears even more remarkable when one recalls the unfavorable composition of the agricultural population by age groups and takes into consideration that this compilation applies to a period of great progress in industry and trade and of severe distress in agriculture. Unfortunately the corresponding data for the whole of the empire are lacking; nevertheless, there is no reason to assume that the results would be substantially different from those of the largest German state. Unfortunately, too, it has not been determined statistically how the birth surpluses are distributed among the different occupational groups. But when one considers that the cities have in effect none of the agricultural population at all, while by far the greatest part of the inhabitants of the countryside pursue agriculture, one may regard as true the fact contested by Brentano that the relative or even absolute decline of the agricultural population impairs the increase in population. In England in this respect, a progressive retardation of the increase in population also is clearly evident. Birth surpluses there amounted during the eighteen-twenties to an average 14 per 1000, during the period 1890 to 1896 to only 11.8 per 1000 of population. The diminished fertility of marriages in France, however, where a larger part of the population than in Germany supports itself in the country, is traceable to causes which, thank God, are not present among us.

Yet not only do proportionally more men come from the agricultural population than from the other, especially the industrial districts, but also among those of the agrarian population subject to military service there is a greater number who are found fit, and these moreover are distinguished in general by a higher degree of war proficiency.

"The fact that the number of those who are fit in relation to the number of those who are subject to military service is greater in the predominantly agrarian regions than in the others," is recognized expressly on page 32 of the work under discussion. The entire greater second part of the work, written by Kuczynski, is devoted on the other hand to the argument that "a considerably greater fitness of the agricultural population is not proved."

Kuczynski bases his considerations upon the results of the German statistics on recruitment. These are published annually by the statistical office of the German Empire in two different compilations. From one of them may be learned how many of those obligated for military service in each army corps district were entered on the basic lists, to which age groups they belonged, how many of them could not be found, failed to appear without excuse, had moved and therefore were liable for service elsewhere, or were excluded as morally unfit. By deducting these four categories from the number of those entered on the basic lists, there follows the number of those obligated for military service, concerning whose physical fitness the recruiting authorities had to decide; and it is then indicated how many of them were rejected, discharged, transferred to the first reserve or to the reserve for replacement, and how many of them, on the other hand, were selected as fit, joined voluntarily, and were superfluous. From the other compilation it may be seen how many recruits from each of the seventy-three higher administrative districts (governmental districts, etc.) of the federal states were placed annually in the army and navy, how many of these possessed formal education, how many did not.

. . . .

Various attempts have been made through comparison of the statistics of recruitment with the overall statistics of population to resolve the question of whether and in what degree the agricultural population excels the industrial, etc., in military fitness. For this purpose the number of those fit for military service, ascertained for every one hundred of those examined for military service over a number of years in the various army corps districts, states, provinces, or administrative districts, have been compared with the total population figures of every district and those of the agricultural, etc., population in them. Against this procedure it has been maintained that, for the purpose of comparisons of this kind, one should group those who have been found militarily fit not according to the districts from which they have been taken, but according to the districts of their birth. In this connection there are further differences of opinion over whether the number of recruits raised should be compared with the population figures of the year in which they were drafted or those of the year of birth.

Well-founded objections arise to each of these methods of comparison; none of the tables projected can produce an adequate picture of the performance of the various occupational classes in military recruitment. Nevertheless it is very noteworthy that in all tables of the above-mentioned work the districts with heavier agrarian population taken as a whole, despite the unfavorable composition by age groups, rank superior to the others in their performance. In some of the tables this superiority does not appear so large as in others, but it is recognizable in all. One needs for this purpose only the figures of the ten or fifteen districts which have the largest rural population, in order to compare them with the corresponding totals of the least agrarian districts.

In my opinion this conclusion is the only significant one to be drawn from the statistics compared. It is not weakened by the fact given prominence by Kuczynski that individual districts which are predominantly industrial appear to excel individual districts which are predominantly rural in regard to the number of recruits supplied. This is explicable by the fact that the physical constitution of the population is not conditioned solely by occupation but that differences in heredity as well as the general conditions of existence in the district are also important. A predominantly agricultural population in a poor mountainous region will often supply fewer men for military recruitment than the same number of people in a flourishing industrial area. Finally, however, there is also a factor which has not been sufficiently appreciated in regard to the influence of industry upon the physical usefulness of the worker for military service, namely the differences among individual branches of industry. The industrial workers who perform a great deal of manual labor, like the iron workers, the smiths, the butchers, etc., are more or less comparable—especially when like carpenters, diggers, etc., they work in the open air—to the agricultural population in physical fitness. The industrial workers, on the other hand, who perform their work in closed rooms without regular muscular exertion lack for the most part the strength and endurance required for military service. And to this latter category belong most of the industrial workers: those of the textile, clothing, foodstuffs, leather, wood, jewelry, toy, chemical, etc., industries. The districts where these branches of industry employ a large proportion of the population produce altogether unsatisfactory recruitment results. The disadvantageous effects of the aforesaid branches of industry upon military recruitment would stand out sharply if the statistics offered any means of establishing precisely how many or how few usable recruits come from the working districts belonging to these industries.

But the statistics do not suffice for this purpose. They do not permit once and for all the numerical establishment of how much the industrial population, in its entirety and in comparison with the agricultural population, shares in the annual provision of troops. Only the superiority of the agricultural population is clear; but it is not known numerically. A corresponding improvement of the statistics on recruitment certainly would be desirable. . . .

. . . .

But statistics surely are not the only source of knowledge. Along with them, experience and sound common sense deserve their due; and both teach us that the army especially draws from the cities the intelligence and mental alertness which have assumed increased value in the conduct of war in modern times; that on the other hand the countryside furnishes the army troops, which are proportionally more numerous and for the most part more qualified in all other respects. On the basis of ample experience, this is the well-established view of all military men, as is the conviction that strong nerves and the moral characteristics which make soldiers fit are more indigenous to the agricultural areas than to the city. The experienced military leader esteems a mixture of urban elements among the troops, but for all situations he trusts these more when the rural element predominates.

The same conclusion must also be drawn by everybody who considers without bias the condition of urban life as it affects the fitness of the population for military service.

. . . .

In Germany the predominant type among the agricultural population is the peasant on his own farm, whereas in industry it is the propertyless wage laborer. The customs and the outlook on life of the agricultural laborers are under the determining influence of the peasant class; in industry there is no middle class of comparable significance, while the social gulf there between employer and worker threatens to widen more and more.

For the development of mind and spirit, the living conditions of the industrial population are generally more favorable than those of the agricultural areas. Of course we recognize, by the conspicuous skill which the Boers despite their lack of military schooling showed on earlier occasions and now exhibit in their present struggle against the English, that agrarian life for the most part is at least no hindrance to the acquisition of mental characteristics suited to war. Such life cultivates an eye for the nature of terrain and this is valuable for the military profession. By contrast, the extensive division of labor causes the occupation of many factory workers to be in no way intellectually stimulating. During work and in the rest periods, however, the workers are always more or less in large groups, whereas the country man is by the nature of his occupation left a great deal to himself. The main point is that the industrial population lives predominantly in the cities and their suburbs; and the fact that more lively intellectual activity prevails there than in the countryside requires no further elaboration and argument.

On the other hand, rural life and agricultural activity are more advantageous to physical health and to the development of moral strength, both of which are auspicious for victory, than urban activity and industrial labor are. The influence of the latter upon the strength and health of mankind has already been referred to; in this respect significant differences exist among the various branches of industry. Also workers' protective legislation has removed or at least reduced many dangers to health in the area of industrial labor. Nevertheless, it cannot be seriously doubted that the occupational activity of the agricultural population promotes physical vigor, endurance, and capacity for resistance, which must be demanded of the soldier, more than the occupation of most industrial workers, especially in the factories. In like manner the leisure activities of the rural population differ from those of the urban population. Much of value has been accomplished lately toward improving the health conditions in the cities through drainage, piping of water, provision for street cleaning, supplying of better air, and so on. More consideration has been given to the improvement of hazardous living conditions, which frequently afflict the poorer classes of people in the cities. But the disadvantages in sanitation which are connected with the fact of many people living closely together, the characteristic mark of the city, can never be completely eliminated. In the countryside as a rule there are fewer sanitary precautions, but the ensuing harm is more limited because the people there live more in the healthful open air and the living quarters are not so cramped as in the cities. The houses stand apart in the country and several families seldom live under one roof. Field work hardens the body; the temptation for pleasure and intemperance is slight in the country; the material life even of the well-to-do peasant is simple and without pretension, free from effeminacy. The farmer's day, despite the most exacting physical labor, runs quietly and evenly. The restless bustle of the age touches him little; it runs its course in the cities, animating and promoting the intellect but making strong and exhausting demands upon the nerves.

Under such circumstances the rural population on the average is more suited physically for bearing privations and hardships than is the urban population employed by industry and is more capable of resisting the pressures of war upon the nerves—unless it is reduced to bitter poverty. Quickly expanding wealth such as can be seen in the industrial and commercial cities in economically favorable periods has not fallen to its lot. But all the more securely will it preserve its superiority in physical vigor and health.

In moral characteristics, too, the rural population is especially suited to military service. It does not participate in the corrupting and socially disruptive dance around the golden calf. The peasant is content with the modest reward of his honest labor; and when this turns out to be more abundant, his way of life and his view of life are scarcely affected. In its quiet, contemplative existence the rural population is less exposed and less susceptible to temptations than the urban. Accustomed to continuous and greater exertions of its strength, it has less longing, after the burden and toil of the day, for pleasures and distractions. These are present only in limited degree; the joy in labor itself and in nature must take their place. This gives a serious bent to the outlook on life, in which the customary, the inbred, and the traditional play a large role, and simple piety thrives. With love for the native soil grows love for the fatherland. The countryman becomes aroused over new ideas with difficulty; raised in the discipline of the home and community, he subordinates himself willingly to legitimate authority, and while stubbornly maintaining his conceptions and rights, he does his duty with devotion, loyalty, and abnegation. From people of this nature develop under proper direction soldiers who are well-disciplined, trustworthy, and brave.

Thus the superior physical and moral fitness of the rural population for war follows as much from the nature of the conditions under which it lives as from the testimony of men entrusted with the practice of military life. Today the military value of the rural population has been brought anew to our minds by the heroic resistance which the Boers, despite the poverty of material means and despite imperfect military organization and training, have been able to offer the vastly superior force of the most wealthy country in the world. No doubt their military fitness has been increased by the necessity of constant preparedness for battle, which in the civilized countries of Europe does not influence the daily life of the people in a comparable manner. Nonetheless there is no doubt that the ability of the Boer states to resist is based primarily upon the agrarian character of the people. This strength would stand out even more sharply if the same age groups which the Boers put in the field had been called up from the London Exchange or from the factory population of the English cities in order to compete with them as militia in hand-to-hand combat. Unfortunately this instructive spectacle has been withheld from us.

To summarize:

Industry and commerce advance well-being and culture and enhance the material power of the state. Of course they also increase the foreign interests which require protection from the state and, along with peaceful relations with other peoples and states, enhance the possibility of international friction. For the expanded responsibilities which consequently devolve upon it, the state can employ only those means of power which are not essential for the protection of the source of its power, which is the very borders of its territory. The last-named responsibility of self-protection not only continues to exist unchanged alongside the new foreign interests, but it gains significance through the fact that industry and trade make the life of the nation more susceptible to destruction through enemy attack, and the increased wealth of the country seldom fails to arouse envy and covetousness abroad.

Now all states are not exposed to enemy attack in the same degree. It has been pointed out already how great an advantage England has in this respect through its insular position. Without the aid of the sea, the means of power which are at its disposal today would not suffice for the defense of its territory, let alone for the maintenance and extension of its power in other parts of the world. In glaring contrast, Germany is separated from the strongest military powers of Europe only by land boundaries difficult to defend while at the same time it is open to attack by an enemy sea power. It has required the greatest mustering of its armed forces at all times to maintain its existence; it still requires this while its expanding industry and commerce create a concurrent daily increase in the significance of its interests abroad which must be protected. The future of Germany depends upon the development of its armed power to keep step with these growing demands.

Thanks to the initiative of Emperor William II we shall soon possess a navy commanding respect. This new creation not only makes considerable demand upon the resources of the empire, but more and more the national interest focuses upon it. Gratifying as the latter phenomenon is in itself, it evokes danger to the undiminished support and further development of the land forces in accordance with the demands of the times. Let us beware of understating their value! Even though without a strong navy we cannot do justice to the expanded national responsibilities which the times pose for us, Germany's security and political influence are based now, as before, primarily upon land forces.

And the backbone of the land forces is agriculture. To abandon it to ruin in order to hasten the development of industry and commerce beyond what is necessary to serve our own needs for industrial products, to receive foreign products in exchange which we need and which we ourselves cannot produce, and finally to assure the livelihood of the expanding population—this is to sacrifice the future of the German nation to the delusive and fleeting grandeur of the present!

10. Local Government

Local Government in Italy (1901)[*]

The conditions of local government in Italy resembled the state described in Baron Sonnino's pessimistic picture of parliamentary practice. Corruption and exploitation in local government reflected abuse in the central organs of government. Liberals in Italy and in other countries rightly believed that the strength of freedom in England rested upon the vigorous public responsibility of borough and county governments. The statement given below offers many clues as to why government in Italy, and by inference that in other countries, failed to reach English standards. The conditions portrayed here cannot be regarded as typical of Europe, but the analysis of them offers a point of departure for discussing such problems as (1) the relation between central and local government; (2) the economic and social situation in which government will readily attend to the welfare of the people, and that in which government will not do so; (3) the political and social significance of taxation and public expenditure—indeed, this document invites consideration of the whole matter of the character of government as an expression of the culture of the people. The close connection in Italy between economic stagnation and political stagnation is evident, and one may infer from this connection that similar economic and social conditions in other countries produce similar political and administrative abuses, that improvement in economic conditions brings progress in political conditions.

The two English scholars who here analyze the Italian local government do not qualify as persons active in the affairs of which they write. The inclusion of their statement is justified by the fact that they gathered their material in large part from interviews with many distinguished Italians—parlia-

[*] Bolton King and Thomas Okey, *Italy Today* (London: James Nisbet and Co., 1901), pp. 263-76.

mentarians, newspaper editors, professors, officials, and economic leaders. The authors quoted here are reporters in the best sense of the word; they give the results of investigations by judicious participants in affairs of local government.

Local government has a more than usual importance in Italy. Municipal life has still much of its historic strength, and when Gino Capponi called Tuscany "an aggregate of communes," he expressed what is more or less true of the whole country. "Often," says a recent writer, "the blood of the middle ages runs in the veins of our communes." To many of the Southern Italians the commune is everything and the State is very little; the commune and its doings and its struggles make a big part of his life, while the far-off Government at Rome vanishes to a speck. The peasant, who will not trouble to vote at a Parliamentary election, cares much to be a village councillor, and in 1889 there were 19,000 farmers or agricultural labourers and 12,000 artisans, who sat in the coveted seat of communal government. The provincial city clings to the glory that has come down from the days of its medieval independence; some were till yesterday the capitals of their little states. Italy has no true metropolis to suck the life of the country to itself. Milan, Turin, Genoa, Florence, Naples, Palermo rival or surpass Rome in manufactures and commerce, in literary and artistic activity, in journalism, in social brilliancy, in their influence on the country's general life. They have their factories, their theatres, their newspapers, their publishers, their exhibitions, which Rome can barely equal. Take a little town like Modena, with a population of 31,000, and we find in it a University, a great Military School, an Academy of Fine Arts, two large Libraries, and a Court of Appeal, besides its own municipal activities.

Nor is there any sign that this social decentralization is diminishing. Unity has centralized the administration and to a certain extent political life; it has centralized nothing else. Climate and geography at present forbid Rome to become a great capital like London or Paris or Berlin. Were Parliamentary life more real, the interest of the country would gravitate more there; but in its present discredit and congestion, municipal reform is the most hopeful channel of social advance, and Italians assert with some exaggeration that all the best public life of the country lies in the municipalities. Certainly in some of the cities there has been of late years a very notable development of municipal activity. But the urgency of local politics lies in the intimate connection between municipal finance and the people's food. The local duties make a big part of the burden of taxation that is crushing the poor. The price of bread and meat, of wine and sugar and coffee, of eggs and cheese and fish, depends to a large extent on the municipal policy of each town. It is this that makes the starving and despairing peasant of the South revolt against his Communal Council, and not against the Government.

The Local Government of Italy, which has changed but little since 1865, does small credit to Italian legislative ability. Perhaps from a concession to a doctrinaire equality, perhaps from sheer lack of constructive capacity, the Italian law gives much the same powers and duties to every commune, large and small. In their relations with the central Government there is little difference between a city of half a million inhabitants and a tiny Alpine hamlet. The great city is subject to irritating and unnecessary interference; the little town or village has powers altogether beyond its capacity, and which only tempt it to extravagance. Each of the 8262 communes has its Council of fifteen to eighty members, according to its size, elected by literates on a lower qualification than the Parliamentary franchise. The term of office is for six years, and one-half of the members go out of office every three years. The Council has only two statutory meetings in the year (though, of course, in the large towns it meets oftener), and in the intervals its work is carried on by a small Junta, which acts as an executive committee to carry out in detail the resolutions of the Council, and draft its budget and by-laws. Every commune has a Syndic for its chief officer, appointed by the Council for three years, and a Secretary, appointed in the first instance for two years and afterwards for periods of not less than six; in all but the smaller communes a person to be eligible for the latter post must, as a rule, have passed through a Lyceum and Technical Institute. Except for electoral purposes, there is no local area corresponding to the English district or French *arrondissement;* in some parts of Italy the communes are themselves districts, each containing several towns or villages. There are sixty-nine provinces, with an average population of about 450,000, each with its machinery analogous to that of the commune—a Council of twenty to sixty members, elected on the same franchise and for the same period, and meeting once a year, nominally, at all events, for a month's session; a Deputation corresponding to the Communal Junta;[1] and a Prefect appointed by the Government, who is assisted by a Provincial Junta of six members, of whom four are appointed by the Council. It will be seen that a large amount of power necessarily passes to the Communal Junta and Provincial Delegation, and their influence is probably greater than that of the Committees of an English local body.

The powers of the Councils are very wide. The compulsory duties of the Communal Councils include the maintenance of streets, communal roads,[2] lighting (where there is any), and markets; all sanitary matters and the provision of burial grounds; elementary education and certain duties in respect of secondary education; the relief of the poor and a general control of local charities; local police and prisons; registration of births and deaths; electoral registration; certain duties in sea-towns in respect of ports and lighthouses; and the maintenance of the fabric of churches, where no other sufficient means are forthcoming. The compulsory duties of the Provincial Councils include the maintenance of provincial roads; the control of river channels and embankments; most secondary and technical education; the maintenance of pauper lunatics; and certain supervisory powers over elementary education and charities. But beyond these compulsory duties, both communes and provinces have almost unlimited permissive powers. Subject to the Prefect's veto, they may undertake any "services or offices of public utility." These often include necessary objects of municipal enterprise. But it means, too,

[1] Members of the Deputation not resident in the chief town of the province may, at the option of the Council, be paid an allowance not exceeding 8s. for each meeting and travelling expenses. Members of the Provincial Junta are paid 8s. to 12s. for each meeting.

[2] Communal, provincial, and national roads are respectively 54, 39, and 7 per cent of the whole.

that a commune sometimes spends more money on its theatre than on its schools,[3] or delights a Southern populace on fête-days with costly illuminations and explosion of petards in the streets at no small risk to the limbs of the crowd and the tottering houses. £1200 is spent on one piece of fireworks to make a Roman holiday. Impecunious local bodies encourage music and the fine arts, have universities without scholars, secondary schools without apparatus, "museums and picture galleries with hardly a local reputation." It is true that the permissive expenditure accounts for only £2,500,000 out of a total local expenditure of £22,000,000, but in the Sicilian communes it covers more than one-fifth, and at the best it is a sum that poverty-stricken Italy can ill afford.

Various minor cures have been suggested, but the obvious and only effective remedy would be to differentiate between the larger and smaller communes and limit the powers of the latter. In place of this simple principle, which has solved the difficulty in England, the Italians have an irritating and cumbersome system of bureaucratic checks. The Prefect is a nominee and officer of the Crown. In the great majority of communes it is only since 1896 that the Syndic has been elective, and he is still not only executive officer of the commune, but a Government official, who during his three years of office can only be removed by permission of the Prefect or for "serious reasons of public order." Neither Prefect nor Syndic can be called to account except by his superiors, or sued save by permission of the Crown—a principle which, however general outside Anglo-Saxon countries, is a grave and standing threat to public liberty. The Prefect and the Provincial Junta have large, and, to a considerable extent, discretionary powers over the resolutions and finances of both Communal and Provincial Councils. There are very weighty objections to the system. It is intolerable that great cities like Milan and Turin should be subordinated to anything less than a Government Department, that they should be at the mercy of an official who,

---

[3] Palermo has spent £360,000 in building two theatres and £20,000 in building new schools, for which there is an urgent need. It is worth noting that when the Milan municipality stopped the subsidy to La Scala, a public agitation compelled them to restore it.

however capable he may be and sometimes is, is a mere local functionary. Like Government Auditors in England, different Prefects may adopt quite diverse standards, and their powers are much wider than those of our Auditors. Perhaps it is even more galling that a small Provincial Junta, representing a district practically dependent on the great city, should be able to override the municipal resolutions. There is a still graver stumbling-block in the Prefect's small reputation for impartiality. He is not only an administrative officer, he is the political agent of the Government; and his political attributes unfit him for any work that requires judicial qualities. If the Government orders him, as it sometimes does, to act illegally towards a commune, he has no option but to obey. The average Prefect represents the prejudices of the ruling classes, and he has seldom much tenderness for Municipal Socialism in any of its forms. Even a Moderate, like Signor Vigoni, the ex-Syndic of Milan, complains bitterly of the official opposition to municipal reform. At Novara the Prefect last year cut out eight-ninths of the sum appropriated by the municipality for the feeding of poor school-children. At Reggio-Emilia his Council quashed the letting of communal land to a Co-operative Society. Two Syndics were suspended last year for permitting official celebrations of the First of May; a Clericalist Syndic was prosecuted for altering the name of a street from "Settembre XX."[4] Among the many Communal Councils that are dissolved every year, the offence is sometimes that they have a Socialist majority or have made themselves unpleasant to the local Deputy. An Under-Secretary in the Home Office lately had a Communal Council dissolved in his own constituency, for supporting the opposition candidate. No doubt the Prefect's interference is often prompted by the partisan central Government. But it were better that the communes should deal directly even with an Italian Government Department than with an irresponsible and often bigoted official. During the last year or two, as the sense of municipal responsibility has spread, a strong movement has been growing up to free the communes from the tutelage alike of Prefect and central Government, and find a better

[4] The date of the capture of Rome in 1870.

safeguard against extravagance in a municipal referendum. A "Communes' League" is making headway, and though many of the larger cities hold aloof and the Government has done its best to check it, it is likely to make itself felt in the near future.

But crass and obstructive as the whole system is, its main social gravity lies in its financial aspect. It is not that either local taxation or indebtedness reach to very imposing figures. The total local expenditure is £22,000,000, or about 14s. per head; the indebtedness in 1896 was over £54,000,000, or £1. 15s. per head, but the valuable communal properties, largely in landed estates, amount to as much. The evil lies in that the communes have copied the State only too faithfully in throwing the burden of taxation on the poor; and the State has made the problem graver by appropriating sources of communal income for its own benefit, while it is ever imposing fresh duties on them, and its grants-in-aid are hardly appreciable. At present the two chief resources of the communes are a tax on land and buildings (*sovrimposta*), which is practically equivalent to our rates, and the local duties (*dazio consumo*) on food and other articles. The former, though in the rural communes it bears hardly on the small farmer, at all events reaches the property-owners in the towns. By the letter of the law it may not exceed a half of the State's land-tax, unless no other funds are forthcoming to enable a commune to execute its statutory duties; but as a matter of fact, the limit is exceeded in the majority of communes, and in seventy-four it is more than five times as high as the State's tax though perhaps in these cases the assessment is a very low one. While the rates are comparatively free from objection, the *dazio consumo* is a terrible tax on food. Every commune may impose a duty on flour, bread, and maccaroni up to 10, or in certain cases 15 per cent. of value; on meat up to ½d. per lb., on wine up to 1½d. per gallon; on almost every other kind of food or drink (except those mentioned below), on soap, paper, firing, forage, building materials, and furniture up to 20 per cent. of value. The "closed communes" (as a rule those with a population exceeding 8000) may impose in addition duties on sugar up to nearly ½d. per lb., on butter up to ⅓d. per lb., and on paraffin up to nearly ¼d. per lb. In the "open" communes (with

populations under 8000) the communal duty is not severe, and in
1897 amounted to less than 9d. per head. But in the 336 closed communes, with a population of about 6,600,000, it amounted to over
16s. per head. At Genoa it reaches £1. 16s. per head, the heaviest
local duty outside Paris, it is said, in Europe. And its incidence inevitably falls mainly on the poor. Careful inquiries made by the
Socialists at Turin and Palermo go to show that at both places, while
the average working man pays nearly 4 per cent. of his income in
local duties, the tradesman with an income of £220 pays 1.4 per
cent., and the rentier with an income of £750 pays .5 per cent.

Rates and *dazio consumo* make up two-thirds of local income, and
the test of a commune's care for its poor may be found in their relative proportion. On the whole of the country the duties are only
slightly heavier than the rates. But in Sicily the duties are more than
twice, and in the South generally nearly twice as high. At Turin in
1898 the rates reached only to one-quarter of the duties; at Palermo
they are at the present time less than a seventh. The disturbances
of 1898 led to a vigorous agitation for the reduction of the duties,
and to some extent it has borne fruit. A law of that year has offered
certain inducements to the communes to repeal the duty on flour
and bread, and other Bills, going further in the same direction, have
been introduced since then. At Bologna and Bergamo the duty has
been abolished. It is no doubt doomed in all the more progressive
municipalities. But the problem how to supply the deficit is a very
thorny one. Little can be raised from most of the minor sources of
income. The tax on dwelling-houses (*valore locativo*) is too unpopular
to be largely adopted. Where the rates are low, they might be increased with advantage, but in many towns they have already reached
a maximum. The impoverished national exchequer cannot at present
make grants-in-aid substantial enough to meet the case of the large
towns. Some new local tax must be found, whose incidence will fall
on the rich, and on personalty in particular. In England personalty
contributes indirectly to local expenditure through the grants-in-aid
from the Imperial Exchequer. In Italy it contributes nothing. Up
to 1891 the communes were allowed to impose a small income-tax,
and men of different parties have advocated a power to reimpose it;
unless it is made progressive, its incidence on small incomes, as im-

posed by the State, is already too heavy to permit of any increase. Some Socialists have suggested a severely graduated family tax, with exemption for the poor. At present the rich are greatly under-taxed. At Turin a family with an income of £40 pays 4.4 per cent. in all kinds of local taxation, while one with an income of £760 pays 1.1 per cent.

Till this is done, till the wealthier classes are made to feel the burden of local taxation themselves, the *dazio consumo* will be "the *deus ex machina* for every commune that spends more than it ought." It is this more than anything else that has made it so easy for the middle classes to exploit local government in their own interest, and in parts of the South has made it a mere instrument to plunder the poor. The same struggle for existence in the middle classes, which has done so much to corrupt the central government, has led to the creation of a host of unnecessary posts under the communes. In the worst days of municipal corruption at Naples, there was one em-ployee to every hundred inhabitants. Sometimes, especially in the South, there are yet graver scandals. Roads are often made at the communal expense for the benefit of individuals. A Sicilian com-mune levied a special rate on land, but exempted all proprietors of more than forty acres. At Palermo a local official put four sons in an orphanage. M. Laveleye quotes the case of a ruined *grand seigneur,* Syndic of his town and an influential Deputy, who gave official ban-quets and dined at the best restaurants, his caterers not daring to send in their bills. The local government of Naples has long been in the hands of a small faction in league with the *camorra,* which plays into the hands of the companies, to whom it has made over electric light and water and tramways. But there is not plunder enough for all the hungry bourgeois, and the fight for bread gives new zest to the hereditary feuds of the small towns. The spoils are to the victors, and, especially since 1876, each shifting of the communal majority means the loss of office to the friends of the vanquished party. In a Sicilian commune not long ago the party in power paid no *dazio consumo;* and in parts of the island it is a recognized custom that those who are in persecute, and occasionally murder, those who are out.

Where these elementary abuses exist, municipal development is impossible. But in the North, and here and there in the South, healthier conditions prevail. There is considerable interest in Municipal Socialism, and some careful study of its development in England and France. The Socialists and progressive Catholics have wisely recognized that at present the municipalities are the best field for their activities. All the democratic parties favour municipalization more or less, not only in the public services, but in the supply of bread. Even the Moderates in towns like Milan and Bologna are prepared to go a long way. In the taking over of public services, in the improvement of the condition of municipal employees, in the erection of workmen's dwellings, in providing free meals for school children, something has already been done. Bologna has recently municipalized its gas; at Turin there are public baths, and the Socialists and Clericalists here have carried a resolution to insert clauses in municipal contracts for a minimum wage and maximum working-day; Rome has made its Tramways Company reduce the hours of drivers and conductors; Reggio-Emilia has started an information office for emigrants; Cremona is taking over a flourishing cooperative bakery for municipal working. At Venice the Commune has cooperated with the Savings Bank in erecting workmen's dwellings. But the best work has been done at Milan, owing in part to Socialist pressure, but carried out by the Moderate majority, before it was ousted two years ago. All the tram lines belong to the municipality; most of them are leased for ten years, but the Council retains considerable powers of control, and takes a rental of £288 per mile and 60 per cent. of the net profits. This in 1899 brought in £40,000, or 25 per cent. of the capital sunk by the municipality. There are halfpenny trams in the morning for workmen, school-teachers, and school-children; 35,000 halfpenny tickets and 145,000 at higher prices are sold every day. The Council itself works a tram line to the cemetery, and takes hearses and mourners free of charge. The gas mains belong to them, and they have made the private company that supplies the gas reduce its charges by over £50,000 a year. There is a municipal water supply, which makes a fair profit; there are municipal slaughter-houses and public baths, the latter being visited in the summer months by 2000 persons a day. The city is now preparing to quarry its own paving-stones. The total expenses of its government are over £900,000.

11. Autocracy and Popular Pressure for Reform

Shipov Talks with Plehve and Witte (July 2-3, 1902)°

The conversations that Shipov, a zemstvo liberal, had with ministers Plehve and Witte show that, constitutionally speaking, Russia in 1902 had not advanced so far along the road to popular participation in government as most German states had by 1819. The reader should try to ascertain where each of the three Russians stood in the line of development from autocracy and absolutism to self-government, and to perceive what forces in the society each counted upon to support his policy. The student should then contrast the conceptions expressed with those of von Gentz, Donoso Cortés and Bismarck, in order to be aware of the wide range of conservative views about the character of government. After reading Shipov's memorandum, one may have the impression that the three Russians did not fully understand the concepts they were using, or realize that they—perhaps our own thinking is too affected by our knowledge of subsequent events—were working in a stifling atmosphere charged with the menace of explosion. The conversations offer examples of how dominant ideas and institutions can be utterly out of keeping with emerging popular forces.

Plehve: I have wished for a long time to make your acquaintance, Dmitri Nikolaevich. I have always been interested in your public activities and I have always respected them. It grieves me, therefore, that one of your latest actions has made it necessary for me to open our conversation in a manner which is not to my liking. First of all I must communicate to you our Sovereign's order. At the end of

° D. N. Shipov, *Vospominaniia i dumy o perezhitom* (Moscow, 1918), pp. 171-97. Quoted in V. I. Gurko, *Features and Figures of the Past: Government and Opinion in the Reign of Nicholas II* (Stanford University Press, 1939), pp. 691-703.

May [1902] you organized a conference of zemstvo men. This conference discussed the participation of the representatives of zemstvo boards in the Gubernia and Uezd Committees on the Needs of Agricultural Industry. When I had full information regarding the sessions of this conference and the program which it had worked out, I made a report to the Sovereign. His Majesty was quite indignant. He considers this conference an attempt to oppose the government and to deprive the uezd and zemstvo committees, which are now being organized, of representatives of zemstvo boards who had been called by Sovereign order to attend these committees. The Sovereign has instructed me to express to you his disapproval and even displeasure [with your recent activities], and to warn you that if other similar conferences are organized by you, he will dismiss you from your position, in spite of the useful work you are performing, and will deprive you permanently of the right to take part in public work.

Shipov: Must I simply take notice of what I have been told? May I give my explanations to Your Excellency?

Plehve: Please tell me everything that might explain your actions.

Shipov: First of all I must say how deeply sorry and even grieved I am at having incurred His Majesty's displeasure. But I feel it my duty to explain that the discussions carried on by the zemstvo men in question were not of the nature later ascribed to them, as Your Excellency has just told me. The discussions which took place at the end of May in Moscow were not different from a number of similar discussions which have been taking place among zemstvo men even since 1895. It has been a custom among zemstvo men, while attending various official congresses . . . . to gather together in order to talk over and exchange views on the most important points pertaining to everyday zemstvo work. In the course of the year such discussions have taken place at the handicraft congress in St. Petersburg and at the congress in Moscow to discuss the prevention of fires. These discussions were primarily concerned with the problem of the participation of representatives of zemstvo boards in the Gubernia and Uezd Committees on the Needs of Agricultural Industry. I will not conceal from you the fact that in the course of these discussions zemstvo men manifested a certain irritation and displeasure; and naturally so, for they could not remain indifferent to the fact that the government had ignored zemstvo institutions when attempting to solve the very important problems of the needs of agriculture. In this mood of irritation many zemstvo men believed that the representatives of the zemstvo boards should refuse to participate actively in the work of the committees to which they had been invited. This opinion met with objections from others, however, and no final decision on this point was made . . . [at that time]. But in view of the seriousness of the matter at issue, the zemstvo men agreed to meet again and to invite other persons to attend their meeting. Accordingly the question was discussed at a conference in May, when the mood of the zemstvo men was calmer. This conference came to the conclusion that, since zemstvo board representatives were called by the Special Conference—which, on its part, was appointed by the Sovereign—to attend the work of the committees, refusal to participate in the work of the committees would be equivalent to a refusal to comply with a Sovereign order. The great majority of zemstvo men present decided, therefore, that the representatives of the zemstvo boards should actively participate in the work of the committees. The minority . . . accepted the decision of the majority . . . . It should be added that all participants in the May conference agreed that the zemstvo men called to take part in the work of the committees were expected to state officially that they were expressing only their personal opinions, and not the opinions of the zemstvo assemblies, as the latter did not select them to represent these assemblies at the committees and did not give them any instructions. The participants in the May conference believed that the needs of agriculture could not be satisfied by individual meaures as long as general conditions tending to retard agricultural development continued to exist . . . . These conditions, common to all gubernias, were unfavorable to the economic prosperity of the rural population, and they were as follows: (1) There exists no legal status for the peasants; (2) the education of the rural population is insufficient; (3) the position of the zemstvos, called upon to assist agricultural industry, is unsatisfactory; (4) the government's financial and economic policies are not satisfactory, consequently the rural population is overburdened with taxation.

It must be clear from what I have just said, first, that from our discussion we hoped to define how the representatives of the boards could best fulfill their duties in the committees; and, second, that we discussed general conditions unfavorable to agriculture and considered them exclusively from the point of view of the needs and well-being of the population. May I take the liberty of asking Your Excellency to communicate to His Majesty my explanations.

Plehve: I shall report to the Emperor all that I have heard from you, but I do not know whether or not His Majesty will alter his earlier opinion. For my part, as Minister of the Interior, I must tell you that your explanations are not entirely satisfactory. The fact that various illegal conferences have been taking place over a period of several years can in no way justify your last conference, as it cannot be considered legal. It is fortunate that in this instance the sensible majority prevailed over the minority, and that the latter submitted to the decision of the former; but it might have happened just the other way . . . . Organizations of this kind cannot be considered legal.

But let us now end the official part of our conversation. I have wished for some time to have a talk with you. So let us now talk as two private individuals. I believe that you and I have much in common, and I think that we both might belong to the same camp. I do not know that this can actually be, but I am very glad to have this opportunity of exchanging views with you. I am in favor of zemstvo institutions, and I am convinced that no state order is possible unless the public is attracted to local self-government. I do not consider it possible to govern a country with the help of an army of officials alone, and I do not consider zemstvo institutions to be incompatible with our political order. On the contrary, I believe that side by side with an autocratic rule there can exist a broadly developed local self-government. Of course, I cannot help thinking that very often zemstvo institutions are inclined to go beyond the limits of their tasks and that sometimes they pursue political aims. In the program of the May conference in Moscow you discussed the legal status of the peasant class. There is no need for me to say that this problem is not involved in the needs of agriculture, although I cannot deny that a certain connection—probably not as close as you are inclined to think—does actually exist between the two problems. But I think it necessary to say that zemstvo institutions do not even confine themselves to a discussion of problems similar to that on peasant status; very often they raise points which directly or indirectly concern the general political order of the country. You must remember very well that when zemstvo assemblies have been approached by the government on important issues—such as the matter of national food supply in the 'seventies, or of local institutions at the time of Count Loris-Melikov in the 'eighties, and so forth—some zemstvos, such as Novgorod and Chernigov, have frequently failed to confine themselves to the questions put to them, and have actually raised the point of a change in our state order. The raising of political questions by zemstvo institutions, whether it is done directly or indirectly, is contrary to the existing political order, and is therefore not only wrong but harmful in so far as actual zemstvo work is concerned. Although I am in favor of zemstvo institutions and am prepared to aid their development, as Minister of the Interior I am obliged to take into account the tendencies manifest in the higher circles, tendencies which zemstvo institutions must also take into consideration. Moreover, the raising by zemstvo people of questions of a political nature encourages tendencies which are unfavorable to any public institution, and are made use of by those who are opposed in general to the principle of local self-government, and I am prepared to establish the necessary contact between the government and public institutions; but in order that this may be possible it is necessary that zemstvo institutions in their turn do not raise any obstacles. It is my opinion that no state order can remain static and that very likely our political order will be replaced by a different one thirty, forty, or fifty years hence (I ask you, please, to see that these words are not repeated); but the raising of this question now is, to say the least, not timely. Such historical development must take place gradually.

Shipov: Allow me to express to you my deep appreciation of the fact that you have considered it possible and necessary to acquaint me so frankly with your ideas on our local self-government and on

its significance in our political order. If you will authorize me to
acquaint my zemstvo comrades in Moscow Gubernia and other gubernias with the content of your remarks, I am sure that a considerable pacification in zemstvo circles will follow and that the zemstvo
people will await more patiently the unfolding of events. Will you
allow me, Your Excellency, to state my own opinion of the significance of our public institutions?

Plehve: I urge you to do so.

Shipov: I am a convinced supporter of the principle of autocracy.
I believe that the autocratic form of government best suits the Russian people. In my view justice can be done and people can be more
secure under autocracy than under a parliamentary régime; that is,
they can be more secure when the autocrat who is the embodiment
and the executor of the people's will realizes his moral responsibility
before his people than when the will of the people is expressed by
an accidental majority and is often the result of a struggle between
various classes or a consequence of the clash of the class and material
interests. I know that people have different opinions on this matter,
and I consider it my duty to express to you my own point of view.
But when I express my devotion to the idea of autocracy, rightly
understood, I cannot identify autocracy with absolutism. I believe
that an autocratic order is compatible with public freedom. What
is more, I believe that under an autocracy a participation of the public
in local self-government on a wide scale is essential. If an autocratic
sovereign takes upon himself to execute his people's will, it is absolutely necessary that he have direct communication with elected
representatives of the people. Only under these circumstances will
the autocratic sovereign be in a position to learn of the needs of the
people and of local situations in general. The difficulties which we
are now experiencing are due exactly to the fact that no contact or
understanding whatever exists between the government and the
public. I am far from saying that our public is blameless; in fact, I
believe that the reason for the present state of affairs lies partly in
the Russian public. Our public is passing through a period of [moral]
sickness—its mood is one of negation; it has few ideals and no stable
opinions. But if you think that public elements should participate in

our state order, it seems to me you must also admit that it is essential for the government to take measures to train the public for partici- pation in the political life of the country. Now this is possible only if the public is organized and if it is attracted to work in government institutions. Yet the gulf that separates government and public has been steadily widening, and this was particularly apparent after the circulation of the memorandum of the Minister of Finance [Witte] entitled "Autocracy and the Zemstvo." In this memorandum the Minister of Finance argued that local self-government is incompati- ble with the idea of autocracy. It would logically follow from this premise that all those who believe in self-government, and who think it their duty to support institutions of local self-government, liberty and independence, are politically unreliable. Can zemstvo men work in peace under such circumstances? Can it be wondered that they become excited? This memorandum was soon followed by several new legislative regulations which seemed to confirm the supposition that the government had accepted the principle outlined in the memorandum . . . . and that it intended actually and consistently to apply the principle. Lastly, the author of the memorandum was appointed chairman of the Special Conference, which considers it possible to ignore zemstvo institutions while discussing such an im- portant matter as the needs of agriculture, a matter which concerns all sides of public life. In making this point I must add that I do not think that zemstvo institutions alone, especially in their present ex- cited frame of mind, are capable of supplying the Special Conference with the information it needs or of expressing absolutely competent opinions. But the need of ascertaining the opinions of public insti- tutions at the present moment is not so much a question of any practical significance as one of principle.

Plehve: In regard to your remarks concerning the memorandum of the Minister of Finance, I must say that no one among the ministers is more convinced of the need for public independence and the de- velopment on a wide scale of public self-government than is S.Y. Witte. The main purpose of the memorandum of which you speak was to assist in the overthrow of my predecessor, I. L. Goremykin, and also to prevent the application of the statute to introduce zemstvo institutions in our borderlands [i.e. the western gubernias]; and with his stand on the latter point I am in absolute agreement. To our great shame we have not succeeded in creating a situation in our borderlands which would make it possible to introduce local self-government there. I am not an admirer of S. Y. Witte's policy (please do not pass this on either), but in all fairness I must say that he is not against public institutions. I admire his genius, thanks to which our finances are in such good condition. I believe that future generations will be grateful to him for what is now being done for them, although I must admit that it represents too heavy a burden for our present taxpayers. I believe it exceedingly useful, therefore, to stress in the memoranda which the representatives of the zemstvo boards intend to present to the local committees the weak points of our financial and economic policies.

Now to return to what you have just said. I agree with you that, at present, contact between the government and the public is lacking. I admit also the necessity of bridging the gulf which exists between these two forces—the government and the public. But I cannot agree with you that under an autocratic régime contact between the government and the representatives of the people is absolutely necessary. I believe that this contact can be made through the officials of the local self-government. Well-informed men who are well acquainted with local conditions and needs can help to establish this contact. Such people would include, for example, chairmen of gubernia zemstvo boards, as they already enjoy the confidence of zemstvo assemblies and are closely associated with zemstvo work. Of course if local interests were actually to be discussed, then the elected representatives of the people would be needed to defend their particular local interests. But the Special Conference does not intend to study local interests. All that the government now needs is well-informed men. Besides, if the principle of the elective representation is adopted, the next step would be the convocation of the *zemskii sobor*.

Shipov: The people who are elected by the zemstvo assemblies to attend to zemstvo self-government do not always have the qualities of well-informed men. Very often the zemstvo assemblies elect to the boards people who have a talent for practical work but may not have the broad outlook or training required for the discussion of state problems. The representation of [class or group] interests has been always alien to the Russian people, and let us hope will always be so. The statute of 1890 concerning zemstvo institutions introduced class groupings in the zemstvo by differentiating between the nobility, merchants, and peasants in the zemstvo assemblies; and what were the results of this innovation? A decline in zemstvo activity as a whole and an apparent apathy in the public mood. But neither the nobility nor the merchants took advantage of the situation to represent their special class interests in zemstvo institutions. As before, these classes continued to be guided in their activities by moral principles, and continued to work together and use whatever means were necessary to satisfy the needs of the less fortunate masses. I am convinced that when zemstvo men are called by Sovereign order to participate in the work of the government, they will try to represent the Russian land and Russian people as a whole and will discuss the only existing national problem, that is, the problem of Russian local people, and will not defend simply their own class interests.

Plehve: In any case the raising of the question of people's representation is untimely. At the present moment only the matter of establishing contact between the government and the official representatives of local government can be considered. I ask you D[mitri] N[ikolaevich] please do not encourage discussions of this nature or of a nature similar to those of which we spoke in the beginning of our conversation. I shall try to call the chairmen of gubernia zemstvo boards to participate in the discussions in the Ministry of the Interior on various points which these institutions are competent to discuss. . . .

I should like to hear your opinion regarding the significance of the so-called "third element" in zemstvo institutions. The contingent of persons invited by the zemstvo to work for it is growing in number and seems to be continually gaining in significance. Yet the great majority of those zemstvo workers are politically unreliable.

Shipov: Speaking to you quite frankly, I must say that it is my deep conviction that the future of zemstvo work rests with the "third element."

Plehve: You don't mean it!

Shipov: I have already had occasion to say that at the present moment no single group in Russia can pretend to have the leading role, and in the future this role can belong only to those public groupings which come to represent the center of the intellectual and spiritual forces of Russia; these forces, I believe, are mainly concentrated in the "third element." Of course, there are people among the "third element" who are politically unreliable—and such people can be found in zemstvo circles also—but it is hardly possible to generalize on this point and speak of the majority of the "third element" as politically unreliable. Besides, it is very necessary to take into account that the prevailing disquiet and excitement in these circles are largely due to the indefinite position of these circles in so far as concerns their status not only in the state but also in the zemstvo. In the majority of cases these people contribute their labor to zemstvo public work quite disinterestedly.

Plehve: As far as their disinterestedness is concerned, I am quite convinced that these people do not serve their material interests, are satisfied with modest salaries, and work unselfishly. Nevertheless, I believe that they are concerned mainly with political aims, that is, the destruction of the present social order.

Shipov: I repeat that among the "third element," just as among the rest of zemstvo people, there are persons whose aims are those of which you have just spoken. But these persons are exceptions. I have worked for a long period of time among the "third element" in the zemstvo, and I must say that the majority of them are Tolstoians in the best sense of the word, that is, in the sense that they feel deeply their moral duty toward their fellow men and wish to contribute to the general good by serving their neighbors rather than by repudiating in its entirety the principle of state order. Taking this moral ideal as their guiding principle, the "third element" is becoming a significant force, especially in zemstvo work. . . .

The next day I visited the Minister of Finance, S.Y. Witte, in compliance with his wish as communicated to me by M. A. Stakhovich. Witte asked me to tell him in detail of my conversation with V. K. Plehve in so far as it concerned the zemstvo May conference. I gave him an account of my visit to V. K. Plehve and then narrated the opinions of the zemstvo men concerning the participation of representatives of zemstvo boards in the work of local committees on the needs of agricultural industry. After this the following conversation took place between us.

Witte: I am very glad that you were so kindly received by the Minister of the Interior. I may have been indirectly responsible for it. I spoke to V[iacheslav] K[onstantinovich] after he had seen M. A. Stakhovich. Even earlier, when it was expected that the zemstvo men intended to organize an obstruction to local committees, I advised V[iacheslav] K[onstantinovich] to let you alone and said that it was not necessary to exaggerate the importance of this matter. Now that it is known that an absolutely correct move in this matter was taken at your conference, I find still less occasion to attach to your meetings the significance which was given them earlier.

I have your program. I may disagree with you on certain points, but that is merely the difference of opinion and convictions. I must also acknowledge that no part of your program goes beyond the points put before the committees. I find the exchange of opinions which took place in Moscow exceedingly useful for [future] work. There is no need for the Special Conference to instruct the local committees to discuss separate points of your program. What is important is to ascertain locally what are the general conditions that are retarding the development of agricultural industry. The discussion of these conditions at the conference of zemstvo men in May in Moscow made it possible to ascertain the public opinion on this point, and consequently has made quite evident the importance of your conference. As chairman of the Special Conference, I consider it my duty to report on it to the Emperor. Tell me, how do you zemstvo people fare and how do you feel?

Shipov: We fare and feel very badly. The zemstvos are surrounded by an atmosphere of distrust which prevents them from working peacefully: they are continually under nervous strain. Instead of quietly attending to zemstvo problems and being concerned with the best methods of doing our work, so that the people will derive most benefit from it, we are obliged to concentrate our attention on other issues and are continually anxious not to arouse the suspicions of the administration; also to avoid various official difficulties which besiege us everywhere. It is impossible to work well when there is no contact or mutual confidence between the government and the public.

Witte: How do you explain the fact that these conditions have recently grown considerably worse?

Shipov: May I speak quite frankly with you?

Witte: I ask you to be quite frank. We talk not as a minister and a chairman of a zemstvo board but as two private individuals.

Shipov: In that case I shall take the liberty of saying that your widely circulated memorandum on the matter of introducing zemstvo institutions in the western regions has been the cause of much disturbance in zemstvo circles.

Witte: Why?

Shipov: In this memorandum it is stated that zemstvo institutions are not compatible with an autocratic order. From this the conclusion was drawn that all persons who support the principle of local self-government and independent zemstvo institutions are politically unreliable. This argument was bound to widen the gulf between the government and the public.

Witte: My memorandum was thoroughly misinterpreted. It does not include anything which should cause dissatisfaction on the part of zemstvo circles. I do not retract what I said in my memorandum; that is, I continue to believe that the two main points of my memorandum are absolutely correct and that their validity cannot be denied by anyone. The first point is that the drawing of the public into the work of the local government will lead to public participation in the central government. This is an axiom which has been proved by the experience of all countries and by the theories of history. No honest-minded person will deny it. In Russia this opinion is also held by such authorities on political science as Gradovsky, Chicherin, and others. Only our dear Aleksei Dmitrievich Obolensky does not agree with me, but he is always beclouded by some theoretical fantasies and believes that the Russians are some very special people, inspired by some special ideals. Of course, I cannot agree with this point of view; I believe that all peoples are alike: English, French, German, Japanese, and Russians! What is good for one people cannot be bad for others!

Shipov (interrupting): Will you allow me to be true to myself and to say that I disagree with you?

Witte: But does the position of the country grow worse when a representative form of government is adopted? Why then should we also refuse to accept it? I state in my memorandum that zemstvo institutions are a historical fact in the political life of the country and that there can be no question of their repudiation; from that I conclude that the participation of the public in local government will lead to its participation in the central government. As a minister I consider it my duty to tell the Emperor this, so that he may be aware of the direction in which the country is going.

My second point is as follows: If we have zemstvo institutions, and if they cannot be done away with, then they must be allowed to live. But actually they are not permitted to live. That is what I explained in my memorandum. Why are zemstvo institutions displeased, why are they disquieted? Because in their present organization they are left without foundation, they are hanging in the air, so to speak (making a movement with his hand). They are separated from the people by a bureaucratic wall, and they feel bureaucratic pressure from above. Zemstvo men ask to be permitted to make contacts with the lower circles of the population, but they are not permitted to do so. They ask permission to join the government machine, and are refused also. . . . Hence they are tossing hither and thither. It is impossible to prevent the inevitable course of political development, but it is possible to retard it. To this end it is necessary to bring zemstvo institutions closer to the people and to assign to them some important tasks. As Minister of Finance, I do not find it possible to accomplish any important economic measures directed to the improvement of the country's general position unless public forces are attracted to participation in this task. To this end, it is necessary that the zemstvos become popular institutions and that everything which separates them from the population be removed. A small zemstvo unit must be created. If under present conditions zemstvos are given numerous and urgent tasks, they will be so busy with them that they will abandon their political pursuits.

Apart from my memorandum, what else is there that is creating dissatisfaction among zemstvo people?

Shipov: After the issuance of your memorandum there began to appear new legislative regulations which, in our opinion, represent the application of the program outlined in your memorandum. Food supply and distribution is being taken out of the hands of zemstvo institutions.

Witte: Here I must agree with you. Such a solution of the question of food supply and distribution was completely wrong. I had foreseen it and had warned D. S. Sipiagin, but I failed to convince him of it. First I insisted and then, I am sorry to say, I gave in. Consequently the work is being done unsatisfactorily and zemstvo institutions are naturally offended. What else?

Shipov: Next the regulation which set the limits of zemstvo taxation.

Witte: Here again is misunderstanding. There is nothing in this law that should offend zemstvo institutions. To have both local and state taxation unlimited is not considered correct or admissible anywhere. The income of the properties taxed can be taken into consideration only to a certain extent. It is at present impossible to settle permanently the limits for zemstvo taxation, that is, until the evaluation work is done; the law of June 12, 1900, is only a temporary measure. If zemstvo institutions find themselves short of funds for their own needs, as a result of setting the limits of zemstvo taxation, the requisite money will be given by the state. Why don't zemstvos use this source? In the state budget for 1901, 500,000 rubles were allocated for this purpose, but the zemstvo institutions used only 50,000. If 500,000 is not sufficient, I am prepared to raise the grant so that it will actually satisfy the requirements.

Shipov: If it were only a question of setting the limit of zemstvo taxation as you have just said, then, of course, such a measure would be correct and could arouse no displeasure on the part of the zemstvos. But the law of June 12, 1900, does not deal with the limit of taxation as a whole. It simply limits to a certain per cent the yearly increase of taxation and in this way interferes with zemstvo independence and the zemstvo's most essential right, namely, its right to impose zemstvo taxes. At the same time zemstvo institutions abstain from using government subsidies in the present situation from fear of losing still more of their independence.

Witte: What else can you point out?

Shipov: Recently the Special Conference on the Needs of Agricultural Industry, of which you are chairman, has found it possible to ignore zemstvo institutions when attempting to solve a very important question which concerns all sides of our national life.

Witte: I ask you to believe in my sincerity. I spoke at the Special Conference in favor of bringing the zemstvo institutions into this work, but I met with objections from D. S. Sipiagin, who was supported by A. S. Ermolov and the majority of the members of the Conference. I found it difficult even to secure the consent of the members of the Conference to the appointment of the committees in their present composition. I considered it necessary to consult zemstvo institutions on the problem which is being studied by the Special Conference, and I foresaw that failure to attract into this work zemstvo institutions would cause public displeasure. But tell me frankly, do you think that zemstvo assemblies are capable of expressing competent opinions and supplying definite suggestions of the essential points in question?

Shipov: Speaking frankly, I must admit that zemstvo assemblies, particularly as they are now composed, would hardly be capable of fulfilling these tasks. Nevertheless, I believe that it is absolutely essential to them to draw them into the discussions on the needs of rural economy, not so much as a matter of practicality, but as a matter of principle and of political consideration.

Witte: I absolutely agree with you on this point. Recently I received a request from the Moscow Gubernia Committee that the zemstvo assemblies be allowed to communicate their opinions on the needs

of agriculture to the Special Conference. I shall pass on this request
to the Conference, but I do not know whether or not the Conference
will find it possible to have it presented to His Majesty. At any rate,
the first sessions of the Conference will not take place before the end
of October or the beginning of November, when the sessions of uezd
assemblies will be ended and when very little time will be left before
the opening of gubernia sessions.

Shipov: Zemstvo assemblies would be willing to call special sessions
in order to discuss this important matter.

Witte then proceeded to ask me about the arrest of some persons
in Moscow whom the police considered politically unreliable, and
whether many such arrests were made, and what impression they
had had on the public. I answered that these arrests were very
numerous in Moscow, and that in the majority of cases there was
nothing against the persons who were arrested. I gave him several
examples of this, and said that such arbitrary acts aroused the anger
even of those who supported law and order. Witte listened to what
I had to say, then mused: "Yet Sipiagin was a good and honest man,
but unfortunately he could see no farther than this" . . . (as he said
this he closed his eyes). With this our conversation ended.

I returned to Moscow in high spirits after my interviews with the
ministers. I wanted to believe that both ministers truly realized the
necessity of making contact with public forces, that a language of
mutual understanding could be found, and that in the near future a
foundation would be laid for the establishment and consolidation of
contact between the government and the public.

On the basis of what the ministers had said, I believed that both
V. K. Plehve and S. Y. Witte had come to realize, perhaps against
their wills, the force of public opinion and the need for making a
contact with these forces which they could no longer ignore. It was
a significant fact that at the time when Sovereign displeasure was
being expressed to the participants in the Zemstvo conference, both
ministers recognized the organization which aimed at zemstvo unification, accepted it as an established fact and spoke to me as its
representative. Even if their words did not actually express their

convictions, it seemed to me that they saw the inevitability of changing their policies. If bridging the gulf which separated the public from government was not the actual wish of the ministers, nevertheless they considered such a measure essential, perhaps in order to save themselves from falling over the precipice. My usual optimism was particularly strong at that time. But it did not last long.

On my return to Moscow I shared my Petersburg impressions first of all with my comrades on the board, and on July 18 I reported my conversations with the ministers to several chairmen of gubernia boards who happened to be in Moscow, and to several zemstvo men who had participated in the May Conference. I said that it was possible to conclude from what had been said, not only by the Minister of Finance but also by the Minister of the Interior, that the reactionary policy of the government was now to be abandoned and that apparently both ministers were prepared to establish contact with the public and consequently paid no attention even to the views of those who were above them. They wished that this change should take place gradually and that zemstvo institutions should raise no obstacles to the carrying out by them of certain measures. The Minister of the Interior thought that an example of such obstacles could be seen in the zemstvo's insistence on participation in the central government and the Special Conference on the Needs of Agricultural Industry. Since I was confident of the sincere desire of the ministers to establish contact with public institutions, I suggested that we cross out for the time being paragraph four of our May program, and in this way show our willingness to make concessions to the government for the sake of realizing our main task: the re-establishment of contact between the government and the public. My suggestion was approved by those present. We also decided to notify the members of all gubernia zemstvos of this decision, and to send them a report of my talks with the ministers. Six persons among us were given this task.

In this way the program we had worked out at the May conference, with paragraph four excluded, served as a guide for the zemstvo representatives in most gubernia and many uezd committees when they prepared their memoranda for the Committee on the Needs of

Agricultural Industry. In this way, too, these committees were supplied with the public opinion on the problem under consideration, a fact which was very important. But the counter-measures and reprisals which were soon put into effect by the local, and particularly the central administration, clearly revealed that both Plehve's and Witte's statements to me of their benevolent intentions in regard to zemstvo institutions and their readiness to establish contact with the public were, to say the least, insincere.

In accordance with S. Y. Witte's wishes, I outlined in detail and sent to him in the form of a letter dated July 18 a plan by which zemstvo assemblies could, at least indirectly, express their opinions on the questions which were considered by the local Committees on the Needs of Agricultural Industry. S. Y. Witte wrote me a short letter, July 31, in which he said that he found it difficult to solve the question I had raised, without having it discussed by the Special Conference which was to start work again in November. It was apparent that this was simply an excuse. . . . I do not know even now whether or not S. Y. Witte discussed this matter with V. K. Plehve as he had promised to do. At any rate, in July the Minister of the Interior sent to all gubernia and uezd marshals of nobility [who were presiding over the local committees] a circular letter containing the statute of the Special Conference on the Needs of Agricultural Industry and stating that the "participation of zemstvo institutions in the study of separate points of the Conference's program was not considered necessary." . . . A little later—in September—the governors, acting in accordance with another circular from the same minister, warned the marshals of nobility of possible attempts on the part of the zemstvo assemblies to discuss the questions connected with the Sovereign's expression of displeasure with the participants of the May conference, and asked the marshals to take all measures necessary to prevent the inclusion of such questions in the agenda of the zemstvo assemblies; should such questions be included, the marshals were asked to delete them from the agenda by virtue of their special authority as chairmen of assemblies.

I shall not discuss here the repressions and prosecutions suffered by the zemstvo representatives for their memoranda to the local committees. . . . I shall limit myself to mentioning facts which concerned the activity of the Moscow gubernia committee alone. . . . [Shipov then relates how at Plehve's orders measures were taken to prevent the Moscow zemstvo institutions from expressing their opinions on the needs of agriculture.]

Such conduct on the part of the Minister of the Interior so soon after our conversation convinced me that I had been wrong to place my confidence in him. It became clear to me that when V. K. Plehve gave me such a kind reception he was endeavoring to attract me into close collaboration with him, intending to buy me off and make use of me in the ministry as a person well acquainted with zemstvo work. On the other hand, as he considered that I was held in certain esteem among zemstvo people, he thought that my collaboration might weaken the public opposition to the government. When he saw that his plans were not materializing, V. K. Plehve had soon changed his attitude toward me, and decided to take every opportunity to bring pressure to bear against me.

[On pages 233-5 of his book, Shipov gives an account of his reelection, on February 14, 1904, to the post of chairman, for the third time, of the Moscow Zemstvo Board and of Plehve's refusal to confirm the election because of Shipov's "political unreliability."]

12. Government and the Industrial Workers

Clemenceau: *Speech on Strikes, Trade Unions, and Socialism* (1906)*

What should the national government do in the event of a large-scale strike in an essential industry? As Minister of the Interior for France, Clemenceau, a liberal Republican with a reputation for being sympathetic to labor, in 1906 faced this question. In a celebrated speech, given in large part below, he answered an attack by the Socialist M. Jaurès. He stated his policy and explained what action he had taken toward the strikers. He criticized socialism and summarized the legislation that the government of the Third Republic had passed in favor of the workers. The list of laws is impressive, even though the Republican government in France had not aided the workers by social legislation nearly so much as had the German and British governments. Clemenceau's account supplements that offered about the position of trade unions by Carl Legien and that about labor conditions in the pre-union stage by Krupskaya. The reader may wonder whether workers of such diverse material and cultural conditions as those in Germany, France, and Russia, to mention only three countries, can be accurately grouped together under the heading of a proletarian class. He may conclude that the labor problem equally concerned the worker, the capitalist-employer, and the state officials. Each of these groups had to adjust to the other and cooperate in working out relations that would further the achievement of a novel industrial society. How far does Clemenceau indicate that they had come by the eve of World War I?

---

* *Journal Officiel, Chambre des Députés,* June 18-19, 1906, pp. 1994-2012.

M. Clemenceau: Having been personally and directly challenged by the Honorable M. Jaurès, I wish at the outset to render full homage to the noble passion for social justice so gloriously animating his eloquence. With an irresistible impulse of idealism he wishes the happiness of all humanity, and we are witnesses that he would spare no effort to assure this happiness.

To the chords of his lyre Amphion modestly erected the walls of Thebes. At the voice of M. Jaurès a still greater miracle takes place! He speaks and all the historical organizations of human societies suddenly collapse. [Applause.]

Whatever social order man has conceived and attempted, whatever justice he has achieved by suffering, sorrow, and blood since the day when he first issued from his cave to conquer the earth, whatever effort for and progress toward a better life (over millions of years) he has made—all becomes dust, all vanishes in smoke. And if your gaze follows this smoke into the heavens, there is a new marvel, for in sumptuous clouds enchanted palaces rise where all human misery is banished. It remains only to fix them in the air and to set their foundations among us for the work of Genesis to be restored forever. [Applause.]

The social evil which Jehovah could not eliminate from his work will have disappeared. Only the evil of the human condition will remain, and this, I assure you, is sufficient.

Alas! While this magnificent mirage unfolds before the charmed eyes of the new creator, I, vacillating mortal that I am, labor miserably in the plain and in the depths of the valley, struggling with an ungrateful soil which yields me a niggardly harvest. Hence the difference between our points of view which his good will has so much difficulty forgiving me for. [Laughter and applause from the Left and the Center.]

M. Jaurès, indeed, threw me a few bouquets; but I soon discovered that it was to sacrifice me the more pompously on the altar of collectivism after having pronounced upon me a pitiless condemnation. [Laughter and applause from the same benches.]

But I do not pride myself upon being one of these noble and resigned victims who stretch out an innocent throat to the sword of Calchas. [New laughter and applause.]

I argue, I struggle, I revolt, and when M. Jaurès tells me that he has conceived a most unfavorable opinion of my policy, I appeal from this judgment to a superior judge, to this Chamber, exponent of a republican country.

Of what am I accused? M. Jaurès reproaches me in harsh words for having rejected and repressed the working class, not more than any other government in France—as some of his colleagues have said, such as M. Paul Constans and M. Vaillant a while ago—but as much as the majority of the reactionary governments of the French Republic. . . .

Where then did I meet the working class? Was it among those panic-stricken unfortunates who were going to pillage and destroy, ravage the homes of their comrades from the mines? Certainly not. I have met miners; but were they in these acts the legitimate representatives of the working class? Were they at this moment committing acts which you who question me could defend? Certainly not.

I know well—and you have done me the favor of agreeing with me—that I would have considered an armed encounter between the troops and the workers on strike as the worst possible disaster. Surely, if you do not do justice to me in this, I shall do it to myself, and that is enough for me. [Applause from the Left.]

I have done everything in the world to avert this catastrophe. Through difficulties such as no other government has met—I speak of those governments with which you compare me so lightly—through these difficulties, by my presence not only in the strikes of the North and the Pas-de-Calais, but in Paris itself (and I will tell you what I have done in Paris), have you not seen that I have striven to show that not for a moment was I of those governments which allowed the panic-stricken unfortunates to take their chance and walk to their death?

No, I wanted to take a personal part insofar as I could do so. . . .

In the North we had 85,000 strikers, in Paris, 115,000; M. Jaurès said 200,000, but everyone knows that he is generous with figures. [Laughter.]

I believe that I may say that it is the largest known strike—at least in a defined territorial area. In America there was a strike of 250,000 men, but it was spread over the immense territory of the United States. In the city of Paris alone we had a strike of 115,000 men, all of whom, I am convinced, were good men, but who at certain times— and they are to be excused, I hasten to say—were not always in a very peaceful mood. . . .

I arrived at Lens as soon as the strike was called because I had something to say to the strikers which I wanted to say myself. In a hundred articles I have always maintained that the government should not send troops preventively on the strike scene before violence has taken place.

I borrowed the argument from Gambetta, who said: "When the troops arrive after a strike is called, it is first the employer who feels supported."

And Gambetta observed that the impartiality of the government thus found itself compromised in the eyes of the workers. . . . It is this conception of Gambetta's which I wished to apply, and it seemed to me that I should first go to explain it to the workers. I arrived at Lens, where the greatest tranquillity reigned everywhere. I went to the town hall of Lens, and had the honor of being received by M. Basly, mayor of Lens, and by his friends. He was in conflict with the anarchists' syndicate; naturally, he advised me against going to the House of the People, which was the meeting place of the anarchists. I went there all the same; it was to speak to them that I had come, and I said to them—not as M. Vaillant makes me say, with a levity which from him astounds me—that no matter what they did they would not see troops in the city of Lens. It would have been simple folly if I had spoken thus I said to them: "Do you want to have a strike without soldiers? Well! That depends upon you. Nothing is easier; you have only to respect order; you have only not to violate the law." And they answered me: "The presence of soldiers is a provocation; that is what has always brought trouble." Well! I told them: "There will be no soldiers . . . unless by acts of violence you oblige me to repress unlawful acts." And I went farther, adding: "However, as there might be certain ones who are interested in trouble-making, during the night I am going to have soldiers brought in who will be installed in the pits, so that there will be no surprise by violence there; they will not go into the streets but will prevent any violence on the part of the ill-disposed; if the machines were to be damaged, it would mean a loss of several months' work for you when you went back to work."

We agreed on this point, and some of the men told me that if there was any damage done to the machinery in the mines, it would be only at the instigation of the companies.

I left with that, and in leaving I said to the prefect: "There will perhaps be a critical hour. If this hour arrives, call me and I will come again. I will again have something to say to the strikers, though it will be for the last time.

This hour came the day when I received a telephone call from the prefect of the Pas-de-Calais, who told me: "The general and I are surrounded in the Lens railroad station. What is to be done?"

The word "surrounded" was not exact, as M. Basly observed immediately; the truth is that without troops, with only a squad or half a squad, the general and the prefect of the Pas-de-Calais found themselves attacked on the railroad line by a considerable mob of strikers.

I left, and while I was en route the troop commanded by Colonel Schwartz, with an admirable stoicism to which I have already rendered homage, undertook to release the prefect of the Pas-de-Calais and the general shut in the station.

. . . .

The question of knowing what orders were given to the troops has been discussed. You will be given them in a short time when I read you the official documents; but I can tell you now that the orders were to exhaust all the resources of patience; then if the lives of the men were in danger to do what was necessary for self-defense. It is obvious that one cannot send soldiers in front of barricades from which stones are thrown at them or from which shots are fired at them and forbid their charging and defending themselves with the arms provided them. But the orders to have patience were multiplied and multiplied to infinity. It was under these conditions that Colonel Schwartz with his troop, and Lieutenant Lautour at his side, left to attack this barricade. And the last word to the prefect in the presence of the general was this: "Colonel, be patient beyond the bounds of reason, but, if necessary, you have the duty to defend yourself." And the colonel left, having had authorization to use his arms. To his great honor, he charged, and he delivered the station, sword in sheath, without having used arms.

Lieutenant Lautour fell at his side, as well as several soldiers; I have the list; if I wanted to make an indictment against the workers, against those whom you call the "working class" and whom I myself call the strikers of Pas-de-Calais, if I wanted to make an indictment against them, as you seem to be expecting, nothing would be simpler; but I know the excuses of these unfortunates, and I am not on this platform to accuse them.

This done, I went to Denain the next day. The city, it must be said, was in the throes of a riot. I had forbidden the troops to come to get me at the station. The colonel came alone and said to me: "There are streets through which we can pass." So we went by certain streets, and I arrived without difficulty at the town hall of Denain. When I had conferred with the civil and military authorities, it was called to my attention that your colleague, M. Selle, mayor of Denain, was at home. He had been the victim of a fight in the strike and was confined to his bed, and I was made to understand that it was my duty to pay him a visit. I went, and while I was with him a mob of about 2,000 or 3,000 men—with many children, I must say—came to beat on the walls of the house to ask me to go to the town hall and listen to the strikers' delegates.

I spoke from the height of the balcony, declaring that I would not go to the town hall from which I had just come; and in fact I believe that if I had done so, considerable trouble would have resulted. I declared that I would go to the station and that I would receive the delegates of the strikers if they wished to go there.

I had a telephone available, and it was suggested that I call the cavalry to clear the square; for, I must admit, the majority of these men were armed with clubs. It is a great error on which you should clearly enlighten the workers, M. Jaurès, to confuse the right to strike and the right to bludgeon. [Applause and laughter.] In our country when a man goes on strike, he believes that he does not accomplish his work completely if he does not carry out a demonstration—we are well aware how it starts, but never know how it will finish—and if some violence is not exerted on those who are not of his opinion.

I then had the door opened and I went down—there was no great merit in this, I assure you—into the midst of the crowd, which did not receive me badly, although several made remarks to me that were almost as disagreeable as those which I received from M. Paul Constans regarding the difficulties caused by bringing the troops to Denain. . . .

I accompanied the mob to the station at Denain. We sent for the delegates of the strikers; they came, and in this station I participated in discussion, listened to their complaints, deliberated with them for more than an hour. I acceded to several of their requests which were just. I refused to withdraw the troops, because the very existence of this mob with clubs showed that the troops were not useless.

Following this discussion the prefect of the North, by my order, made certain overtures to the metallurgical companies which did not want to maintain relations with the striking unions and which, on my demand, consented to deliberate with them on the next day. I ask you in good faith, M. Jaurès, is all of this from a man who nourishes homicidal projects against the working class? It is from a Republican who is trying to fulfill his duty as Minister of the Interior, charged with maintaining the social order, when the social order is troubled not by the working class but by certain members of the working class, which cannot be the same thing in your eyes.

That is not all. The next day, at the station in Lens, acting on a telegram from me, the directors of the mines met, and I had a conference with them. M. Basly's union, at my summons, met in another room at the station because the employers' group and the workers' union did not want to meet one another. I spent my time going from one room to the other to find a means of reconciliation. Is this the act of a man inspired with hostile sentiments against the working class, a man who desires to curb it, to repress it in its legitimate aspirations? ["Very good! Very good!" from the Left.]

The following day the negotiations continued at the prefecture of Arras. As M. Basly said, the workers met in one room, the employers in another. I spent my afternoon there, and it was during one of these trips which I made from the employers to the workers that I was approached by the private secretary of the prefect, who told me: "M. Minister, Captain Lesage, surrounded in the police station of Liévin, asks your authorization to fire on the mob to free himself."

Gentlemen, I observed the 18th of March at first hand, and that was a terrible day in my life; I do not believe that I have received a more heart-rending blow than when they came to ask me at the prefecture of Arras, not knowing what was happening at Liévin, for authorization to fire on unarmed men.

My answer was what it should have been. I did not wish to give the order they requested of me. I said that Captain Lesage had received very precise instructions which allowed him to use arms only if the lives of his men were threatened, that from the prefecture of Arras I could not judge what was happening on the public square of Liévin, that it was for the captain to judge the situation and to act on his responsibility, but that I advised him again to use the greatest prudence.

The telephone was cut off while I was giving this answer; and two hours later Captain Lesage was able to free himself without having to fire a shot. [Applause.]

. . . .

Ask the Parisian strikers if they have learned the path to the Minister of the Interior. There is not a trade union, there is not a group of strikers who have not been received when they have asked to see me. My door has always been as open, also, to the employers as to the workers.

I received them all, I listened to them all. I held discussions with everyone. I had the disputing parties brought together for talks. At the time of the diggers' strike, which could have resulted in difficulties for the municipal administration in the construction of the subway, I called into my office the prefect of the Seine and his directors, the president of the municipal council, the chairman, all those who could negotiate with the strikers. I must say that after the negotiations, which lasted sometimes until midnight, it happened that strikers, perhaps at the end of their arguments—I do not want to insist on that—left, slamming the door and saying disagreeable things to us. But until that time they had not stopped telling us: "At least we thank you for having received us and having listened to us."

Are those, I repeat, the acts of a man who represses the working class?

You have said to me, M. Jaurés, using a bit of psychological fakery, that I must have become angry when comparing my helplessness to construct the new city with the power of idealistic construction of which you have given proof ["Very good!" and laughter from Left, Center and Right], and that this anger decided me to send the troops against the strikers.

I assure you that I acknowledge myself beaten on this point. I yield before it. Certainly your power of construction goes much beyond even the power of destruction with which you have so well reproached me. ["Very good!" and laughter from the same benches.] No, I did not get angry; I sent the troops only gradually, according to need.

When the outbursts started, I sent a greater number of soldiers, in such a way that the troops were everywhere in possession of the ground which they occupied and were not in danger of being overcome.

I sent some more; and the more I sent, the more it proved that they were necessary and that I should send still more until the riot was broken. [Applause from the Left, Center, and Right.]

While the strike was following its course in Paris, other conflicts broke out at many points, and my attention was focused upon various places where there were disturbances. There was not a single one of these disturbances reported and personally investigated on which a contradictory report was not presented to me either by the plaintiff or by the prefecture of police.

Often I recognized that a striker was right; sometimes the policemen were punished.

.   .   .   .

It happened that the prefect of police, to whom I give credit and who conducted himself admirably in these circumstances, said to me: "Be careful, M. Minister. If we continue thus, our agents will no longer arrest anyone." I answered: "Let us continue to decide in favor of those who are in the right, and against those who are wrong." And the prefect of police obeyed.

Is that the work of a man who is fighting against the working class? It should be clearly understood that all of us are here to pursue our education in liberty and that the men entrusted with repression have special need of that education. Could I be behind each of them? Could M. Lépine? Assuredly not. Their education had to go forward; I had to formulate my instructions to M. Lépine so that he could express his own to his agents; I had to conceive a strike theory.

I will read you my instructions in a while if you will listen to me. M. Lépine talked the matter over with me and understood my ideas, and he had to make himself understood by his agents. All of this took several days, during which the events of which I was just speaking took place. . . .

I thought that my acts would speak for me. I thought that the hour would come when I could explain myself face to face with my adversaries. This hour has arrived, and I use it to say first that I consider the persecutors of the workers to be those who encourage them in the foolish idea that the interests of the working class are being promoted wherever there is a lawless worker. The persecutors are those who indicate to the workers that their enemy is the very government charged with maintaining order in the interest of society, since only within the framework of law can the emancipation of the workers come about. [Lively applause.]

I say that those who act against the working class are those who encourage it to believe that it can do no wrong and that it may oppress its oppressors.

I say that those who act against the working class are those who delay its education [new applause], for education is not a matter of words, as pedagogues profess and believe; education is achieved by deeds. We shall know that the working class is worthy to govern in a democracy, as you desire and I myself heartily wish, on the day when it will freely conform its acts to the justice it demands.

This is the kind of education which it must be given. Nothing is learned from speeches; if speeches could teach the world, the Sermon on the Mount would have been realized long ago. [Laughter and applause.]

I attempted to contribute to this education; and as I have said before, M. Jaurès, neither at Lens nor at Denain did I find you as a fellow-laborer. I am not complaining, of course, but yet with the great and legitimate authority that you have, if your word had been joined with mine, who knows how many dangers might have been avoided?

Here now is my dispatch on the subject of strikes to all the prefects of France:

I remind you that in case of a strike in your department, your double objective should be to safeguard equally the liberty to work and the liberty to strike.

It is not at all my desire that troops of infantry or cavalry appear on the premises of the strike as a preventive measure when the strike is called, as used to be done.

You should bring these troops to the vicinity of the strike, concealing their presence as much as possible, and make advance arrangements for their prompt requisition.

If order is menaced, they should arrive during the night to occupy either the mine head or the workshops, workyards or factories, where they will remain concealed. Only if order is disturbed will they be put into action.

To insure order and carry out the patrols which appear necessary to you, you will first of all call up the total strength of the *gendarmerie* at your disposition, and if it is insufficient, detachments of cavalry. You should always tell me exactly what arrangements you have made, what effective strength you intend to employ, and how you will distribute it at the points to be protected, should the occasion arise. Please acknowledge the receipt of these instructions.

And here finally are the instructions of the prefect of the North to the troops. I cannot read all of it to you, as it is too long a document; but I want to read the beginning and the end to indicate its character. These instructions were drawn up with my approval.

The troops have been requisitioned:
1. to protect the liberty to work;
2. to protect people and property;

3. to reestablish and to assure public order compromised by the uprising.

The right to strike is a right which all workers may freely exercise; it is permissible for them to try to persuade their comrades by public meetings, private conversations, or visits to their homes; in short by all the legal means of regular propaganda. But, under the pretext of striking, acts of pillage and riot are committed everywhere. The government is firmly resolved to put a stop to this. It has called on the army and counts upon its prudent and firm help.

I believe it necessary to define with the greatest possible precision in what manner and to what extent I expect cooperation from the troops which I have requisitioned.

First: Protection of the right to work. All workers who go to the pits or to the factories to work, alone or in groups, will be vigorously protected against all those who prevent them from so doing by intimidation, threats, or violence. Those who are forced to join the strikers or to carry flags or handbills should be immediately set free. The arrival and departure of these workers should be closely supervised and protected.

Second: Protection of persons and property. The pits, the factories, the dwellings of engineers or employers, and the houses of the workers who work will be especially protected against attack by the rioters.

And to conclude:

The government relies upon the prudence and the firmness of the officers and soldiers. The latitude which I give them by covering them with my personal responsibility, far from inciting them to excessive action, will lead them, I am certain, to face with coolness, moderation, and courage any event which may take place.

. . . .

It is not the working class against whom I take action but those who pretend without mandate to speak in its name and who try to put me in the wrong when they know that I am right.

. . . .

M. Jaurès, speaking of the dispatch of troops as a result of the great anger that he supposed I experienced because of my powerlessness to erect my own city of God, said that the fight between the two unions had been the pretext. M. Jaurès knows better than I do that the matter does not concern two unions but two parties, the Socialist party to which he belongs, and the anarchist or syndicalist group. He has thus defended the syndicalist group apropos of May 1. It is nonetheless true that the fight between the two parties in the North was bitter.

In an article M. Basly called the anarchists apologists of burglary; he complained that we called in unattached libertarians ready for anything to destroy what they call in their picturesque language "the syndicate of money-guzzlers." With all due respect, it was the Socialist group.

It was M. Basly who wrote this under his signature, and in the journal *Réveil du Nord*, which is one of the principal organs of the Socialist party. [Denials from the extreme Left.]

M. Feron: It is the custom to repudiate journals, depending upon the circumstances.

M. Clemenceau: I did not say these words by chance. I am a friend of the director, the Honorable M. Delesalle, and I have always considered him . . . .

M. Delory: This journal is not controlled by the party. [Exclamations.] . . . .

M. Clemenceau: Does that mean that the members of the party are not independent? What do I hear? Are there Socialists who are not independent? And it is a Socialist who says that! [Laughter and applause from a great number of benches. Interruptions from the extreme Left.] I know that catholic Socialism has its protestants. I have no qualification to express my opinion on the more or less great orthodoxy of M. Delesalle.

M. Jules-Louis Breton: Delesalle is an excellent Socialist!

M. Alexander Zevaes: He was the assistant to M. Delory.

M. Clemenceau: Well, gentlemen, listen to the manner in which this excellent Socialist spoke of the anarchists and the syndicalist party, in an article entitled "The role of the Anarchists."

It will be said that the band of wretched anarchists sent to the Pas-de-Calais by the General Confederation of Labor did not miss a chance to sow seeds of discord among the miner proletariat and traitorously attacked from behind the brave representatives of the miners' union while they were resisting the exploiting and lying companies.

The referendum had destroyed them, and at the same time that the Levys and the Sorgues fled toward Paris, the Monattes and the Delzants went elsewhere to try their talents for spreading propaganda, arson, burglary, and mendicity by force.

Today, thanks to their arousing inflammable pitboys (these are the young laborers who work in the mines), inexperienced young people, the formerly calm emancipation movement of the miners has taken on the aspect of a disordered invasion by barbarians; because of the exhortations of this horde of bandits, sent to the North by the union of unnamable professions of Paris, public sympathy bit by bit is turning away from the miners' strike; and simultaneously, to the great joy of the companies, the government has had to issue orders for repression such as it refused at the beginning. . . .

They have never lost an opportunity of fomenting violence and pillage in the ranks of the strikers every time the delegates of the workers went to Paris to try to carry the day in conferences with employers; they tried, these strangers to the mines, to set off angry explosions whose results compromised success, as on the day when the employers, gathered in Paris to seek a solution, abruptly separated at the news of the pillage of the Reumaux house.

We know what they are worth from the undeniably true report presented to the municipal council of Paris which states that the enormous subsidy turned over to them was diverted from the workers' organizations and used for the most vicious orgies and the most disgraceful debaucheries.

And further:

Deprived of official money, they have nevertheless found the means of spreading in France millions of stamped propaganda handbills advocating desertion before the enemy; this represented an expense of at least 300,000 francs.

Where did the money come from? Is it necessary to ask, when on the eve of elections the forces of reaction need to frighten the hesitant and timorous electors?

[Applause and laughter from the Left.]

In reading this text I thought of the reprimands which the Honorable M. Jaurès has loudly addressed to me from this tribune. He reproached me—these are the textual words—"with having without serious evidence stamped with moral decay and suspicion the chiefs of the workers' movement on the eve of the great legal combat that the workers were going to carry out." This was apropos of the conspiracy.

Allow me to say that it seems to me that the court at Béthune, in arresting the men accused by the Socialist journal *Réveil du Nord,* has done nothing but follow the information given it by the Socialists . . . .

M. Jaurès: Then you make arrests on the strength of a newspaper article?

M. Clemenceau: Your interruption astonishes me. I have arrested no one; that is not in my power.

M. Jaurès: I speak of the court at Béthune.

M. Clemenceau: You interrupt readily, but I am going to answer.

I had no one arrested. I transmitted to the public prosecutor of the Republic the police dossiers which were in my possession, and I feel no embarrassment in telling you that these dossiers had nothing in particular against the members of the General Confederation of Labor. These men were arrested nevertheless. I learned of their arrest, as you did, from the newspapers. But when I find that the accusation of having distributed money in the strikes in the interest of reactionaries, which is the reason for these men's arrest, has been mentioned in the principal Socialist journal in the North, I have the right to turn toward you who reproach me for having stamped these same men with disgrace, and say to you: "It is you who have first stamped them with disgrace in accusing them of being bandits, the apostles of burglary and pillage, and in affirming that they had received considerable sums from reactionary sources."

I know very well that after the election harmony was preached, and at Saint-Mandé a great reconciliation was proclaimed. The answer of the anarchists was not so pleasant as could have been expected. M. Griffuelhes himself . . . .

M. Walter: He is not an anarchist!

M. Clemenceau: M. Griffuelhes himself, speaking of this banquet (and specifying that he went there only with a press card) wrote jokingly: "I went there to receive arrows; I received flattery." And he concluded: "A strong desire for reconciliation comes from the declaration given at the banquet. The desire is certainly not shared in the workers' groups."

M. Edouard Vaillant: Reconciliation is nonetheless very necessary.

M. Clemenceau: That is possible, but I have shown that your advances were not very well received. In any case, the assertion of M. Jaurès that the fight between the Socialists and anarchists had served as the pretext to send the troops is not justified by any known fact . . . .

I must speak of the first of May since you have done so. You said that we took precautions which were not justified.

These precautions were clothed with an exceptional character. There was a moment when, all alone in my office objectively seeking where my duty lay, I asked myself if I could take the responsibility of calling all those troops whose presence in Paris has justifiably shocked you, or if I could run the risk of abandoning the capital of the Republic to the terrible emergency which seemed to menace it. I asked myself the question. There are moments in life when one must have the courage to make a decision and abide by it. It seemed to me that I would seriously fail in duty to my country, to Republican ideas, if at such a time I made Paris run the risk of riot, the consequences of which were not easy to predict.

I know very well that you have told me there was no danger. But these things are said at the tribune afterwards when there is no longer any danger. [Applause from the Left and Center.] As for myself, my responsibility obliged me to state my position beforehand. And if peace had been disturbed, if the uprisings had taken place with all their consequences, you would perhaps have been the first to turn against me, not in public but in private conversation.

I shall tell you the reasons which decided me; I shall tell you honestly.

The demonstration of the first of May was organized by the General Confederation of Labor; and the Socialist party, according to

M. Vaillant, was only the collaborator. With the General Confederation of Labor it is quite natural that in such circumstances we attempt first of all to find out what it represents and what it desires. Here is an article by M. Lagardelle, one of the most prominent theoreticians of the revolutionary syndicalist movement, appearing in the April issue of the *Mouvement Socialist*:

The parliamentary socialists and the democrats strive to conquer the state. . . .

This casts blame on you, M. Jaurès.

M. Jaurès: We are blamed on many sides!

M. Clemenceau: Then feel sorry for me! [Laughter.]

The revolutionary syndicalists attempt to disorganize it [the state], the better to destroy it.

There is a program of action.

We thus understand the difference in their action with respect to the unions of civil servants and the strikes of employees or workers of the state.

Doubtless for the unions the struggle against the state as employer also aims to improve the situation of the workers and employees, which it utilizes. But this is only a subordinate activity. To ruin the hierarchy, to break the tie of dependence which binds it; to wipe out the tremendous power of the major instrument of bourgeois domination: that is the meaning of the war which is beginning against the state and its subordinates.

The anti-militaristic and anti-patriotic propaganda also has no other meaning. It is neither the fear of military service nor the fear of war which is at the basis of it. The objectives are the breaking up of the army and the destruction of nationalism, for the institution of the army and the sentiment of nationalism are the foundation of the state.

I thus found myself in the presence of a tremendous demonstration, organized by men who profess the theories which you have just heard, by the men whom you have defended in the tribune in unmistakable terms. You have told us that they "prepared a movement completely free from any order of violence." Those are your own words.

Gentlemen, listen to the words supposedly free of any order of violence, as M. Jaurès alleges.

The delegates of the building workers—painters, laborers, masons, roofers, locksmiths, etc., who at present form a total of 25,000 strikers—met at 8:30 in the great hall, which was full. They established their claims anew: an eight-hour day, with eight francs' pay, weekly rest, and suppression of competitive wage bargaining. The meeting ended at midnight with the vote for the following agenda of the day.

The striking building workers—painters, laborers, masons, roofers, locksmiths, etc., numbering 3000—assembled for action in the great hall at the call of the building committee, after having listened to the various comrades in regard to the tactics for united action; they pledged to go at six o'clock in the morning to permanent headquarters to form mixed patrols with the mission of ferreting out all the renegades of every trade guild by every possible means.

If this is not violence, I really do not know what it is! [Laughter and applause from the Left.] When an organization which declares that its aim is the destruction of the state organizes an action like the one just indicated and declares that it is going to win by every possible method, even a modest bourgeois minister may be a bit suspicious.

That is what happened to me; I became suspicious [Laughter], and the result was that there were some arrests on the Place de la République. You have said 800. Your figures usually need to be revised.

There were 650 persons arrested; we found 33 former convicts and 76 foreigners; that makes about 100 demonstrators who would have done well not to be there. [Laughter.]

M. Jules Coutant: And is that the fault of the workers?

M. Clemenceau: It is because it was not the fault of the workers that I defended the workers against you. [Applause from the Left and the Center.]

M. Jules Coutant: It is quite the contrary.

M. Clemenceau: You needed victims, and as you had none, you invented them. I read in *Humanité* that one had died; I read in *Humanité* that there were some dead which I was hiding.

I shuddered. The Minister of the Interior hiding cadavers! In the words of *Humanité*:

The Minister of the Interior put the last straw on the heap of his baseness, in creating a plot where deceit vies with hate to discredit the organization of the General Confederation of Labor and malign its comrades, such as Griffuelhes and Lévy....

These are the men of whom M. Delesalle spoke so well a while ago.

He has the cynicism to present as workers the worst enemies of the working class; to crown this arbitrariness, he delivered Paris, placed in a state of siege, to the rage of Lépine, who, on the first of May, had his day of blood. Eight hundred arrests were announced, but who will count the wounded? Who will count the dead who are hidden?

[Interruptions from the extreme Left.]

When they write that some are dead, they should at least prove it. It was never verified because it could not be verified.

Now, before concluding this report, which I have tried to make as clear and unbiased as possible, I must observe that it was inevitable that the Socialist party should reproach me and the government for the acts described, since its principle is to defend not the working class but the workers' agitators, no matter who they are and what they do.

This is what M. H. Bracke, one of the most distinguished members of the University, was writing so kindly in *Humanité*.

Has there ever been a more reactionary ministry in the full sense of the word than the one containing the cream of the radicals, the Sarriens and the Clemenceaus, and even an erstwhile Socialist, M. Briand? Has there ever been one more hostile to the working class and to socialism?

Better informed, we perceive that the radical bourgeois will stop at nothing, not even at the suppression of universal suffrage, to retain political power, the bulwark of his economic exploitation.

[Laughter and exclamation from the Left and Center. "Very good! Very good!" from various benches of the extreme Left.]

"Very good," you say; I have just demonstrated the contrary by facts, and I defy you to refute me on this point.

A bit farther M. Révelin, still in *Humanité,* reproached us for having governed France as Russia was governed before the Duma. Do you still approve? And to crown all, the same M. Révelin as a supreme insult reproached us for being prejudiced in favor of order.

This prejudice I have. Here is a point of conflict on which it is possible to reason. I fear no idea, I retreat before no proposition, if it is open to reason; but I say that (especially if you who interrupt us have conceived the ambitious projects which you revealed the other day) you have no less need for order than ourselves, for nothing may take place in any society if legal order is not maintained. [Lively applause from a great number of benches.]

I believe that I have demonstrated the inanity of the reproaches which were addressed to me by the Honorable M. Jaurès concerning the acts of my administration with respect to the strikes. . . .

It remains for me to show the contradiction of ideas which has dictated our evaluations of the two sides.

First of all, concerning the strikes themselves, I find myself in opposition to the Honorable M. Jaurès on a fundamental point.

I am of the opinion that any man who needs to work and who finds work has the right to work. [Applause from the Left, Center, and Right.] I am of the opinion that society and the public authority have the duty of assuring him the exercise of this right.

Eighteen months or two years ago I had a discussion on this point in the press with M. Jaurès, and this is how I know the singular opinion which he holds. M. Jaurès denies this right without any ambiguity. He wrote: "I admit that I am stupified when suddenly M. Clemenceau invokes the supposed right of workers to replace other workers on strike as a form of the right of livelihood."

And continuing his demonstration, my adversary observes that while I seek to assure the worker's right to a living, I put obstacles in the way of the strikers' exercise of the right to a living. That is certainly your argument, my dear colleague.

I take the liberty of answering that the comparison is not an exact one. First of all, I do not pretend to suppress vital competition with universal laws. I believe that vital competition is a phenomenon which should be regulated by social laws. I believe that as much as possible we should attempt to correct through law the fundamental evil in nature, but I believe at the same time that this is possible only if we establish our social organization on the only solid basis, the inalienable rights of all men.

The situation between the two competitors is not equal. It is inexact to say that both fight for the right to livelihood. The worker who demands work, who seeks it and finds it, fights for a living, to assure his own life and that of his family. But we cannot say that the worker who abandons his position for a higher wage fights for his life . . . .

I maintain that the worker who goes on strike is moved by the idea of bettering his situation, and this is legitimate.

But it often happens, as in the strikes in Paris, that the workers who go on strike to improve their situation are obliged by unforeseen circumstances to return to work under the conditions that they had disdained. It is thus inexact to say that they were fighting for a living. Moreover, one day in my office in Paris when I was talking with construction workers and excavators on strike, a great number of them told me in the presence of witnesses (the prefect of the Seine, the directors, and the president of the municipal council, who could support my testimony): "We do not fight for an increase in wages; we are fighting for a shorter work day."

That is legitimate; they are exercising a right. I am not their adversary. Insofar as I could, I helped them in this demand. But I ask you, gentlemen, the question which I vainly asked M. Jaurès in the press.

I have seen certain strikes at first hand in which my sentiments were on the side of the strikers; but I cannot hide the fact that I found myself terribly embarrassed when I heard a man who was reproached for presenting himself for hire answer: "You go on strike in order to gain a higher wage. We do not say that you are wrong. Only, we have wives and children and we have earned nothing for three months. Work is offered us. Will you nourish our little ones if we refuse?"

If you refuse the right of the employers to replace the workers on strike and the right of the free workers to present themselves for hire, as M. Jaurès clearly did in his thesis, what will you do with the women and children whom you will deprive of nourishment? That is the question which is asked; I await the answer and well believe that I shall wait for it a long time. [Laughter and applause from the Left and the Center.]

It is unnecessary to say that in his answer the Honorable M. Jaurès has explained to me that this conflict will not exist in his future society; he has indicated to me in broad outline, as he usually does, under what conditions the conflict may be alleviated. I do not disagree, but as we still need six months to know the conditions of the future city, I demand that I be told today how to resolve the conflict which confronts me in the present social plight.

I have naturally tried to inform myself about this matter through the election programs of the Socialist party. I have here a great number of manifestos—all very interesting, incidentally, some demanding reforms which I would be prepared to adopt for my own—but I addressed myself especially to the program of the Socialist party. The Socialist party published a program for the use of all its candidates, as is perfectly natural. . . .

Here is what I find in the manifesto. First of all, a statement of doctrine: "The only way of freeing yourselves is to substitute collective property for capitalistic property." The consequences of this affirmation are not reasoned out; the means of bringing this substitution about are not proposed. But at least the affirmation of the principle is contained in the declaration.

What reforms are to result from this affirmation of principle?

Here they are:

Limitation of the working day to eight hours.

Extension of the right to organize to all the employees of the state, the department, and the commune.

Social insurance against all the risks of unemployment and sickness.

Progressive tax on income and inheritance.

Return to the nation of the monopolies which capital has made its greatest fortresses.

Voting by list with proportional representation.

This is very bourgeois. [Laughter and applause from the Left and the Center. Noise from the extreme Left.] And when, after explaining his program, M. Jaurès asked me what mine is, I had some difficulty resisting the temptation to answer: "You know my program very well—it is in your pocket, you have taken it from me."

M. Jaurès: Very good. We take note of it.

M. Clemenceau: What! Really! You take note of the fact that I support the eight-hour day in principle!

From the extreme Left: In principle.

M. Clemenceau: Naturally in principle. I do not believe that any among you can run the risk of economic catastrophe by suddenly replacing the eleven-hour day with the eight-hour day. As for myself, I would not be ready for it now, but I am ready to orient myself as soon as possible and even immediately toward this final result, the eight-hour day.

You will observe that I believe in the progressive income tax. But, M. Jaurès, your interruption astonished me. In 1885 in this Chamber you voted against the progressive income tax, and in the name of this changing infallibility you reproach me for having remained faithful to all my convictions! I say then that the practical program is ours; I am for the return to the nation of the great monopolies which are held by private industry today. But we must understand each other. . . .

If you think that I meant to say that at a moment's notice I am prepared to bring in a bill to force the return to the nation of all the monopolies held by private industry, you are mistaken; that is not my idea. I meant to say that I am ready to start the work today—for example, by purchasing railroad companies.

Some of you amuse yourselves in the corridors by saying that we have forgotten to mention in our statement this or that reform, and that it is a document of no importance. M. Jaurès has spoken of it to me with consummate disdain. I accept his disdain calmly; however, if someday we need to organize—I do not say a collectivist society—but organize for socializing the means of production to a greater extent than exists today, at least we shall have posed the question leading to this result, depending upon the advance in education and culture of the workers. ["Very good! Very good!" from the Left.]

Is this then nothing? You have not said a word about it. The result is that when we compare the two manifestoes we discover that the ministerial declaration is notably more socialistic than the collectivist declaration. [Applause and laughter from the Left.]

That said, I should recognize that you have formed an organization before whose principle my bourgeois mentality would retreat. I want to speak of what we call unification. Unification is in my eyes nothing more than a sort of catholicization of Socialism. [Applause from the Left.] It is the seizure by a governing oligarchy of the workers' democracy trying to emancipate itself.

It is the revival of the old mentality which, to assure the triumph of the Gospel, made the promise of liberty the most terrible instrument of authority against the free development of the individual. [Applause from the same benches.]

. . . .

It was not only the Catholic Pope who was vanquished at the last elections; it was the spirit of oppression, the spirit of dogmatism, in all walks of life. The dogmatic spirit was driven from the purely intellectual domain, and it is not we who will seek to reestablish it in the economic dogma.

Finally we get to the questions which were raised on this tribune by the Honorable M. Jaurès. I ask his permission not to discuss at this time the reasons which brought him to adopt his famous decree of expropriation against all citizens.

First he judged the present society on the basis of two sets of figures, one showing extreme wealth, the other extreme misery. I find the criticism a bit improvised; a complicated organism may not be judged by two sets of figures. In addition, I find that so serious a discussion is not appropriate in an interpellation because it demands too much elaboration. It cannot be avoided, it must take place; but it must take place fully, and I hope that, thanks to M. Jaurès, as soon as he has completed the bills with which he is now busy, we may initiate a debate worthy of this important question.

I cannot tell whether this organization will be an organization of progress, as M. Jaurès believes, or one of regression. I will only point out that he was seriously mistaken when he gave us to understand implicitly that the demands which the agrarian party made on the Duma in Russia were entering into his conception. Quite the contrary; there is social property which is in the process of disappearing and individual property which is in the process of being created. [Applause. Interruption from the extreme Left.]

Finally, against his conclusion I have an argument, *a priori* assuredly, but one which does not seem to me without value. It is that he brings us an absolute. He totally abolishes human misery, and this is a considerable accomplishment; but once he achieves his organization it seems that the evolution of man and human society is stopped. I am suspicious of a system which does not leave room for indefinite evolution of the human spirit.

M. Paul Constans: No one ever said that!

M. Clemenceau: I know very well that M. Jaurès did not say it in these terms; he could not say it, for he has too scientific a mind for that; but it is a question of knowing whether such would be the result of his conceptions; that is what we shall discuss. Individual property has evolved; it will evolve for a long time. The relationship between individual and social property will not remain as it now is; and when I say that, I say nothing that cannot be approved by any one.

It is agreed that this is an open question. We shall discuss it as much as you like. Meanwhile, I wish especially to point out the sophism upon which you have established your right of expropriation. You have shown us both extreme wealth and extreme poverty; you have promised us that in six months you would find the way to remedy the evil you point out, and you have concluded: "Would not this society be better, more just and more humane? Reply before casting blame!"

M. Jaurès, there are more than two hypotheses to submit to this Chamber. Between the actual society of today and yours, between these two extremes, there are an infinite number of social conceptions which may be developed. [Applause.]

You make the task too easy. Admitting even that your criticisms are well founded, that present society is as bad as you say it is (and I am not one of those who pretend that it is very good, as you well know), admitting further that the society which you have conceived is actually realizable, you have omitted a point worth considering. We have more than a choice between the society which you promise and the society of today. There are an infinite number of other hypotheses; and later when I speak to you of the projects of social order which this much-abused middle-class Republic has nevertheless brought about, I shall show you without difficulty that the social régime of today is not the social régime of twenty years ago, that it is indeed founded upon absolutely different principles.

Therefore I cannot admit that you give us the choice only between these two hypotheses, and that you have said the last word when you say to us: "Beware! If you do not accept my project, the human mind is bankrupt." M. Jaurès, it is not necessary to confound the bankruptcy of the human spirit with the bankruptcy of M. Jaurès's spirit.

Is this type of ideal society which you offer us new? Who has not dreamed of a future society? I am myself capable of dreaming of it with you whenever you please. Only it is not yet demonstrated— the demonstration will be your responsibility later—that this dream is worthy of discussion by a deliberative assembly. An ideal society has been the eternal subject of the dreams of all Asia. Jesus, the last of a long line of prophets, because He thought that He could achieve an entire new order of humanity through words, . . . saw His direct disciples reestablish in His name the society of violence and blood against which he had protested. . . . . Your victory will be no greater than His. I do not believe that the day will come when you will have temples throughout the extent of civilized lands, in which your words will daily be repeated to a throng of eager listeners. You will certainly not have greater success than this, and when you note that the material success of Christianity resulted only in the moral failure of the words of Christ (that is to say, in a state of affairs which only reproduced the old order which He had wished to destroy)—allow me not to wish you this victory.

America is still full of mystic societies which seek the realization of the City of God on earth. I have often heard in the forests of New England predictions which are not appreciably different from yours.

In 1848 the Republic believed itself to be on the eve of the great day, and we saw many builders of future cities. Recall the sessions of the Constituent and Legislative Assemblies when Pierre Leroux, Victor Considérant, or Proudhon explained, as you will do soon, plans of the new society. A great number declared themselves in favor of the suppression of individual property. Long before them Thomas More, at the beginning of the sixteenth century, had condemned individual property in terms more definitive than any you could employ. These men were not inferior to you. Where are they now? Search for them. [Interruptions from the extreme Left.]

You have replaced them, as others will presently replace you.

The truth is that we must distinguish two things in the social organization, man and environment. Theoretically, it seems more simple to reform the environment; everyone goes about it with pleasure. But if you consider that the environment of the social organization is and can be only the product of successive human conceptions, you will see that to modify the social organization arbitrarily without bothering to find out if man can adapt himself to it can lead only to the most marked disorder. [Applause from the Left.] Thus, even for those who hope to remake the social organization, everything first of all goes back to the elemental reform of the individual. [New applause from the same benches.]

If you reform the individual, if you apply yourselves principally to the reform of human personality, man will know for himself how to find the form of organization which suits him, without bothering about your theories or your prophecies. They certainly cannot be realized, because you cannot, unless you are yourself a divinity, anticipate the result of human evolution.

I do not know the results of your labors, but I can say that when you have given us the form of the new society, you will have to present a new man to live in the society created in your brain. I say that the present-day man is not the one you need to live in that society. This morning, in a remarkable article by M. Paul Boncour in *L'Aurore,* this question was put to you; and since you will reply to me, I beg you to answer it:

I ask M. Jaurès whether he sincerely believes that at the present moment or even in a long time the working class will be in a position to assume the entire direction of industrial, agricultural, and commercial affairs.

. . . .

You pretend to construct the future at once; we construct the man who will construct the future, and we thereby accomplish a phenomenon much greater than yours. We are not constructing a man expressly for our city; we take man as he is, from his primitive caves, still perfectly hewn in his cruelty, in his goodness, in his egoism, in his altruism, in the pathos of the evils he endures and the evils to which he himself subjects his kind.

We accept him as fallible, contradictory, groping toward he knows not what better things, and we enlighten him and broaden his mind. We mitigate the evil and fortify the good in him, and we liberate him. We lead him, after he has departed from the bestial régime of force, toward a greater and greater approximation of true justice. [Lively applause from the Left and from various benches of the Center.] And every day brings a little more unselfishness, a little more nobility, goodness, beauty, a little more new power over himself and the external world. It is our ideal to magnify man, the reality rather than the dream, whereas you enclose yourself and all mankind with you in the narrow sphere of an anonymous collective absolutism. We place our ideal in the beauty of individualism, in the splendor of the expansion of the individual in a society which rules him only to develop him more fully.

Cannot this ideal withstand comparison with yours, over which it has the advantage of being already on the way to realization?

You have pathetically invoked the example of the great revolutionaries and have said to us: "Do as they did and make a decision."

By the controversies which we have had in the press, you can see already that in what concerns me I have made my decision, not against you but against your ideas, and in favor of the society sprung from the French Revolution.

The development of this society of the French Revolution in justice and liberty is our entire program, and this program we oppose fearlessly to your authoritative and dogmatic conceptions.

The French Revolution never desired the things you wish for; it wanted the direct opposite. It drew up the Rights of man, proclaimed the liberty and sovereignty of the individual and, having proclaimed it, began to realize it. And you, only slightly emancipated even in revolt, seek a return to dogmatic unity at the moment when it is bankrupt.

And now you have spoken to me of my program of 1885!

If I were in your position, the answer would be only too easy. In 1885 you were against social reforms; and, because we have demanded social reforms, in the name of the changes which have taken place in your mind you ask that there should be no changes in mine. Well, by chance I have not changed. We have shown the people this ideal, the elimination of the wage-earner classes; personally I have not deviated from that, and I do not see why I should change, although I do not, as you do, decree this elimination by yet-unknown methods. We all know that we have simply outlined what should be achieved by increasing cooperation—by the fusing, I could say—of labor and capital, and this cooperation should be possible as the education of the workers increases, a goal toward which we all strive.

I believe that is clear enough. And if I apply this principle to the present situation, what do I see?

We have just had elections which were a great triumph for the republican idea. What was the significance of these elections? First, that the Republic was forever beyond all challenge and that the anti-republican parties were decreed henceforth impotent, that they must renounce forever the reestablishment of the old régime on the ruins of the Republic. This is the first conclusion on which we should be unanimous—including even these gentlemen [the Right]; I expect no less of their good faith—to abide by the verdict of the electors. You see that there is no protest. . . .

The second point is that the nation desired the clerical question to be settled in the future in the liberal sense. Clerical oppression has run its course. . . . . Privileges from the state for the profit of the Church have disappeared; the Church will no longer obtain from us, the French state, the financial cooperation or the privileges on which up to now it has insisted.

These are the two points which were brought to light by the verdict of universal suffrage.

Finally, it was again clearly indicated by our examination of the movement which has taken place in all factions and of the nuances of opinion within the Republican party, that the greatest hour for social justice has arrived. Here is the third point on which the elections threw light.

As to methods, everyone knows that the electors have left to us the care of finding them, and it could not be otherwise. These methods are not new; they are known. I found them a while ago in the Socialist manifesto; and I found them before in the declaration of the Government. I do not have to go back to them.

And now you tell us that this declaration is weak. I admit it willingly. But I point out to you that we are a Government for but a day and that you are deputies for only four years, and if in four years we could realize half this program, I myself would feel great pride.

While you have not yet succeeded in making your collectivist program live, we on the other side have succeeded in making our program of social amelioration live. And here I must declare that I protest against a phrase of M. Jaurès, who spoke to us of the most numerous class, the workers' class, "to whom almost everything has been refused."

M. Jaurès, I need revenge. I am going to inflict upon you the reading of these reforms which the bourgeois Republicans have carried out in favor of the working class, to whom you maintain that we have refused almost everything.

This document is a bit long, but the longer it is the more you will be disconcerted. And yet I have kept back a great number of the laws. . . . .

First, to do it well, we must mention all the laws of liberty, for these are in my opinion the foundation of the laws of social emancipation, and all the laws of education, for without democratic education social emancipation would be only a word. The working class could rise to power for a day; it would soon see itself hurled to the bottom of the abyss. There is nothing durable in the reforms which we are making if we do not manage to perfect, to improve man and to kindle in him the democratic spirit.

Consequently I have the right to put in the first rank of social reform the laws of liberty and the laws of education . . . . I read:

Law of April 9, 1881, creating the postal savings bank.

Law of February 16, 1883, making labor inspectors responsible for the execution of the law of September 9, 1848, regarding the length of the work day for adults.

M. Dubois: At twelve hours!

M. Clemenceau: We shall soon be down to ten hours. Has this been done without the legislature?

Law of March 21, 1884, authorizing the creation of the professional trade associations.

. . . .

Law of July 20, 1886, reorganizing the retirement funds for old age.

Law of July 24, 1887, for protection of badly treated or morally abandoned children.

Law of December 27, 1890, on the contract for hiring and on the relationship between the agents of the railroads and the companies (first, establishing for workers, without clearly fixing it, a right to indemnity in case of firing by an employer hiring without a set length of time; second, prescribing the submission to ministerial approval of statutes for aid and retirement funds of the railroad companies).

Law of July 20, 1891, creating a labor office.

Law of November 2, 1892, on the work of children, minor girls, and women in industry. Duration of the working day: ten hours for those up to sixteen years of age, eleven hours for those from sixteen to eighteen. Night work is prohibited for males less than eighteen years old and for women of all ages (although it is authorized in factories operating continuously, for a maximum of seven hours out of twenty-four). Weekly rest and rest on legal holidays. The age of entry of children into mines is raised to thirteen years, and underground work remains prohibited for women. The departmental inspectors become state civil servants, and inspection personnel is made up of eleven divisional inspectors and ninety-two inspectors of the departments.

Law of December 27, 1892, organizing optional conciliation and arbitration in matters of collective dispute between the employers and employees.

Law of June 12, 1893, concerning the hygiene and security of workers in industrial establishments.

Law of July 15, 1893, organizing free medical help.

Law of August 1, 1893, modifying the law of July 24, 1867 on associations and notably facilitating the formation of cooperative societies by lowering the nominal established issue price of stocks.

Law of June 29, 1894, organizing compulsory retirement assistance for mine workers, completed by the law of July 16, 1896.

Law of November 30, 1894, on low-cost housing, completed by the law of March 31, 1896.

Law of January 12, 1895, protecting the salaries and the small wages of workers and employees against attachments.

Law of April 5, 1898, a new organic law for societies of mutual aid.

Law of April 9, 1898, on work accidents.

Three decrees of August 10, 1890, on work conditions in markets, passed in the name of the state, departments, communes, and charitable establishments (Millerand decrees). These decrees assure the workers in state enterprises: (1) weekly rest for the employees as well as for the workers; (2) protection against the competition of foreign labor; (3) a minimum salary; (4) the limitation of the working day. These arrangements, compulsory for government employment, may be recorded in the account book of the work of the departments, communes, and charitable establishments.

Decree of September 1, 1899, reorganizing the superior council of labor. This council is reorganized on the basis of election. The employers' and workers' members, previously chosen by the minister, are to be elected in the future. The employer members will be elected by the Chambers of Commerce and the councils of the Conciliation Board, and the worker members by the unions and the councils of the Conciliation Board.

Law of March 30, 1900, amending the law of November 2, 1892, on child labor and the labor of minor girls and women in industrial establishments (Millerand-Colliard). This law established the ten-hour working day from April 1, 1904, for children and women as well as for adults working on the same industrial premises. Previously the law of 1892 fixed eleven hours for women and ten hours for children. Adults referred to in the law of 1900 were subject only to the law of 1848 and could consequently work twelve hours.

Law of July 1, 1901, on the union contract. This law, which established freedom of association, was utilized for the formation of associations by certain professions which remained outside the application of the law of 1884 on professional associations.

Law of March 14, 1904, relative to the hiring of employees and workers of both sexes and all professions. This law permits the abolition of the employment agencies, solving a question confronting the Assembly, since 1898.

Law of May 9, 1905, amending the law of July 8, 1890, on the delegates for the security of mine workers. This law assures to the miners' delegates compensation sufficient for them not to have to work in the mine to assure their existence.

Law of June 29, 1905, relative to the duration of work in the mines. This law gradually reduces to eight the hours of work in the mines.

Law of July 14, 1905, relative to obligatory assistance to the aged, infirm, and incurably ill.

Law of November 14, 1905, supporting the opening of supplementary credits by virtue of the budget of 1905, with the intention of reducing the working day in state industry.

Law of April 2, 1906, concerning the participation of the delegates for the security of the mine workers in retirement and assistance funds.

Finally, workers' retirement, which was voted by the Chamber and which is at this hour before the Senate.

Well, gentlemen, I ask you at what previous time such legislative work has been accomplished in twenty-five years. I do not claim that we could not have done better. I do not claim, either, that there is not much more left to do—but I say that when such an effort has been put forth by a series of Republican assemblies, you do not have the right to turn upon them and say that they have done nothing or almost nothing for the working class. [Applause from the Left and the Center.]

I have not claimed this group of social reforms for the benefit of any party in this Chamber. ["Very good! Very good!" from the Left

and Center.] I have not said a word to this effect, and it is very easy
to answer me about what I have not said.

I have said before, and I repeat, that this bourgeois organization
which you reproach as incapable of giving any satisfaction to the
workers has answered you in advance by facts. It is nothing to vote
these laws. One still has to be capable of living them, of putting them
into practice, and of deriving the sum of benefits which they contain.
When a parliament such as this one comes from the electoral meetings and puts social questions first on the agenda, it gives an assur-
ance of its good will which you could not fail to recognize. Yet you
receive it badly and respond to it badly when you say that you can
do nothing for the working class through the present organization.

Your accusation is in words; our answer is in facts.

Even in your party, men are found who have my point of view;
one of those here, M. Varenne, an integral Socialist, I believe, has
recently written in the *Lanterne* an article from which I take the
following passage: "As to the social transformation which doubtless
is the long-range"—he does not ask for six months—"but unchanging
aim in our platform, it is not enough to announce it and to erect the
image in the foreground like a kind of scarecrow. The essential
thing is to prepare for it by education and organization."

That is the whole program of the Radical party.

My answer is: "If this education comes in its own time when the
proletariat is enlightened and disciplined enough. . . ."—that is what
I said myself when I said that it was not enlightened or disciplined
enough at the present time to find a place in the organization which
you have conceived—"when the proletariat is enlightened and disciplined enough to assume the responsibility for directing production,
the transformation, matured by long evolution, will take place without violence and almost without effort. Political democracy will develop freely into social democracy. By universal suffrage, which con-
secrates the political sovereignty of the citizens, the workers will
have conquered economic sovereignty."

I have, incidentally, another authority to cite which is no less
important. It is perhaps yet more important than yours; it is from a
man whom you know well, M. Edouard Bernstein.

M. Bernstein, in a book entitled *Socialism théorique et la social démocratie practique,* has written the following:

What social democracy will have to do for a long time yet instead of speculating on the great catastrophe of Karl Marx, the revolution, is to organize politically and prepare the working class for democracy. It must fight for all the reforms in the state suitable for raising the working class and for transforming the institution of the state in a democratic sense. . . .

["Very good! Very good!" from the extreme left.]

There is nothing there which is not simply a statement of the republican doctrine.

. . . And as I am absolutely convinced that it is impossible to skip the periods important in the evolution of peoples, I attach the greatest significance to the present duty of social democracy, to the struggle for the political rights of the workers, to the political activity of the workers in the interest of their class, as well as to the work of their economic organization. It is in this sense that I once wrote that for me the movement is everything and that what we usually call the final aim of socialism is nothing.

Here we are in full agreement. The final aim of socialism is nothing, and the movement in the direction of social justice is everything. It is one of your own who said it. It is the program of the Radical party, and I believe that I may say that it is even the program of the Government.

We do not need you to recall our program to us; we do not need you to ask us whether we mean to apply it. Our only reason for being on these benches is action, action which dispels uncertainty, which does away with weakness, which rules and disciplines the will of the strong.

By action we have overcome the oppression of the Church. By action we shall suppress the economic oppression of existing privileges. We have delivered the soul, and we shall deliver the body.

Have confidence, man of little faith who misunderstands the work of the Republic in which you were a worthy laborer. Because we do not think alike, is that a reason to hate one another? That is a residue of religious mentality.

For myself, I have no dogmatic condemnation to pronounce against you, and it makes little difference to me that you have this or that idealistic conception of the future. If we understand each other we can collaborate in common political action in this Assembly, on the condition that your collaboration be sincere and complete, excluding the idea of abandoning us to budgetary expediency.

You say that the moment is decisive for the Radical party. We know it! But allow me to say that it is also decisive for the Socialist party, which is not entirely a unified party in spite of what you say. It is necessary to make reforms or resort to revolution. We have made reforms. We wish to continue them. Are you ready to aid us? Let us work together!

If you are willing to work with us, here is our hand outstretched to you and your electors.

If not, let each follow his own destiny. Without you we shall try to be adequate to the task. We shall bravely carry the day's responsibilities, and for the rest we place ourselves before the enlightened impartiality of the Chamber and the republican country. [Lively and prolonged applause from a great number of benches on the Left and in the Center.]

13. Nationalism in Action

Program of the Society of National Defense
[*Narodna Odbrana*] (1911)*

This statement, issued as a pamphlet by the Executive Committee of the *Narodna Odbrana,* a Serbian patriotic society, explains not the theory but the organization and practice that nationalists developed in order to achieve their objective. The theory of nationalism becomes more understandable in this form than it does by the exposition of abstractions alone. It is evident from the pamphlet that in order to be able to aggrandize their own nation, nationalists must arouse the people to a sense of identification with this aim. As in the case of imperialism, nationalism can succeed only when internal conditions in a country or nation are closely related to foreign policy. The program of the *Narodna Odbrana* could with appropriate change of names be duplicated in the writings of nationalists in any country. It is preferred over the statements of Fichte, Mazzini, Barrès, and others because, like Hitler's *Mein Kampf* of a later period, it states a program that was actually being carried out.

I. The Rise and Activity of the First *Narodna Odbrana*

The Serbian people has endured during its existence many difficult and bitter days. Among these days is September 24, 1908, when Austria-Hungary illegally annexed Bosnia and Herzegovina. This day can be compared to the worst days of our past. It was especially painful for the Serbian people in that it came at a time when more

* *Narodna Odbrana Izdanje Stredisnog Odbora Odbrane* (Belgrade, 1911), translated into German and printed in *Die Kriegsschuldfrage* (Berlin, 1927), V, 192-225.

fortunate peoples had already completed their national unification and had created large states, and when culture and freedom were presumed to be at their peak.

At such a time Austria-Hungary oppressed along with other peoples several million Serbs, whom she penalizes and seeks to alienate from us. They may not openly call themselves Serbs, and may not adorn their homes with the Serbian flag; they may not trade freely, cultivate their soil, erect Serbian schools, openly celebrate the feast of the patron saint [Slava], and may not sing of Kossowo or of Prince Marko and Milosch Obilitsch. Only such a state, only an Austria-Hungary, could carry through such an annexation.

1. Rise of the Organization and Its Program

The annexation of Bosnia and Herzegovina not only aroused Serbia and Montenegro; it aroused all Serbs, and one can say all of Europe as well.

After the proclamation of annexation the situation was such that it appeared impossible for the matter to end peacefully. The continual rolling of drums, the shrilling of trumpets, and the daily proclamations and excited telegrams indicated war. Our land was in feverish excitement, meetings were held everywhere, and the people demanded war. In these serious times and under these conditions the *Narodna Odbrana* [Society of National Defense] was founded. The aroused nationalistic masses asked that words be translated into deeds, that all necessary preparations for war be made, that the great national will to sacrifice be organized. Overnight, simultaneously in various cities, through the will and determination of the national masses, the *Narodna Odbrana* was created. Urged on by the will of the people, the leading citizens came together in Schabatz, Nisch, and other places to found committees of defense. Such a committee was chosen also in Belgrade early in October, 1908, at a meeting of leading citizens assembled at the City Hall. Because it was for the defense and protection of the people, the committee was called the Society of National Defense, or *Narodna Odbrana*, as in the previously mentioned cities.

The full committee was set up at the session of October 8, when the program which had been worked out by the provisional committee was adopted. In accordance with this program the *Narodna Odbrana* accepted the duty of:

1. arousing national consciousness, spurring it on, and strengthening it;
2. taking up the registration and acceptance of volunteers;
3. building volunteer branches and preparing for armed action;
4. collecting voluntary gifts of money and supplies in kind for the realization of the goals;
5. organizing free corps for special and independent guerrilla warfare, arming and training these groups;
6. carrying out defensive action for the Serbian people in every direction.

Even before the *Narodna Odbrana* was organized, similar committees had grown up in the interior of the country. Therefore, in order better to carry out its purpose, the *Narodna Odbrana* proceeded to get in touch with the others and to found more groups wherever they did not yet exist. The founding and the program of this committee were so enthusiastically greeted by the people that within three weeks the entire country was organized like one group under the slogan: "All for the Serbian people and the fatherland!"

The enthusiasm was so great that committees were founded in places where no one had expected it. In less than a month, 223 committees and almost as many branch committees were set up in cities and villages. Committees were founded even abroad. In part this was done on the initiative of the Belgrade committee; but even without it, in a good many places outside Serbia either committees or branch committees were founded to work for the goals of national defense.

2. The Work of the Organization

It was a pleasure to see with what speed the work of these quickly organized groups for national defense advanced. The various committees competed with one another in their eagerness to act. Each strove to show itself the most useful for the country and for the common cause. Especially to be praised are the committees of

Schabatz, Nisch, Tjupraja, Valjevo, and Vranja. So it was in Serbia itself, and so it was everywhere abroad where committees and branch organizations were set up.

A. ACTIVITY FOR PREPARING THE VOLUNTEERS AND FREE CORPS [*Komitadschis*] AND ASSEMBLING MATÉRIEL CONTRIBUTIONS

A major task for the *Narodna Odbrana* was the reception of volunteers and the collecting of matériel to outfit them. The people participated gladly in fulfilling both needs. Those who did not belong to the army came forward as volunteers, and anyone who could not be taken into the volunteers gave his last penny. In a short time an entire army of volunteers assembled, and there was likewise a mass of matériel. Single districts and counties placed at the service of the committees large sums for outfitting volunteers (e.g., the county of Smederevo contributed 20,000 dinars); others at the instigation of the committees bought machine guns for their regiments, and so on. Almost everyone made material sacrifices.

In addition to Serbia, volunteers from Austria-Hungary, Russia, Germany, Bulgaria, Turkey, Greece, Italy, and other countries, mostly from Italy and Russia, came forward. There were not only individual and small groups but even mass volunteering of two thousand or more people. For example, a telegram came from Moscow asking permission for 10,000 volunteers to set out for Serbia, and a similar one came from Italy. Many of the communications are very interesting. A lawyer who, as a youth in 1876 had been a volunteer on the Drina, wrote in his letter: "Even if I am gray and in my sixties, I feel strong enough to stand with right against injustice. I know the plains of Matschva, the waves of the Drina, the mountains of Herzegovina; and my heart will not leave me in peace until I make my way there again with my rifle in my hand and, if fate wills, spill my blood and the blood of your enemies." To develop the volunteers into fighters, the central committee and the committees in the interior organized student and guard companies in which active and enthusiastic officers of the Serbian army led the drill, although they were forbidden to do so. Many officers preferred punishment to remaining away from these practice hours.

From the ranks of the volunteers the *Narodna Odbrana* organized a free corps of some hundreds of men. These men were drilled in the use of weapons and explosives of all kinds, so that they could do the enemy the greatest possible harm whatever means might be chosen. These were to be the vanguard of our regiments and to spread fear and confusion in the rear of the enemy. . . .

The guerrilla group also had a laboratory for all kinds of explosives, where carefully chosen free corpsmen practiced making bombs and other explosives so that later they could operate on the battlefield by themselves. It was wonderful to watch the twelve young men (mostly university students) make bombs and bomb ingredients in a narrow cellar room in a little Serbian town. What a joy for them when they succeeded independently in finishing a bomb! Not the demands of their studies or the threat of the police or the warnings of their parents were able to separate this inspired group of young Serbs, who gathered like falcons from all sides to prepare themselves for the most desperate deeds in behalf of the Serbian cause. To this end they, with their master Pepek, refused to be deterred from their work in the cellar room until certain events which were unfortunate for us brought affairs to an end. . . .

B. THE OTHER ACTIVITY OF THE *Narodna Odbrana*

The *Narodna Odbrana* worked zealously and successfully for the spread of patriotic feeling and for the awakening of the people to Austria's hostile role toward Serbia. There were conferences, lectures, and meetings held for discussion of the Serbian question, especially the issues of the Serbian territories, the Serbian nation, and the injustice done to Serbia and the entire Serbian people by Austria's annexation of Bosnia and Herzegovina. To this end special newspapers also were established as organs of the *Narodna Odbrana;* in every printed line they encouraged the people and aroused them to the struggle against Austria. The following newssheets especially stood out: the *Narodna Odbrana* of the Schabatz committee, *Prve zrtue* [i.e., *The First Sacrifices*] of the Valjovo committee, *Singjelic* of the Nisch committee, *Momcilo* of the Pirot committee, *Narodna Odbrana* of the Negot committee, and many others. Among these publications also belongs a book written by the central committee, *On the Austro-Hungarian Army*, of which 8,000 copies (in two editions) were circulated.

The righteous cause of the Serbs had its protagonists in all the newspapers of the capital. The papers spread propaganda in favor of the ideas of the *Narodna Odbrana* and supported it at every opportunity; it is under great obligation to them for their activity in lightening tasks and overcoming obstacles. The *Narodna Odbrana* was similarly active abroad through its committees and branch committees.

Many of the more prominent European newspapers represented very vigorously the righteous cause of the Serbs and accused Austria-Hungary of greed. Some Italian, English, French, and Russian journals in particular spoke out in our favor.

A great part in these successes was played by other organizations which similarly placed themselves at the service of the *Narodna Odbrana* in winning public opinion in their countries over to the Serbian cause. Here we are in debt especially to the patriotic organizations of Italy, in the first place to the Garibaldians, whose leader General Garibaldi personally offered to come to our help at the head of his numerous Red Shirts. We must also emphasize especially the relations with our American brothers, who have joined together there for activity in behalf of the Serbian cause. The committee which they founded issued a call to action, addressed to all Serbs in the United States, and grouped them around the central committee with its strongholds in New York and Chicago. The *Narodna Odbrana* kept in touch with this committee by letter and through confidential agents. Our cause in America was excellently represented by the Serb newspapers, *Balkan* in Chicago and *Borba Balkana* [*The Struggle of the Balkan*] in St. Louis.

3. Cessation of Activity

The entire activity of the *Narodna Odbrana*, which can only be briefly sketched here because of lack of space and because not all of what was done can be discussed, came to an end with the recognition by the Great Powers of the annexation of Bosnia and Herzegovina. Serbia then stood alone. In the interest of her further existence and influence she had to await events, to sheath her drawn sword in order to be able to use it with greater force and skill at the first opportunity.

The Belgrade *Narodna Odbrana* expressed to all volunteers, corporations, and individuals its thanks for their support, dismissed the guerrillas, stopped the gathering of matériel, and entered upon a reorganization of its program. The branch committees were maintained and with them began a new activity—to prepare the country, strengthen our society, and make us all ready, in case of a new opportunity like the annexation, to unroll the old red flag of war with greater strength and success.

The transition of the former *Narodna Odbrana* to its new activity and the nature of the new activity are discussed elsewhere in detail. It is our duty here to thank again, with all our hearts and in the name of the holy goals which the old organization served, all those who supported these by their activity and to urge them to devote themselves with similar earnestness to the new activity. The new work occupies only an interim period of preparation in the service of the same ideal toward which the new *Narodna Odbrana* is striving with the same slogan as before: "All for the Serbian people and the fatherland."

II. THE NEW CONTEMPORARY *Narodna Odbrana*

1. Its Rise and Program

The annexation of Bosnia and Herzegovina showed, first, that Serbia is not ready for the struggle which circumstances are pressing upon her and, second, that the struggle which Serbia has to carry on is much more serious and difficult than we thought before the annexation. Recognition of these facts brought the leaders of the *Narodna Odbrana* to the decision not to dissolve the organization but to preserve it. The annexation was only one among several blows which our enemies had already directed against us or which were still to come. So that a new attack would not catch us so unprepared, it was necessary to arm—to work. The lack of preparedness which appeared at the time of the annexation was not only "military"; it was of a general nature, involving our whole nation. Today's army is the people. Guns and cannon alone do not make a good army. To succeed in war our people must understand about arms, must know that (and why) it has to go to war; it must have a strong national consciousness; it must have a high cultural level; it must not be split by internal enmities; it must be healthy and strong economically. All this is necessary in order to wage a war with rifles and cannon. In addition there is still another consideration: *What we call peace is no peace, since this time of peace is a condition of war.* Among peoples competing with one another, there is never peace. The struggle by force of arms represents for them only a moment when everything is staked on one card in order to force a solution. Until then the weapons are their schools, books, commerce, industry; there is need for care of the health and physical well-being of the people, for national progress in every direction.

The one like the other—the preparation for war as well as the struggle in time of peace—must be the concern not merely of the state but also of each individual and of all society. In addition to giving our resources to the state because of the law, we must all work for it of our own free will. All peoples think and act in this way, and we must too; we must do so all the more in that we are in a much more difficult position than any other people. That we saw this and understood it was in part the result of the surprise we felt at the annexation. It gave the impetus for the first organization in behalf of national defense, and its results produced the second such organization, since naturally these considerations influenced the direction in which the new activity of the *Narodna Odbrana* developed. The activity advocated by the new organization aims at the preparation of the people for a struggle in all phases of national endeavor in accordance with modern demands. First of all comes the strengthening of national consciousness, the development of physical culture, improvement of the economic and physical welfare of the people, its cultural betterment, and so on, insofar as the individual and society can and must cooperate with the state in all these respects. So much in general for the program of the new *Narodna Odbrana*. In the following sections we shall emphasize and clarify our new activity in more detail.

2. Bringing Together the Forces Working Voluntarily among the People

When at the end of the annexation crisis we had to decide about the need for a rebirth of the *Narodna Odbrana*, we knew that the main lines of our thinking were nothing new; even before the attempts at annexation in Serbia justified our aims, there was indeed much which was accomplished. There were groups for furthering physical culture, for promoting the economic progress of the people, for improving the health of the people and awakening them in general; also, other humanitarian organizations grew up, as well as various patriotic societies for women.

The members of all these groups, as well as many persons working independently, developed a notable readiness to sacrifice; nevertheless, the men of the *Narodna Odbrana* had to admit, as they set new goals for the organization, that these groups and persons had not reached the expected success in their work, especially because they were separated, were without connection with one another, and were working without mutual cooperation—even frequently were at odds as, for example, in the feud between the Sokol and the Duschan Silni [two large Serbian gymnastic organizations].

All work for the development of physical culture, for the improvement of the health of the people, of the cultural and economic level, of the national consciousness, and so on, has the same goal—the strengthening of the people and of the state. A separation can and should be allowed only insofar as the division of labor demands it; otherwise, all our efforts should go forward simultaneously, mutually supporting each other and led by the spirit of accepted, united endeavor.

The *Narodna Odbrana* recognized this, and therefore it emphasized the drawing together, the cooperation and organization of all the effective forces among the people, in order to bring about voluntary sacrifice as one of the first points on its new program.

Divided, dispersed, shattered—in its external and internal relations—our people were surprised by the annexation and powerless to offer resistance. The annexation taught us what is needed, namely unity of the people, unification in thought and action in the widest sense of the word. There had been enough feuds and splits. There must be unity in every possible field of endeavor. The *Narodna Odbrana* used its understanding of the general situation first of all in the area of voluntary activity, where it could most easily be put into practice. In addition to arousing private initiative, its goal was to give to our uprooted society a living example of the love and harmony in which we too could work together.

The local committees of the *Narodna Odbrana* which had existed at the time of the annexation were perfect for this purpose. At that time they already included voluntary workers in various branches of their activity. In the spirit of their task, the committees were now to be broadened and the individual volunteers still outside them were to be assimilated in order to secure unity of ideas and harmony of operation. This was done, and so today virtually all committees of the *Narodna Odbrana* are places of discussion and understanding and of the mutual fraternal effort of all voluntary workers for the Serbian people's welfare. Where they are not yet so they must become so; all branches of private activity are equally welcome. Every single part of this activity can advance in each locality only if the entire locality becomes eager for this advance. One of the first tasks of the *Narodna Odbrana* is to encourage every opportunity to advance, relying upon the combined efforts of all workers in every locality.

3. The Struggle Against Political and Personal Dissension

The organization was conscious of the fact that Serbia's previous failures or slight successes had been caused in large part by the fact that our national social order (not only in Serbia but in all the Serbian south) is at odds with itself in every respect, and especially in the political field. As a result of this situation, the *Narodna Odbrana* could not stop at gathering the forces of private initiative; it had to wage war upon the enmities existing generally among us. By bringing together the various members of each committee, it had done away with feuds in a part of public life; but that was not enough. To stop these feuds meant improvement on the one hand at the expense of more significant considerations on the other hand. Certainly a harmonious and unified private initiative is a great gain; but it is a temporary one if we retain our former enmity in other respects, especially politically. That is one point, and secondly there is a great question as to whether private endeavor can be unified at all if there is no diminution of civil strife elsewhere. In a word, the one does not go without the other. A true Serbian Society of National Defense must take up the struggle against the civil strife among us Serbs in general, and first of all against political enmities as the strongest and most dangerous of all.

In the committees of the *Narodna Odbrana,* men from all political parties work together as members. Many of them are among the most influential and respected of politicians within their own parties. The struggle of the society against feuds, therefore, is not directed against the parties or against politics. The *Narodna Odbrana* knows well that the life of the state and of the people today is not possible without political parties. Thus it does not make war against political parties. What it is fighting is the exaggerated exploitation of our political life, the use of politics for selfish individualistic ends—insofar as this occurs, and we all know that it does occur.

What the *Narodna Odbrana* demands and preaches, what it fights for and will fight for, is patience in all aspects of our life and the subordination of the individual to the commonweal. The society is of the belief that all of us, including all political parties, must serve only Serbia and the Serbs; it maintains, that is, that the fatherland and the Serbian people as a whole must come before everything else, even parties.

According to the view of the *Narodna Odbrana,* political parties must function not as hostile camps for destroying political opponents, but as groups competing in the service of the country and nation. The society wants to maintain and enhance that spirit of love and reconciliation which was awakened in Serbia by the annexation. In striving for this, the *Narodna Odbrana* remains true to itself, since this spirit of reconciliation has made its existence possible. In accordance with the principles to which it owes its rise and with the tasks which circumstances lay upon it, the society strives honorably to fulfill these tasks. Accordingly, it accepts as a great and important task the promotion of cooperation, brotherly love, and toleration of all Serbians in all fields, including insofar as possible the field of politics as well.

4. Agitation among All Groups

Before the annexation, private activity among the people in the fields of physical culture, health, cultural progress, etc., was only weakly developed. This condition resulted not only from the lack of unity of the workers but also from the paucity of propaganda. Thus all efforts were confined to a small circle and did not penetrate into the broad masses.

When the *Narodna Odbrana* set for itself all the tasks mentioned, it recognized, along with the need for unification of the forces for work, the need to spread agitation for its goals among the masses, into the cities and villages, and to arouse the people directly, by means of public meetings and lectures at which the members of our committee would appear as agitators in behalf of all aspects of our endeavor.

If anything is to be achieved among the people, agitation must be carried on by the spoken and written word; the spoken word is always more effective.

The *Narodna Odbrana,* convinced of the magnitude of our national need and the necessity for the speediest possible relief, has made its task the seizing of many present or future national opportunities. Thus it must take advantage of the most significant means for the successful development of its action, namely agitation in meetings and lectures in order to reach the widest possible audience of the people through the spoken word.

The agitation which the society undertook for the Sokols, for the shooting clubs, for public health, and for the strengthening of national consciousness is of extraordinary importance. This agitation has been a main factor in the success of the organization, whose entire activity would have otherwise only marked time.

Therefore, agitation for the goals of the *Narodna Odbrana* among the broad masses will not cease as long as the society exists; in fact, it will be stronger and livelier than ever. Its aim is to win over to our goals every man in Serbia, from the palace to the hut, from the youngest to the oldest. Along with bringing together private workers and carrying on the struggle against civil strife, the *Narodna Odbrana* considers the widest possible agitation for its ends among the masses of the people as its strongest means of activity and its best hope of success.

III. The Three Main Tasks

The new *Narodna Odbrana* has chosen for its main tasks some activities in which, before the annexation, private endeavor was either not at all active or was so only with small success, and in which even today it is weakest, although in view of our conditions the strongest activity is desirable. In the first place belongs:

1. The Strengthening of National Consciousness

Along with many evils, the annexation also brought us some good in that it aroused our thinking and showed us our many mistakes. Among other things, we were taught by the annexation that our people in Serbia were not so nationally conscious as is necessary in a country which, as a small independent territory with three million inhabitants, represents the hope and protection of seven million enslaved Serbian people.

Not only in the broad lower classes of the peasantry, but even among the ranks of the intelligent there is only limited understanding of how things stand with our people across the frontier. In Serbia no one knows as much as he should about Bosnia, Herzegovina, Croatia, Dalmatia, the Banat, the Batschka, Old Serbia, and Macedonia. The terms "Sojka," "Precanin," "Schwaba," "Bosniak," "Zinzar," "Schop," "Arnaut," and "Turke" are used seriously among all people of Serbian nationality. Our society does not feel its Serbian identity sufficiently, does not know its national strength, is not conscious enough of its duties as a Serbian people. Of all this we are not so much aware as a people should be under the most favorable circumstances possible, let alone a people like ours chosen to be a Piedmont.

For all these reasons the *Narodna Odbrana,* if it is to strengthen our people physically and economically, had to and has to strive to raise the level of our internal, spiritual, moral life and so seek first of all to strengthen Serbian national consciousness.

As its first, most sacred, and most important goal the *Narodna Odbrana* undertakes the awakening, unfolding, strengthening, and developing of Serbian nationalism from city to city, from village to village, from house to house, from man to man, and from greybeard to child. Our goal is a nationally conscious and proud Serbia. We wish to create such a Serbia as quickly as possible. Only such a country is worthy to bear the name Serbia; only such a country will have the power to withstand all the difficulties which rise up around us; only a country proud of its Serbian identity and highly conscious of it will be able to bear the sacrifices demanded in freeing and uniting an entire people.

Only when Serbian national consciousness bursts into flame can the popular will be kindled for all the other tasks of the *Narodna Odbrana*. Therefore the society places before all else the task of strengthening the national consciousness.

2. Furthering Physical Development

From such experiences as those we have had with mustering, we know that our youth is largely deficient physically as a result of our great indifference toward bodily development.

While among other peoples in all places, on Sundays and holidays and even on work days the crack of rifles and the joyful cry of the Sokol resound, our effeminate society hardly bothers about physical or military exercise and spends its entire free time sitting in the coffee houses or dozing at home. Many of our villages and towns have no sport organization at all. Only a very few Serbs of either sex are members of sport groups; likewise, only a few of our wealthy people are founders and patrons of patriotic organizations. Weakness and indifference to the common good have overcome all classes of our society.

We know that a people able to meet the struggles facing Serbia cannot be created out of young people with pale faces and narrow chests who look like old men, and such young people we meet everywhere. Yet we are not concerned about the fatal results of our lack of action. Officers, priests, teachers, professors, and other officials are far too little interested in physical exercise, as are businessmen, industrial leaders, and others. Not only do they avoid sports; they ridicule those who disturb our sleepy world and who want to spur us on to exercise.

The annexation found us unprepared in everything, most lamentably of all in the field of physical conditioning. The honor of Serbian physical culture was almost at an end! In as short a time as possible this situation must be changed by means of enthusiastic, well thought-through, and persistent effort.

The *Narodna Odbrana* will fight with all available means for the development and the progress of physical improvement in Serbia, and especially of the shooting and gymnastic groups. This will be its second main task. Its activity will develop in two directions: one part influencing society and the people by arousing a feeling for sports and by founding sport organizations even in the smallest Serbian villages; the other affecting the state, the government, and the national parliament, from which must be demanded the introduction of compulsory military education into all schools, and material aid to private initiative.

Parallel with these efforts in behalf of physical culture, agitation for the creation of a strong army must also be spread among the masses. A love for the military profession must be aroused, as well as love and a spirit of sacrifice for the fatherland. In special sections in this book we shall speak again of the close connection between the *Narodna Odbrana* and separate branches of physical exercise.

3. The Introdudction of New Methods of Work

The difficult conditions in which our people finds itself, and of which we have been seriously conscious only since the annexation, demand of us the deepest earnestness in fulfilling the tasks which various organizations and committees offer to individual initiative. To work for physical education and other goals cannot be a subject merely of conversation and must not serve to satisfy our vanity or provide a means of distraction. We must not concern ourselves with it only temporarily, but must show the enthusiasm and seriousness suitable for this great, important, and holy work.

We must not be ashamed to speak of Sokols, shooting societies, and popular gatherings; we must personally sacrifice time and money for this by giving up many pleasures. We must not avoid the small villages and cities but be proud to go there in order to serve the rebirth of our people. The *Narodna Odbrana* demands of the members of the groups and committees that they assume not just places of honor but the actual responsibility of accomplishing the work to be done. For an educated Serb the worthiest and best spot, the first to which every young Serb must devote himself and to which he must remain true late into life, is contact with the people in the lowest ranks, in the farthest villages, in the smallest towns where folk knowledge and national progress have progressed least. There he must work as a teacher, religious leader, county or municipal official. By means of promoting an effort of this kind for the commonweal, by popularizing these ideas among wide ranks of the people through lectures and meetings, through simultaneously arousing equal enthusiasm for all kinds of activity, the *Narodna Odbrana* transplants into our social order completely new methods of developing the work of private initiative.

Instead of concentrating upon a few persons, as previously, this work will be a common, great, national pursuit; from an unpurposeful activity carried on only occasionally and almost as a sport, we must create a powerful and enthusiastic national movement. The introduction of new methods to further the efforts of private endeavor is vital to the success of the entire activity of the *Narodna Odbrana* and belongs among the first tasks of our new activity.

IV. Rifle Clubs and the *Narodna Odbrana*

The work of physical development is so important in a country like Serbia that we must speak of it again, especially in regard to the most important branches of exercise. Let us begin with the shooting clubs.

Throughout the existence of the world there has been and will be war among peoples. In this struggle, "no one has the right to rely upon hope—only upon God and his own strength."

Struggles between nations and states are always eventually decided by wars, and the wars are conducted with firearms.

The firing of weapons is today one of the most important means of carrying on warfare. Thus all peoples, all states, all thinking men in the entire world devote the greatest care to this matter. In the countries which have the greatest cultural development and the longest period of military service, practice in shooting is most common. Although the period of military service lasts only two or three years in such countries, everywhere there are shooting clubs where young and old may practice. From examples given elsewhere, everyone can see for himself how much is sacrificed throughout the world for the sake of practice in shooting.

If this is the situation in other countries, we are right in demanding that even more be done here for shooting practice than is done elsewhere, because we live in a country of peasants where the term of military service is only six months and where enemies surround us. The *Narodna Odbrana* demands that there be no Serb in Serbia who is not a member of a shooting club, that no hamlet be without a shooting society. Compulsory rifle practice is to be introduced into all schools, and the state must support the shooting clubs in such numbers as to make Serbia into one great rifle center, where on Sundays and holidays the Serbian rifle shot will echo from mountain to mountain and from one end of Serbia to the other.

If a new blow like the annexation should come, a new Serbia would rise up to meet it, a Serbia in which every Serbian boy and old man is a rifleman. We shall discuss further, in various places in this book, all that the *Narodna Odbrana* has done and intends to do to improve the quality of shooting. It is apparent from all that we say, however, that improvement of our marksmanship must be one of our first tasks.

V. GYMNASTIC SOCIETIES [*Sokols*]

Like all other forms of life, peoples too are defeated in the struggle for existence if they do not have the strength to endure. Everything which is weak and unhealthy is destroyed in competition, and only what is healthy, strong, and adaptable lives on. The history of those peoples which have disappeared and of those which still survive attests to this law of nature. From history we see that the decline of a people first began when immorality and indolence appeared, when good customs and a sound way of life were abandoned.

The history of the Serbian and Turkish peoples confirms this law. The Turks, better organized militarily, stronger in numbers, and fanatic in belief, destroyed the Serbian state when it was weakened internally and broken by the conflicts between Serbian feudal lords. But how do the Turks fare today? Once the strongest people in the world, the Turks today are the "sick man" of the Bosporus. This the Turks have become because they lacked the ability to endure the struggle with more powerful, healthier, more advanced peoples. What has all this to do with the Serbian Sokol?

In the south the old Turks are already retreating; only a part of our peoples still groans under their yoke; but from the north come new Turks, more fearsome and dangerous than the old ones. Culturally superior and economically strong, our northern enemies turn upon us. They want to rob us of freedom and language, tread upon us, destroy us. Already we perceive signs of the coming struggle; the Serbian people face the question: "To be or not to be?" And now the time has come for the institution of the Serbian Sokols. That is the demand of the hour, the order of national defense.

Only a sound, powerful, nationally conscious, and well-organized people is capable of defense, of war, and of victory.

This truth the Serbian Sokols have written on their flags and they announce it to the people. This truth they want to translate into fact.

The Serbian Sokol movement wants to strengthen everyone who joins—all Serbian brothers and sisters. It wants to awaken in each Serb pride in and consciousness of our national strength, so that we may embark upon the struggle as a powerful and conscious people with confidence in national victory and without fear for the future of the nation. That is what the Serbian Sokols want; that is their goal. . . .

The idea of the Serbian Sokol is the idea of the Serbian people. The Sokol idea coincides in its aims with the aims of the Serbian people. In the ideal of the Sokol the Serbian ideal becomes realized, because it unites in this ideal all its members irrespective of where they live. It is a powerful weapon which must be extended to all groups of the people.

Without troubling themselves about the political and religious convictions of their members, without paying attention to class or rank, the Sokols draw in young Serbs, both male and female, for the purpose of physical and moral training in the interest of national cultural development.

The Sokols' goal in promoting physical exercise is not the further holding of exhibitions to arouse wonder at the skill displayed; the exercises and entire organization of the Sokols exist instead to develop strong and hardy men and women, beautiful in growth and form, of free, courageous, and independent spirit—good patriots, who not only love their country but also are able to defend it in the hour of need.

The Serbian Sokol ideal is a great one because it is the national ideal. To make it a reality all Serbs must rally to the Sokols. Our people are in danger. We all must harness our strength, must develop every muscle, must illuminate every part of the brain. Through the tireless effort of us all, the Serbian Sokols will give the Serbian people a healthy, strong, nationally conscious, and well-organized nation, a nation that will not be defeated but will triumph in the struggle for national survival.

Thus the realization of the ideal of the Serbian Sokols is one of the first goals of national defense rightly understood.

VI. The Olympic Club and the *Narodna Odbrana*

The idea of physical development has already gained wide acceptance in the world. In connection with it comes the holding of competitive games. The French were among the first to institute numerous contests in shooting and marching, and they attained great success in this project. Individual corporations and wealthy persons put up prizes and do so even now. The Germans, the Swedes, the English, and the Americans do the same and have even surpassed the French in some respects. The ancient heroic Greeks, Macedonians, and Romans owed their success in large part to their strong youths. The Olympic games near Mt. Olympus in honor of the god Zeus were the most important among the national celebrations of the Greeks. Spectators from all Greek lands streamed to these games. The prizes in the contests honored not only the winner but his native city as well. The winner was glorified in song and crowned with wreaths. The

Greeks already in those times gave the highest honor to speed in running, and their great hero Achilles was known as "the swift-of-foot."

The Olympic games which we have today for competition in running and other sports are named in honor of the Greeks, who three thousand years ago understood the importance of physical training better than do many modern nations, among these unfortunately the Serbs.

When, because of the annexation of Bosnia and Herzegovina, we Serbs first awoke to the need for an armed Serbian nation, a few citizens founded the Olympic Club in Belgrade for the purpose of gaining wide support for competitive games.

The goal of the Olympic Club is not to found Sokols or shooting societies; it aims rather to support these by arousing an interest in physical exercise among the people through competitive games, since naturally competition arouses a great need for the members of competing groups to train themselves. Thus the Club asks its members to direct the people into the Sokols and rifle clubs. Since the Olympic Club is concerned with military considerations, it will most certainly help to raise the number of trained fighters among the people. Prizes given in all fields stimulate the desire for success. The higher the prize the greater the effort; and thus the club has provided prizes, for without prizes in all fields there can be no competition.

Those are the foundations upon which the Olympic Club is built. In order to persuade as many people as possible to take part in the competitive games, clubs must be founded in every district, in every county, and in every community to hold meets at least once a year (first in marching and riflery) and to give the victors prizes contributed by patriotic citizens. In those places where no physical exercise is pursued, the Olympic Clubs are necessarily the forerunners of the Sokols and shooting organizations, but where those already exist they are their helpers.

In cooperative and complementary effort with the other sport organizations, but above all with the *Narodna Odbrana,* they will raise the level of useful sport and suppress the harmful. With the development of their activity the clubs will change from being social and simple to being more practical and complex. If the number of competitors in the games is to increase, as a means of furthering the glory of our arms, our minds must be roused from their previous indifference. Two or three energetic men in a town or village will suffice to advance the cause, if they will give at most one week a year to the Olympic Club. Their trouble will be small, yet it will have results of great value. Through small sacrifices they will help to bring our physical condition to the peak necessary if it is to measure up to the goals of the Society.

VII. What We Aim At in Our Lectures

Up to now the lectures of the *Narodna Odbrana* have been more or less propaganda talks. In them the program of our new activity has been developed. In every lecture the annexation, the activity of our former organization and the tasks of the present one have been discussed. But in addition to such lectures, even at the beginning, other speeches have discussed individual questions, as for example the protection of health, the fight against illiteracy, the furnishing of the peasant house, the meaning of the rifle clubs, and so on. The lectures of the *Narodna Odbrana* will never cease to be propaganda for our cause, but they will constantly develop more in the direction of individual subjects concerning the varied questions of our social and national life. We must hold talks in city and country, in the smallest hamlet, without fanfare, in quietness and modesty. We do not seek a huge audience at the talks; a small but serious group is enough, since we want not display but earnest work.

The *Narodna Odbrana* wants to maintain by means of the lectures a continuous school for teaching the people all its tasks. It intends to carry on agitation by means of its lectures, to inspire and win over people to its tasks, to instruct them in what it wants to impart. The lectures are planned to serve as a kind of voluntary adult education, enabling the listeners according to their preparation to receive instruction about various problems. Moreover, these lectures must be a guiding light in Serbian Piedmont, the country which is the guardian of the old Serbian idea and bearer and executor of the Serbian ideal, an eternal light fed by the flames of Serbian love and kindling Serbian hearts for the Serbian nation and the holy Serbian cause.

Of such a nature are the lectures of the *Narodna Odbrana!* They are a mighty lever for us. Our organization has been principally dependent upon them for its previous success; and if it continues with them, its success will be even greater. One cannot imagine the activity of the *Narodna Odbrana* without the lectures.

VIII. The Work of Women in the *Narodna Odbrana*

In view of the work it has before it, the *Narodna Odbrana* counts on the women as well as the men.

In the struggles of all peoples the women have won great fame for themselves, in the fields of national independence, national welfare, and progress, among the Italians, French, Poles, and other peoples; and the national struggles of the Czechs and Slovenes today illustrate the same fact.

The Serbian woman is equally able to support the Serbian man in the national effort. Already, through the various women's organizations, she is taking part in the work for national welfare; there is no welfare work which can be carried out without the help of our women. The *Narodna Odbrana* already keeps a certain connection with these groups (namely, with the Circle of Serb Sisters) and owes to them many of its successes.

The *Narodna Odbrana* demands of the women nothing which they do not understand or are unaccustomed to doing. It wants simply to strengthen them in their previous work and to arouse still more love among them for it, and especially to encourage them in the work of raising the cultural level of our peasant women and girls and thus of freeing them from ignorance and superstition. The women working with us must help to interest the peasant woman in our goals, for the peasant woman is mother of us all and yet is in the worst condition.

The Narodna Odbrana has taken representatives of the women's groups into its committees. It emphasizes in its lectures its need for the cooperation of the Serbian women and girls. So it has opened its ranks to the Serbian woman and hopes that the help which it is already receiving from her will be constantly greater and more successful. In addition to taking part in the gathering of contributions, participating in festivals, and caring for the female youth, we are thinking here also of the participation of our women and girls which is needed in the work of the Sokols and shooting groups. Alongside the Serbian man of sound body and mind must stand the Serbian woman, also of sound body and mind—the falcon and its mate.

The *Narodna Odbrana* will for its part gladly support the entrance of our women into all fields of our endeavor; but especially it wishes to bring the influence of the educated Serbian woman to bear on the forgotten peasant woman. Although our women with rare exceptions have not concerned themselves in this matter, we consider it of primary importance and value in the service of our people and of our country.

The help given by the Serbian mother, wife, sister, and daughter to the *Narodna Odbrana* constitutes a great force, and we want it to be a constantly greater one.

IX. SMALL TASKS OF THE *Narodna Odbrana*

Every great work is built of a number of smaller ones. The more civilized peoples of the world have long recognized this in their national effort. Among them, especially among the Germans and Czechs, each small piece of work is valued for the fame and pride and high usefulness connected with it.

In invoking the term "small work," we mean that we work little by little but all together, that each one in his turn devotes a few days to the task with steady attention and without pause. Small work is the modest, unseen, inconspicuous effort of the individual and of societies on a small scale, comprising a substantial harvest when the fruits are added up. It is the work of the Sokol; of the practice hours of the marksman who does not miss a time; of the enthusiastic teacher who all through the year, without anyone's hearing of it outside school, teaches women and girls to read; of the teacher who does the same among the men; of the young university student, priest, or teacher who founds in his village an agricultural cooperative, a reading room, or a library; of the young professor or the doctor of the small town who in the course of the year in the villages of his district gives some twenty lectures about the duties of a citizen and a Serb, about health, physical culture, the value of literacy, and so on.

It is small work when each of us with modesty and enthusiasm plows his furrow without taking his eye from the plow. Small work is a powerful weapon in the struggle of the Czechs, of the Germans, and of the other civilized peoples, and it is time that we here in the Balkans, we who have so much fallow land before us, recognize the value of work on a small scale.

It is especially important that the Serbs learn to honor small tasks. For we are a stormy southern people inclined toward noisy competition and big words, and unaccustomed to modest small tasks.

By means of spreading the idea of inspired and persevering small work, the *Narodna Odbrana* brings a wave of love and trust to the most neglected members of our society, brings life and work to the most remote corners of our country. Small work brings us all together, binds us to one idea, makes us alike, destroys barriers, unifies all our powers, in that it draws in the small, lends meaning to the least, assembles all in one spirit, for one goal, for one end—the freedom and unification of our people.

Acceptance of the principle of small work means that even the child with the Sokol feather in his hat, the high-school girl taking subscriptions for a needed primer, the peasant helping to pay the expenses for a shooting match, the high-school boy with the badge of an anti-alcoholic, each can feel himself a worthy worker for the creation of national freedom and national happiness, not to mention the adult citizens and intelligent officials, the workers in the cultural, national, and patriotic institutes. The advantage of such a conception, the extent to which the morals and self-confidence of the people can be raised, cannot be described in words.

"Small work" is the result of a progressive conception of life and society. Big talk is to be replaced by practical effort. Stone laid upon stone makes the palace, says our proverb. Small work aims at the same. Instead of noisy speeches about great things it demands great works in small compass; instead of empty speechmaking about Duschan's great empire it wants to make a small Duschan's empire in every village; before we unify all Serbs, we must unify each Serbian village in one thought, one effort. We can make every Serbian house into a small Serbian castle, every Serbian village into a small fortress, every Serbian town into a small empire of Serbian consciousness, Serbian knowledge, Serbian strength. The modest small work still despised by us today has to perform these worthy tasks, these great goals, in order to bring about the steeling of the powers of the people, in order to promote organization, health, the abolition of illiteracy and alcoholism, and so forth.

By raising small goals to great tasks and giving to very modest activity the significance of holy work, the *Narodna Odbrana* is carrying through a small revolution of the spirit in accordance with its conception of the duties and of the importance of national work.

To preach "small work" as a mighty means for regenerating our society must be one of the first tasks of the *Narodna Odbrana*.

X. The Renaissance of Society

If one takes everything into consideration, it is apparent that our present social order does not measure up to the serious demands of the times and its tasks.

Our people is not healthy enough, not rich enough; its national duties are not sufficiently well known; it is not hard-working and thrifty enough, not well enough grounded in the use of weapons and not well enough furnished with arms, is indifferent and neglectful; in fact, it is not equal to its present duties.

What is true of our people in general is especially applicable to its understanding. Understanding is the guide of a people. Much of the weakness from which we suffer would quickly disappear if understanding were spread among the people to assist in the effort toward improvement. If we are not to be destroyed, we must try to steer our life into a better course; we must strive to regenerate our entire society and above all our understanding.

The entire activity of the *Narodna Odbrana* is directed toward changing all of us—society, the people, Serbia, Serbdom. Every single task of the *Narodna Odbrana* involves a change and rebirth in every part of our national life, and all the tasks together work toward the renaissance of the whole.

The *Narodna Odbrana* wants to create a new Serbia, a new race, new men, a new Serbian understanding. Only new men will be able, in spite of all the difficulties of our position, to beat back all the dangers threatening Serbia and Serbdom and to lead our people along the road to success and victory. Our entire program, with all its many facets and goals, may be expressed in one word: Rebirth. The *Narodna Odbrana* seeks the rebirth of the state and of the people, of our entire present society. All its activity is designed to reach this goal. In order to work successfully toward this purpose, however, the members of our committees, as well as all our workers and agitators, must be able to appear before society as newly transformed persons.

Prior to the metamorphosis of others, we must renew ourselves; before we speed the rebirth of the world, we must first complete it in ourselves. That is a natural and logical demand. Only he who is deeply convinced himself that the condition of Serbdom is very serious and that work such as the *Narodna Odbrana* preaches is needed, and who cannot live without this conviction, is the kind of worker that we need; only he will understand how to agitate for our ideas. He serves the ideals by fulfilling all their demands, and so he will inspire the confidence of others.

A change within all society and first of all within the minds and hearts of its members is thus the goal toward which our entire activity is striving.

A true worker of the *Narodna Odbrana* must experience an inner change, must develop himself into a new man in the spirit of the ideas announced by the movement, must be an enthusiastic worker and fighter, and must bear the torch before his people and daily set an example in carrying out our program.

The aim of the *Narodna Odbrana* is the complete regeneration of society, the creation of new, better Serbs in accordance with all the demands of the new time—an objective which will in its fuller conception take much time and work. In a smaller degree, however, it must succeed even today. These first new men of today must be the first enthusiastic workers.

XI. New Serbian National Heroes [*Obilitsche* and *Singjelitsche*]

It is quite wrong to think Kossowo[1] once existed, is past, and that

[1] The Turks crushed the Serbian-Albanian-Croatian army at Kossowo in 1389 and conquered the country, but a Serb hero of the battle succeeded in penetrating the Turkish line and slaying the Sultan. The anniversary of the battle and of the assassination became the great Serbian national holiday.

today it must simply be avenged. Kossowo is still among us, or, to put it differently, we are today in the middle of Kossowo, and we are not avenging it but fighting on its battlefield.

The Serbian people are always fighting the battle of Kossowo, only the battlefield changes form. Our present Kossowo is the darkness and ignorance in which the Serbs live. Barbarism of every kind, unhygienic conditions, lack of national consciousness, party and other feuds—these are the Turks of today against whom we must set out to a new Kossowo. These internal causes of a new Kossowo are considerable; there are external causes too, however, beyond our boundaries in the north and west—the Germans, the Austrians, and the Swabians with their drive toward our Serb and Slavic south. Darkness and ignorance among our people within and the German invasion from outside are the new Turks whom we must meet today on the Serb battlefield of Kossowo and with whom we have to resume the struggle for the Serbian name and Serbian freedom.

The freedom of a people is just as incomplete when it is in bondage to ignorance as when it is in physical bondage. Man can be enserfed also to errors, prejudices, ignorance, love of drink, barbarism. War must be waged against all these evils. Just as we once rebelled against the Turks, we must now rebel against these evil national conditions and fight for freedom from them.

The view that there is war only when the guns thunder and the rifles crack is a false one. Among nations there is never peace, but always a condition of war; life goes forward under the sign of struggle. Even today in the middle of peace the Serbs are waging a desperate war. Woe to him who does not know it. This war is our present fight for our soil, our health, civilization, knowledge, schools, physical culture—as we have described it already in the section "The New Contemporary *Narodna Odbrana.*"

The *Narodna Odbrana,* convinced of this conception of our present position, expects that it will find among the unknown teachers and priests, among the students, merchants, and other modest workers displaying private initiative in all directions, new heroes such as are demanded by today's Kossowo, today's war for our freedom. Milosch Obilitsch fought his way through Turkish swords and lances to the tent of Mured to murder him. Our new contemporary hero, whether teacher or priest or some other national worker, must make his way through insults, humiliations, and injustice in order to drive darkness and ignorance from the soul of the people. Singjelitsch in the defense of the newly created Serbia blew himself and his companions up along with the breastwork. The national worker today must often sacrifice his personal happiness and his family in order to agitate day by day for the freeing of our society from the sins of disease, poverty, lack of national consciousness, and so on.

The struggle for the benefits of civilization demands heroism no less than does war. A good Sokol or shooting club is not easy to build. To give lecture after lecture in towns and villages in an atmosphere of lack of understanding, antagonism, and disfavor, to break a lance untiringly for this or that noble thought of national rebirth—this means being a hero. Work in behalf of the cooperative, the association for popular health, and every other similar affair is bound up with physical, spiritual, moral, and material sacrifice. This is equally true in our territories outside, in Turkey and Austria-Hungary, where officials persecute such people and bring them to prison and the gallows. Just as the lance-splintering battle of Kossowo produced an Obilitsch and the struggle on the Tschegar a Singjelitsch, this war against darkness and ignorance and for light and knowledge, the true freedom, must give us similar heroes.

The *Narodna Odbrana* does not doubt that in the struggle of guns and rifles in which we are to engage against the Germans and our other enemies, our people will produce a whole line of heroes. But we are not satisfied with that. We regard the present supposed peace as war and we demand heroes for the struggle which we must conduct today within Serbia and beyond its boundaries.

By this demand the *Narodna Odbrana* emphasizes to the highest degree how important to the country the struggle asked of us is, and how glorious and honorable a task it is to be a fighter of the *Narodna Odbrana*.

XII. The Union with Brothers and Friends

The preservation of the tie with our brothers abroad, both near and far, and with our other friends in the world is one of the principal activities of the *Narodna Odbrana*.

When the *Narodna Odbrana* uses the word "nation" it means our entire people, not only the Serbs in Serbia. It rejoices over every advance which our brothers abroad make toward the goals developed here, and wishes their private initiative to unfold as much as possible. For this part of our people, private endeavor is indeed the only salvation; these Serbs are entirely dependent on self-help, whereas those in Serbia have the state to care for them. The *Narodna Odbrana* hopes that its activity in Serbia will strongly encourage our brothers abroad to support private initiative more actively, so that the new national uprising may be sufficiently effective everywhere to create a strong national defense for all Serbian areas. If such is not the case, the national defense will not be complete.

The maintenance of the tie with our brothers abroad requires us to arrange for frequent meetings with them wherever they are and to cultivate such meetings among ourselves in Serbia. These gatherings do not need to be huge and noisy; the quieter and more frequent they are, the more they will lead to mutual acquaintance and union.

The *Narodna Odbrana* has kept up all the ties which it established during the annexation period with peoples friendly to us. It is doing its best to maintain these and has succeeded in its effort to strengthen them further.

The maintenance of relations with our brothers abroad requires that the *Narodna Odbrana* help every Serb, Croat, and Slovene who comes to Serbia. It must also welcome every stranger who comes among us as a friend in order to inform himself about our conditions. Our effort to inform friendly nations about our national situation must be constantly pursued if it is to be advantageous to us.

The *Narodna Odbrana* follows carefully all events among all Serbs, ready to intervene at any time for the just and holy national cause. If events call for action, then our efforts to keep alive our ties with our brothers and friends across the borders of Serbia will prove useful and productive.

We must keep our people here in Serbia informed about events among our brothers abroad and about conditions among our friends. We must be active and persistent in this work, because our people in Serbia must be thoroughly informed about the situation among our brothers and must know about our friends too. Only an exact knowledge in both cases can give us the needed information about our national strength and make us acquainted with the entire truth about our national situation and our task.

XIII. Two Important Tasks

In conclusion, we want to mention two more important tasks of the *Narodna Odbrana,* and with them we will close the part of our pamphlet setting forth our program.

The *Narodna Odbrana* maintains that the annexation of Bosnia and Herzegovina is clearly an invasion of our country from the north; thus it regards Austria as our principal and greatest enemy and so represents it to our people. The exposition of this idea is in no way fanaticism or chauvinism but a healthy and entirely understandable task, an elementary duty, a need exactly like that to impress the fact that two times two makes four.

The Serbs have never hated for the mere sake of hating, but they have always loved freedom and independence. We have already said in another place that, just as once the Turks from the south pressed upon us, now the Austrians from the north are coming. If the *Narodna Odbrana* is preaching the need for a struggle with Austria, it is but proclaiming the sacred truth which arises out of our national position. If hate and fanaticism develop, they are but natural phenomena which come as results and not as an end. For us the goal is our existence, our freedom. If hate against Austria breaks out, we are not the ones who have sown it; Austria is the sower of the hate, through her action against us which forces us to struggle until she is destroyed.

Today everywhere a new concept of nationalism has become prevalent. Nationalism (the feeling of nationality) is no longer a historical or poetical feeling, but the true practical expression of life. Among the French, Germans, and English, and among all other civilized peoples, nationalism has grown into something quite new; in it lies the concept of bread, space, air, commerce, competition in everything. Only among us is it still in the old form; that is, it is the fruit of spiritual suffering rather than of reasonable understanding and national advantage. If we speak of freedom and union, we parade far too much the phrases "breaking our chains" and "freeing the slaves"; we call far too much upon our former Serbian glory and think too little of the fact that the freeing of subjected areas and their union with Serbia are necessary to our citizens, our merchants, and our peasants on the grounds of the most elementary needs of culture and trade, of food and space. If one were to explain to our sharp-eyed people our national task as one closely connected with the needs of everyday life, our people would take up the work in a greater spirit of sacrifice than is today the case. We must tell our people that the freedom of Bosnia is necessary, not just because of their feeling of sympathy with their brothers who suffer there, but also because of commerce and its connection with the sea; national union is necessary because of the stronger development of a common culture. The Italians welcome the conquest of Tripoli not just because of the glory to be won by the success of their arms, but especially because of the advantage they hope to gain by annexing Tripoli. Our people must adopt a more realistic attitude toward politics. We must show them how we would stand culturally and economically if we were united into one state and were in as favorable a position commercially as that of Timok in relation to the Adriatic. . . .

Along with the task of explaining to our people the danger threatening us from Austria, the *Narodna Odbrana* has also the other important tasks of explaining to them, while preserving our holy national memories, this new, healthy, fruitful conception of nationalism, and of convincing them to work for national freedom and unity.

XIV. Conclusion

The old *Narodna Odbrana* was called into being on account of the annexation. When we saw that there would be no war, the organization ceased its original activity relating to the crisis of annexation and turned to the new activity demanded by its holy mission as national defender. The lesson that had been learned from the annexation was that we must prepare ourselves as thoroughly as possible, with all the strength and persistence we can command. The state is to prepare its forces administratively; and parallel with its effort, private initiative is to prepare itself by means of its voluntary strength. Let us prepare, let us prepare unceasingly for the struggle which the annexation foreshadows. To activate these private efforts, to assemble and to concentrate them is what the *Narodna Odbrana* has undertaken; it will rouse them where they have become weak, plant them where they are lacking, conciliate them where they are feuding. The preparation and strengthening of Serbia in all fields of national life and of national effort is our working program. The *Narodna Odbrana* is the same as it was in the annexation period, adapting its work to the changing times and situations while maintaining all its previous ties. It still is a source of protection and is national in scope. Around its banner the citizens of Serbia gather today as they did during the annexation. Then we called for war, but now we call for work. Then we wanted meetings, demonstrations, volunteers, guerrillas, rifles, and bombs; today we want quiet, fanatical, untiring effort and responsibility as a preparation for the struggle which will come with guns and cannons.

The change which took place in Serbia after the annexation is in great part due to the efforts of the *Narodna Odbrana*. As a true national defender, our organization will endure to the end; and if the end comes, if a situation obtains like that at the time of the annexation, thanks to its present activity the *Narodna Odbrana* will face the task which it will have to fulfill then with a tenfold greater ability than it had at the time of the annexation. Through its present activity it is preparing itself and the country for the real function for which it has come into being.

All in all, the *Narodna Odbrana* aims through its work to advance upon the enemy on the day of reckoning with a sound, nationally conscious, and internally reconciled Serbian people, a nation of Sokols, rifle clubs, heroes—in fact, the fear and terror of the enemy—reliant front-rank fighters and executors of Serbia's holy cause.

If this succeeds, all will be well for us; woe to us if we fail.